THE **ELEVENTH** DOCTOR

DOCTOR WHO

ARCHIVES

VOLUME 2

TITAN
COMICS

TITAN COMICS

Collection Editor
Andrew James
Assistant Collection Editor
Kirsten Murray
Collection Designer
Rob Farmer
Senior Editor
Steve White

Titan Comics Editorial
Lizzie Kaye, Tom Williams
Production Assistant Peter James
Production Supervisors Maria Pearson, Jackie Flook
Production Manager Obi Onuora
Studio Manager Selina Juneja
Senior Sales Manager Steve Tothill
Brand Manager, Marketing Lucy Ripper
Senior Marketing & Press Officer Owen Johnson
Direct Sales & Marketing Manager Ricky Claydon
Commercial Manager Michelle Fairlamb
Publishing Manager Darryl Tothill
Publishing Director Chris Teather
Operations Director Leigh Baulch
Executive Director Vivian Cheung
Publisher Nick Landau

Cover By
Tommy Lee Edwards
Original Series Edits By
Denton J. Tipton

BBC WORLDWIDE

Director of Editorial Governance
Nicolas Brett
**Director of Consumer Products
And Publishing**
Andrew Moultrie
Head of UK Publishing
Chris Kerwin
Publisher
Mandy Thwaites
Publishing Co-Ordinator
Eva Abramik

Special thanks to
Steven Moffat, Brian Minchin, Matt Nicholls,
James Dudley, Edward Russell, Derek Ritchie,
Scott Handcock, Kirsty Mullan,
Kate Bush, Julia Nocciolino, Ed Casey,
Marcus Wilson and Richard Cookson
for their invaluable assistance.

 THE **ELEVENTH** DOCTOR

DOCTOR WHO ARCHIVES

DOCTOR WHO: THE ELEVENTH DOCTOR
ARCHIVES OMNIBUS VOL. 2
ISBN: 9781782767695
Published by Titan Comics, a division of Titan
Publishing Group, Ltd. 144 Southwark Street, London,
SE1 0UP.

Contains material originally published as Doctor Who
Series 2 #13-16, Series 3 #1-12 and the 2012 Special.

A CIP catalogue record for this title is available from the
British Library. First edition: December 2015.

10 9 8 7 6 5 4 3 2 1

Printed in China. TC00956.

Titan Comics does not read or accept unsolicited
DOCTOR WHO submissions of ideas, stories or artwork.

www.titan-comics.com

CONTENTS

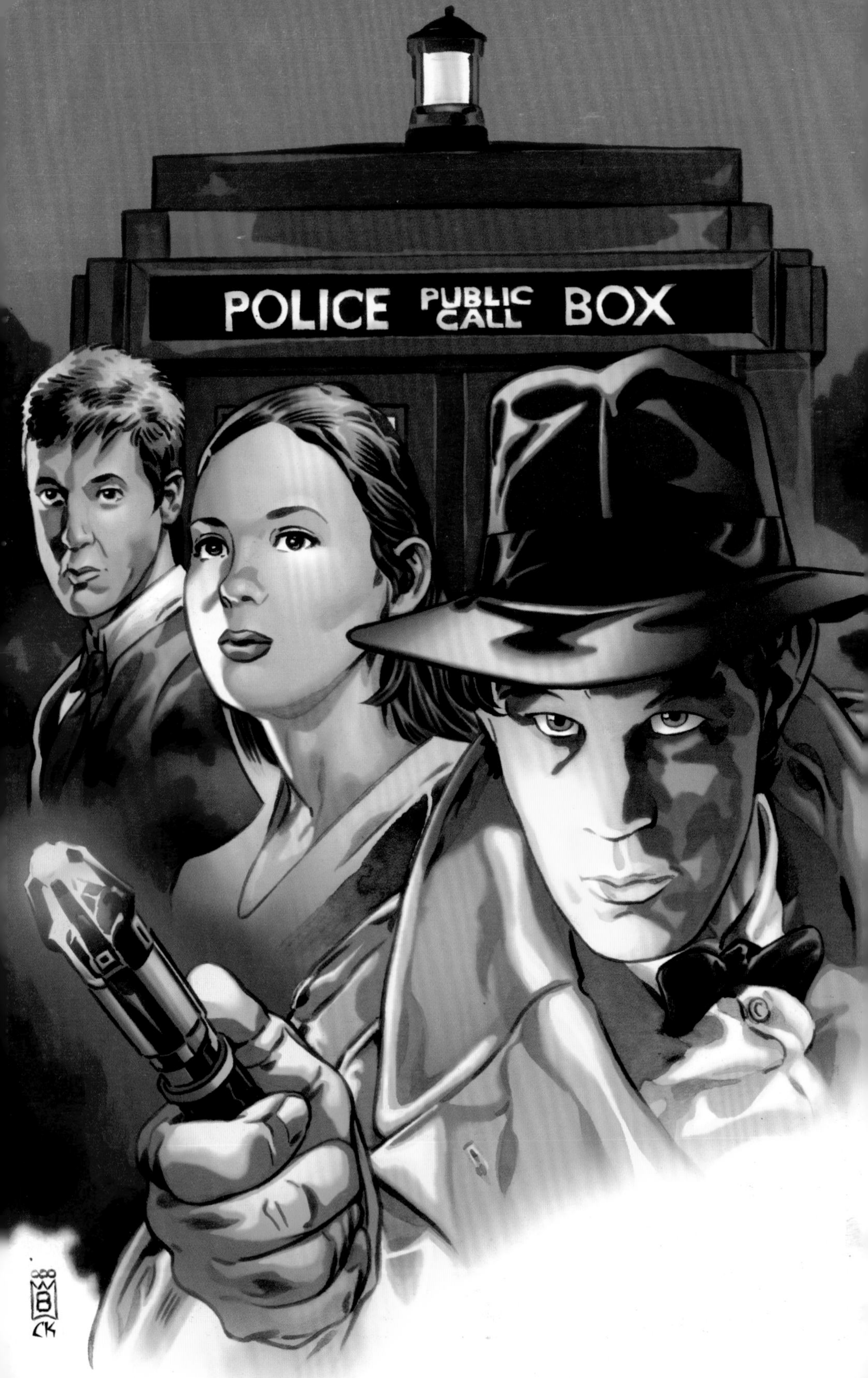
POLICE PUBLIC CALL BOX

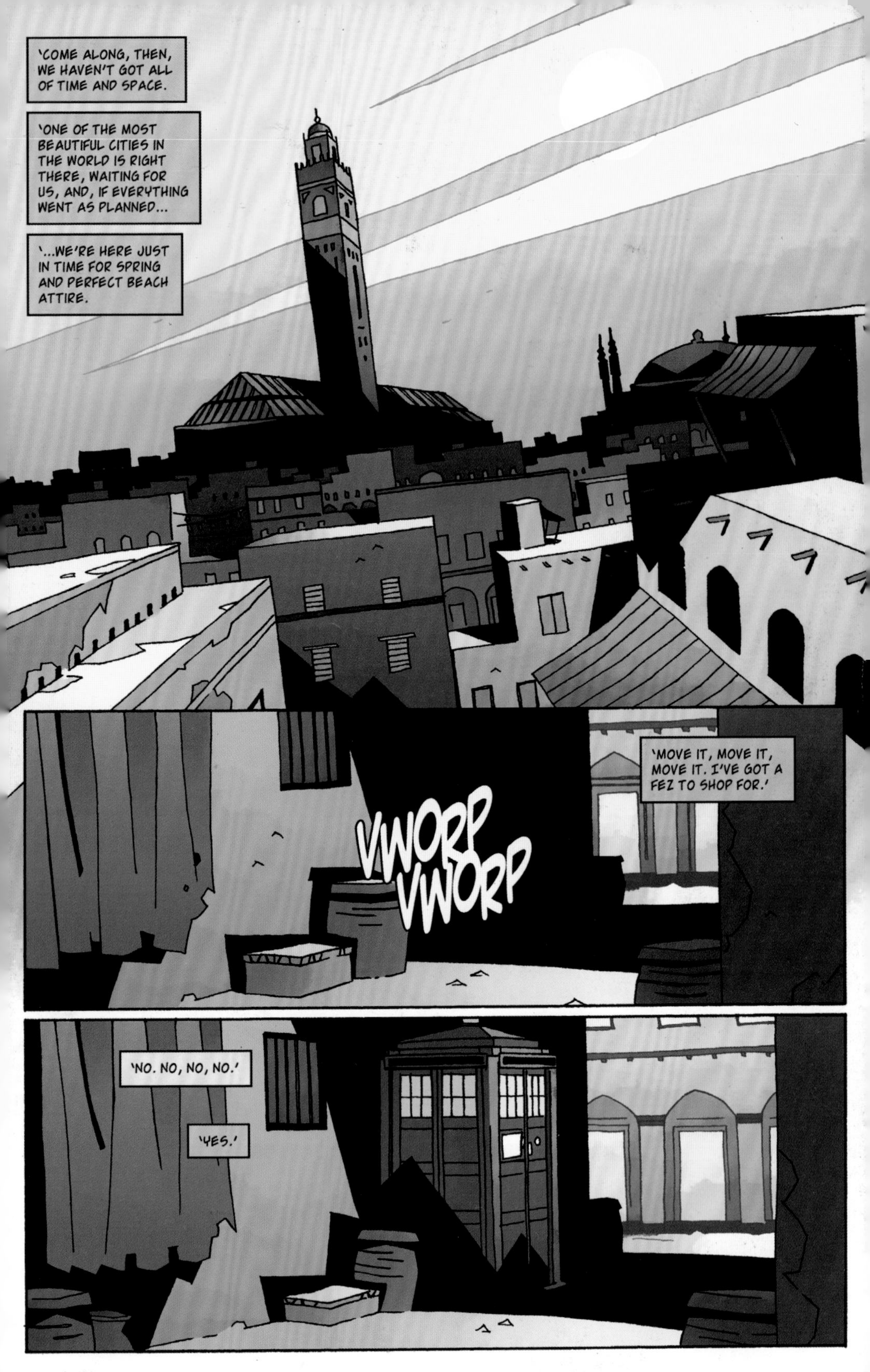
'COME ALONG, THEN, WE HAVEN'T GOT ALL OF TIME AND SPACE.
'ONE OF THE MOST BEAUTIFUL CITIES IN THE WORLD IS RIGHT THERE, WAITING FOR US, AND, IF EVERYTHING WENT AS PLANNED...
'...WE'RE HERE JUST IN TIME FOR SPRING AND PERFECT BEACH ATTIRE.
VWORP VWORP
'MOVE IT, MOVE IT, MOVE IT. I'VE GOT A FEZ TO SHOP FOR.'
'NO. NO, NO, NO.'
'YES.'

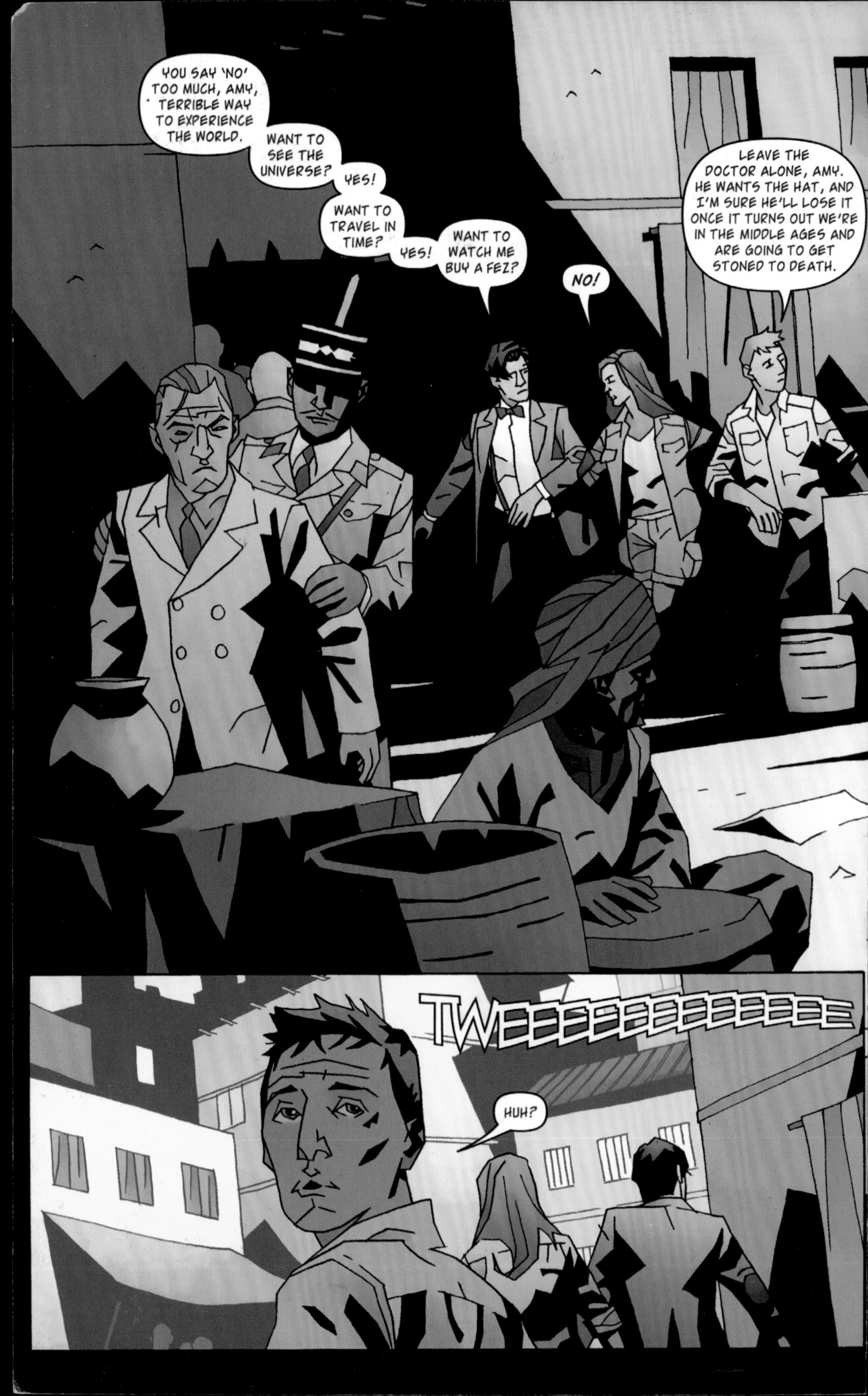
YOU SAY 'NO' TOO MUCH, AMY, TERRIBLE WAY TO EXPERIENCE THE WORLD.
WANT TO SEE THE UNIVERSE?
YES!
WANT TO TRAVEL IN TIME?
YES!
WANT TO WATCH ME BUY A FEZ?
NO!
LEAVE THE DOCTOR ALONE, AMY. HE WANTS THE HAT, AND I'M SURE HE'LL LOSE IT ONCE IT TURNS OUT WE'RE IN THE MIDDLE AGES AND ARE GOING TO GET STONED TO DEATH.
TWEEEEEEEEEEEEEEE
HUH?

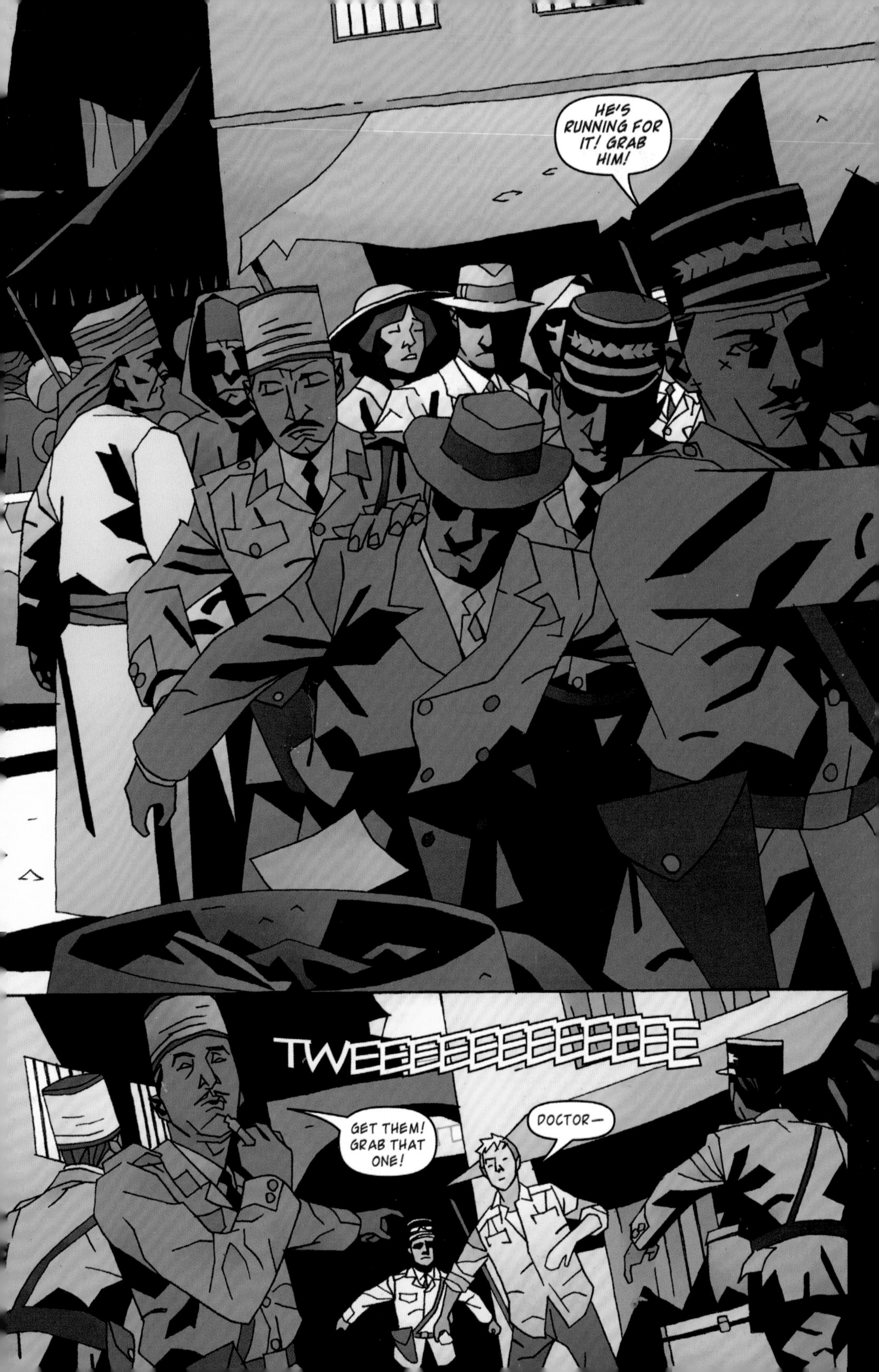
HE'S RUNNING FOR IT! GRAB HIM!
TWEEEEEEEEEEEEEEE
GET THEM! GRAB THAT ONE!
DOCTOR—

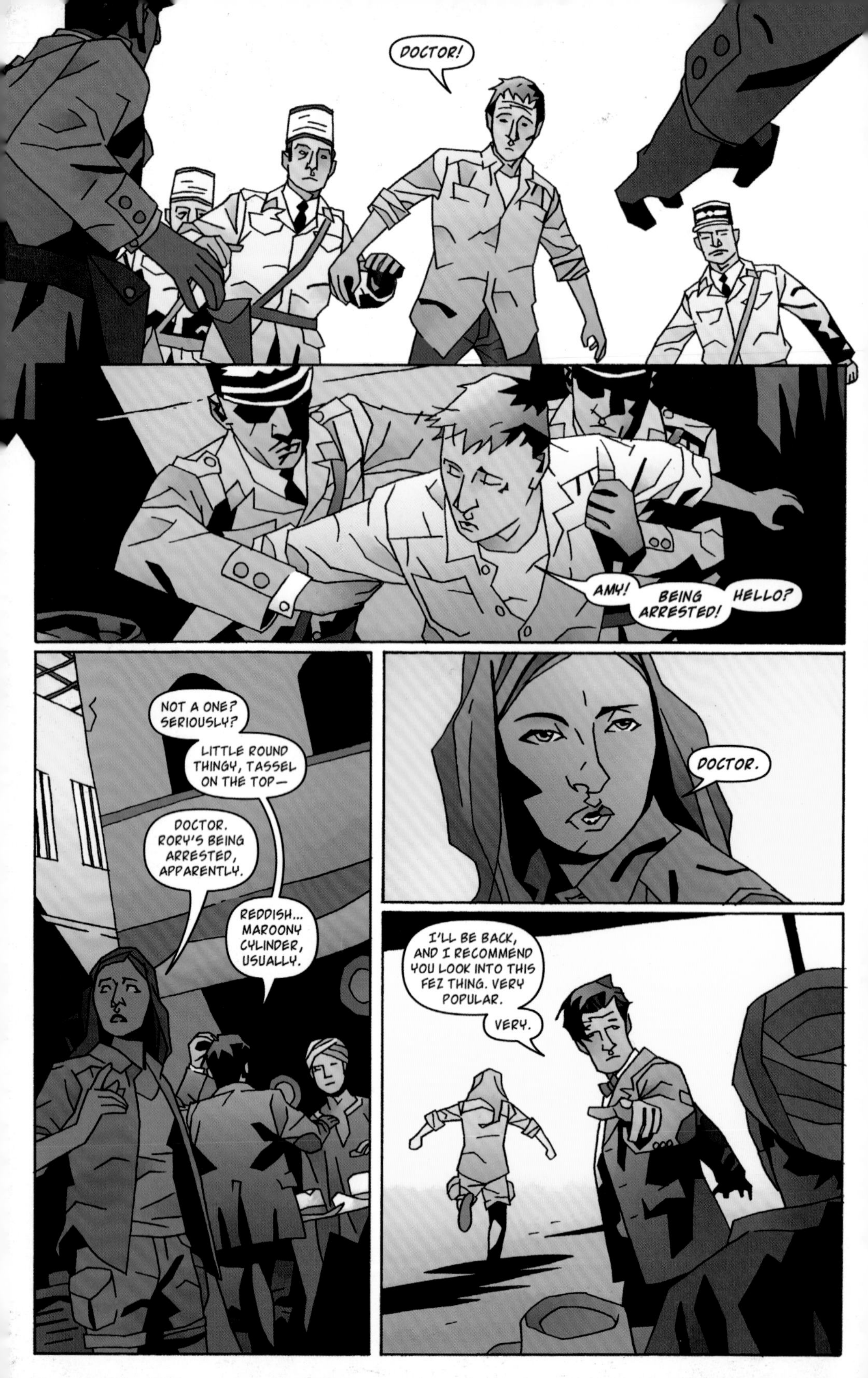
DOCTOR!
AMY!
BEING ARRESTED!
HELLO?
NOT A ONE? SERIOUSLY?
LITTLE ROUND THINGY, TASSEL ON THE TOP—
DOCTOR. RORY'S BEING ARRESTED, APPARENTLY.
REDDISH... MAROONY CYLINDER, USUALLY.
DOCTOR.
I'LL BE BACK, AND I RECOMMEND YOU LOOK INTO THIS FEZ THING. VERY POPULAR.
VERY.

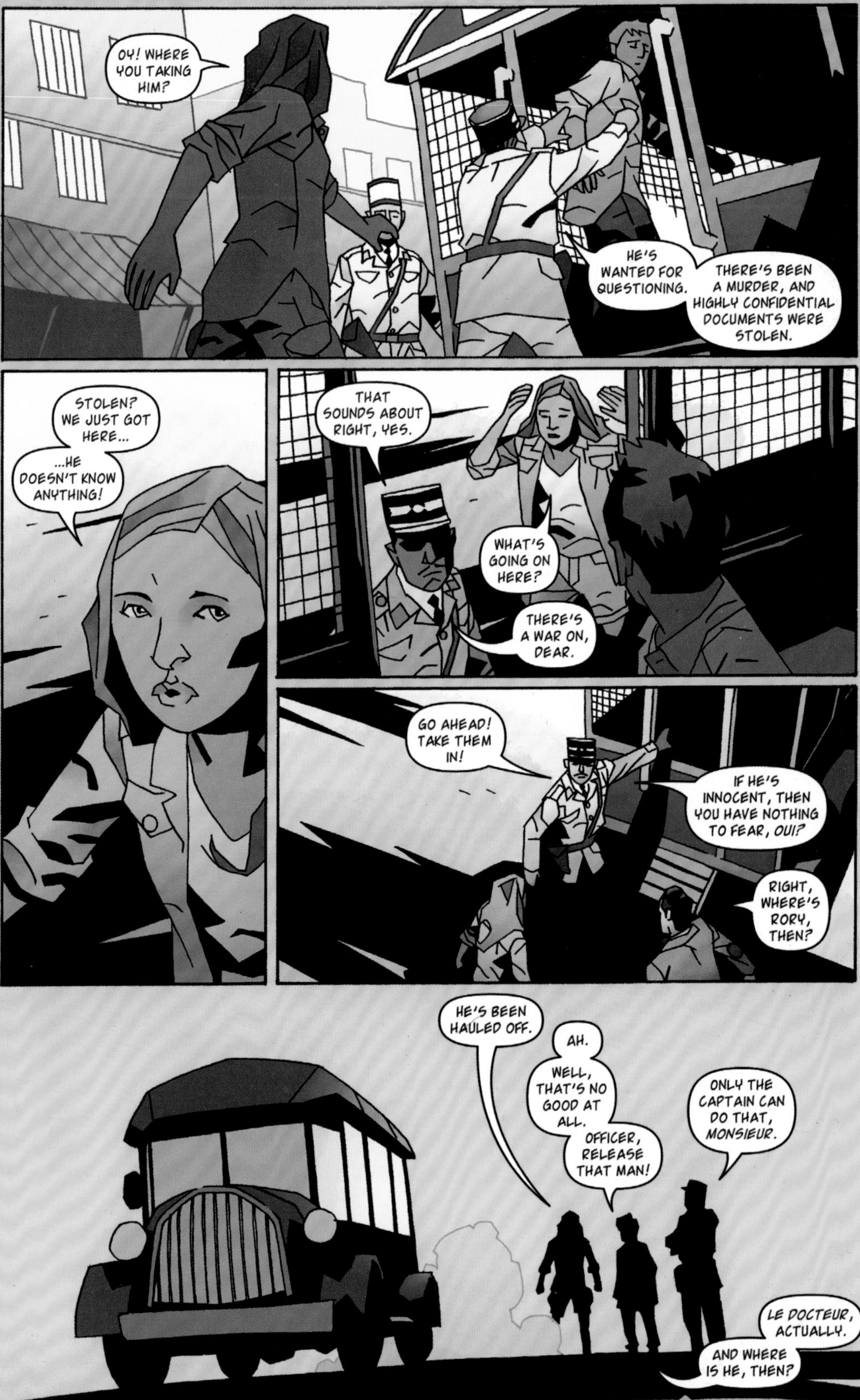
OY! WHERE YOU TAKING HIM?
HE'S WANTED FOR QUESTIONING.
THERE'S BEEN A MURDER, AND HIGHLY CONFIDENTIAL DOCUMENTS WERE STOLEN.
STOLEN? WE JUST GOT HERE...
...HE DOESN'T KNOW ANYTHING!
THAT SOUNDS ABOUT RIGHT, YES.
WHAT'S GOING ON HERE?
THERE'S A WAR ON, DEAR.
GO AHEAD! TAKE THEM IN!
IF HE'S INNOCENT, THEN YOU HAVE NOTHING TO FEAR, OUI?
RIGHT, WHERE'S RORY, THEN?
HE'S BEEN HAULED OFF.
AH.
WELL, THAT'S NO GOOD AT ALL.
OFFICER, RELEASE THAT MAN!
ONLY THE CAPTAIN CAN DO THAT, MONSIEUR.
LE DOCTEUR, ACTUALLY.
AND WHERE IS HE, THEN?

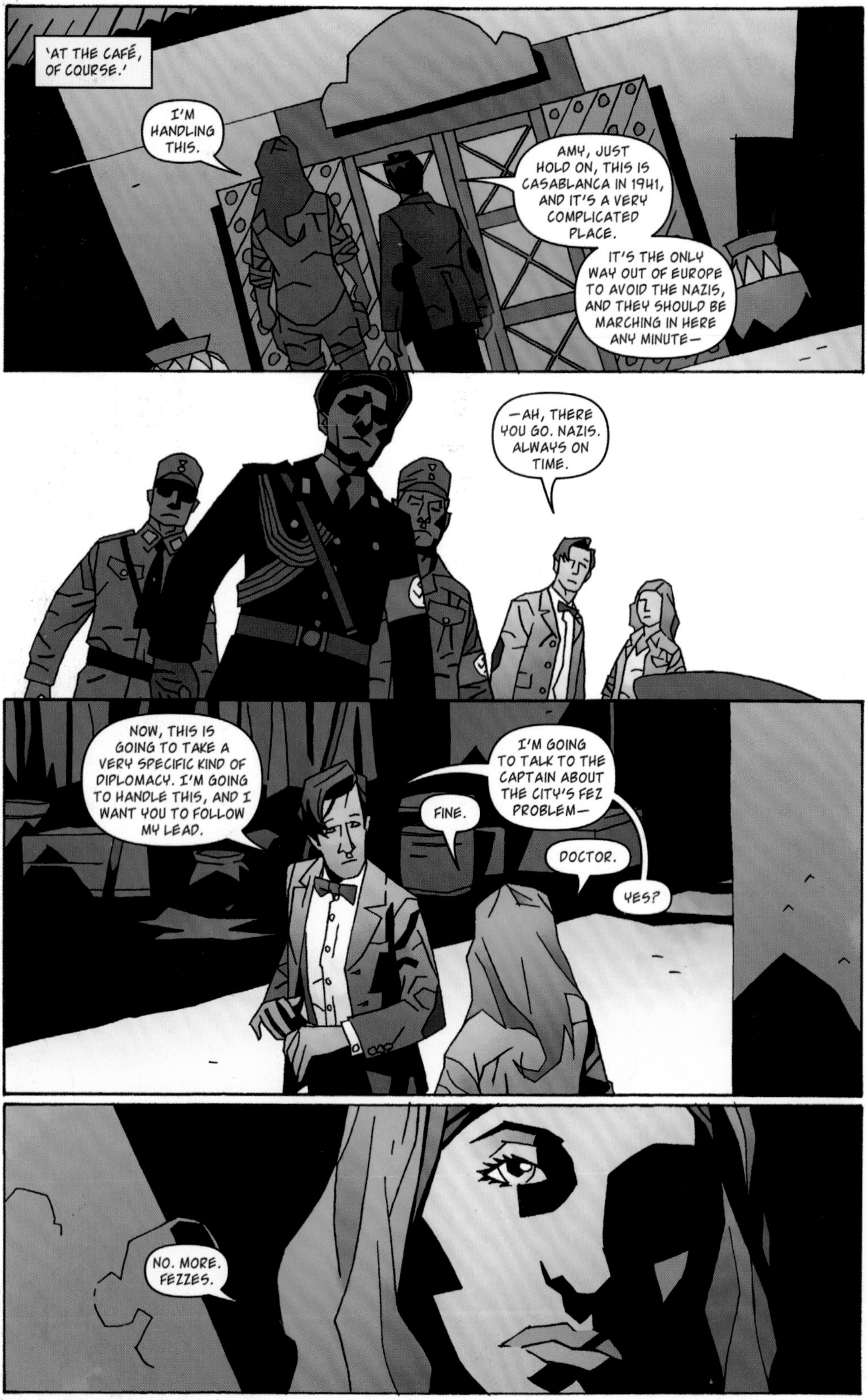
'AT THE CAFÉ, OF COURSE.'
I'M HANDLING THIS.
AMY, JUST HOLD ON, THIS IS CASABLANCA IN 1941, AND IT'S A VERY COMPLICATED PLACE.
IT'S THE ONLY WAY OUT OF EUROPE TO AVOID THE NAZIS, AND THEY SHOULD BE MARCHING IN HERE ANY MINUTE—
—AH, THERE YOU GO. NAZIS. ALWAYS ON TIME.
NOW, THIS IS GOING TO TAKE A VERY SPECIFIC KIND OF DIPLOMACY. I'M GOING TO HANDLE THIS, AND I WANT YOU TO FOLLOW MY LEAD.
FINE.
I'M GOING TO TALK TO THE CAPTAIN ABOUT THE CITY'S FEZ PROBLEM—
DOCTOR.
YES?
NO. MORE. FEZZES.

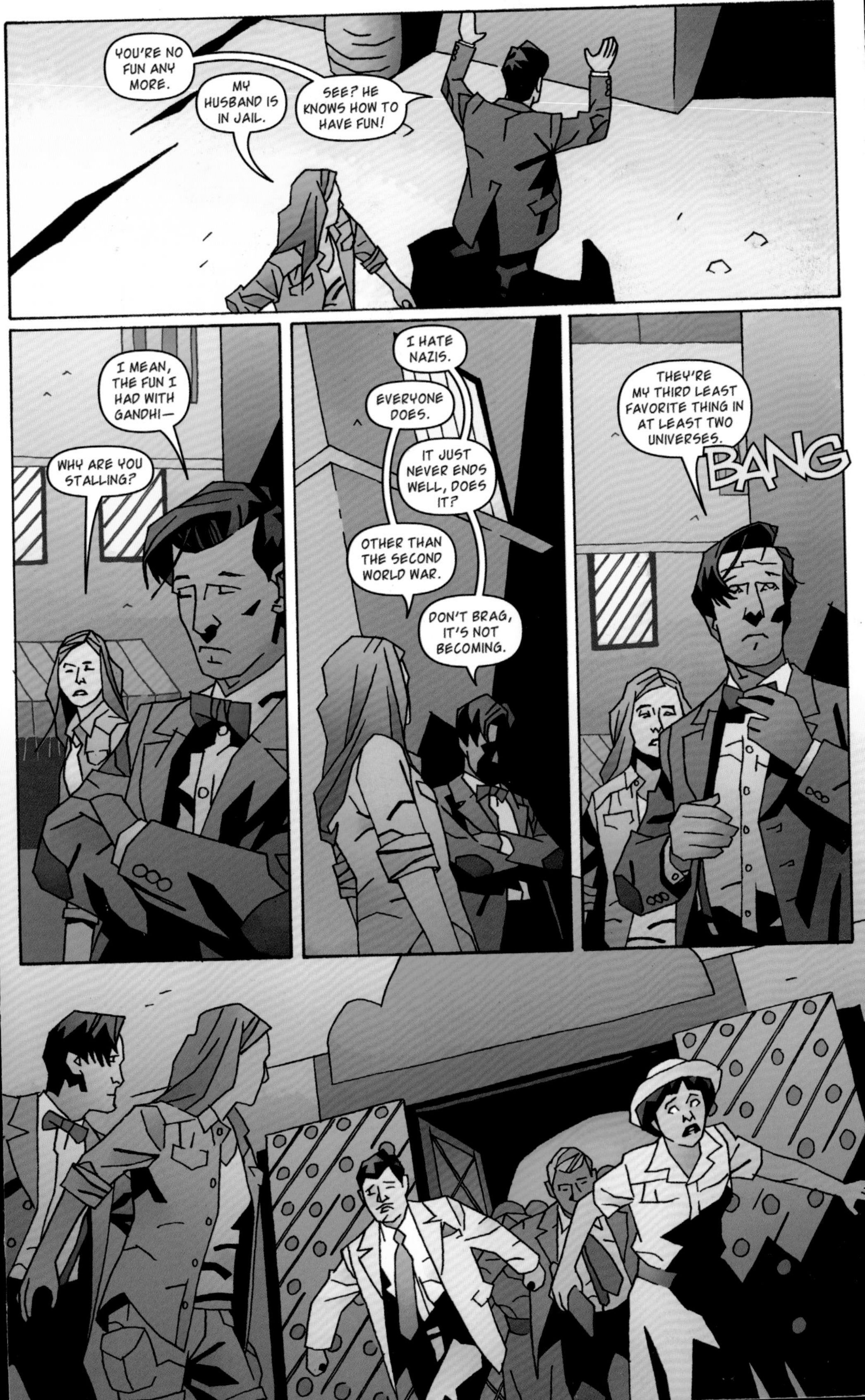

YOU'RE NO FUN ANY MORE.
SEE? HE KNOWS HOW TO HAVE FUN!
MY HUSBAND IS IN JAIL.
I MEAN, THE FUN I HAD WITH GANDHI—
WHY ARE YOU STALLING?
I HATE NAZIS.
EVERYONE DOES.
IT JUST NEVER ENDS WELL, DOES IT?
OTHER THAN THE SECOND WORLD WAR.
DON'T BRAG, IT'S NOT BECOMING.
THEY'RE MY THIRD LEAST FAVORITE THING IN AT LEAST TWO UNIVERSES.
BANG

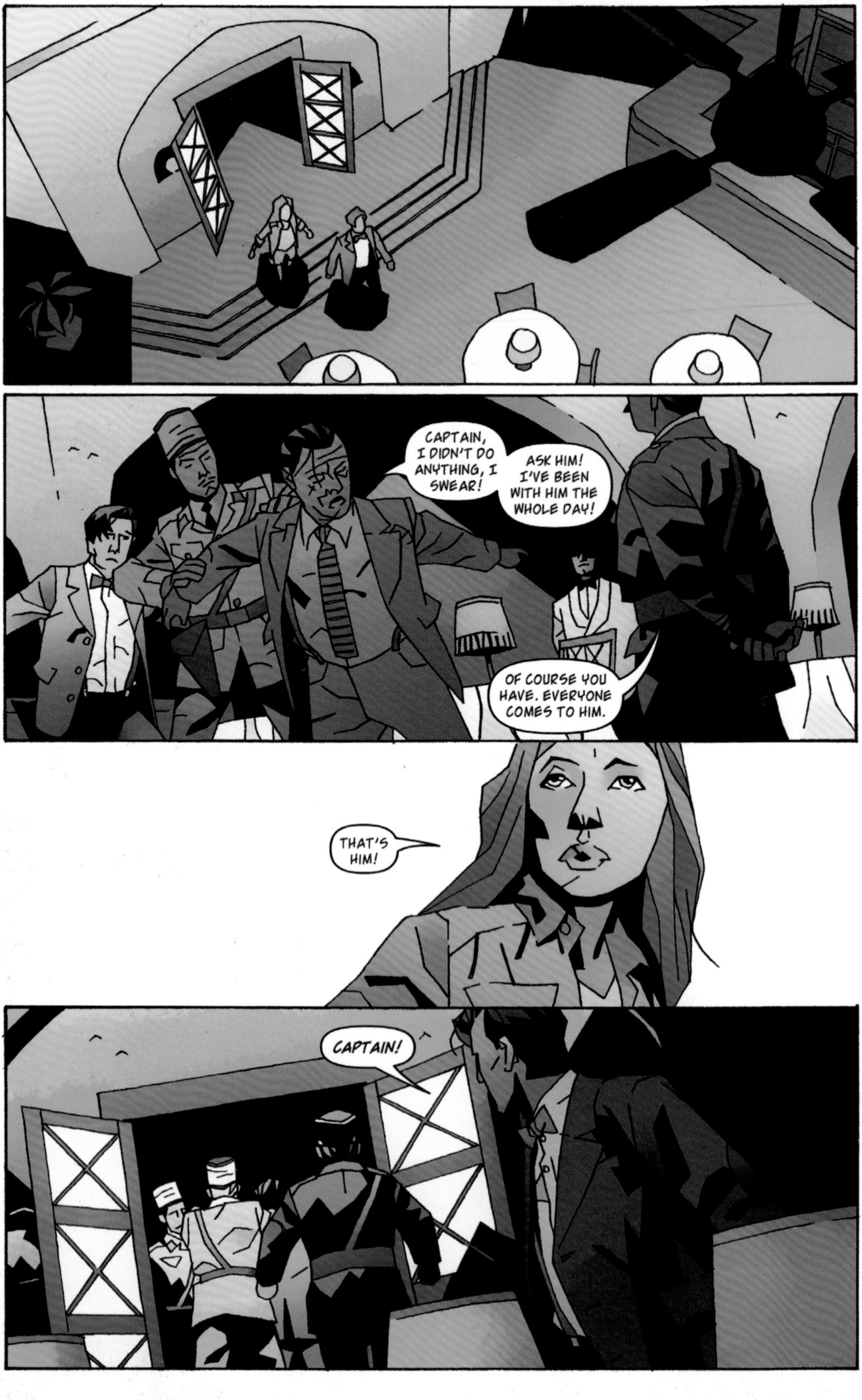
CAPTAIN, I DIDN'T DO ANYTHING, I SWEAR!
ASK HIM! I'VE BEEN WITH HIM THE WHOLE DAY!
OF COURSE YOU HAVE. EVERYONE COMES TO HIM.
THAT'S HIM!
CAPTAIN!

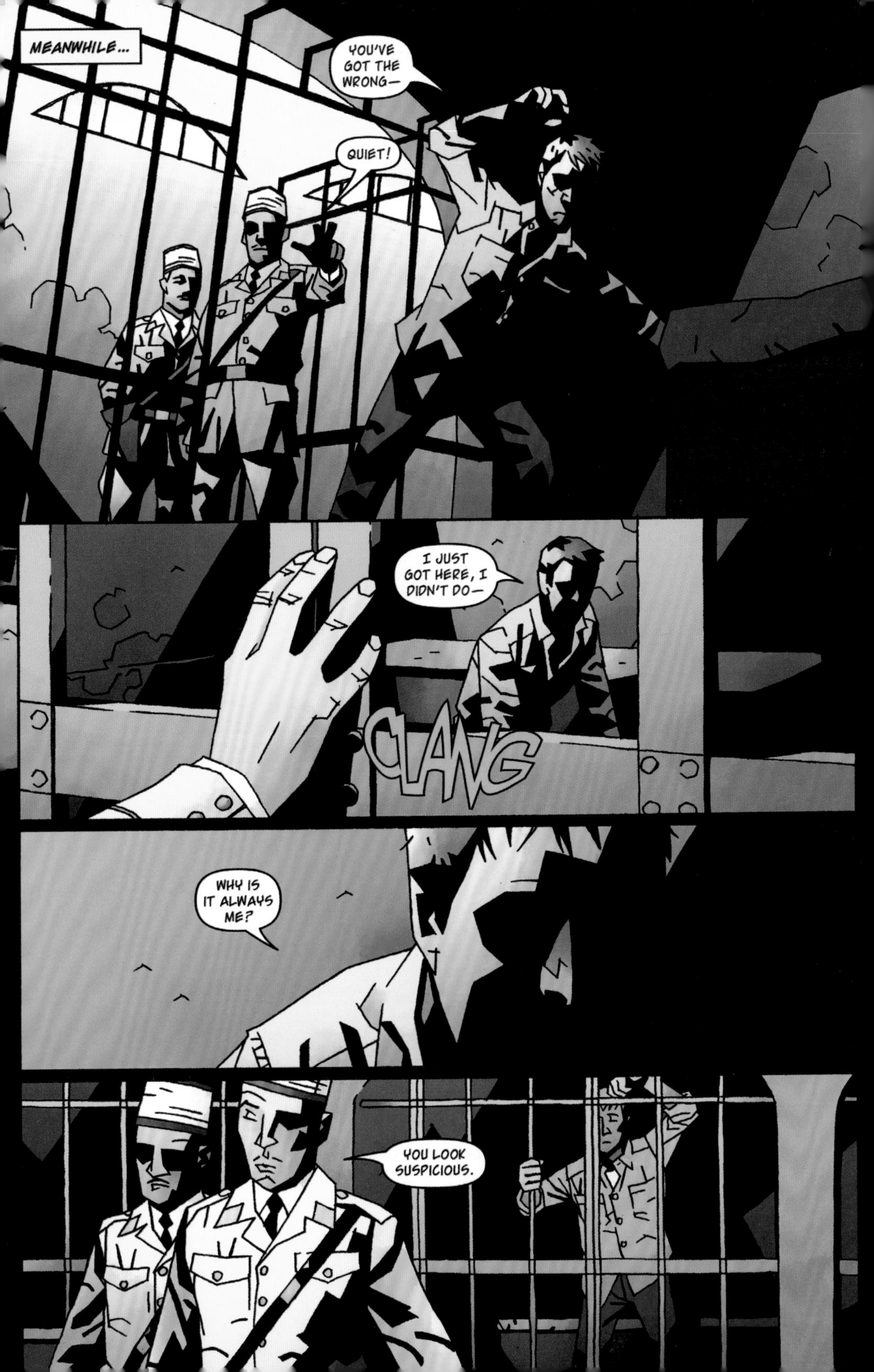
MEANWHILE...
YOU'VE GOT THE WRONG—
QUIET!
I JUST GOT HERE, I DIDN'T DO—
CLANG
WHY IS IT ALWAYS ME?
YOU LOOK SUSPICIOUS.

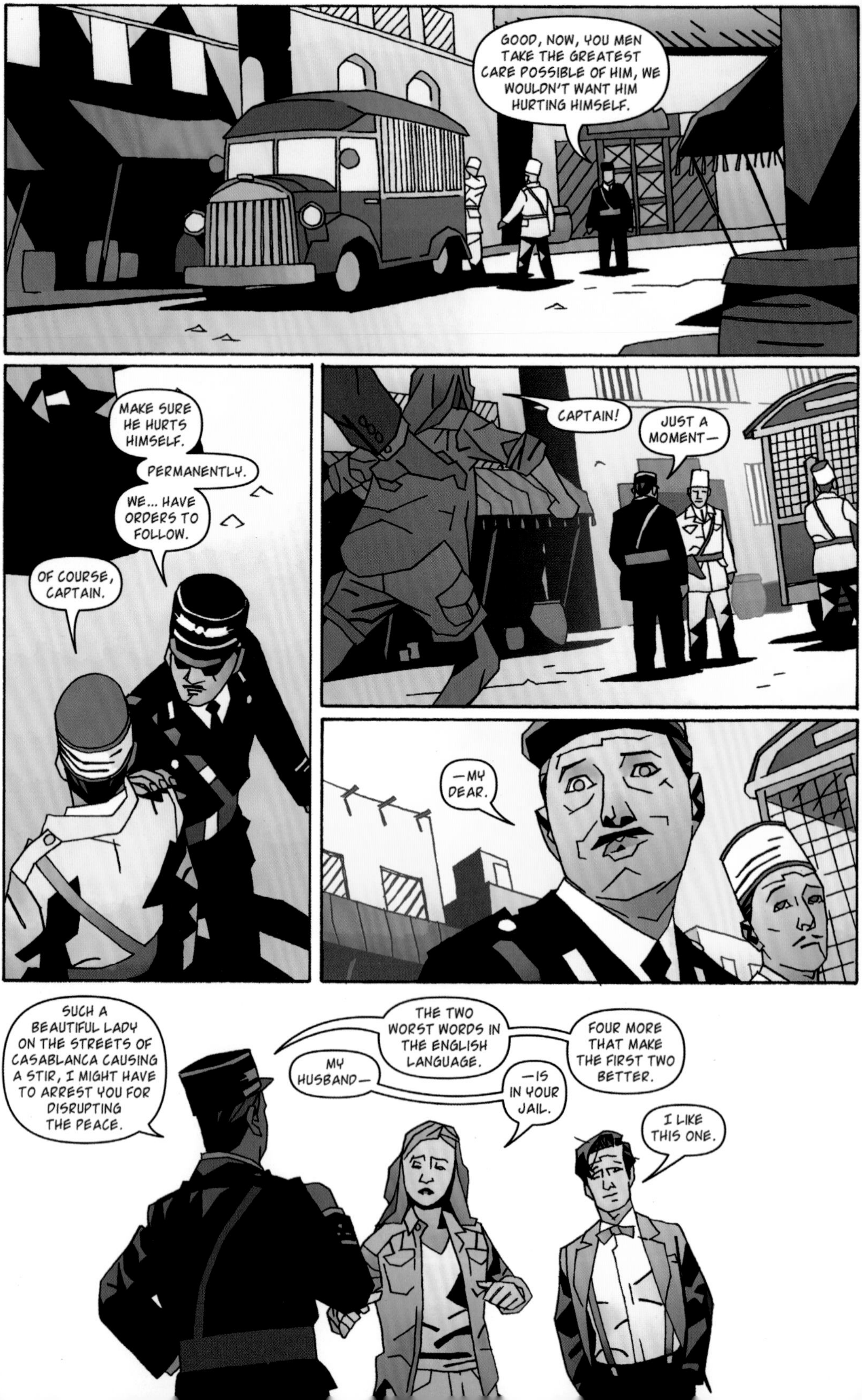
GOOD, NOW, YOU MEN TAKE THE GREATEST CARE POSSIBLE OF HIM, WE WOULDN'T WANT HIM HURTING HIMSELF.
MAKE SURE HE HURTS HIMSELF.
PERMANENTLY.
WE... HAVE ORDERS TO FOLLOW.
OF COURSE, CAPTAIN.
CAPTAIN!
JUST A MOMENT—
—MY DEAR.
SUCH A BEAUTIFUL LADY ON THE STREETS OF CASABLANCA CAUSING A STIR, I MIGHT HAVE TO ARREST YOU FOR DISRUPTING THE PEACE.
MY HUSBAND—
THE TWO WORST WORDS IN THE ENGLISH LANGUAGE.
—IS IN YOUR JAIL.
FOUR MORE THAT MAKE THE FIRST TWO BETTER.
I LIKE THIS ONE.

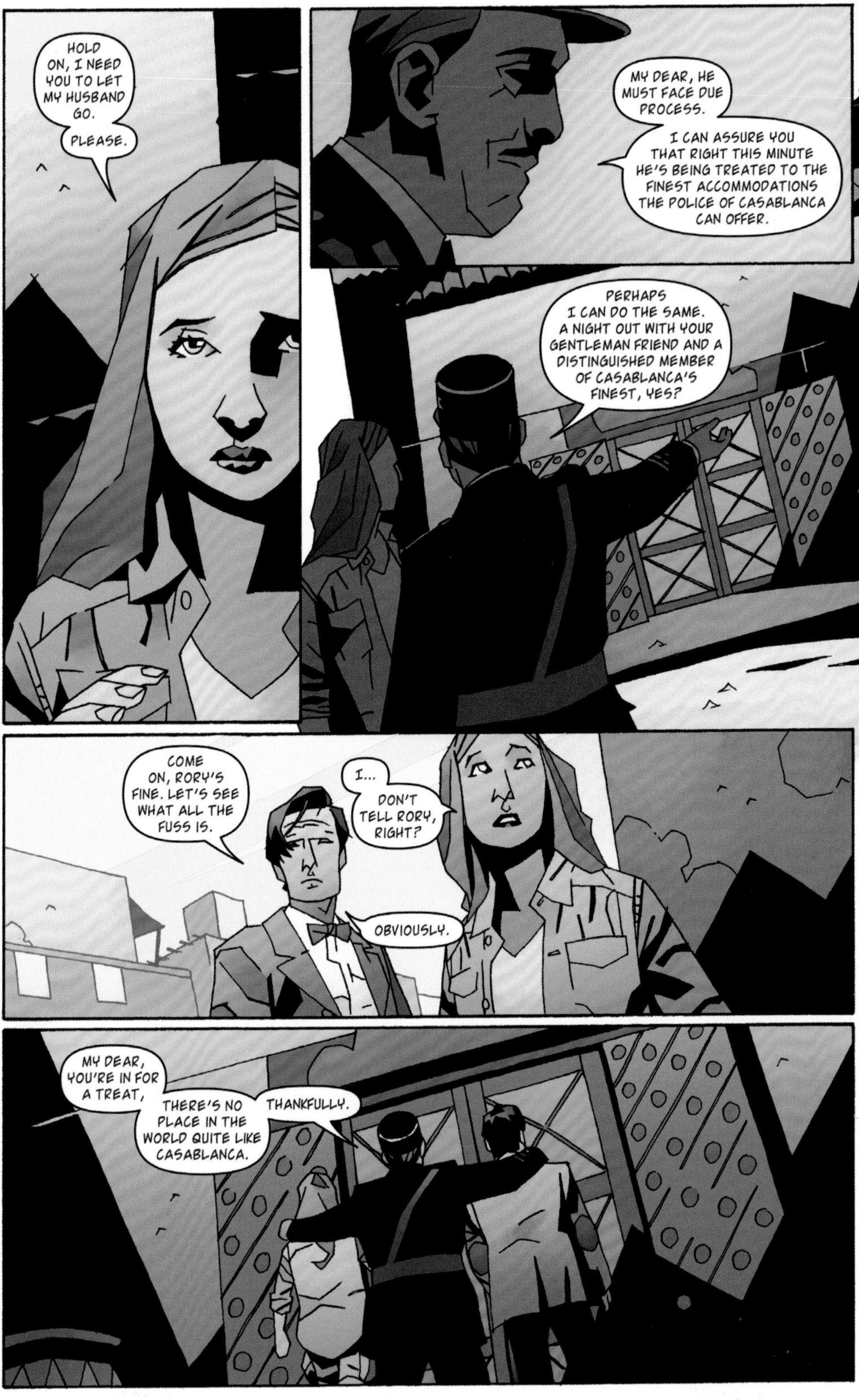
HOLD ON, I NEED YOU TO LET MY HUSBAND GO.
PLEASE.
MY DEAR, HE MUST FACE DUE PROCESS.
I CAN ASSURE YOU THAT RIGHT THIS MINUTE HE'S BEING TREATED TO THE FINEST ACCOMMODATIONS THE POLICE OF CASABLANCA CAN OFFER.
PERHAPS I CAN DO THE SAME. A NIGHT OUT WITH YOUR GENTLEMAN FRIEND AND A DISTINGUISHED MEMBER OF CASABLANCA'S FINEST, YES?
COME ON, RORY'S FINE. LET'S SEE WHAT ALL THE FUSS IS.
I...
DON'T TELL RORY, RIGHT?
OBVIOUSLY.
MY DEAR, YOU'RE IN FOR A TREAT,
THERE'S NO PLACE IN THE WORLD QUITE LIKE CASABLANCA.
THANKFULLY.

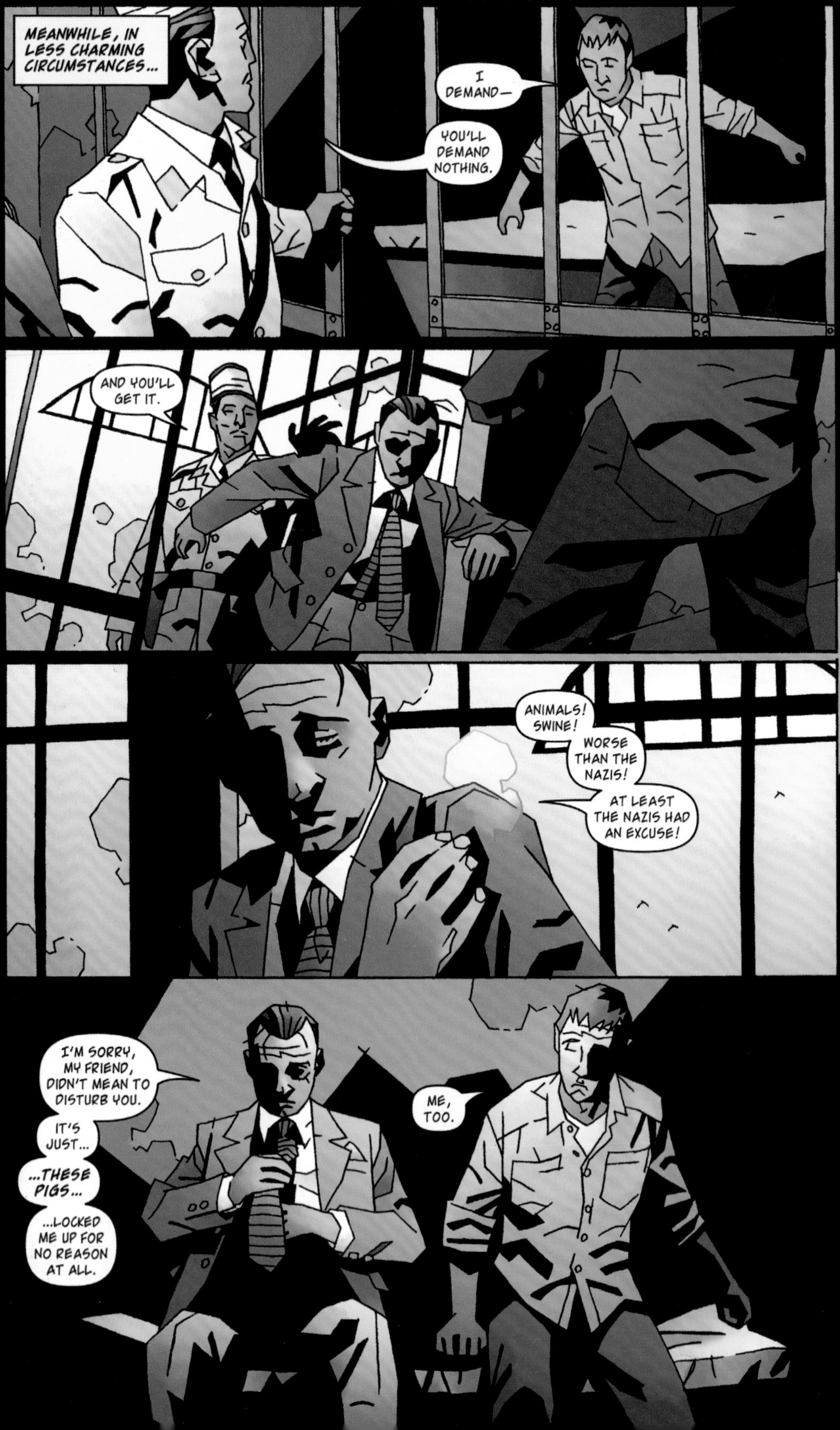
MEANWHILE, IN LESS CHARMING CIRCUMSTANCES...
I DEMAND—
YOU'LL DEMAND NOTHING.
AND YOU'LL GET IT.
ANIMALS! SWINE!
WORSE THAN THE NAZIS!
AT LEAST THE NAZIS HAD AN EXCUSE!
I'M SORRY, MY FRIEND, DIDN'T MEAN TO DISTURB YOU.
IT'S JUST...
...THESE PIGS...
...LOCKED ME UP FOR NO REASON AT ALL.
ME, TOO.

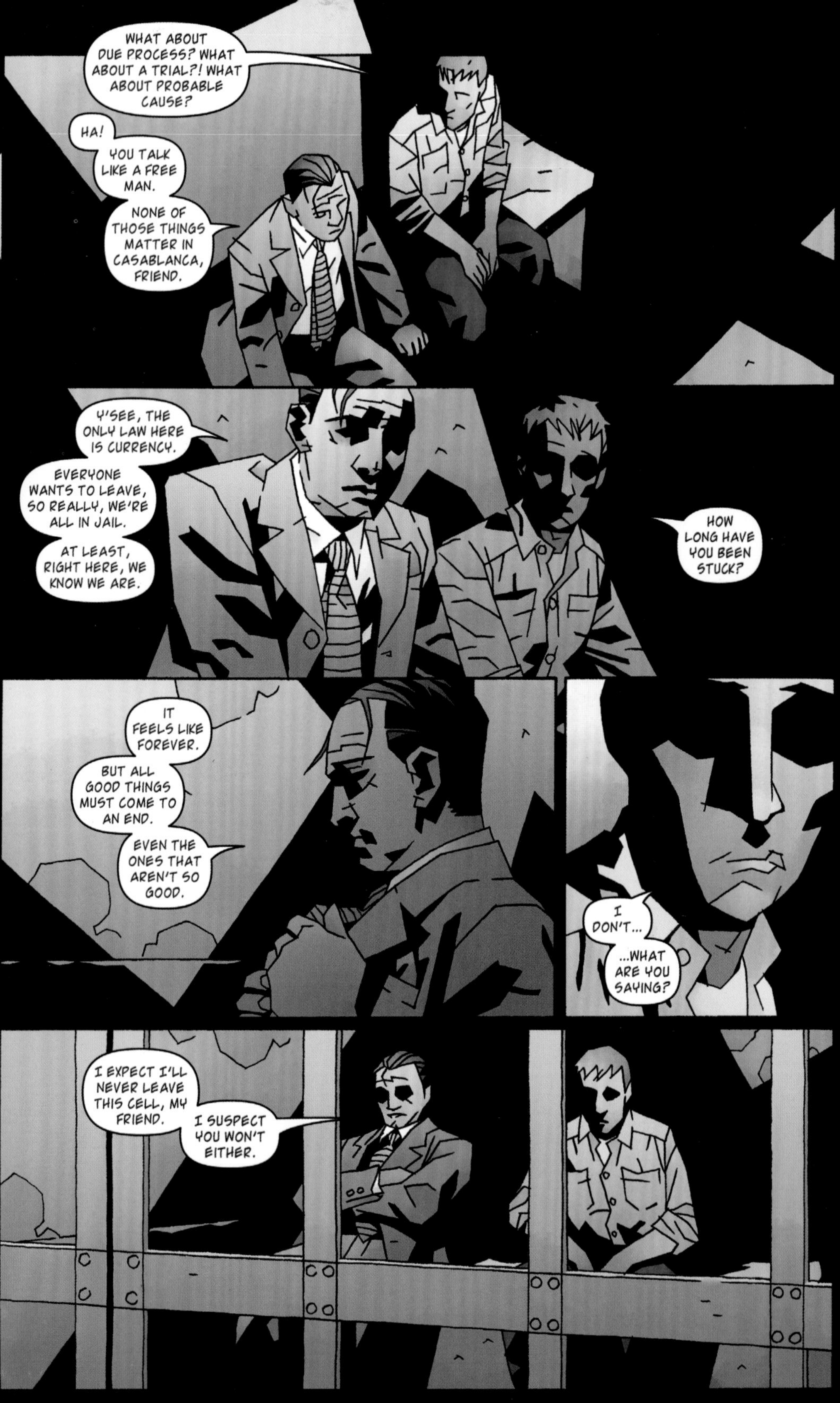
WHAT ABOUT DUE PROCESS? WHAT ABOUT A TRIAL?! WHAT ABOUT PROBABLE CAUSE?
HA!
YOU TALK LIKE A FREE MAN.
NONE OF THOSE THINGS MATTER IN CASABLANCA, FRIEND.
Y'SEE, THE ONLY LAW HERE IS CURRENCY.
EVERYONE WANTS TO LEAVE, SO REALLY, WE'RE ALL IN JAIL.
AT LEAST, RIGHT HERE, WE KNOW WE ARE.
HOW LONG HAVE YOU BEEN STUCK?
IT FEELS LIKE FOREVER.
BUT ALL GOOD THINGS MUST COME TO AN END.
EVEN THE ONES THAT AREN'T SO GOOD.
I DON'T...
...WHAT ARE YOU SAYING?
I EXPECT I'LL NEVER LEAVE THIS CELL, MY FRIEND.
I SUSPECT YOU WON'T EITHER.

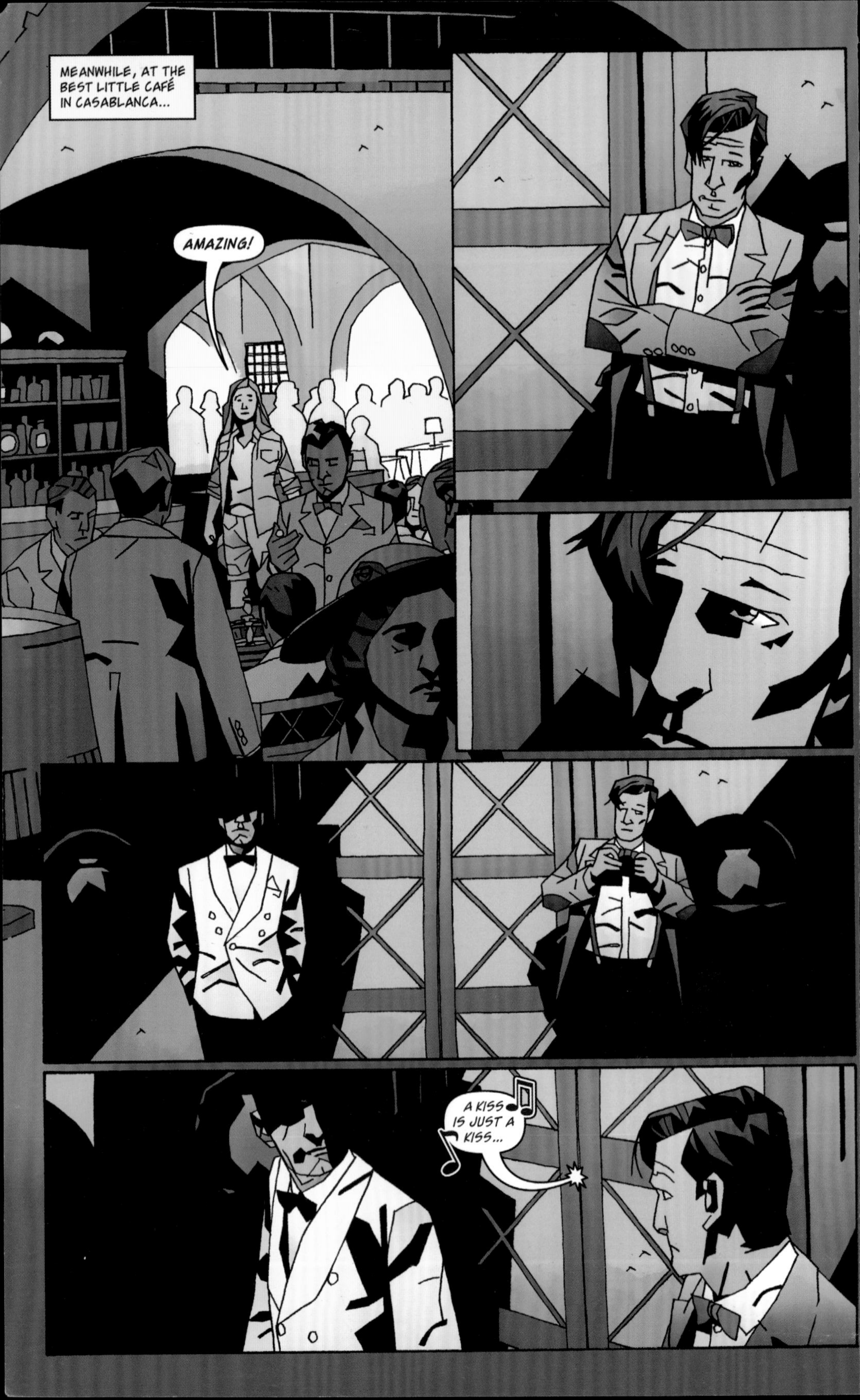
MEANWHILE, AT THE BEST LITTLE CAFÉ IN CASABLANCA...
AMAZING!
A KISS IS JUST A KISS...

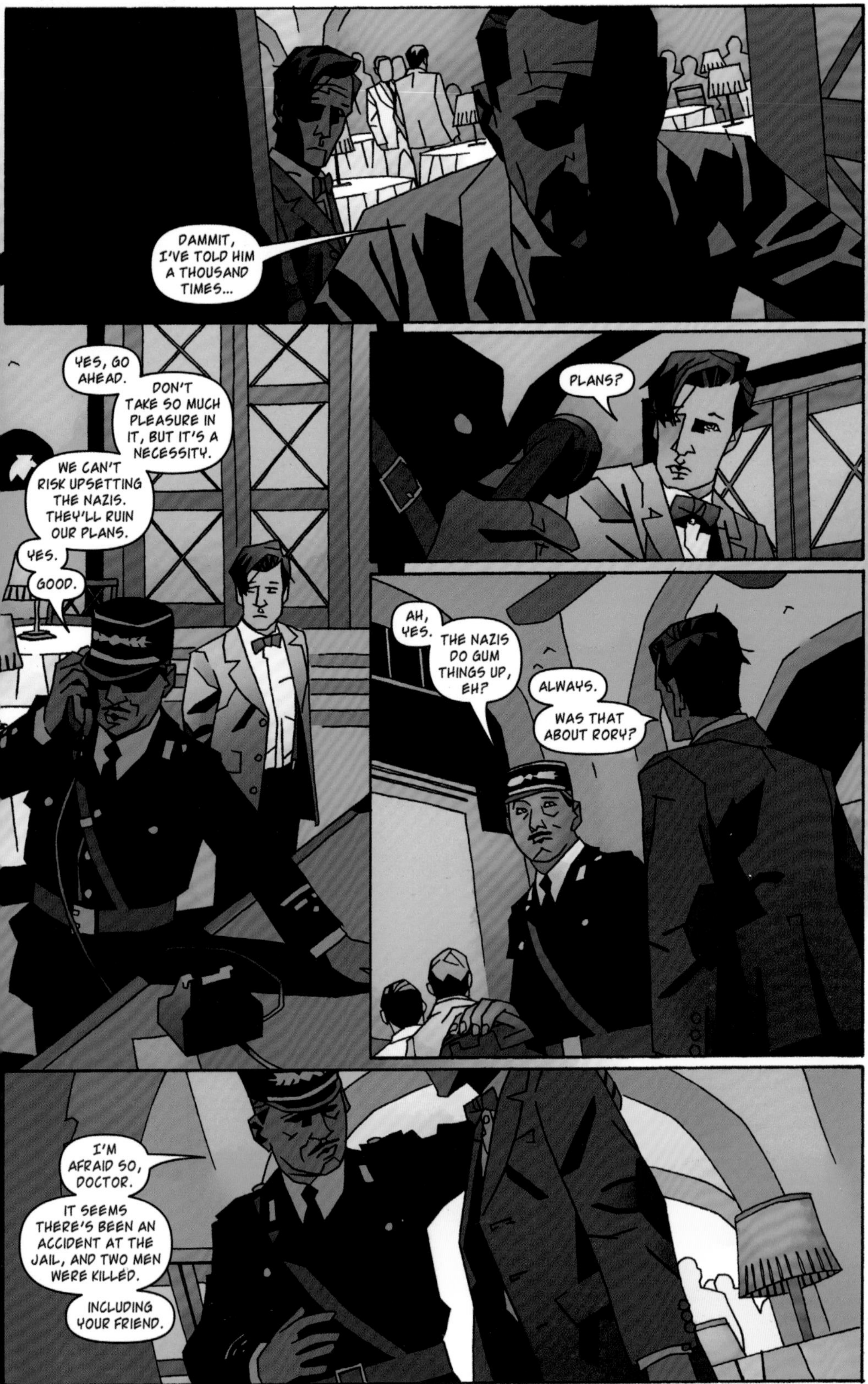
DAMMIT, I'VE TOLD HIM A THOUSAND TIMES...
YES, GO AHEAD.
DON'T TAKE SO MUCH PLEASURE IN IT, BUT IT'S A NECESSITY.
WE CAN'T RISK UPSETTING THE NAZIS. THEY'LL RUIN OUR PLANS.
YES.
GOOD.
PLANS?
AH, YES.
THE NAZIS DO GUM THINGS UP, EH?
ALWAYS.
WAS THAT ABOUT RORY?
I'M AFRAID SO, DOCTOR.
IT SEEMS THERE'S BEEN AN ACCIDENT AT THE JAIL, AND TWO MEN WERE KILLED.
INCLUDING YOUR FRIEND.

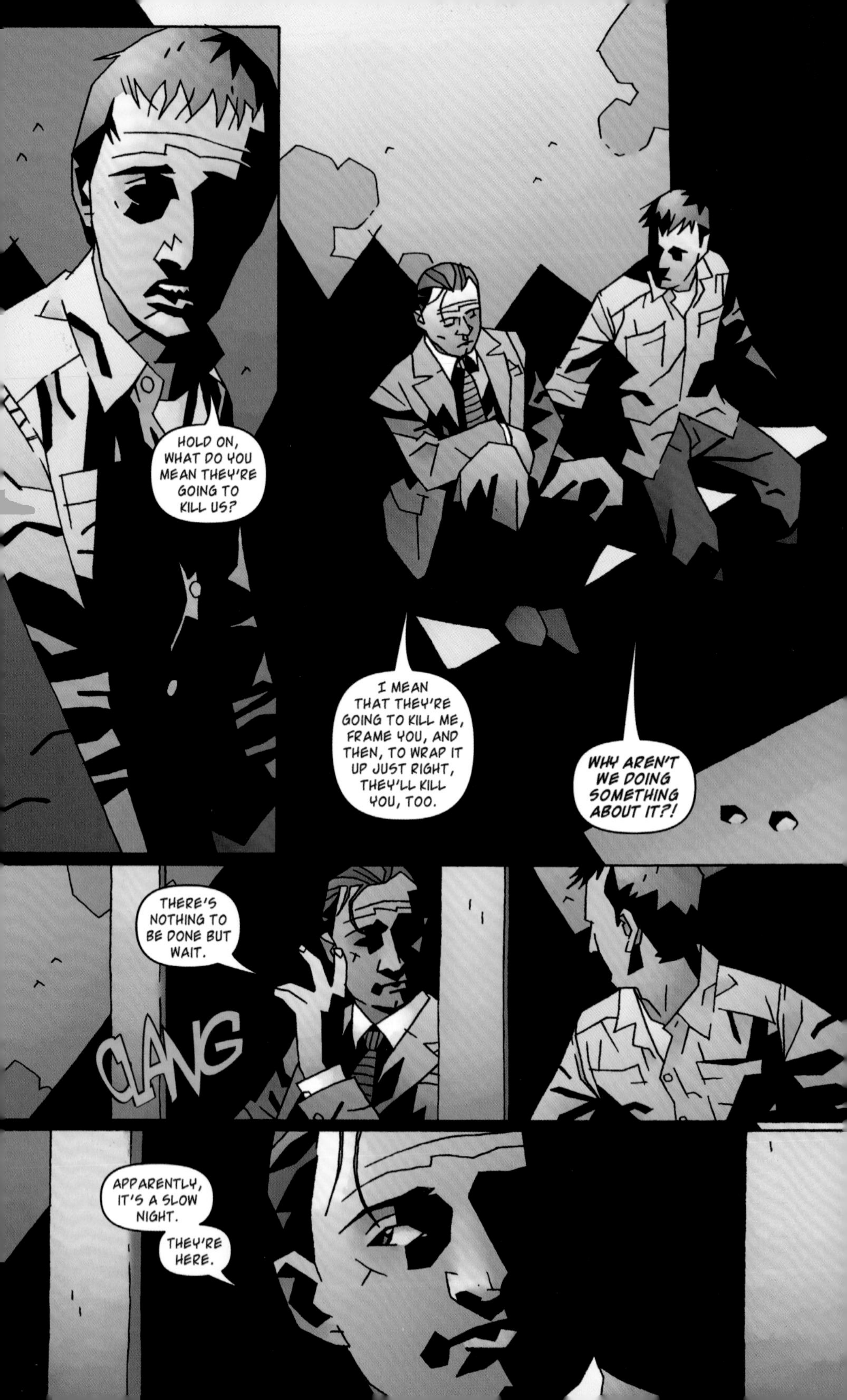
HOLD ON, WHAT DO YOU MEAN THEY'RE GOING TO KILL US?
I MEAN THAT THEY'RE GOING TO KILL ME, FRAME YOU, AND THEN, TO WRAP IT UP JUST RIGHT, THEY'LL KILL YOU, TOO.
WHY AREN'T WE DOING SOMETHING ABOUT IT?!
THERE'S NOTHING TO BE DONE BUT WAIT.
CLANG
APPARENTLY, IT'S A SLOW NIGHT.
THEY'RE HERE.

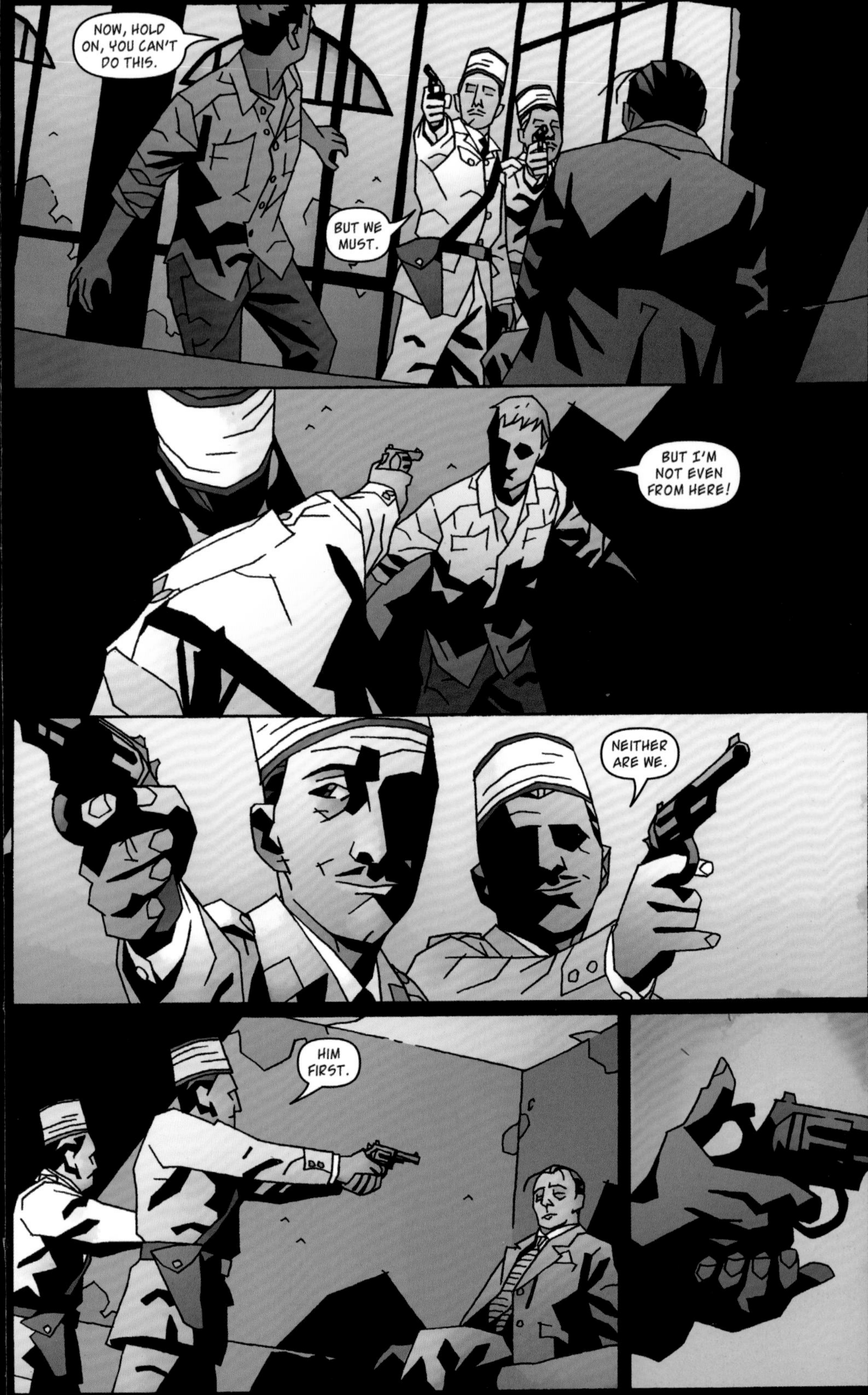
NOW, HOLD ON, YOU CAN'T DO THIS.
BUT WE MUST.
BUT I'M NOT EVEN FROM HERE!
NEITHER ARE WE.
HIM FIRST.

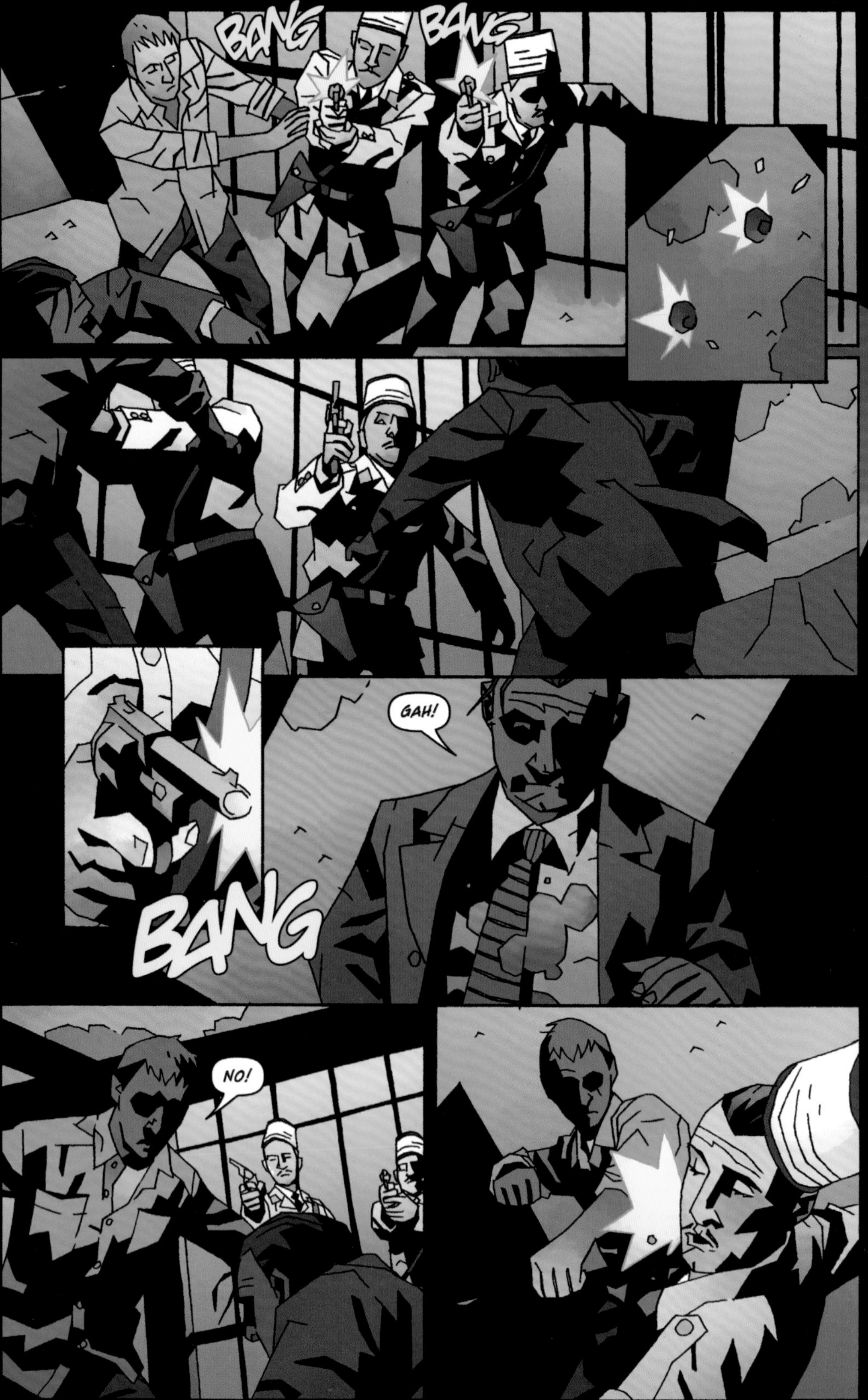
BANG
BANG
GAH!
BANG
NO!

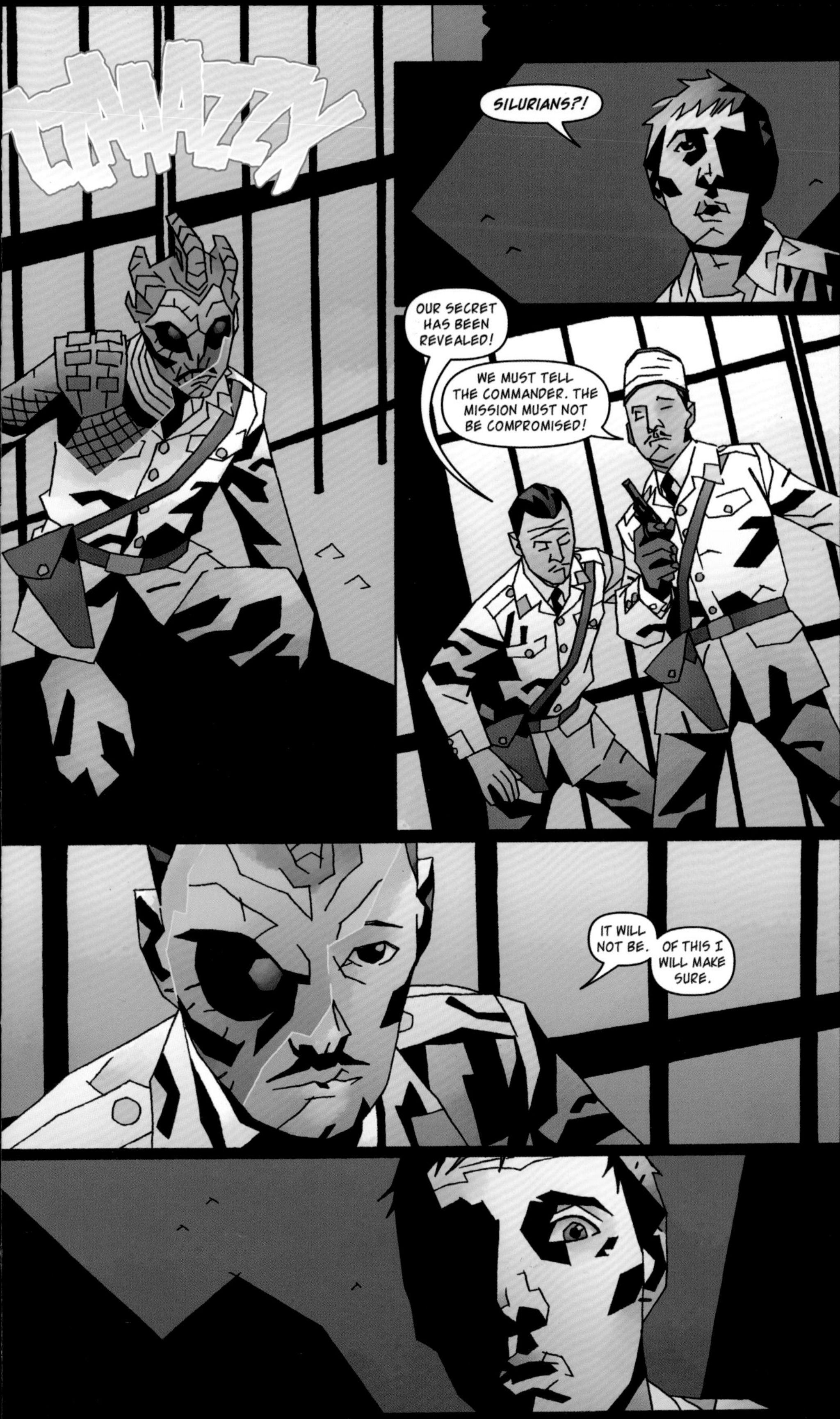
SILURIANS?!
OUR SECRET HAS BEEN REVEALED!
WE MUST TELL THE COMMANDER. THE MISSION MUST NOT BE COMPROMISED!
IT WILL NOT BE.
OF THIS I WILL MAKE SURE.

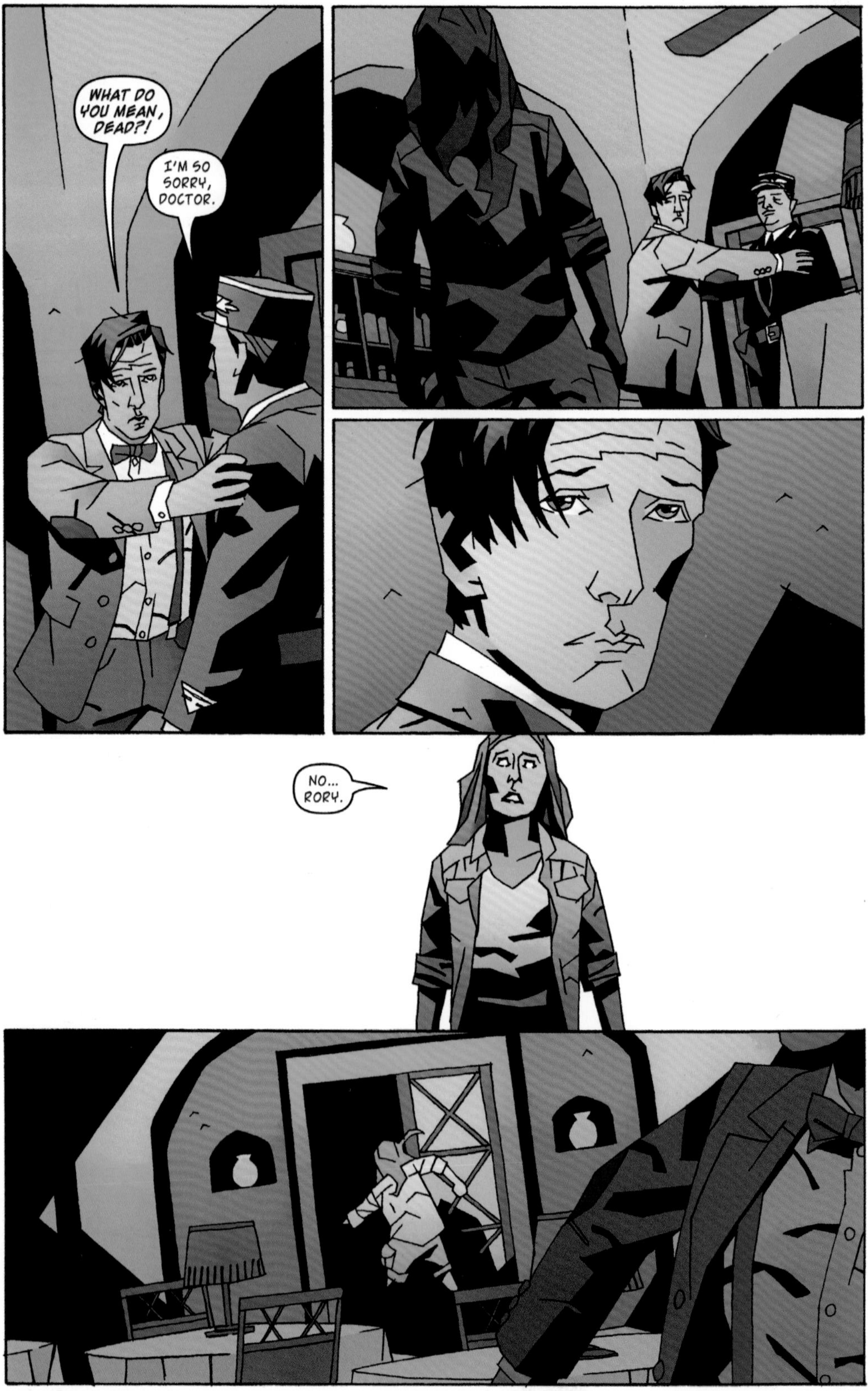
WHAT DO YOU MEAN, DEAD?!
I'M SO SORRY, DOCTOR.
NO... RORY.

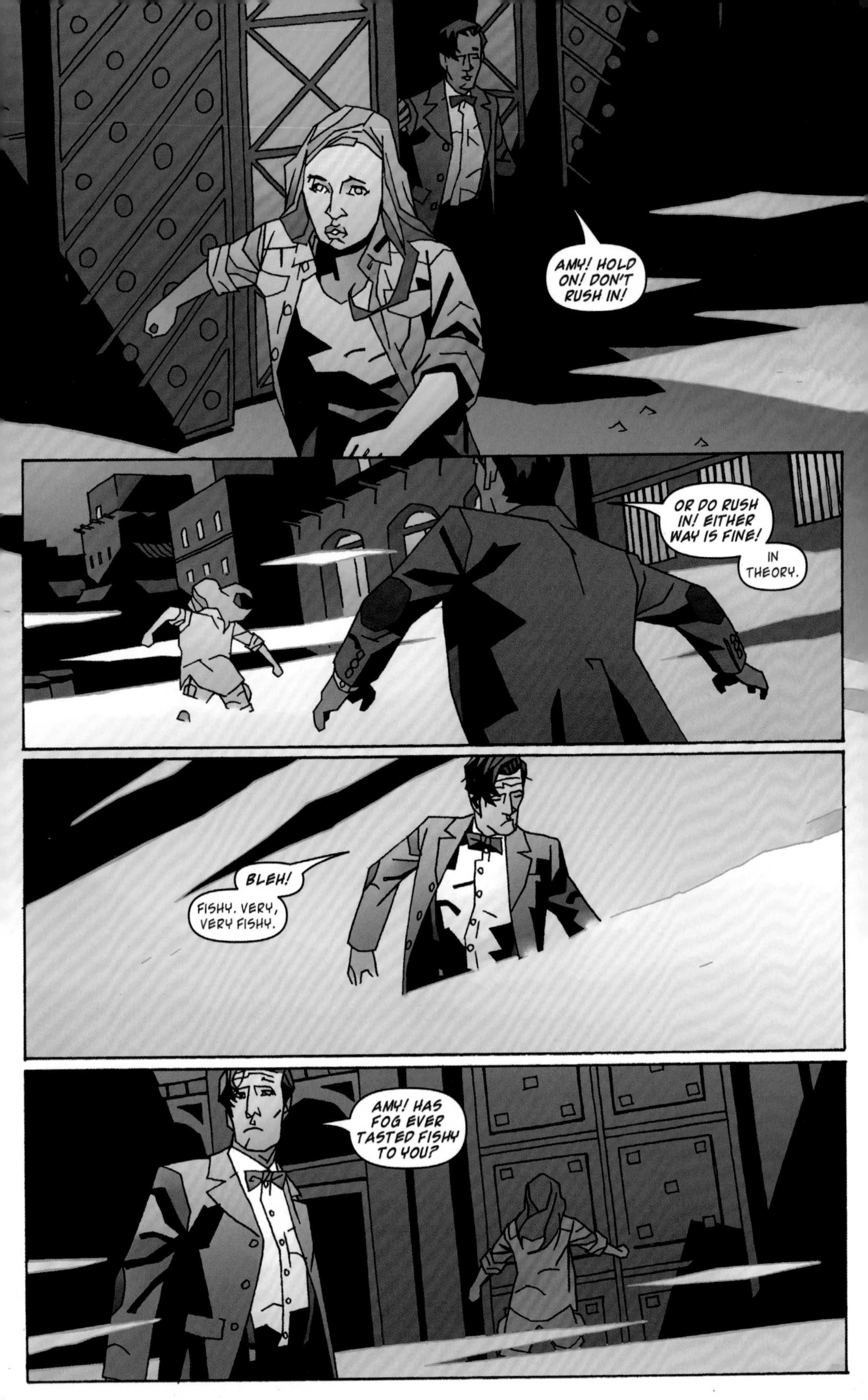
AMY! HOLD ON! DON'T RUSH IN!
OR DO RUSH IN! EITHER WAY IS FINE!
IN THEORY.
BLEH!
FISHY. VERY, VERY FISHY.
AMY! HAS FOG EVER TASTED FISHY TO YOU?

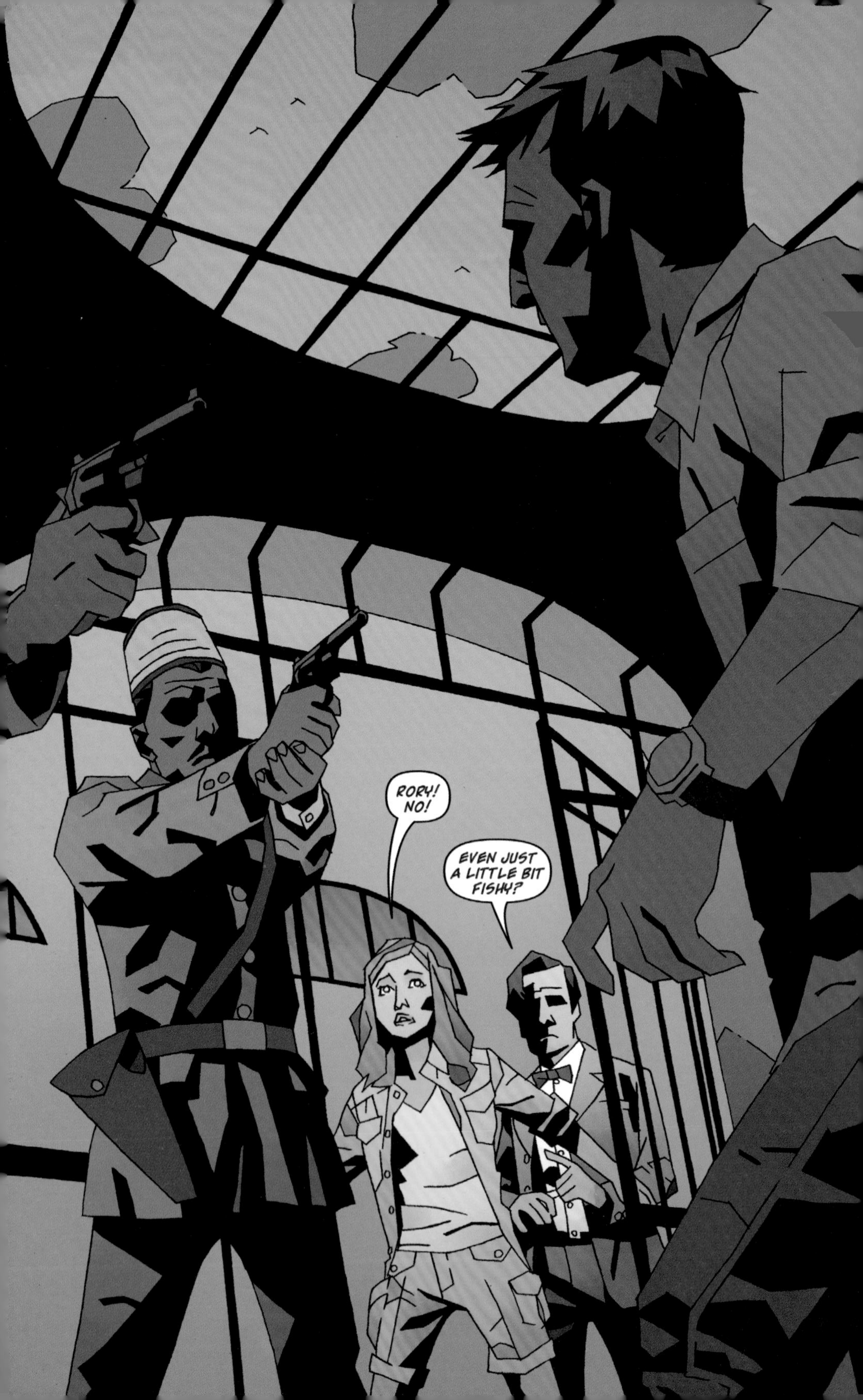
RORY! NO!
EVEN JUST A LITTLE BIT FISHY?

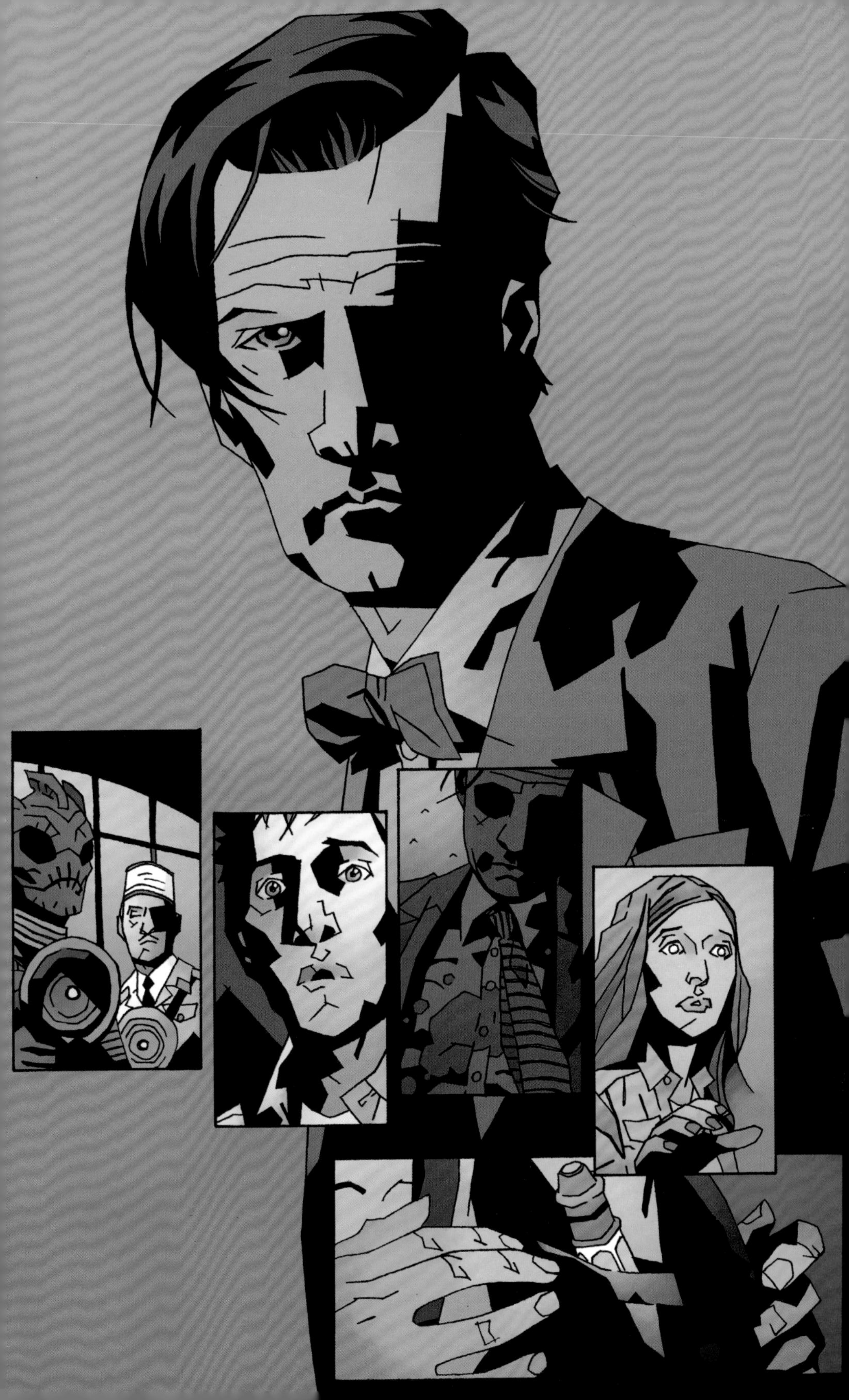

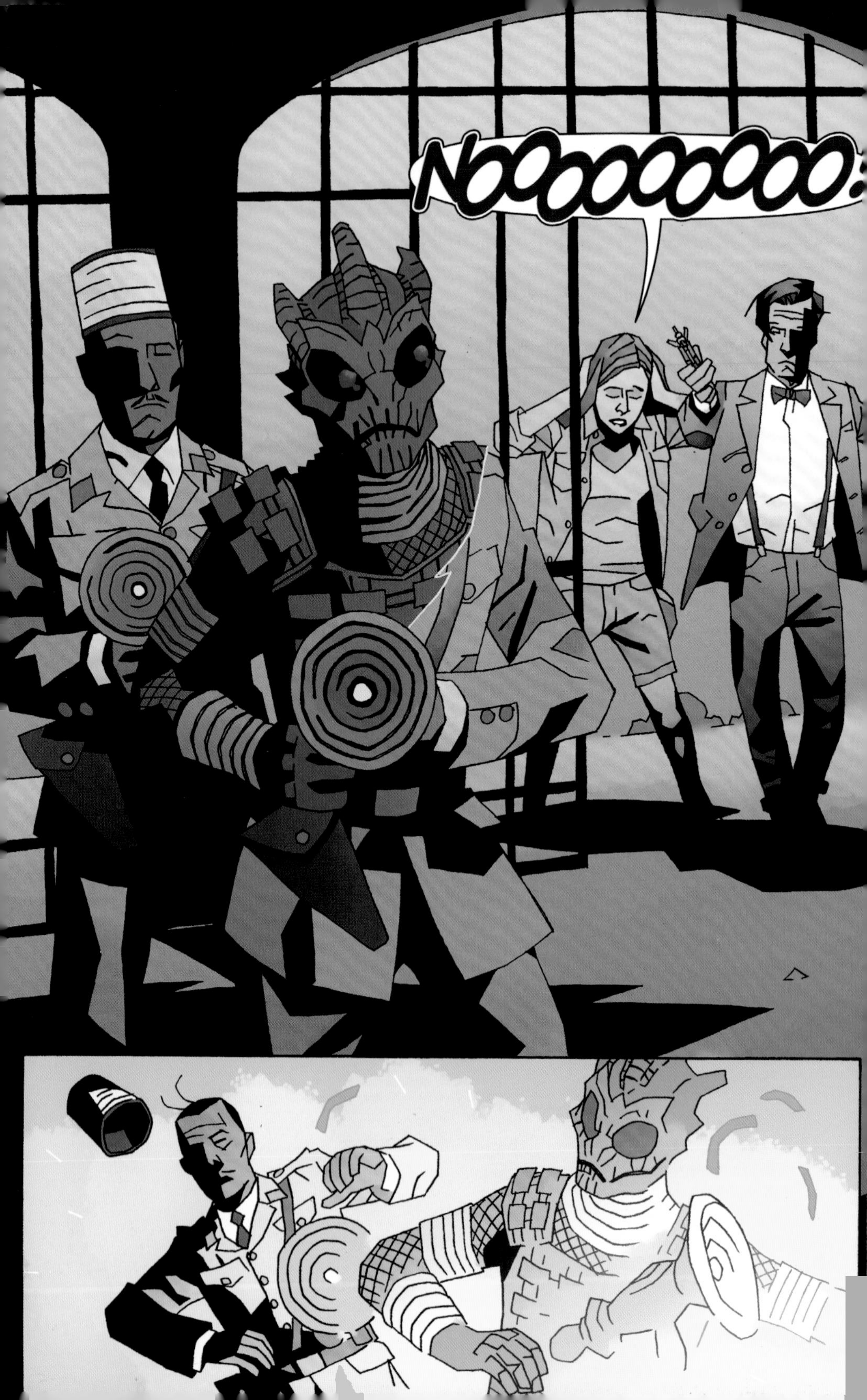
NOOOOOOOOOO!

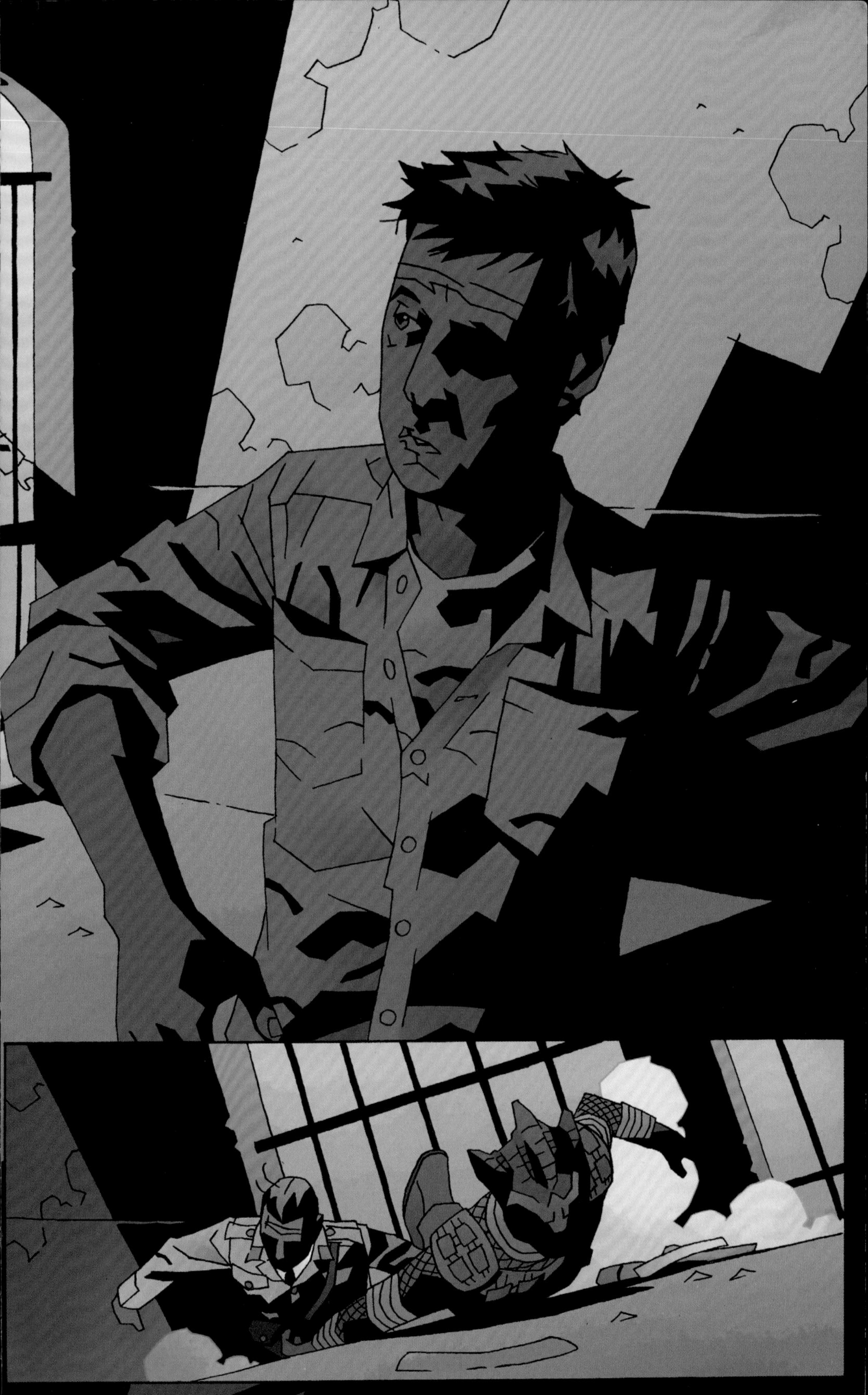

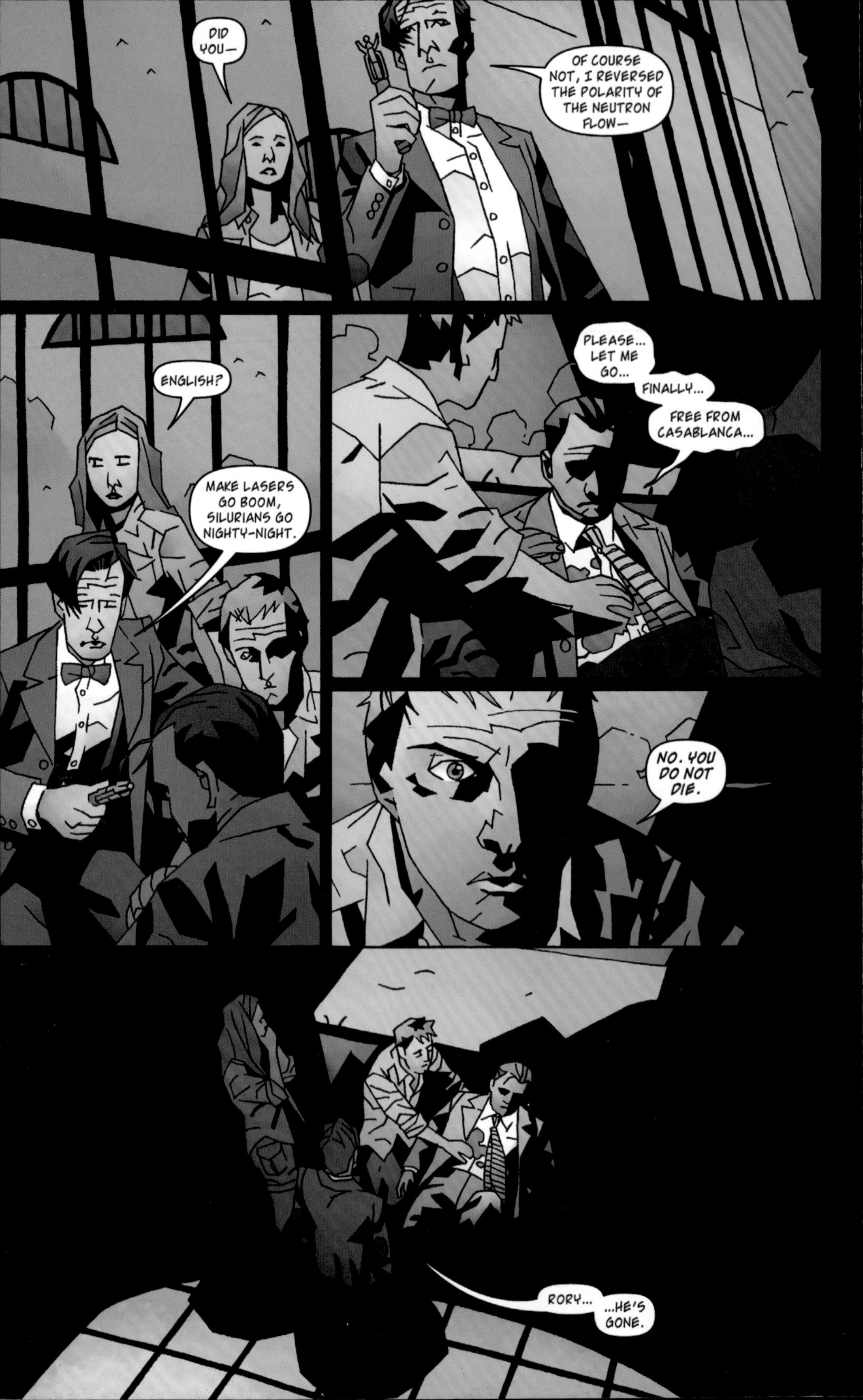

DID YOU—
OF COURSE NOT, I REVERSED THE POLARITY OF THE NEUTRON FLOW—
ENGLISH?
MAKE LASERS GO BOOM, SILURIANS GO NIGHTY-NIGHT.
PLEASE... LET ME GO...
FINALLY...
FREE FROM CASABLANCA...
NO. YOU DO NOT DIE.
RORY...
...HE'S GONE.

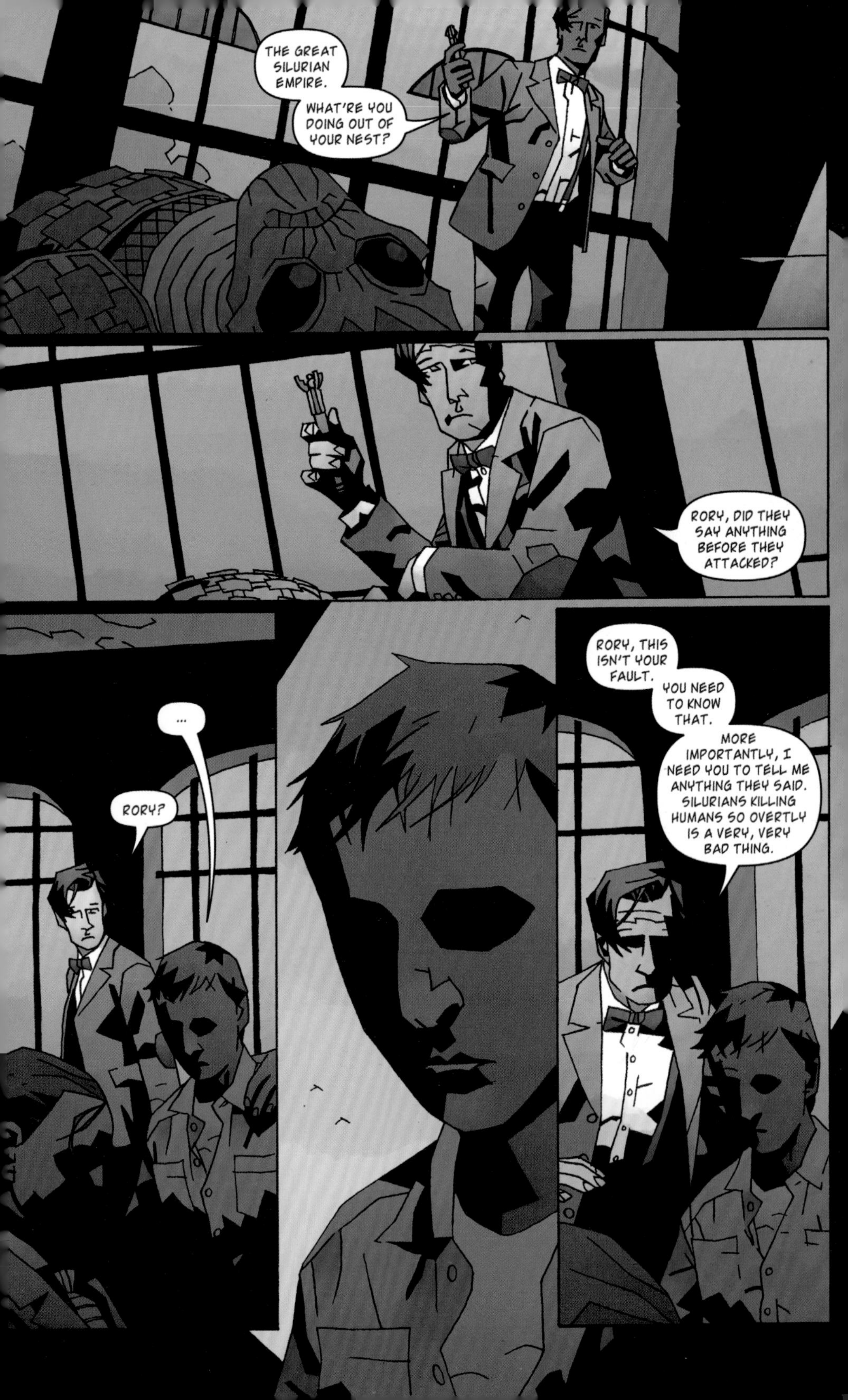
THE GREAT SILURIAN EMPIRE.
WHAT'RE YOU DOING OUT OF YOUR NEST?
RORY, DID THEY SAY ANYTHING BEFORE THEY ATTACKED?
...
RORY?
RORY, THIS ISN'T YOUR FAULT.
YOU NEED TO KNOW THAT.
MORE IMPORTANTLY, I NEED YOU TO TELL ME ANYTHING THEY SAID. SILURIANS KILLING HUMANS SO OVERTLY IS A VERY, VERY BAD THING.

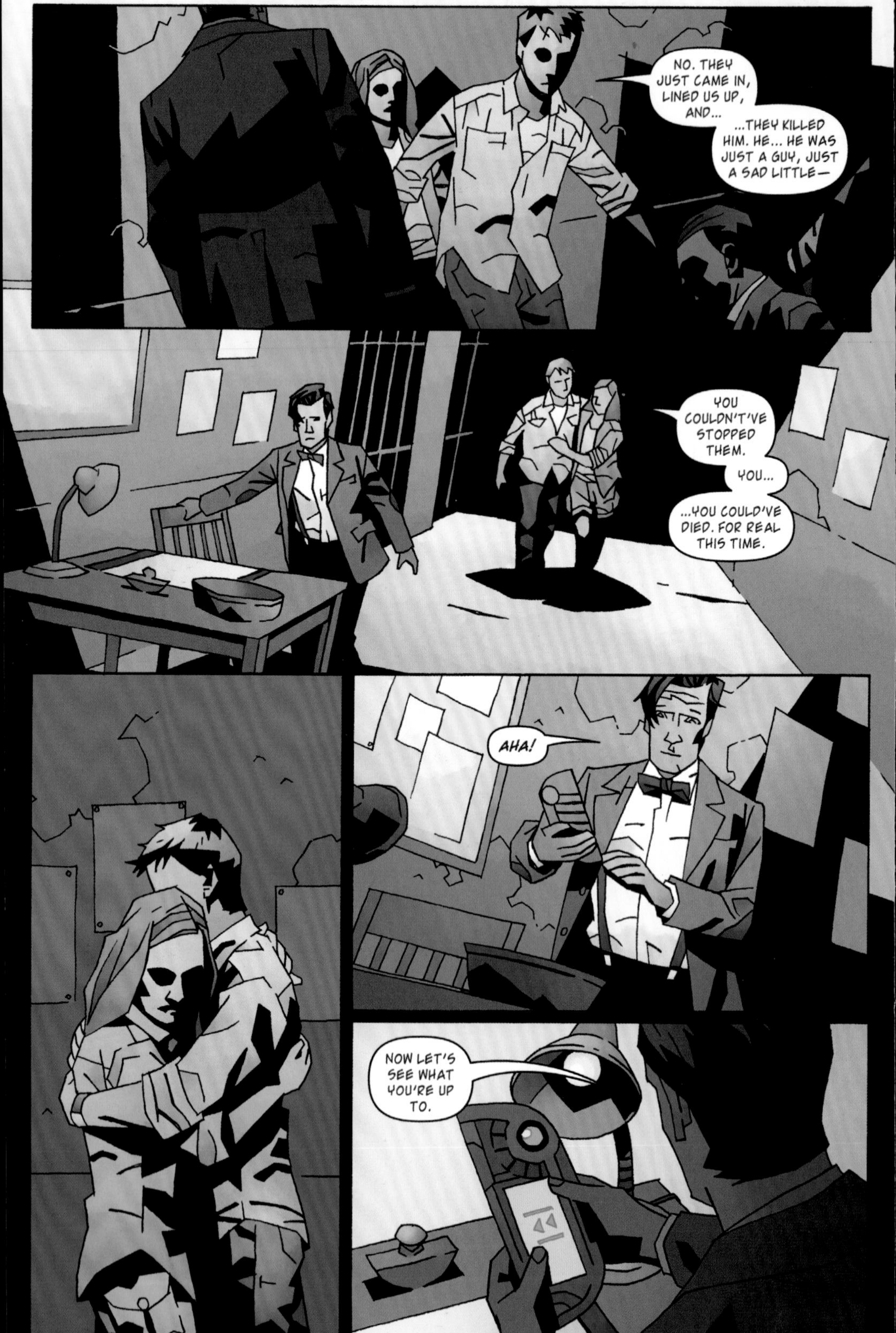
NO. THEY JUST CAME IN, LINED US UP, AND...
...THEY KILLED HIM. HE... HE WAS JUST A GUY, JUST A SAD LITTLE—
YOU COULDN'T'VE STOPPED THEM.
YOU...
...YOU COULD'VE DIED. FOR REAL THIS TIME.
AHA!
NOW LET'S SEE WHAT YOU'RE UP TO.

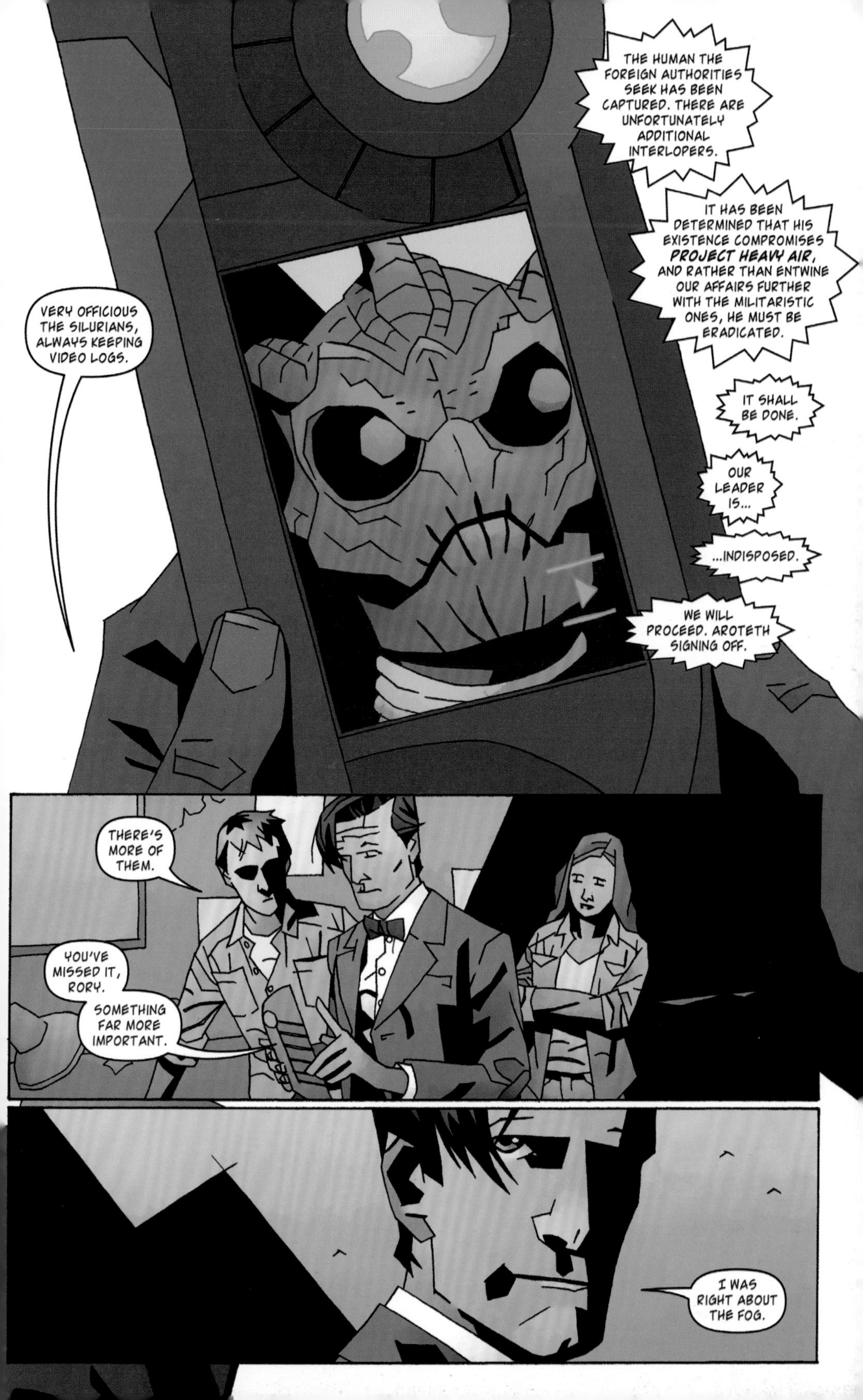
THE HUMAN THE FOREIGN AUTHORITIES SEEK HAS BEEN CAPTURED. THERE ARE UNFORTUNATELY ADDITIONAL INTERLOPERS.
IT HAS BEEN DETERMINED THAT HIS EXISTENCE COMPROMISES PROJECT HEAVY AIR, AND RATHER THAN ENTWINE OUR AFFAIRS FURTHER WITH THE MILITARISTIC ONES, HE MUST BE ERADICATED.
VERY OFFICIOUS THE SILURIANS, ALWAYS KEEPING VIDEO LOGS.
IT SHALL BE DONE.
OUR LEADER IS...
...INDISPOSED.
WE WILL PROCEED. AROTETH SIGNING OFF.
THERE'S MORE OF THEM.
YOU'VE MISSED IT, RORY.
SOMETHING FAR MORE IMPORTANT.
I WAS RIGHT ABOUT THE FOG.

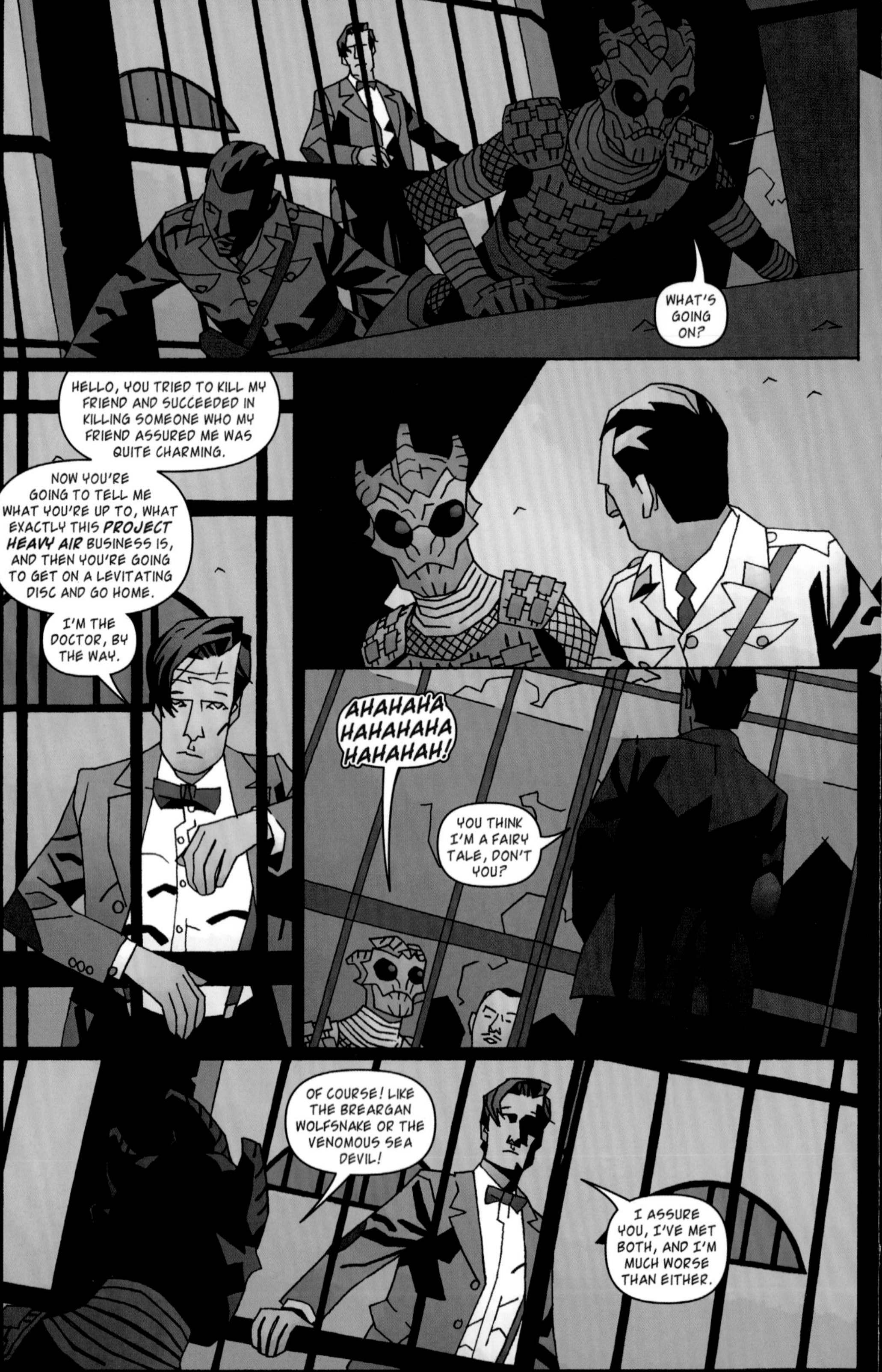
WHAT'S GOING ON?
HELLO, YOU TRIED TO KILL MY FRIEND AND SUCCEEDED IN KILLING SOMEONE WHO MY FRIEND ASSURED ME WAS QUITE CHARMING.
NOW YOU'RE GOING TO TELL ME WHAT YOU'RE UP TO, WHAT EXACTLY THIS PROJECT HEAVY AIR BUSINESS IS, AND THEN YOU'RE GOING TO GET ON A LEVITATING DISC AND GO HOME.
I'M THE DOCTOR, BY THE WAY.
AHAHAHA HAHAHAHA HAHAHAH!
YOU THINK I'M A FAIRY TALE, DON'T YOU?
OF COURSE! LIKE THE BREARGAN WOLFSNAKE OR THE VENOMOUS SEA DEVIL!
I ASSURE YOU, I'VE MET BOTH, AND I'M MUCH WORSE THAN EITHER.

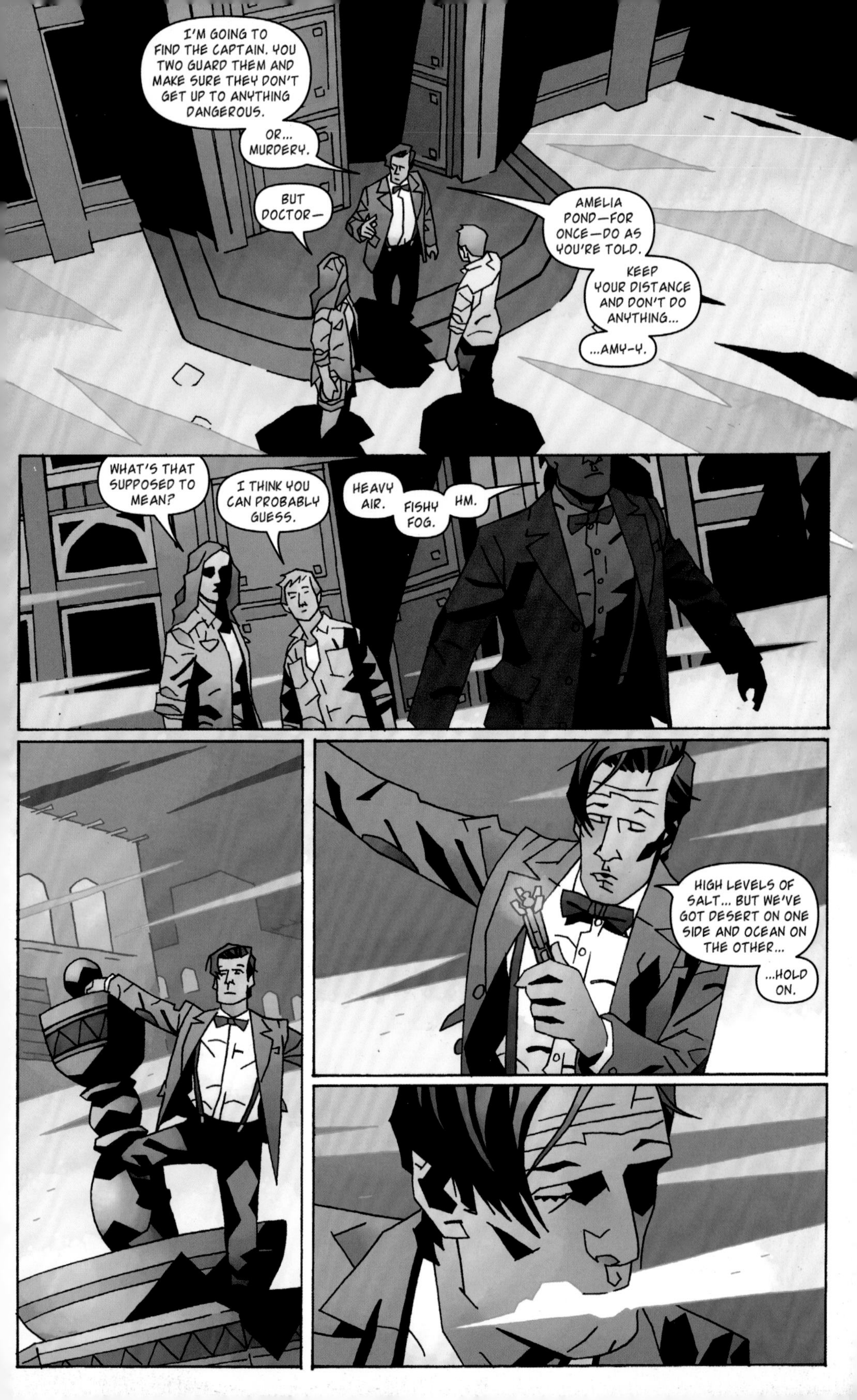
I'M GOING TO FIND THE CAPTAIN. YOU TWO GUARD THEM AND MAKE SURE THEY DON'T GET UP TO ANYTHING DANGEROUS.
OR... MURDERY.
BUT DOCTOR—
AMELIA POND—FOR ONCE—DO AS YOU'RE TOLD.
KEEP YOUR DISTANCE AND DON'T DO ANYTHING...
...AMY-Y.
WHAT'S THAT SUPPOSED TO MEAN?
I THINK YOU CAN PROBABLY GUESS.
HEAVY AIR.
FISHY FOG.
HM.
HIGH LEVELS OF SALT... BUT WE'VE GOT DESERT ON ONE SIDE AND OCEAN ON THE OTHER...
...HOLD ON.

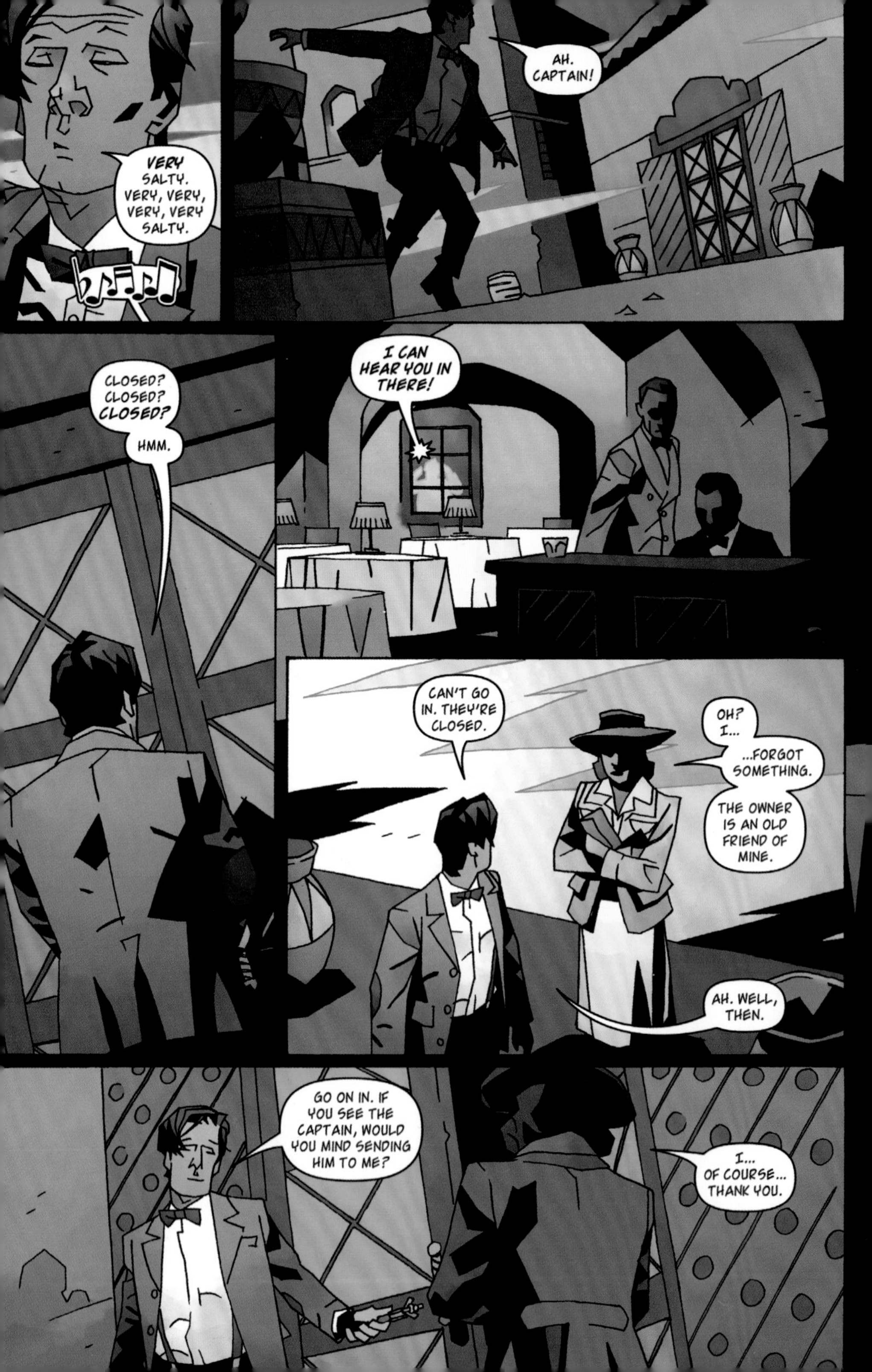
VERY SALTY. VERY, VERY, VERY, VERY SALTY.
AH. CAPTAIN!
CLOSED? CLOSED? CLOSED?
HMM.
I CAN HEAR YOU IN THERE!
CAN'T GO IN. THEY'RE CLOSED.
OH? I...
...FORGOT SOMETHING.
THE OWNER IS AN OLD FRIEND OF MINE.
AH. WELL, THEN.
GO ON IN. IF YOU SEE THE CAPTAIN, WOULD YOU MIND SENDING HIM TO ME?
I... OF COURSE... THANK YOU.

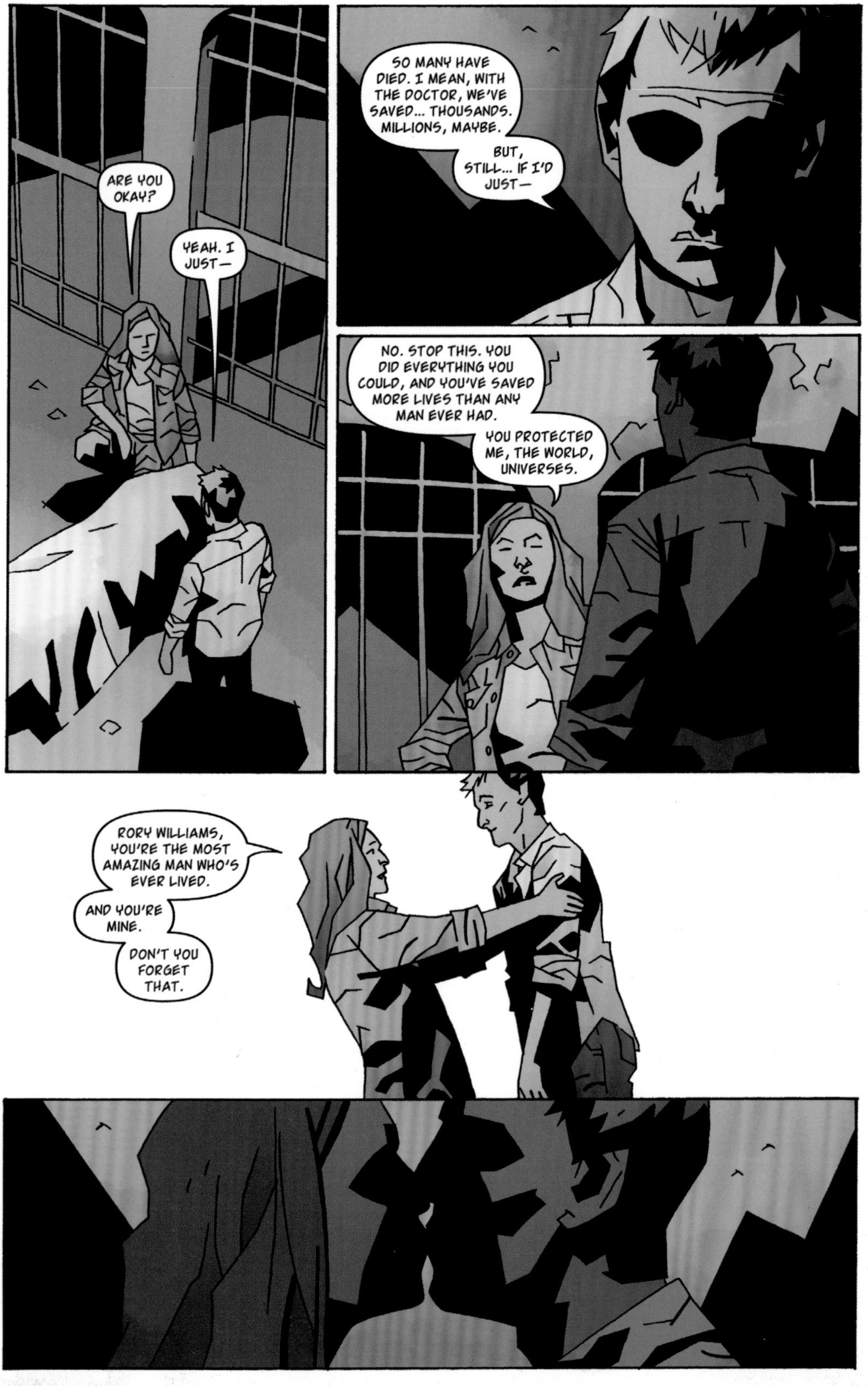
ARE YOU OKAY?
YEAH. I JUST—
SO MANY HAVE DIED. I MEAN, WITH THE DOCTOR, WE'VE SAVED... THOUSANDS. MILLIONS, MAYBE.
BUT, STILL... IF I'D JUST—
NO. STOP THIS. YOU DID EVERYTHING YOU COULD, AND YOU'VE SAVED MORE LIVES THAN ANY MAN EVER HAD.
YOU PROTECTED ME, THE WORLD, UNIVERSES.
RORY WILLIAMS, YOU'RE THE MOST AMAZING MAN WHO'S EVER LIVED.
AND YOU'RE MINE.
DON'T YOU FORGET THAT.

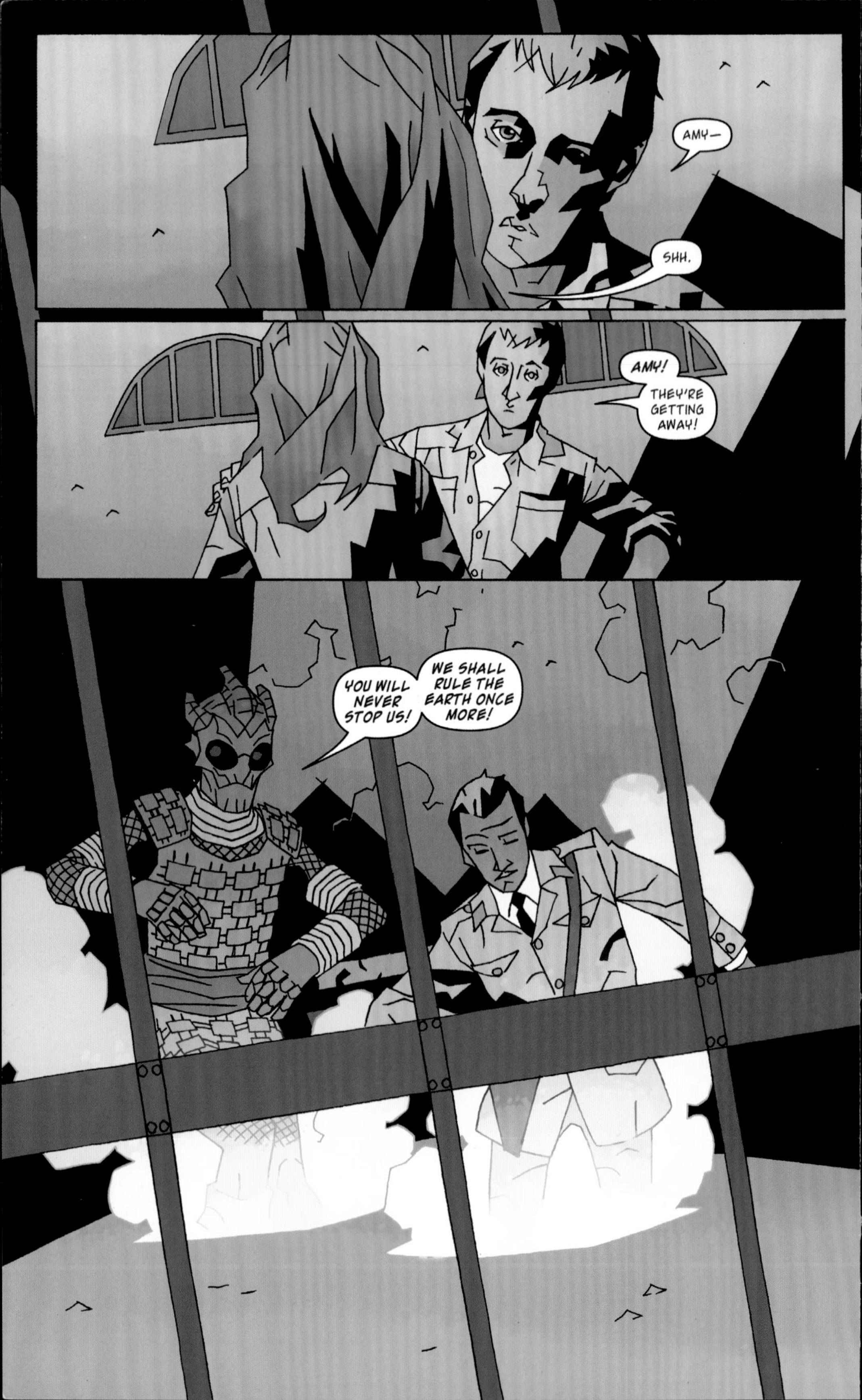
AMY—
SHH.
AMY!
THEY'RE GETTING AWAY!
YOU WILL NEVER STOP US!
WE SHALL RULE THE EARTH ONCE MORE!

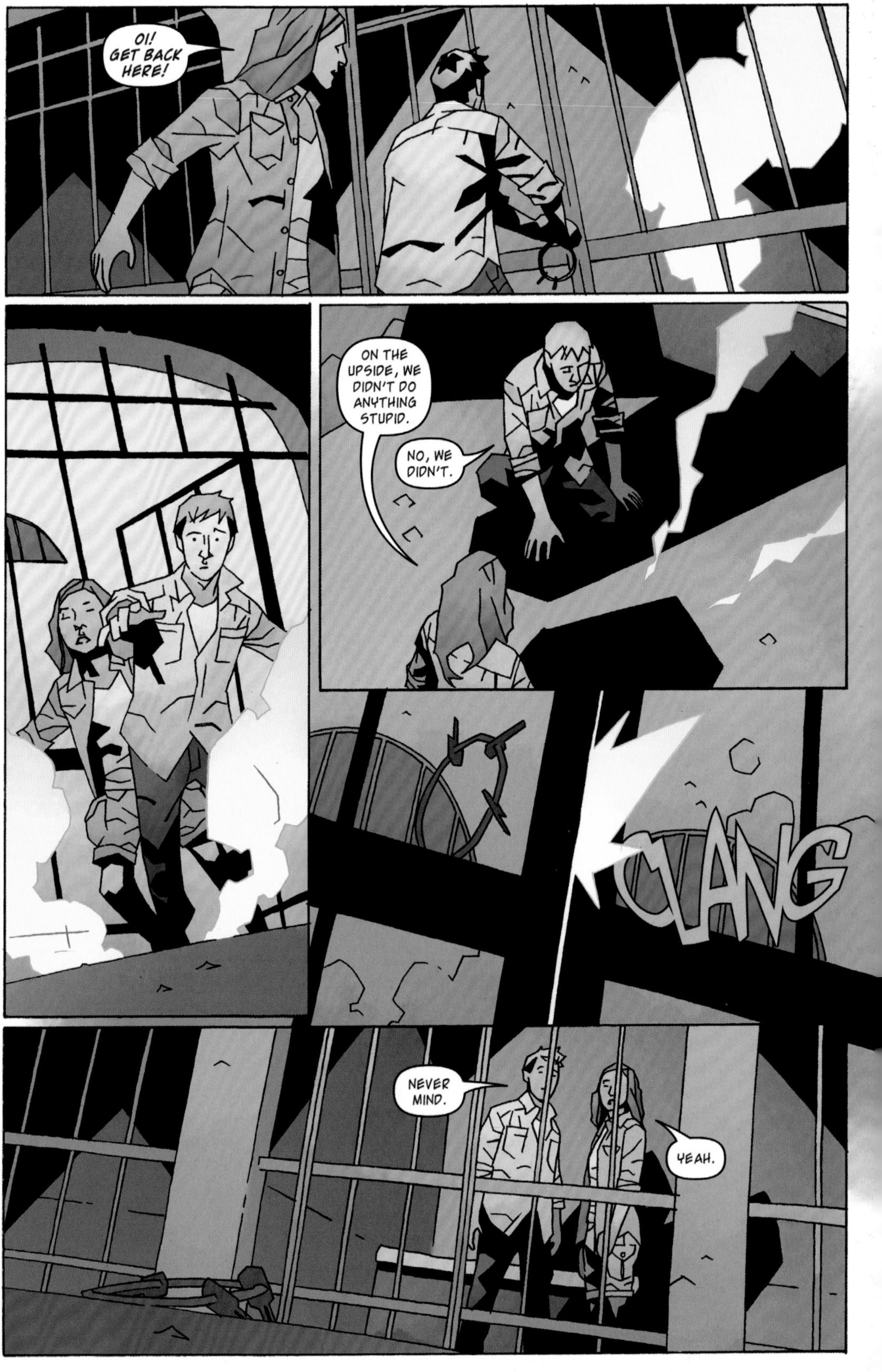

OI! GET BACK HERE!
ON THE UPSIDE, WE DIDN'T DO ANYTHING STUPID.
NO, WE DIDN'T.
CLANG
NEVER MIND.
YEAH.

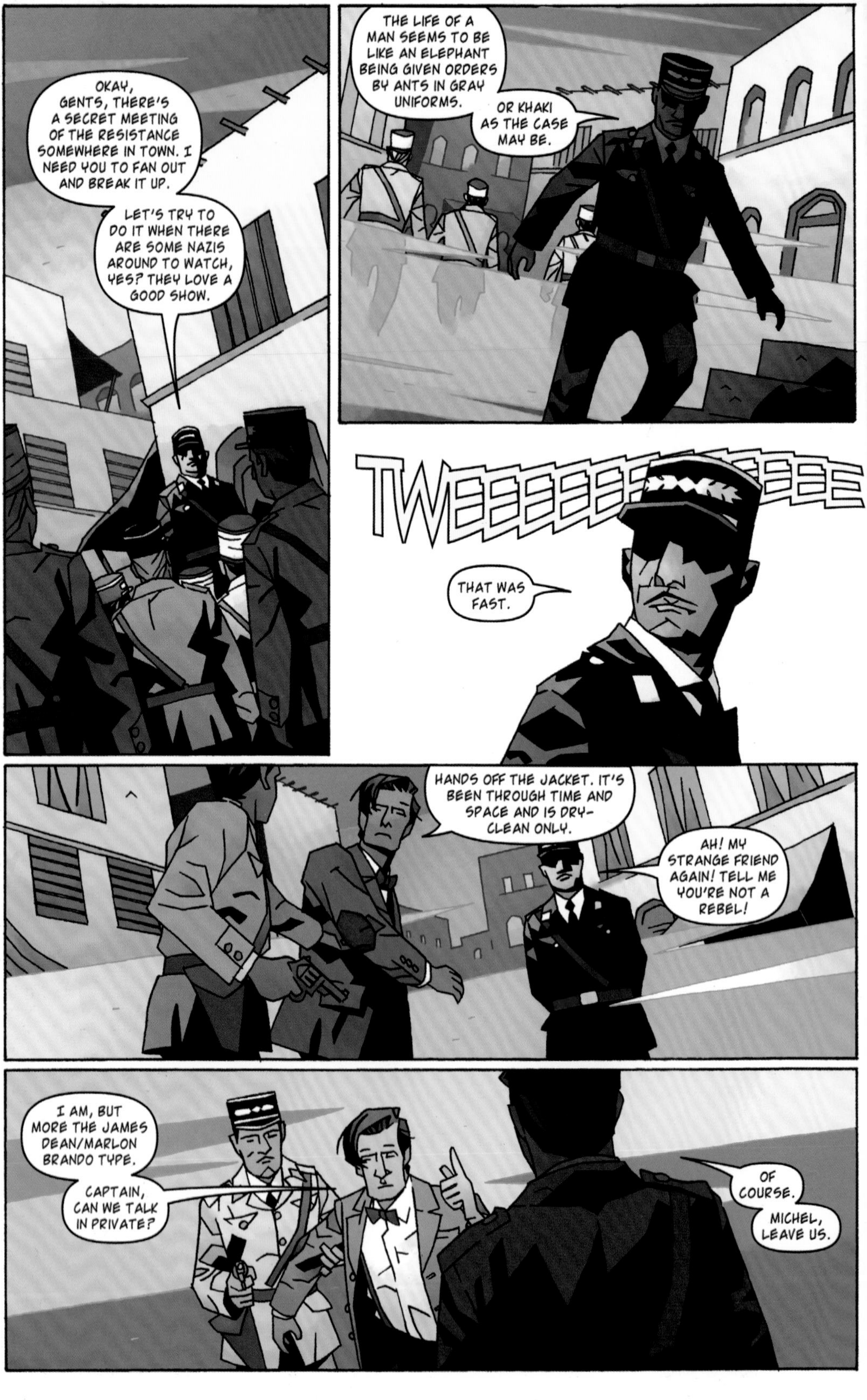
OKAY, GENTS, THERE'S A SECRET MEETING OF THE RESISTANCE SOMEWHERE IN TOWN. I NEED YOU TO FAN OUT AND BREAK IT UP.
LET'S TRY TO DO IT WHEN THERE ARE SOME NAZIS AROUND TO WATCH, YES? THEY LOVE A GOOD SHOW.
THE LIFE OF A MAN SEEMS TO BE LIKE AN ELEPHANT BEING GIVEN ORDERS BY ANTS IN GRAY UNIFORMS.
OR KHAKI AS THE CASE MAY BE.
TWEEEEEEEEEEEEEEE
THAT WAS FAST.
HANDS OFF THE JACKET. IT'S BEEN THROUGH TIME AND SPACE AND IS DRY-CLEAN ONLY.
AH! MY STRANGE FRIEND AGAIN! TELL ME YOU'RE NOT A REBEL!
I AM, BUT MORE THE JAMES DEAN/MARLON BRANDO TYPE.
CAPTAIN, CAN WE TALK IN PRIVATE?
OF COURSE.
MICHEL, LEAVE US.

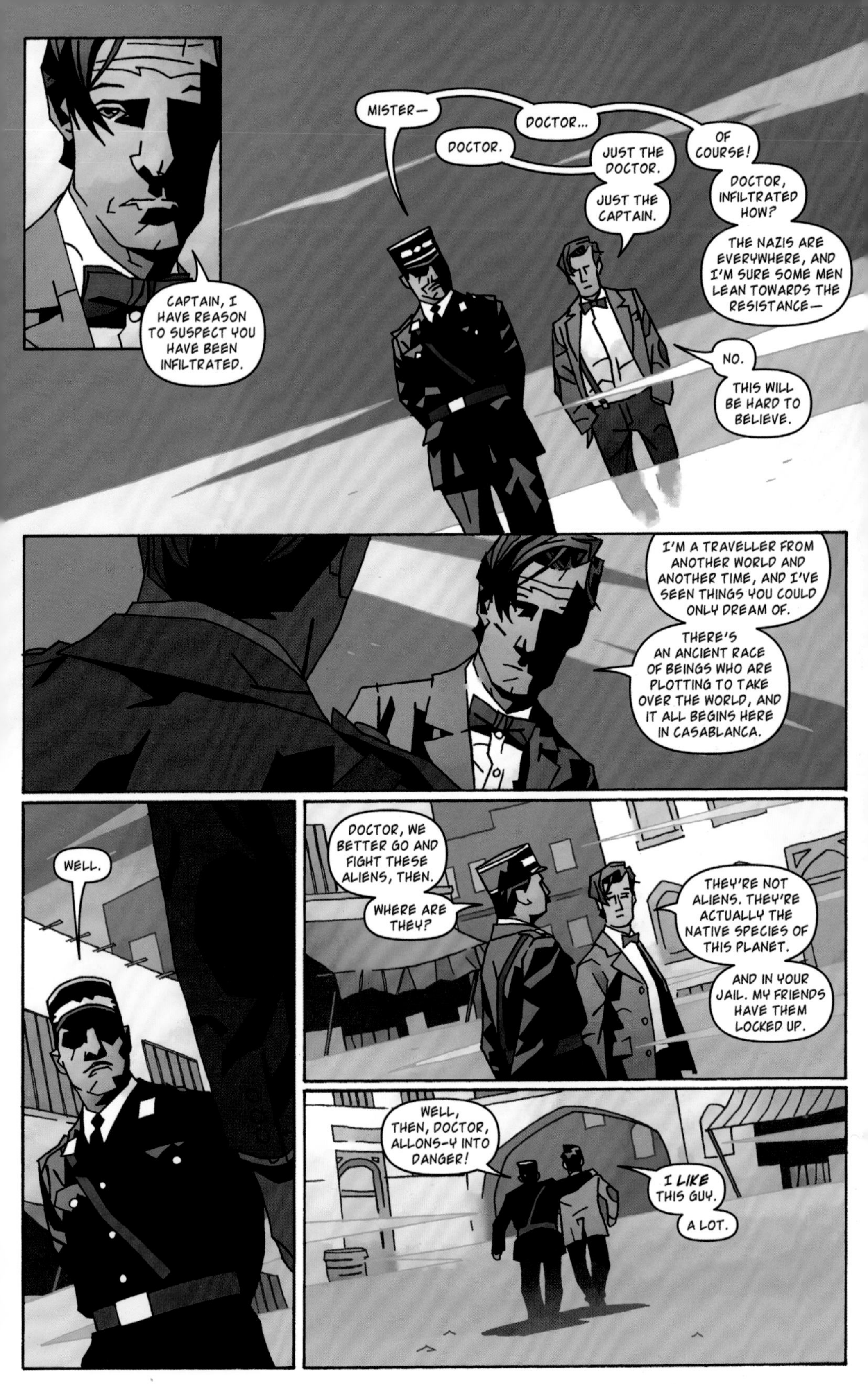
CAPTAIN, I HAVE REASON TO SUSPECT YOU HAVE BEEN INFILTRATED.
MISTER—
DOCTOR...
OF COURSE!
DOCTOR.
JUST THE DOCTOR.
JUST THE CAPTAIN.
DOCTOR, INFILTRATED HOW?
THE NAZIS ARE EVERYWHERE, AND I'M SURE SOME MEN LEAN TOWARDS THE RESISTANCE—
NO.
THIS WILL BE HARD TO BELIEVE.
I'M A TRAVELLER FROM ANOTHER WORLD AND ANOTHER TIME, AND I'VE SEEN THINGS YOU COULD ONLY DREAM OF.
THERE'S AN ANCIENT RACE OF BEINGS WHO ARE PLOTTING TO TAKE OVER THE WORLD, AND IT ALL BEGINS HERE IN CASABLANCA.
WELL.
DOCTOR, WE BETTER GO AND FIGHT THESE ALIENS, THEN.
WHERE ARE THEY?
THEY'RE NOT ALIENS. THEY'RE ACTUALLY THE NATIVE SPECIES OF THIS PLANET.
AND IN YOUR JAIL. MY FRIENDS HAVE THEM LOCKED UP.
WELL, THEN, DOCTOR, ALLONS-Y INTO DANGER!
I **LIKE** THIS GUY.
A LOT.

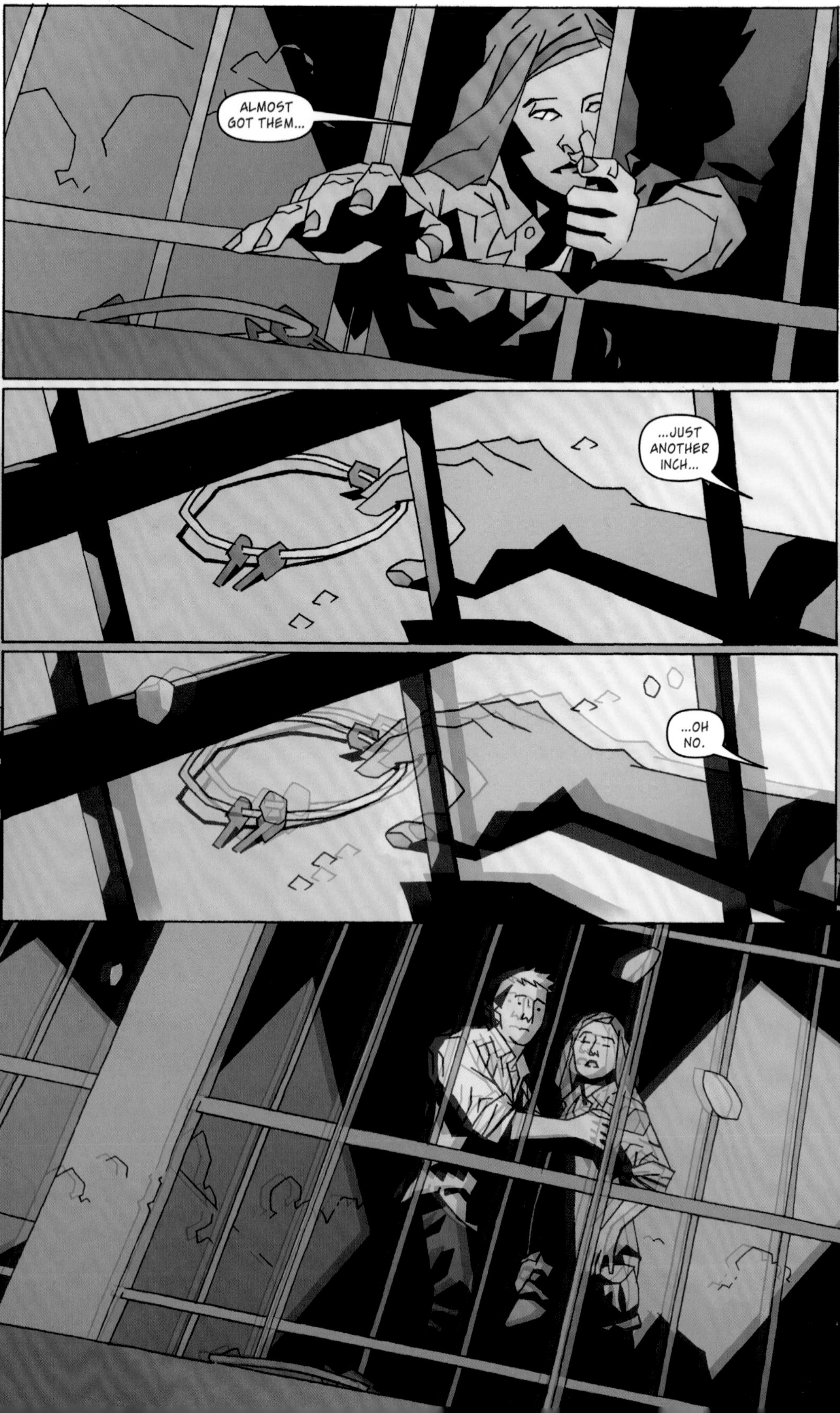
ALMOST GOT THEM...
...JUST ANOTHER INCH...
...OH NO.

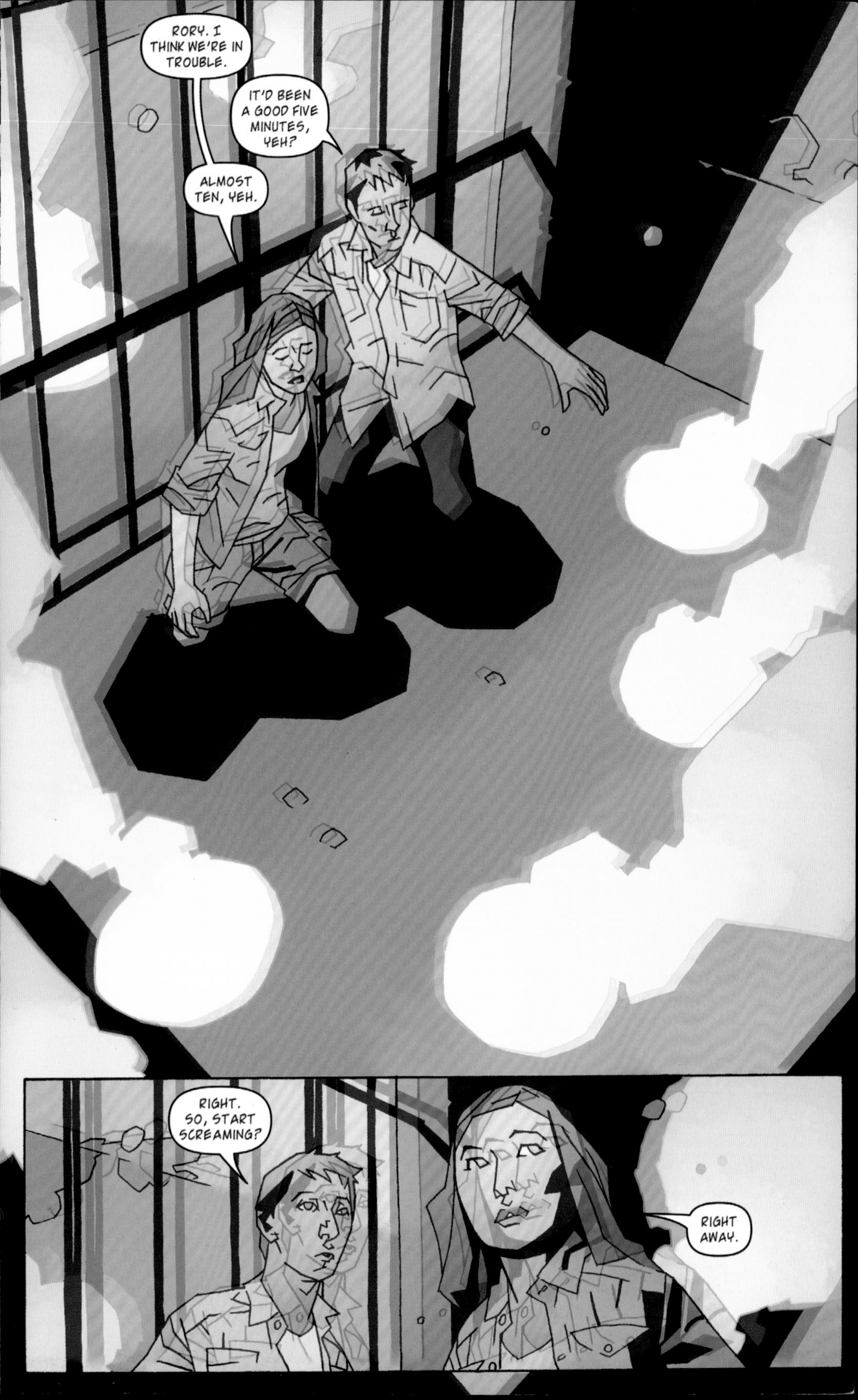
RORY. I THINK WE'RE IN TROUBLE.
IT'D BEEN A GOOD FIVE MINUTES, YEH?
ALMOST TEN, YEH.
RIGHT. SO, START SCREAMING?
RIGHT AWAY.

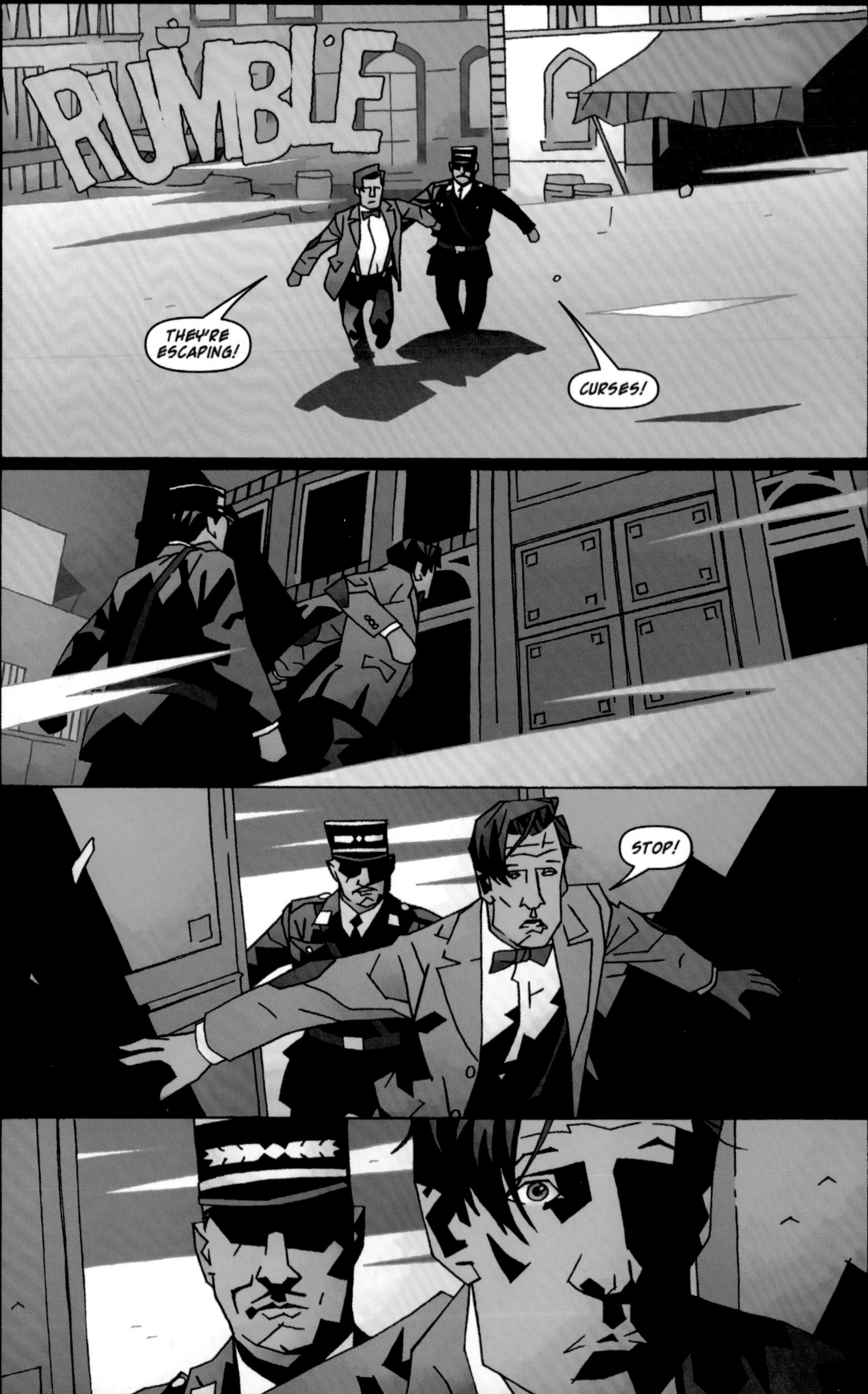
RUMBLE
THEY'RE ESCAPING!
CURSES!
STOP!

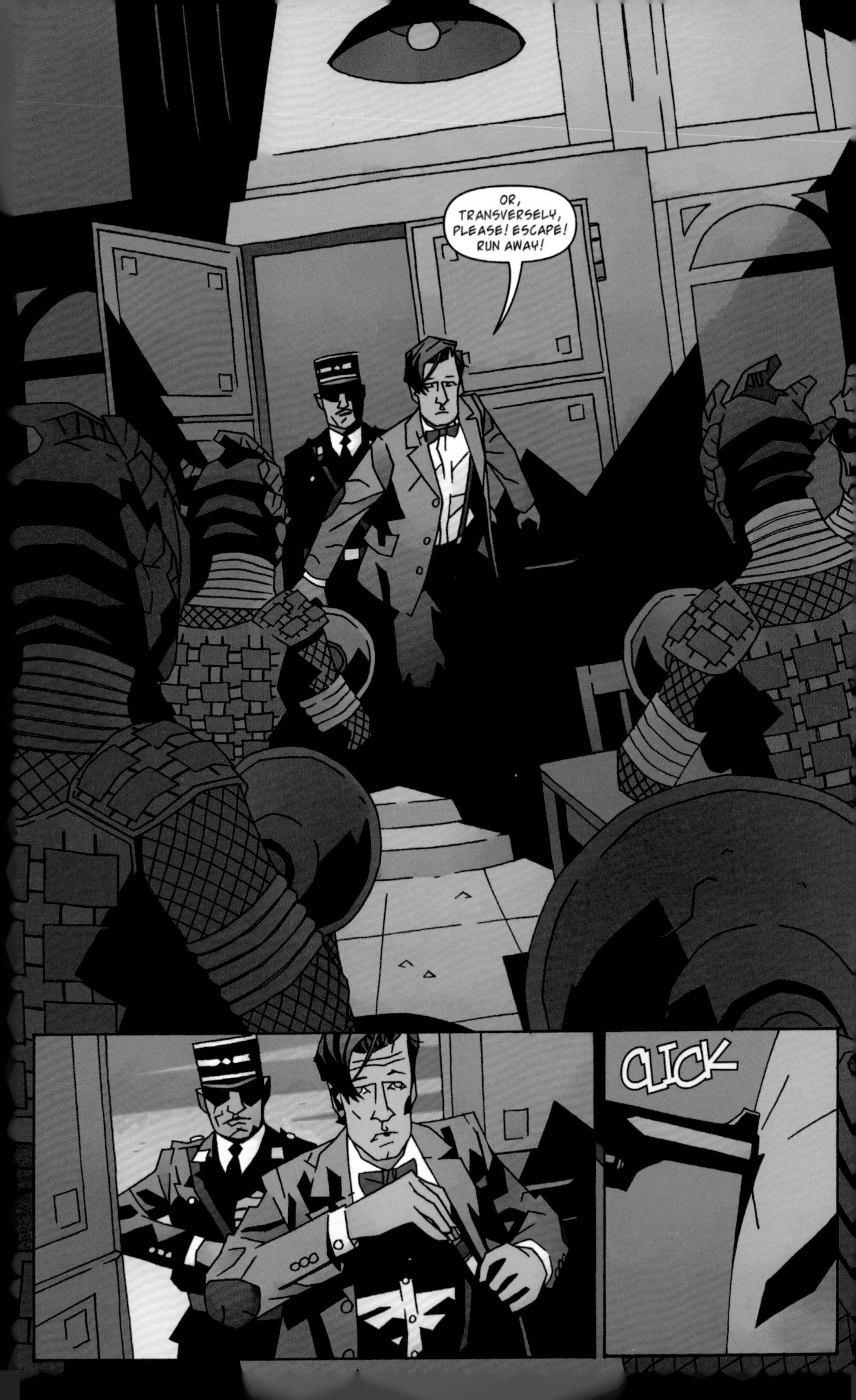
OR, TRANSVERSELY, PLEASE! ESCAPE! RUN AWAY!
CLICK

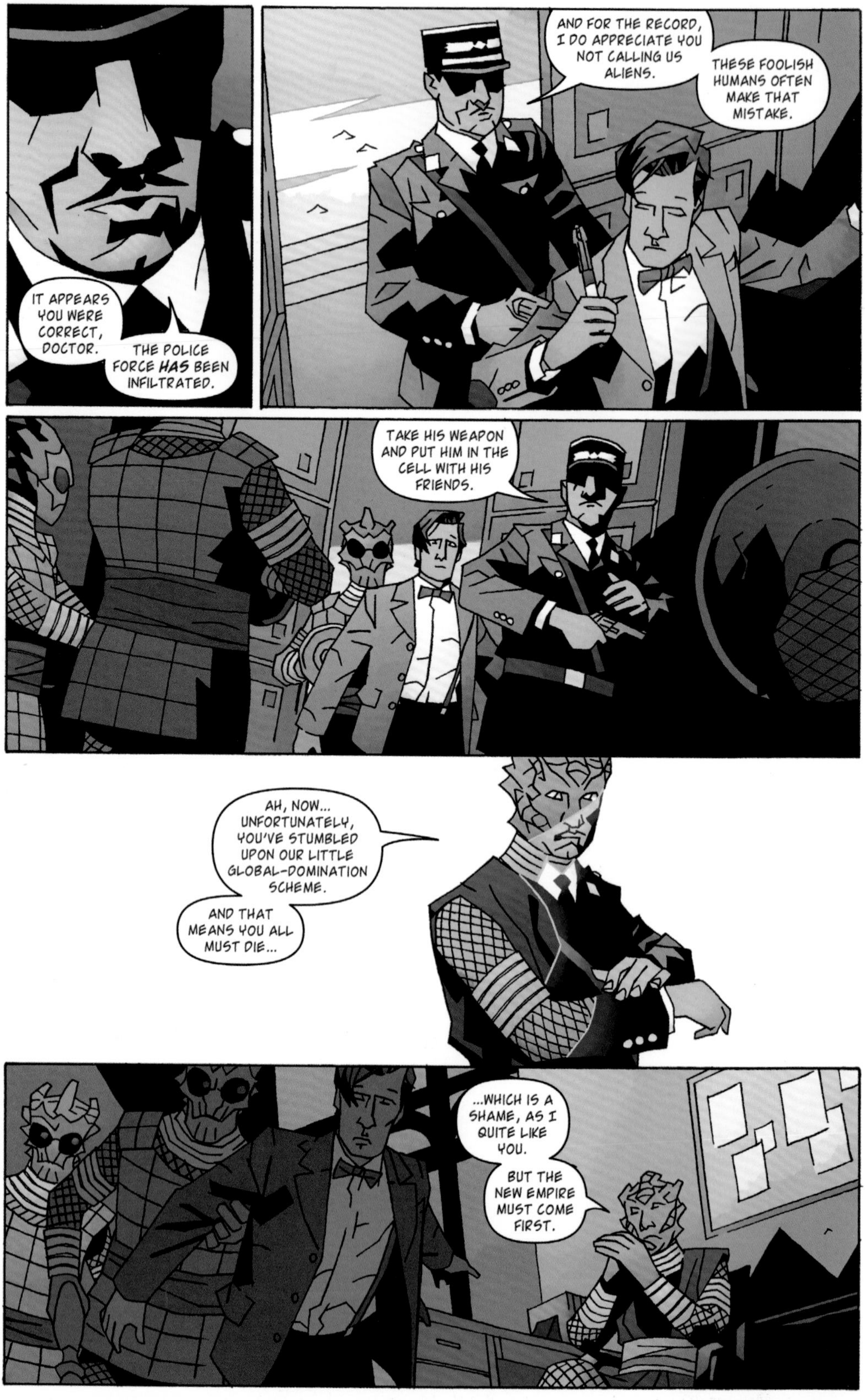
IT APPEARS YOU WERE CORRECT, DOCTOR.
THE POLICE FORCE HAS BEEN INFILTRATED.
AND FOR THE RECORD, I DO APPRECIATE YOU NOT CALLING US ALIENS.
THESE FOOLISH HUMANS OFTEN MAKE THAT MISTAKE.
TAKE HIS WEAPON AND PUT HIM IN THE CELL WITH HIS FRIENDS.
AH, NOW... UNFORTUNATELY, YOU'VE STUMBLED UPON OUR LITTLE GLOBAL-DOMINATION SCHEME.
AND THAT MEANS YOU ALL MUST DIE...
...WHICH IS A SHAME, AS I QUITE LIKE YOU.
BUT THE NEW EMPIRE MUST COME FIRST.

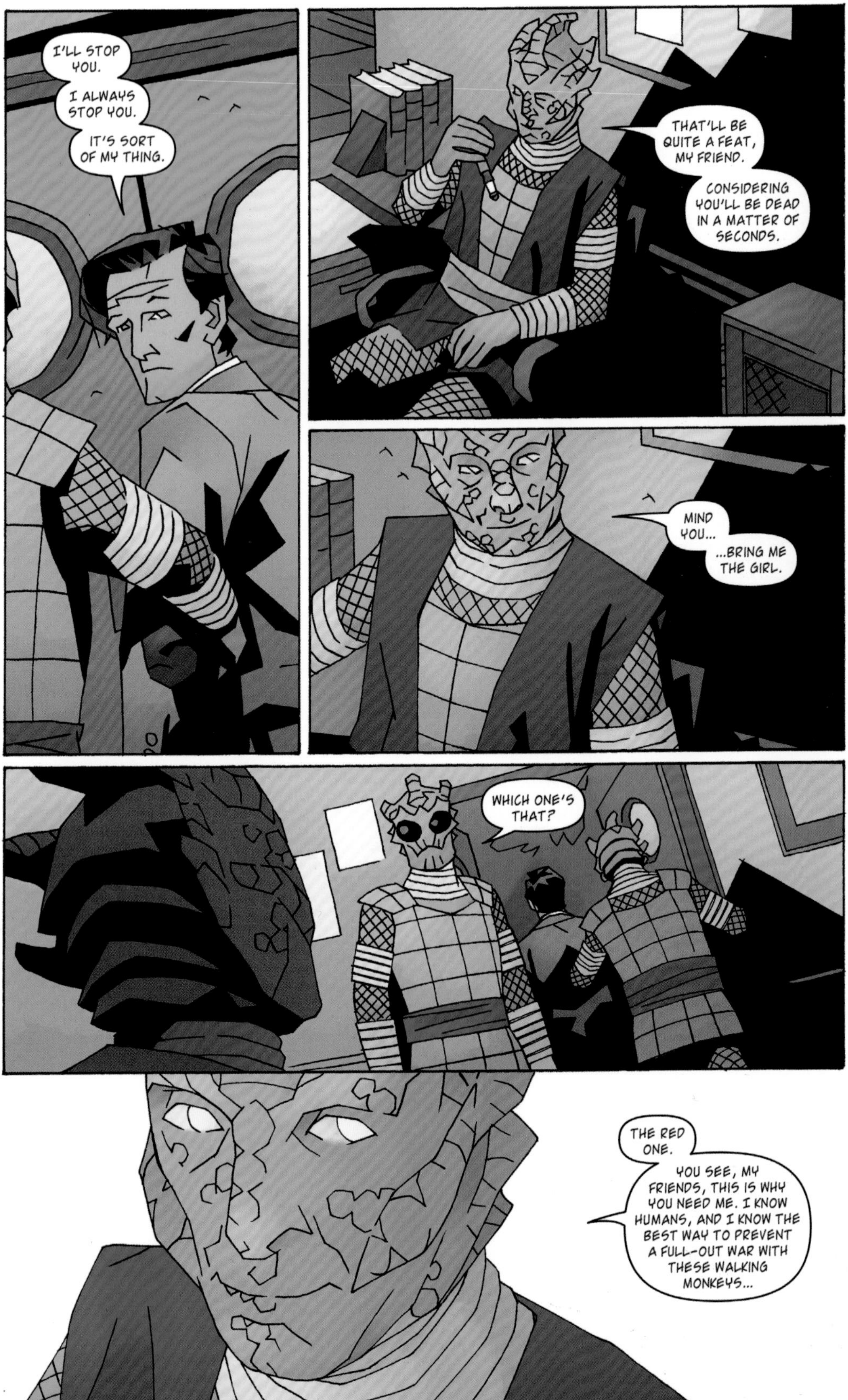
I'LL STOP YOU.
I ALWAYS STOP YOU.
IT'S SORT OF MY THING.
THAT'LL BE QUITE A FEAT, MY FRIEND.
CONSIDERING YOU'LL BE DEAD IN A MATTER OF SECONDS.
MIND YOU...
...BRING ME THE GIRL.
WHICH ONE'S THAT?
THE RED ONE.
YOU SEE, MY FRIENDS, THIS IS WHY YOU NEED ME. I KNOW HUMANS, AND I KNOW THE BEST WAY TO PREVENT A FULL-OUT WAR WITH THESE WALKING MONKEYS...

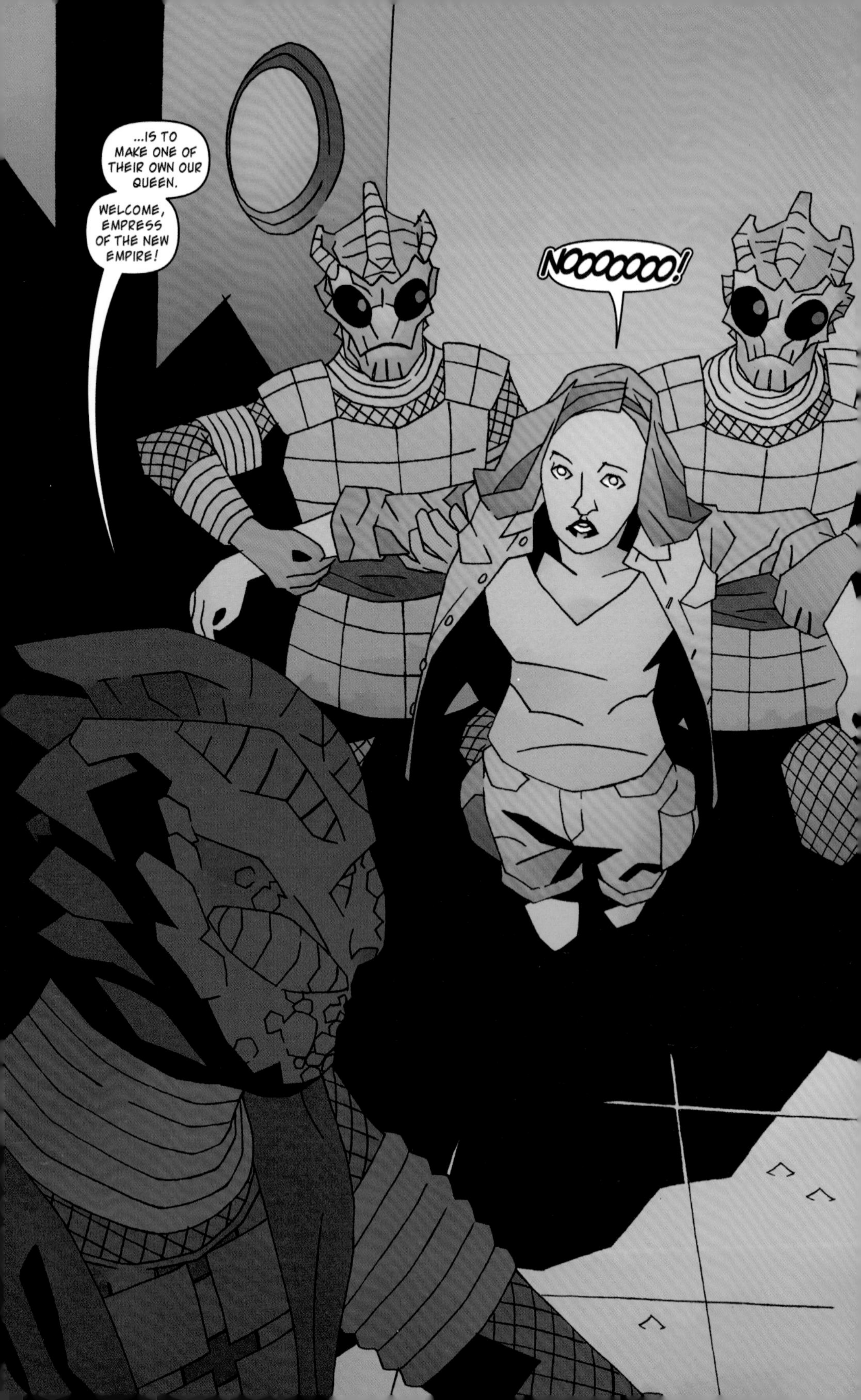
...IS TO MAKE ONE OF THEIR OWN OUR QUEEN.
WELCOME, EMPRESS OF THE NEW EMPIRE!
NOOOOOOO!

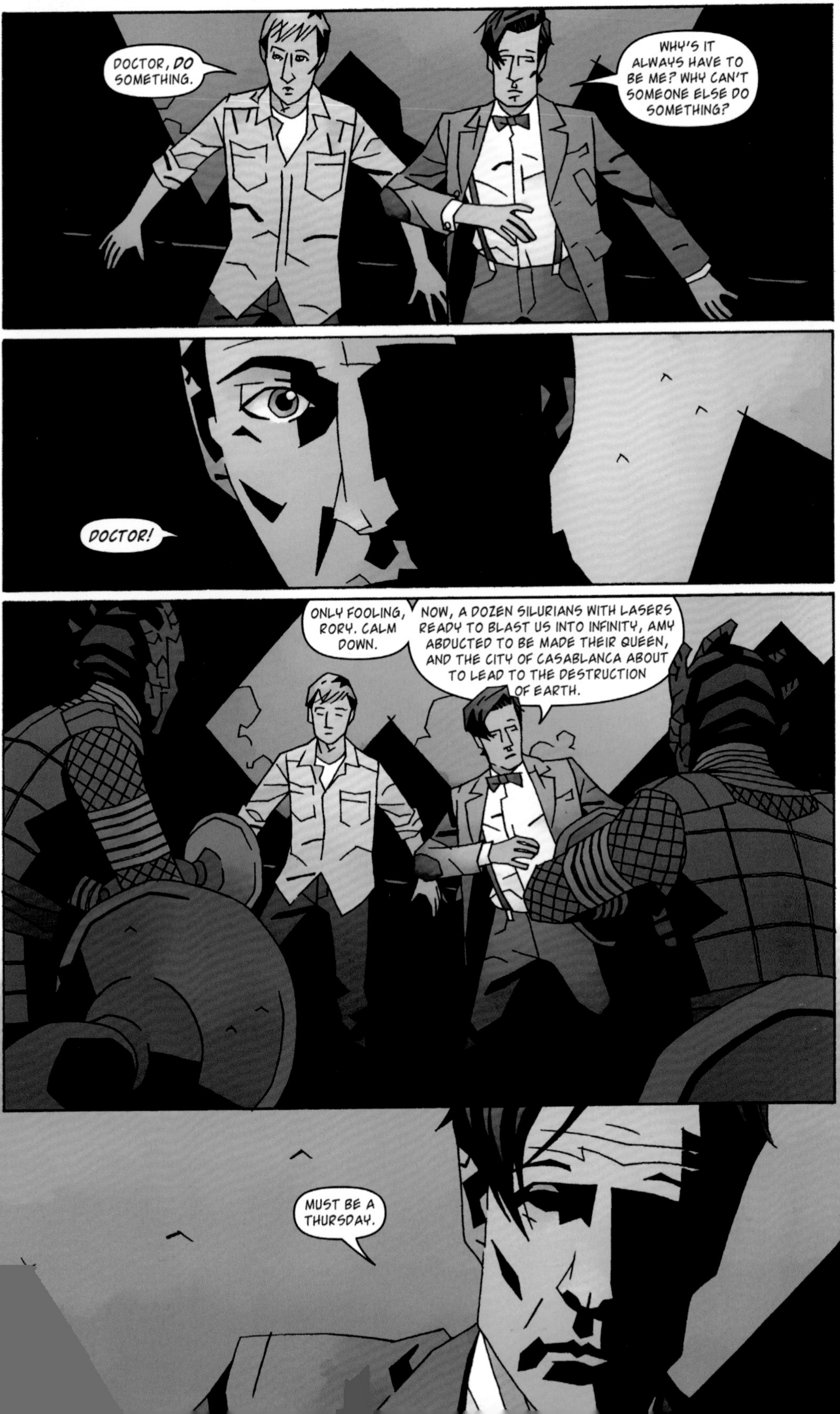
DOCTOR, DO SOMETHING.
WHY'S IT ALWAYS HAVE TO BE ME? WHY CAN'T SOMEONE ELSE DO SOMETHING?
DOCTOR!
ONLY FOOLING, RORY. CALM DOWN.
NOW, A DOZEN SILURIANS WITH LASERS READY TO BLAST US INTO INFINITY, AMY ABDUCTED TO BE MADE THEIR QUEEN, AND THE CITY OF CASABLANCA ABOUT TO LEAD TO THE DESTRUCTION OF EARTH.
MUST BE A THURSDAY.

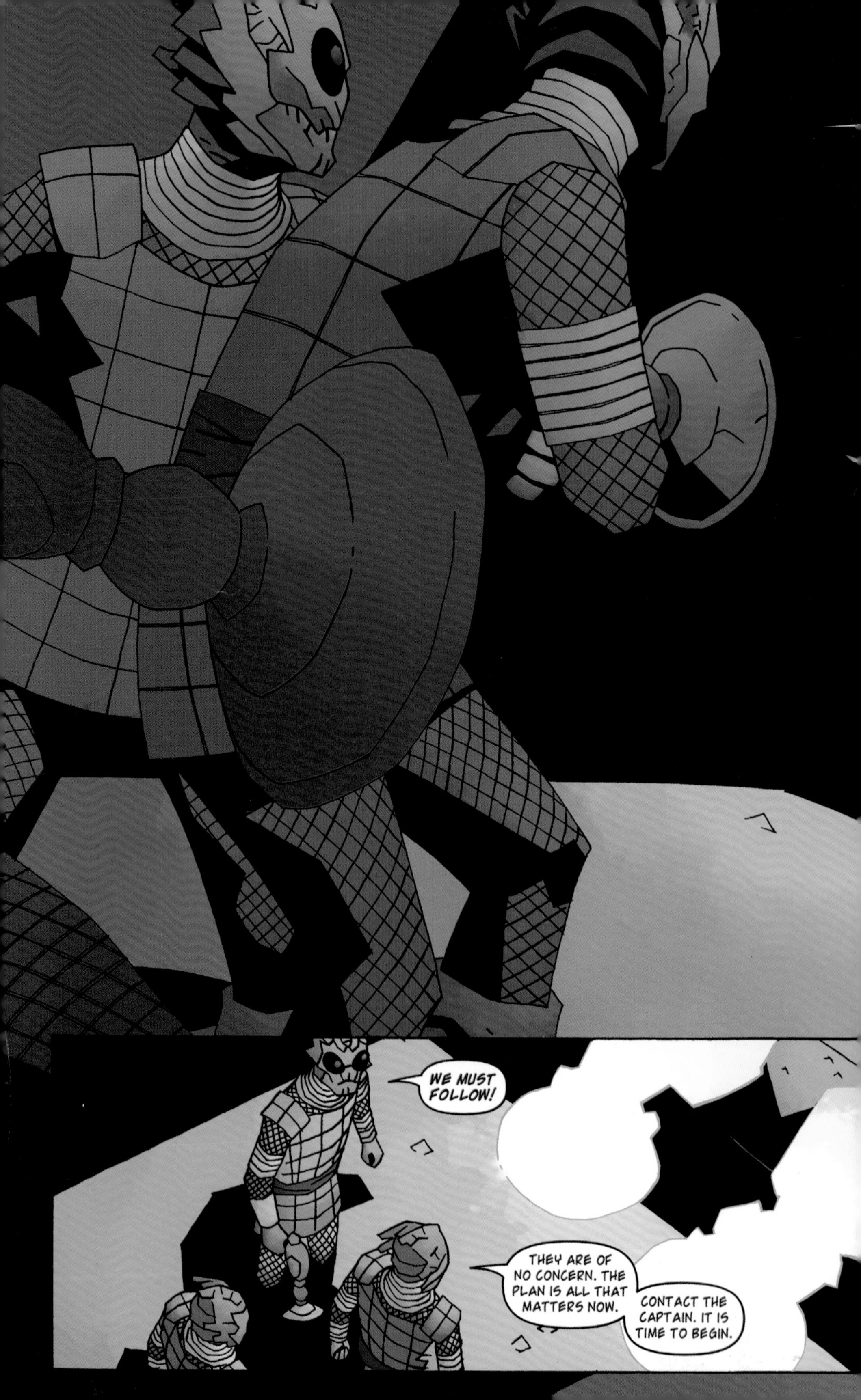
WE MUST FOLLOW!
THEY ARE OF NO CONCERN. THE PLAN IS ALL THAT MATTERS NOW.
CONTACT THE CAPTAIN. IT IS TIME TO BEGIN.

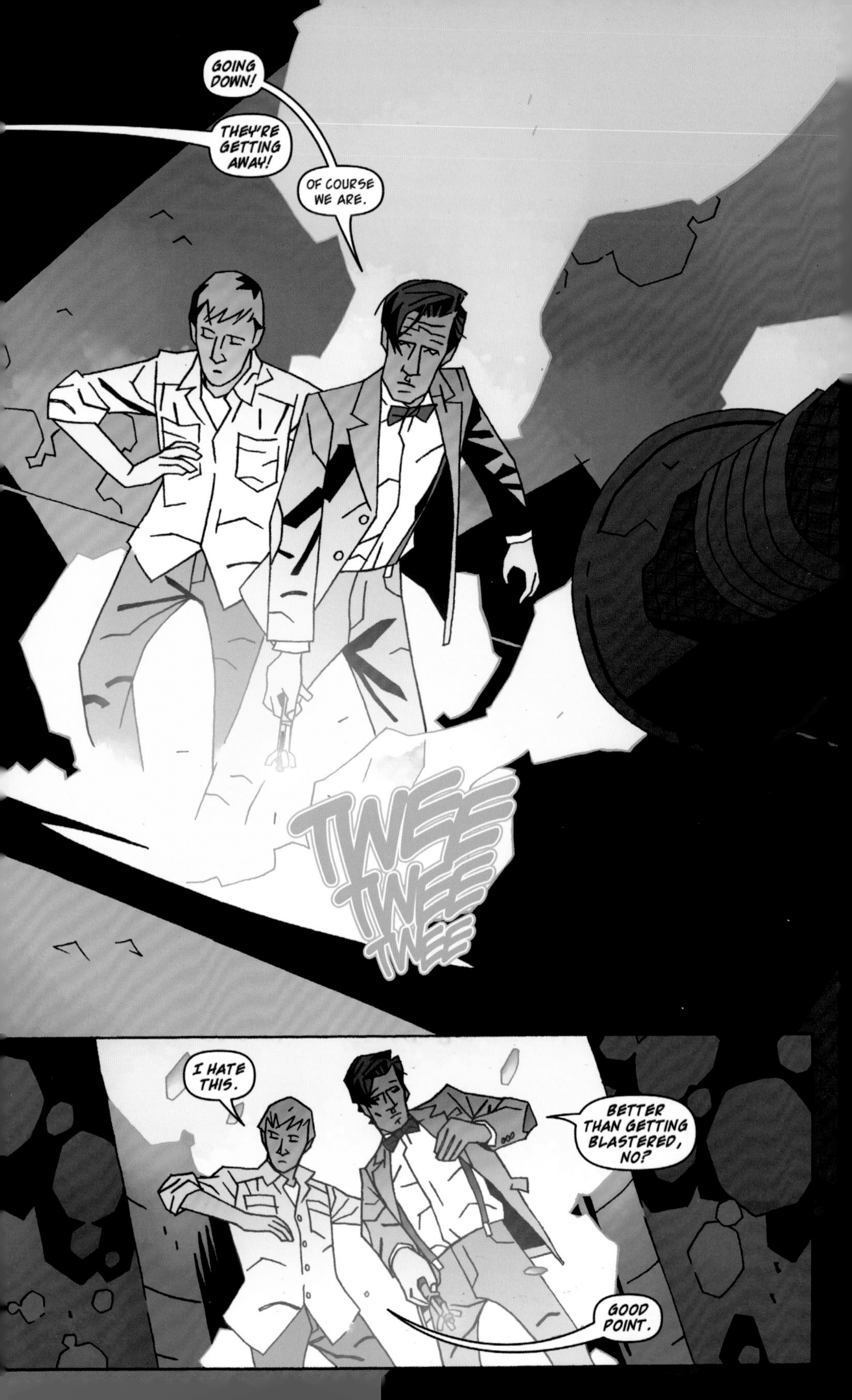
GOING DOWN!
THEY'RE GETTING AWAY!
OF COURSE WE ARE.
TWEE
TWEE
TWEE
I HATE THIS.
BETTER THAN GETTING BLASTERED, NO?
GOOD POINT.

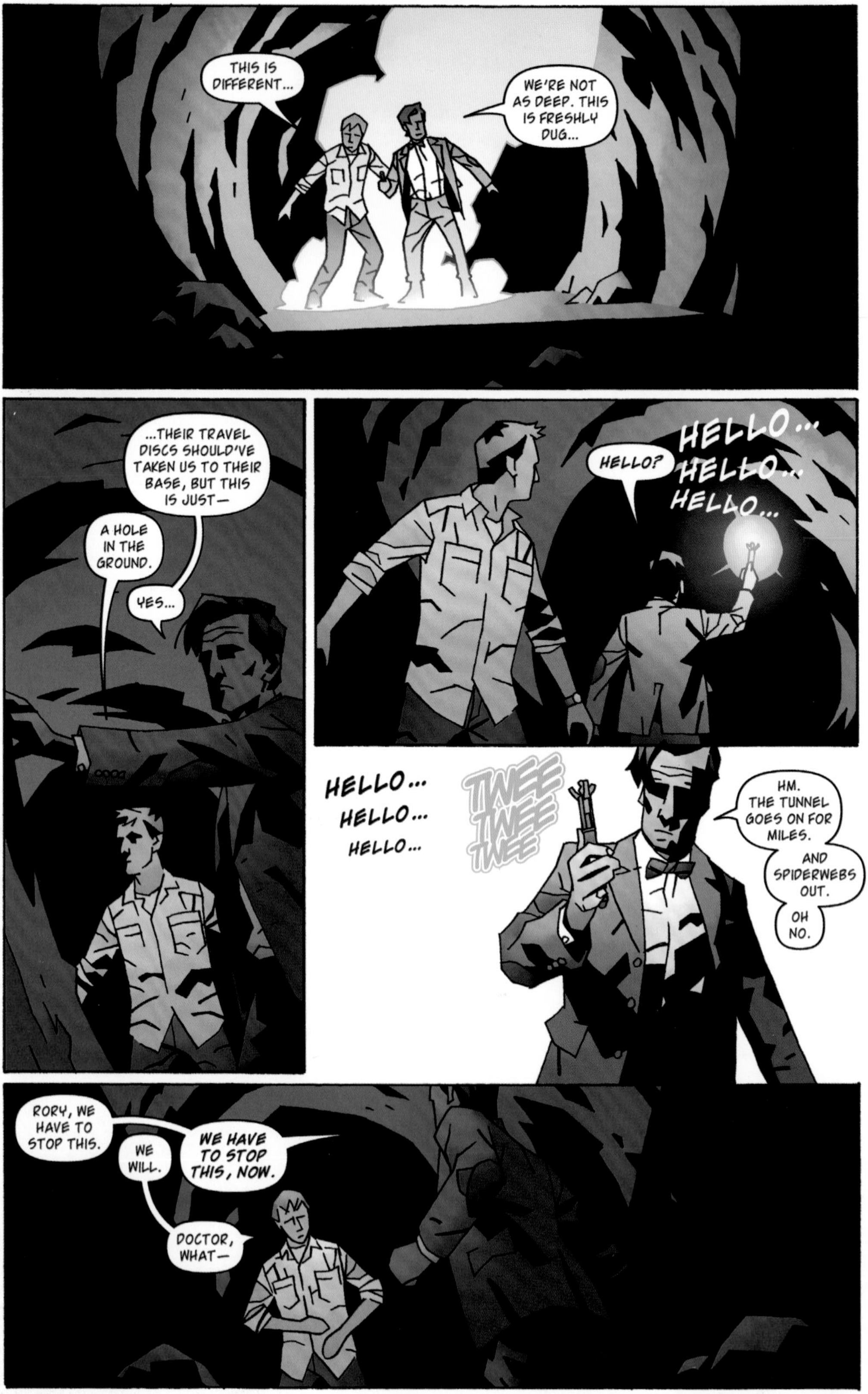
THIS IS DIFFERENT...
WE'RE NOT AS DEEP. THIS IS FRESHLY DUG...
...THEIR TRAVEL DISCS SHOULD'VE TAKEN US TO THEIR BASE, BUT THIS IS JUST—
A HOLE IN THE GROUND.
YES...
HELLO?
HELLO... HELLO... HELLO...
HELLO... HELLO... HELLO...
TWEE TWEE TWEE
HM. THE TUNNEL GOES ON FOR MILES.
AND SPIDERWEBS OUT.
OH NO.
RORY, WE HAVE TO STOP THIS.
WE HAVE TO STOP THIS, NOW.
WE WILL.
DOCTOR, WHAT—

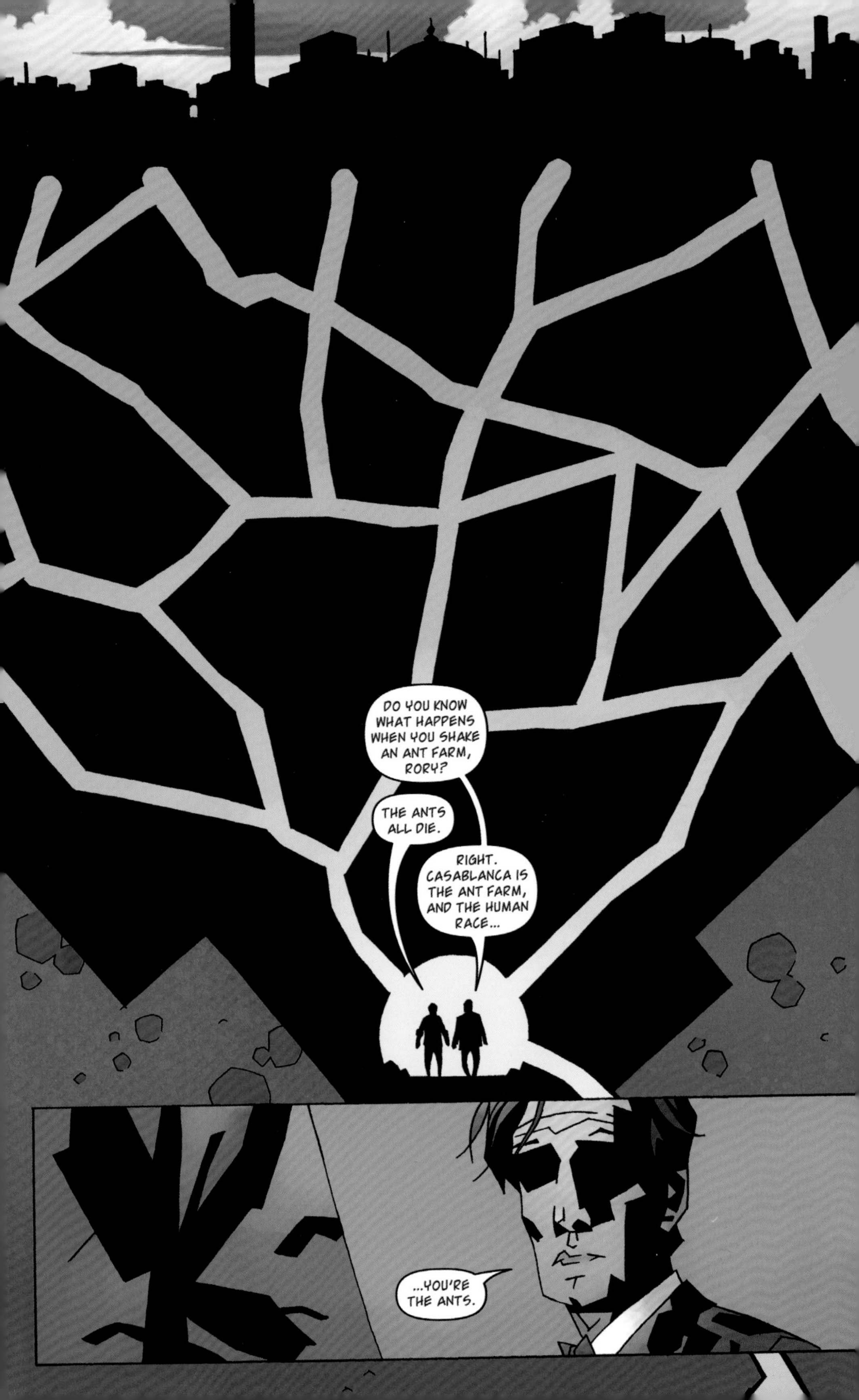
DO YOU KNOW WHAT HAPPENS WHEN YOU SHAKE AN ANT FARM, RORY?
THE ANTS ALL DIE.
RIGHT. CASABLANCA IS THE ANT FARM, AND THE HUMAN RACE...
...YOU'RE THE ANTS.

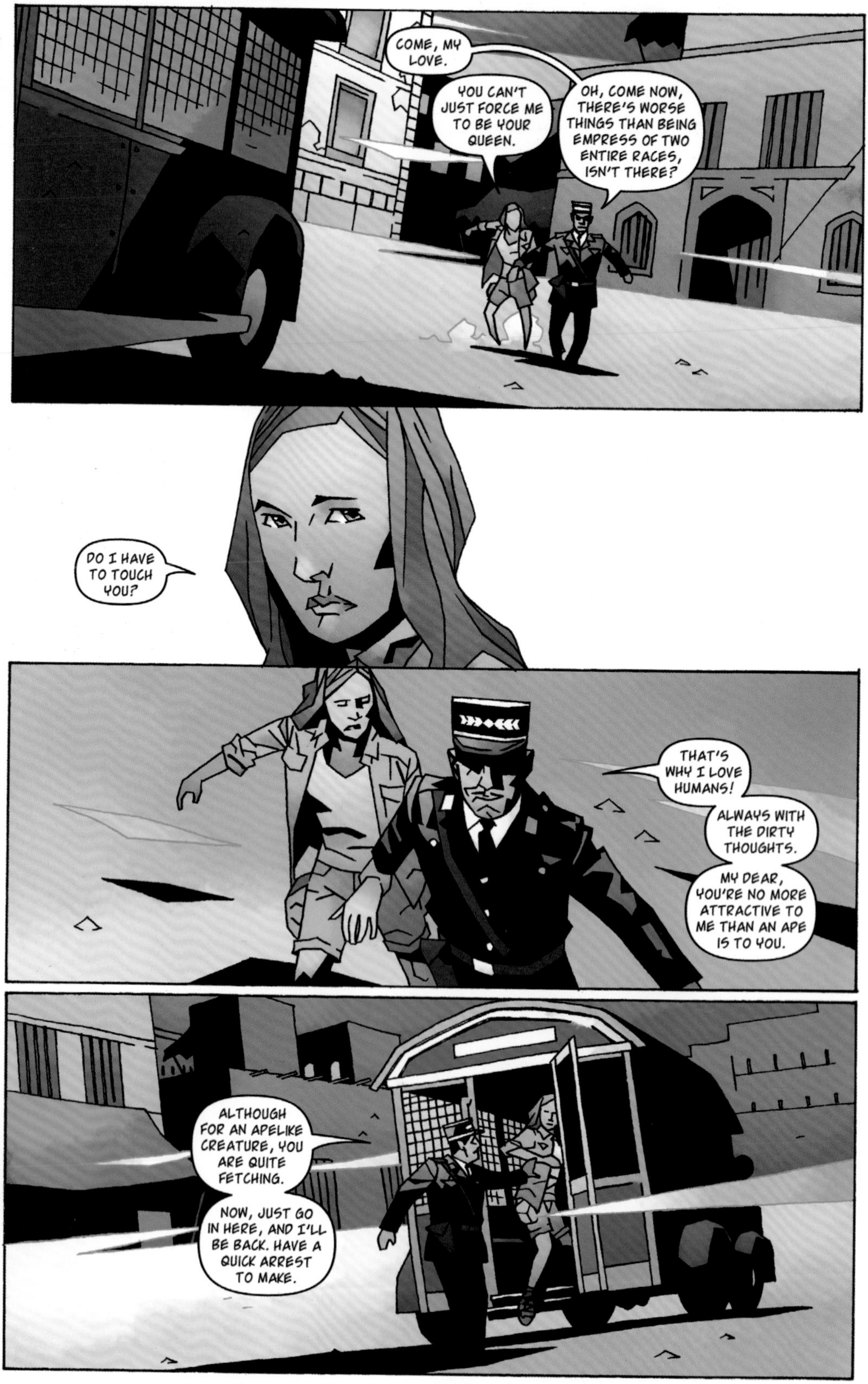
COME, MY LOVE.
YOU CAN'T JUST FORCE ME TO BE YOUR QUEEN.
OH, COME NOW, THERE'S WORSE THINGS THAN BEING EMPRESS OF TWO ENTIRE RACES, ISN'T THERE?
DO I HAVE TO TOUCH YOU?
THAT'S WHY I LOVE HUMANS!
ALWAYS WITH THE DIRTY THOUGHTS.
MY DEAR, YOU'RE NO MORE ATTRACTIVE TO ME THAN AN APE IS TO YOU.
ALTHOUGH FOR AN APELIKE CREATURE, YOU ARE QUITE FETCHING.
NOW, JUST GO IN HERE, AND I'LL BE BACK. HAVE A QUICK ARREST TO MAKE.

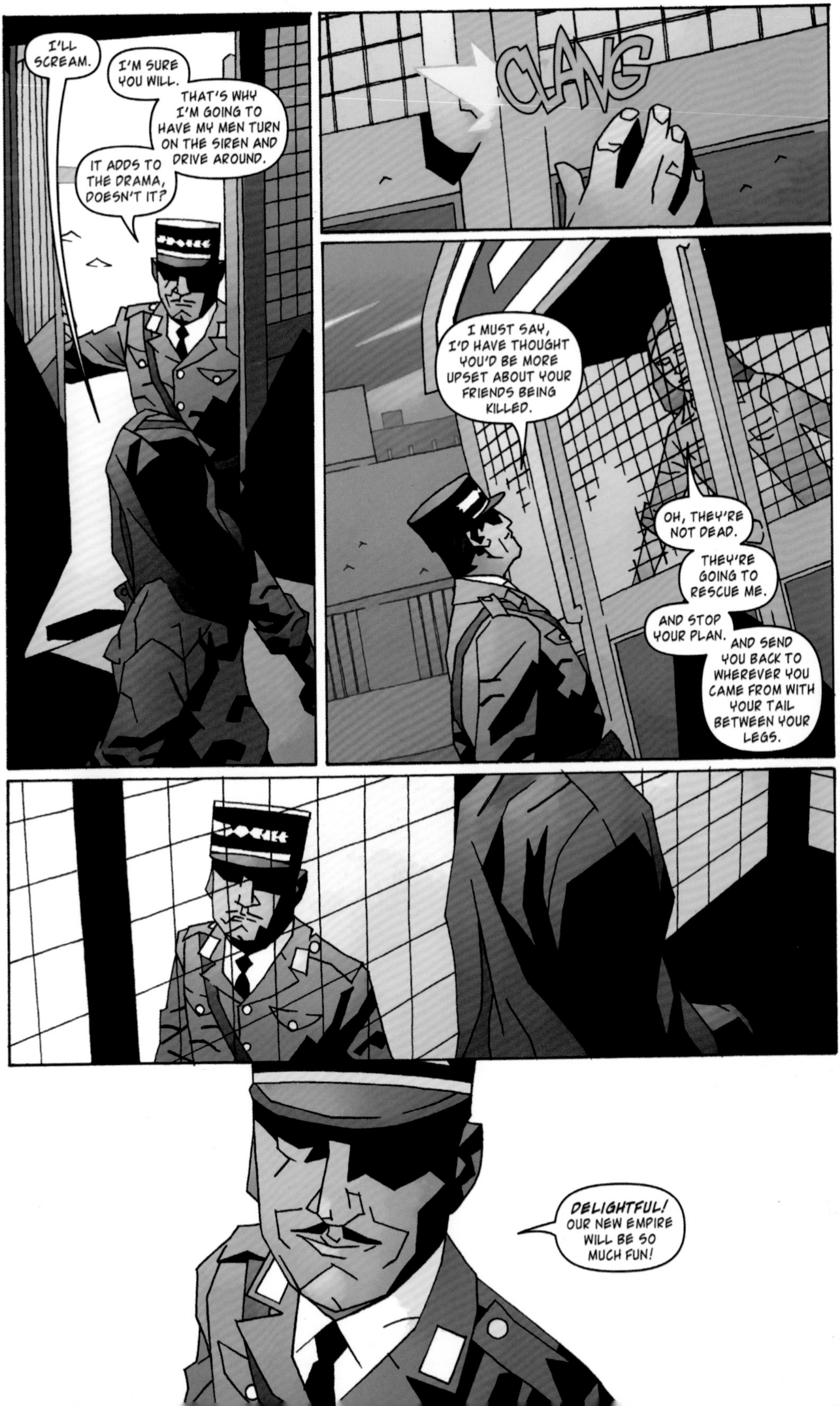
I'LL SCREAM.
I'M SURE YOU WILL.
THAT'S WHY I'M GOING TO HAVE MY MEN TURN ON THE SIREN AND DRIVE AROUND.
IT ADDS TO THE DRAMA, DOESN'T IT?
CLANG
I MUST SAY, I'D HAVE THOUGHT YOU'D BE MORE UPSET ABOUT YOUR FRIENDS BEING KILLED.
OH, THEY'RE NOT DEAD.
THEY'RE GOING TO RESCUE ME.
AND STOP YOUR PLAN.
AND SEND YOU BACK TO WHEREVER YOU CAME FROM WITH YOUR TAIL BETWEEN YOUR LEGS.
DELIGHTFUL! OUR NEW EMPIRE WILL BE SO MUCH FUN!

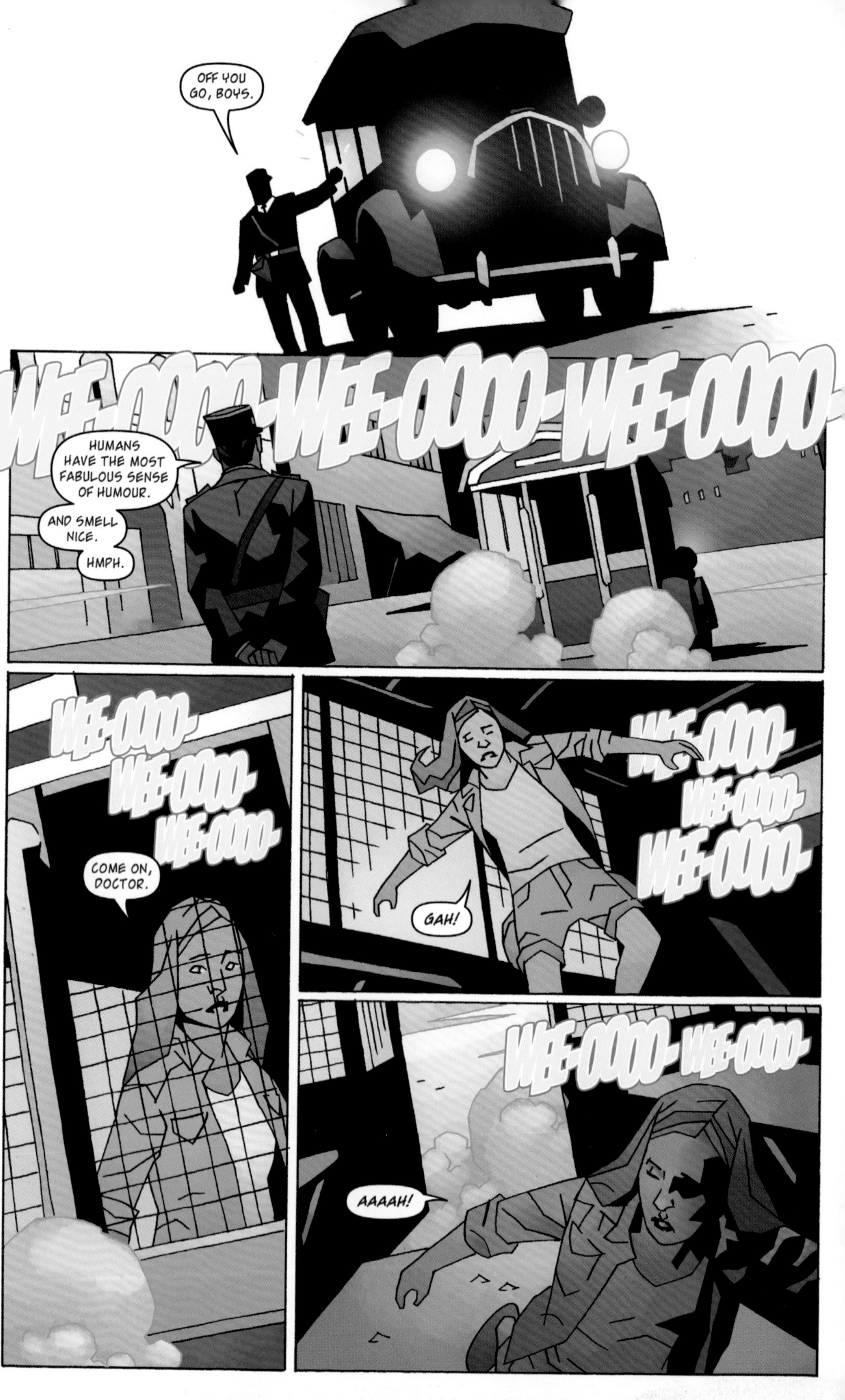

OFF YOU GO, BOYS.
WEE-OOOO-WEE-OOOO-WEE-OOOO-
HUMANS HAVE THE MOST FABULOUS SENSE OF HUMOUR.
AND SMELL NICE.
HMPH.
WEE-OOOO-
WEE-OOOO-
WEE-OOOO-
COME ON, DOCTOR.
WEE-OOOO-
WEE-OOOO-
WEE-OOOO-
GAH!
WEE-OOOO-WEE-OOOO-
AAAAH!

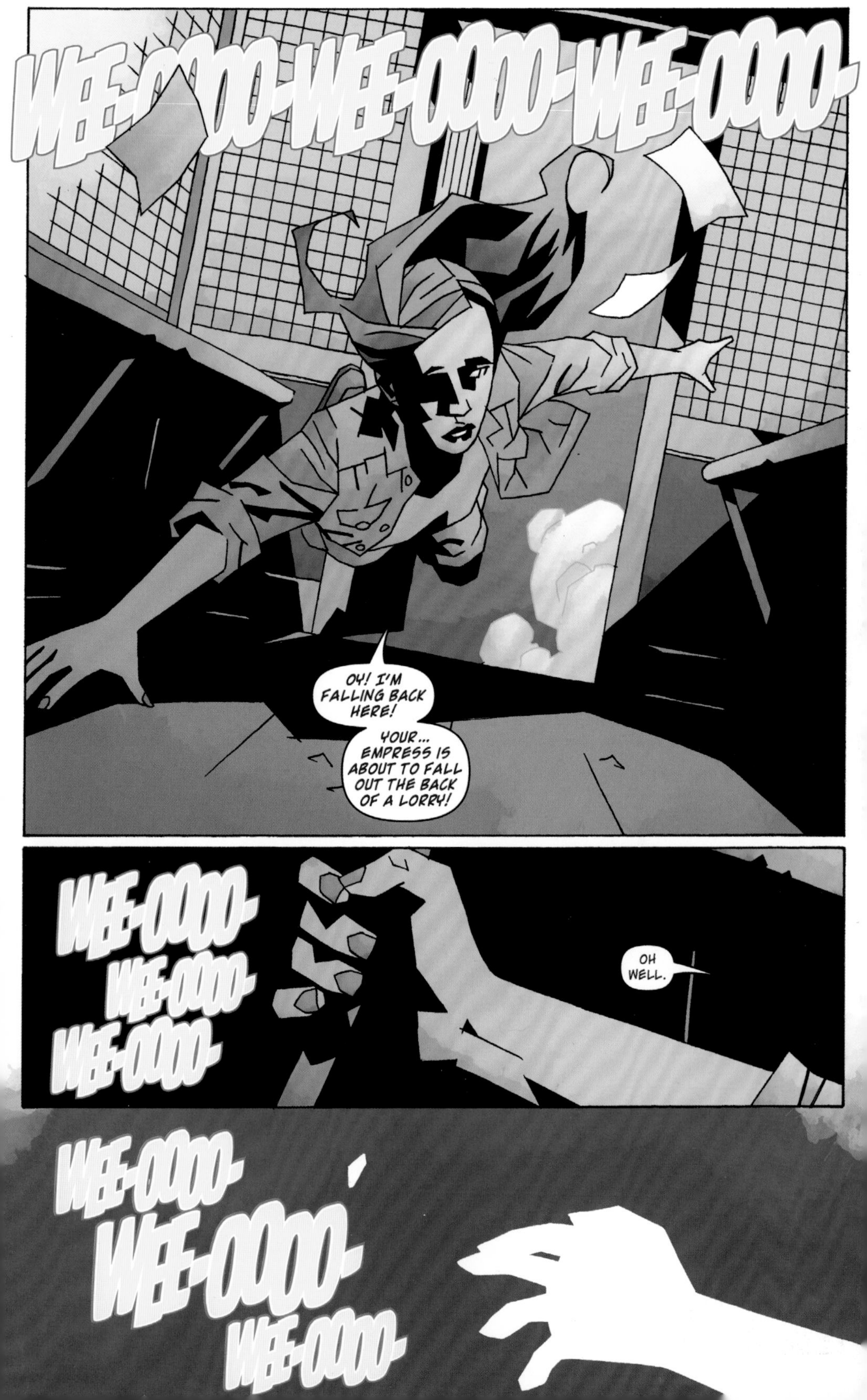
WEE-OOOO-WEE-OOOO-WEE-OOOO-
OY! I'M FALLING BACK HERE!
YOUR... EMPRESS IS ABOUT TO FALL OUT THE BACK OF A LORRY!
WEE-OOOO-
WEE-OOOO-
WEE-OOOO-
OH WELL.
WEE-OOOO-
WEE-OOOO-
WEE-OOOO-

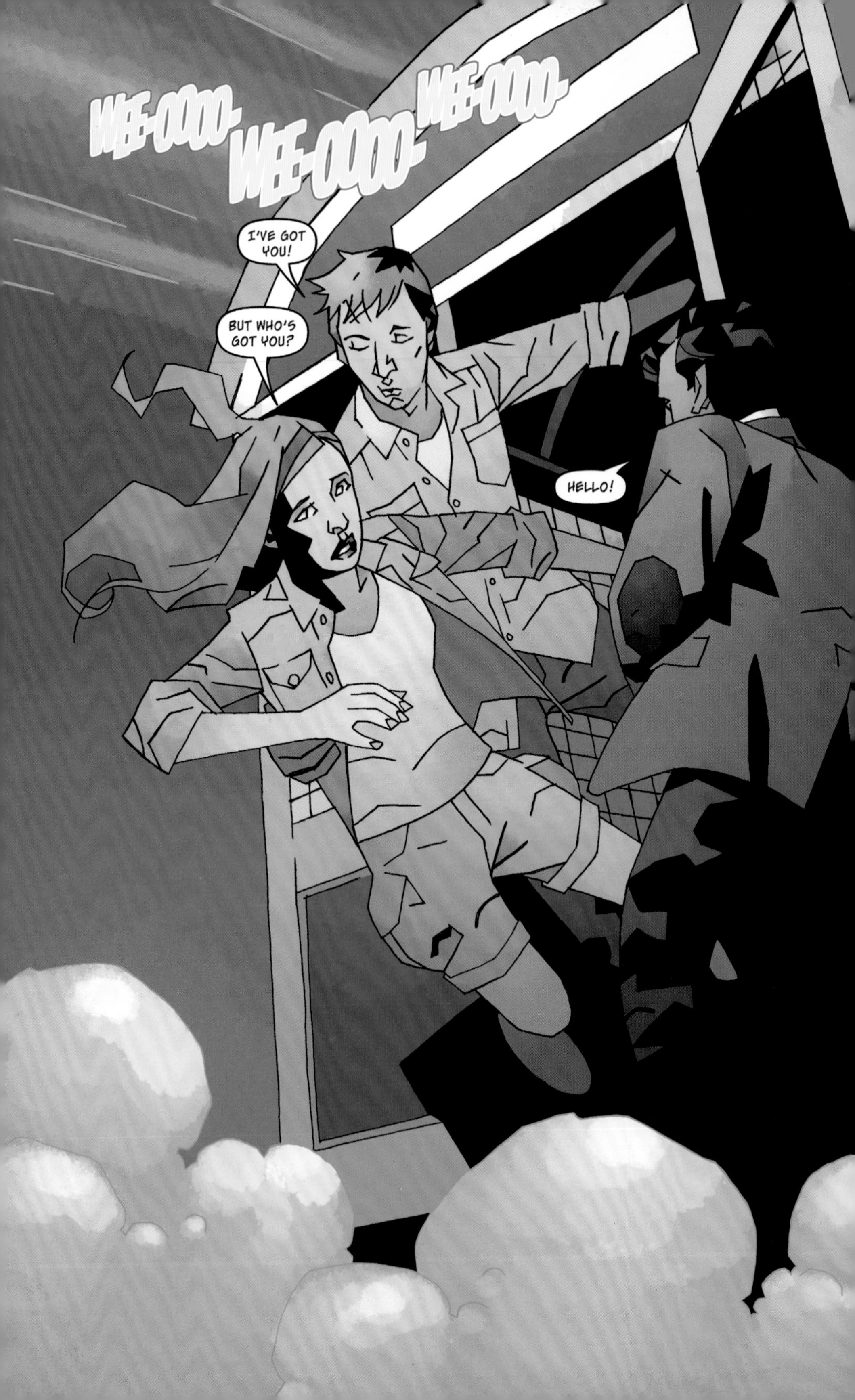
WEE-OOOO-
WEE-OOOO-
WEE-OOOO-
I'VE GOT YOU!
BUT WHO'S GOT YOU?
HELLO!

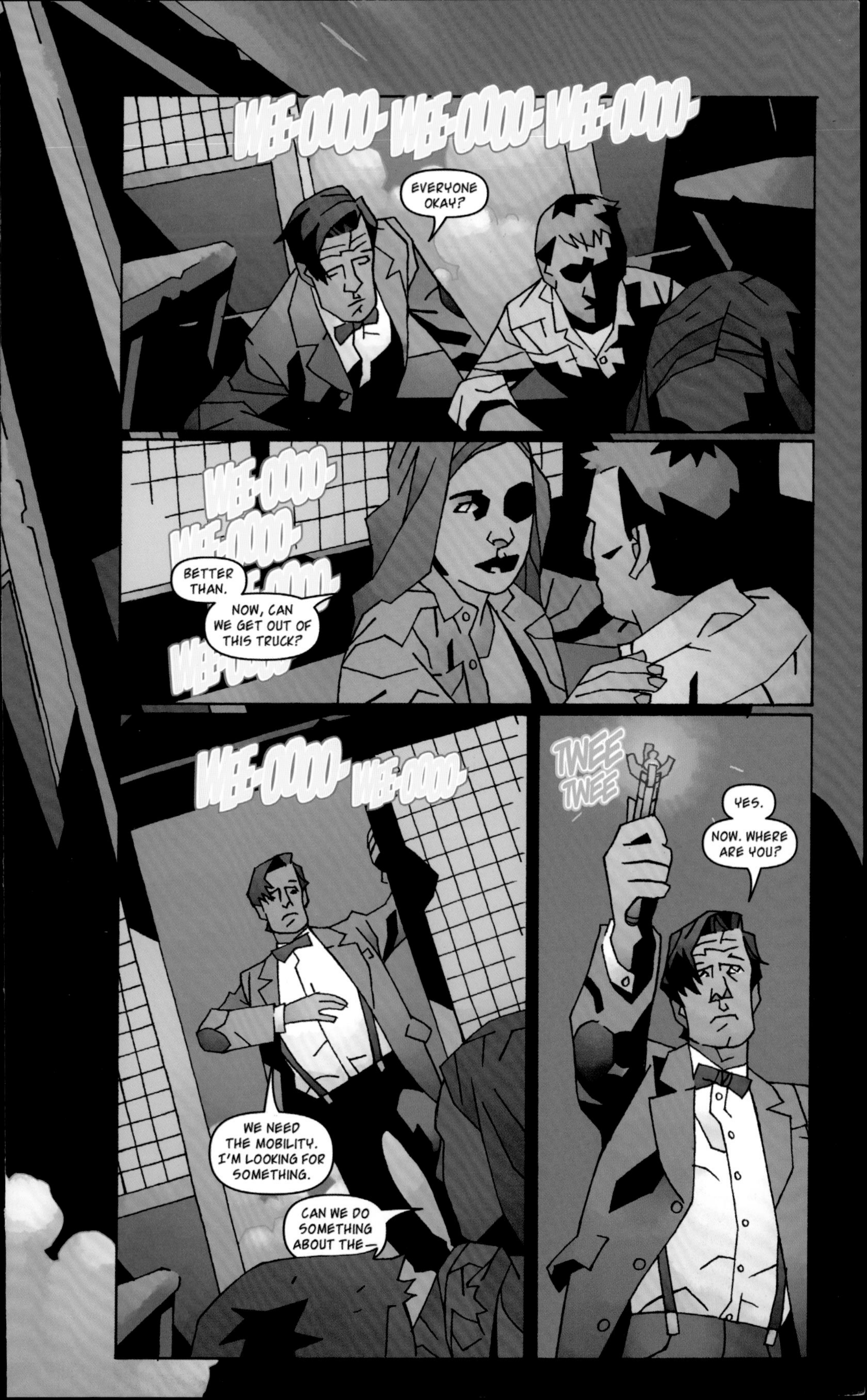
WEE-OOOO-WEE-OOOO-WEE-OOOO-
EVERYONE OKAY?
WEE-OOOO-
WEE-OOOO-
WEE-OOOO-
WEE-OOOO-
BETTER THAN.
NOW, CAN WE GET OUT OF THIS TRUCK?
WEE-OOOO-WEE-OOOO-
WE NEED THE MOBILITY. I'M LOOKING FOR SOMETHING.
CAN WE DO SOMETHING ABOUT THE—
TWEE TWEE
YES.
NOW. WHERE ARE YOU?

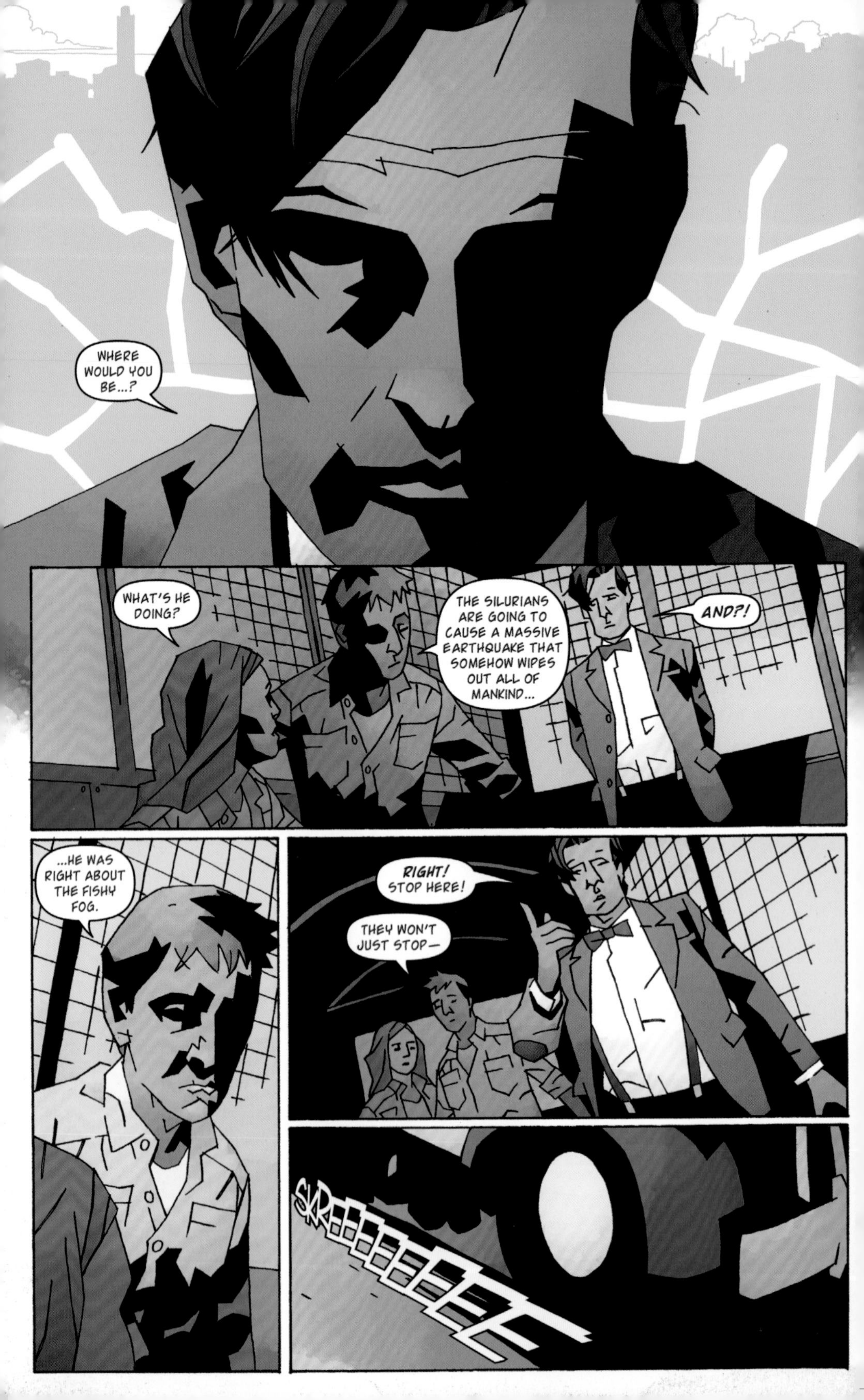
WHERE WOULD YOU BE...?
WHAT'S HE DOING?
THE SILURIANS ARE GOING TO CAUSE A MASSIVE EARTHQUAKE THAT SOMEHOW WIPES OUT ALL OF MANKIND...
AND?!
...HE WAS RIGHT ABOUT THE FISHY FOG.
RIGHT! STOP HERE!
THEY WON'T JUST STOP—
SKREEEEEEEEEE

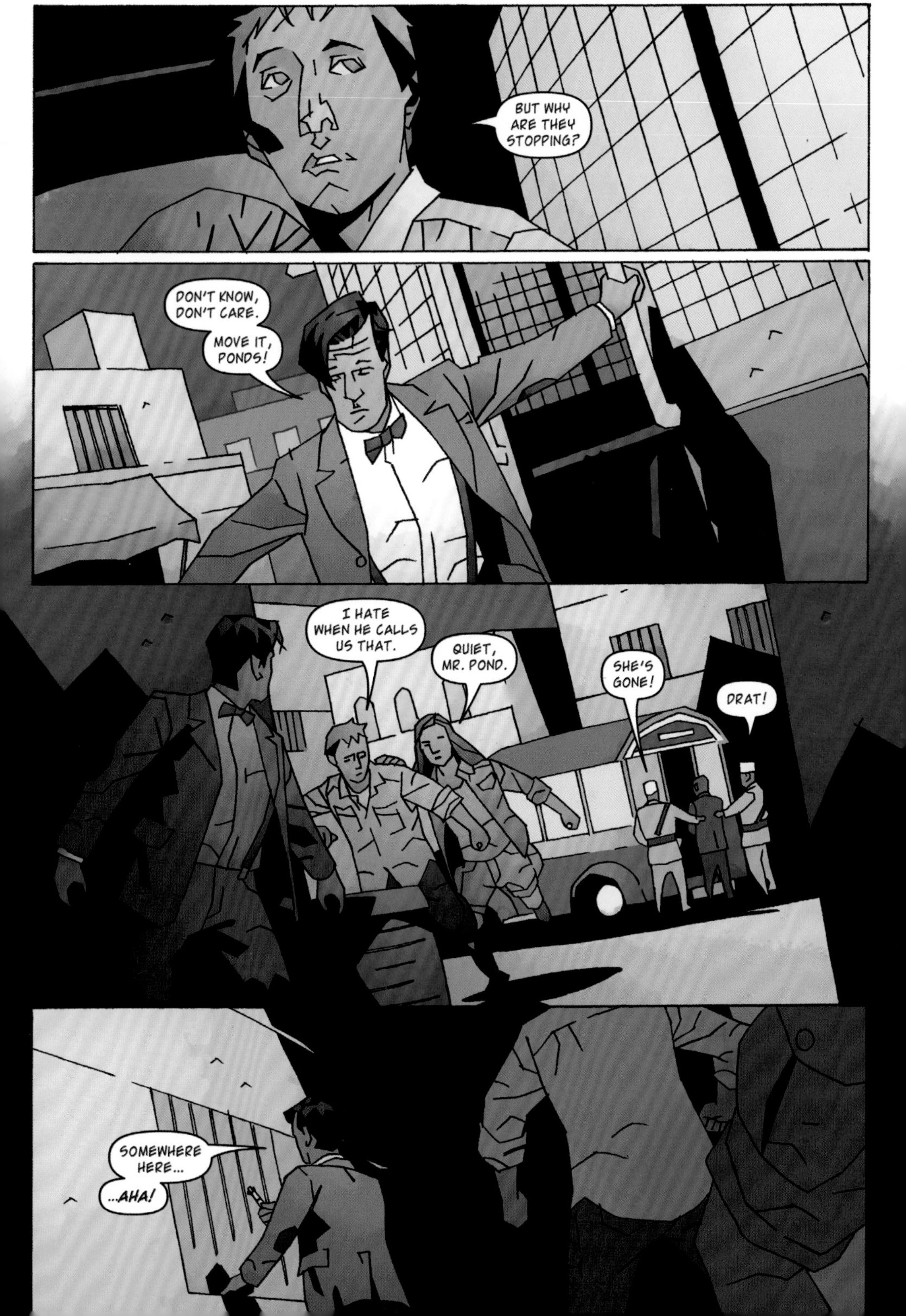
BUT WHY ARE THEY STOPPING?
DON'T KNOW, DON'T CARE.
MOVE IT, PONDS!
I HATE WHEN HE CALLS US THAT.
QUIET, MR. POND.
SHE'S GONE!
DRAT!
SOMEWHERE HERE...
...AHA!

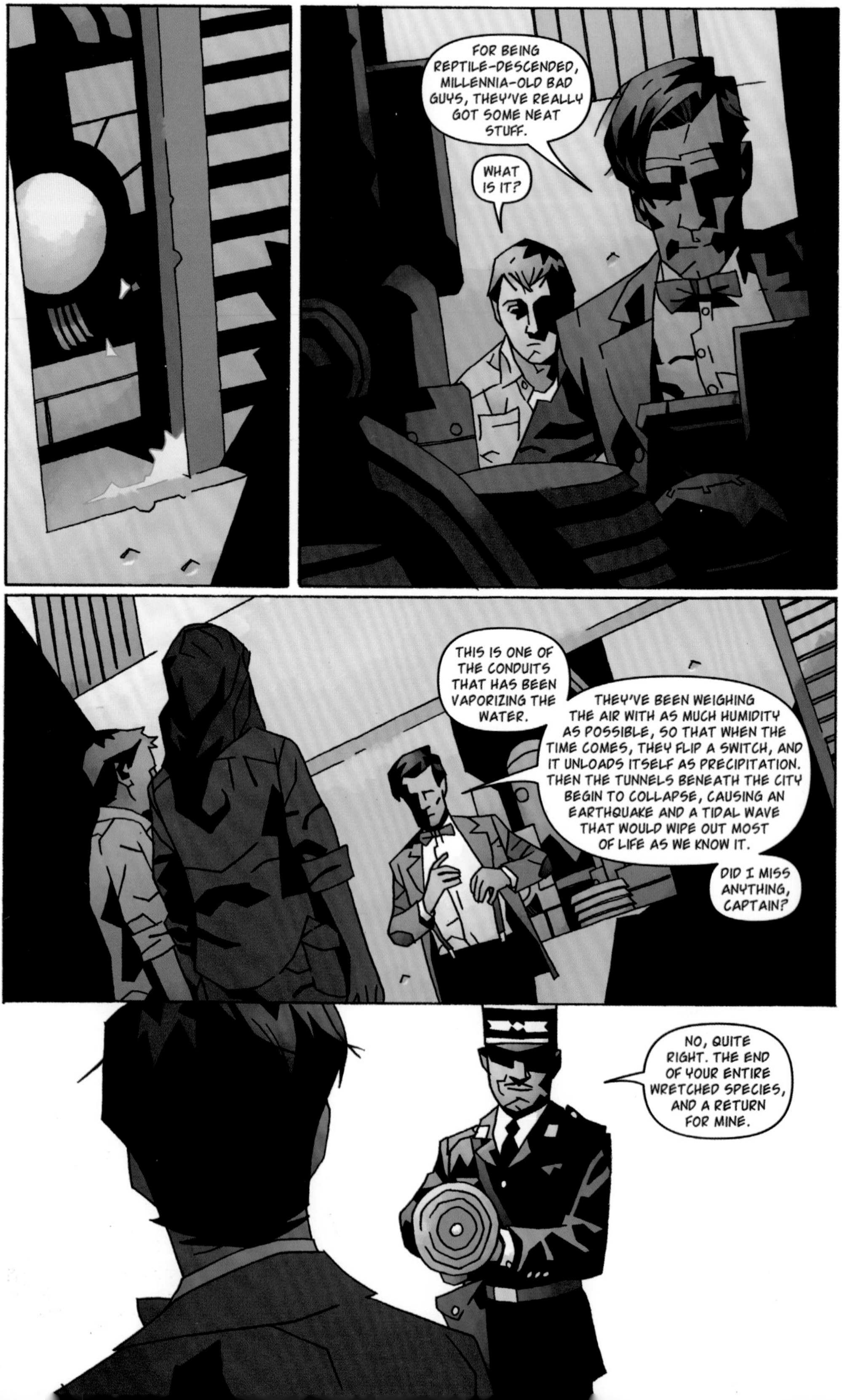
FOR BEING REPTILE-DESCENDED, MILLENNIA-OLD BAD GUYS, THEY'VE REALLY GOT SOME NEAT STUFF.
WHAT IS IT?
THIS IS ONE OF THE CONDUITS THAT HAS BEEN VAPORIZING THE WATER.
THEY'VE BEEN WEIGHING THE AIR WITH AS MUCH HUMIDITY AS POSSIBLE, SO THAT WHEN THE TIME COMES, THEY FLIP A SWITCH, AND IT UNLOADS ITSELF AS PRECIPITATION. THEN THE TUNNELS BENEATH THE CITY BEGIN TO COLLAPSE, CAUSING AN EARTHQUAKE AND A TIDAL WAVE THAT WOULD WIPE OUT MOST OF LIFE AS WE KNOW IT.
DID I MISS ANYTHING, CAPTAIN?
NO, QUITE RIGHT. THE END OF YOUR ENTIRE WRETCHED SPECIES, AND A RETURN FOR MINE.

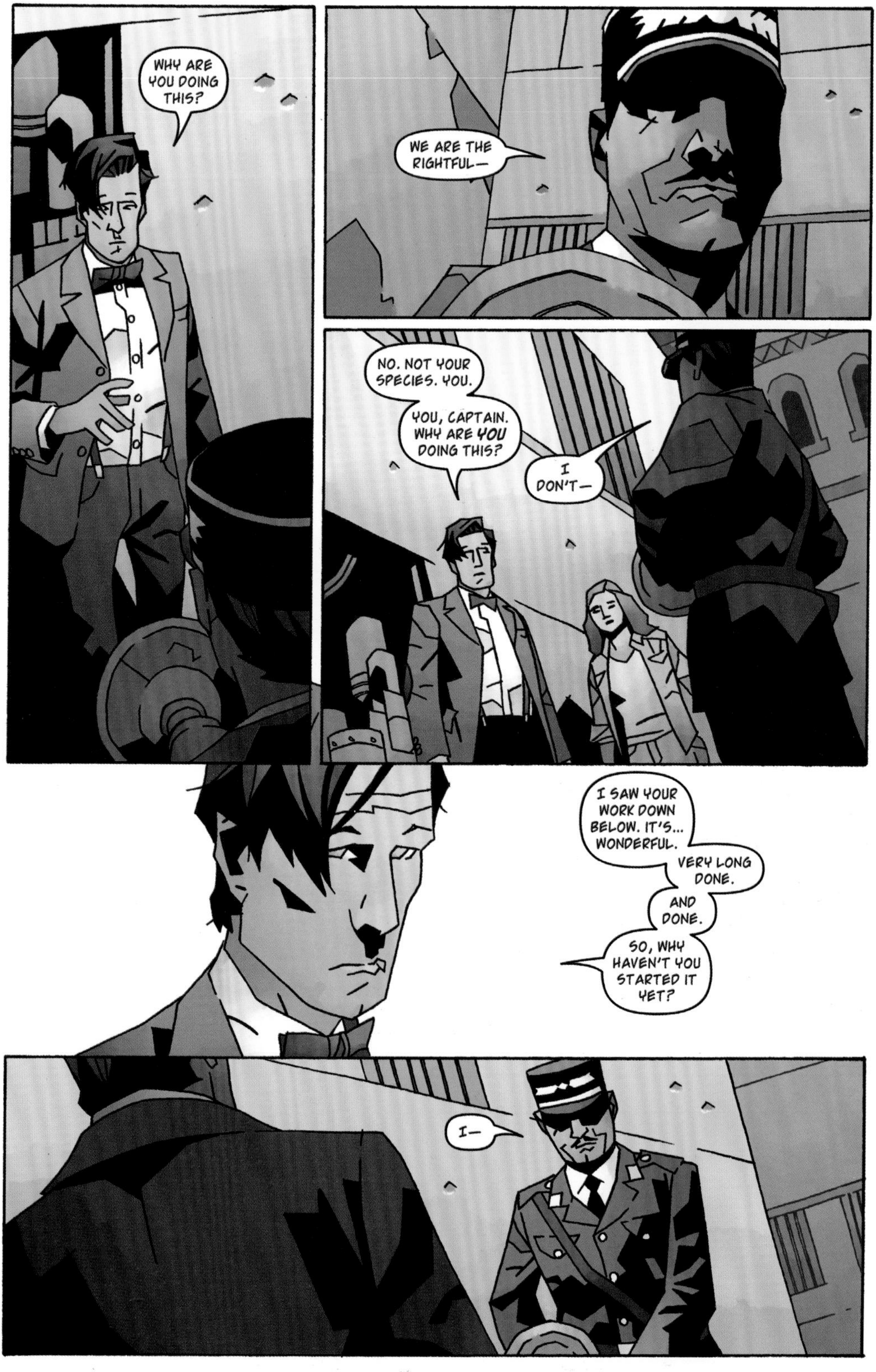
WHY ARE YOU DOING THIS?
WE ARE THE RIGHTFUL—
NO. NOT YOUR SPECIES. YOU.
YOU, CAPTAIN. WHY ARE YOU DOING THIS?
I DON'T—
I SAW YOUR WORK DOWN BELOW. IT'S... WONDERFUL.
VERY LONG DONE.
AND DONE.
SO, WHY HAVEN'T YOU STARTED IT YET?
I—

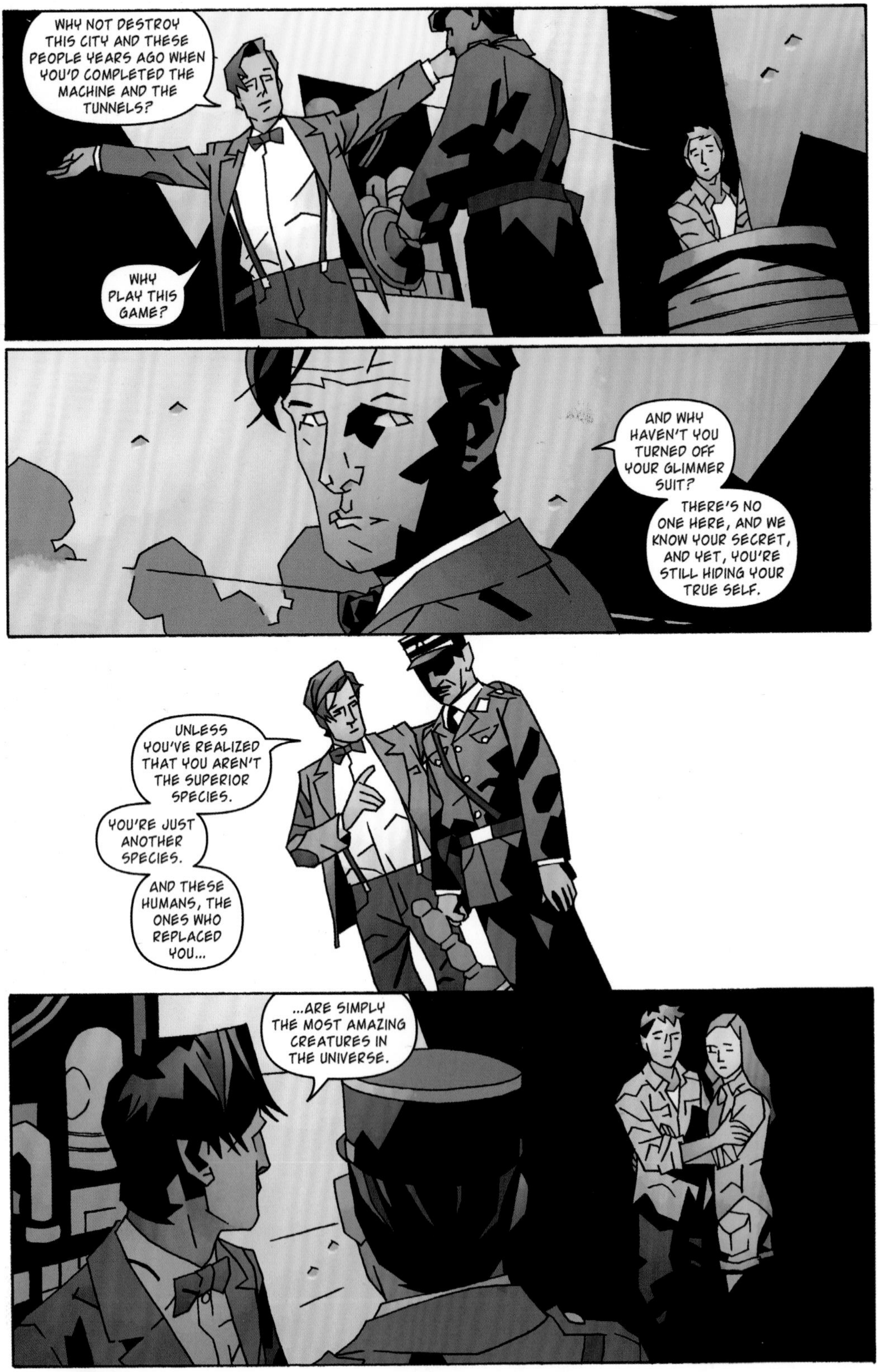
WHY NOT DESTROY THIS CITY AND THESE PEOPLE YEARS AGO WHEN YOU'D COMPLETED THE MACHINE AND THE TUNNELS?
WHY PLAY THIS GAME?
AND WHY HAVEN'T YOU TURNED OFF YOUR GLIMMER SUIT?
THERE'S NO ONE HERE, AND WE KNOW YOUR SECRET, AND YET, YOU'RE STILL HIDING YOUR TRUE SELF.
UNLESS YOU'VE REALIZED THAT YOU AREN'T THE SUPERIOR SPECIES.
YOU'RE JUST ANOTHER SPECIES.
AND THESE HUMANS, THE ONES WHO REPLACED YOU...
...ARE SIMPLY THE MOST AMAZING CREATURES IN THE UNIVERSE.

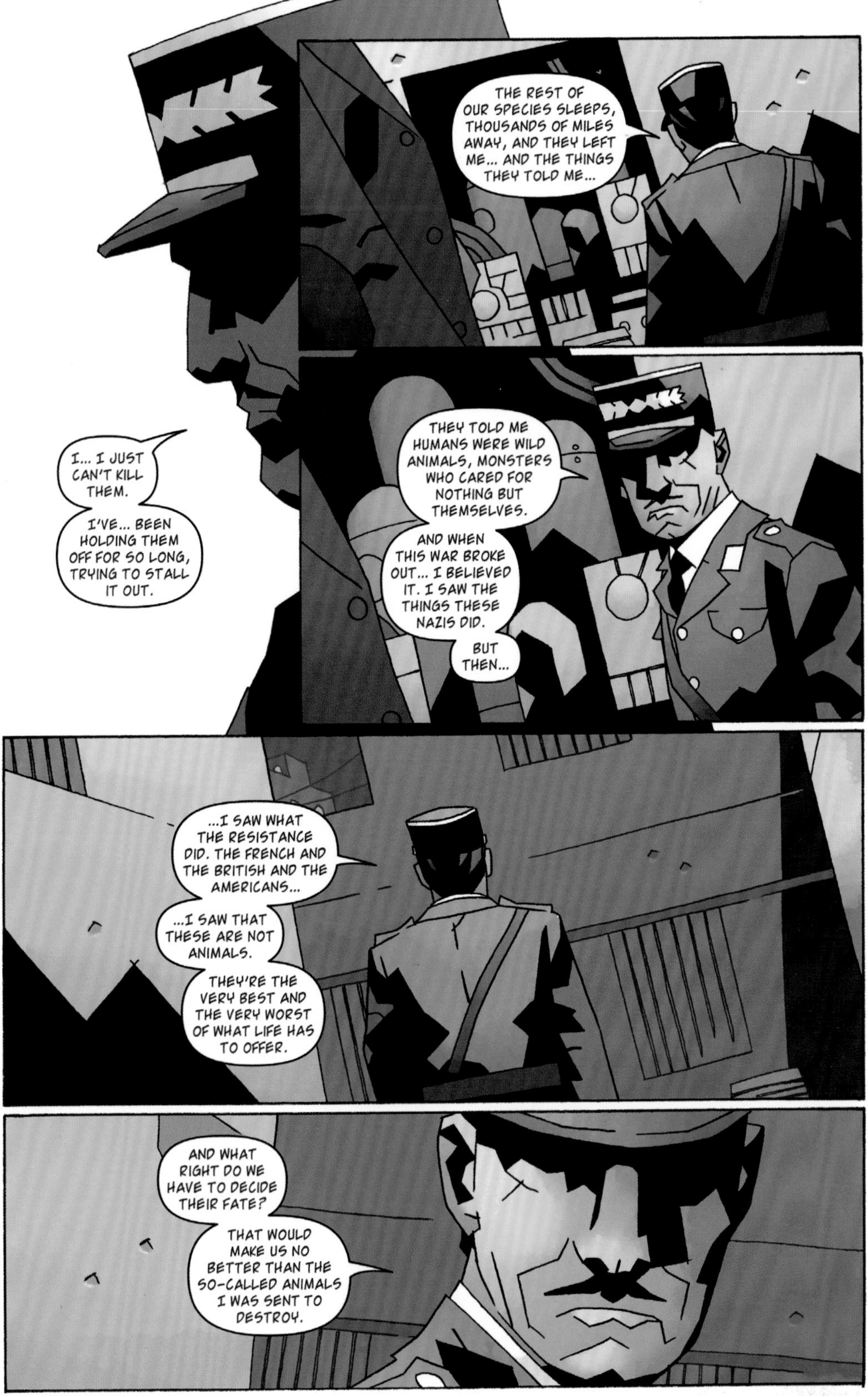
THE REST OF OUR SPECIES SLEEPS, THOUSANDS OF MILES AWAY, AND THEY LEFT ME... AND THE THINGS THEY TOLD ME...
THEY TOLD ME HUMANS WERE WILD ANIMALS, MONSTERS WHO CARED FOR NOTHING BUT THEMSELVES.
AND WHEN THIS WAR BROKE OUT... I BELIEVED IT. I SAW THE THINGS THESE NAZIS DID.
BUT THEN...
I... I JUST CAN'T KILL THEM.
I'VE... BEEN HOLDING THEM OFF FOR SO LONG, TRYING TO STALL IT OUT.
...I SAW WHAT THE RESISTANCE DID. THE FRENCH AND THE BRITISH AND THE AMERICANS...
...I SAW THAT THESE ARE NOT ANIMALS.
THEY'RE THE VERY BEST AND THE VERY WORST OF WHAT LIFE HAS TO OFFER.
AND WHAT RIGHT DO WE HAVE TO DECIDE THEIR FATE?
THAT WOULD MAKE US NO BETTER THAN THE SO-CALLED ANIMALS I WAS SENT TO DESTROY.

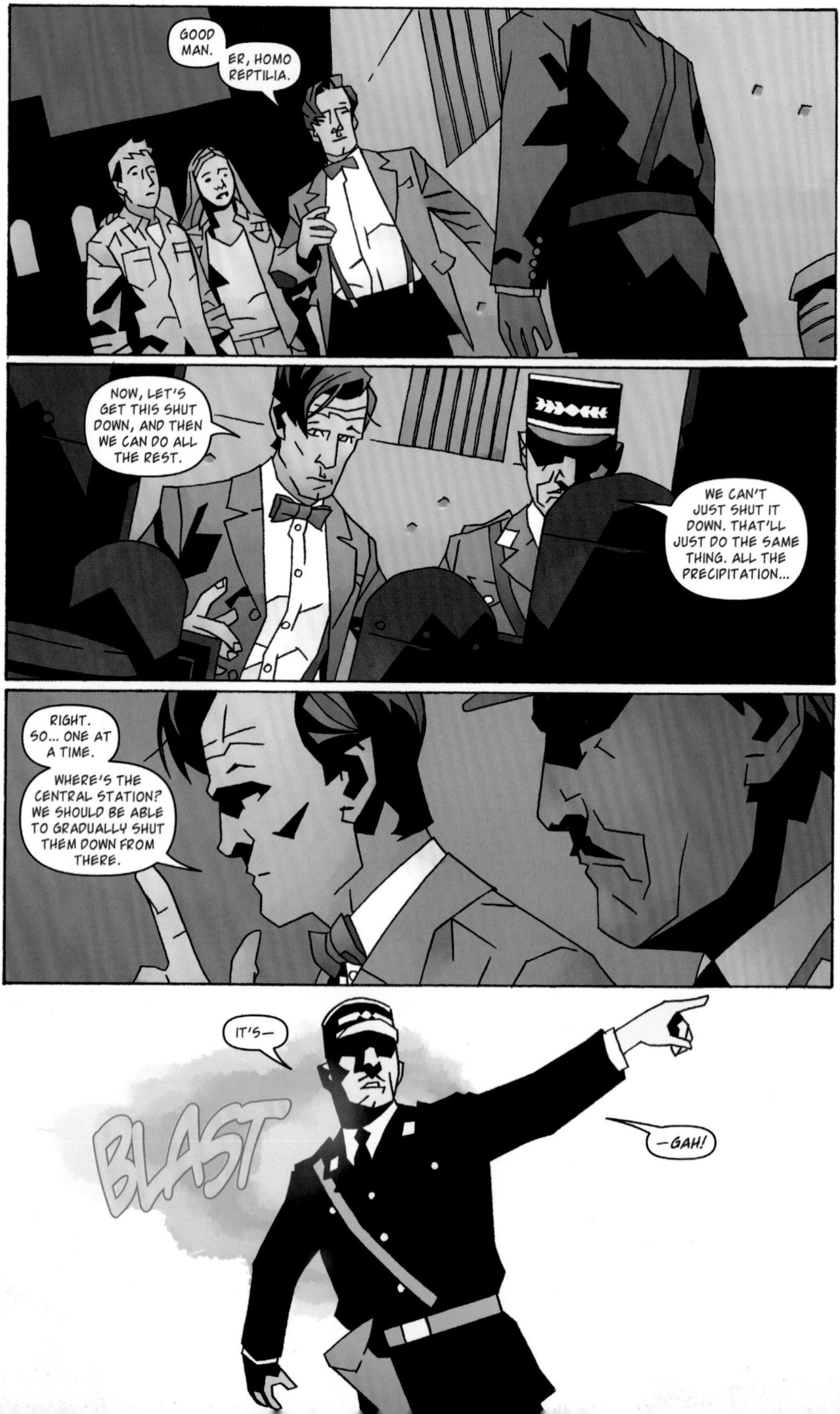
GOOD MAN.
ER, HOMO REPTILIA.
NOW, LET'S GET THIS SHUT DOWN, AND THEN WE CAN DO ALL THE REST.
WE CAN'T JUST SHUT IT DOWN. THAT'LL JUST DO THE SAME THING. ALL THE PRECIPITATION...
RIGHT. SO... ONE AT A TIME.
WHERE'S THE CENTRAL STATION? WE SHOULD BE ABLE TO GRADUALLY SHUT THEM DOWN FROM THERE.
IT'S—
BLAST
—GAH!

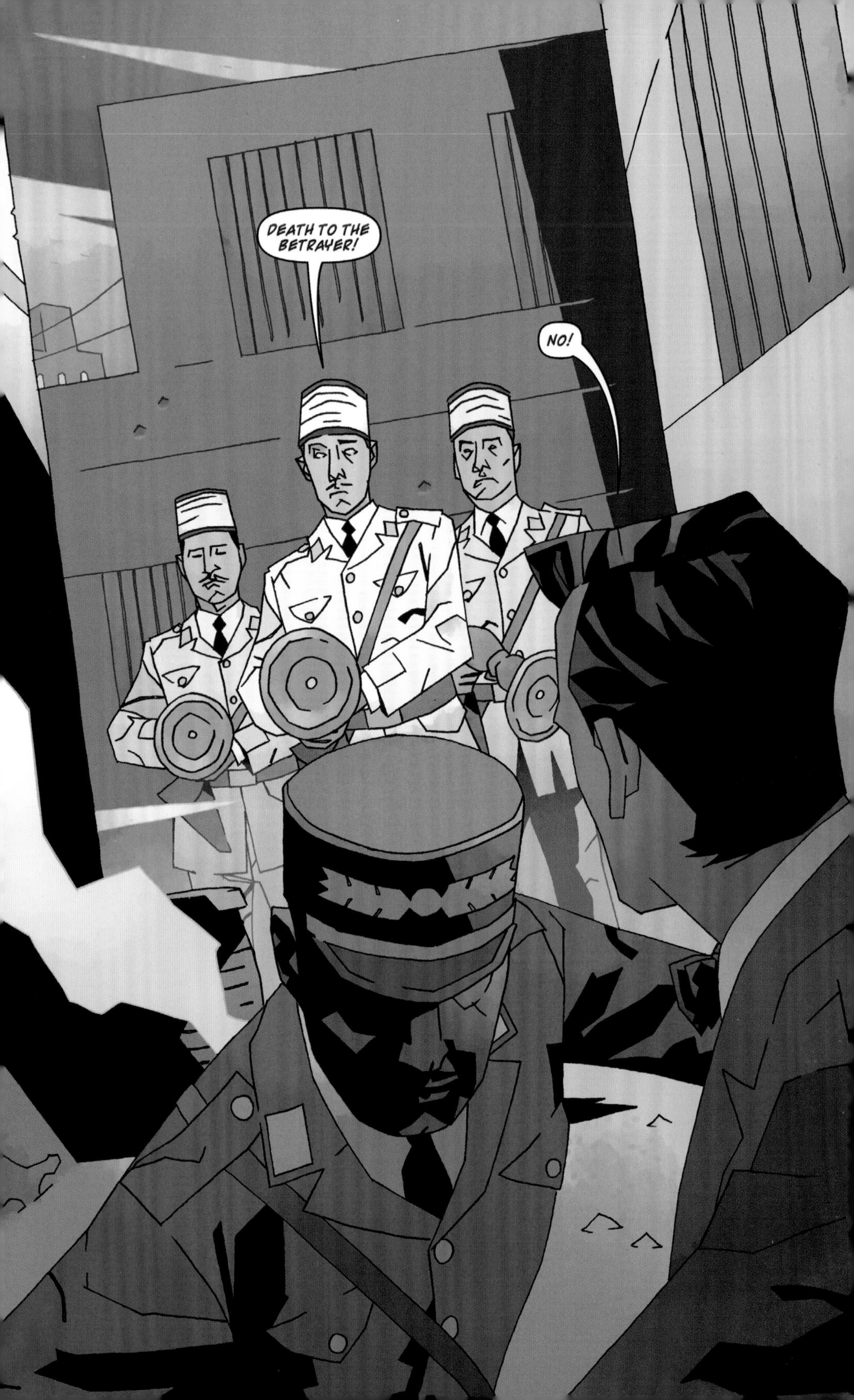
DEATH TO THE BETRAYER!
NO!

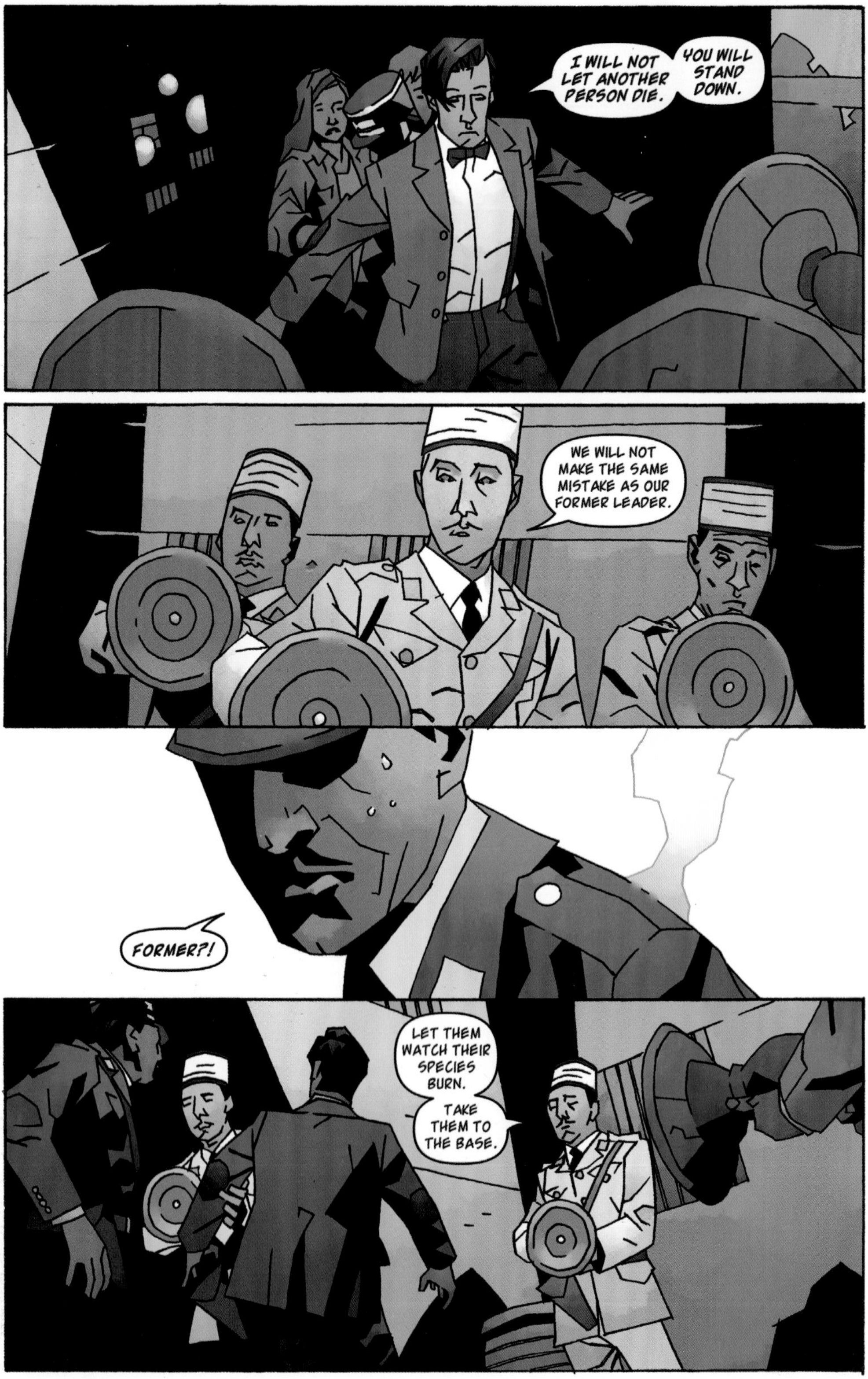
I WILL NOT LET ANOTHER PERSON DIE.
YOU WILL STAND DOWN.
WE WILL NOT MAKE THE SAME MISTAKE AS OUR FORMER LEADER.
FORMER?!
LET THEM WATCH THEIR SPECIES BURN.
TAKE THEM TO THE BASE.

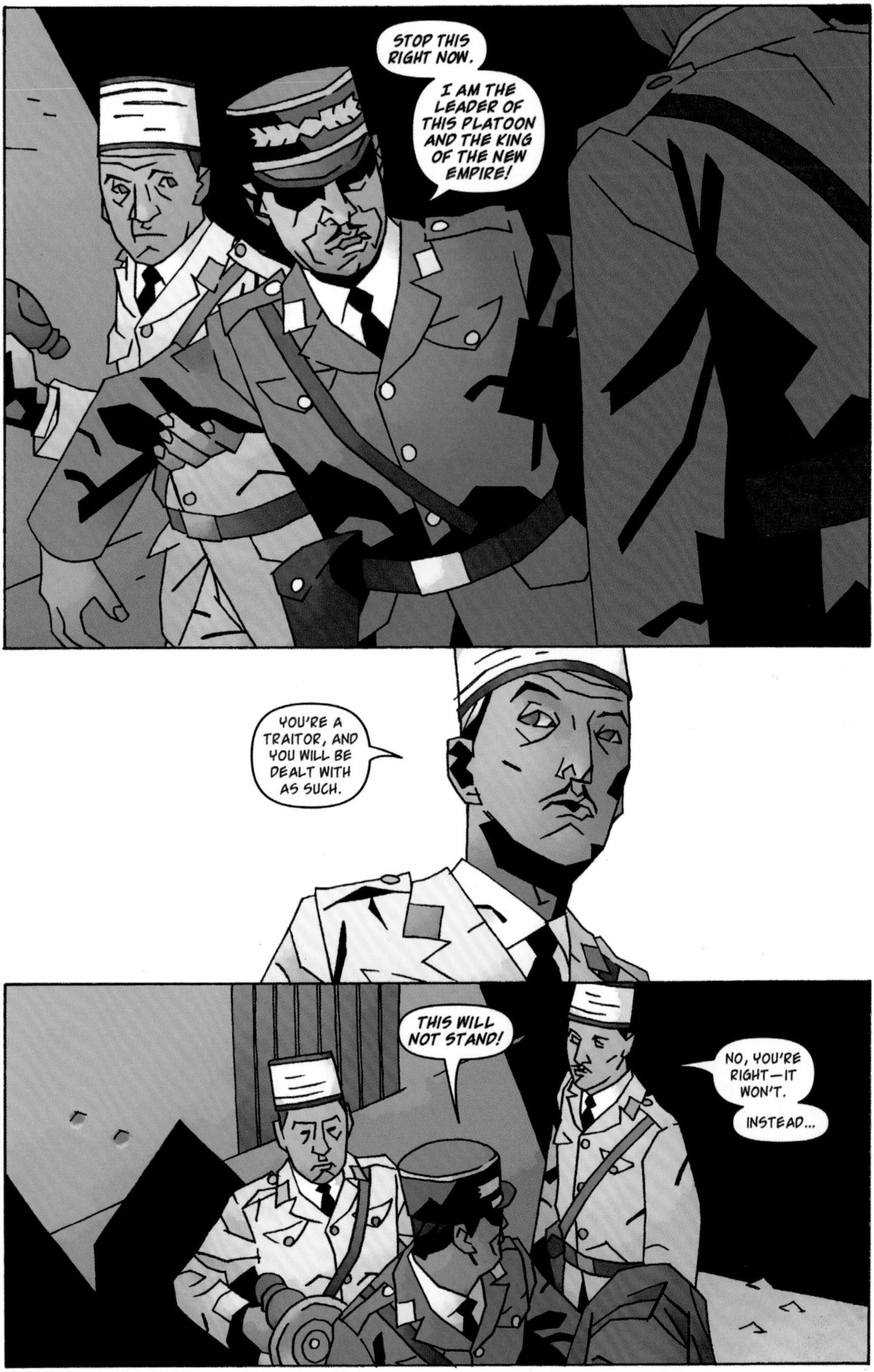
STOP THIS RIGHT NOW.
I AM THE LEADER OF THIS PLATOON AND THE KING OF THE NEW EMPIRE!
YOU'RE A TRAITOR, AND YOU WILL BE DEALT WITH AS SUCH.
THIS WILL NOT STAND!
NO, YOU'RE RIGHT—IT WON'T.
INSTEAD...

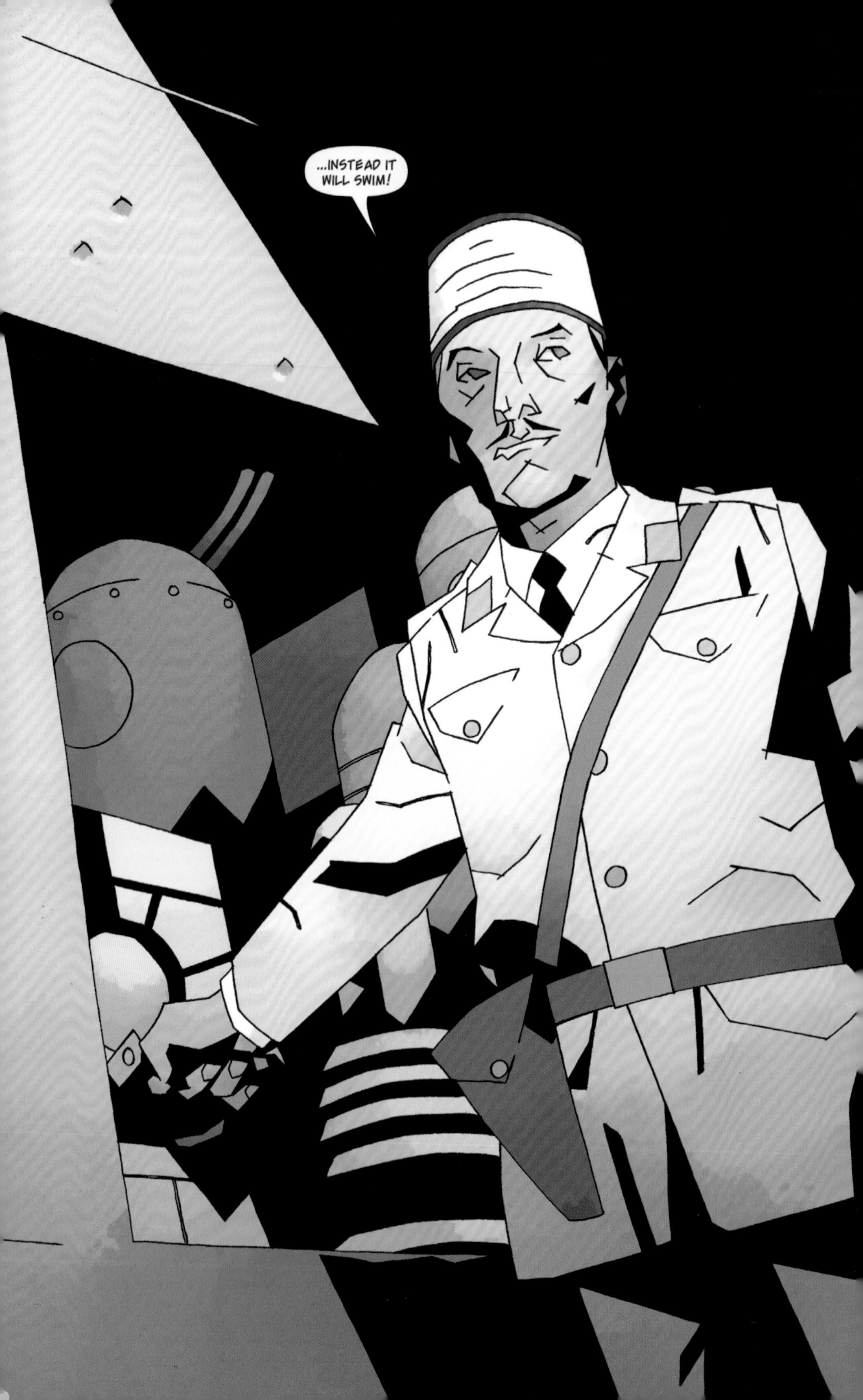
...INSTEAD IT WILL SWIM!

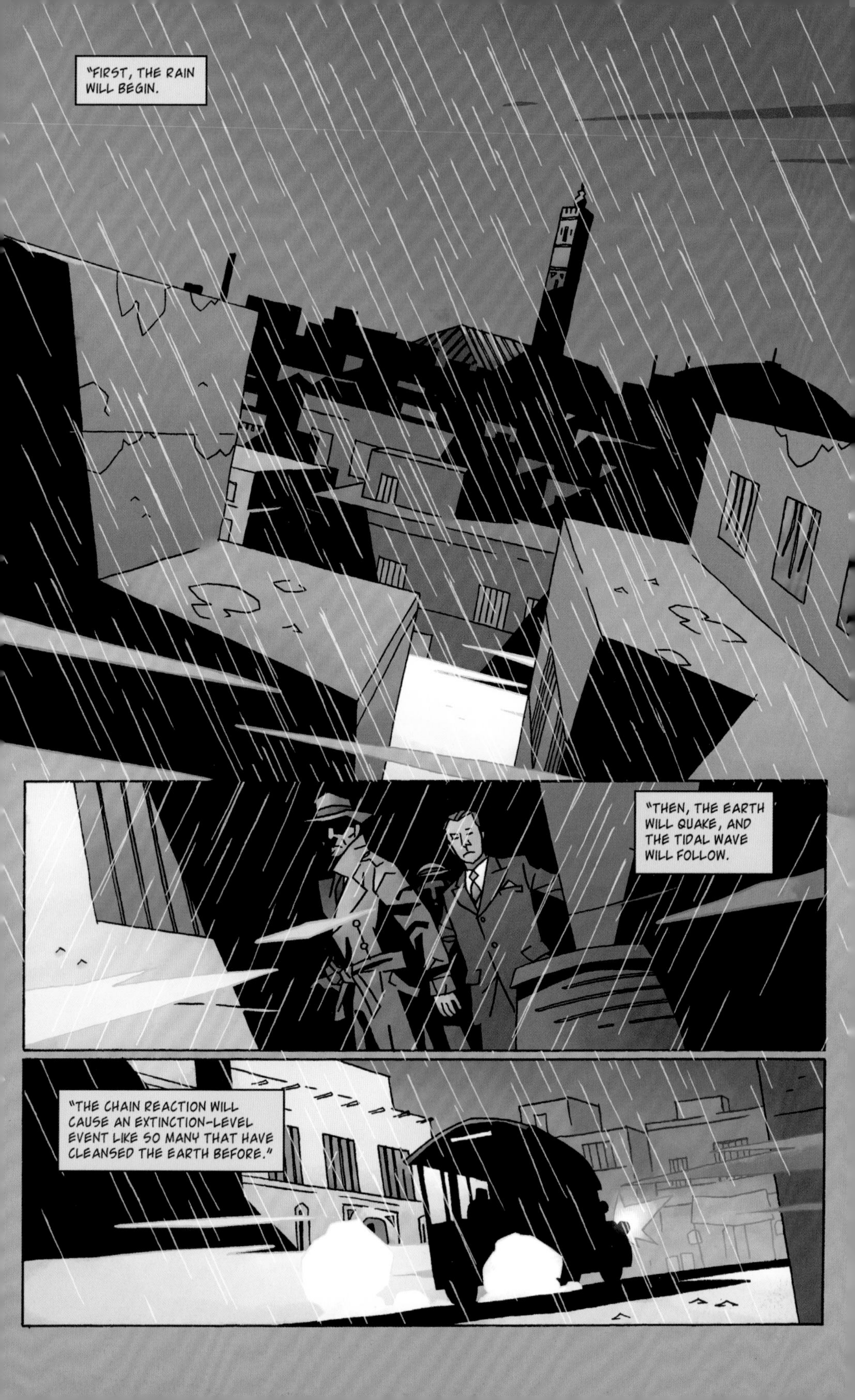
"FIRST, THE RAIN WILL BEGIN.
"THEN, THE EARTH WILL QUAKE, AND THE TIDAL WAVE WILL FOLLOW.
"THE CHAIN REACTION WILL CAUSE AN EXTINCTION-LEVEL EVENT LIKE SO MANY THAT HAVE CLEANSED THE EARTH BEFORE."

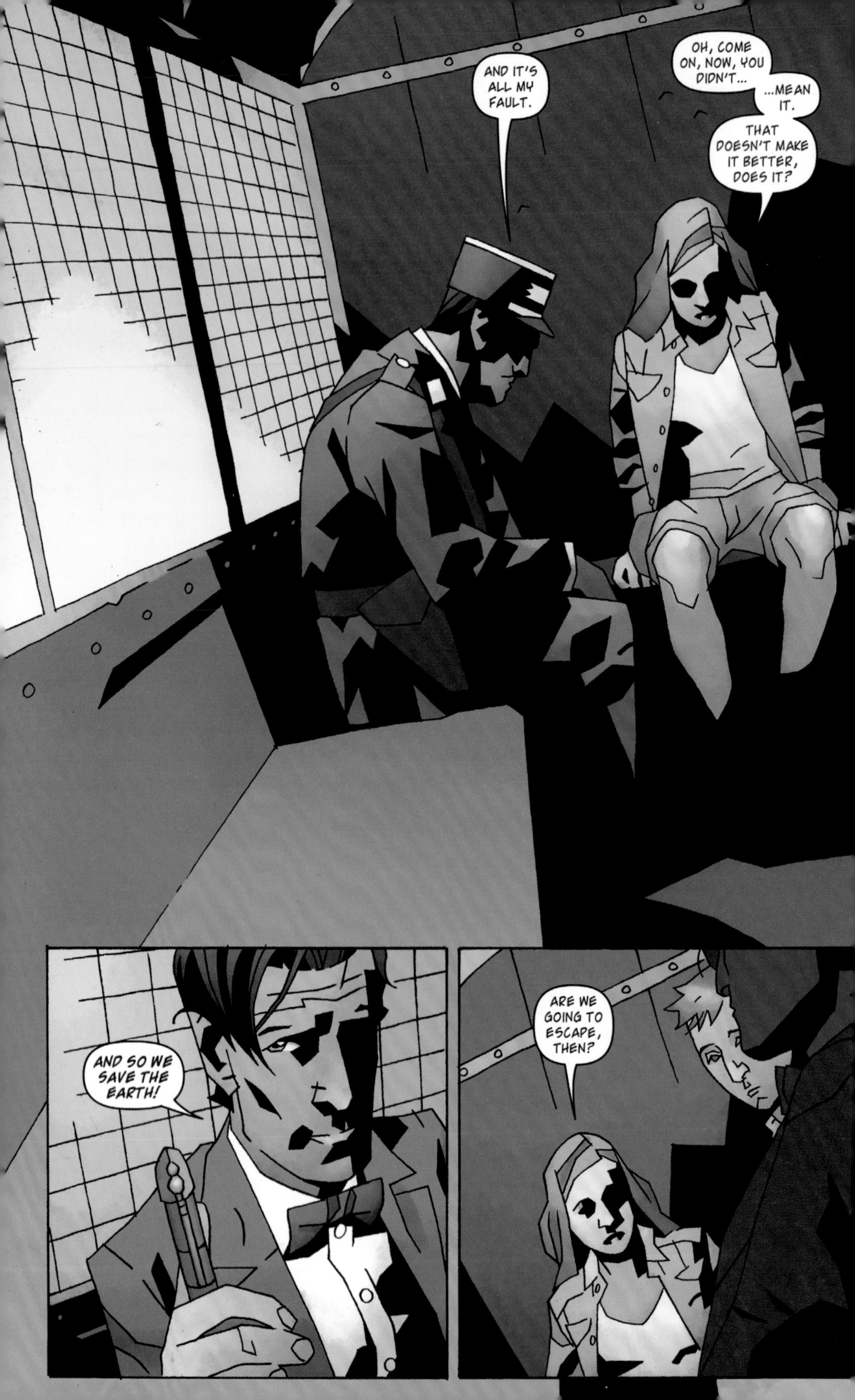
AND IT'S ALL MY FAULT.
OH, COME ON, NOW, YOU DIDN'T...
...MEAN IT.
THAT DOESN'T MAKE IT BETTER, DOES IT?
AND SO WE SAVE THE EARTH!
ARE WE GOING TO ESCAPE, THEN?

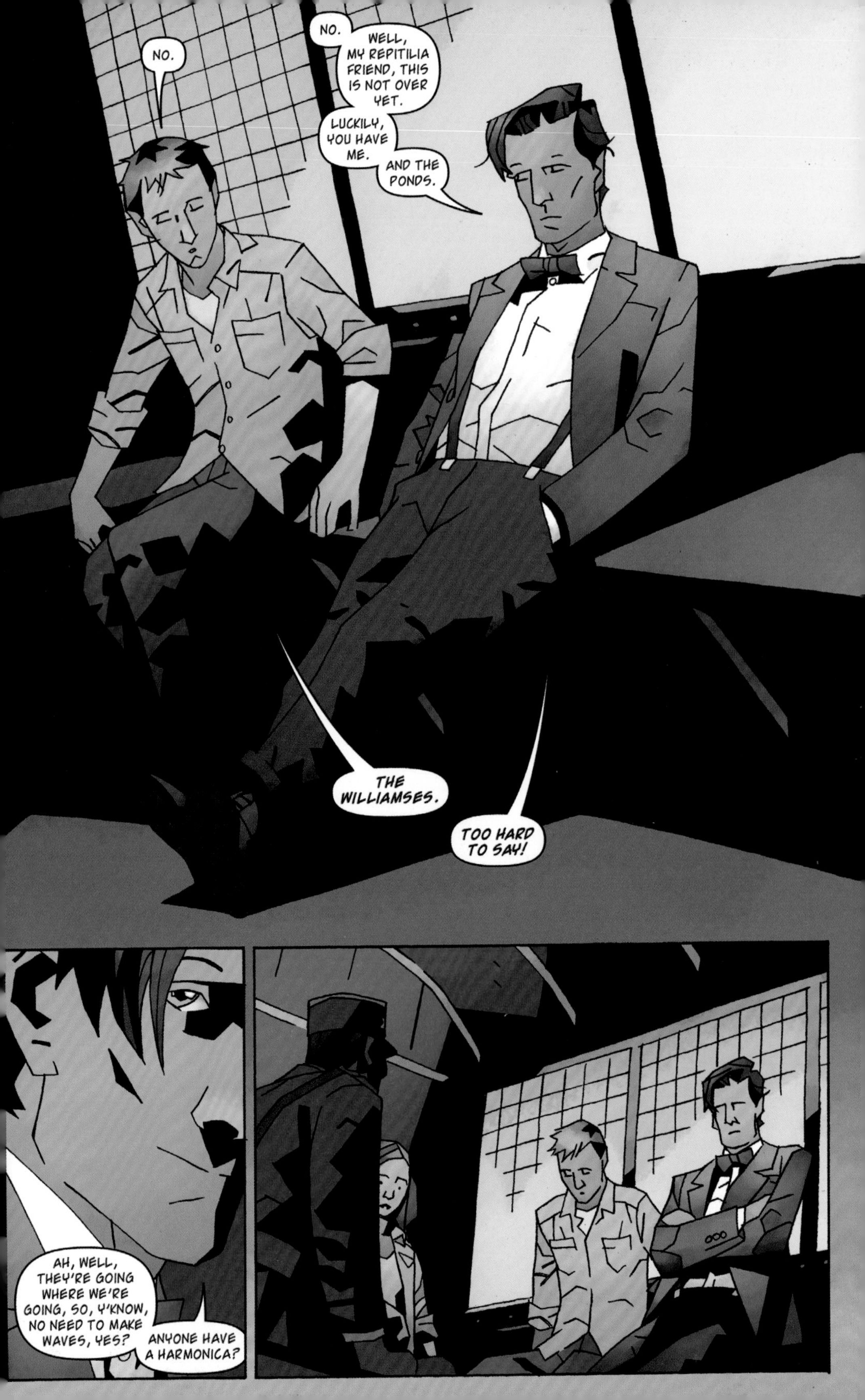
NO.
NO.
WELL, MY REPITILIA FRIEND, THIS IS NOT OVER YET.
LUCKILY, YOU HAVE ME.
AND THE PONDS.
THE WILLIAMSES.
TOO HARD TO SAY!
AH, WELL, THEY'RE GOING WHERE WE'RE GOING, SO, Y'KNOW, NO NEED TO MAKE WAVES, YES?
ANYONE HAVE A HARMONICA?

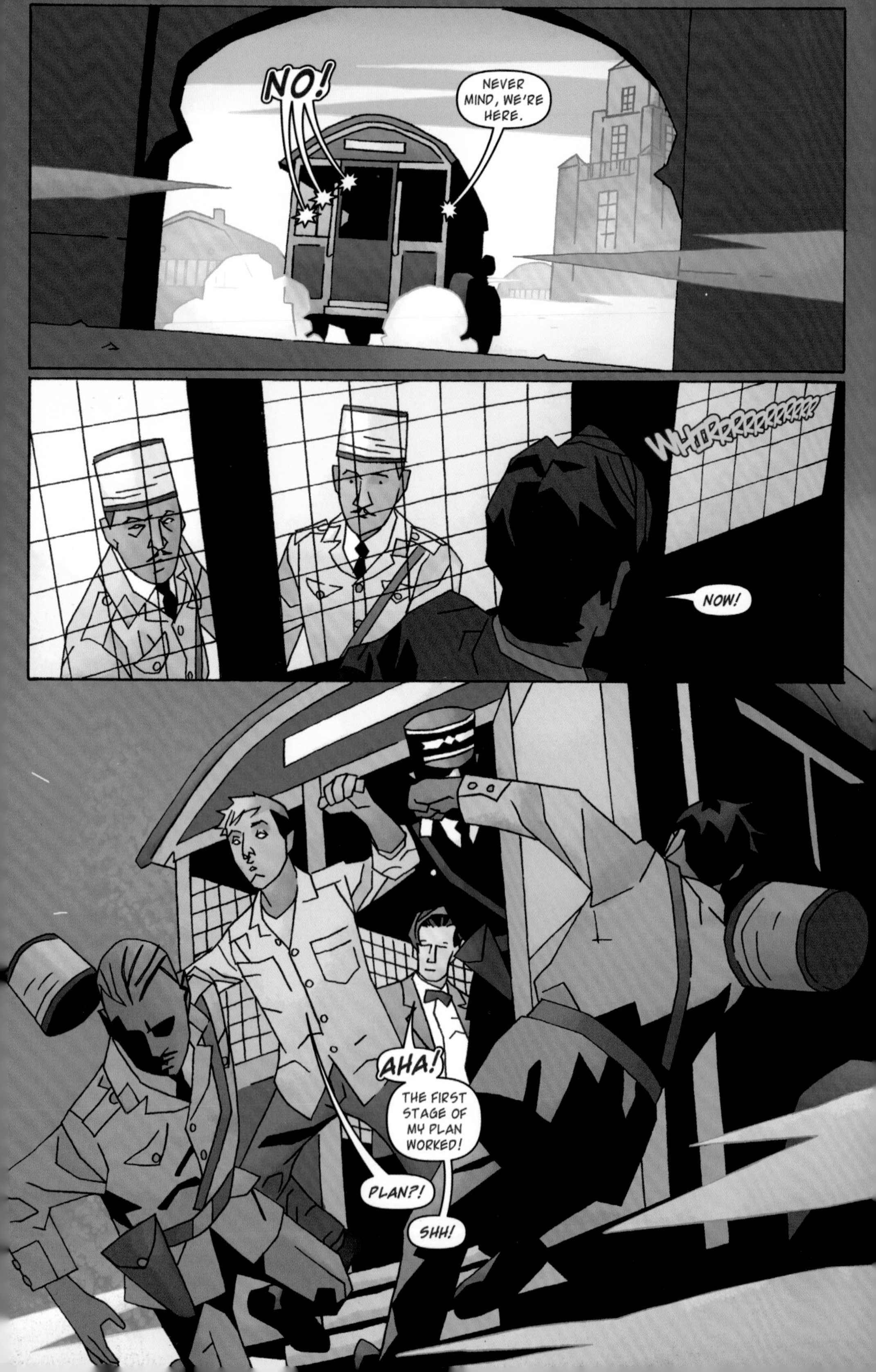
NO!
NEVER MIND, WE'RE HERE.
WHIRRRRRRRRRR
NOW!
AHA!
THE FIRST STAGE OF MY PLAN WORKED!
PLAN?!
SHH!

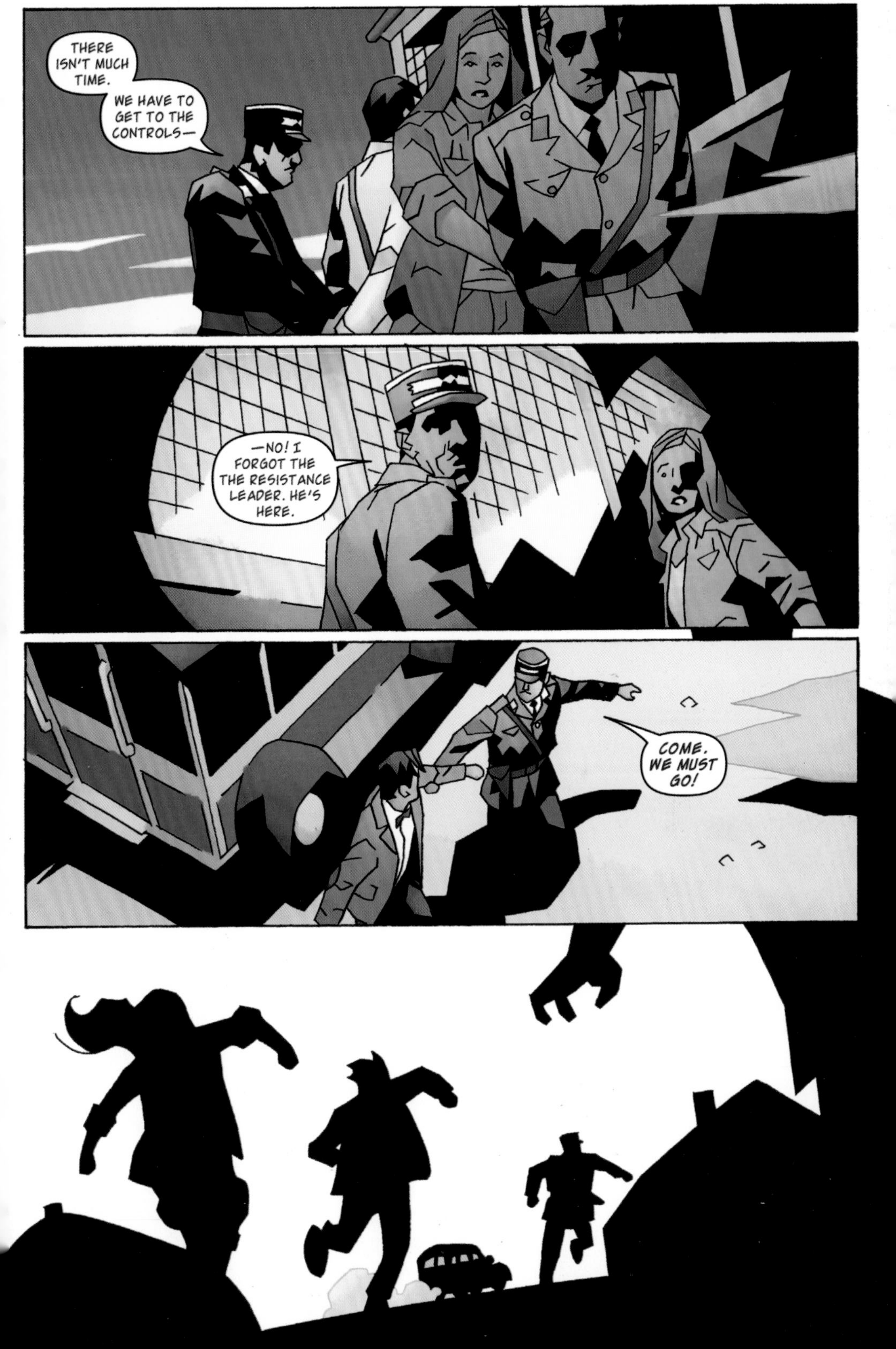
THERE ISN'T MUCH TIME.
WE HAVE TO GET TO THE CONTROLS—
—NO! I FORGOT THE THE RESISTANCE LEADER. HE'S HERE.
COME. WE MUST GO!

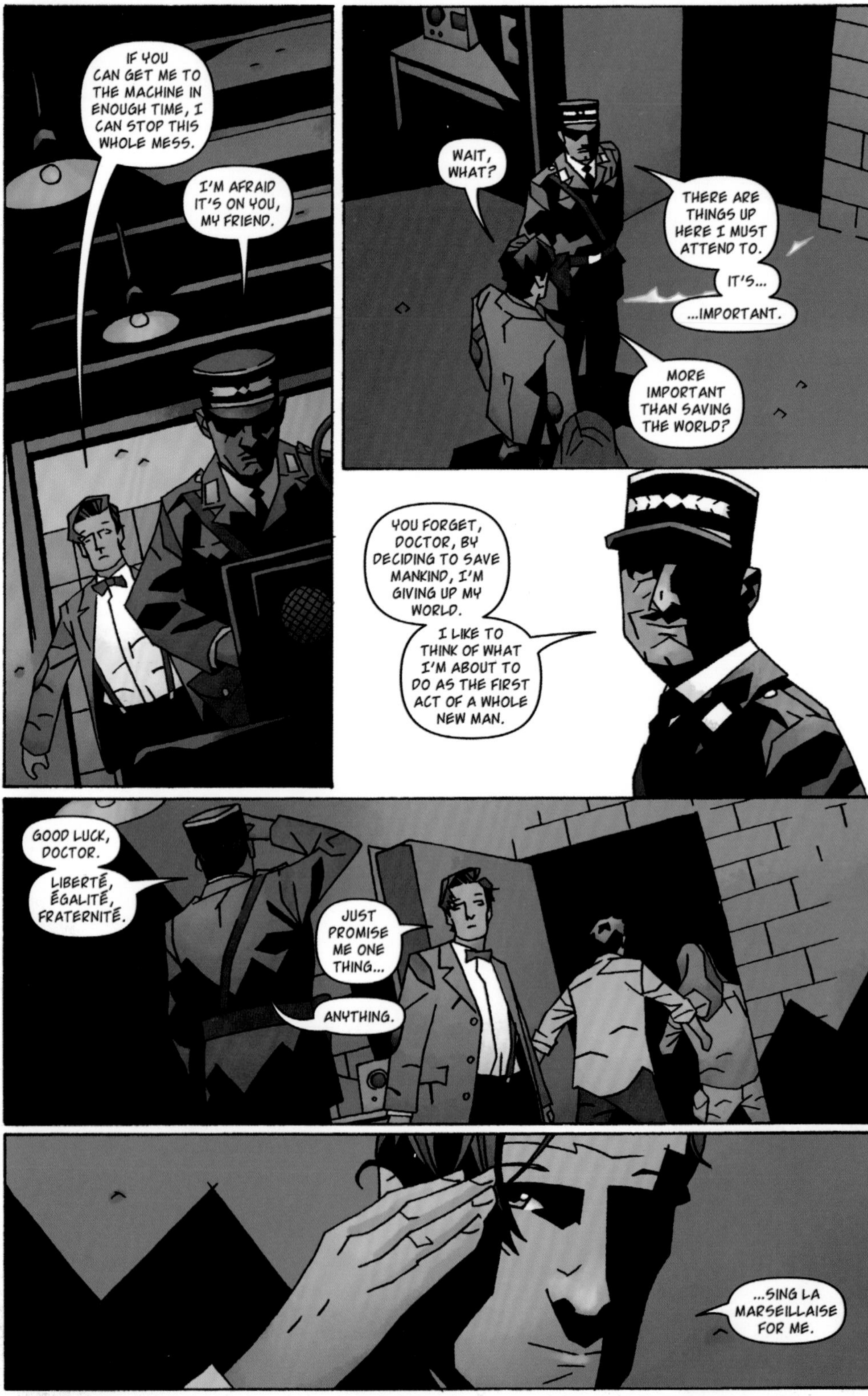
IF YOU CAN GET ME TO THE MACHINE IN ENOUGH TIME, I CAN STOP THIS WHOLE MESS.
I'M AFRAID IT'S ON YOU, MY FRIEND.
WAIT, WHAT?
THERE ARE THINGS UP HERE I MUST ATTEND TO.
IT'S...
...IMPORTANT.
MORE IMPORTANT THAN SAVING THE WORLD?
YOU FORGET, DOCTOR, BY DECIDING TO SAVE MANKIND, I'M GIVING UP MY WORLD.
I LIKE TO THINK OF WHAT I'M ABOUT TO DO AS THE FIRST ACT OF A WHOLE NEW MAN.
GOOD LUCK, DOCTOR.
LIBERTÉ, ÉGALITÉ, FRATERNITÉ.
JUST PROMISE ME ONE THING...
ANYTHING.
...SING LA MARSEILLAISE FOR ME.

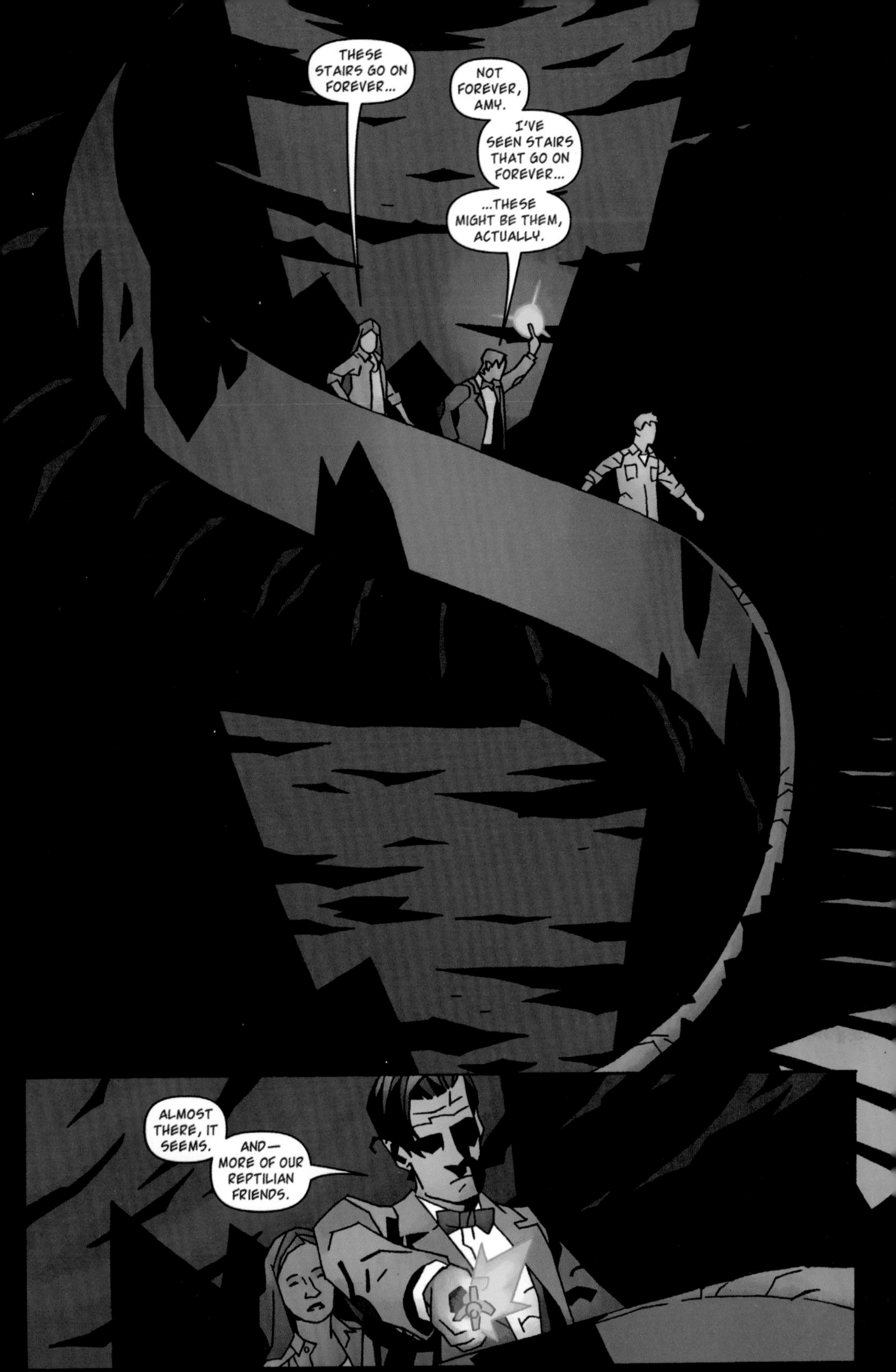
THESE STAIRS GO ON FOREVER...
NOT FOREVER, AMY.
I'VE SEEN STAIRS THAT GO ON FOREVER...
...THESE MIGHT BE THEM, ACTUALLY.
ALMOST THERE, IT SEEMS.
AND— MORE OF OUR REPTILIAN FRIENDS.

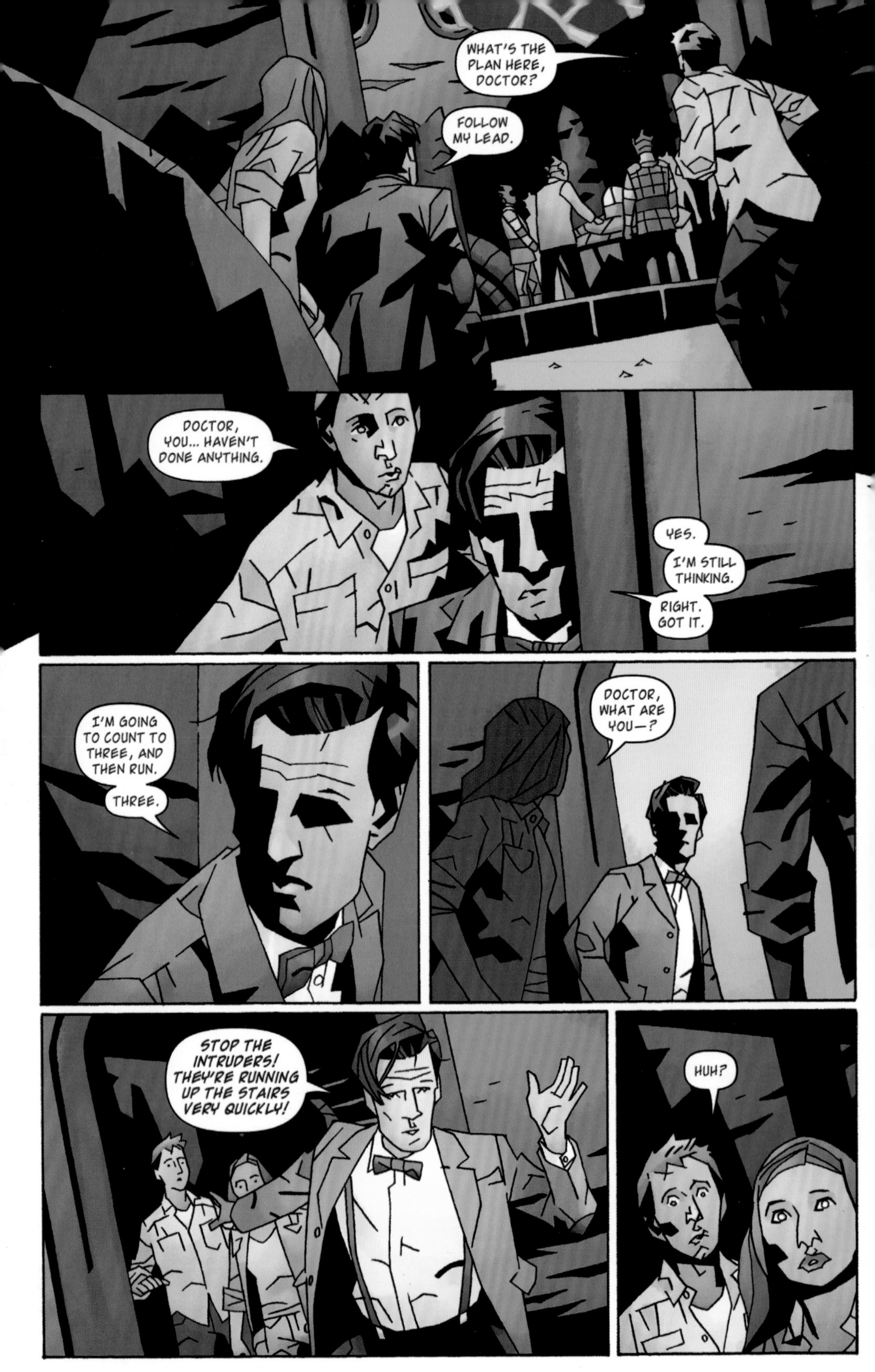
WHAT'S THE PLAN HERE, DOCTOR?
FOLLOW MY LEAD.
DOCTOR, YOU... HAVEN'T DONE ANYTHING.
YES.
I'M STILL THINKING.
RIGHT. GOT IT.
I'M GOING TO COUNT TO THREE, AND THEN RUN.
THREE.
DOCTOR, WHAT ARE YOU—?
STOP THE INTRUDERS! THEY'RE RUNNING UP THE STAIRS VERY QUICKLY!
HUH?

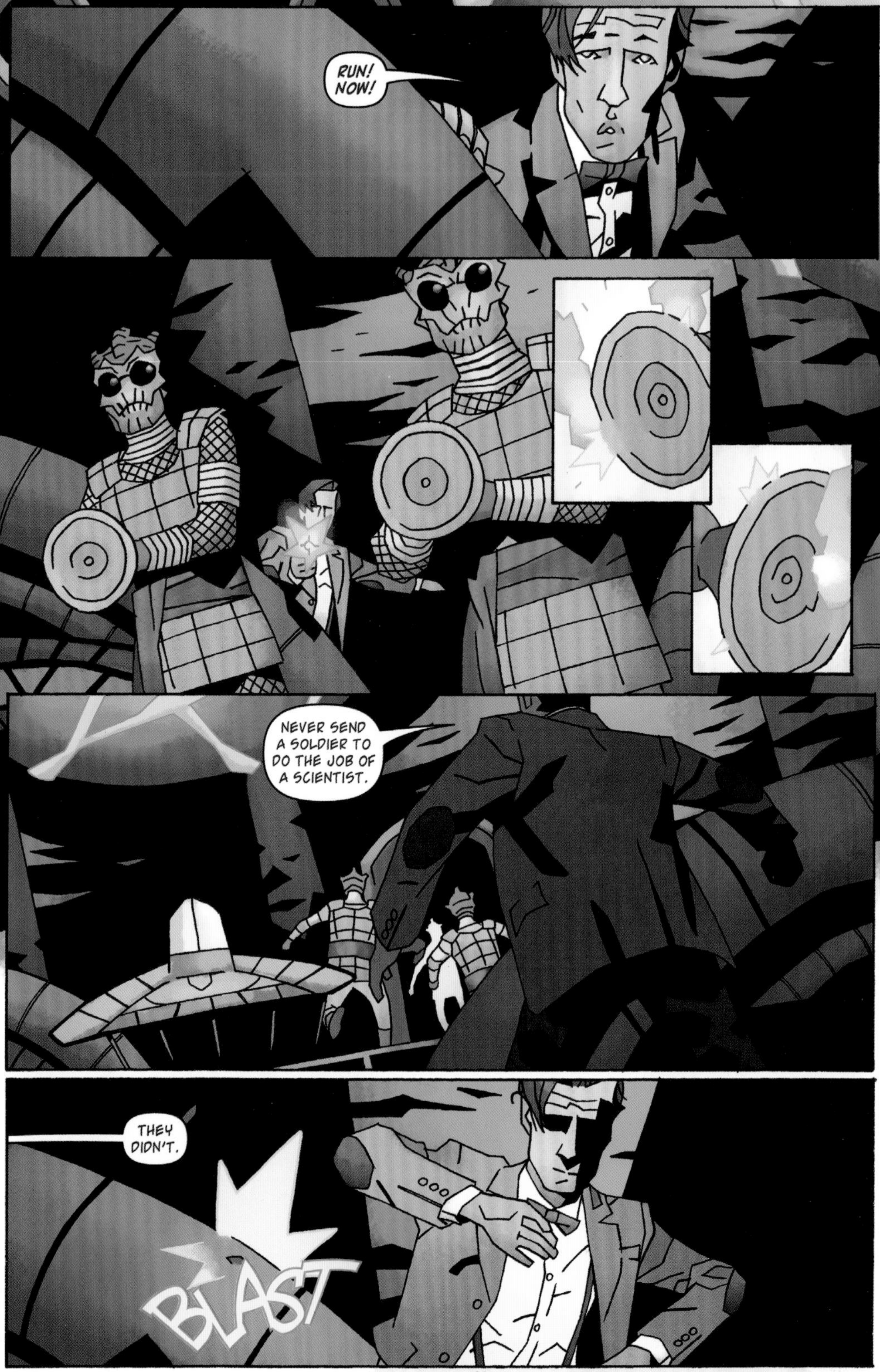
RUN! NOW!
NEVER SEND A SOLDIER TO DO THE JOB OF A SCIENTIST.
THEY DIDN'T.
BLAST

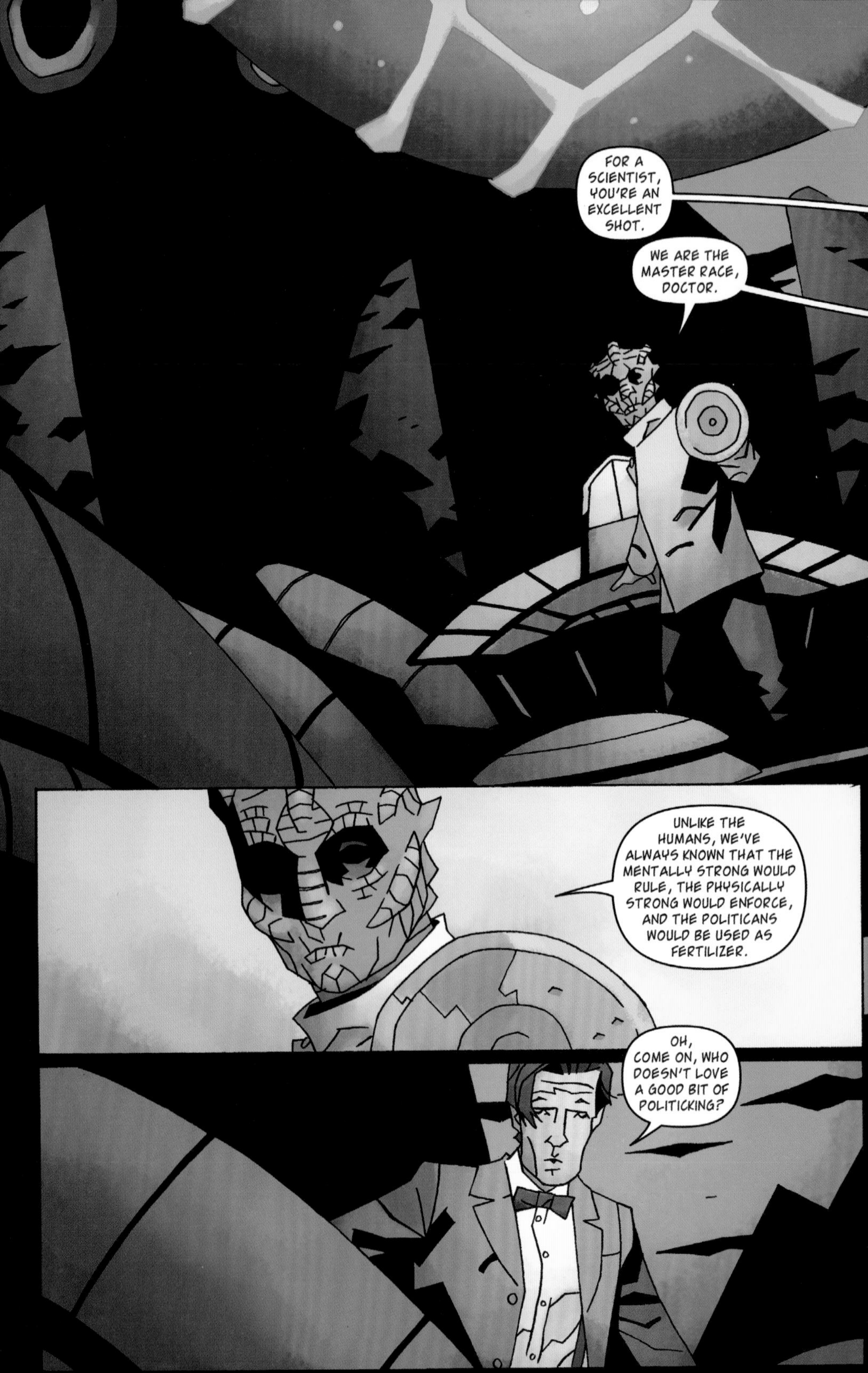
FOR A SCIENTIST, YOU'RE AN EXCELLENT SHOT.
WE ARE THE MASTER RACE, DOCTOR.
UNLIKE THE HUMANS, WE'VE ALWAYS KNOWN THAT THE MENTALLY STRONG WOULD RULE, THE PHYSICALLY STRONG WOULD ENFORCE, AND THE POLITICANS WOULD BE USED AS FERTILIZER.
OH, COME ON, WHO DOESN'T LOVE A GOOD BIT OF POLITICKING?

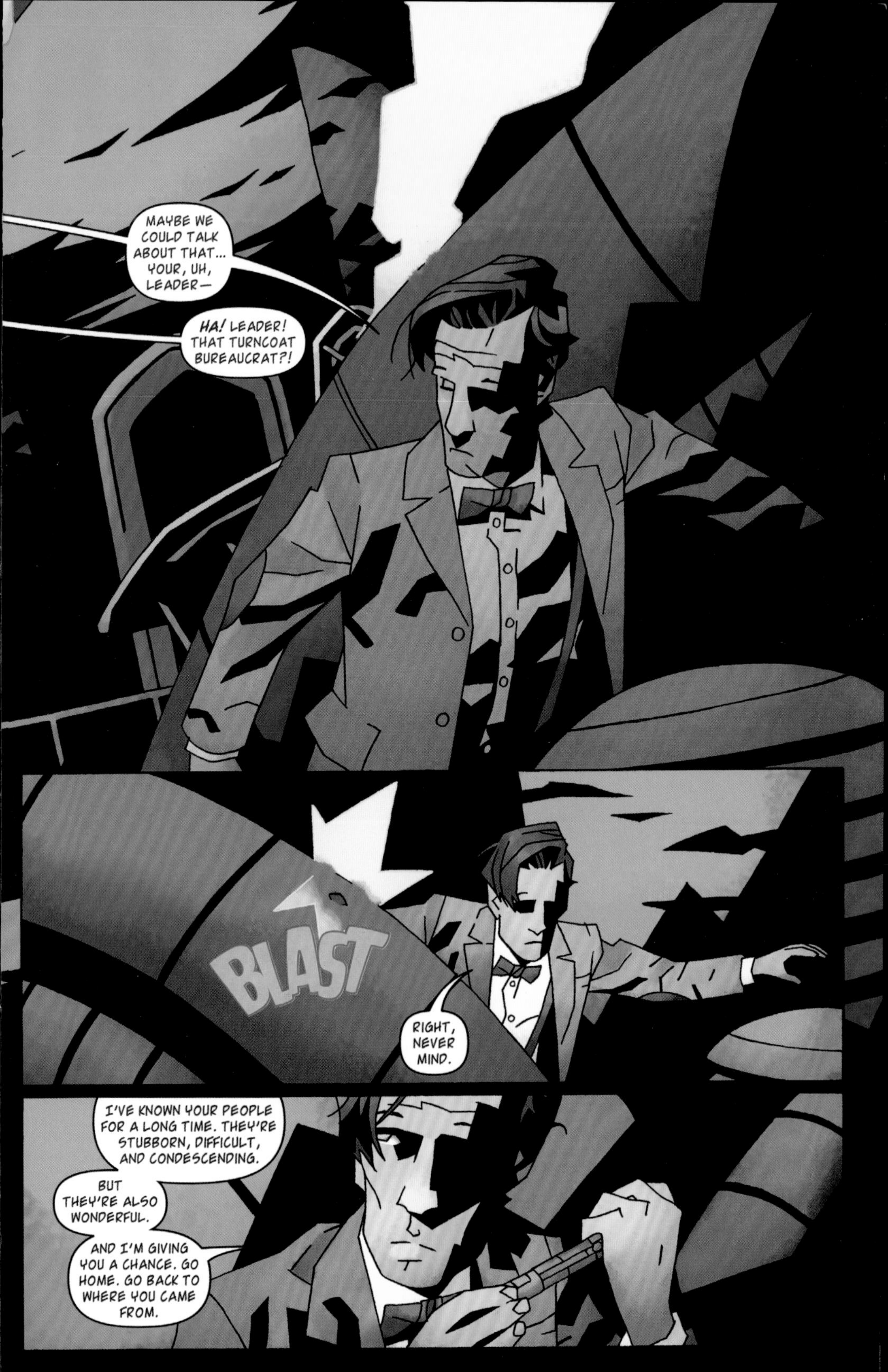
MAYBE WE COULD TALK ABOUT THAT... YOUR, UH, LEADER—
HA! LEADER! THAT TURNCOAT BUREAUCRAT?!
BLAST
RIGHT, NEVER MIND.
I'VE KNOWN YOUR PEOPLE FOR A LONG TIME. THEY'RE STUBBORN, DIFFICULT, AND CONDESCENDING.
BUT THEY'RE ALSO WONDERFUL.
AND I'M GIVING YOU A CHANCE. GO HOME. GO BACK TO WHERE YOU CAME FROM.

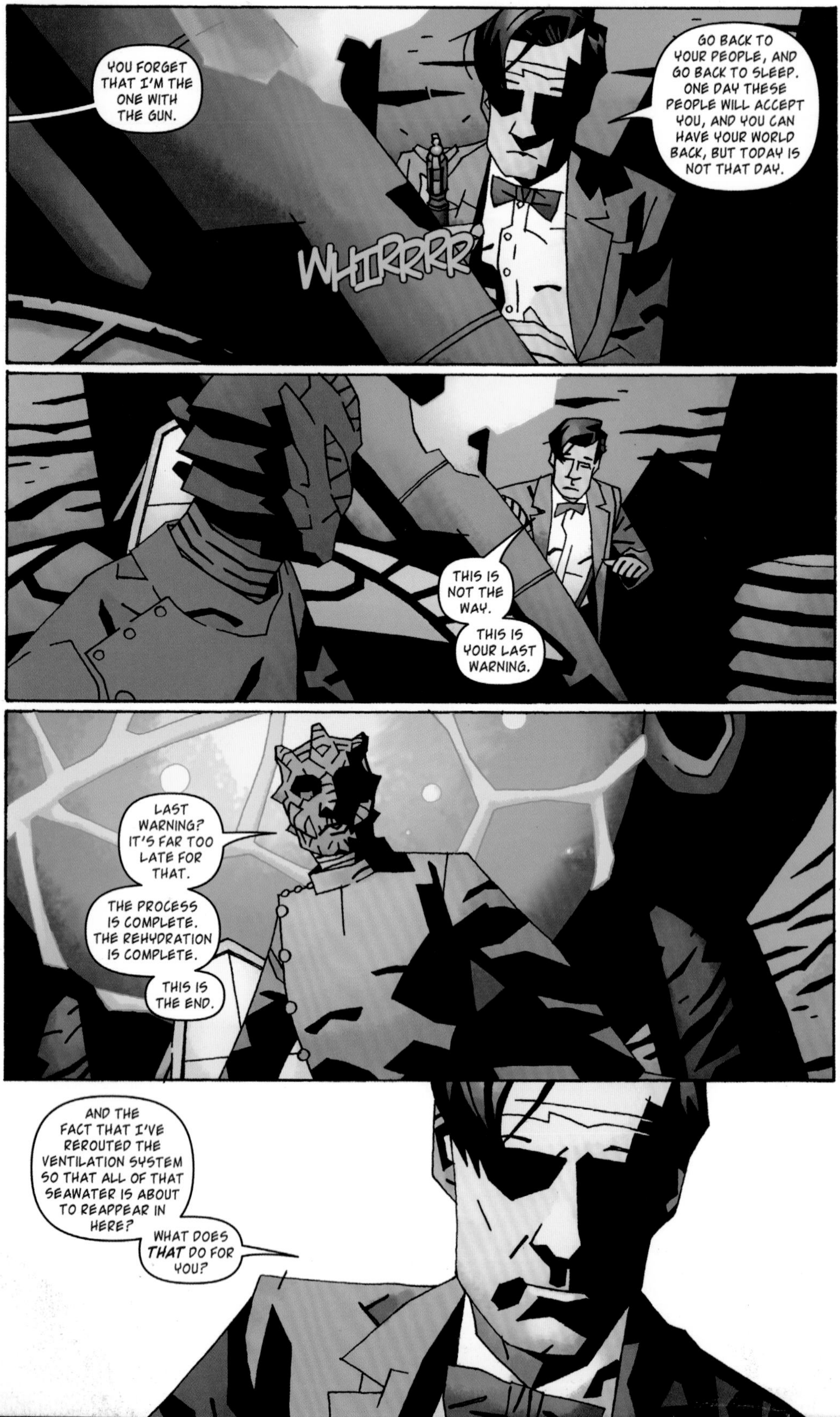

YOU FORGET THAT I'M THE ONE WITH THE GUN.
GO BACK TO YOUR PEOPLE, AND GO BACK TO SLEEP. ONE DAY THESE PEOPLE WILL ACCEPT YOU, AND YOU CAN HAVE YOUR WORLD BACK, BUT TODAY IS NOT THAT DAY.
WHIRRRR
THIS IS NOT THE WAY.
THIS IS YOUR LAST WARNING.
LAST WARNING? IT'S FAR TOO LATE FOR THAT.
THE PROCESS IS COMPLETE. THE REHYDRATION IS COMPLETE.
THIS IS THE END.
AND THE FACT THAT I'VE REROUTED THE VENTILATION SYSTEM SO THAT ALL OF THAT SEAWATER IS ABOUT TO REAPPEAR IN HERE?
WHAT DOES *THAT* DO FOR YOU?

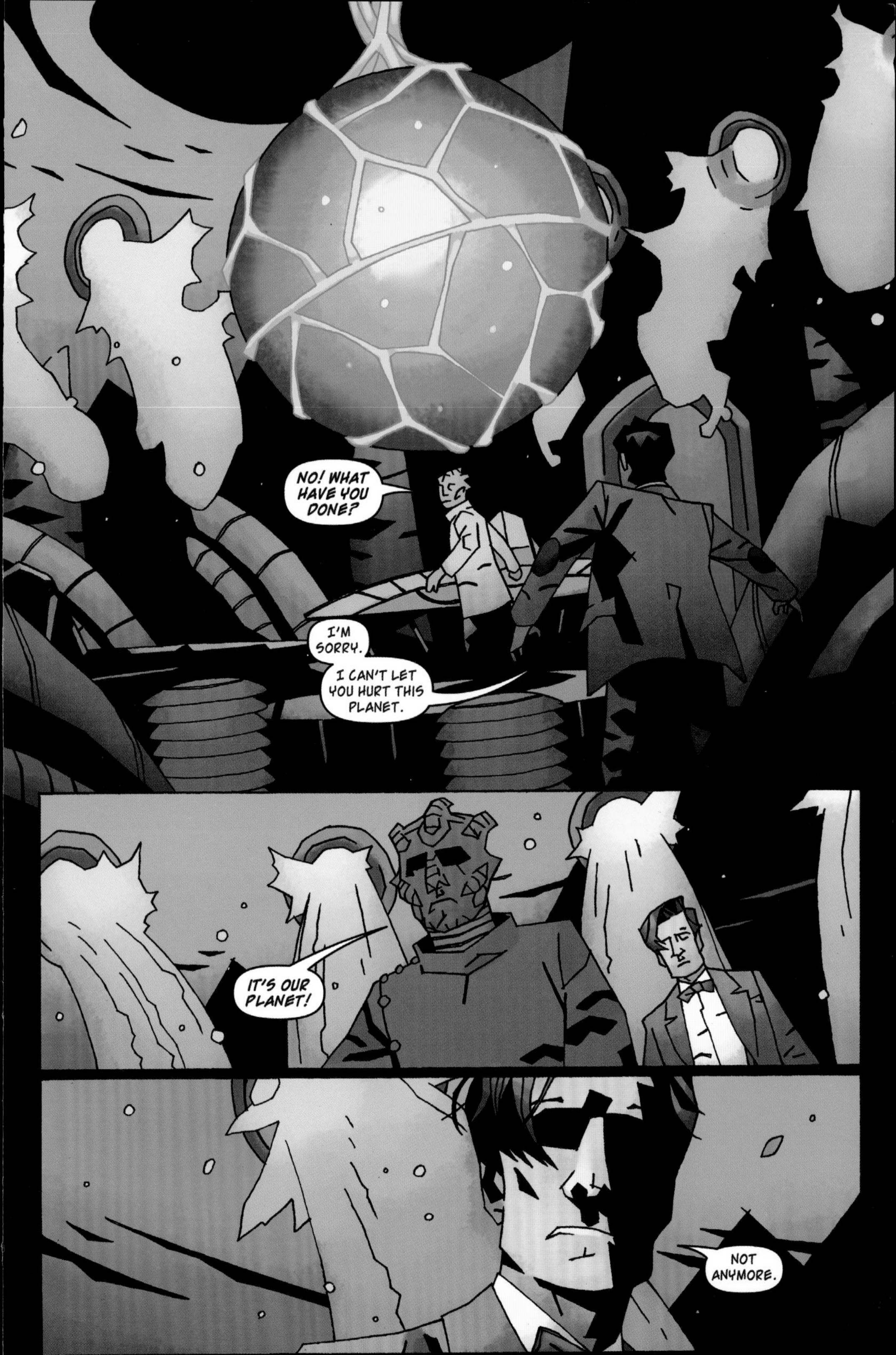
NO! WHAT HAVE YOU DONE?
I'M SORRY.
I CAN'T LET YOU HURT THIS PLANET.
IT'S OUR PLANET!
NOT ANYMORE.

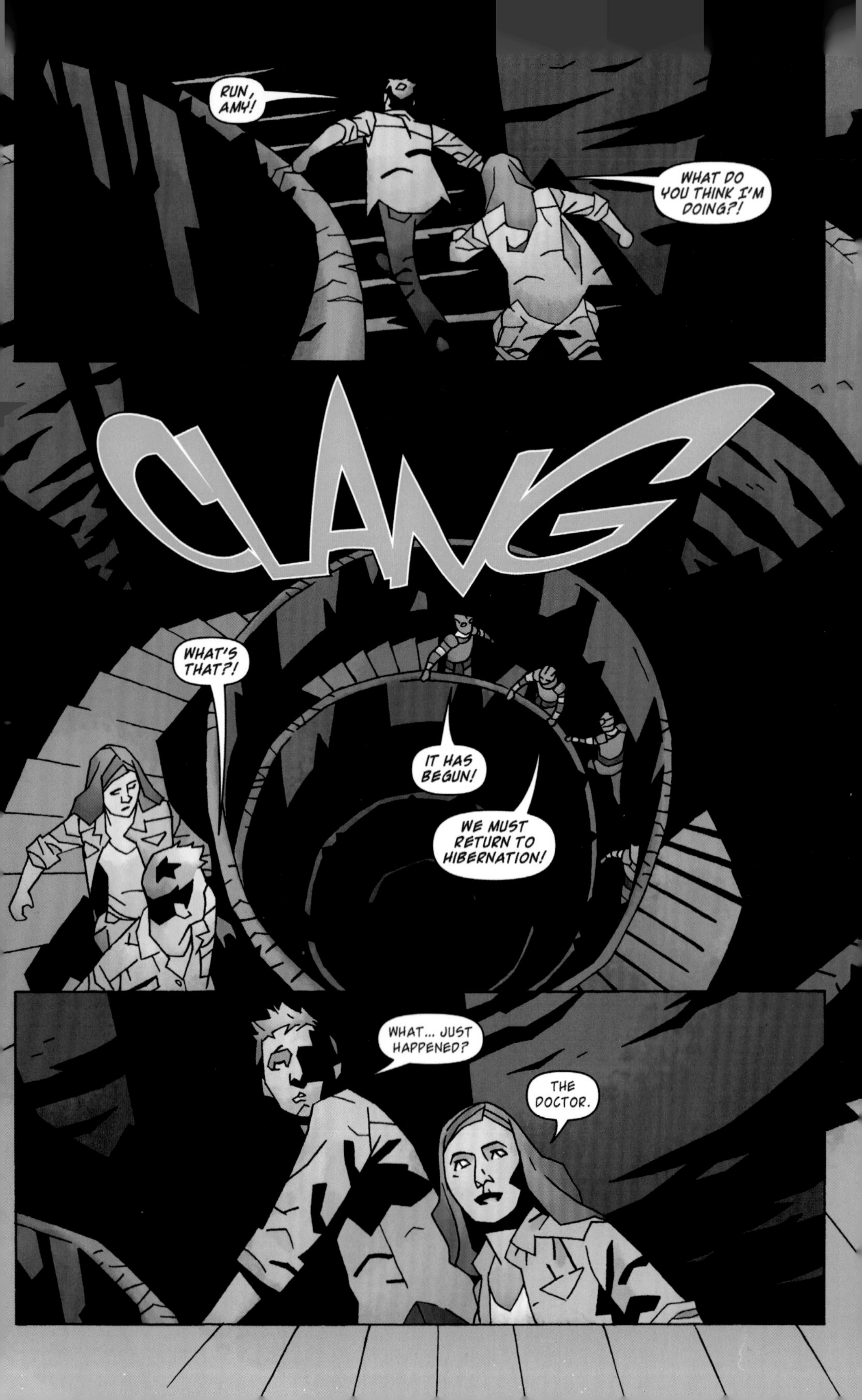
RUN, AMY!
WHAT DO YOU THINK I'M DOING?!
CLANG
WHAT'S THAT?!
IT HAS BEGUN!
WE MUST RETURN TO HIBERNATION!
WHAT... JUST HAPPENED?
THE DOCTOR.

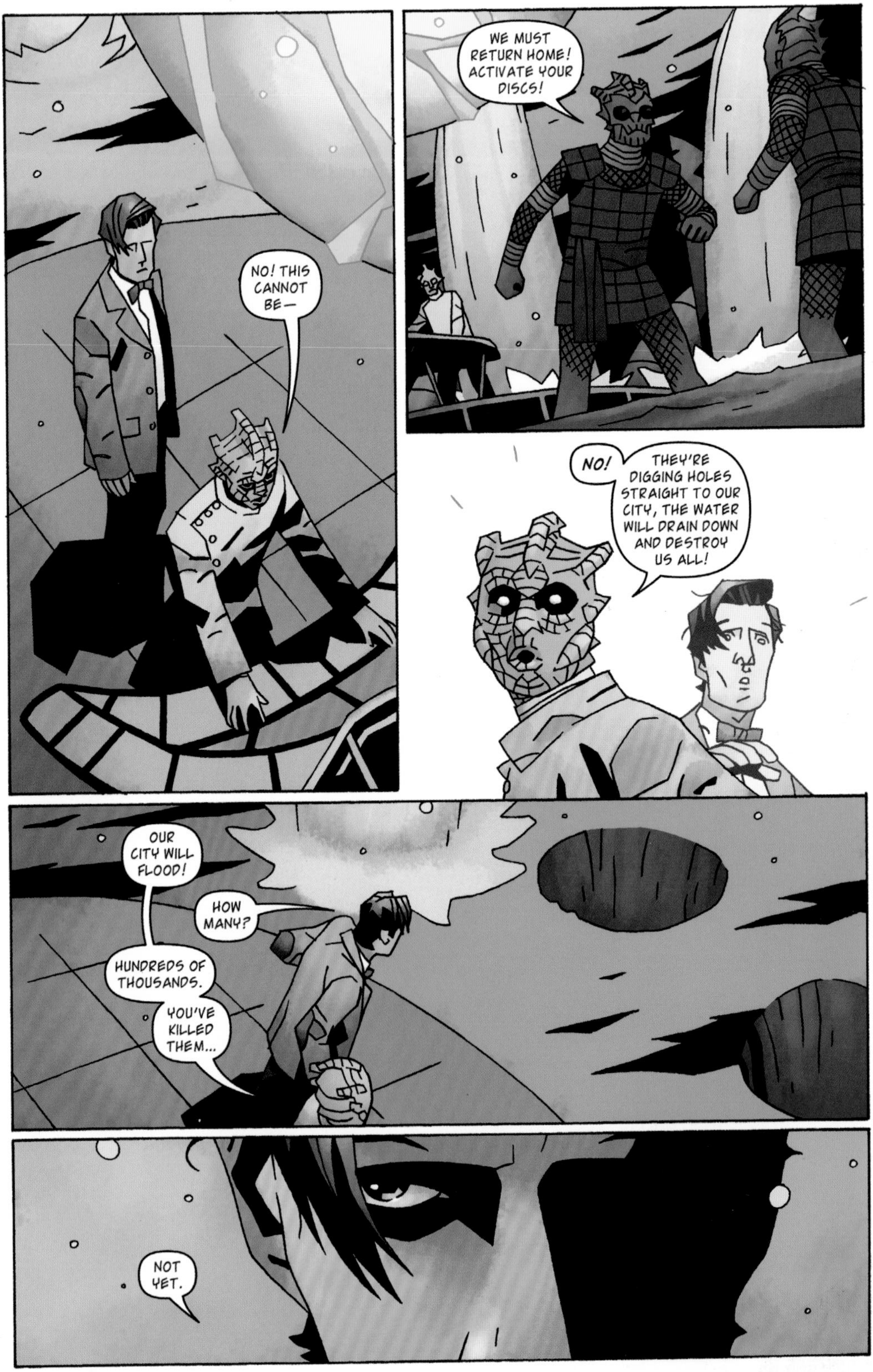
NO! THIS CANNOT BE—
WE MUST RETURN HOME! ACTIVATE YOUR DISCS!
NO!
THEY'RE DIGGING HOLES STRAIGHT TO OUR CITY, THE WATER WILL DRAIN DOWN AND DESTROY US ALL!
OUR CITY WILL FLOOD!
HOW MANY?
HUNDREDS OF THOUSANDS.
YOU'VE KILLED THEM...
NOT YET.

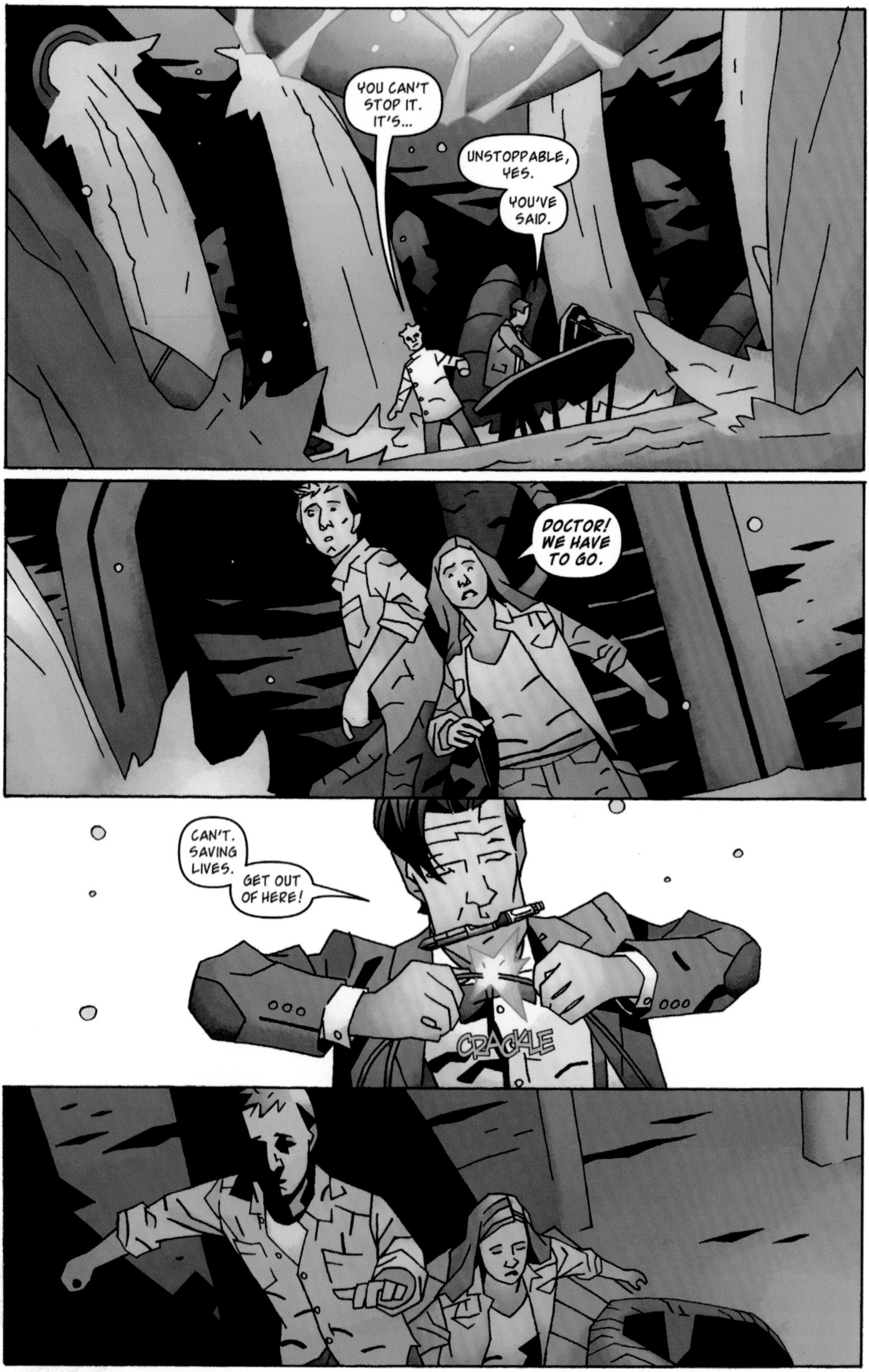
YOU CAN'T STOP IT. IT'S...
UNSTOPPABLE, YES.
YOU'VE SAID.
DOCTOR! WE HAVE TO GO.
CAN'T. SAVING LIVES.
GET OUT OF HERE!
CRACKLE

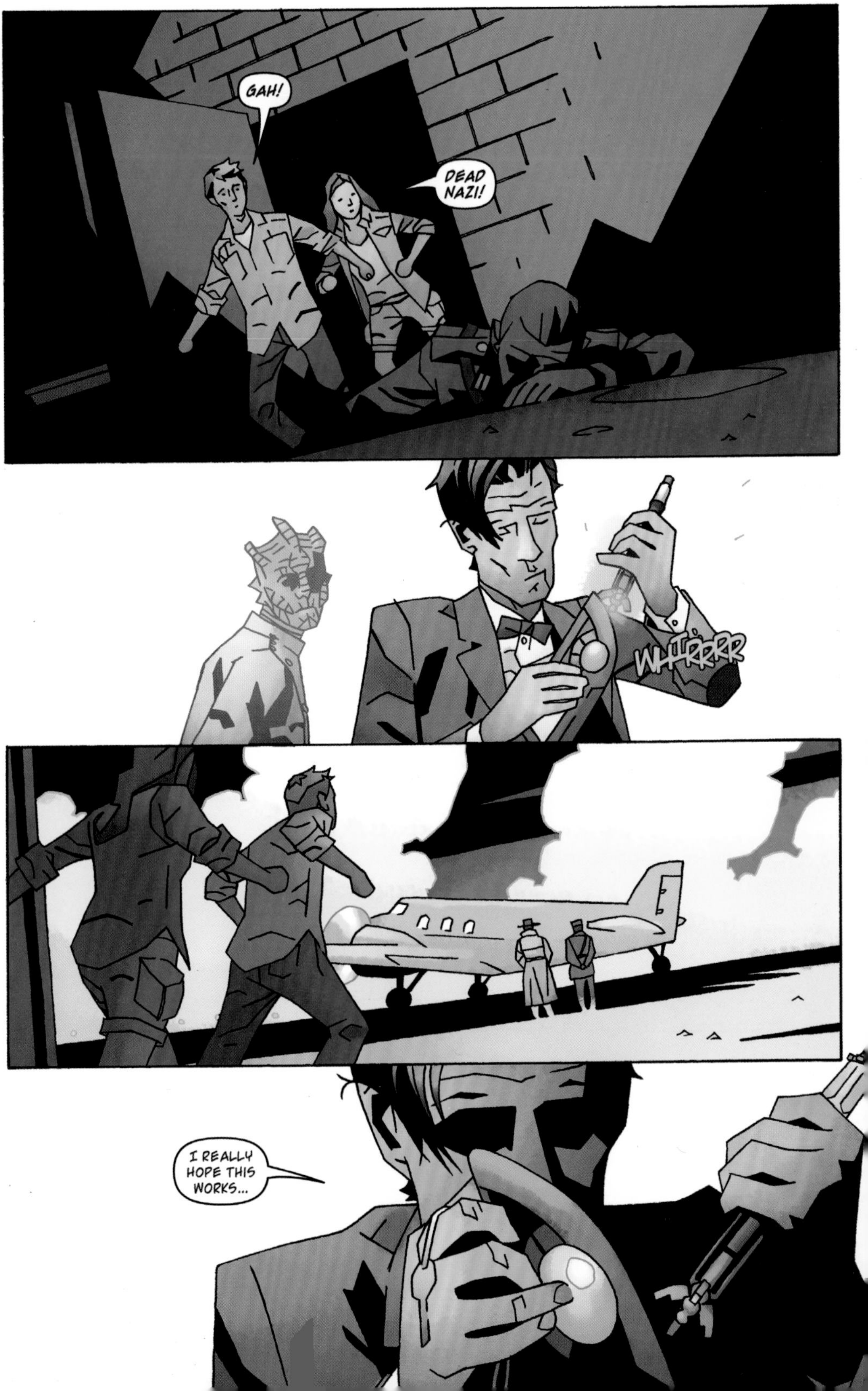
GAH!
DEAD NAZI!
WHIRRRR
I REALLY HOPE THIS WORKS...

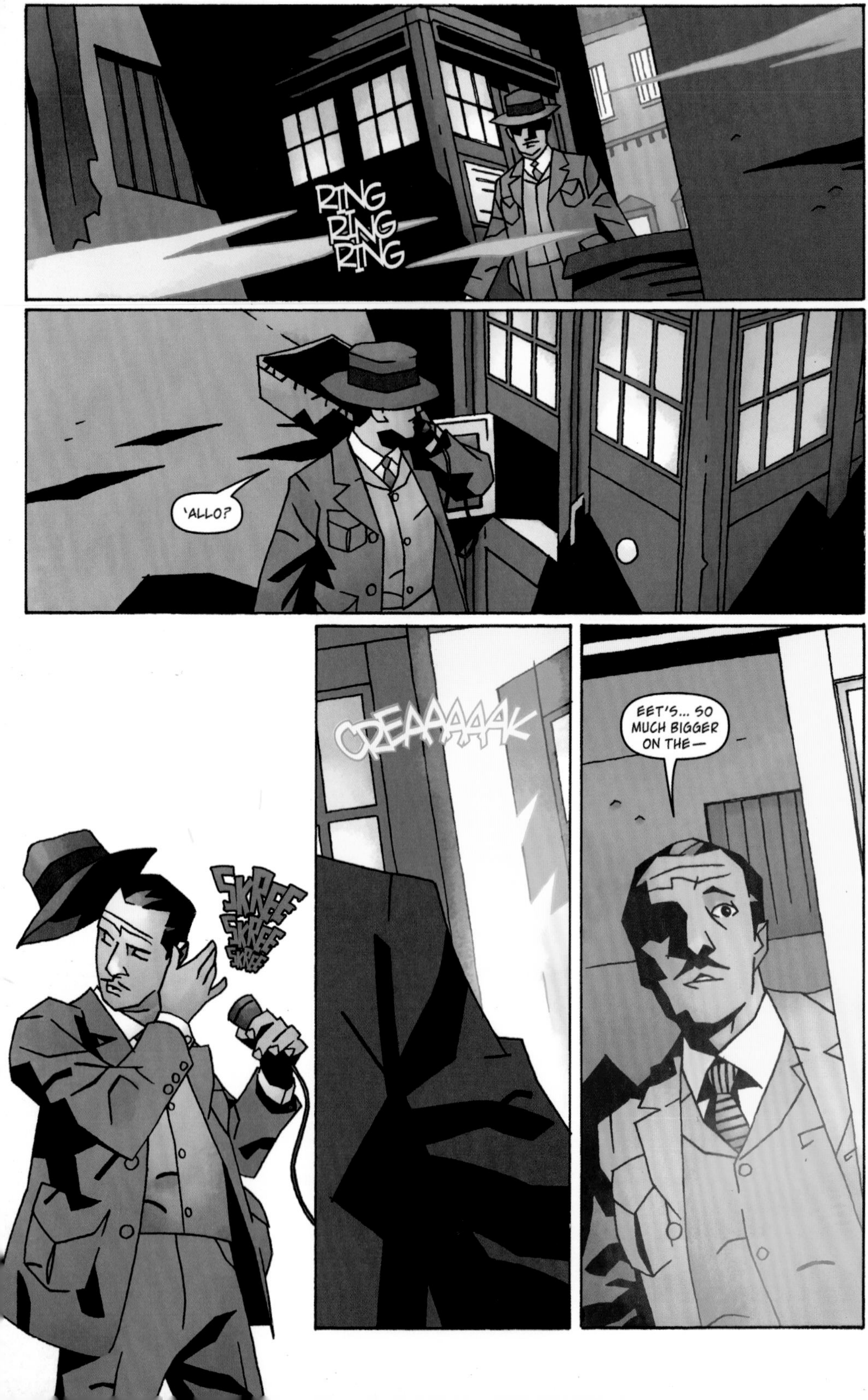
RING
RING
RING
'ALLO?
SKREE
SKREE
SKREE
CREAAAAAK
EET'S... SO MUCH BIGGER ON THE—

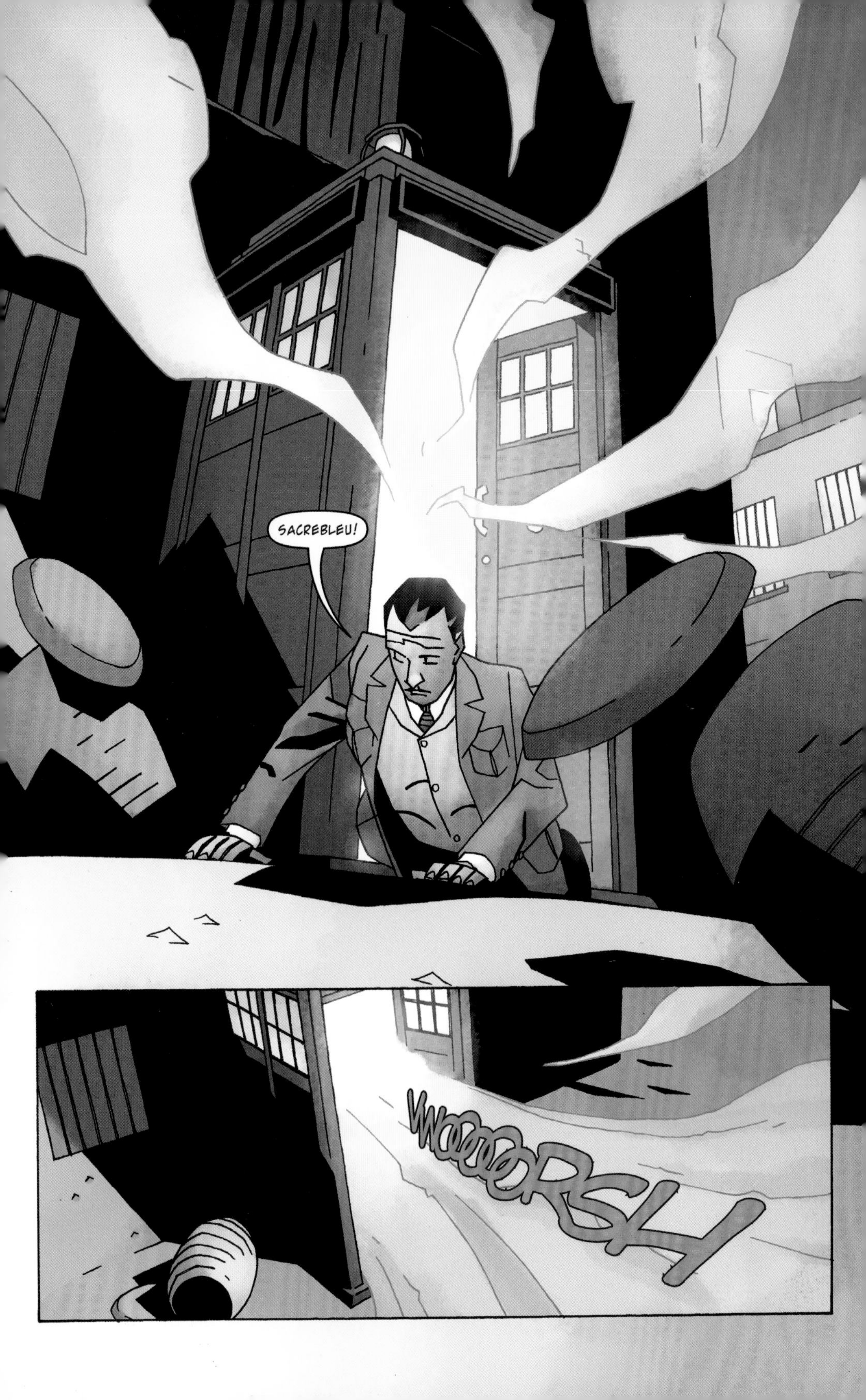
SACREBLEU!
VWOOOORSH

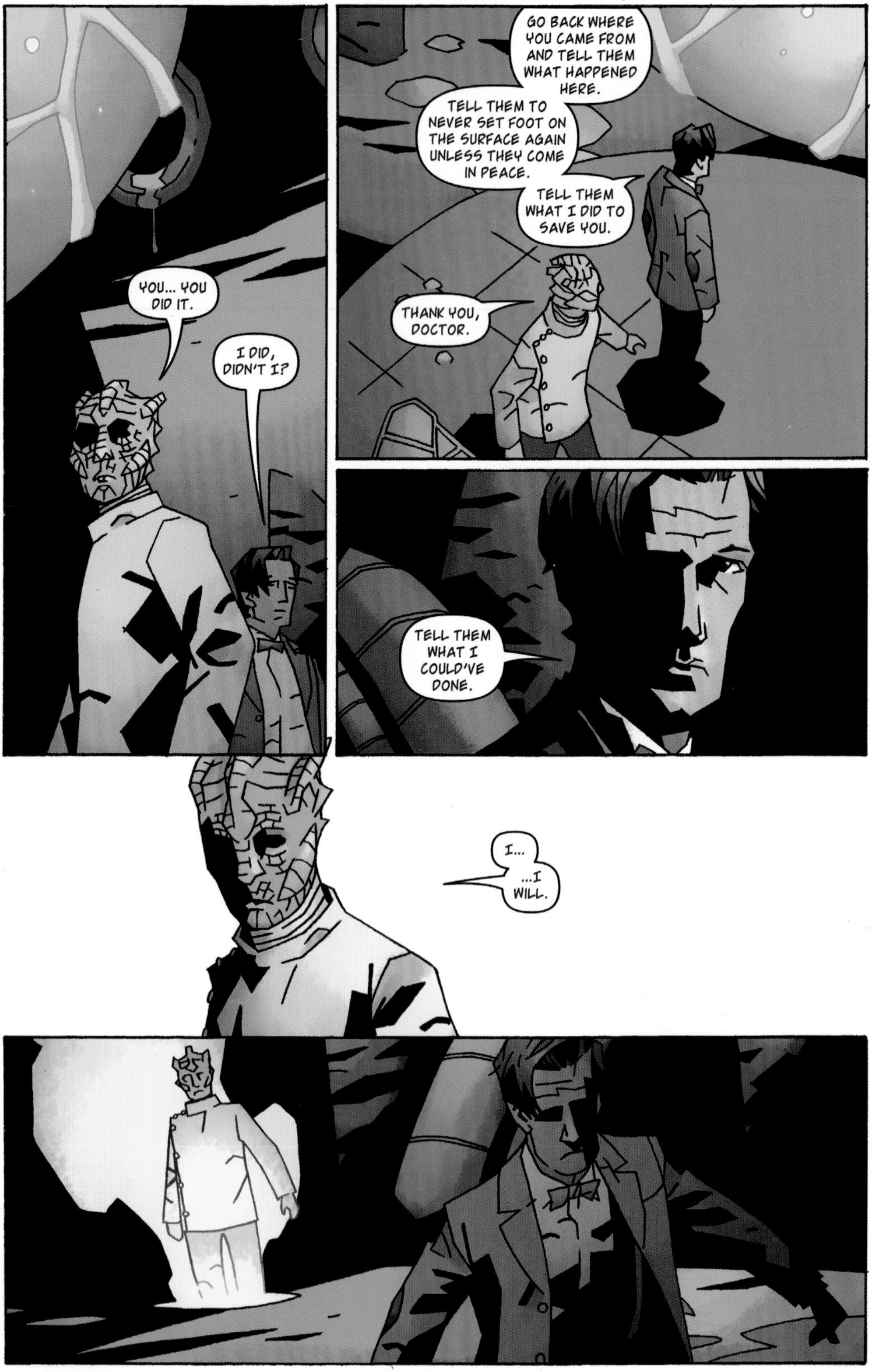
YOU... YOU DID IT.
I DID, DIDN'T I?
GO BACK WHERE YOU CAME FROM AND TELL THEM WHAT HAPPENED HERE.
TELL THEM TO NEVER SET FOOT ON THE SURFACE AGAIN UNLESS THEY COME IN PEACE.
TELL THEM WHAT I DID TO SAVE YOU.
THANK YOU, DOCTOR.
TELL THEM WHAT I COULD'VE DONE.
I...
...I WILL.

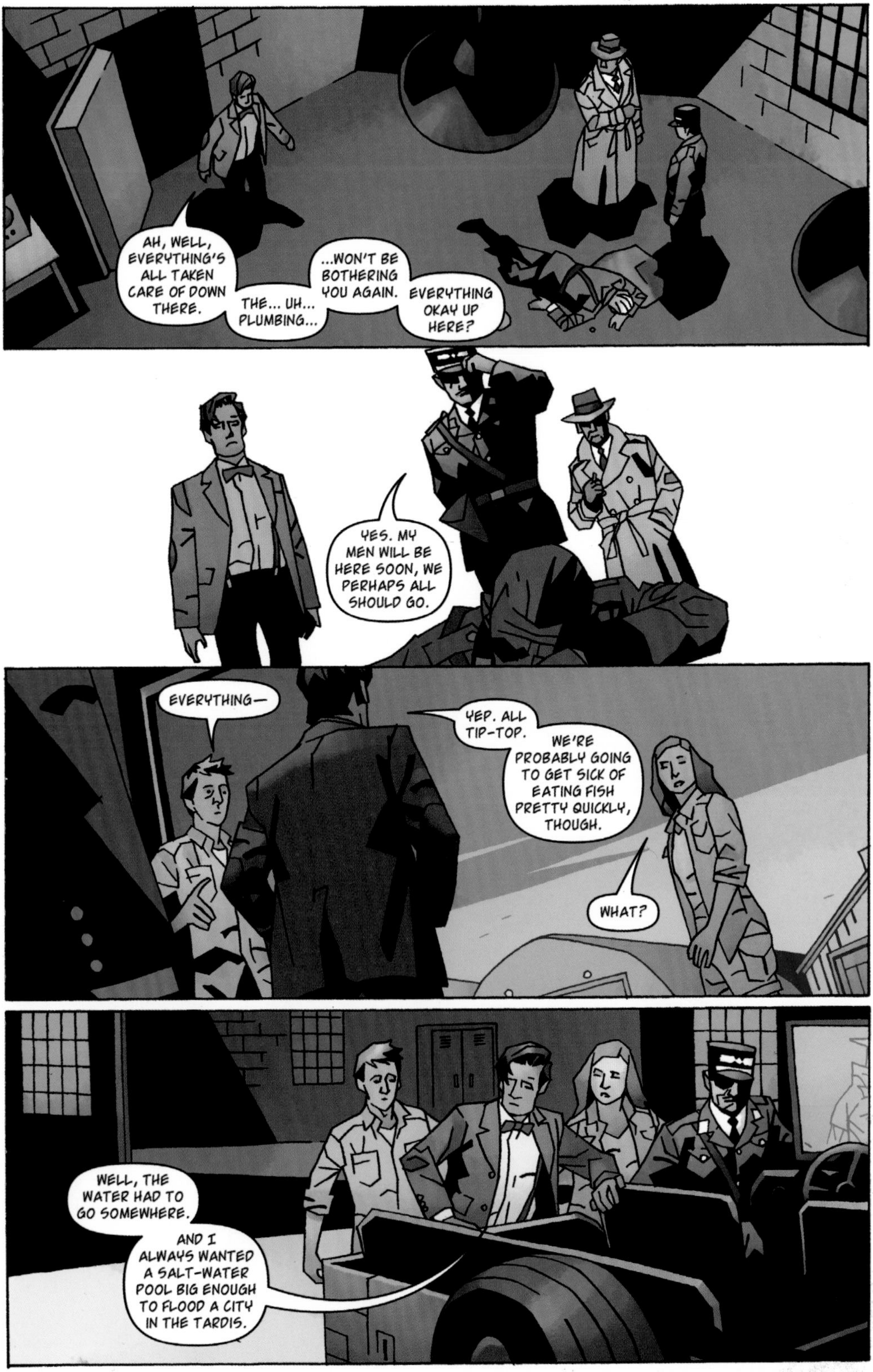
AH, WELL, EVERYTHING'S ALL TAKEN CARE OF DOWN THERE.
THE... UH... PLUMBING...
...WON'T BE BOTHERING YOU AGAIN.
EVERYTHING OKAY UP HERE?
YES. MY MEN WILL BE HERE SOON, WE PERHAPS ALL SHOULD GO.
EVERYTHING—
YEP. ALL TIP-TOP.
WE'RE PROBABLY GOING TO GET SICK OF EATING FISH PRETTY QUICKLY, THOUGH.
WHAT?
WELL, THE WATER HAD TO GO SOMEWHERE.
AND I ALWAYS WANTED A SALT-WATER POOL BIG ENOUGH TO FLOOD A CITY IN THE TARDIS.

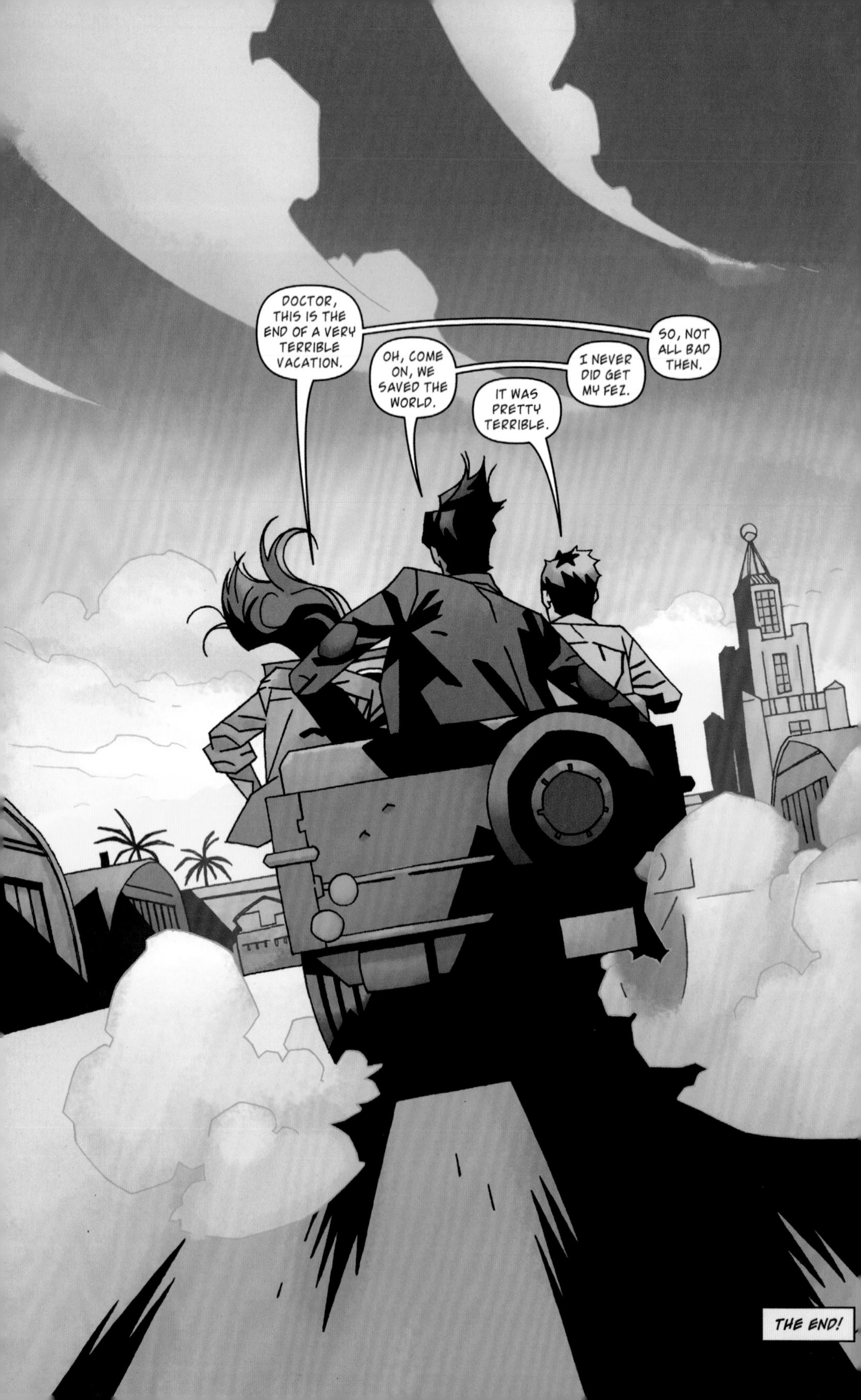
DOCTOR, THIS IS THE END OF A VERY TERRIBLE VACATION.
OH, COME ON, WE SAVED THE WORLD.
IT WAS PRETTY TERRIBLE.
I NEVER DID GET MY FEZ.
SO, NOT ALL BAD THEN.
THE END!

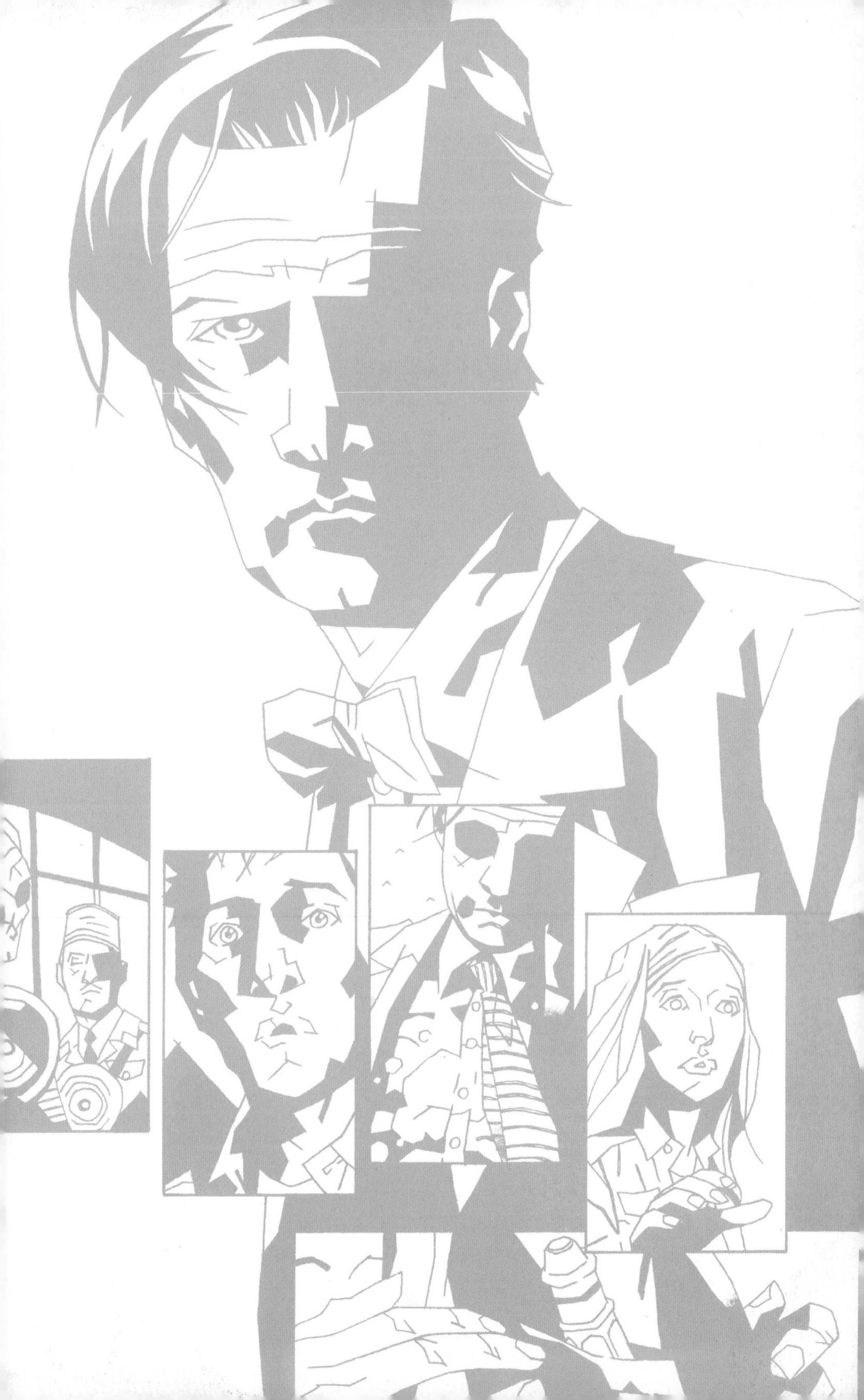

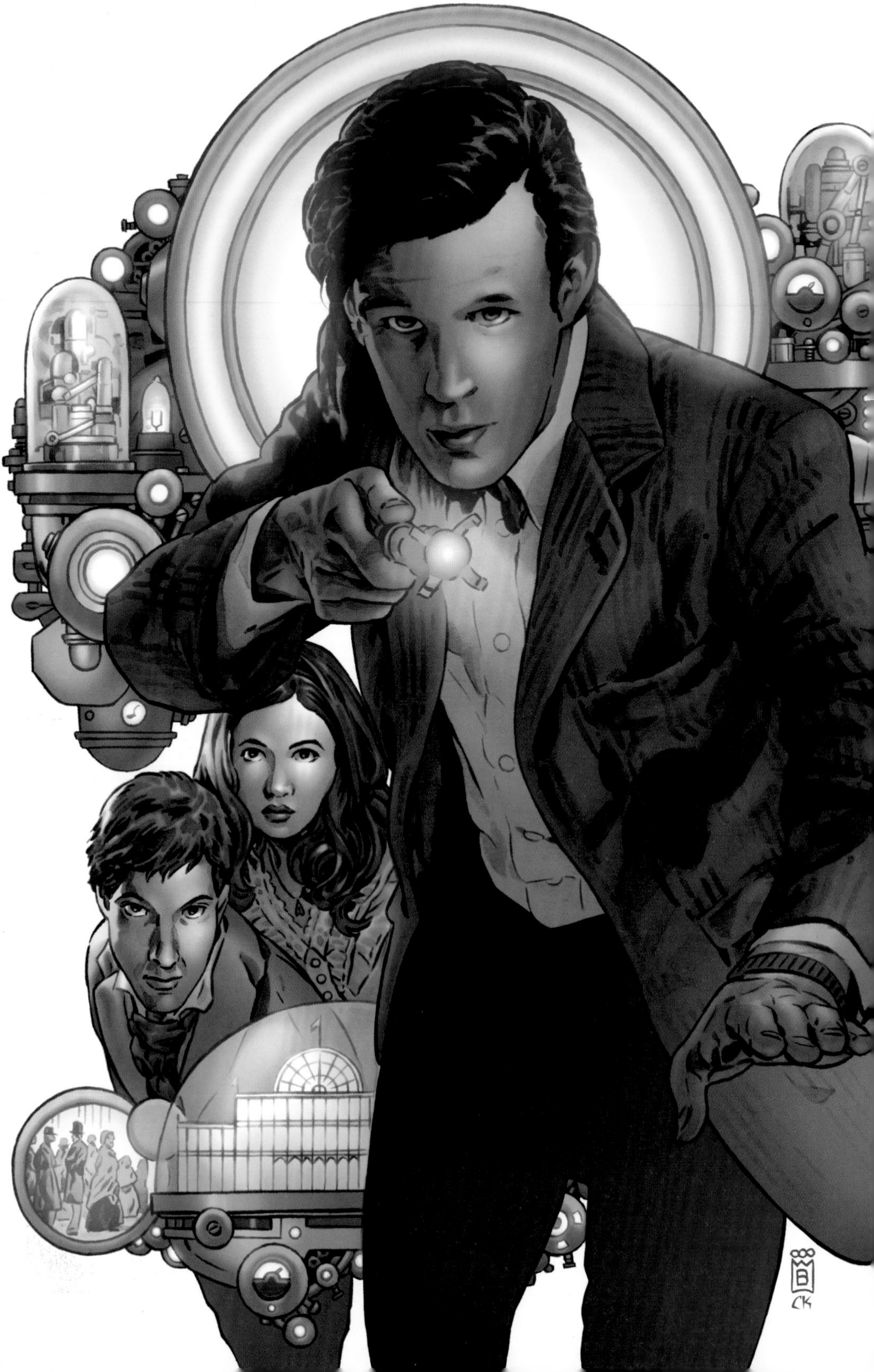

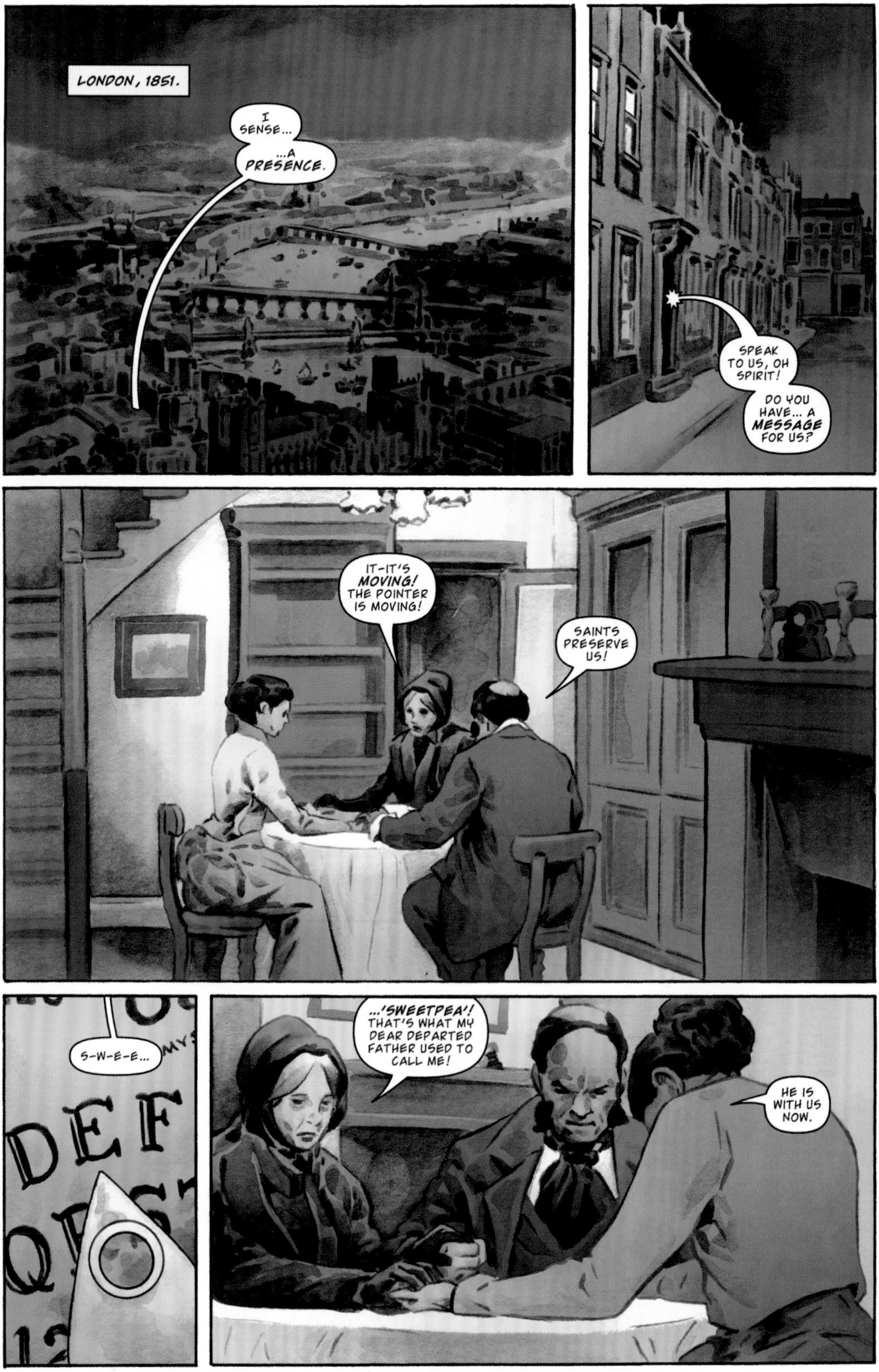
LONDON, 1851.
I SENSE...
...A PRESENCE.
SPEAK TO US, OH SPIRIT!
DO YOU HAVE... A MESSAGE FOR US?
IT-IT'S MOVING! THE POINTER IS MOVING!
SAINTS PRESERVE US!
S-W-E-E...
DEF
...'SWEETPEA'! THAT'S WHAT MY DEAR DEPARTED FATHER USED TO CALL ME!
HE IS WITH US NOW.

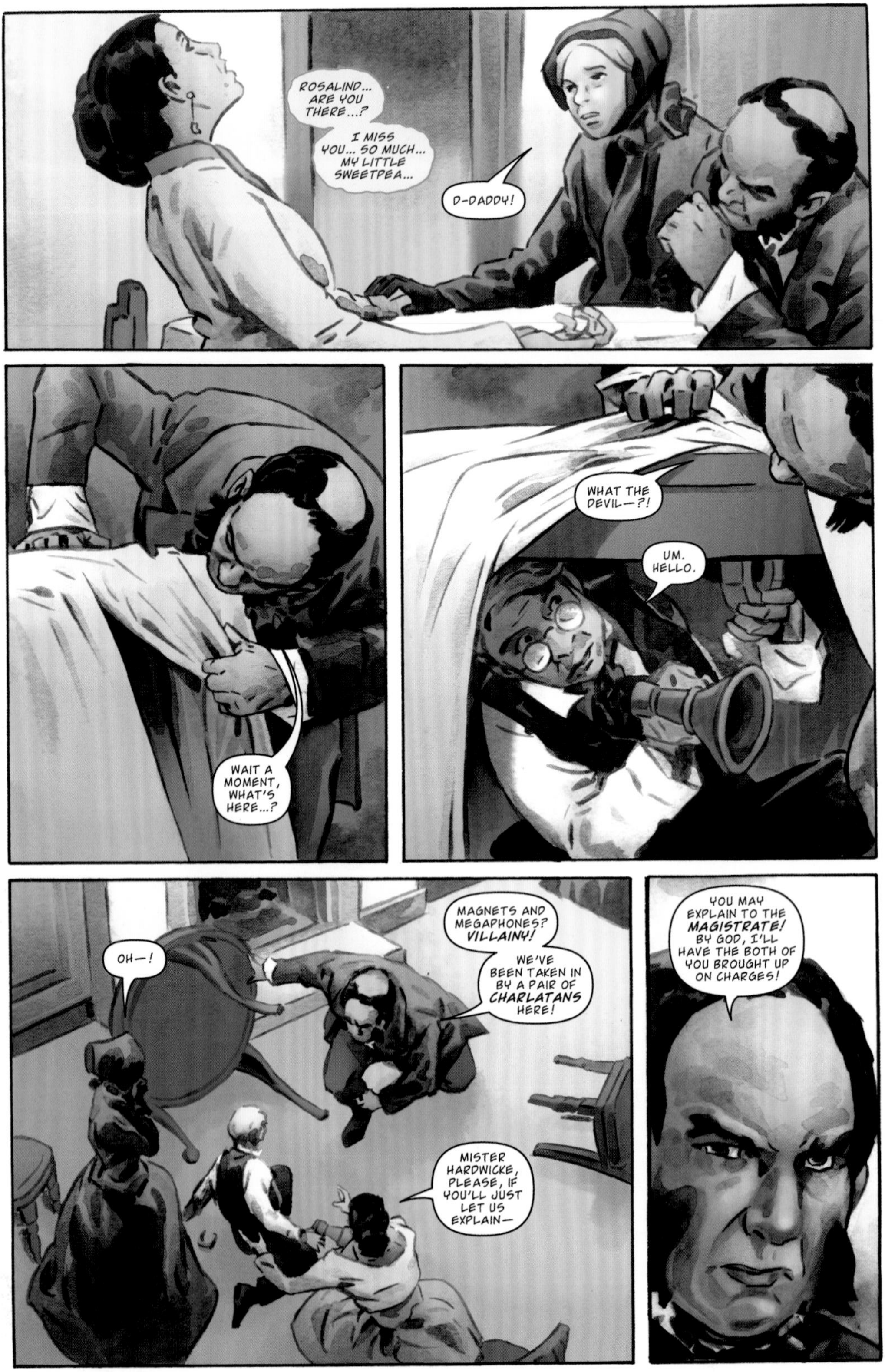
ROSALIND... ARE YOU THERE...?
I MISS YOU... SO MUCH... MY LITTLE SWEETPEA...
D-DADDY!
WAIT A MOMENT, WHAT'S HERE...?
WHAT THE DEVIL—?!
UM. HELLO.
OH—!
MAGNETS AND MEGAPHONES? ***VILLAINY!***
WE'VE BEEN TAKEN IN BY A PAIR OF ***CHARLATANS*** HERE!
MISTER HARDWICKE, PLEASE, IF YOU'LL JUST LET US EXPLAIN—
YOU MAY EXPLAIN TO THE ***MAGISTRATE!*** BY GOD, I'LL HAVE THE BOTH OF YOU BROUGHT UP ON CHARGES!

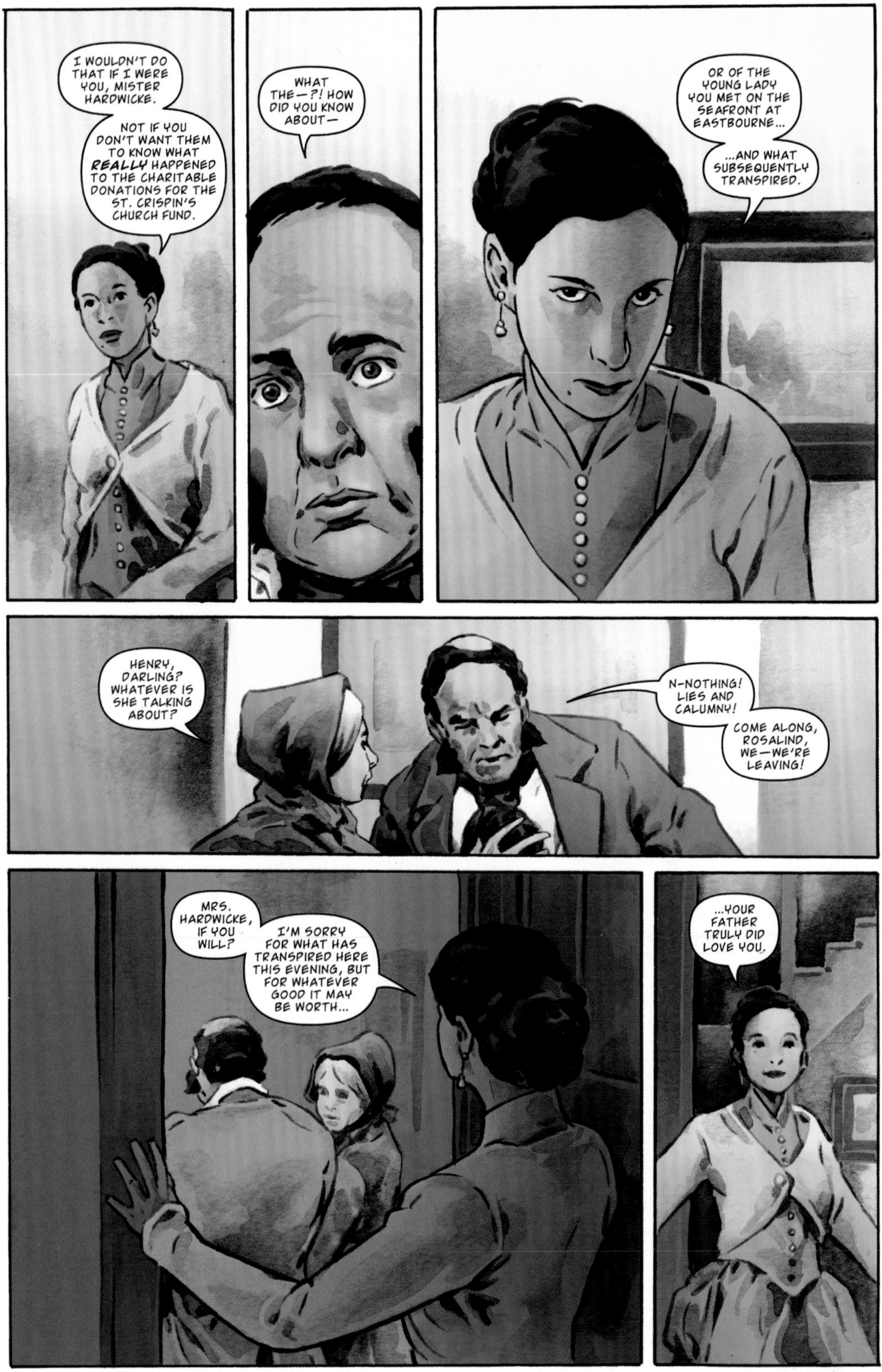
I WOULDN'T DO THAT IF I WERE YOU, MISTER HARDWICKE.
NOT IF YOU DON'T WANT THEM TO KNOW WHAT REALLY HAPPENED TO THE CHARITABLE DONATIONS FOR THE ST. CRISPIN'S CHURCH FUND.
WHAT THE—?! HOW DID YOU KNOW ABOUT—
OR OF THE YOUNG LADY YOU MET ON THE SEAFRONT AT EASTBOURNE...
...AND WHAT SUBSEQUENTLY TRANSPIRED.
HENRY, DARLING? WHATEVER IS SHE TALKING ABOUT?
N-NOTHING! LIES AND CALUMNY!
COME ALONG, ROSALIND, WE—WE'RE LEAVING!
MRS. HARDWICKE, IF YOU WILL?
I'M SORRY FOR WHAT HAS TRANSPIRED HERE THIS EVENING, BUT FOR WHATEVER GOOD IT MAY BE WORTH...
...YOUR FATHER TRULY DID LOVE YOU.

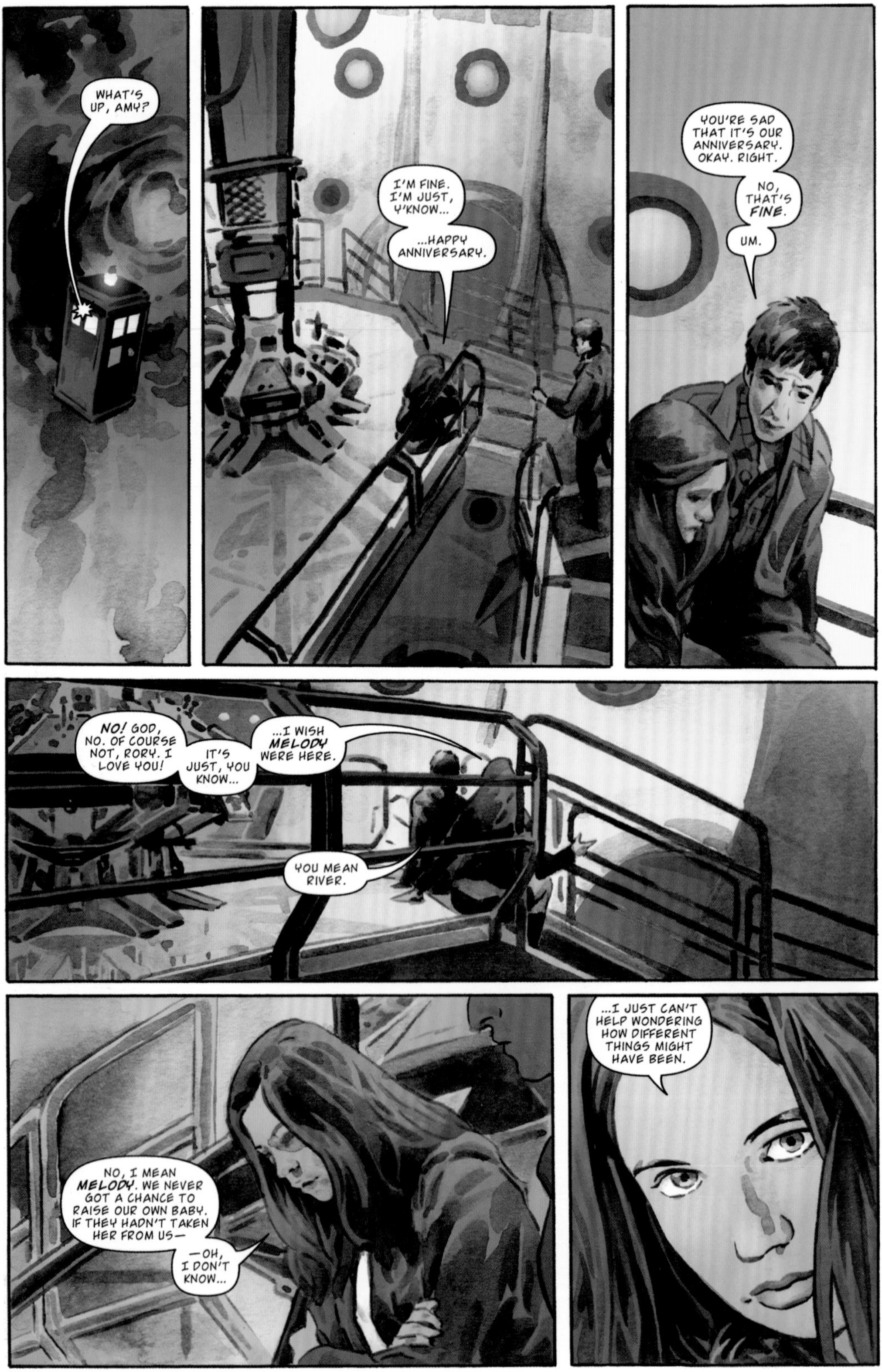
WHAT'S UP, AMY?
I'M FINE. I'M JUST, Y'KNOW...
...HAPPY ANNIVERSARY.
YOU'RE SAD THAT IT'S OUR ANNIVERSARY. OKAY. RIGHT.
NO, THAT'S FINE.
UM.
NO! GOD, NO. OF COURSE NOT, RORY. I LOVE YOU!
IT'S JUST, YOU KNOW...
...I WISH MELODY WERE HERE.
YOU MEAN RIVER.
NO, I MEAN MELODY. WE NEVER GOT A CHANCE TO RAISE OUR OWN BABY. IF THEY HADN'T TAKEN HER FROM US—
—OH, I DON'T KNOW...
...I JUST CAN'T HELP WONDERING HOW DIFFERENT THINGS MIGHT HAVE BEEN.

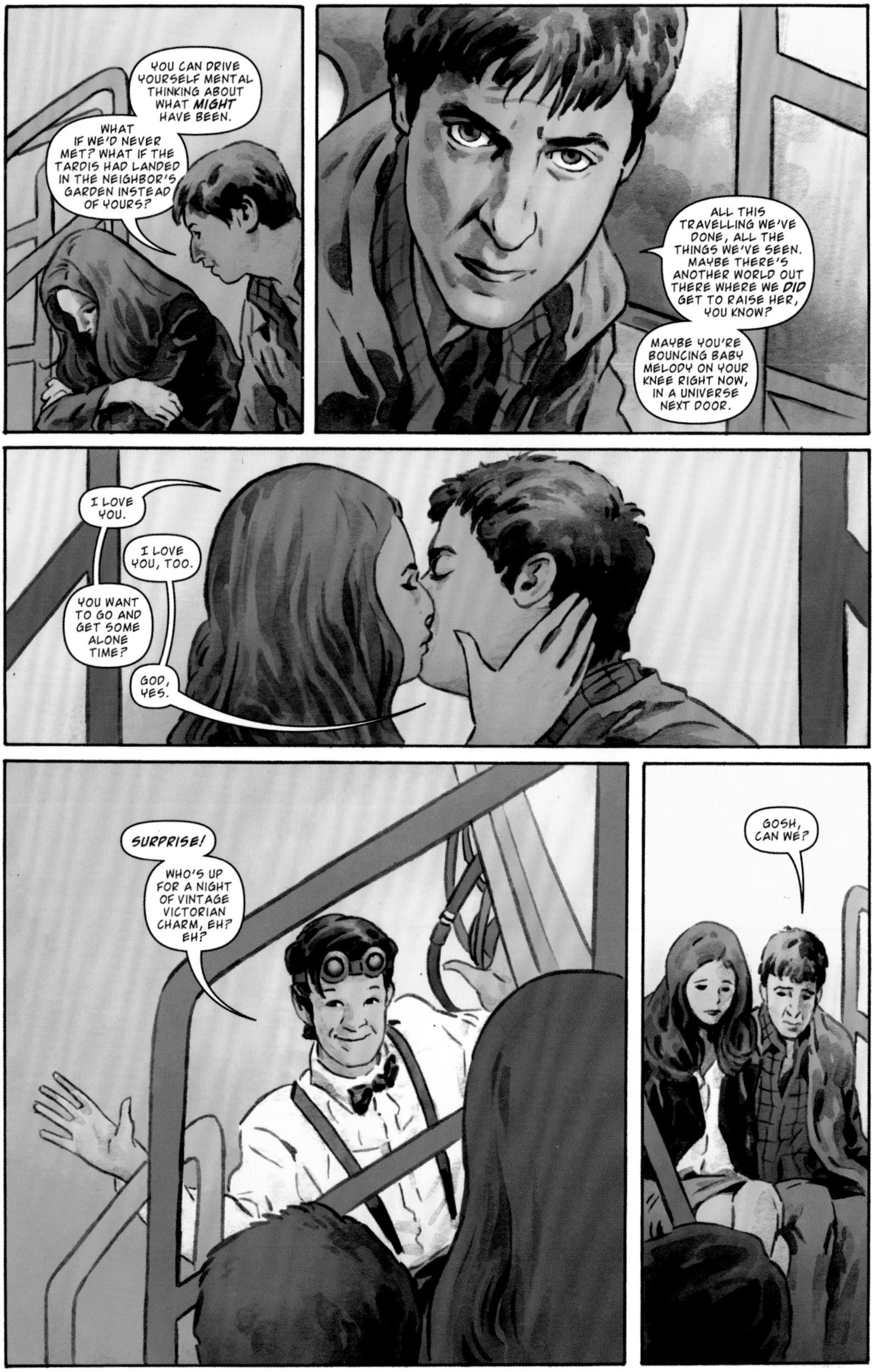
YOU CAN DRIVE YOURSELF MENTAL THINKING ABOUT WHAT MIGHT HAVE BEEN.
WHAT IF WE'D NEVER MET? WHAT IF THE TARDIS HAD LANDED IN THE NEIGHBOR'S GARDEN INSTEAD OF YOURS?
ALL THIS TRAVELLING WE'VE DONE, ALL THE THINGS WE'VE SEEN. MAYBE THERE'S ANOTHER WORLD OUT THERE WHERE WE DID GET TO RAISE HER, YOU KNOW?
MAYBE YOU'RE BOUNCING BABY MELODY ON YOUR KNEE RIGHT NOW, IN A UNIVERSE NEXT DOOR.
I LOVE YOU.
I LOVE YOU, TOO.
YOU WANT TO GO AND GET SOME ALONE TIME?
GOD, YES.
SURPRISE!
WHO'S UP FOR A NIGHT OF VINTAGE VICTORIAN CHARM, EH? EH?
GOSH, CAN WE?

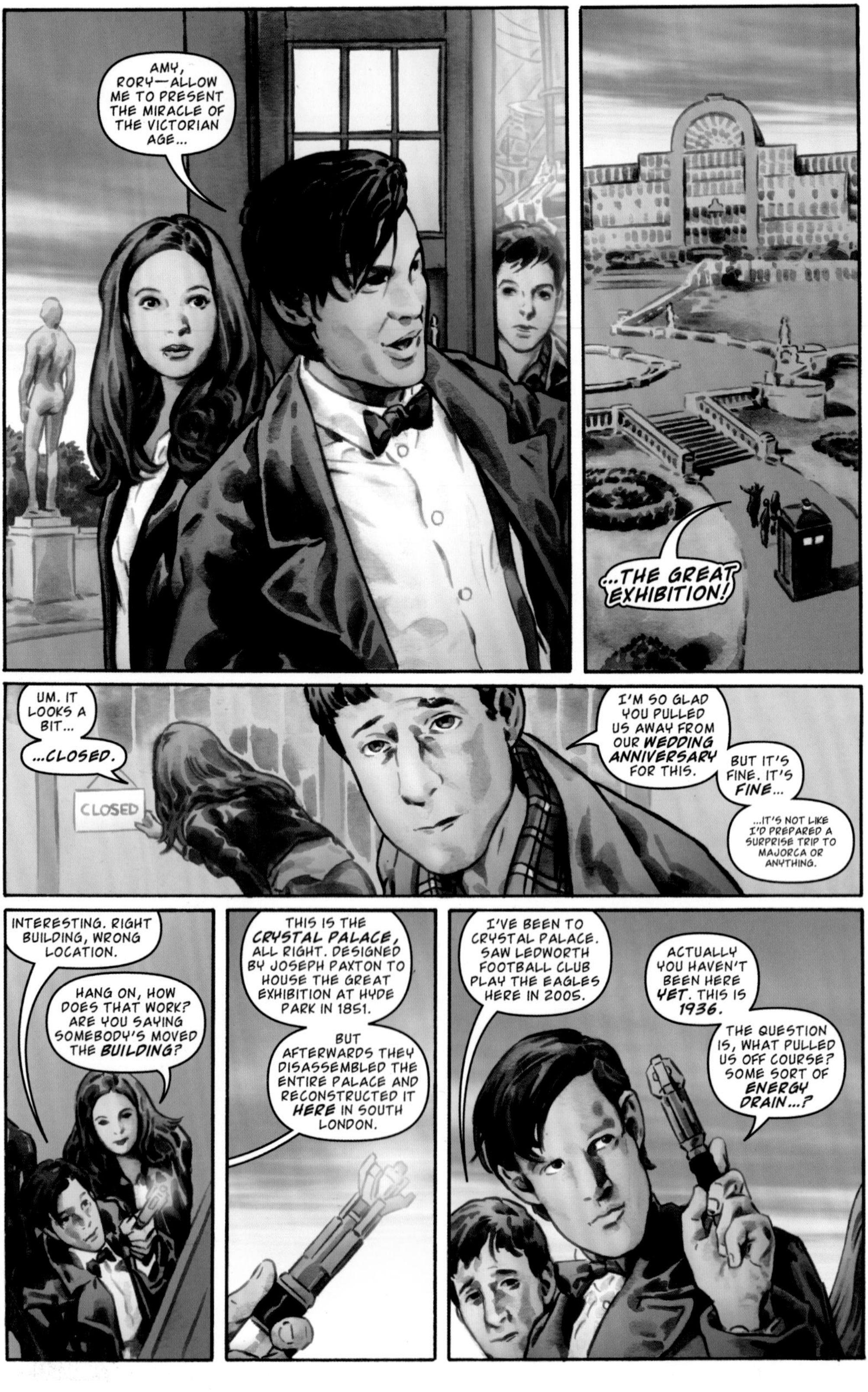
AMY, RORY—ALLOW ME TO PRESENT THE MIRACLE OF THE VICTORIAN AGE...
...THE GREAT EXHIBITION!
UM. IT LOOKS A BIT...
...CLOSED.
CLOSED
I'M SO GLAD YOU PULLED US AWAY FROM OUR WEDDING ANNIVERSARY FOR THIS.
BUT IT'S FINE. IT'S FINE...
...IT'S NOT LIKE I'D PREPARED A SURPRISE TRIP TO MAJORCA OR ANYTHING.
INTERESTING. RIGHT BUILDING, WRONG LOCATION.
HANG ON, HOW DOES THAT WORK? ARE YOU SAYING SOMEBODY'S MOVED THE BUILDING?
THIS IS THE CRYSTAL PALACE, ALL RIGHT. DESIGNED BY JOSEPH PAXTON TO HOUSE THE GREAT EXHIBITION AT HYDE PARK IN 1851.
BUT AFTERWARDS THEY DISASSEMBLED THE ENTIRE PALACE AND RECONSTRUCTED IT HERE IN SOUTH LONDON.
I'VE BEEN TO CRYSTAL PALACE. SAW LEDWORTH FOOTBALL CLUB PLAY THE EAGLES HERE IN 2005.
ACTUALLY YOU HAVEN'T BEEN HERE YET. THIS IS 1936.
THE QUESTION IS, WHAT PULLED US OFF COURSE? SOME SORT OF ENERGY DRAIN...?

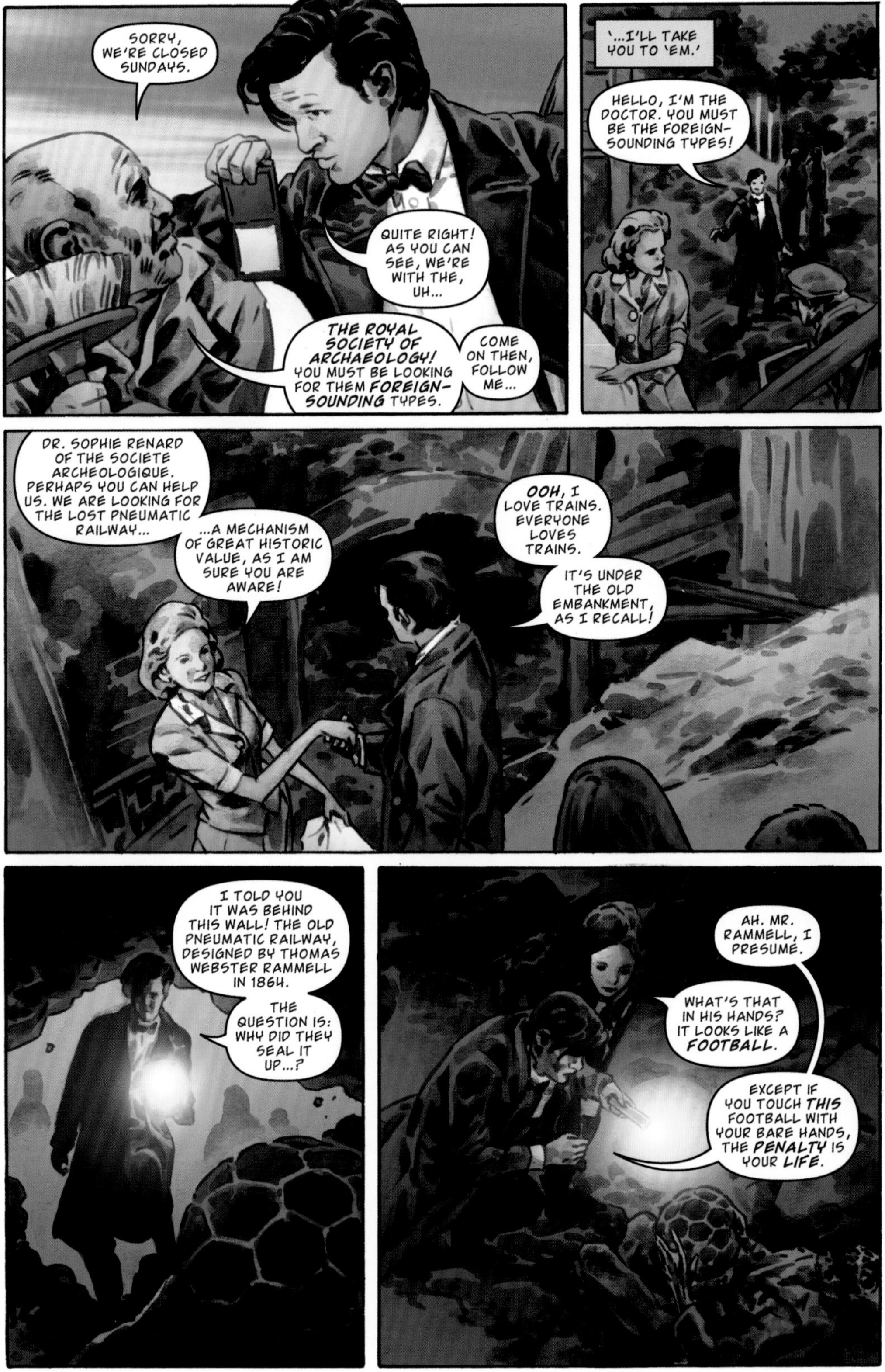
SORRY, WE'RE CLOSED SUNDAYS.
QUITE RIGHT! AS YOU CAN SEE, WE'RE WITH THE, UH...
THE ROYAL SOCIETY OF ARCHAEOLOGY! YOU MUST BE LOOKING FOR THEM FOREIGN-SOUNDING TYPES.
COME ON THEN, FOLLOW ME...
'...I'LL TAKE YOU TO 'EM.'
HELLO, I'M THE DOCTOR. YOU MUST BE THE FOREIGN-SOUNDING TYPES!
DR. SOPHIE RENARD OF THE SOCIETE ARCHEOLOGIQUE. PERHAPS YOU CAN HELP US. WE ARE LOOKING FOR THE LOST PNEUMATIC RAILWAY...
...A MECHANISM OF GREAT HISTORIC VALUE, AS I AM SURE YOU ARE AWARE!
OOH, I LOVE TRAINS. EVERYONE LOVES TRAINS.
IT'S UNDER THE OLD EMBANKMENT, AS I RECALL!
I TOLD YOU IT WAS BEHIND THIS WALL! THE OLD PNEUMATIC RAILWAY, DESIGNED BY THOMAS WEBSTER RAMMELL IN 1864.
THE QUESTION IS: WHY DID THEY SEAL IT UP...?
AH. MR. RAMMELL, I PRESUME.
WHAT'S THAT IN HIS HANDS? IT LOOKS LIKE A FOOTBALL.
EXCEPT IF YOU TOUCH THIS FOOTBALL WITH YOUR BARE HANDS, THE PENALTY IS YOUR LIFE.

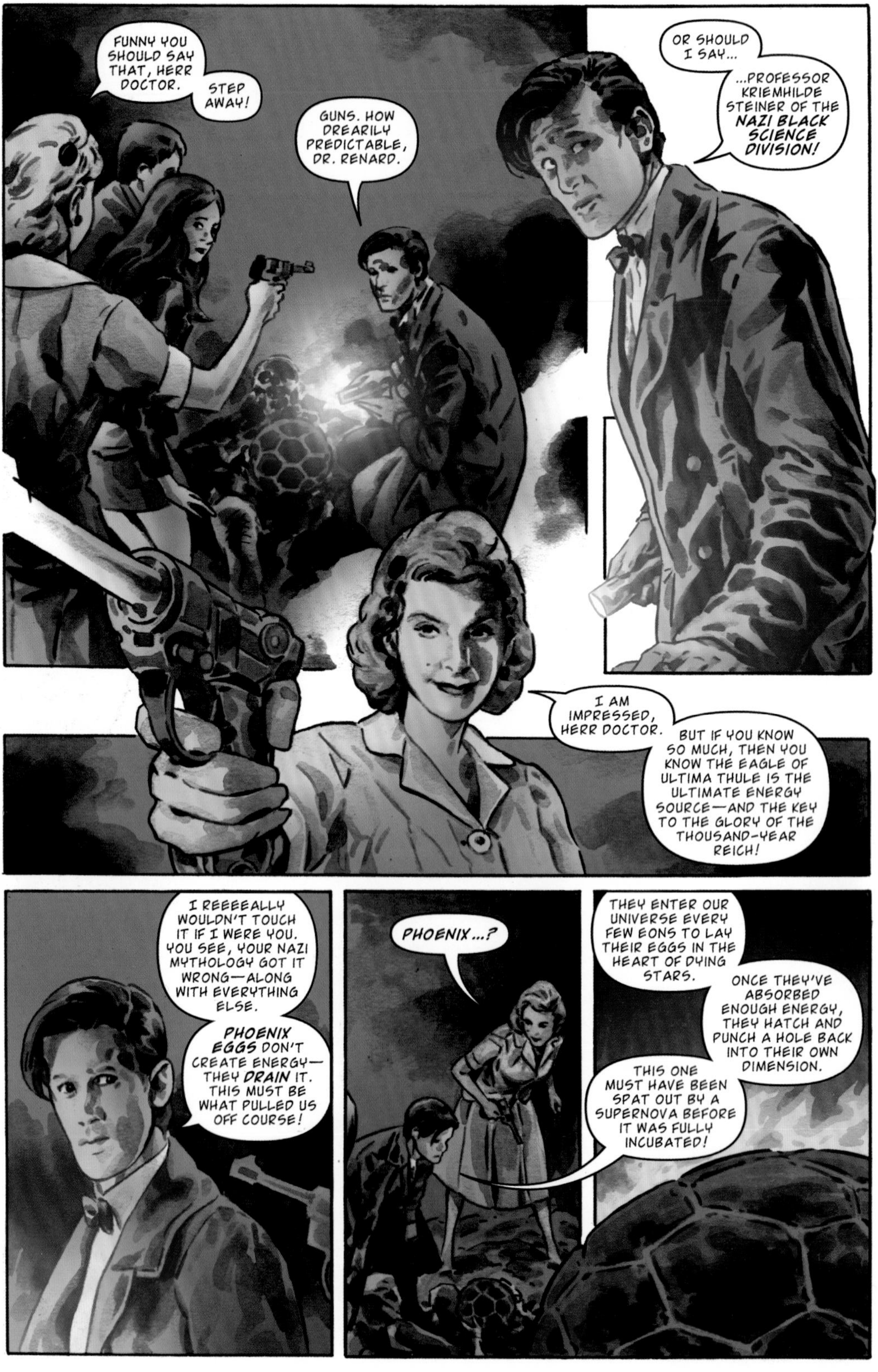
FUNNY YOU SHOULD SAY THAT, HERR DOCTOR.
STEP AWAY!
GUNS. HOW DREARILY PREDICTABLE, DR. RENARD.
OR SHOULD I SAY...
...PROFESSOR KRIEMHILDE STEINER OF THE **NAZI BLACK SCIENCE DIVISION!**
I AM IMPRESSED, HERR DOCTOR.
BUT IF YOU KNOW SO MUCH, THEN YOU KNOW THE EAGLE OF ULTIMA THULE IS THE ULTIMATE ENERGY SOURCE—AND THE KEY TO THE GLORY OF THE THOUSAND-YEAR REICH!
I REEEEEALLY WOULDN'T TOUCH IT IF I WERE YOU. YOU SEE, YOUR NAZI MYTHOLOGY GOT IT WRONG—ALONG WITH EVERYTHING ELSE.
PHOENIX EGGS DON'T CREATE ENERGY—THEY ***DRAIN*** IT. THIS MUST BE WHAT PULLED US OFF COURSE!
PHOENIX...?
THEY ENTER OUR UNIVERSE EVERY FEW EONS TO LAY THEIR EGGS IN THE HEART OF DYING STARS.
ONCE THEY'VE ABSORBED ENOUGH ENERGY, THEY HATCH AND PUNCH A HOLE BACK INTO THEIR OWN DIMENSION.
THIS ONE MUST HAVE BEEN SPAT OUT BY A SUPERNOVA BEFORE IT WAS FULLY INCUBATED!

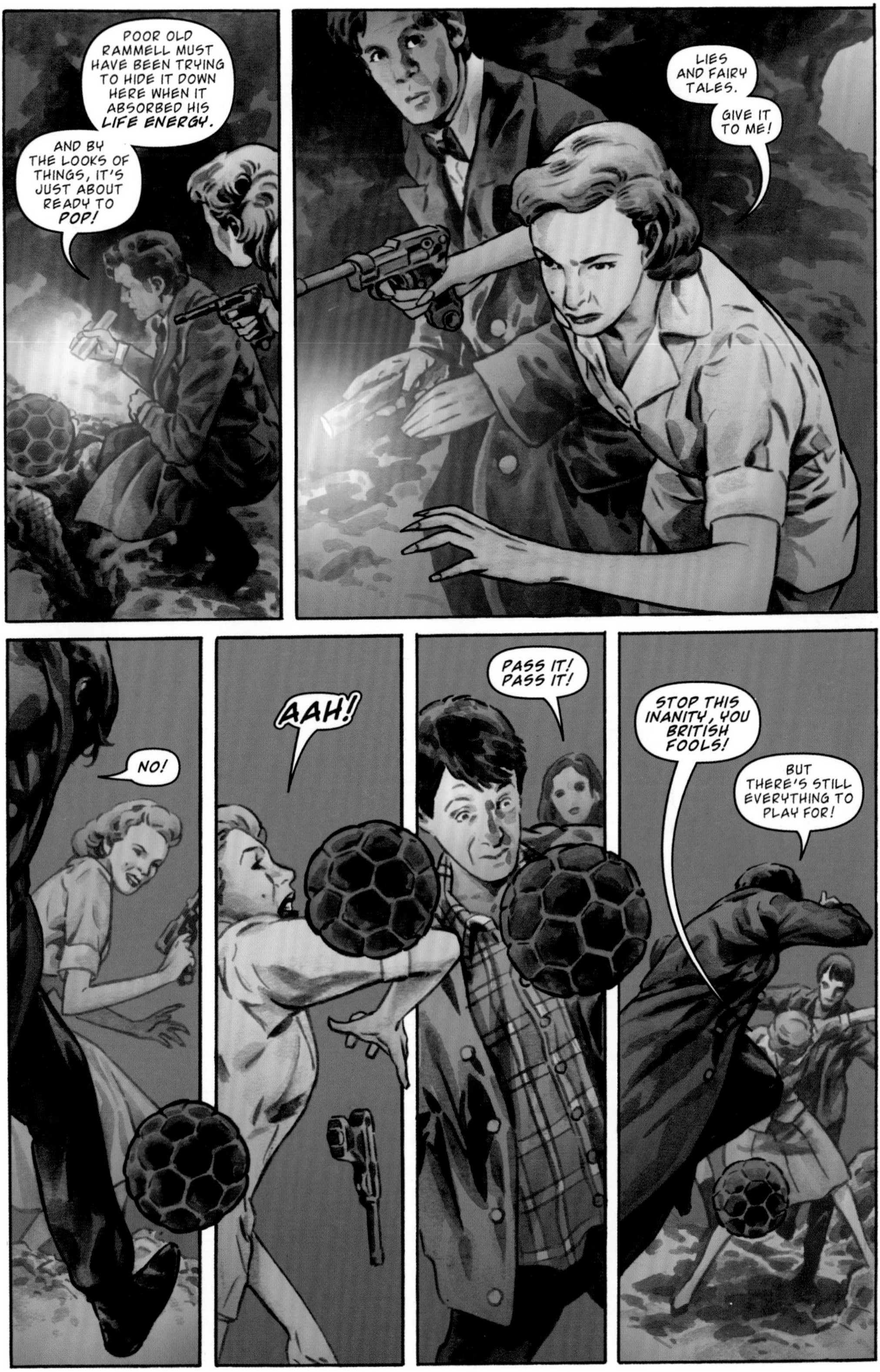
POOR OLD RAMMELL MUST HAVE BEEN TRYING TO HIDE IT DOWN HERE WHEN IT ABSORBED HIS LIFE ENERGY.
AND BY THE LOOKS OF THINGS, IT'S JUST ABOUT READY TO POP!
LIES AND FAIRY TALES.
GIVE IT TO ME!
NO!
AAH!
PASS IT! PASS IT!
STOP THIS INANITY, YOU BRITISH FOOLS!
BUT THERE'S STILL EVERYTHING TO PLAY FOR!

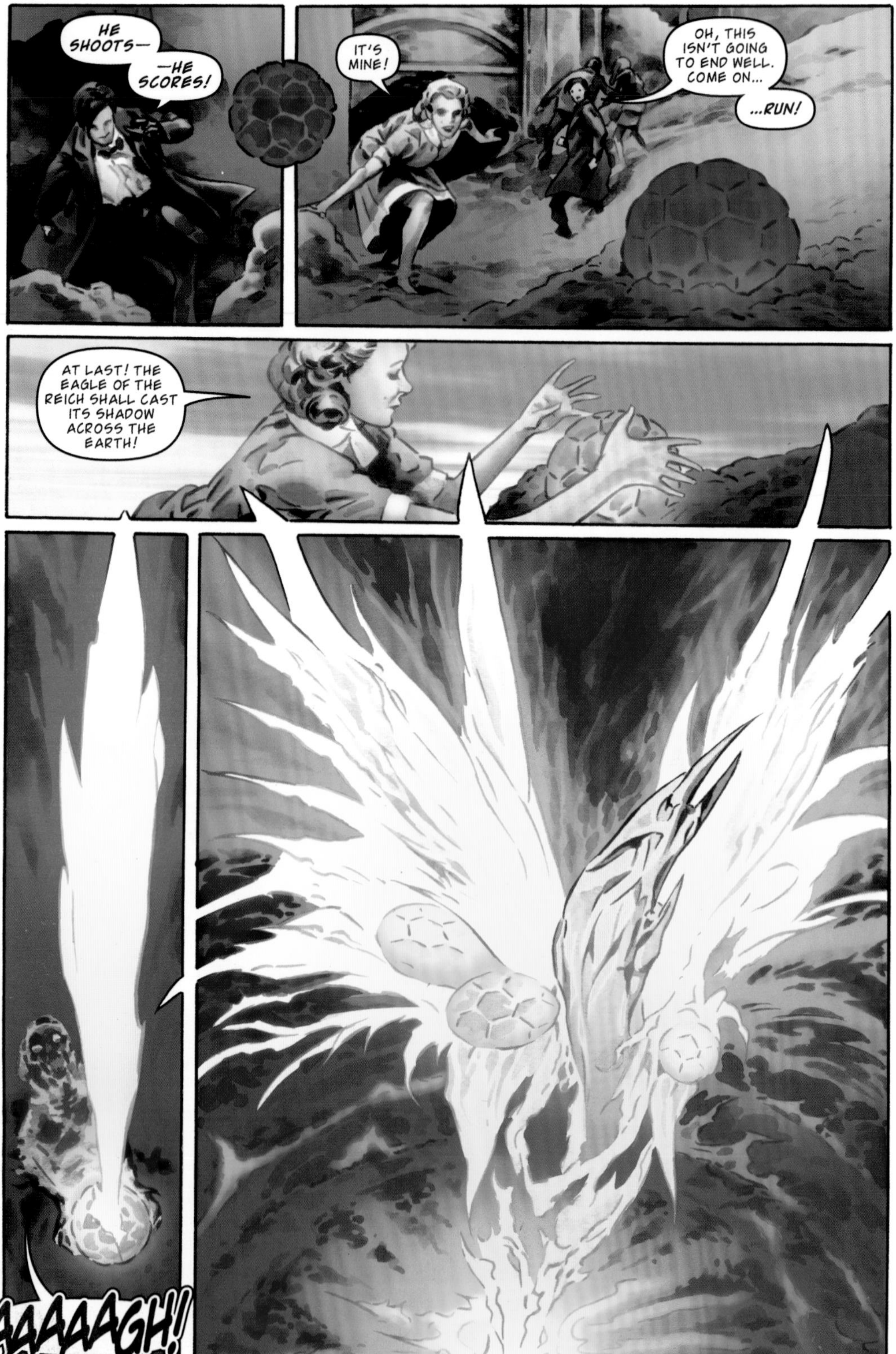
HE SHOOTS—
—HE SCORES!
IT'S MINE!
OH, THIS ISN'T GOING TO END WELL. COME ON...
...RUN!
AT LAST! THE EAGLE OF THE REICH SHALL CAST ITS SHADOW ACROSS THE EARTH!
AAAAAGH!

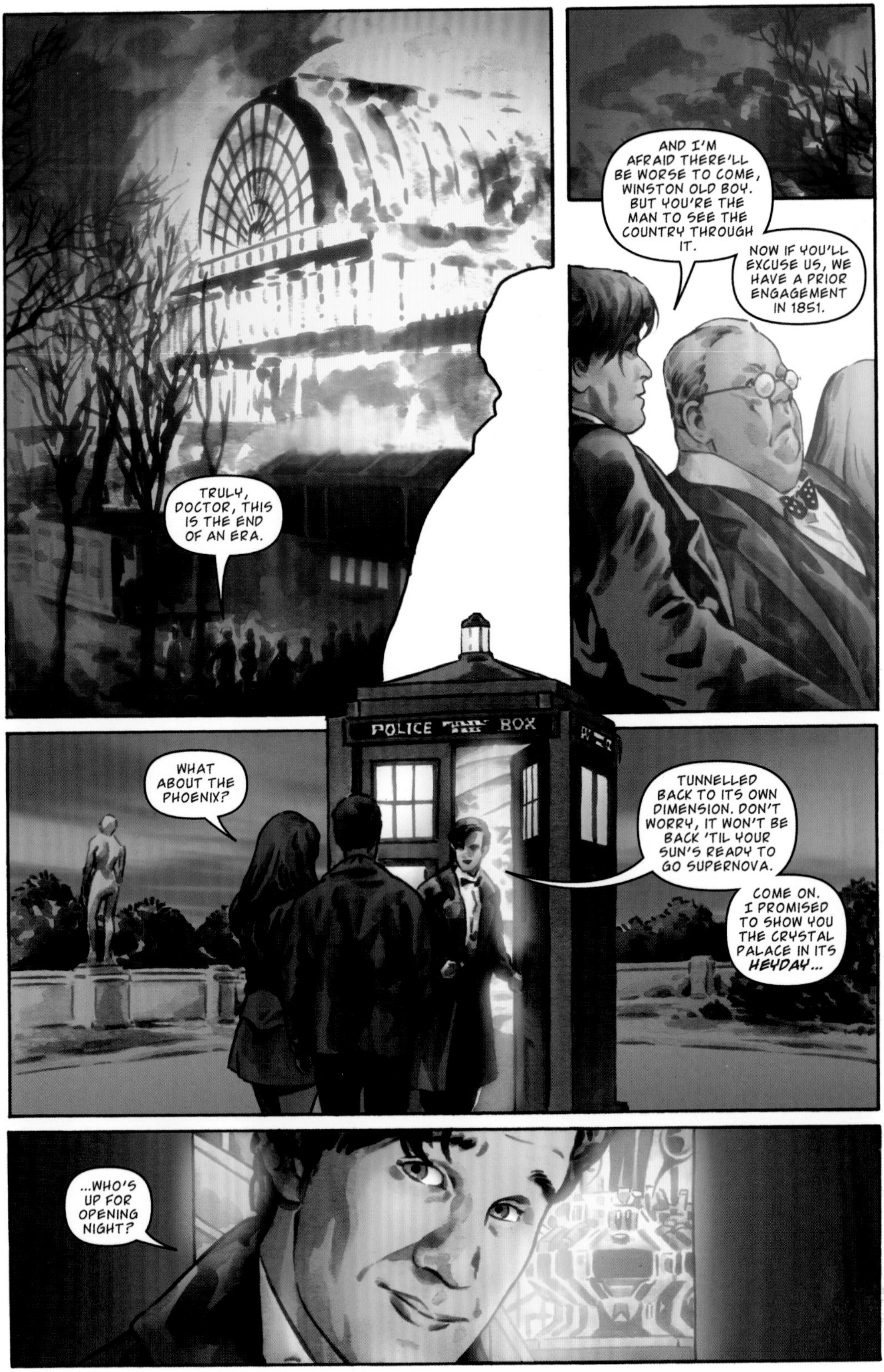
TRULY, DOCTOR, THIS IS THE END OF AN ERA.
AND I'M AFRAID THERE'LL BE WORSE TO COME, WINSTON OLD BOY. BUT YOU'RE THE MAN TO SEE THE COUNTRY THROUGH IT.
NOW IF YOU'LL EXCUSE US, WE HAVE A PRIOR ENGAGEMENT IN 1851.
POLICE BOX
WHAT ABOUT THE PHOENIX?
TUNNELLED BACK TO ITS OWN DIMENSION. DON'T WORRY, IT WON'T BE BACK 'TIL YOUR SUN'S READY TO GO SUPERNOVA.
COME ON. I PROMISED TO SHOW YOU THE CRYSTAL PALACE IN ITS HEYDAY...
...WHO'S UP FOR OPENING NIGHT?

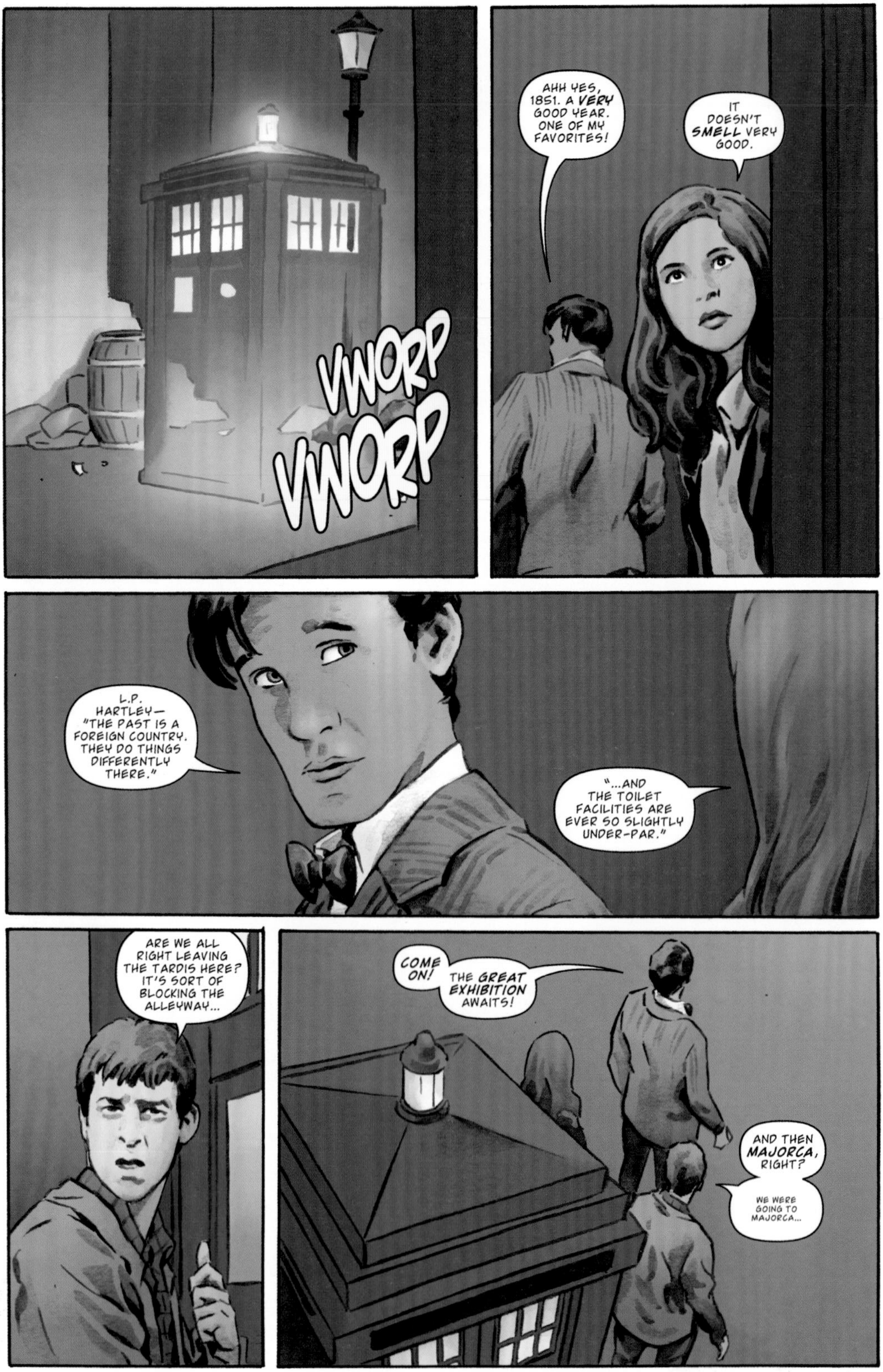
VWORP
VWORP
AHH YES, 1851. A VERY GOOD YEAR. ONE OF MY FAVORITES!
IT DOESN'T SMELL VERY GOOD.
L.P. HARTLEY— "THE PAST IS A FOREIGN COUNTRY. THEY DO THINGS DIFFERENTLY THERE."
"...AND THE TOILET FACILITIES ARE EVER SO SLIGHTLY UNDER-PAR."
ARE WE ALL RIGHT LEAVING THE TARDIS HERE? IT'S SORT OF BLOCKING THE ALLEYWAY...
COME ON!
THE GREAT EXHIBITION AWAITS!
AND THEN MAJORCA, RIGHT?
WE WERE GOING TO MAJORCA...

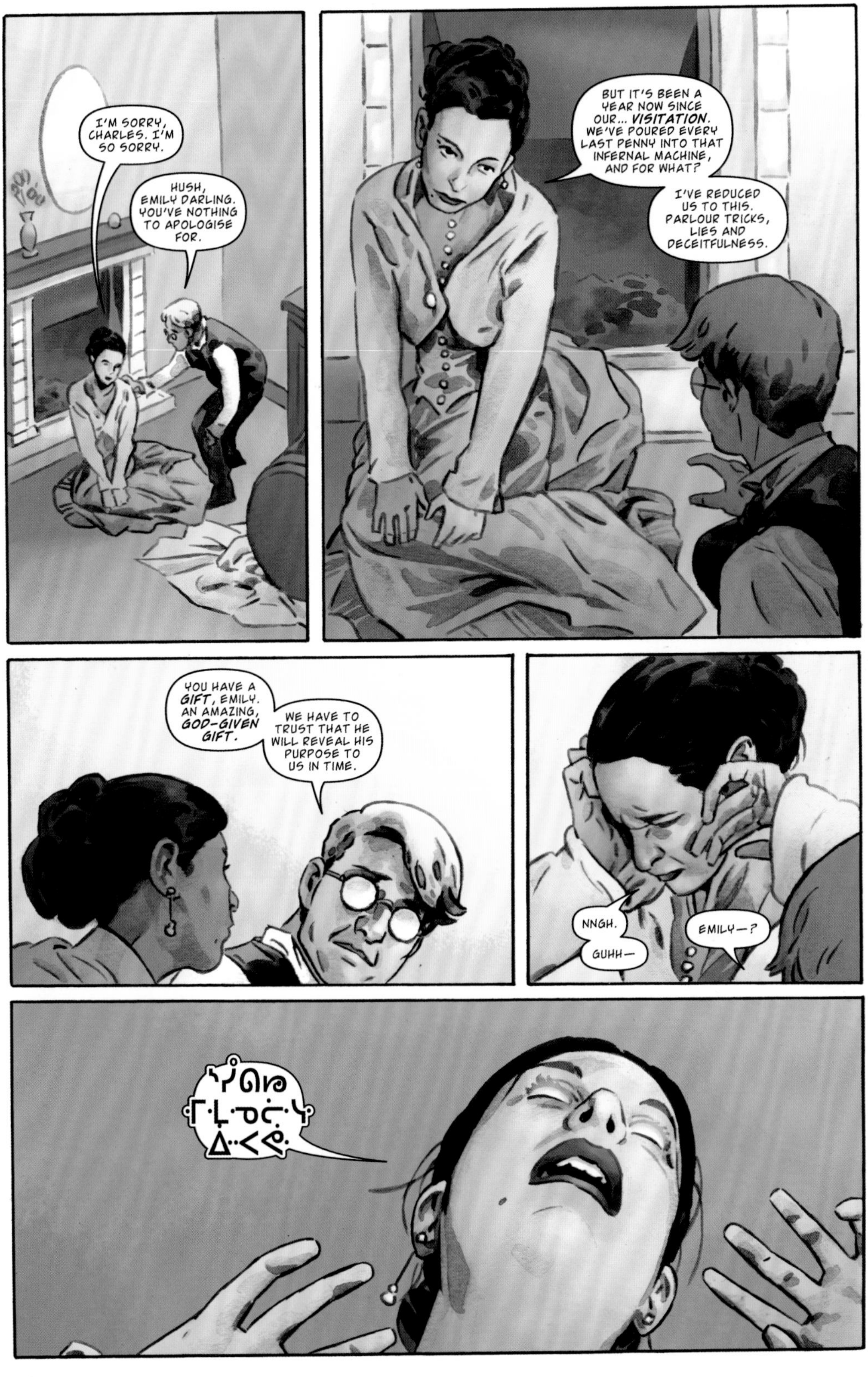
I'M SORRY, CHARLES. I'M SO SORRY.
HUSH, EMILY DARLING. YOU'VE NOTHING TO APOLOGISE FOR.
BUT IT'S BEEN A YEAR NOW SINCE OUR... VISITATION. WE'VE POURED EVERY LAST PENNY INTO THAT INFERNAL MACHINE, AND FOR WHAT?
I'VE REDUCED US TO THIS. PARLOUR TRICKS, LIES AND DECEITFULNESS.
YOU HAVE A GIFT, EMILY. AN AMAZING, GOD-GIVEN GIFT.
WE HAVE TO TRUST THAT HE WILL REVEAL HIS PURPOSE TO US IN TIME.
NNGH.
GUHH—
EMILY—?

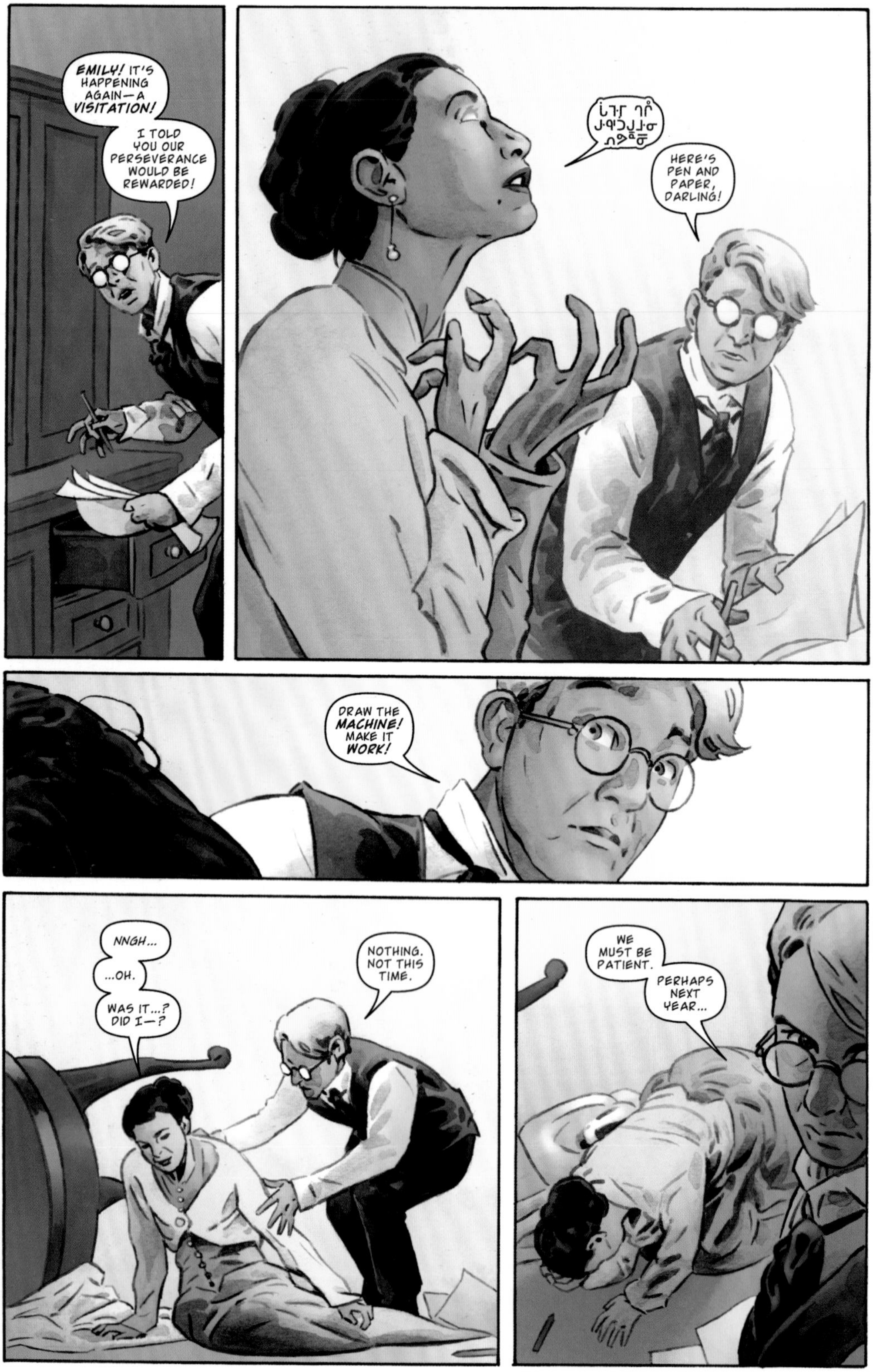
EMILY! IT'S HAPPENING AGAIN—A VISITATION!
I TOLD YOU OUR PERSEVERANCE WOULD BE REWARDED!
HERE'S PEN AND PAPER, DARLING!
DRAW THE MACHINE! MAKE IT WORK!
NNGH...
...OH.
WAS IT...? DID I—?
NOTHING. NOT THIS TIME.
WE MUST BE PATIENT.
PERHAPS NEXT YEAR...

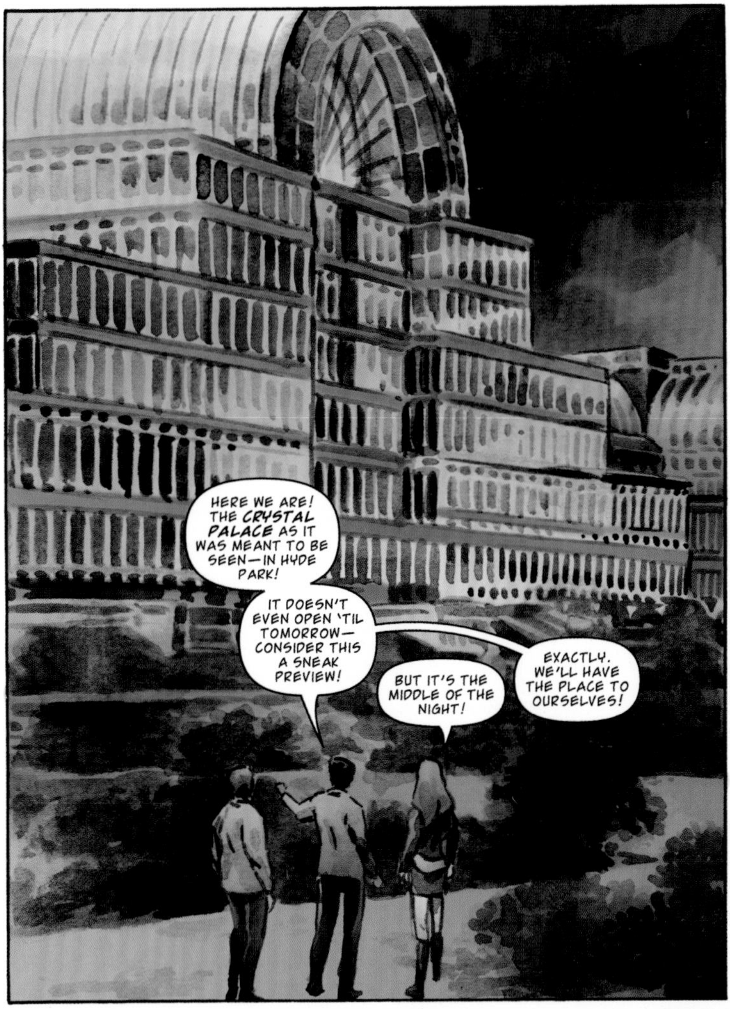
HERE WE ARE! THE CRYSTAL PALACE AS IT WAS MEANT TO BE SEEN—IN HYDE PARK!
IT DOESN'T EVEN OPEN 'TIL TOMORROW—CONSIDER THIS A SNEAK PREVIEW!
EXACTLY. WE'LL HAVE THE PLACE TO OURSELVES!
BUT IT'S THE MIDDLE OF THE NIGHT!

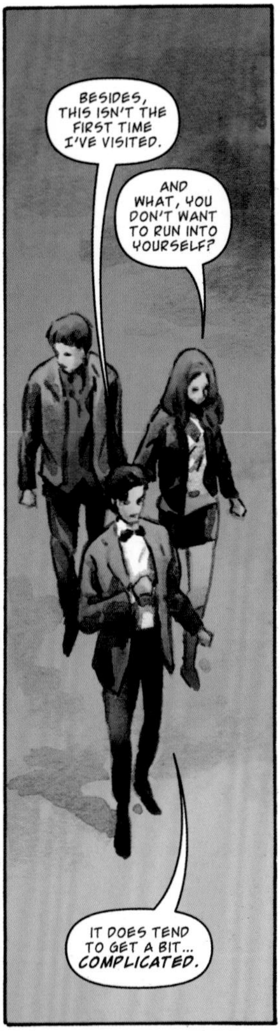
BESIDES, THIS ISN'T THE FIRST TIME I'VE VISITED.
AND WHAT, YOU DON'T WANT TO RUN INTO YOURSELF?
IT DOES TEND TO GET A BIT... COMPLICATED.

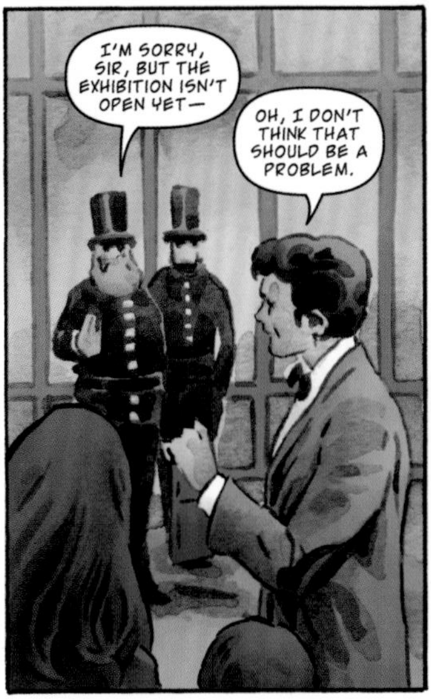
I'M SORRY, SIR, BUT THE EXHIBITION ISN'T OPEN YET—
OH, I DON'T THINK THAT SHOULD BE A PROBLEM.

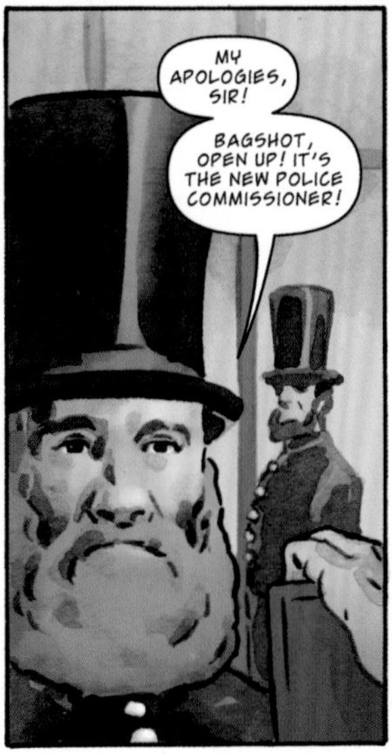
MY APOLOGIES, SIR!
BAGSHOT, OPEN UP! IT'S THE NEW POLICE COMMISSIONER!

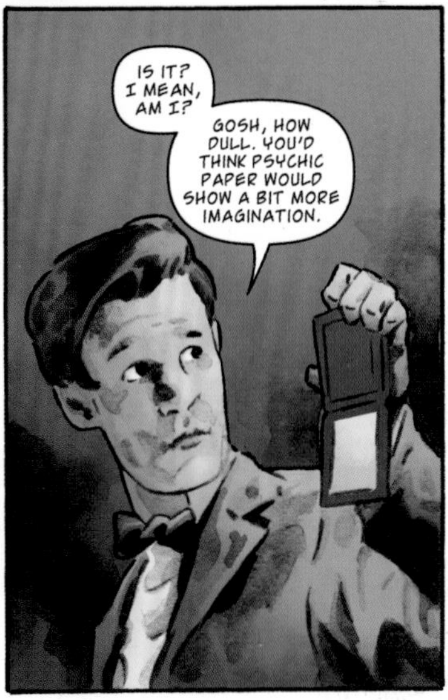
IS IT? I MEAN, AM I?
GOSH, HOW DULL. YOU'D THINK PSYCHIC PAPER WOULD SHOW A BIT MORE IMAGINATION.

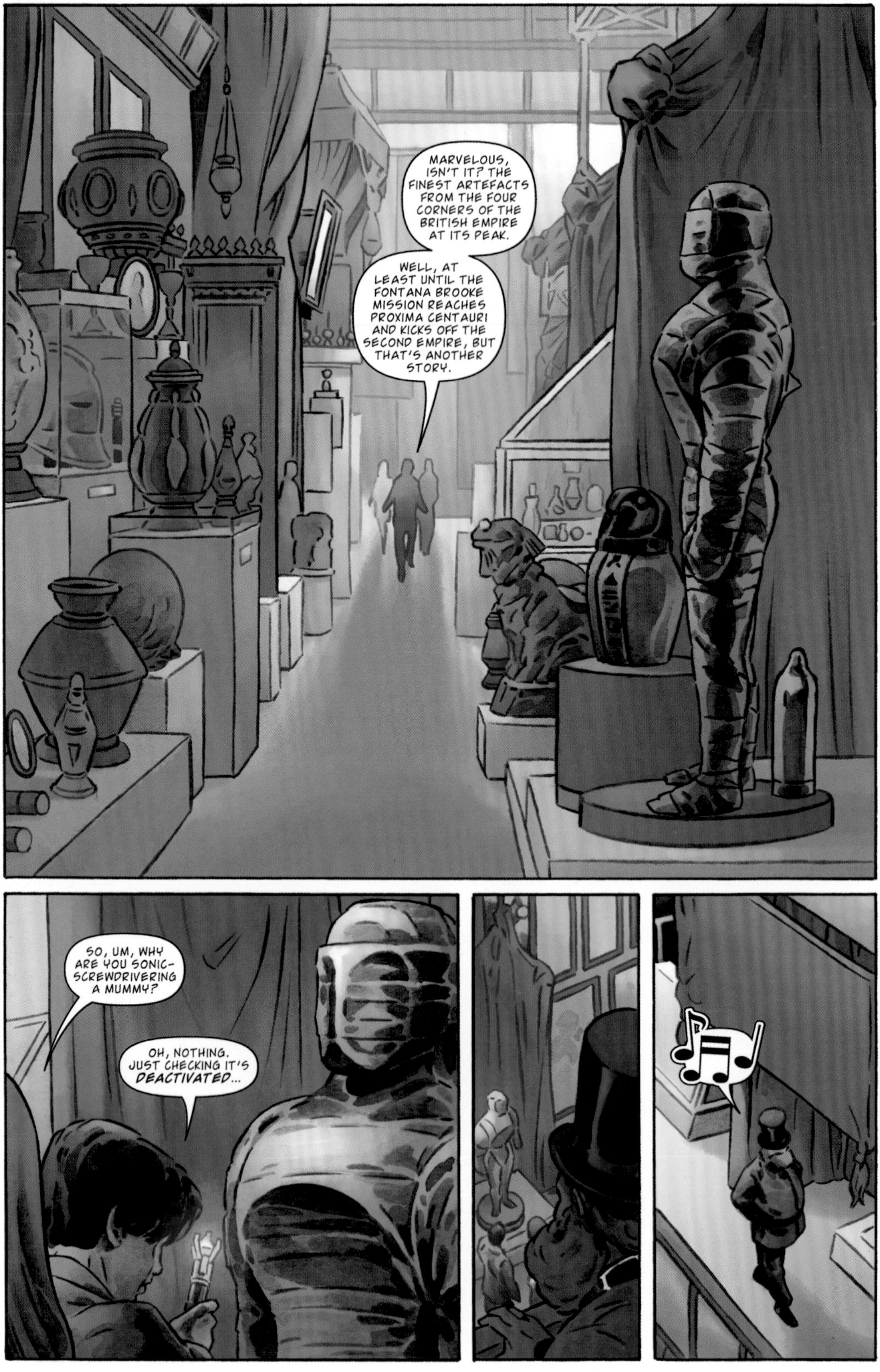
MARVELOUS, ISN'T IT? THE FINEST ARTEFACTS FROM THE FOUR CORNERS OF THE BRITISH EMPIRE AT ITS PEAK.
WELL, AT LEAST UNTIL THE FONTANA BROOKE MISSION REACHES PROXIMA CENTAURI AND KICKS OFF THE SECOND EMPIRE, BUT THAT'S ANOTHER STORY.
SO, UM, WHY ARE YOU SONIC-SCREWDRIVERING A MUMMY?
OH, NOTHING. JUST CHECKING IT'S *DEACTIVATED*...

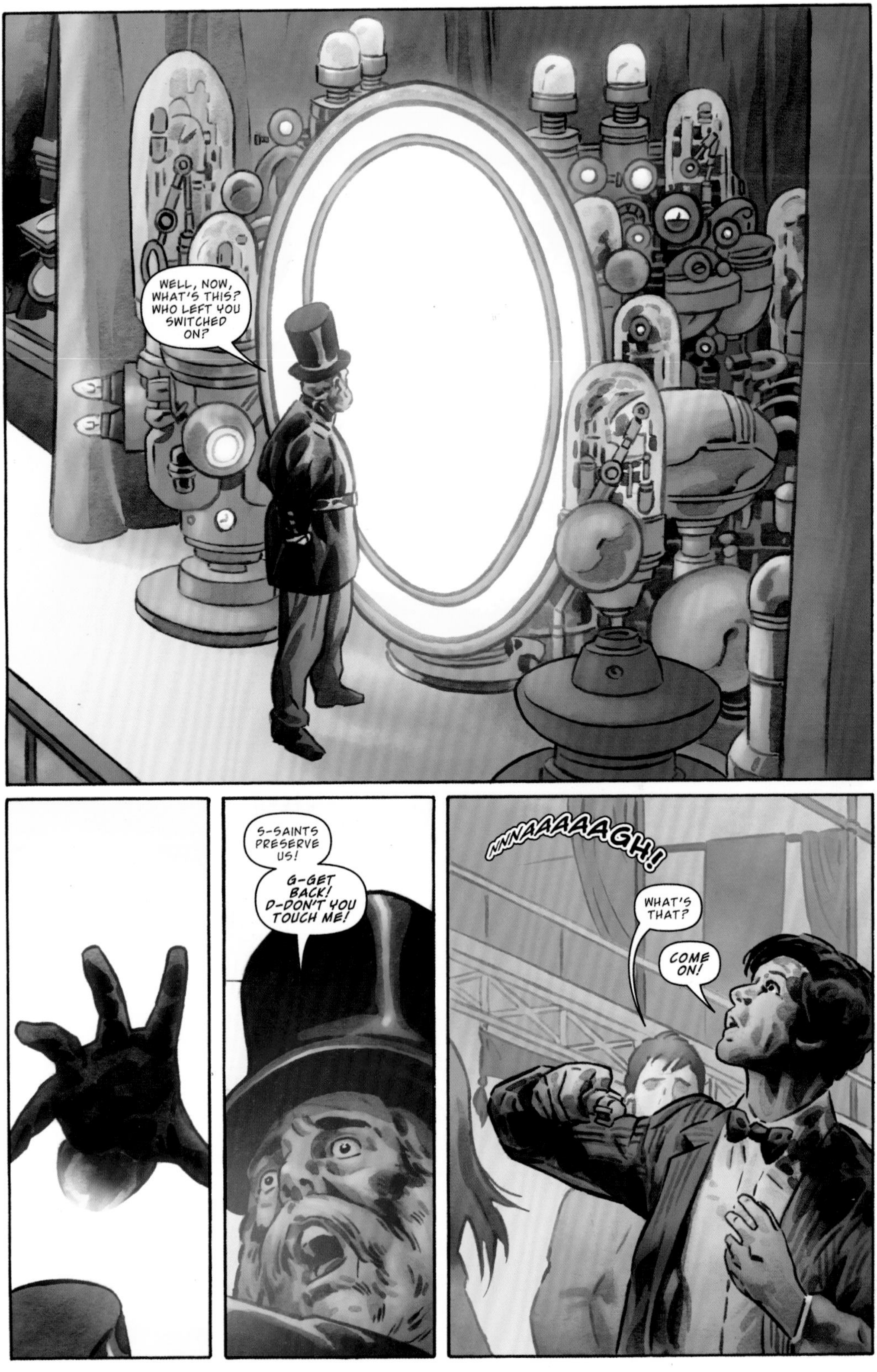
WELL, NOW, WHAT'S THIS? WHO LEFT YOU SWITCHED ON?
S-SAINTS PRESERVE US!
G-GET BACK! D-DON'T YOU TOUCH ME!
NNNAAAAAAGH!
WHAT'S THAT?
COME ON!

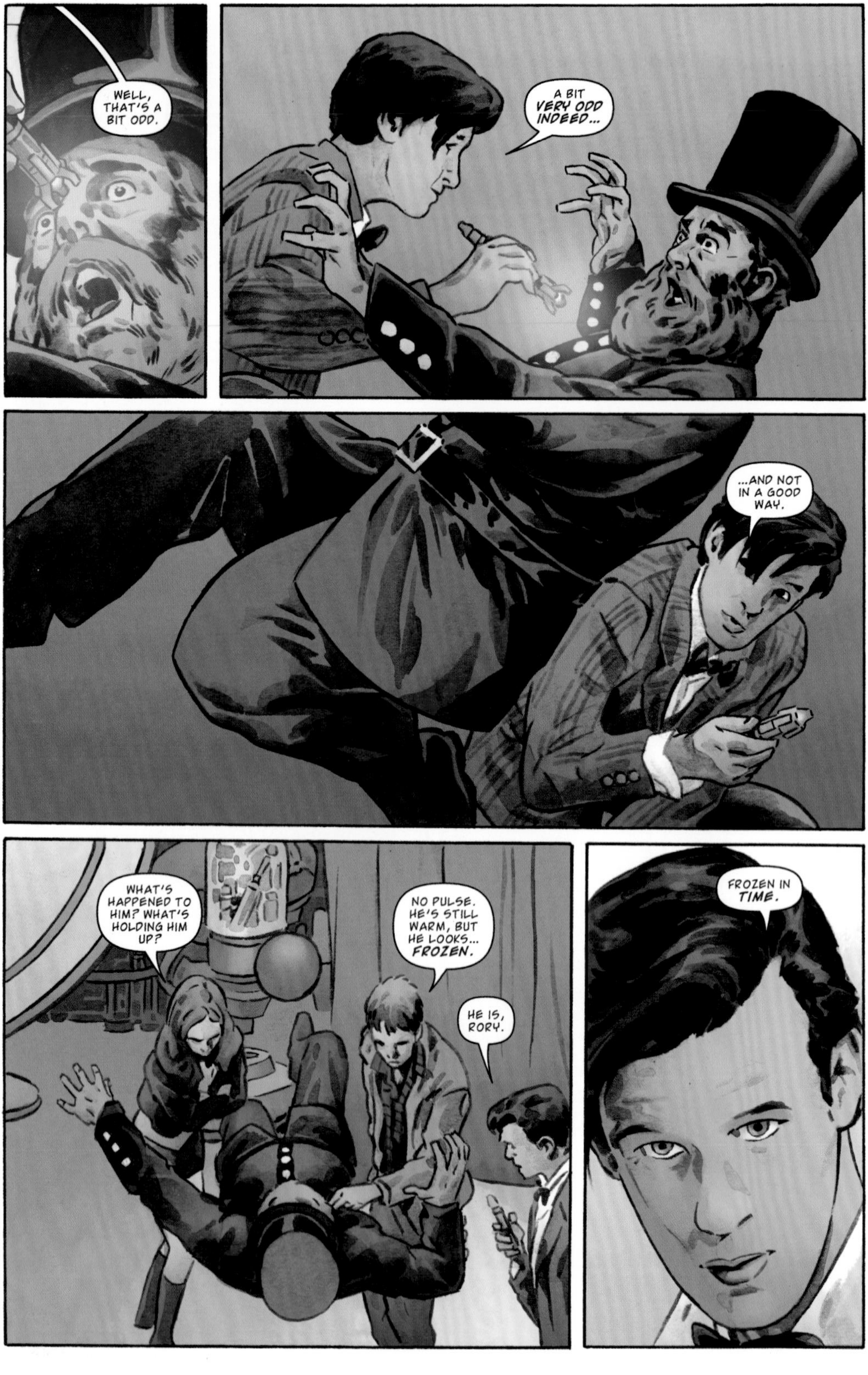
WELL, THAT'S A BIT ODD.
A BIT VERY ODD INDEED...
...AND NOT IN A GOOD WAY.
WHAT'S HAPPENED TO HIM? WHAT'S HOLDING HIM UP?
NO PULSE. HE'S STILL WARM, BUT HE LOOKS... FROZEN.
HE IS, RORY.
FROZEN IN TIME.

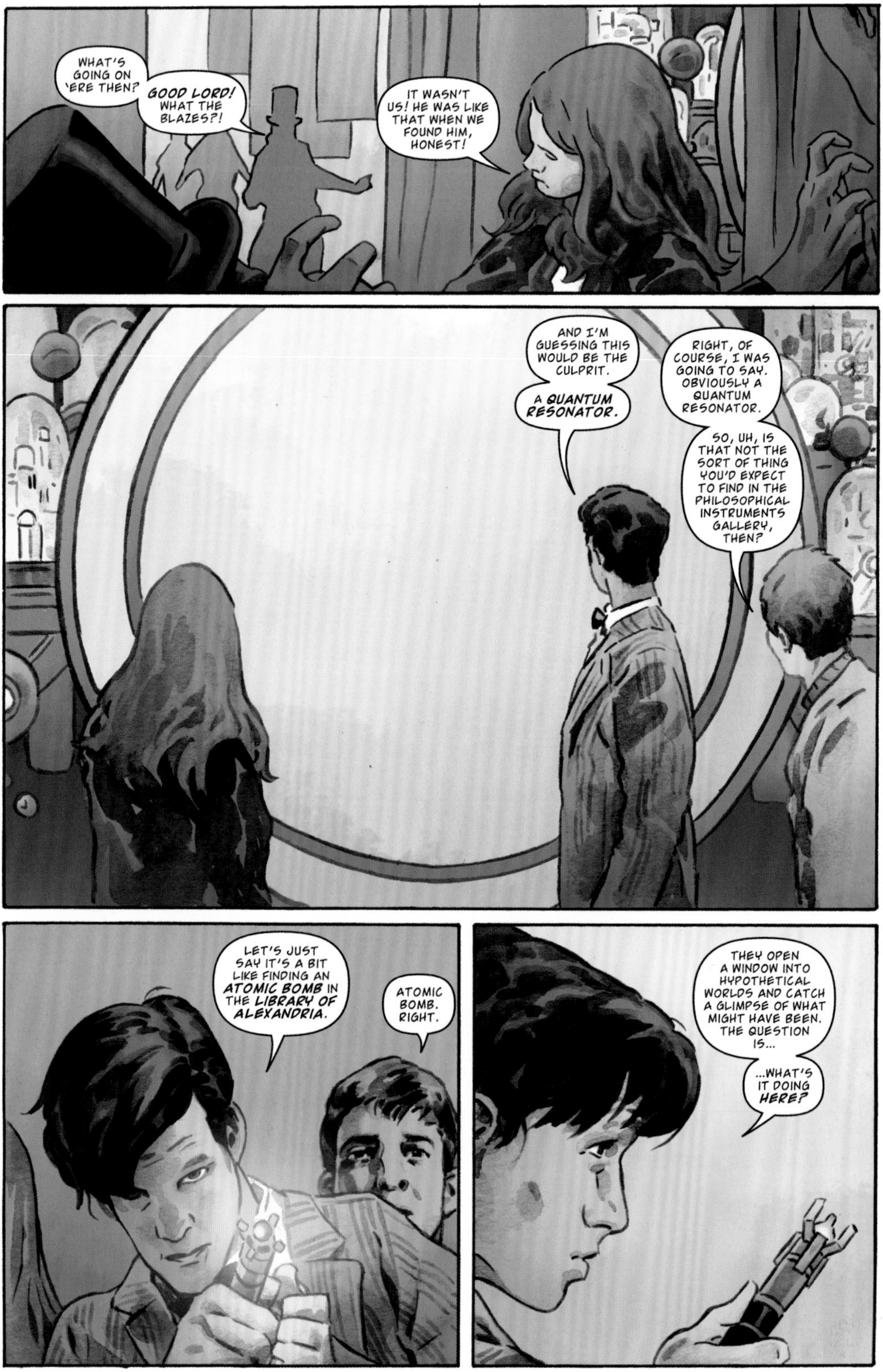
WHAT'S GOING ON 'ERE THEN?
GOOD LORD! WHAT THE BLAZES?!
IT WASN'T US! HE WAS LIKE THAT WHEN WE FOUND HIM, HONEST!
AND I'M GUESSING THIS WOULD BE THE CULPRIT.
A QUANTUM RESONATOR.
RIGHT, OF COURSE, I WAS GOING TO SAY. OBVIOUSLY A QUANTUM RESONATOR.
SO, UH, IS THAT NOT THE SORT OF THING YOU'D EXPECT TO FIND IN THE PHILOSOPHICAL INSTRUMENTS GALLERY, THEN?
LET'S JUST SAY IT'S A BIT LIKE FINDING AN ATOMIC BOMB IN THE LIBRARY OF ALEXANDRIA.
ATOMIC BOMB. RIGHT.
THEY OPEN A WINDOW INTO HYPOTHETICAL WORLDS AND CATCH A GLIMPSE OF WHAT MIGHT HAVE BEEN. THE QUESTION IS...
...WHAT'S IT DOING HERE?

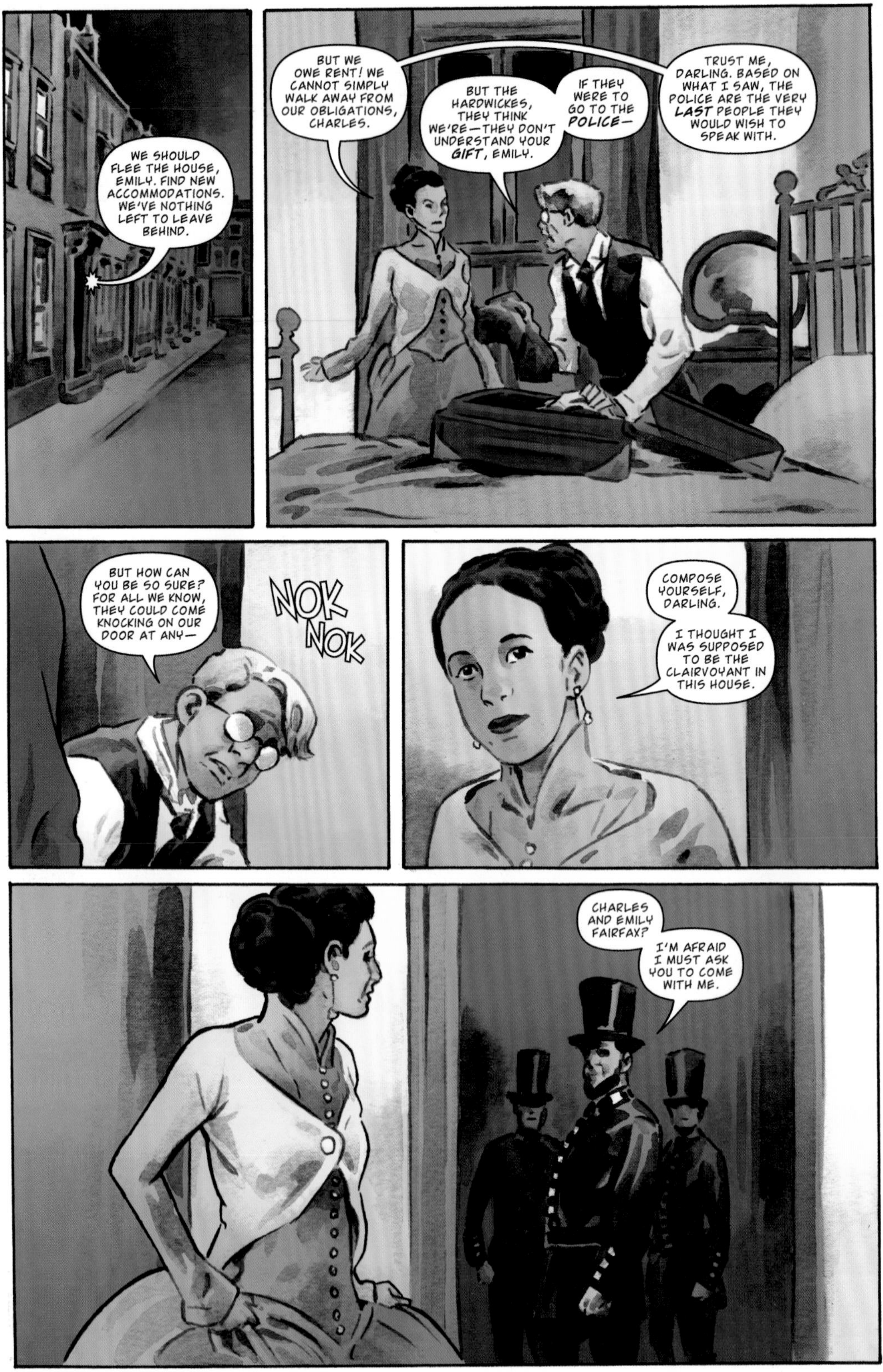
WE SHOULD FLEE THE HOUSE, EMILY. FIND NEW ACCOMMODATIONS. WE'VE NOTHING LEFT TO LEAVE BEHIND.
BUT WE OWE RENT! WE CANNOT SIMPLY WALK AWAY FROM OUR OBLIGATIONS, CHARLES.
BUT THE HARDWICKES, THEY THINK WE'RE—THEY DON'T UNDERSTAND YOUR GIFT, EMILY.
IF THEY WERE TO GO TO THE POLICE—
TRUST ME, DARLING. BASED ON WHAT I SAW, THE POLICE ARE THE VERY LAST PEOPLE THEY WOULD WISH TO SPEAK WITH.
BUT HOW CAN YOU BE SO SURE? FOR ALL WE KNOW, THEY COULD COME KNOCKING ON OUR DOOR AT ANY—
NOK NOK
COMPOSE YOURSELF, DARLING.
I THOUGHT I WAS SUPPOSED TO BE THE CLAIRVOYANT IN THIS HOUSE.
CHARLES AND EMILY FAIRFAX?
I'M AFRAID I MUST ASK YOU TO COME WITH ME.

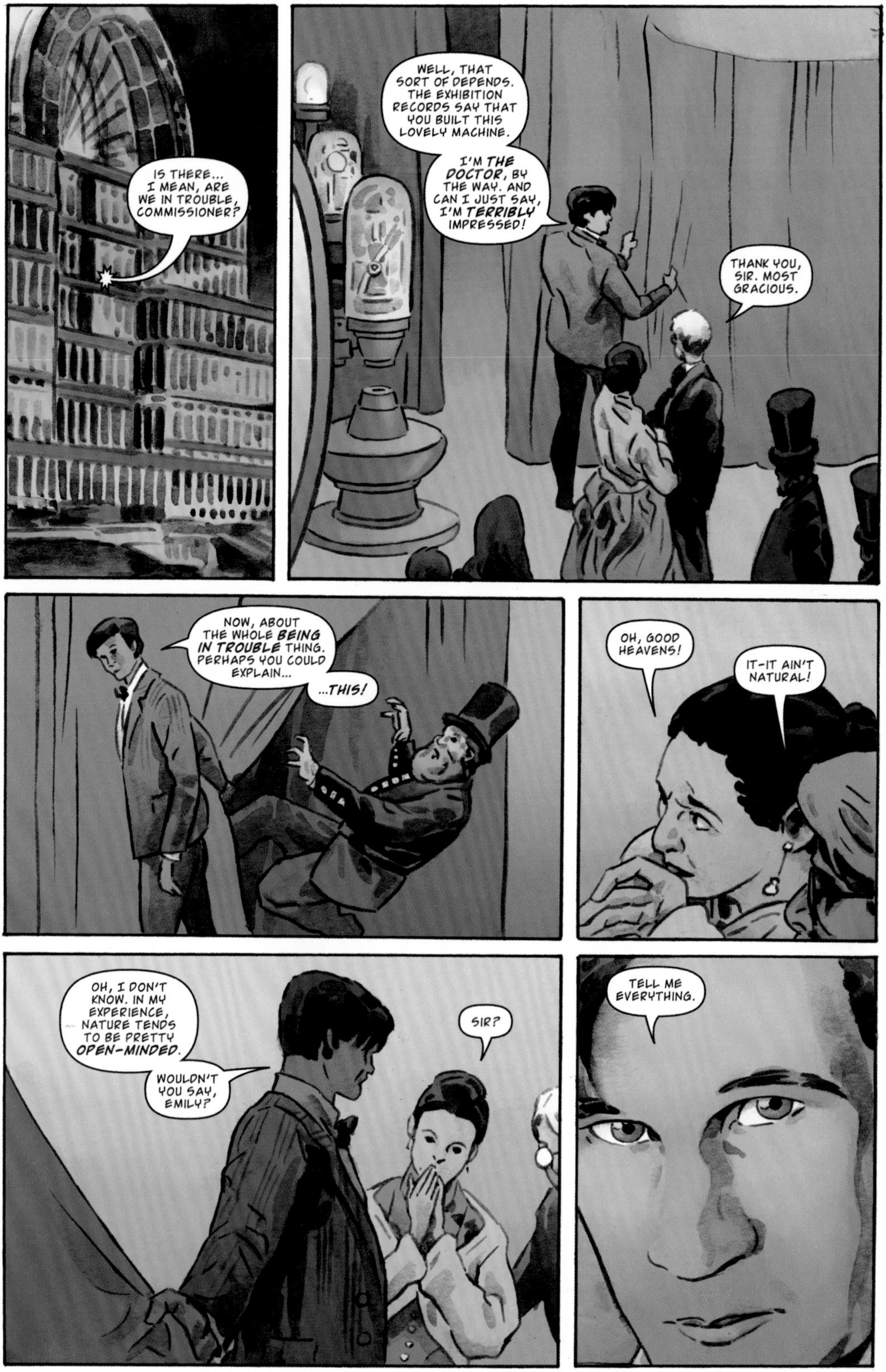
IS THERE... I MEAN, ARE WE IN TROUBLE, COMMISSIONER?
WELL, THAT SORT OF DEPENDS. THE EXHIBITION RECORDS SAY THAT YOU BUILT THIS LOVELY MACHINE.
I'M THE DOCTOR, BY THE WAY. AND CAN I JUST SAY, I'M TERRIBLY IMPRESSED!
THANK YOU, SIR. MOST GRACIOUS.
NOW, ABOUT THE WHOLE BEING IN TROUBLE THING. PERHAPS YOU COULD EXPLAIN...
...THIS!
OH, GOOD HEAVENS!
IT-IT AIN'T NATURAL!
OH, I DON'T KNOW. IN MY EXPERIENCE, NATURE TENDS TO BE PRETTY OPEN-MINDED.
WOULDN'T YOU SAY, EMILY?
SIR?
TELL ME EVERYTHING.

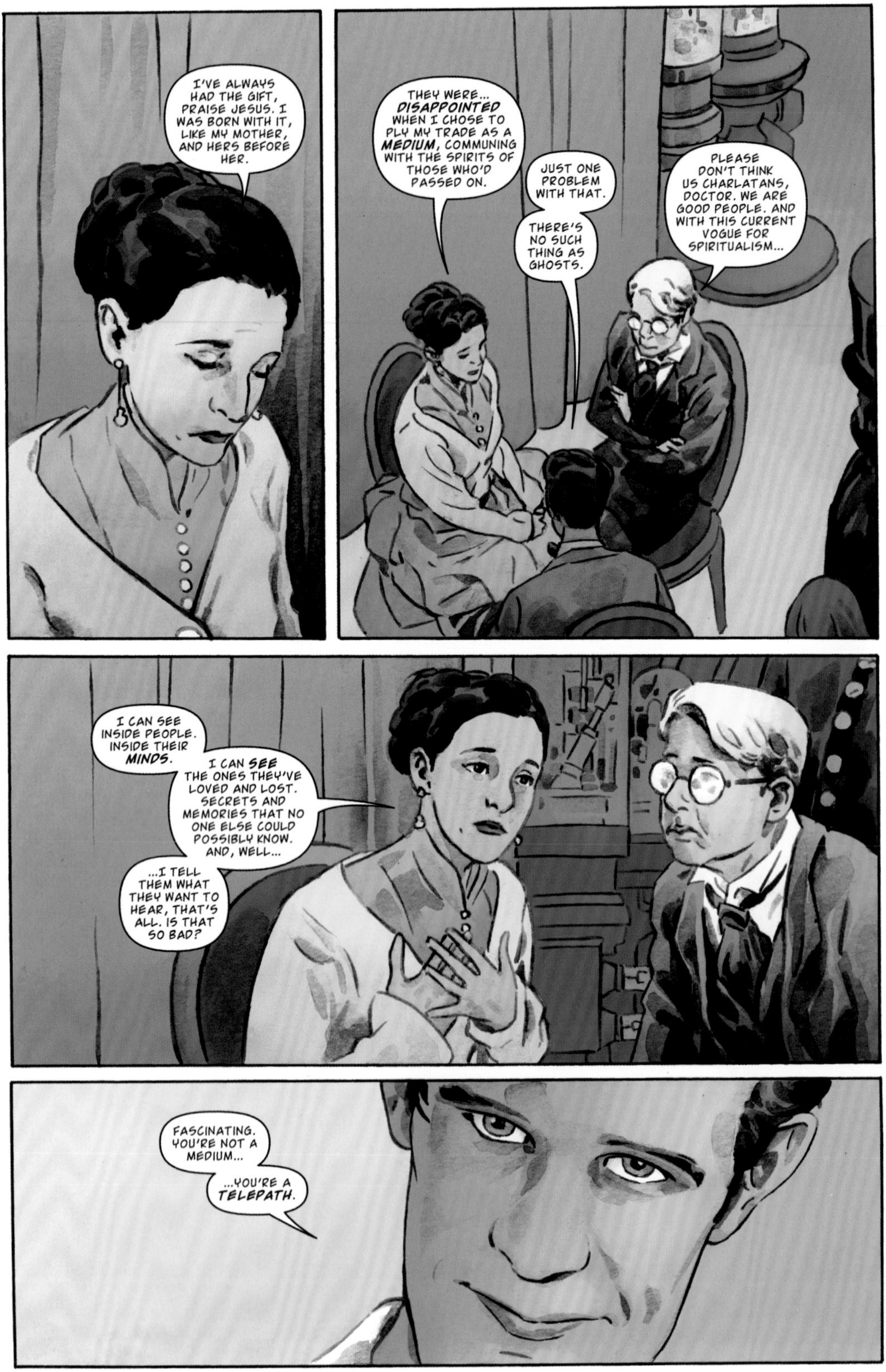
I'VE ALWAYS HAD THE GIFT, PRAISE JESUS. I WAS BORN WITH IT, LIKE MY MOTHER, AND HERS BEFORE HER.
THEY WERE... DISAPPOINTED WHEN I CHOSE TO PLY MY TRADE AS A MEDIUM, COMMUNING WITH THE SPIRITS OF THOSE WHO'D PASSED ON.
JUST ONE PROBLEM WITH THAT.
THERE'S NO SUCH THING AS GHOSTS.
PLEASE DON'T THINK US CHARLATANS, DOCTOR. WE ARE GOOD PEOPLE. AND WITH THIS CURRENT VOGUE FOR SPIRITUALISM...
I CAN SEE INSIDE PEOPLE. INSIDE THEIR MINDS.
I CAN SEE THE ONES THEY'VE LOVED AND LOST. SECRETS AND MEMORIES THAT NO ONE ELSE COULD POSSIBLY KNOW. AND, WELL...
...I TELL THEM WHAT THEY WANT TO HEAR, THAT'S ALL. IS THAT SO BAD?
FASCINATING. YOU'RE NOT A MEDIUM...
...YOU'RE A TELEPATH.

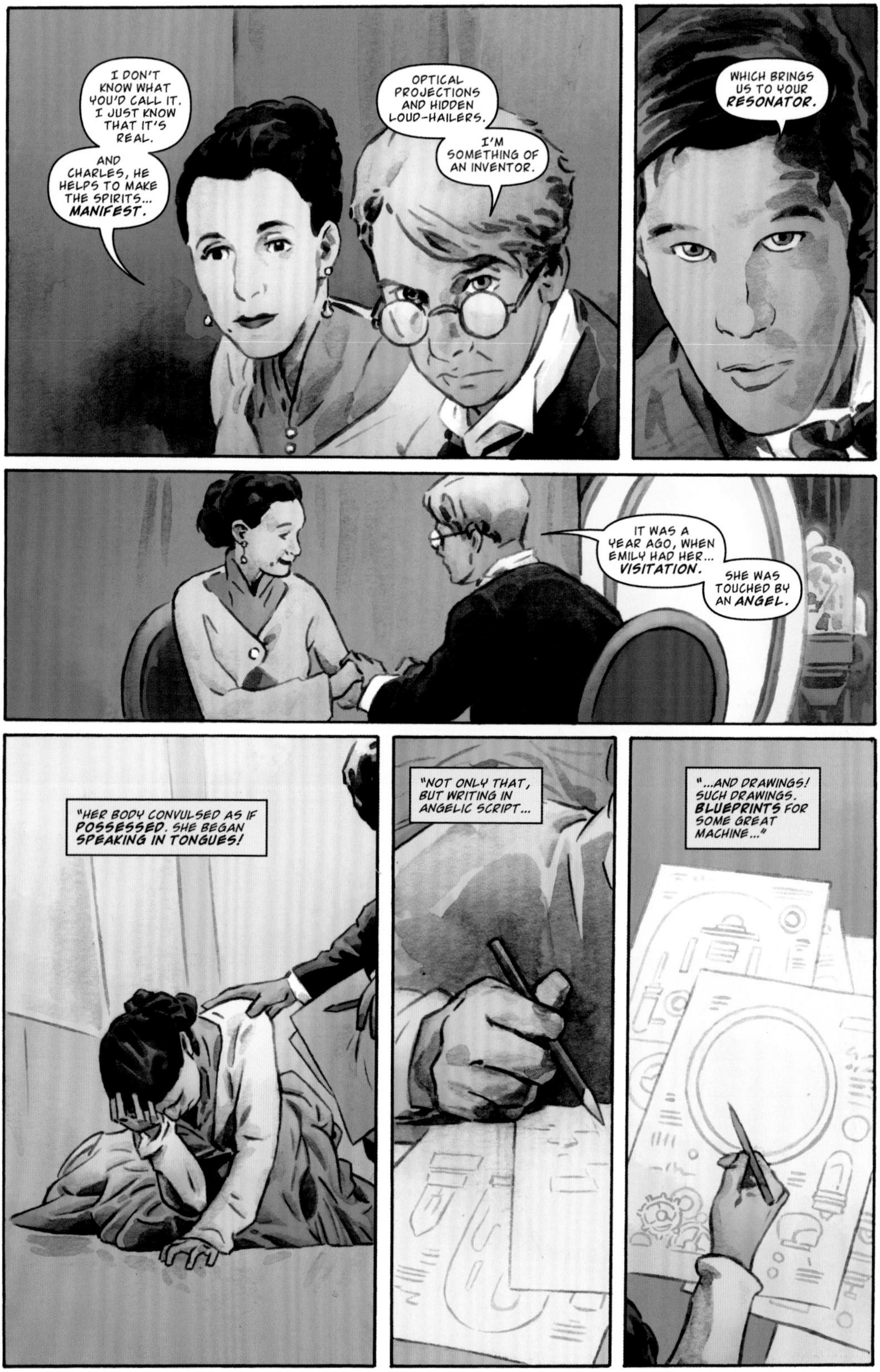
I DON'T KNOW WHAT YOU'D CALL IT. I JUST KNOW THAT IT'S REAL.
AND CHARLES, HE HELPS TO MAKE THE SPIRITS... MANIFEST.
OPTICAL PROJECTIONS AND HIDDEN LOUD-HAILERS.
I'M SOMETHING OF AN INVENTOR.
WHICH BRINGS US TO YOUR RESONATOR.
IT WAS A YEAR AGO, WHEN EMILY HAD HER... VISITATION.
SHE WAS TOUCHED BY AN ANGEL.
"HER BODY CONVULSED AS IF POSSESSED. SHE BEGAN SPEAKING IN TONGUES!
"NOT ONLY THAT, BUT WRITING IN ANGELIC SCRIPT...
"...AND DRAWINGS! SUCH DRAWINGS. BLUEPRINTS FOR SOME GREAT MACHINE..."

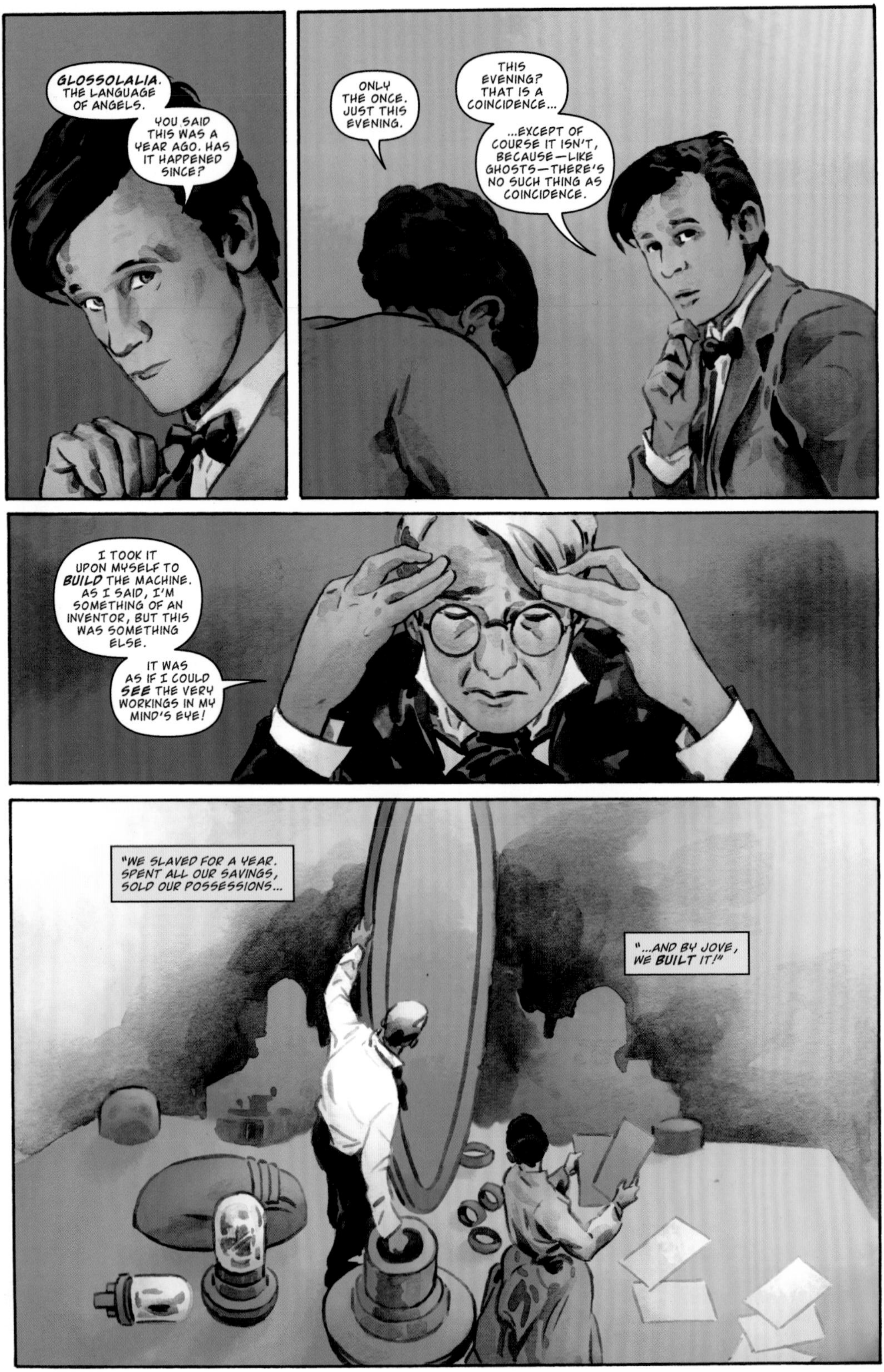

GLOSSOLALIA. THE LANGUAGE OF ANGELS.
YOU SAID THIS WAS A YEAR AGO. HAS IT HAPPENED SINCE?
ONLY THE ONCE. JUST THIS EVENING.
THIS EVENING? THAT IS A COINCIDENCE...
...EXCEPT OF COURSE IT ISN'T, BECAUSE—LIKE GHOSTS—THERE'S NO SUCH THING AS COINCIDENCE.
I TOOK IT UPON MYSELF TO BUILD THE MACHINE. AS I SAID, I'M SOMETHING OF AN INVENTOR, BUT THIS WAS SOMETHING ELSE.
IT WAS AS IF I COULD SEE THE VERY WORKINGS IN MY MIND'S EYE!
"WE SLAVED FOR A YEAR. SPENT ALL OUR SAVINGS, SOLD OUR POSSESSIONS...
"...AND BY JOVE, WE BUILT IT!"

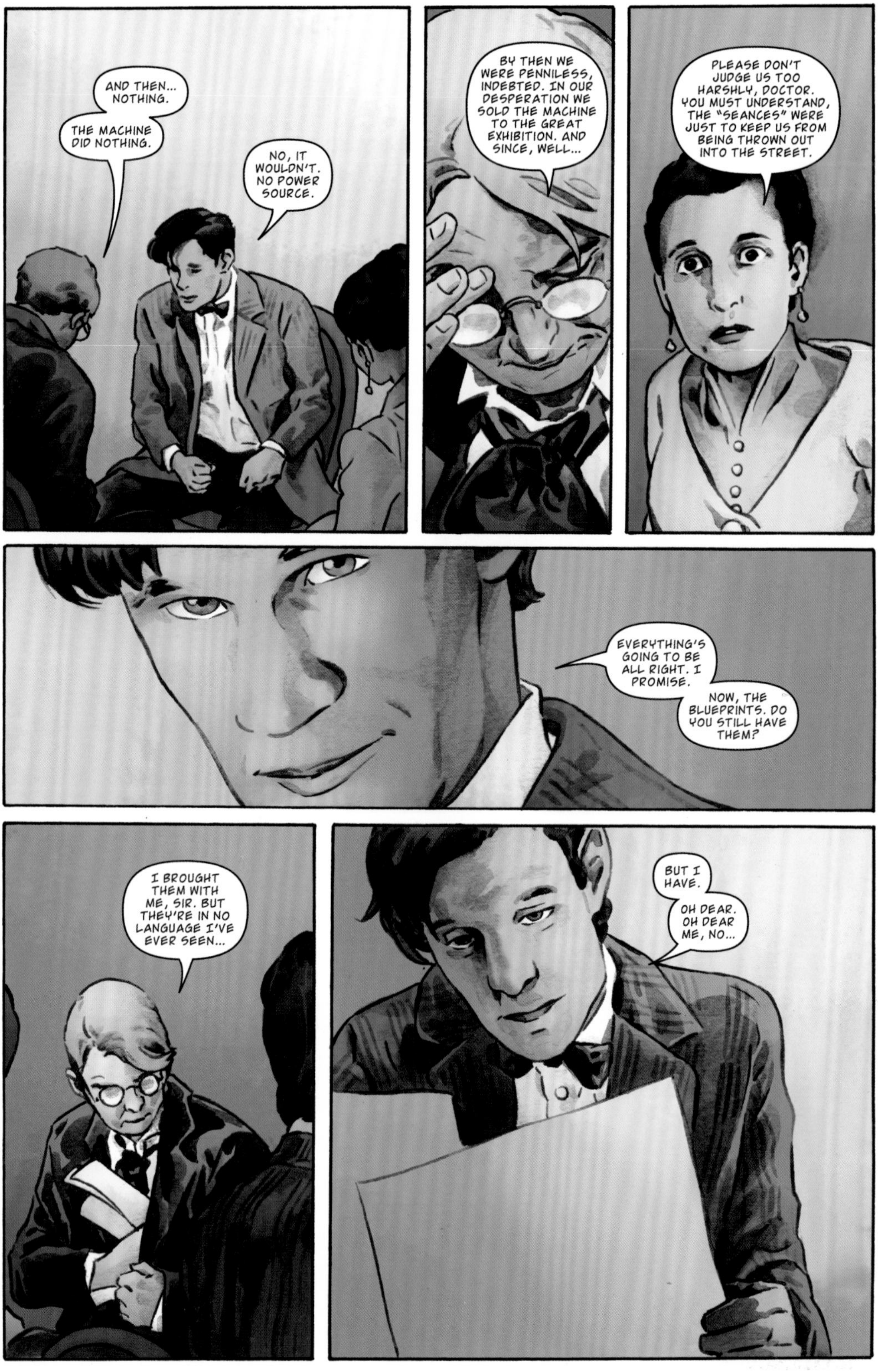
AND THEN... NOTHING.
THE MACHINE DID NOTHING.
NO, IT WOULDN'T. NO POWER SOURCE.
BY THEN WE WERE PENNILESS, INDEBTED. IN OUR DESPERATION WE SOLD THE MACHINE TO THE GREAT EXHIBITION. AND SINCE, WELL...
PLEASE DON'T JUDGE US TOO HARSHLY, DOCTOR. YOU MUST UNDERSTAND, THE "SEANCES" WERE JUST TO KEEP US FROM BEING THROWN OUT INTO THE STREET.
EVERYTHING'S GOING TO BE ALL RIGHT. I PROMISE.
NOW, THE BLUEPRINTS. DO YOU STILL HAVE THEM?
I BROUGHT THEM WITH ME, SIR. BUT THEY'RE IN NO LANGUAGE I'VE EVER SEEN...
BUT I HAVE.
OH DEAR. OH DEAR ME, NO...

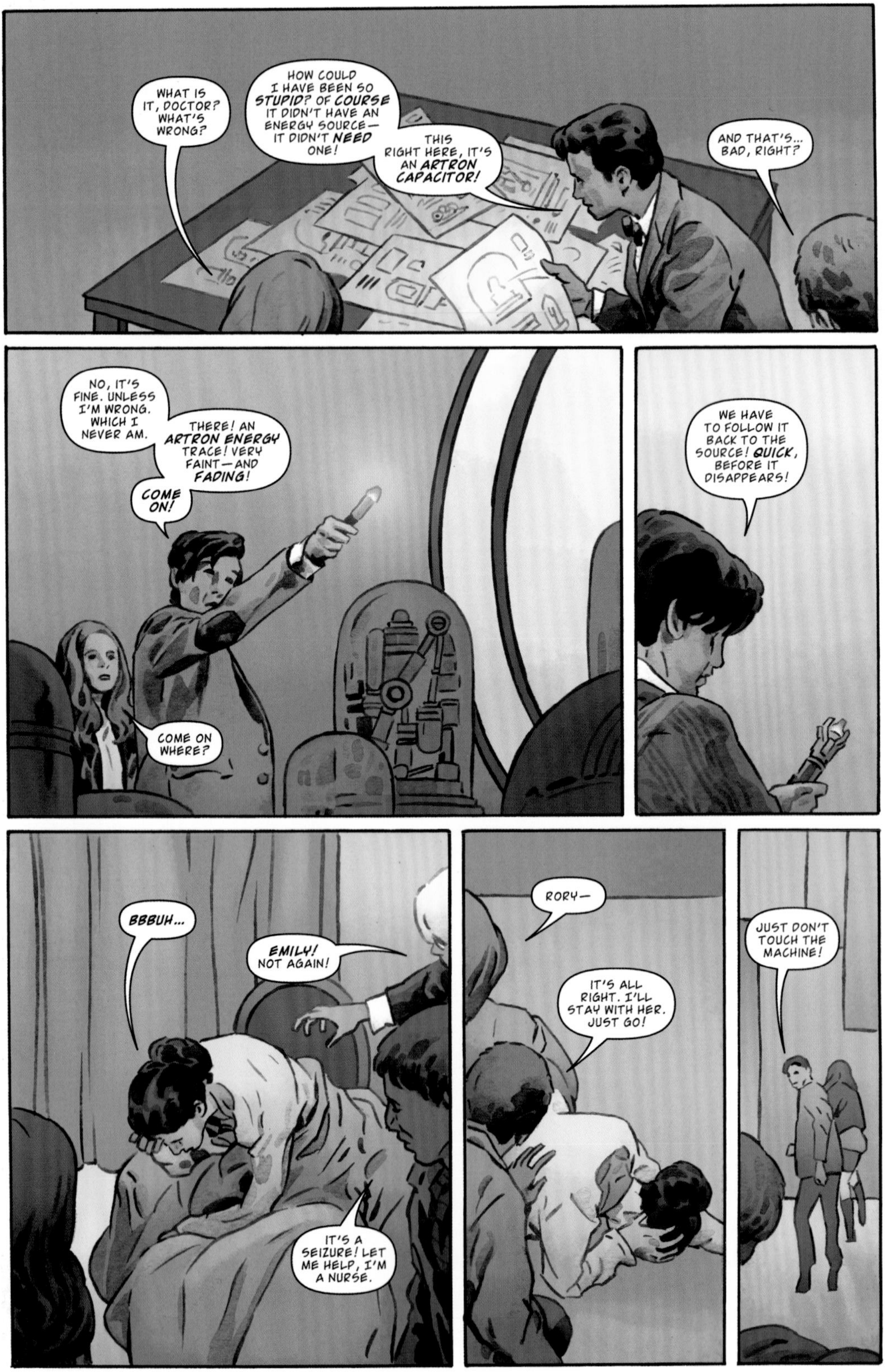
WHAT IS IT, DOCTOR? WHAT'S WRONG?
HOW COULD I HAVE BEEN SO STUPID? OF COURSE IT DIDN'T HAVE AN ENERGY SOURCE— IT DIDN'T NEED ONE!
THIS RIGHT HERE, IT'S AN ARTRON CAPACITOR!
AND THAT'S... BAD, RIGHT?
NO, IT'S FINE. UNLESS I'M WRONG. WHICH I NEVER AM.
THERE! AN ARTRON ENERGY TRACE! VERY FAINT—AND FADING!
COME ON!
COME ON WHERE?
WE HAVE TO FOLLOW IT BACK TO THE SOURCE! QUICK, BEFORE IT DISAPPEARS!
BBBUH...
EMILY! NOT AGAIN!
IT'S A SEIZURE! LET ME HELP, I'M A NURSE.
RORY—
IT'S ALL RIGHT. I'LL STAY WITH HER. JUST GO!
JUST DON'T TOUCH THE MACHINE!

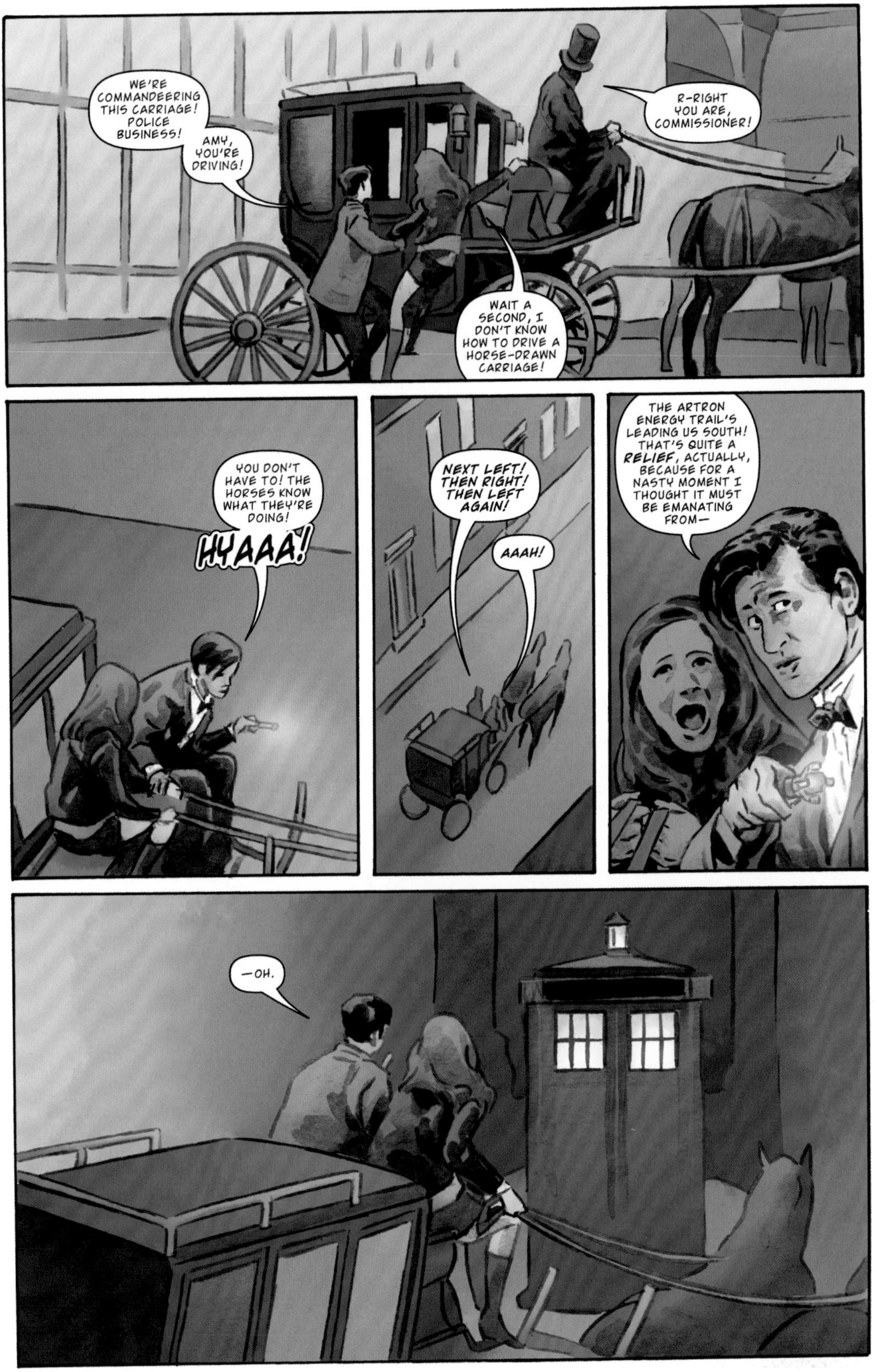
WE'RE COMMANDEERING THIS CARRIAGE! POLICE BUSINESS!
AMY, YOU'RE DRIVING!
R-RIGHT YOU ARE, COMMISSIONER!
WAIT A SECOND, I DON'T KNOW HOW TO DRIVE A HORSE-DRAWN CARRIAGE!
YOU DON'T HAVE TO! THE HORSES KNOW WHAT THEY'RE DOING!
HYAAA!
NEXT LEFT! THEN RIGHT! THEN LEFT AGAIN!
AAAH!
THE ARTRON ENERGY TRAIL'S LEADING US SOUTH! THAT'S QUITE A RELIEF, ACTUALLY, BECAUSE FOR A NASTY MOMENT I THOUGHT IT MUST BE EMANATING FROM—
—OH.

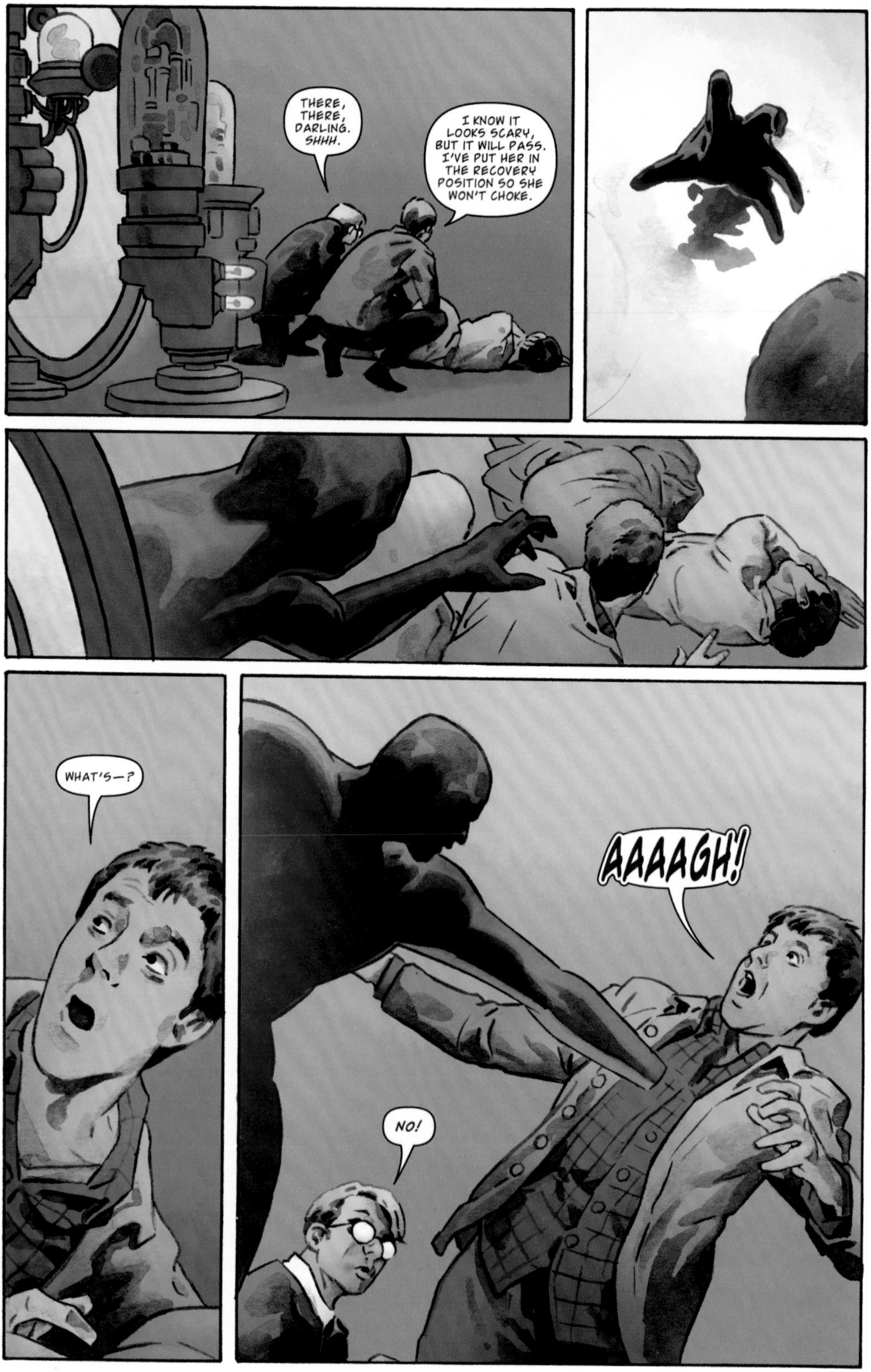
THERE, THERE, DARLING. SHHH.
I KNOW IT LOOKS SCARY, BUT IT WILL PASS. I'VE PUT HER IN THE RECOVERY POSITION SO SHE WON'T CHOKE.
WHAT'S—?
AAAAGH!
NO!

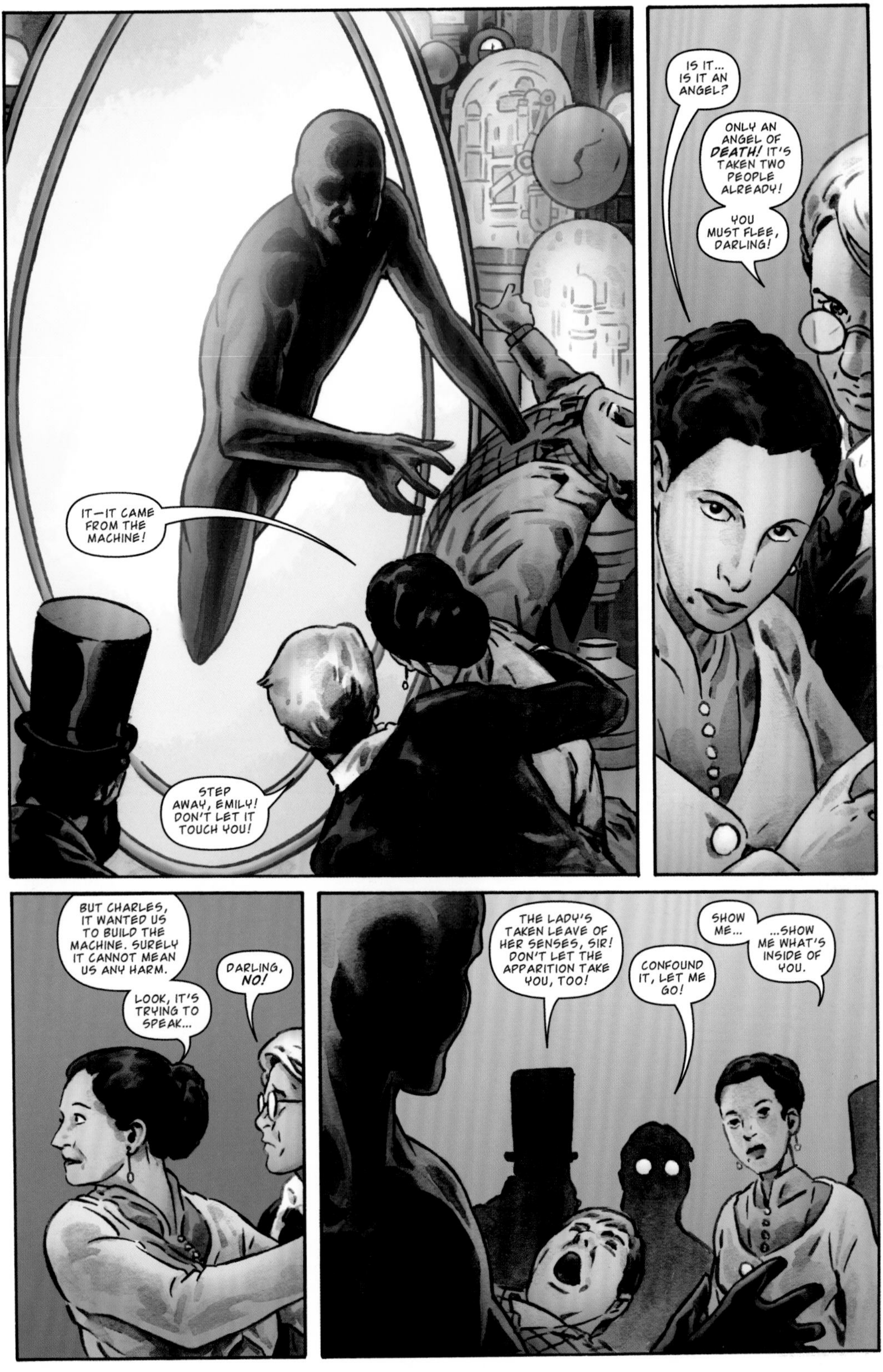
IT—IT CAME FROM THE MACHINE!
STEP AWAY, EMILY! DON'T LET IT TOUCH YOU!
IS IT... IS IT AN ANGEL?
ONLY AN ANGEL OF ***DEATH!*** IT'S TAKEN TWO PEOPLE ALREADY!
YOU MUST FLEE, DARLING!
BUT CHARLES, IT WANTED US TO BUILD THE MACHINE. SURELY IT CANNOT MEAN US ANY HARM.
LOOK, IT'S TRYING TO SPEAK...
DARLING, ***NO!***
THE LADY'S TAKEN LEAVE OF HER SENSES, SIR! DON'T LET THE APPARITION TAKE YOU, TOO!
CONFOUND IT, LET ME GO!
SHOW ME...
...SHOW ME WHAT'S INSIDE OF YOU.

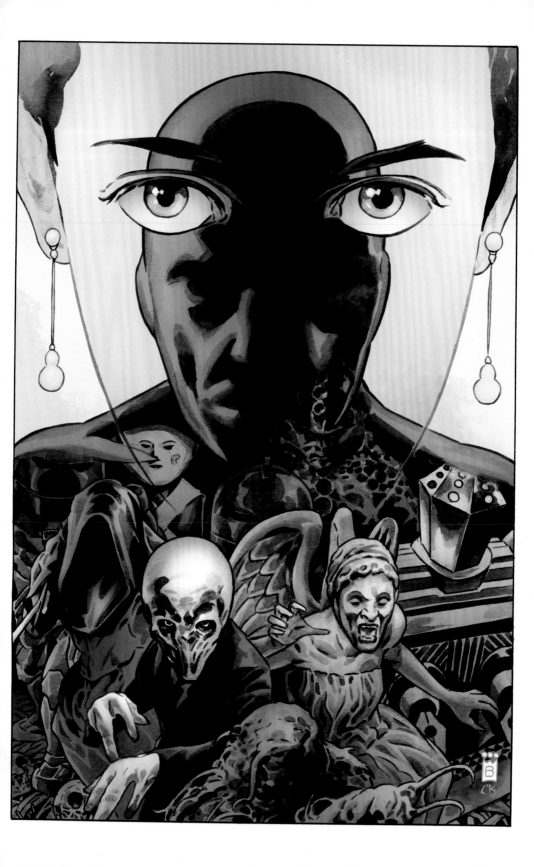

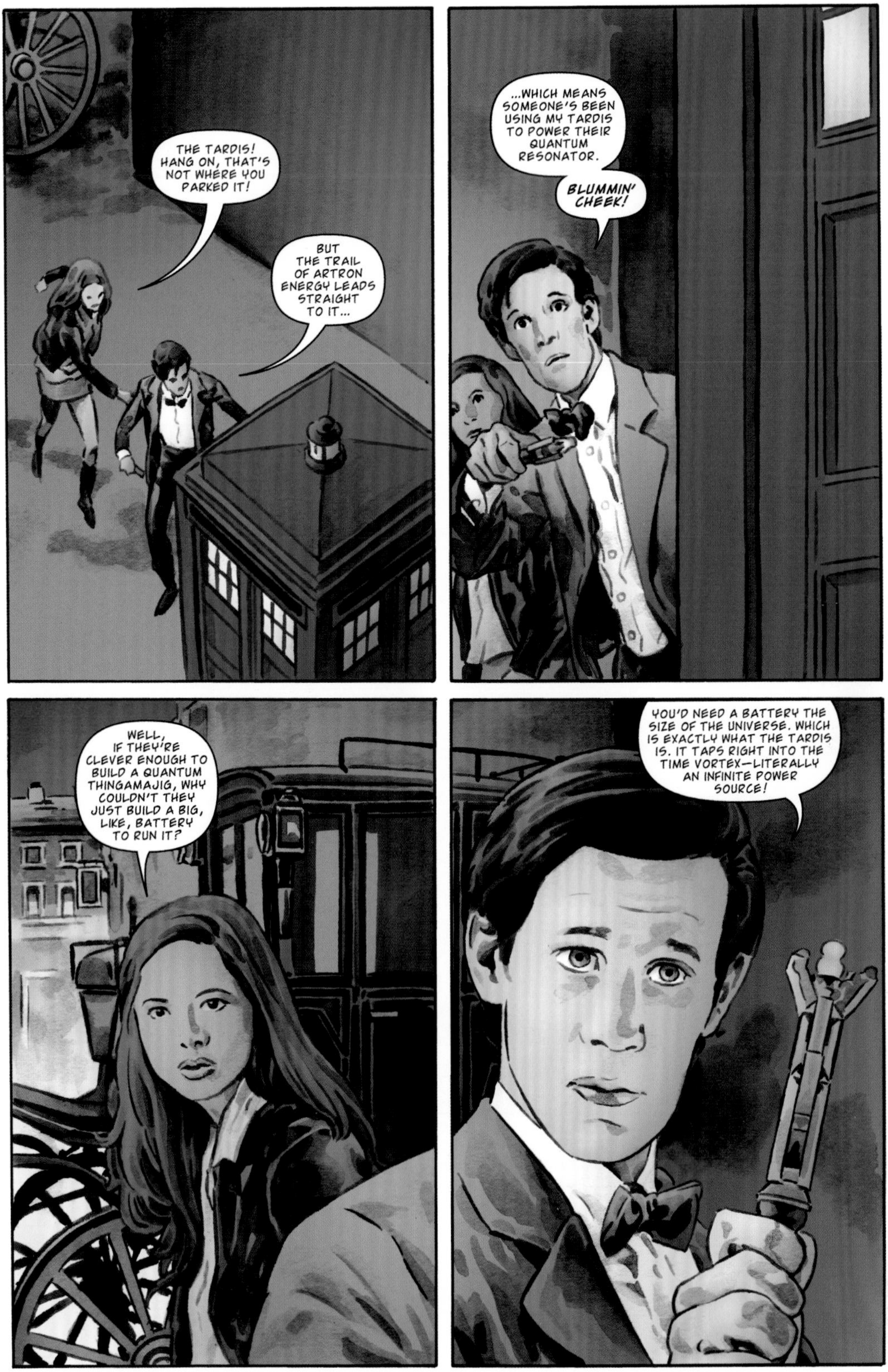
THE TARDIS! HANG ON, THAT'S NOT WHERE YOU PARKED IT!
BUT THE TRAIL OF ARTRON ENERGY LEADS STRAIGHT TO IT...
...WHICH MEANS SOMEONE'S BEEN USING MY TARDIS TO POWER THEIR QUANTUM RESONATOR.
BLUMMIN' CHEEK!
WELL, IF THEY'RE CLEVER ENOUGH TO BUILD A QUANTUM THINGAMAJIG, WHY COULDN'T THEY JUST BUILD A BIG, LIKE, BATTERY TO RUN IT?
YOU'D NEED A BATTERY THE SIZE OF THE UNIVERSE. WHICH IS EXACTLY WHAT THE TARDIS IS. IT TAPS RIGHT INTO THE TIME VORTEX—LITERALLY AN INFINITE POWER SOURCE!

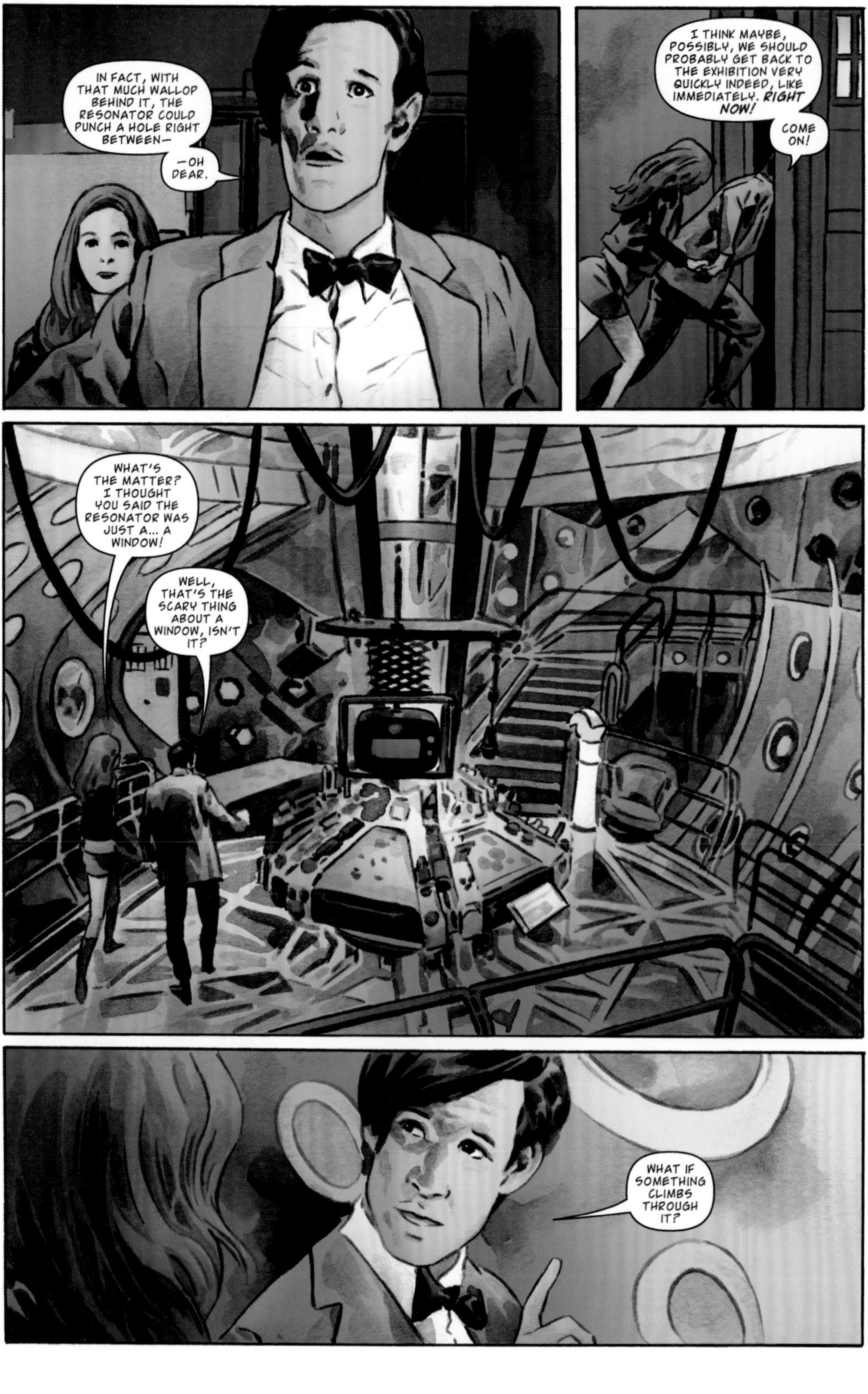
IN FACT, WITH THAT MUCH WALLOP BEHIND IT, THE RESONATOR COULD PUNCH A HOLE RIGHT BETWEEN—
—OH DEAR.
I THINK MAYBE, POSSIBLY, WE SHOULD PROBABLY GET BACK TO THE EXHIBITION VERY QUICKLY INDEED, LIKE IMMEDIATELY. ***RIGHT NOW!***
COME ON!
WHAT'S THE MATTER? I THOUGHT YOU SAID THE RESONATOR WAS JUST A... A WINDOW!
WELL, THAT'S THE SCARY THING ABOUT A WINDOW, ISN'T IT?
WHAT IF SOMETHING CLIMBS THROUGH IT?

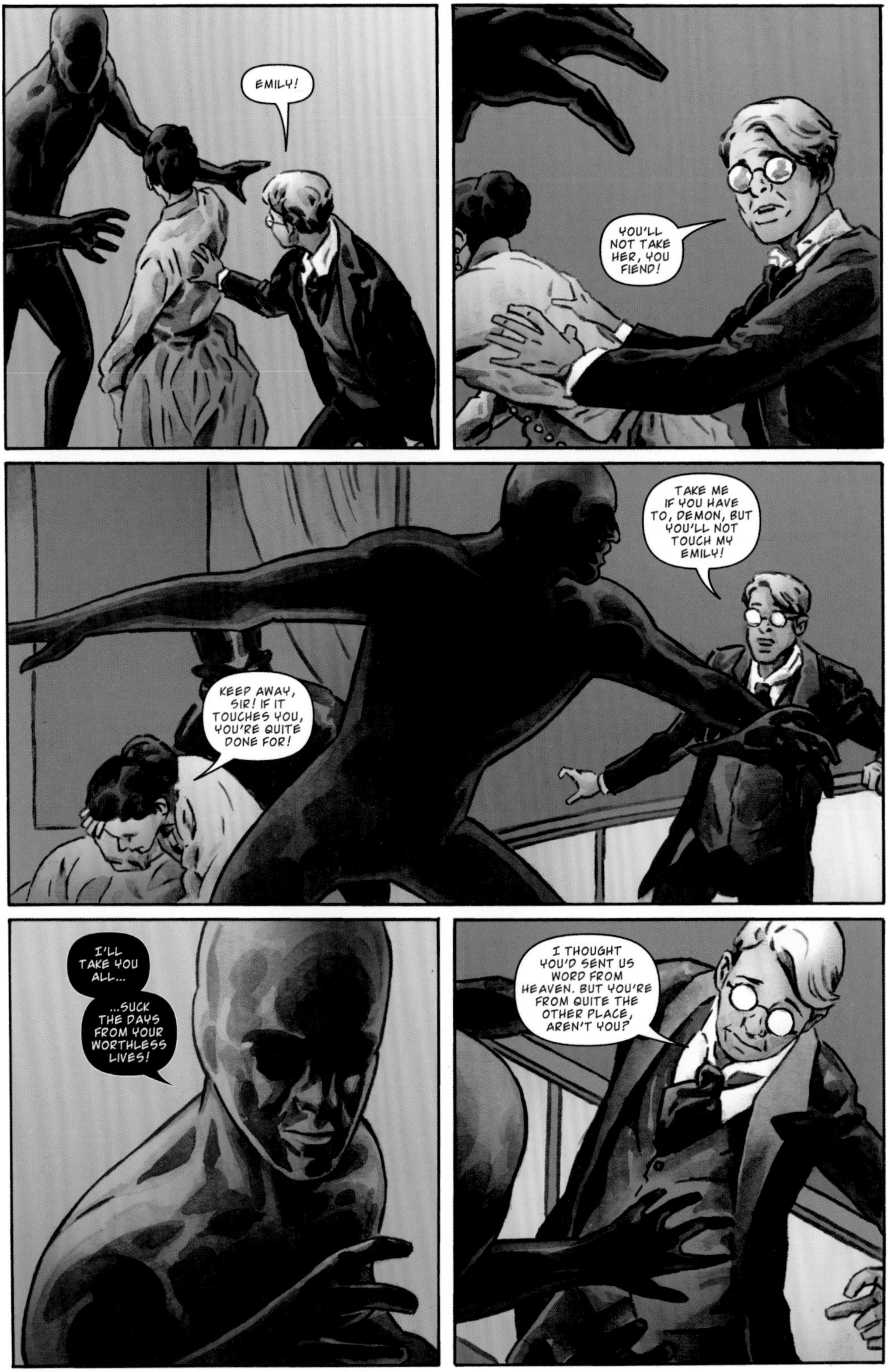
EMILY!
YOU'LL NOT TAKE HER, YOU FIEND!
TAKE ME IF YOU HAVE TO, DEMON, BUT YOU'LL NOT TOUCH MY EMILY!
KEEP AWAY, SIR! IF IT TOUCHES YOU, YOU'RE QUITE DONE FOR!
I'LL TAKE YOU ALL...
...SUCK THE DAYS FROM YOUR WORTHLESS LIVES!
I THOUGHT YOU'D SENT US WORD FROM HEAVEN. BUT YOU'RE FROM QUITE THE OTHER PLACE, AREN'T YOU?

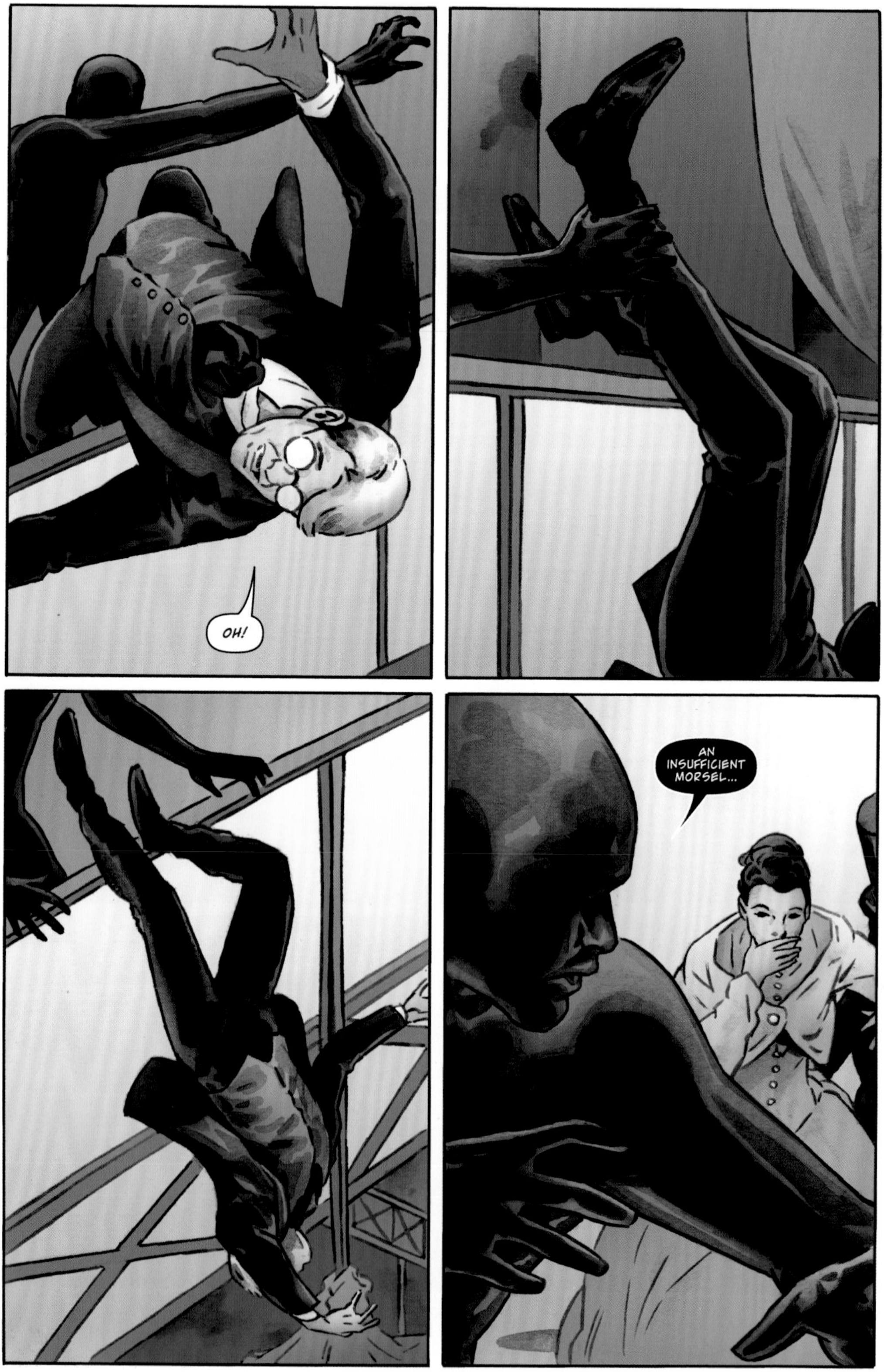
OH!
AN INSUFFICIENT MORSEL...

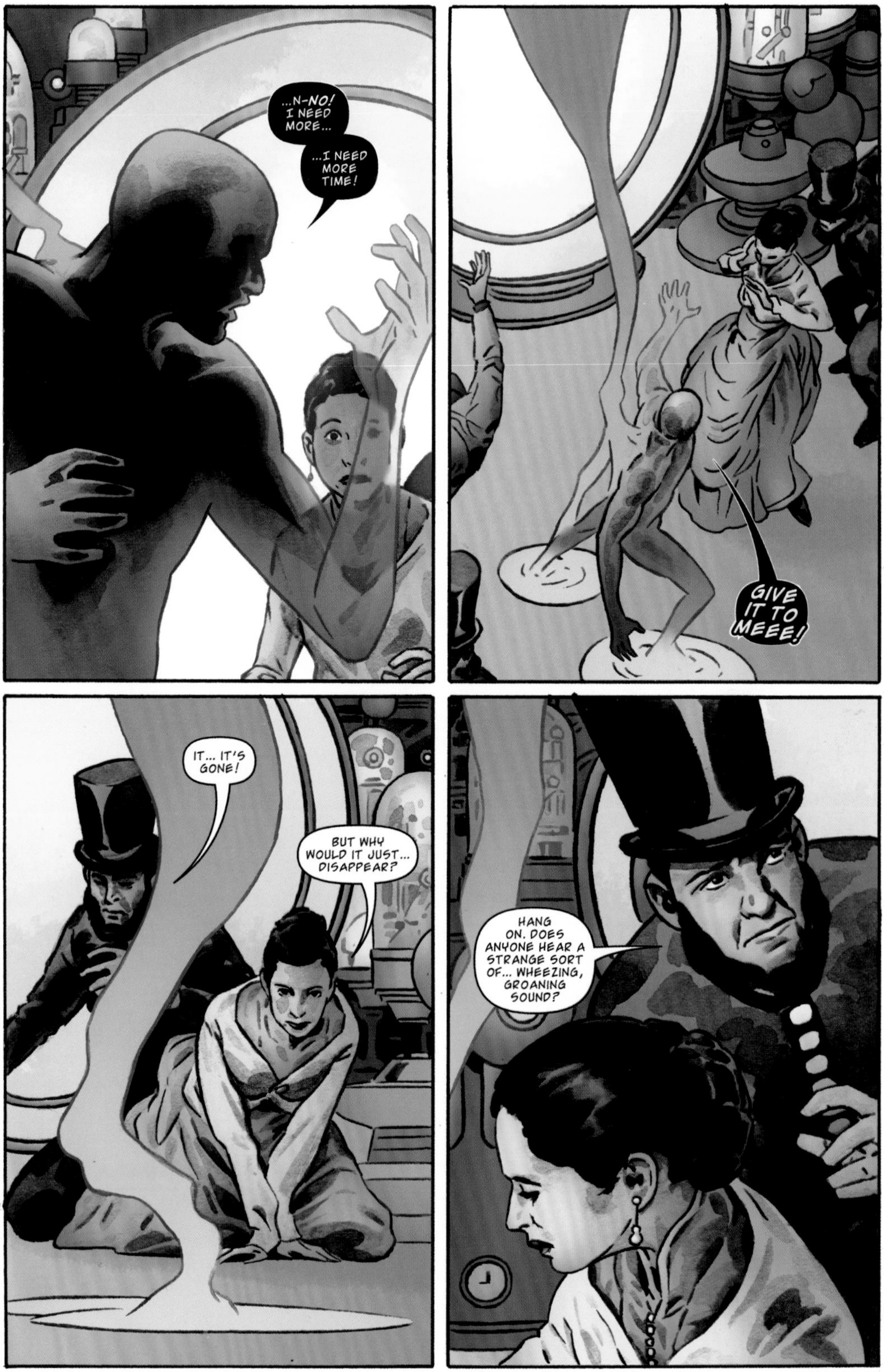
...N-NO! I NEED MORE...
...I NEED MORE TIME!
GIVE IT TO MEEE!
IT... IT'S GONE!
BUT WHY WOULD IT JUST... DISAPPEAR?
HANG ON. DOES ANYONE HEAR A STRANGE SORT OF... WHEEZING, GROANING SOUND?

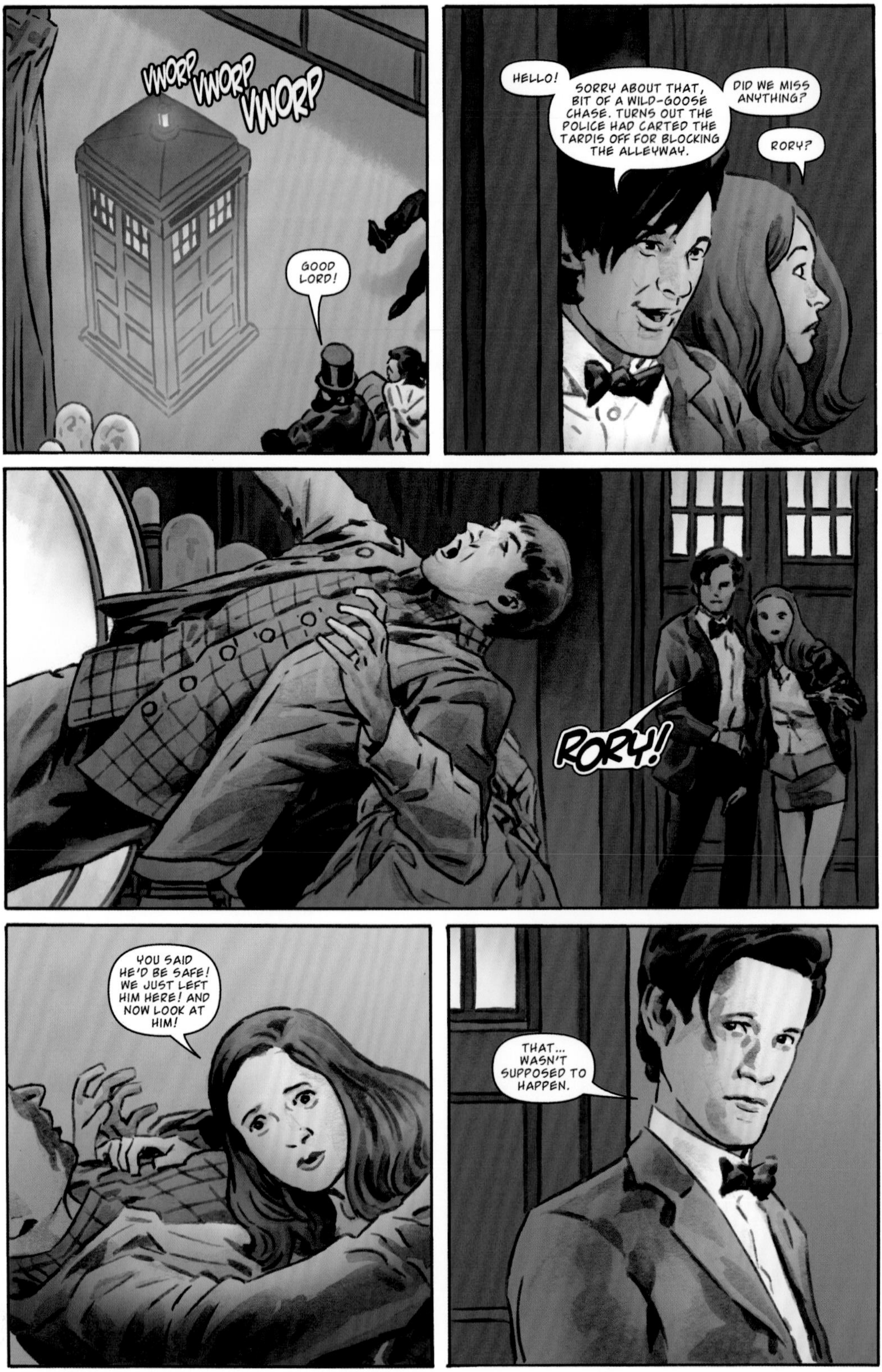
VWORP VWORP VWORP
GOOD LORD!
HELLO!
SORRY ABOUT THAT, BIT OF A WILD-GOOSE CHASE. TURNS OUT THE POLICE HAD CARTED THE TARDIS OFF FOR BLOCKING THE ALLEYWAY.
DID WE MISS ANYTHING?
RORY?
RORY!
YOU SAID HE'D BE SAFE! WE JUST LEFT HIM HERE! AND NOW LOOK AT HIM!
THAT... WASN'T SUPPOSED TO HAPPEN.

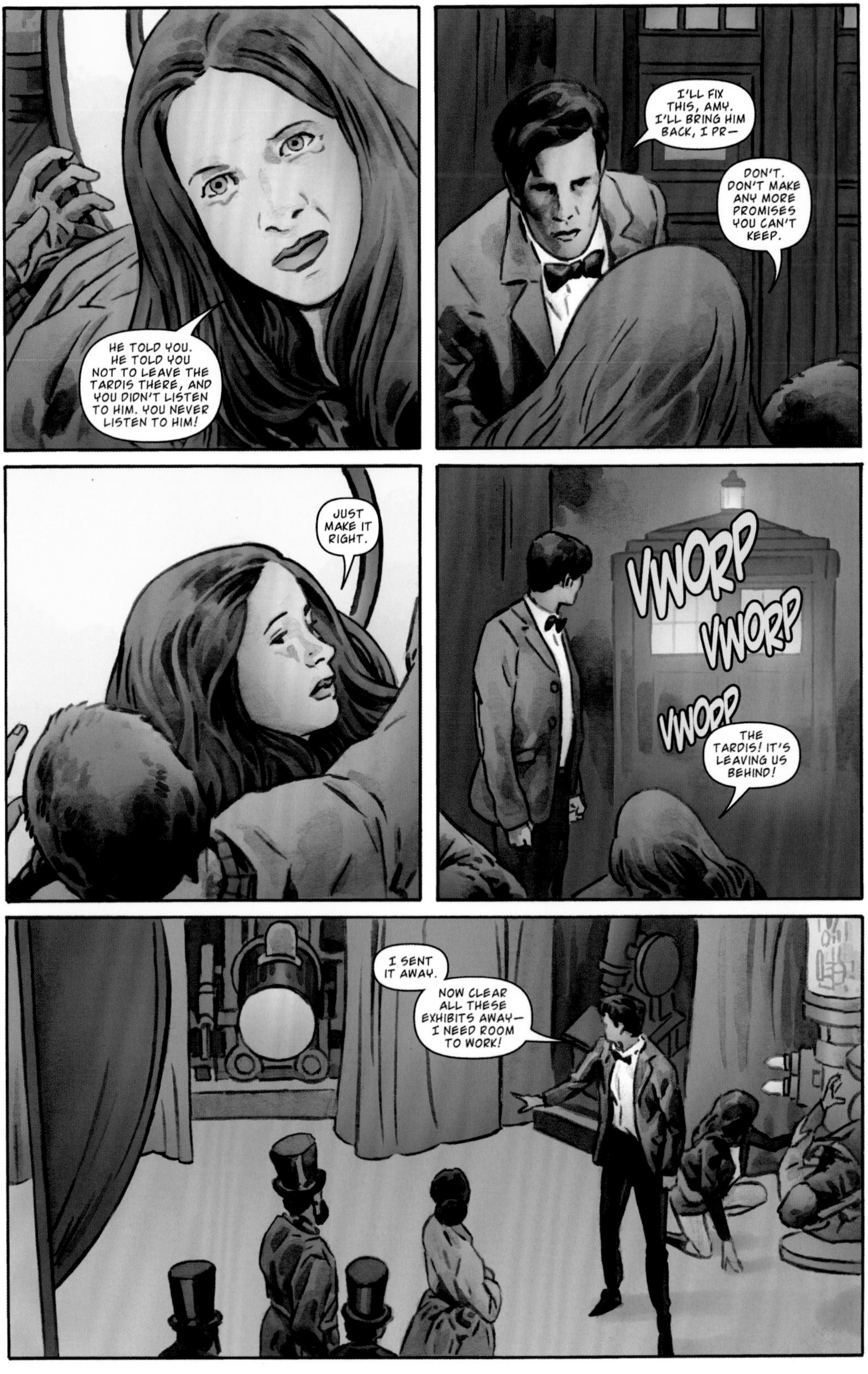
HE TOLD YOU. HE TOLD YOU NOT TO LEAVE THE TARDIS THERE, AND YOU DIDN'T LISTEN TO HIM. YOU NEVER LISTEN TO HIM!
I'LL FIX THIS, AMY. I'LL BRING HIM BACK, I PR—
DON'T. DON'T MAKE ANY MORE PROMISES YOU CAN'T KEEP.
JUST MAKE IT RIGHT.
VWORP
VWORP
VWORP
THE TARDIS! IT'S LEAVING US BEHIND!
I SENT IT AWAY.
NOW CLEAR ALL THESE EXHIBITS AWAY— I NEED ROOM TO WORK!

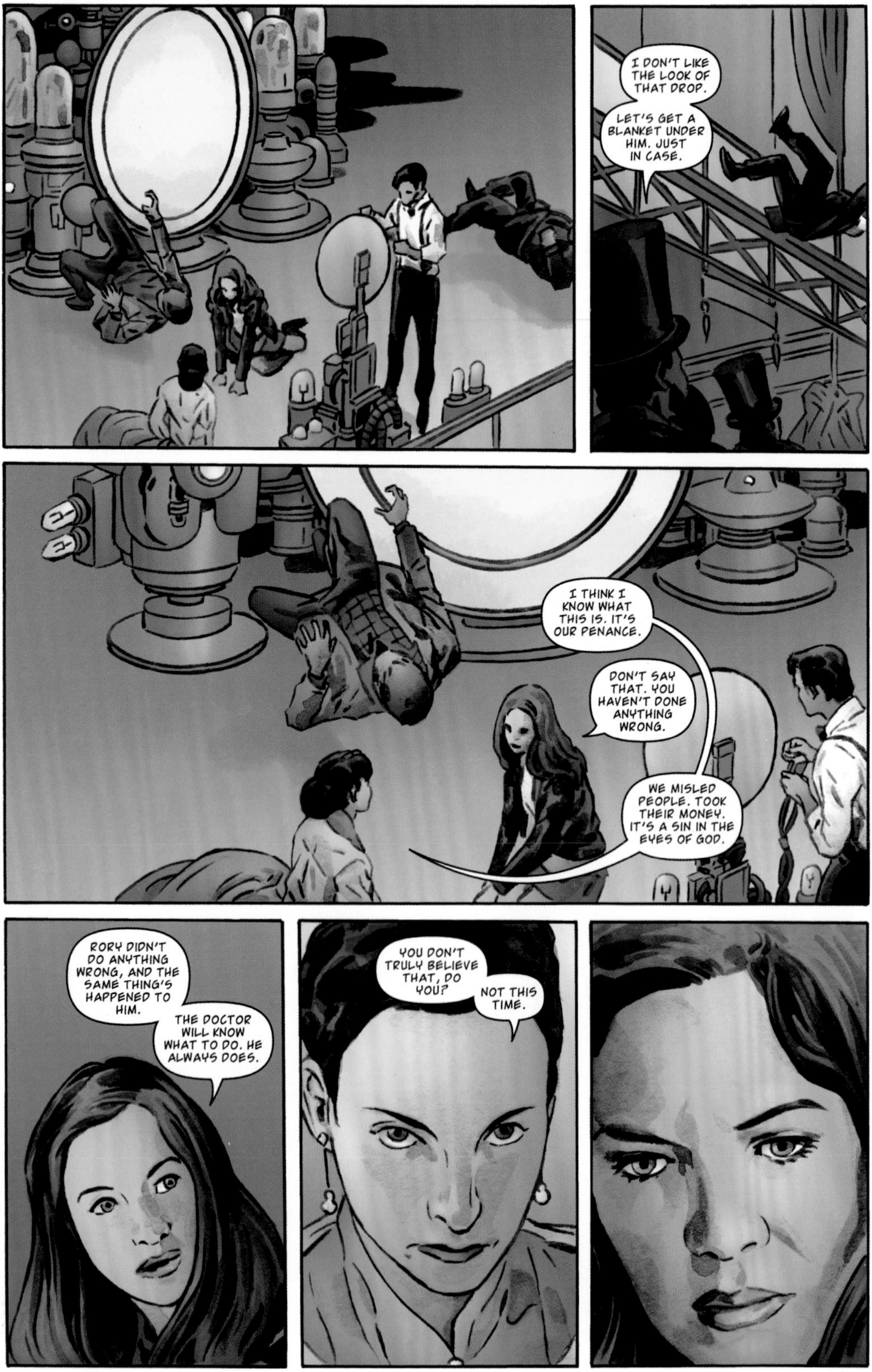
I DON'T LIKE THE LOOK OF THAT DROP.
LET'S GET A BLANKET UNDER HIM. JUST IN CASE.
I THINK I KNOW WHAT THIS IS. IT'S OUR PENANCE.
DON'T SAY THAT. YOU HAVEN'T DONE ANYTHING WRONG.
WE MISLED PEOPLE. TOOK THEIR MONEY. IT'S A SIN IN THE EYES OF GOD.
RORY DIDN'T DO ANYTHING WRONG, AND THE SAME THING'S HAPPENED TO HIM.
THE DOCTOR WILL KNOW WHAT TO DO. HE ALWAYS DOES.
YOU DON'T TRULY BELIEVE THAT, DO YOU?
NOT THIS TIME.

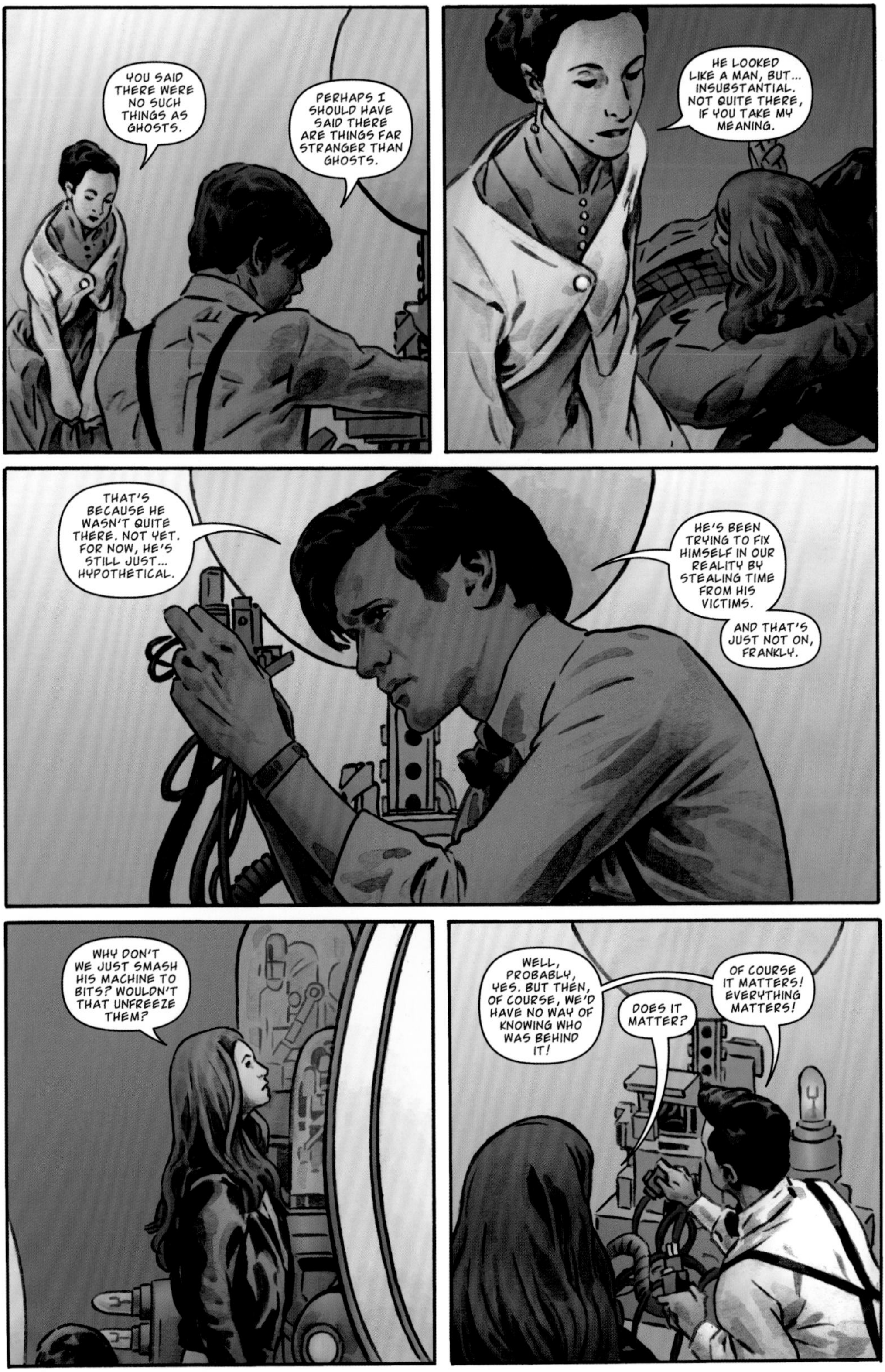
YOU SAID THERE WERE NO SUCH THINGS AS GHOSTS.
PERHAPS I SHOULD HAVE SAID THERE ARE THINGS FAR STRANGER THAN GHOSTS.
HE LOOKED LIKE A MAN, BUT... INSUBSTANTIAL. NOT QUITE THERE, IF YOU TAKE MY MEANING.
THAT'S BECAUSE HE WASN'T QUITE THERE. NOT YET. FOR NOW, HE'S STILL JUST... HYPOTHETICAL.
HE'S BEEN TRYING TO FIX HIMSELF IN OUR REALITY BY STEALING TIME FROM HIS VICTIMS.
AND THAT'S JUST NOT ON, FRANKLY.
WHY DON'T WE JUST SMASH HIS MACHINE TO BITS? WOULDN'T THAT UNFREEZE THEM?
WELL, PROBABLY, YES. BUT THEN, OF COURSE, WE'D HAVE NO WAY OF KNOWING WHO WAS BEHIND IT!
DOES IT MATTER?
OF COURSE IT MATTERS! EVERYTHING MATTERS!

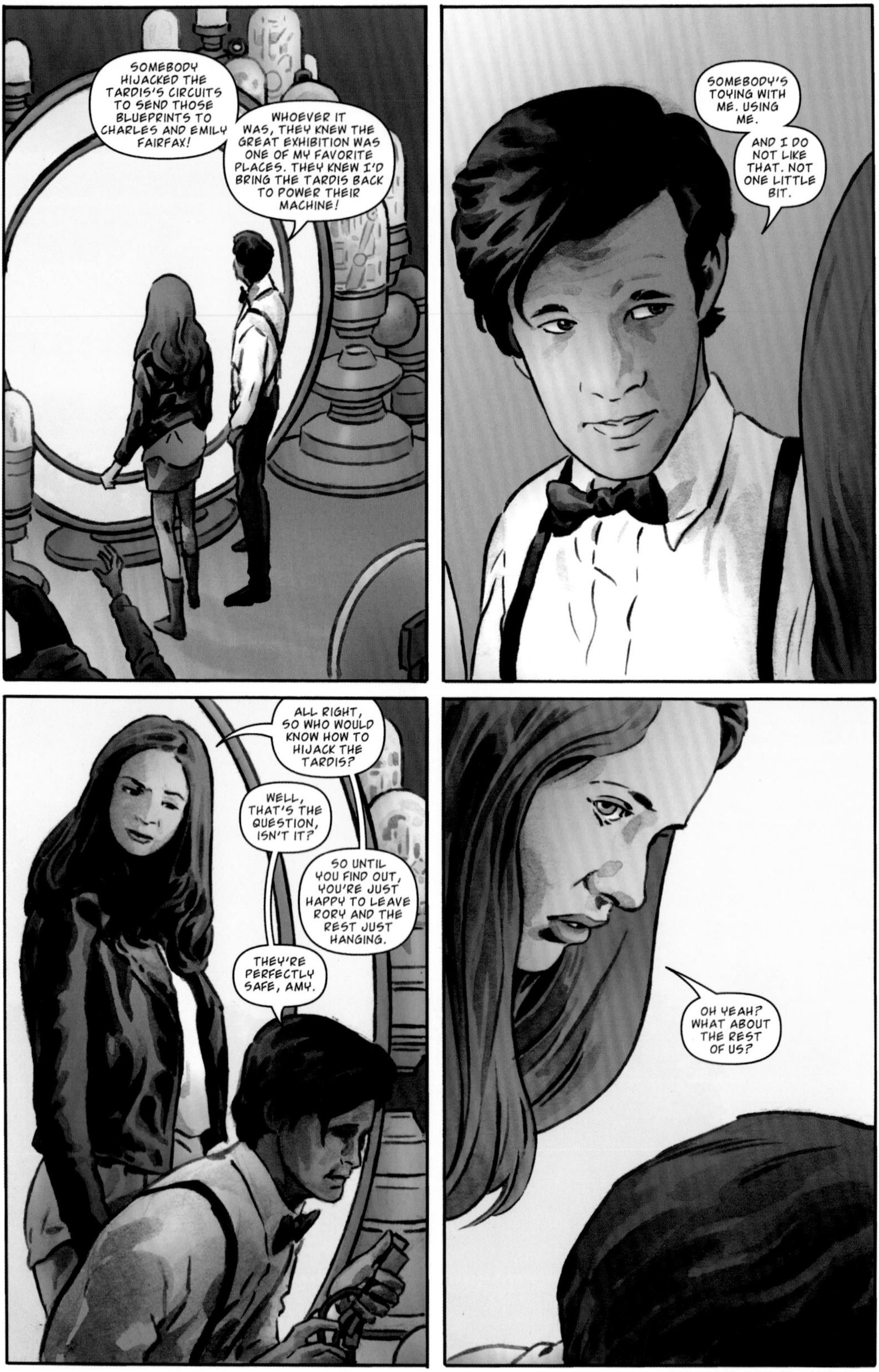
SOMEBODY HIJACKED THE TARDIS'S CIRCUITS TO SEND THOSE BLUEPRINTS TO CHARLES AND EMILY FAIRFAX!
WHOEVER IT WAS, THEY KNEW THE GREAT EXHIBITION WAS ONE OF MY FAVORITE PLACES. THEY KNEW I'D BRING THE TARDIS BACK TO POWER THEIR MACHINE!
SOMEBODY'S TOYING WITH ME. USING ME.
AND I DO NOT LIKE THAT. NOT ONE LITTLE BIT.
ALL RIGHT, SO WHO WOULD KNOW HOW TO HIJACK THE TARDIS?
WELL, THAT'S THE QUESTION, ISN'T IT?
SO UNTIL YOU FIND OUT, YOU'RE JUST HAPPY TO LEAVE RORY AND THE REST JUST HANGING.
THEY'RE PERFECTLY SAFE, AMY.
OH YEAH? WHAT ABOUT THE REST OF US?

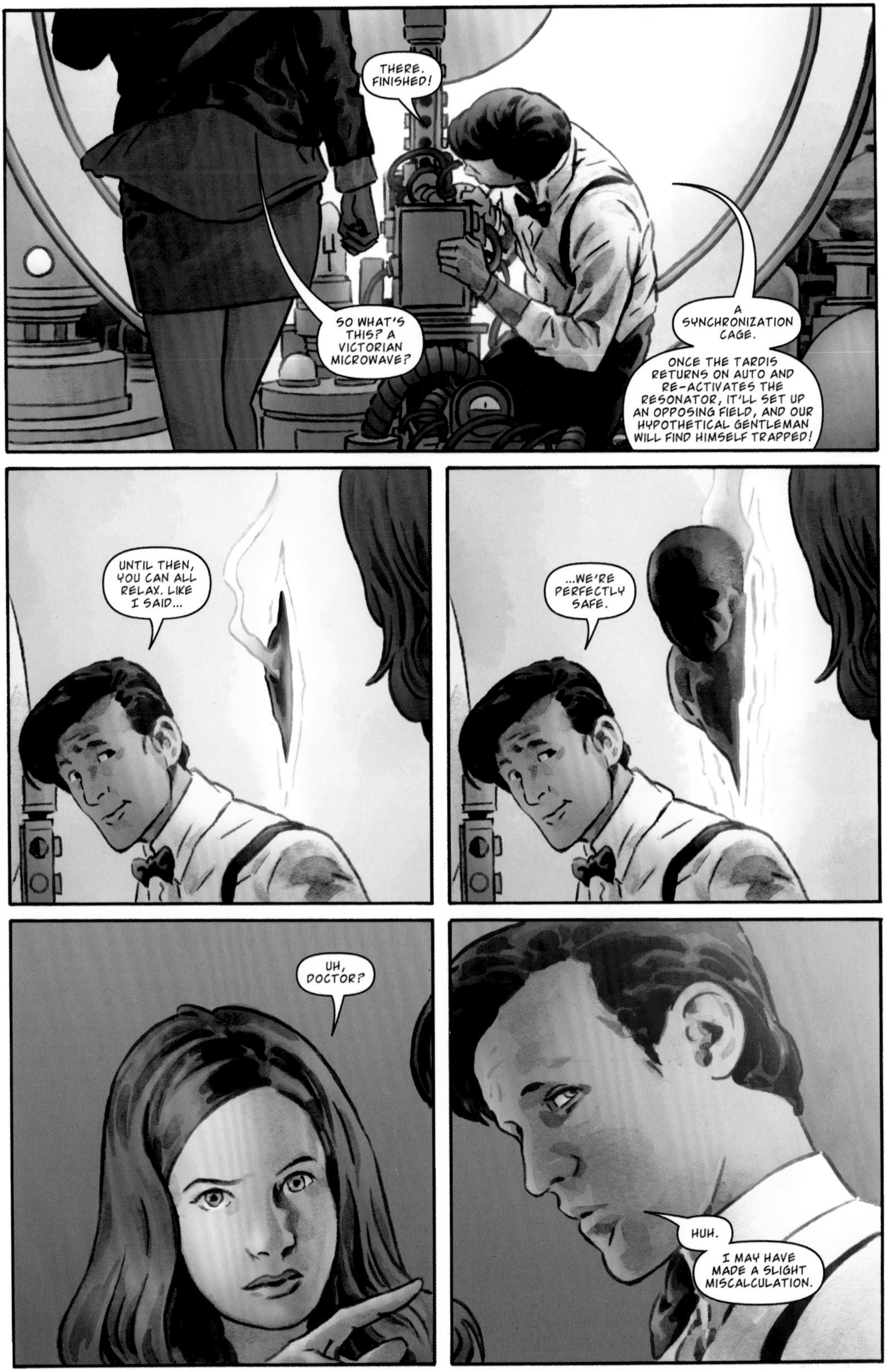
THERE. FINISHED!
SO WHAT'S THIS? A VICTORIAN MICROWAVE?
A SYNCHRONIZATION CAGE.
ONCE THE TARDIS RETURNS ON AUTO AND RE-ACTIVATES THE RESONATOR, IT'LL SET UP AN OPPOSING FIELD, AND OUR HYPOTHETICAL GENTLEMAN WILL FIND HIMSELF TRAPPED!
UNTIL THEN, YOU CAN ALL RELAX. LIKE I SAID...
...WE'RE PERFECTLY SAFE.
UH, DOCTOR?
HUH.
I MAY HAVE MADE A SLIGHT MISCALCULATION.

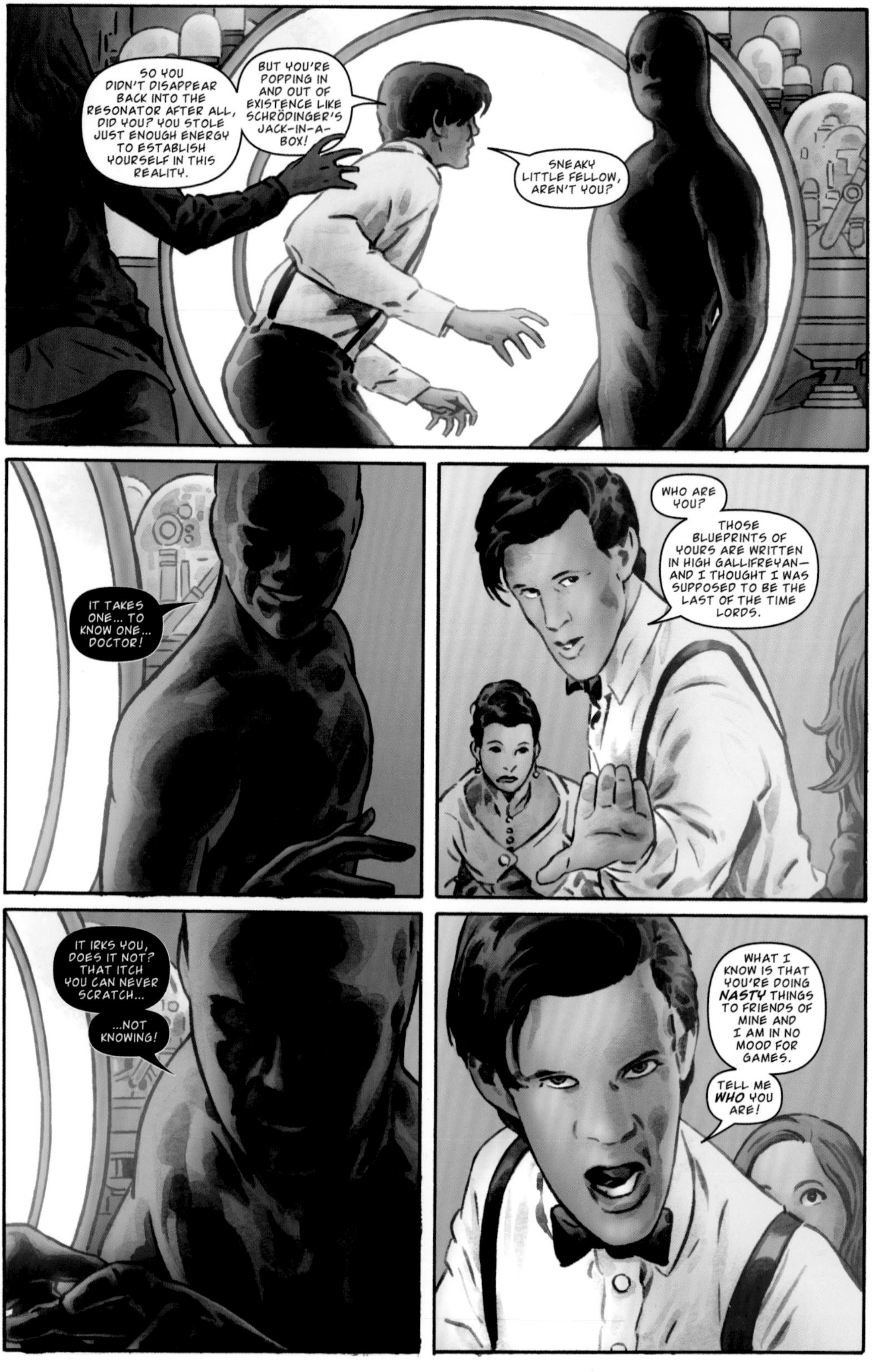
SO YOU DIDN'T DISAPPEAR BACK INTO THE RESONATOR AFTER ALL, DID YOU? YOU STOLE JUST ENOUGH ENERGY TO ESTABLISH YOURSELF IN THIS REALITY.
BUT YOU'RE POPPING IN AND OUT OF EXISTENCE LIKE SCHRÖDINGER'S JACK-IN-A-BOX!
SNEAKY LITTLE FELLOW, AREN'T YOU?
IT TAKES ONE... TO KNOW ONE... DOCTOR!
WHO ARE YOU?
THOSE BLUEPRINTS OF YOURS ARE WRITTEN IN HIGH GALLIFREYAN—AND I THOUGHT I WAS SUPPOSED TO BE THE LAST OF THE TIME LORDS.
IT IRKS YOU, DOES IT NOT? THAT ITCH YOU CAN NEVER SCRATCH...
...NOT KNOWING!
WHAT I KNOW IS THAT YOU'RE DOING **NASTY** THINGS TO FRIENDS OF MINE AND I AM IN NO MOOD FOR GAMES.
TELL ME **WHO** YOU ARE!

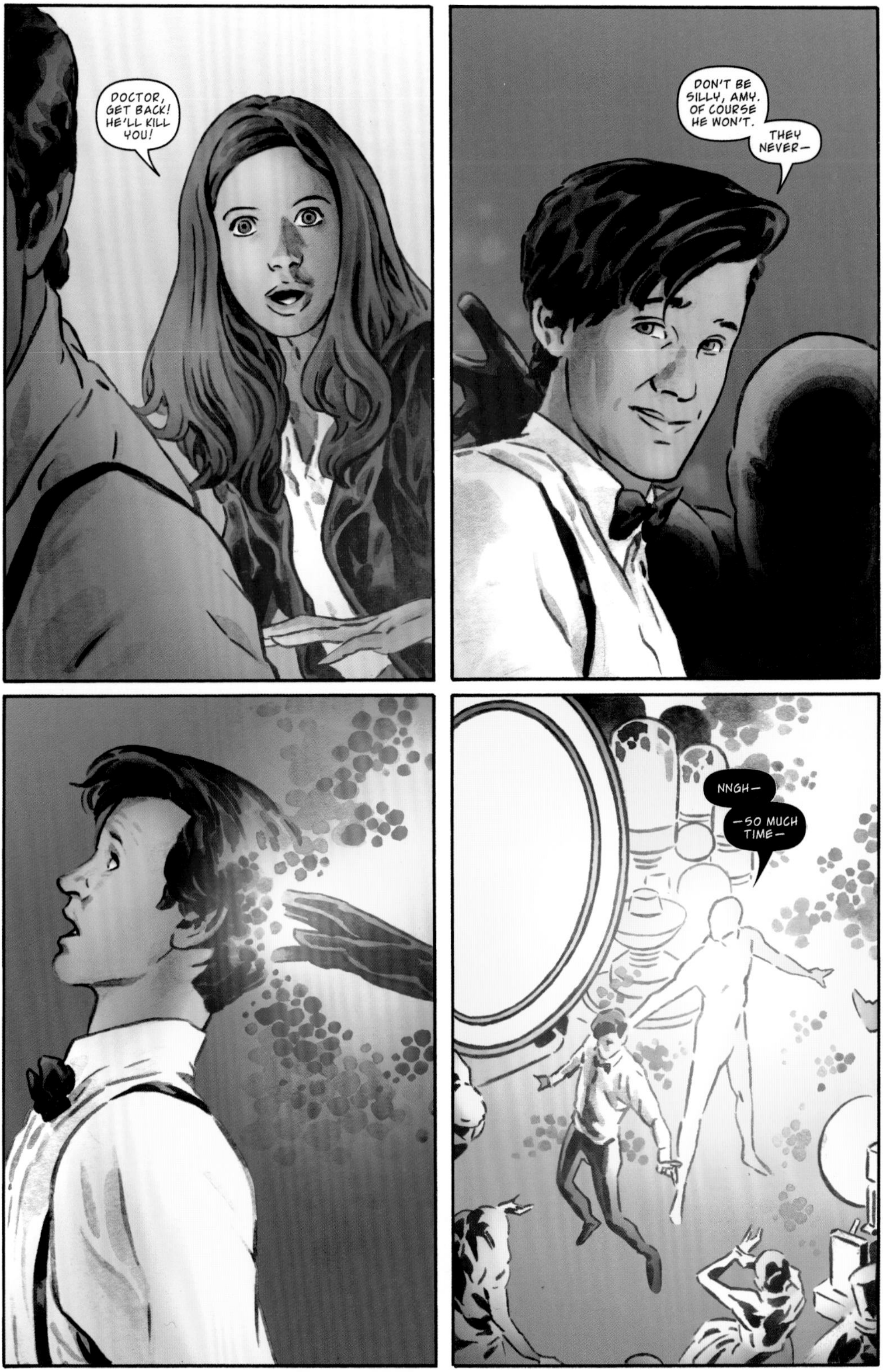
DOCTOR, GET BACK! HE'LL KILL YOU!
DON'T BE SILLY, AMY. OF COURSE HE WON'T.
THEY NEVER—
NNGH—
—SO MUCH TIME—

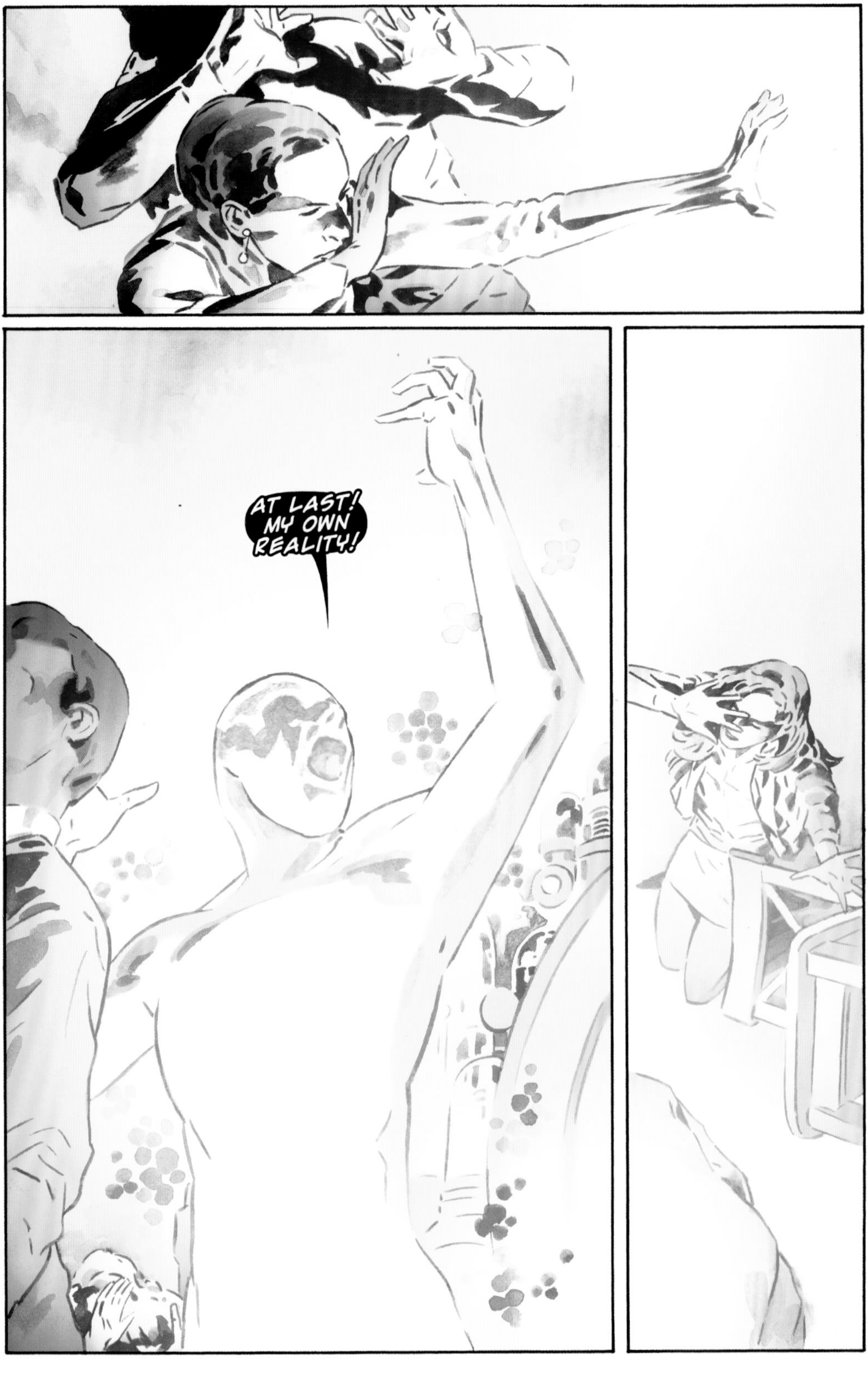
AT LAST! MY OWN REALITY!

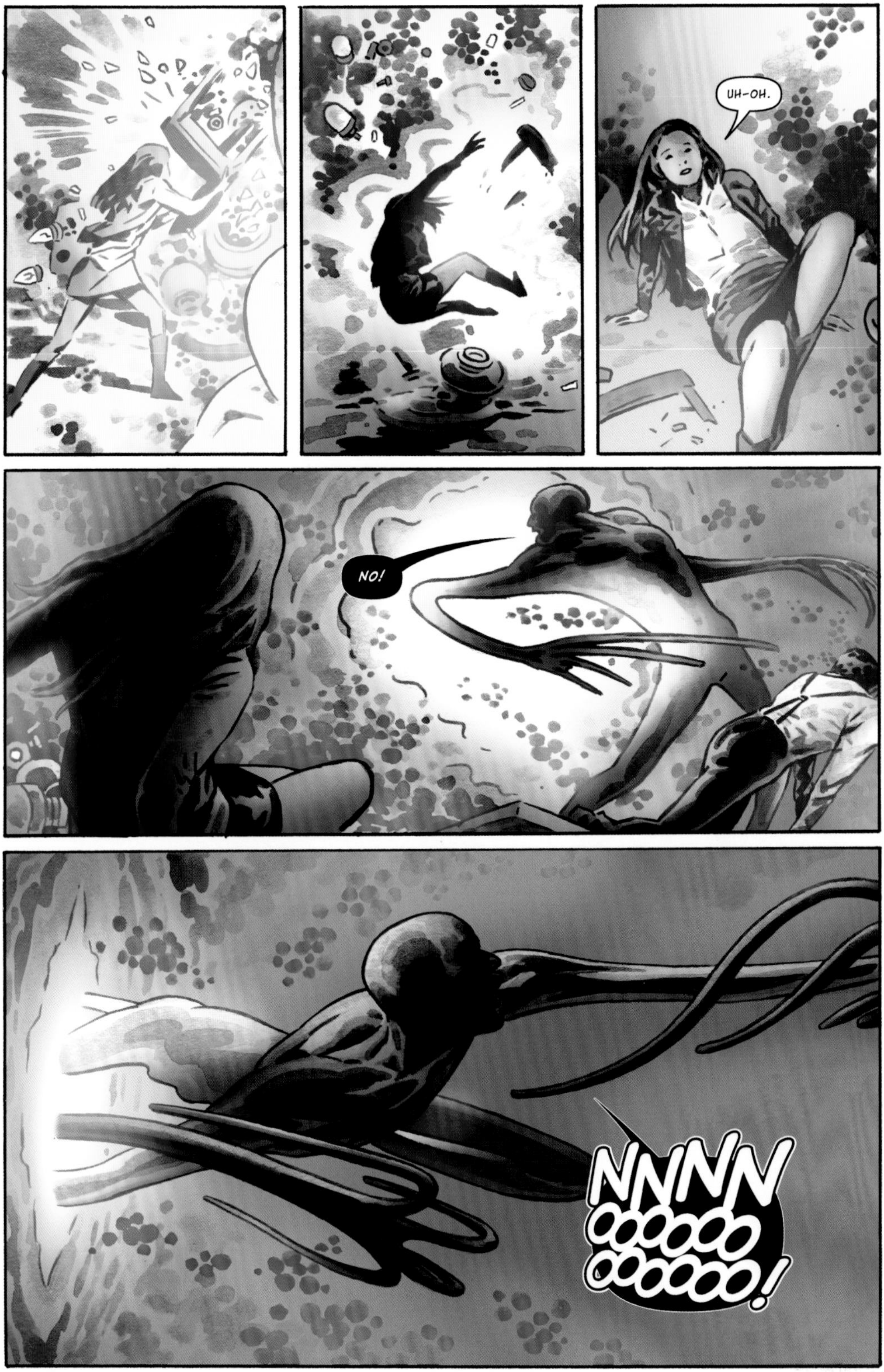
UH-OH.
NO!
NNNNOOOOOOOOOOO!

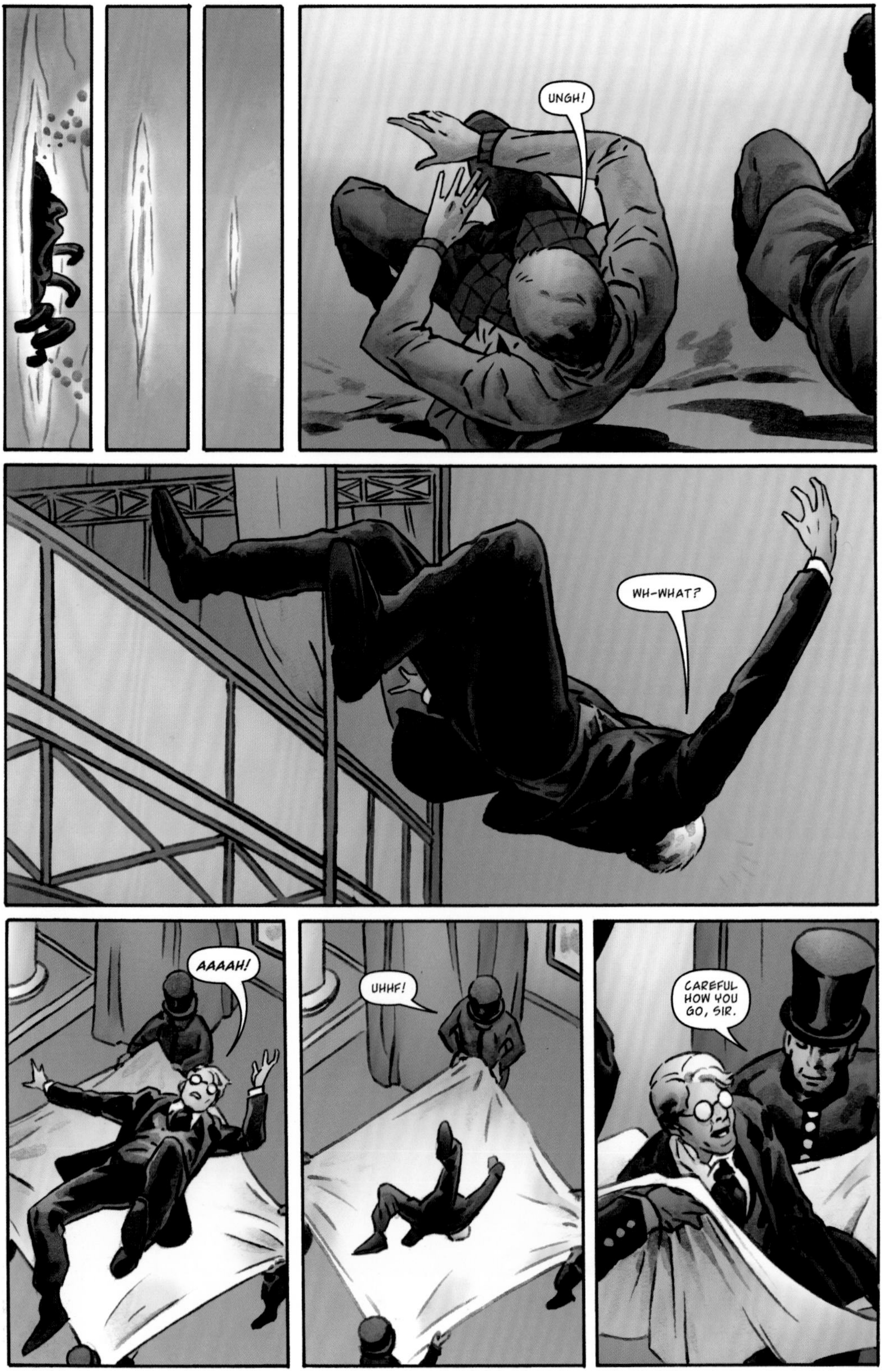
UNGH!
WH-WHAT?
AAAAH!
UHHF!
CAREFUL HOW YOU GO, SIR.

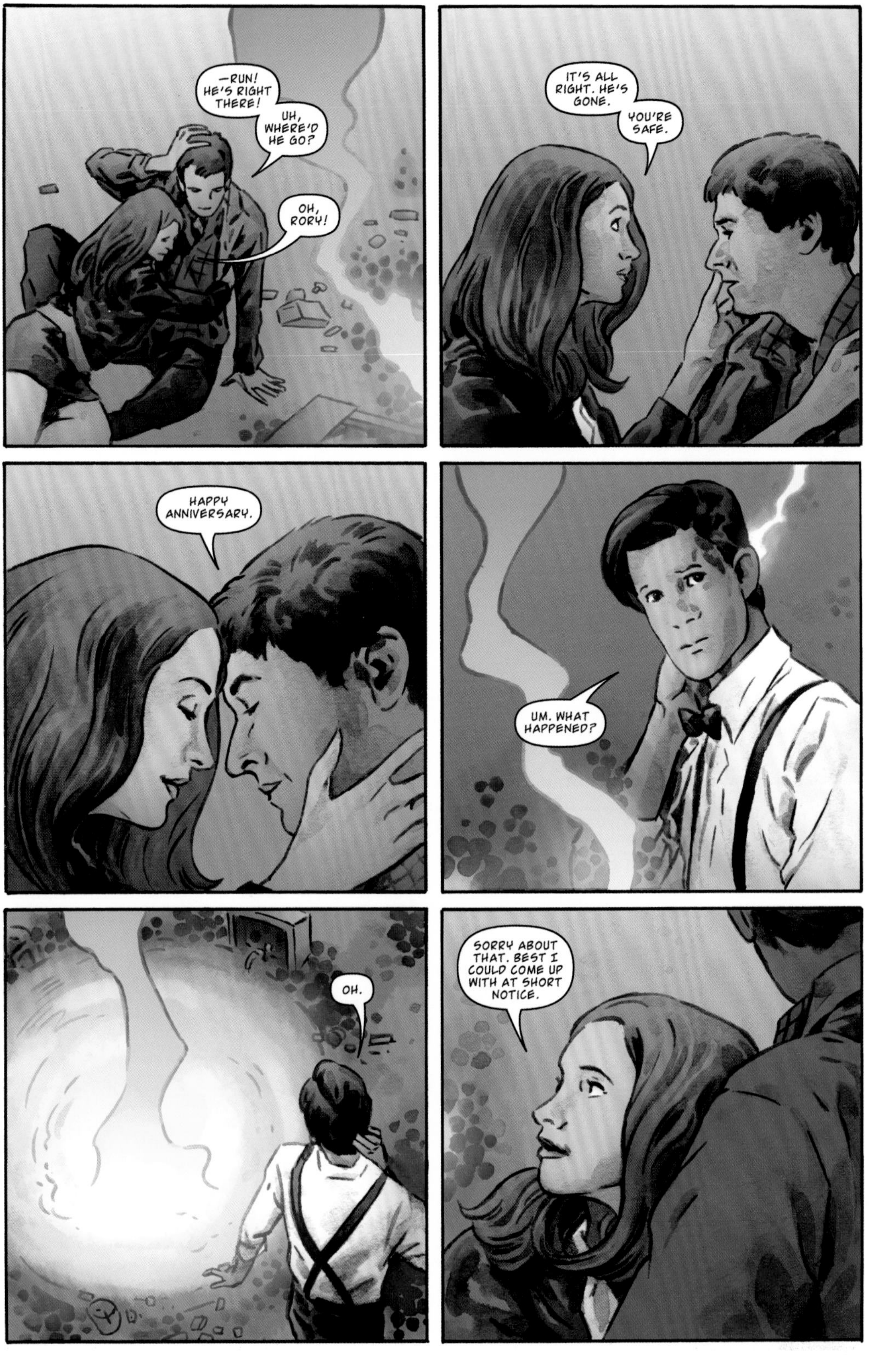
—RUN! HE'S RIGHT THERE!
UH, WHERE'D HE GO?
OH, RORY!
IT'S ALL RIGHT. HE'S GONE.
YOU'RE SAFE.
HAPPY ANNIVERSARY.
UM. WHAT HAPPENED?
OH.
SORRY ABOUT THAT. BEST I COULD COME UP WITH AT SHORT NOTICE.

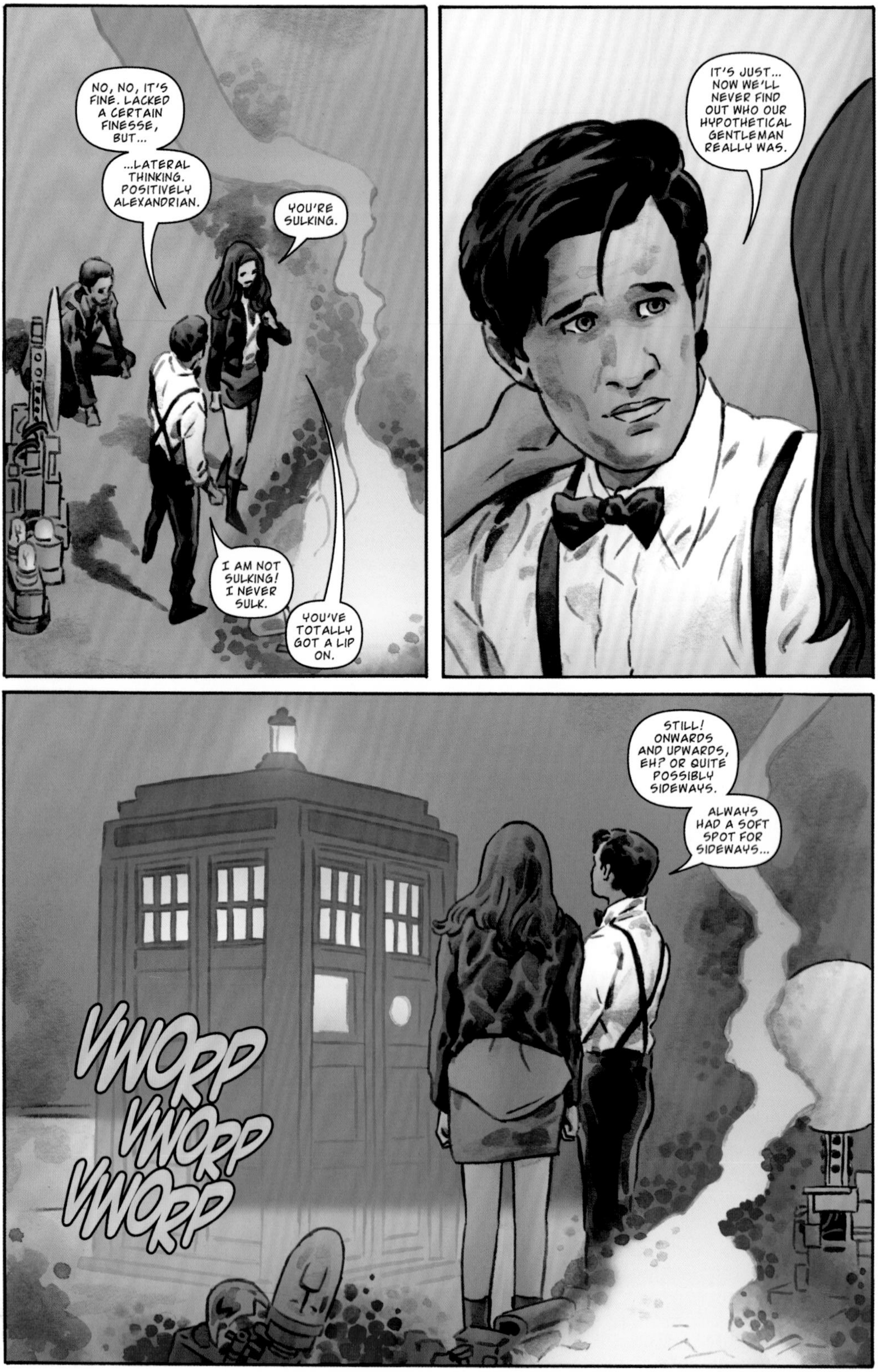

NO, NO, IT'S FINE. LACKED A CERTAIN FINESSE, BUT...
...LATERAL THINKING. POSITIVELY ALEXANDRIAN.
YOU'RE SULKING.
I AM NOT SULKING! I NEVER SULK.
YOU'VE TOTALLY GOT A LIP ON.
IT'S JUST... NOW WE'LL NEVER FIND OUT WHO OUR HYPOTHETICAL GENTLEMAN REALLY WAS.
STILL! ONWARDS AND UPWARDS, EH? OR QUITE POSSIBLY SIDEWAYS.
ALWAYS HAD A SOFT SPOT FOR SIDEWAYS...
VWORP VWORP VWORP

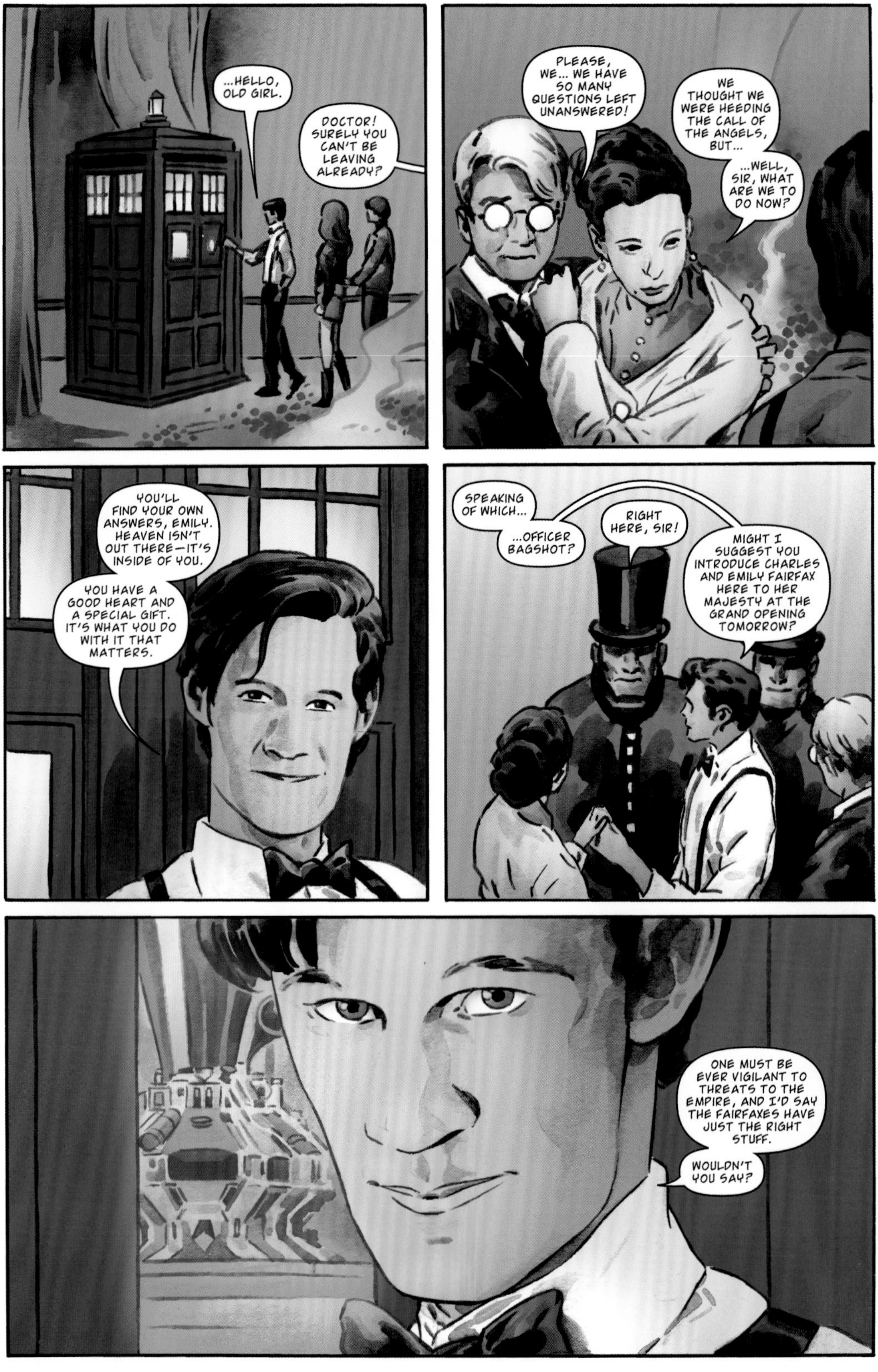
...HELLO, OLD GIRL.
DOCTOR! SURELY YOU CAN'T BE LEAVING ALREADY?
PLEASE, WE... WE HAVE SO MANY QUESTIONS LEFT UNANSWERED!
WE THOUGHT WE WERE HEEDING THE CALL OF THE ANGELS, BUT...
...WELL, SIR, WHAT ARE WE TO DO NOW?
YOU'LL FIND YOUR OWN ANSWERS, EMILY. HEAVEN ISN'T OUT THERE—IT'S INSIDE OF YOU.
YOU HAVE A GOOD HEART AND A SPECIAL GIFT. IT'S WHAT YOU DO WITH IT THAT MATTERS.
SPEAKING OF WHICH...
...OFFICER BAGSHOT?
RIGHT HERE, SIR!
MIGHT I SUGGEST YOU INTRODUCE CHARLES AND EMILY FAIRFAX HERE TO HER MAJESTY AT THE GRAND OPENING TOMORROW?
ONE MUST BE EVER VIGILANT TO THREATS TO THE EMPIRE, AND I'D SAY THE FAIRFAXES HAVE JUST THE RIGHT STUFF.
WOULDN'T YOU SAY?

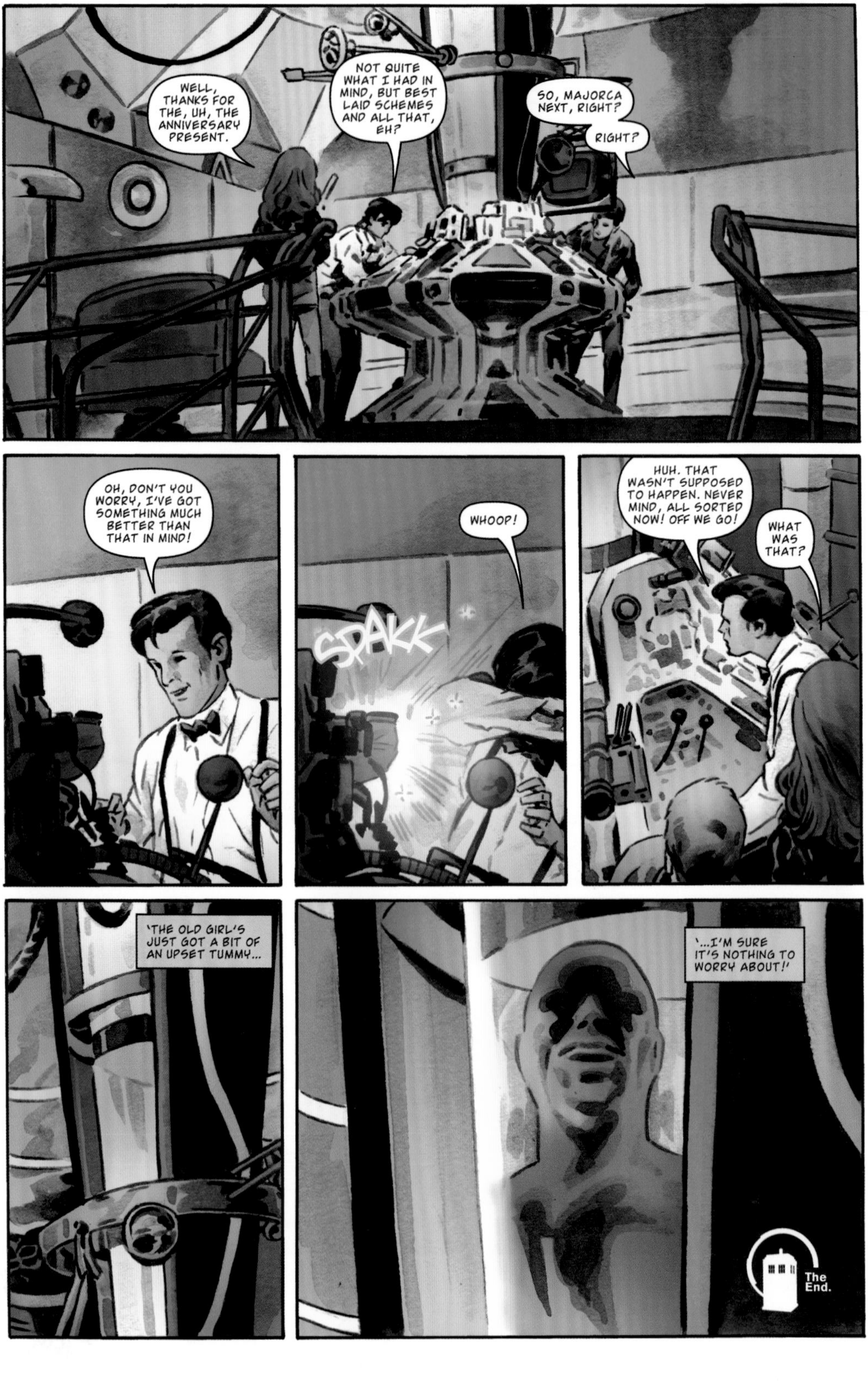
WELL, THANKS FOR THE, UH, THE ANNIVERSARY PRESENT.
NOT QUITE WHAT I HAD IN MIND, BUT BEST LAID SCHEMES AND ALL THAT, EH?
SO, MAJORCA NEXT, RIGHT?
RIGHT?
OH, DON'T YOU WORRY, I'VE GOT SOMETHING MUCH BETTER THAN THAT IN MIND!
WHOOP!
SPAKK
HUH. THAT WASN'T SUPPOSED TO HAPPEN. NEVER MIND, ALL SORTED NOW! OFF WE GO!
WHAT WAS THAT?
'THE OLD GIRL'S JUST GOT A BIT OF AN UPSET TUMMY...
'...I'M SURE IT'S NOTHING TO WORRY ABOUT!'
The End.

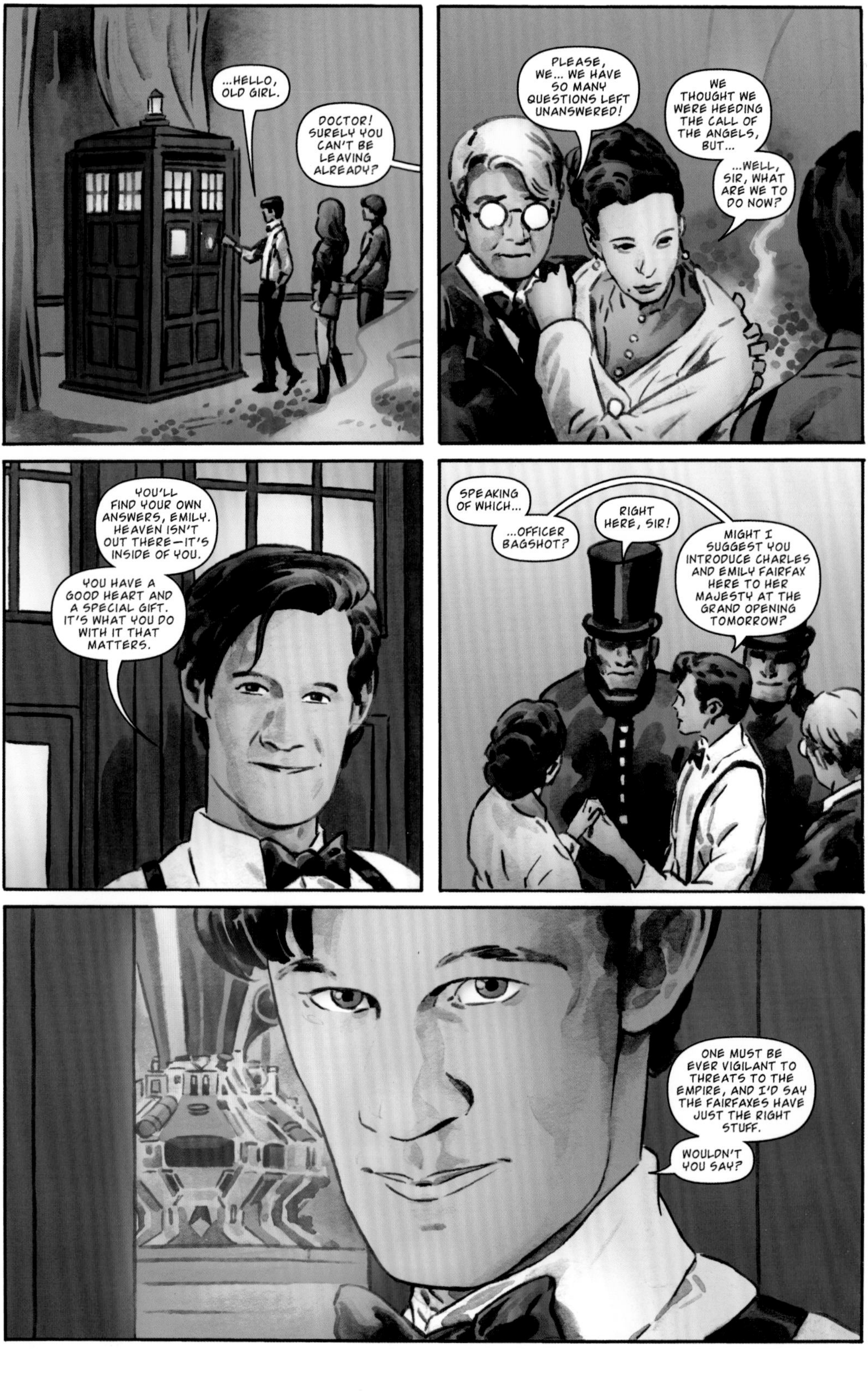
...HELLO, OLD GIRL.
DOCTOR! SURELY YOU CAN'T BE LEAVING ALREADY?
PLEASE, WE... WE HAVE SO MANY QUESTIONS LEFT UNANSWERED!
WE THOUGHT WE WERE HEEDING THE CALL OF THE ANGELS, BUT...
...WELL, SIR, WHAT ARE WE TO DO NOW?
YOU'LL FIND YOUR OWN ANSWERS, EMILY. HEAVEN ISN'T OUT THERE—IT'S INSIDE OF YOU.
YOU HAVE A GOOD HEART AND A SPECIAL GIFT. IT'S WHAT YOU DO WITH IT THAT MATTERS.
SPEAKING OF WHICH...
...OFFICER BAGSHOT?
RIGHT HERE, SIR!
MIGHT I SUGGEST YOU INTRODUCE CHARLES AND EMILY FAIRFAX HERE TO HER MAJESTY AT THE GRAND OPENING TOMORROW?
ONE MUST BE EVER VIGILANT TO THREATS TO THE EMPIRE, AND I'D SAY THE FAIRFAXES HAVE JUST THE RIGHT STUFF.
WOULDN'T YOU SAY?

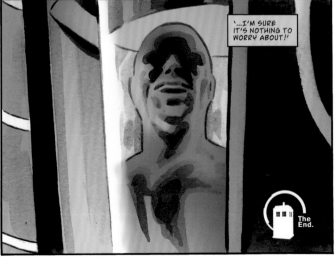

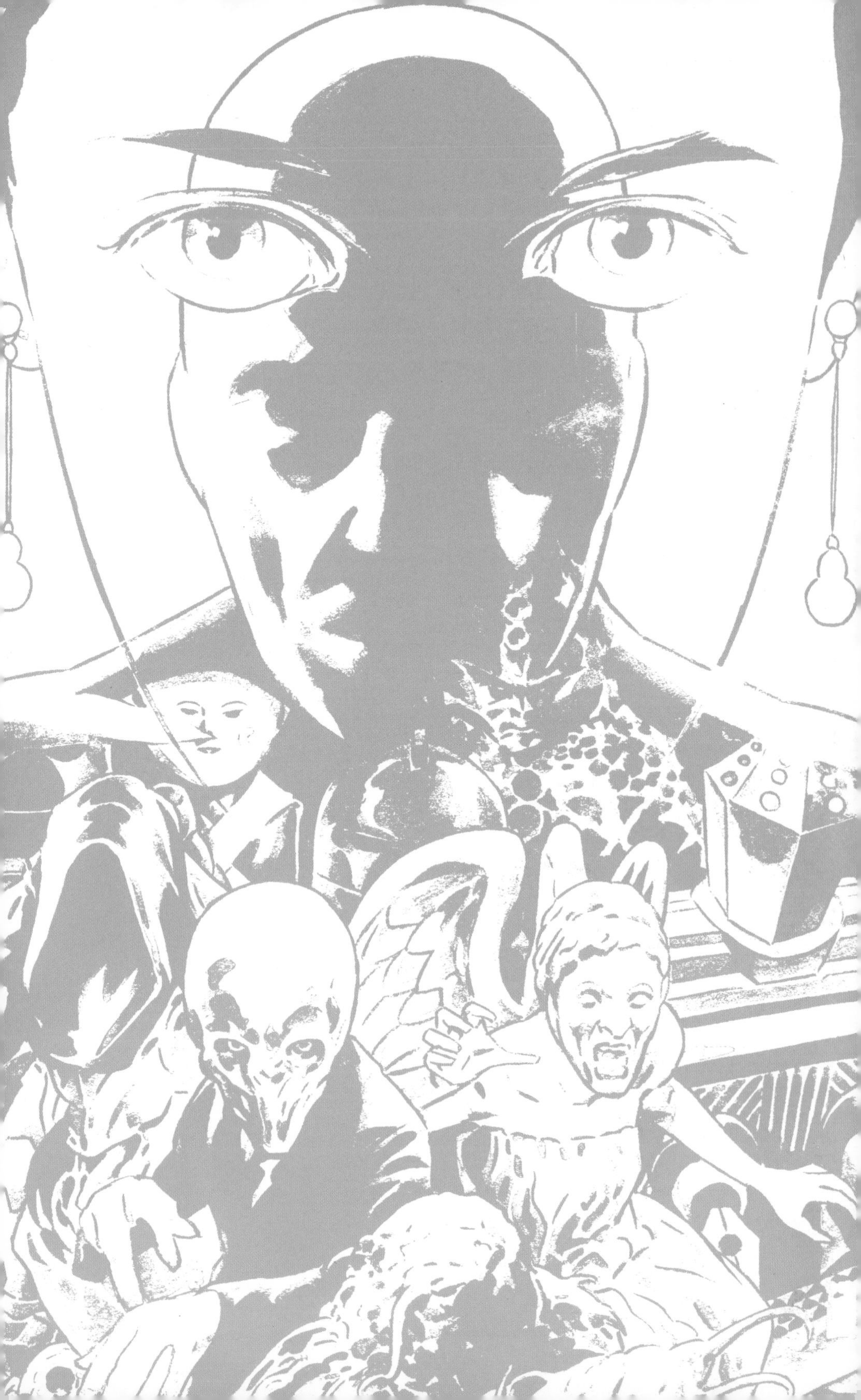

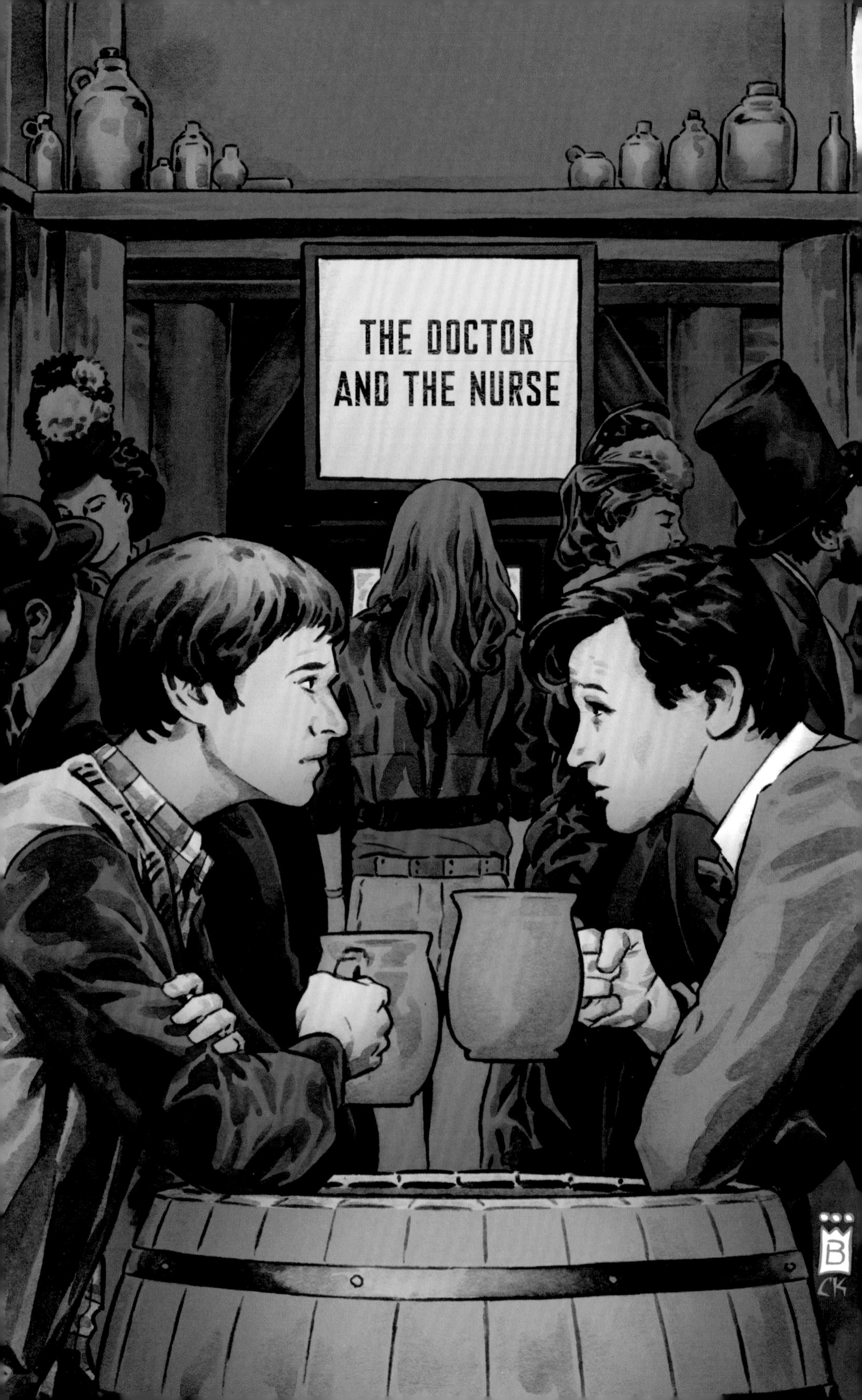
THE DOCTOR
AND THE NURSE

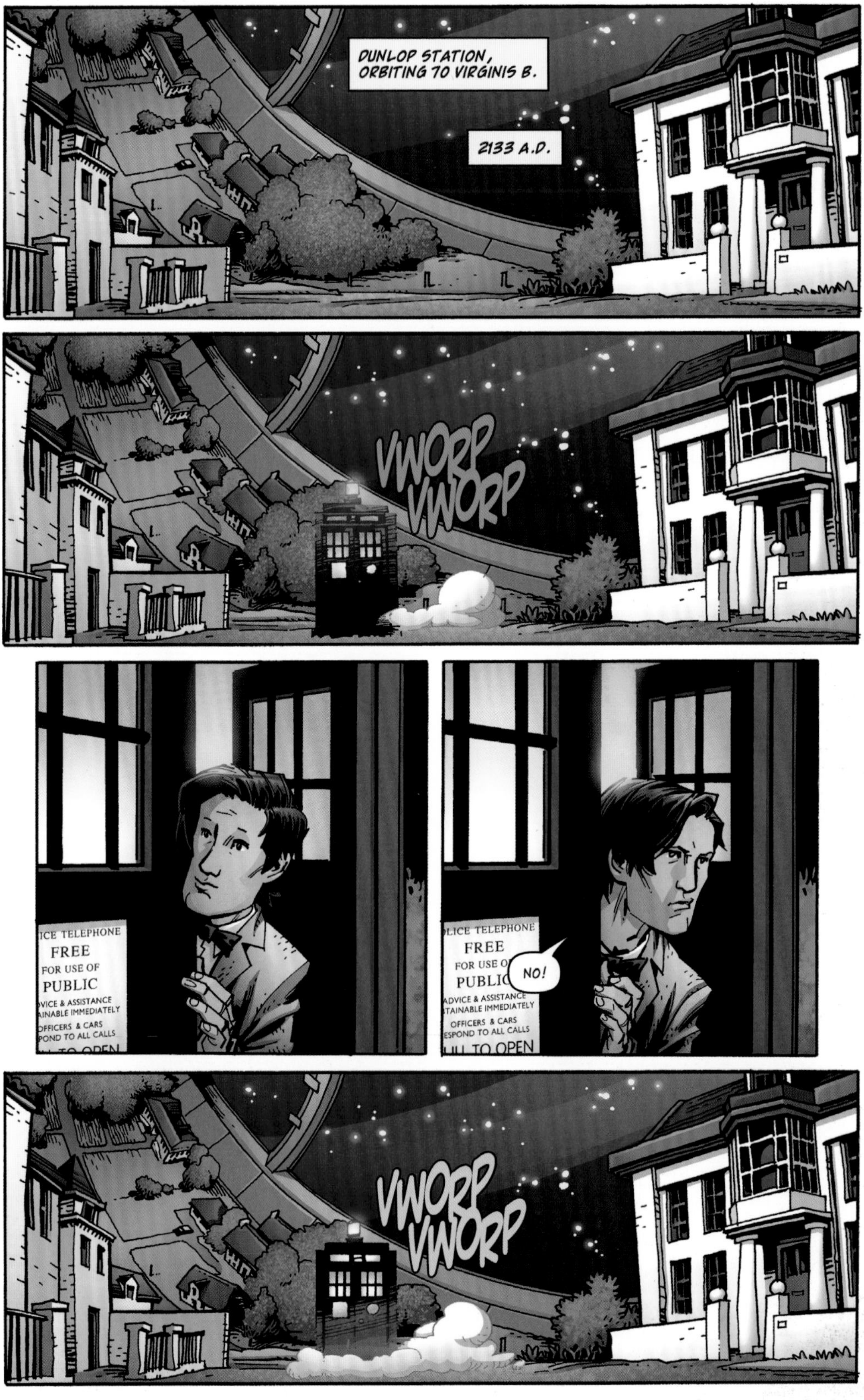
DUNLOP STATION, ORBITING 70 VIRGINIS B.
2133 A.D.
VWORP VWORP
POLICE TELEPHONE
FREE
FOR USE OF
PUBLIC
ADVICE & ASSISTANCE OBTAINABLE IMMEDIATELY
OFFICERS & CARS RESPOND TO ALL CALLS
NO!
VWORP VWORP

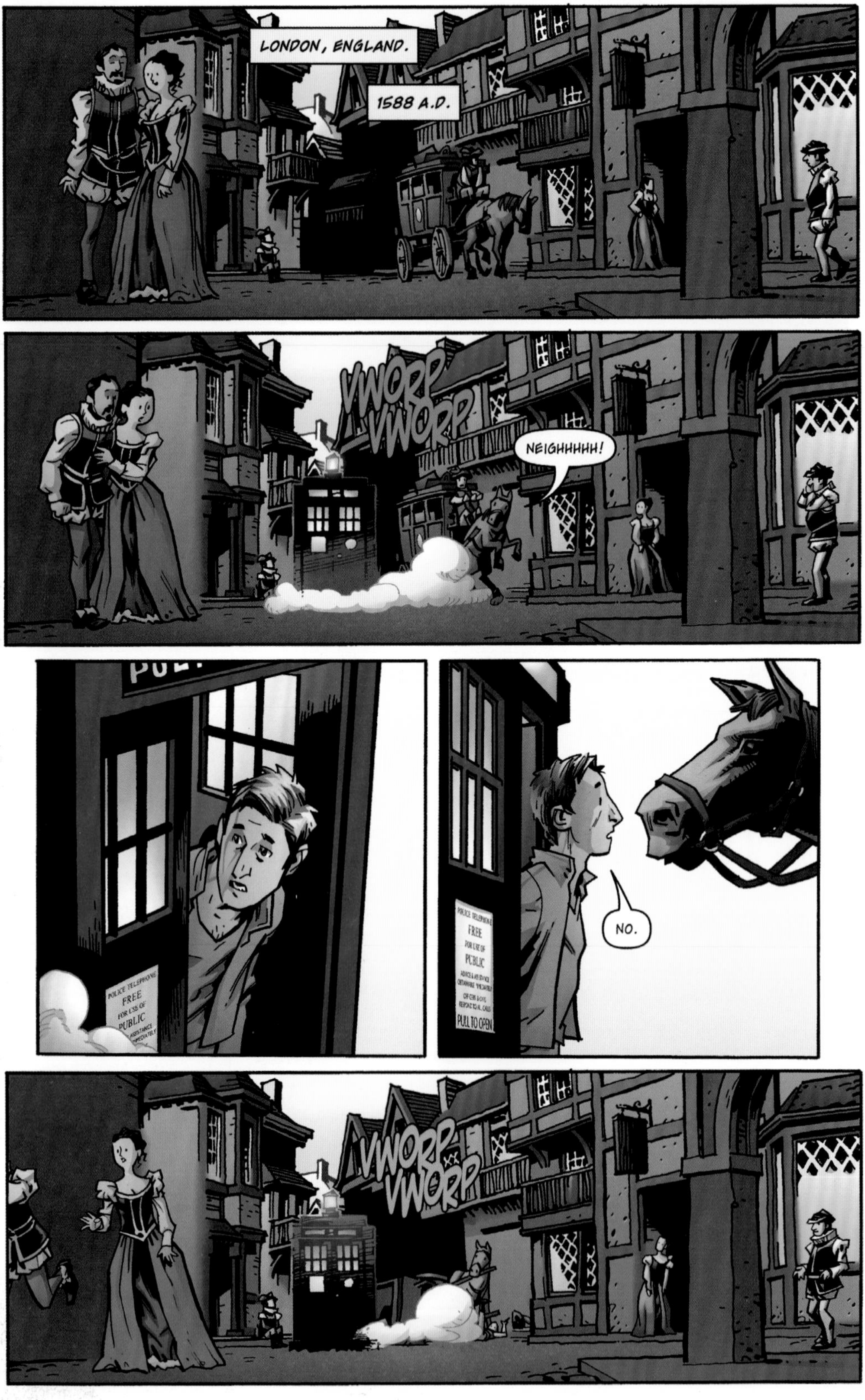
LONDON, ENGLAND.
1588 A.D.
VWORP VWORP
NEIGHHHHH!
POLICE TELEPHONE FREE FOR USE OF PUBLIC
POLICE TELEPHONE FREE FOR USE OF PUBLIC
PULL TO OPEN
NO.
VWORP VWORP

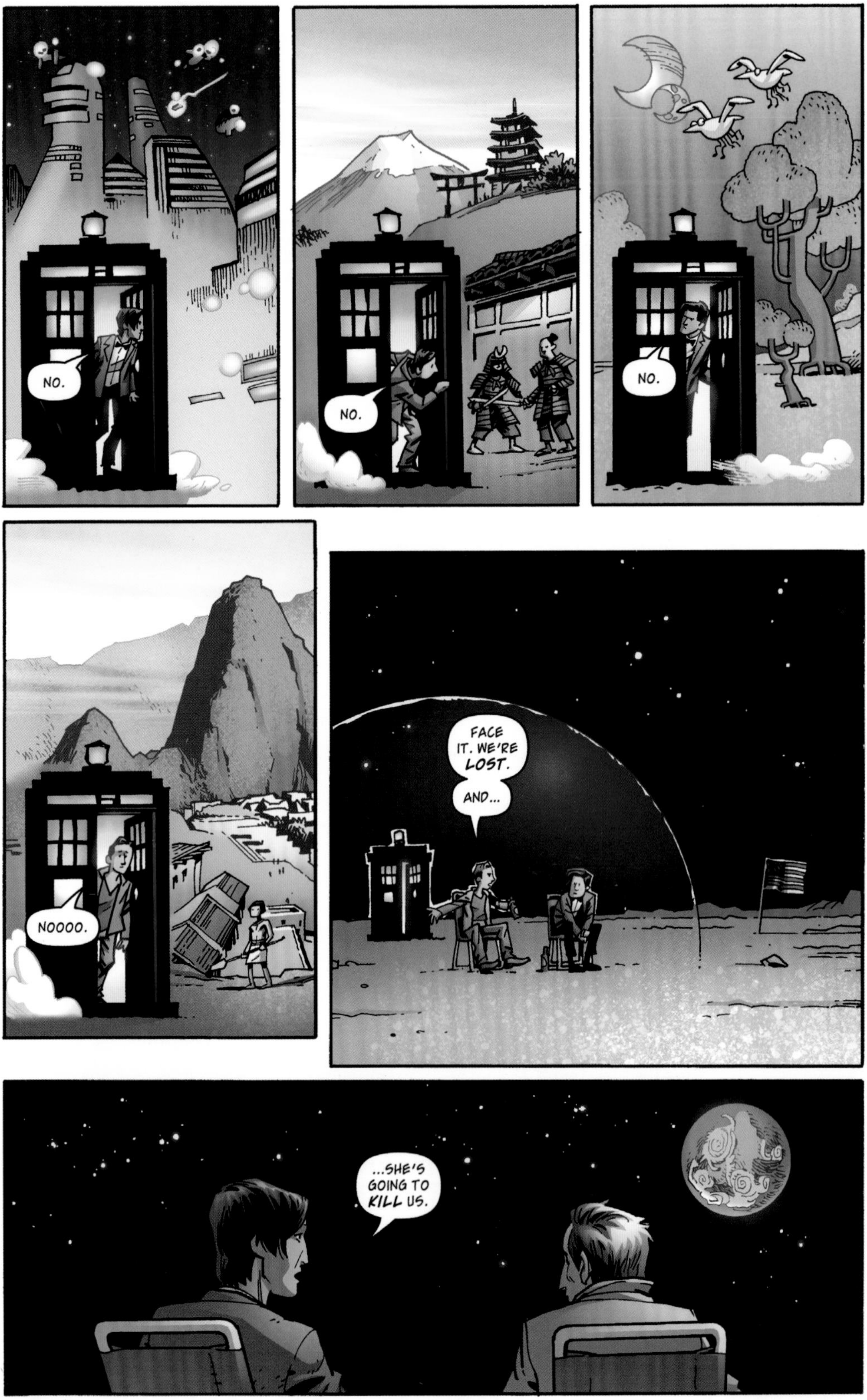
NO.
NO.
NO.
NOOOO.
FACE IT. WE'RE LOST.
AND...
...SHE'S GOING TO KILL US.

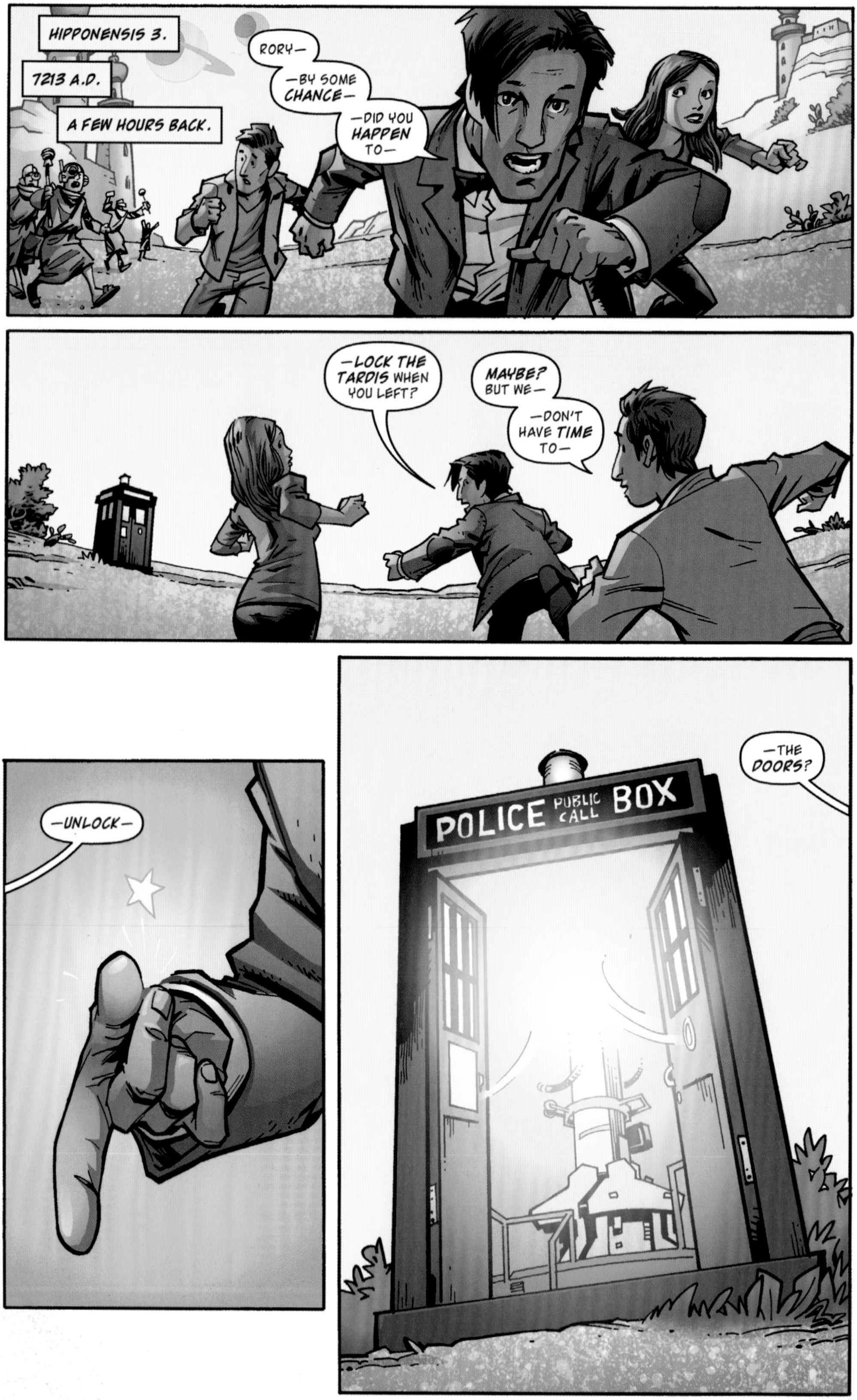
HIPPONENSIS 3.
7213 A.D.
A FEW HOURS BACK.
RORY—
—BY SOME CHANCE—
—DID YOU HAPPEN TO—
—LOCK THE TARDIS WHEN YOU LEFT?
MAYBE? BUT WE—
—DON'T HAVE TIME TO—
—UNLOCK—
—THE DOORS?
POLICE PUBLIC CALL BOX

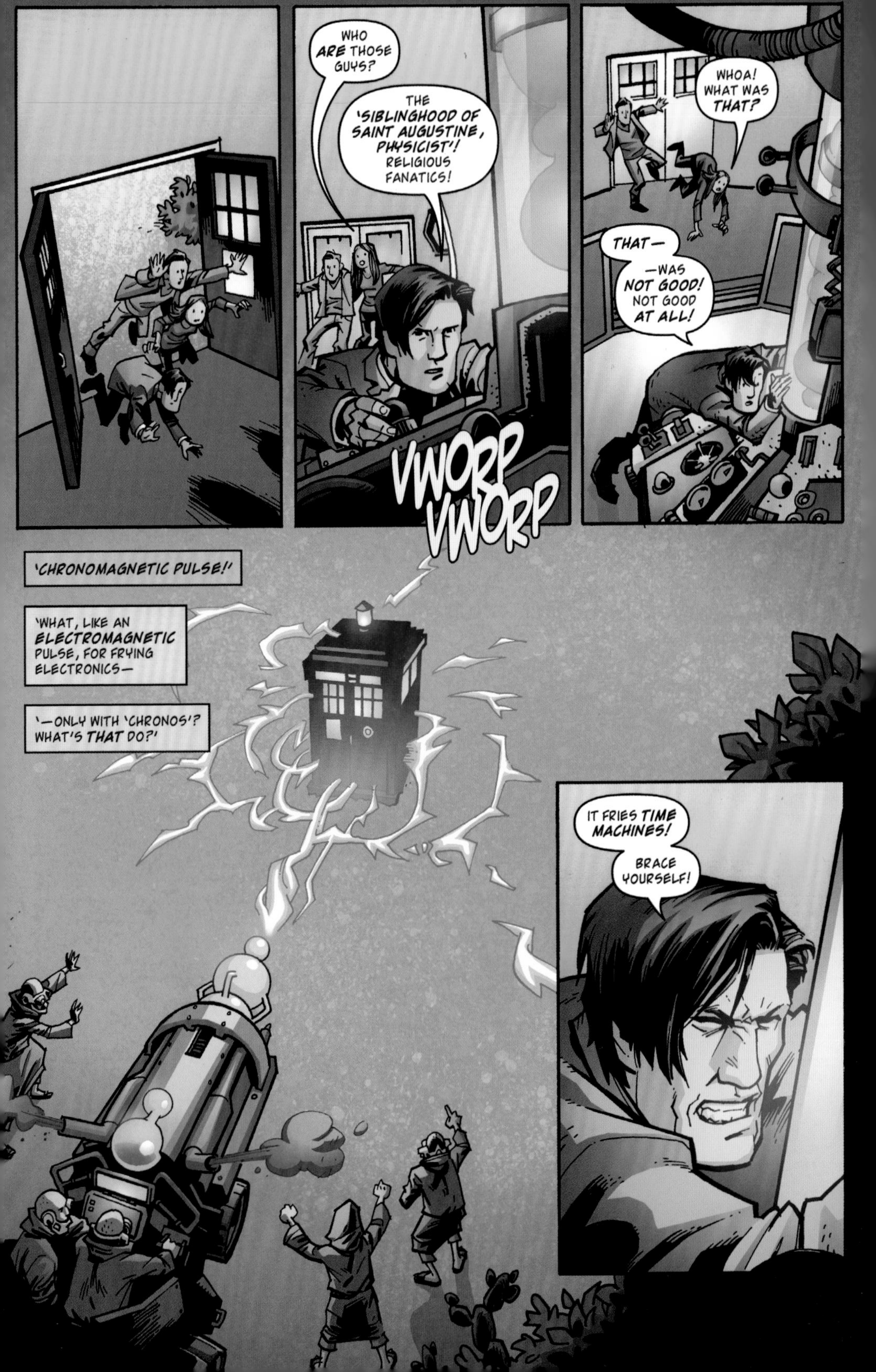
WHO ARE THOSE GUYS?
THE 'SIBLINGHOOD OF SAINT AUGUSTINE, PHYSICIST'! RELIGIOUS FANATICS!
VWORP VWORP
WHOA! WHAT WAS THAT?
THAT—
—WAS NOT GOOD! NOT GOOD AT ALL!
'CHRONOMAGNETIC PULSE!'
'WHAT, LIKE AN ELECTROMAGNETIC PULSE, FOR FRYING ELECTRONICS—
'—ONLY WITH 'CHRONOS'? WHAT'S THAT DO?'
IT FRIES TIME MACHINES!
BRACE YOURSELF!

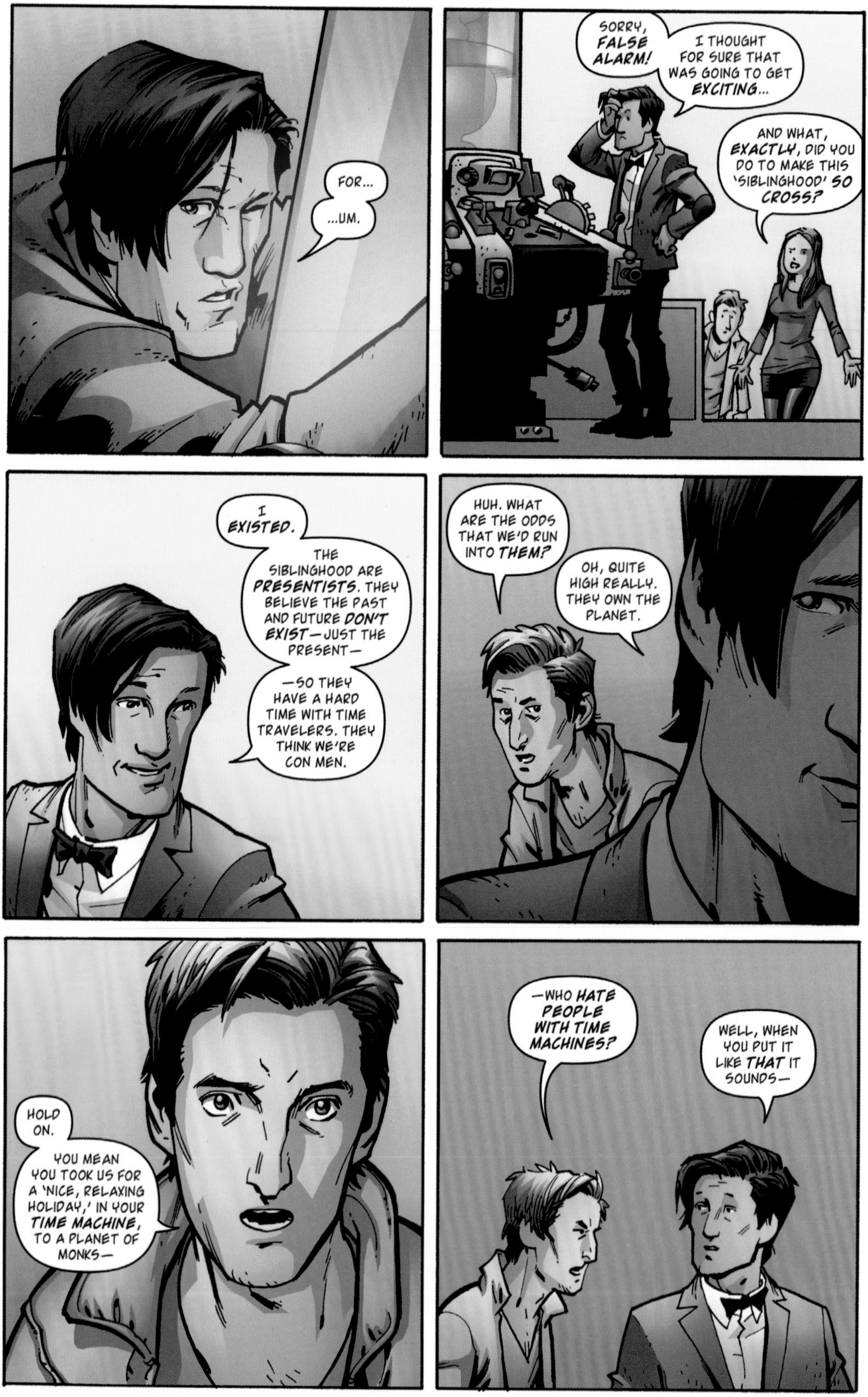
FOR...
...UM.
SORRY, FALSE ALARM!
I THOUGHT FOR SURE THAT WAS GOING TO GET EXCITING...
AND WHAT, EXACTLY, DID YOU DO TO MAKE THIS 'SIBLINGHOOD' SO CROSS?
I EXISTED.
THE SIBLINGHOOD ARE PRESENTISTS. THEY BELIEVE THE PAST AND FUTURE DON'T EXIST—JUST THE PRESENT—
—SO THEY HAVE A HARD TIME WITH TIME TRAVELERS. THEY THINK WE'RE CON MEN.
HUH. WHAT ARE THE ODDS THAT WE'D RUN INTO THEM?
OH, QUITE HIGH REALLY. THEY OWN THE PLANET.
HOLD ON.
YOU MEAN YOU TOOK US FOR A 'NICE, RELAXING HOLIDAY,' IN YOUR TIME MACHINE, TO A PLANET OF MONKS—
—WHO HATE PEOPLE WITH TIME MACHINES?
WELL, WHEN YOU PUT IT LIKE THAT IT SOUNDS—

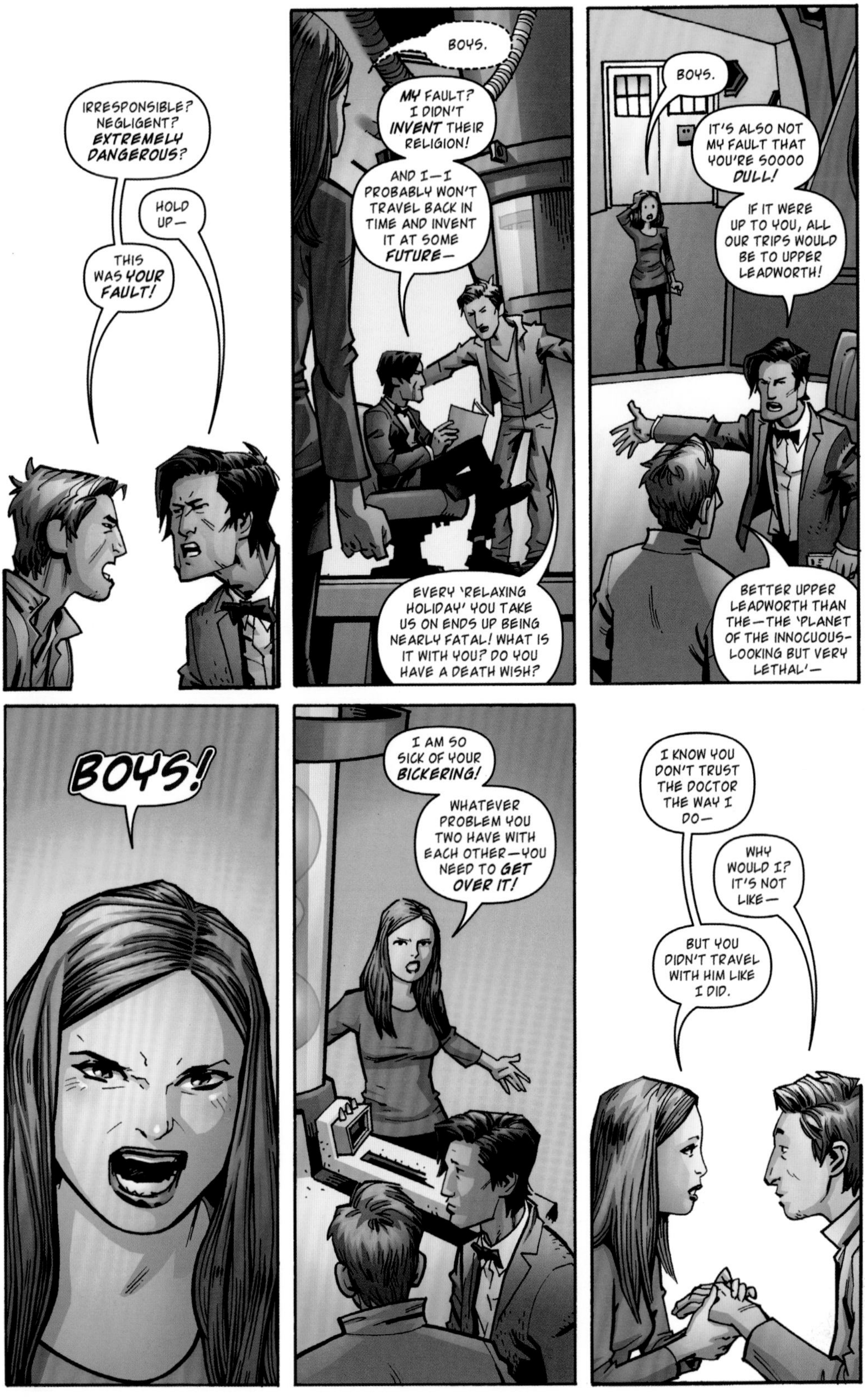
IRRESPONSIBLE? NEGLIGENT? EXTREMELY DANGEROUS?
HOLD UP—
THIS WAS YOUR FAULT!
BOYS.
MY FAULT? I DIDN'T INVENT THEIR RELIGION!
AND I—I PROBABLY WON'T TRAVEL BACK IN TIME AND INVENT IT AT SOME FUTURE—
EVERY 'RELAXING HOLIDAY' YOU TAKE US ON ENDS UP BEING NEARLY FATAL! WHAT IS IT WITH YOU? DO YOU HAVE A DEATH WISH?
BOYS.
IT'S ALSO NOT MY FAULT THAT YOU'RE SOOOO DULL!
IF IT WERE UP TO YOU, ALL OUR TRIPS WOULD BE TO UPPER LEADWORTH!
BETTER UPPER LEADWORTH THAN THE—THE 'PLANET OF THE INNOCUOUS-LOOKING BUT VERY LETHAL'—
BOYS!
I AM SO SICK OF YOUR BICKERING!
WHATEVER PROBLEM YOU TWO HAVE WITH EACH OTHER—YOU NEED TO GET OVER IT!
I KNOW YOU DON'T TRUST THE DOCTOR THE WAY I DO—
WHY WOULD I? IT'S NOT LIKE—
BUT YOU DIDN'T TRAVEL WITH HIM LIKE I DID.

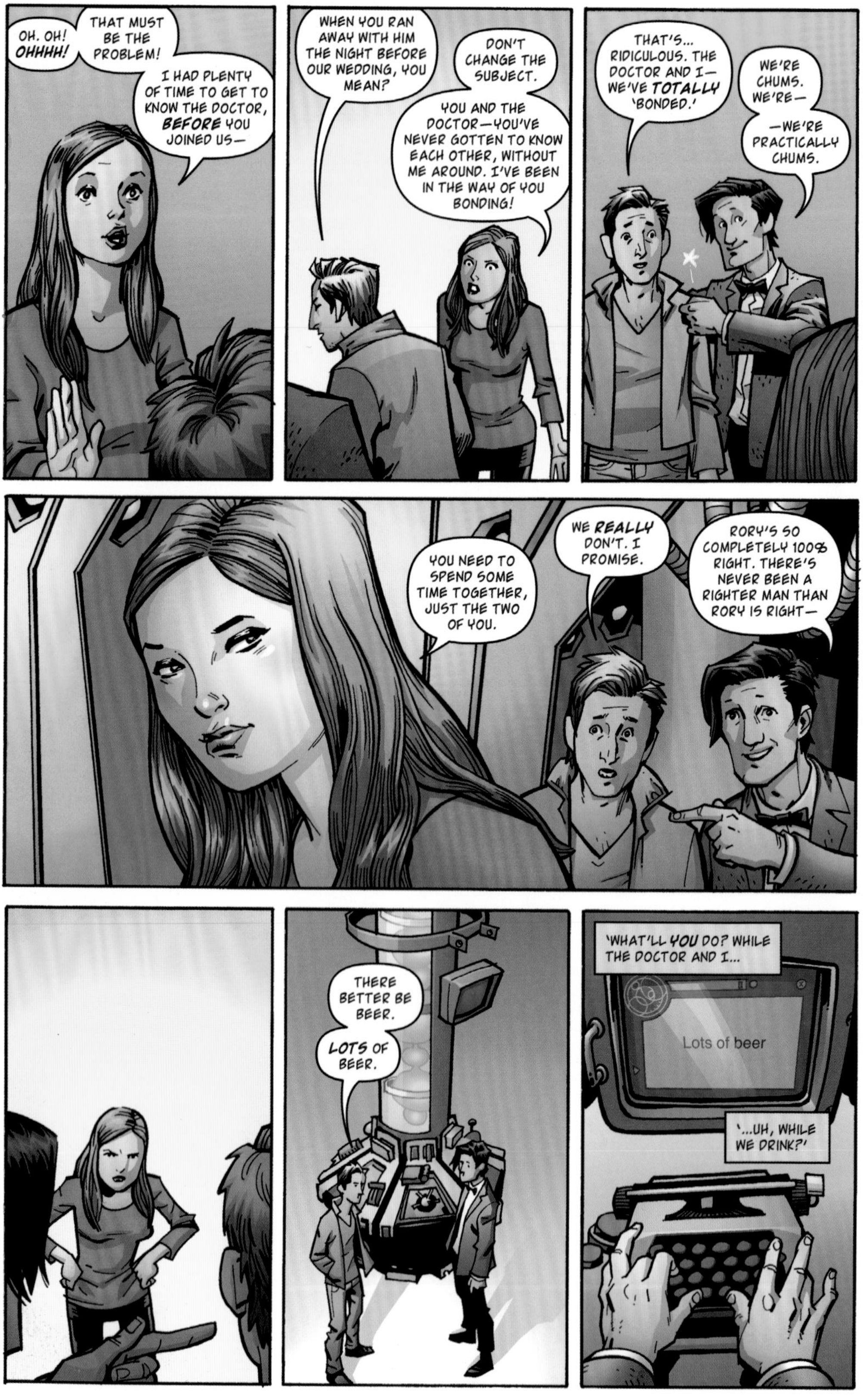
OH. OH! **OHHHH!**
THAT MUST BE THE PROBLEM!
I HAD PLENTY OF TIME TO GET TO KNOW THE DOCTOR, **BEFORE** YOU JOINED US—
WHEN YOU RAN AWAY WITH HIM THE NIGHT BEFORE OUR WEDDING, YOU MEAN?
DON'T CHANGE THE SUBJECT.
YOU AND THE DOCTOR—YOU'VE NEVER GOTTEN TO KNOW EACH OTHER, WITHOUT ME AROUND. I'VE BEEN IN THE WAY OF YOU BONDING!
THAT'S... RIDICULOUS. THE DOCTOR AND I— WE'VE **TOTALLY** 'BONDED.'
WE'RE CHUMS. WE'RE—
—WE'RE PRACTICALLY CHUMS.
YOU NEED TO SPEND SOME TIME TOGETHER, JUST THE TWO OF YOU.
WE **REALLY** DON'T. I PROMISE.
RORY'S SO COMPLETELY 100% RIGHT. THERE'S NEVER BEEN A RIGHTER MAN THAN RORY IS RIGHT—
THERE BETTER BE BEER.
LOTS OF BEER.
'WHAT'LL **YOU** DO? WHILE THE DOCTOR AND I...
Lots of beer
'...UH, WHILE WE DRINK?'

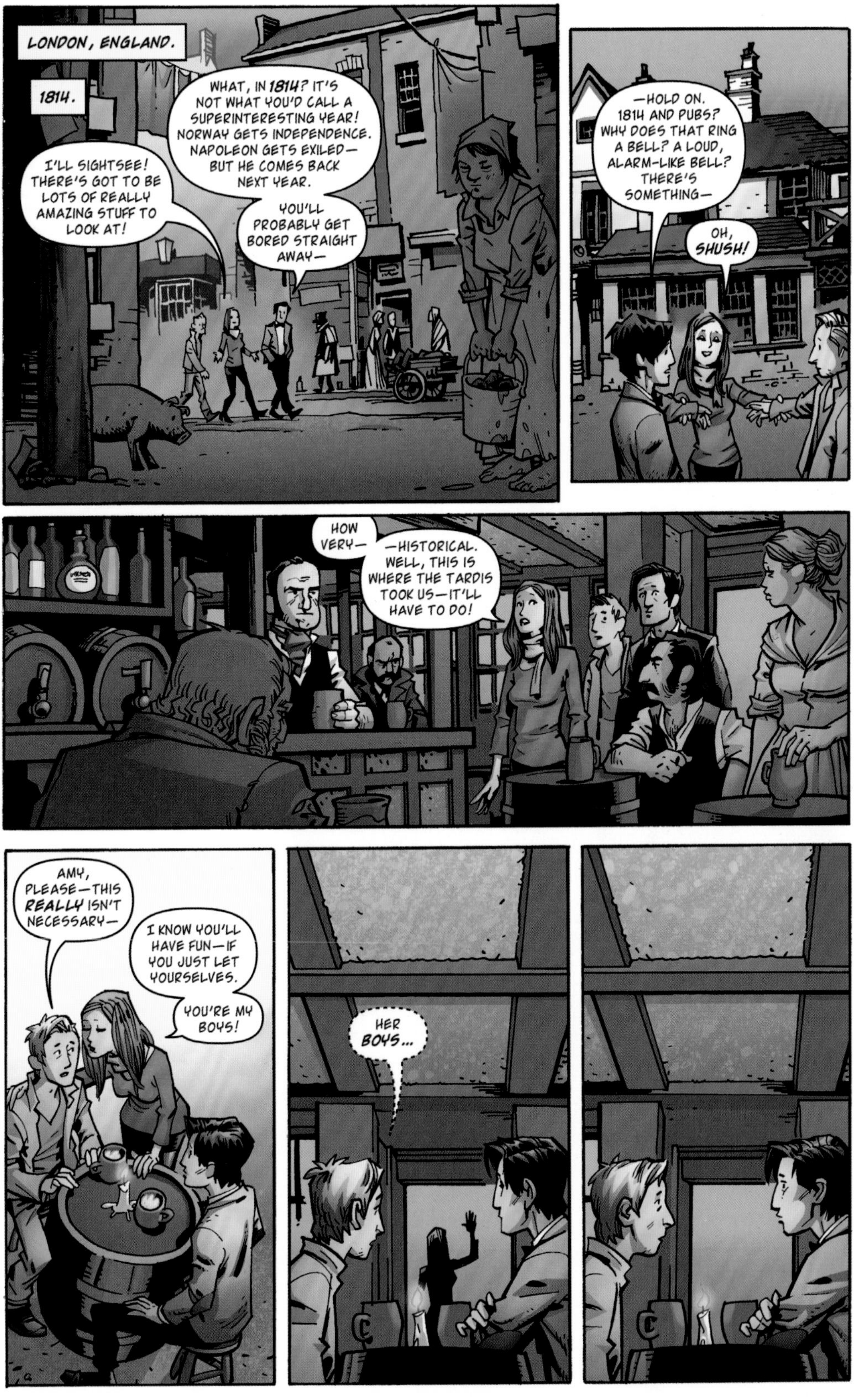
LONDON, ENGLAND.
1814.
I'LL SIGHTSEE! THERE'S GOT TO BE LOTS OF REALLY AMAZING STUFF TO LOOK AT!
WHAT, IN 1814? IT'S NOT WHAT YOU'D CALL A SUPERINTERESTING YEAR! NORWAY GETS INDEPENDENCE. NAPOLEON GETS EXILED— BUT HE COMES BACK NEXT YEAR.
YOU'LL PROBABLY GET BORED STRAIGHT AWAY—
—HOLD ON. 1814 AND PUBS? WHY DOES THAT RING A BELL? A LOUD, ALARM-LIKE BELL? THERE'S SOMETHING—
OH, SHUSH!
HOW VERY—
—HISTORICAL. WELL, THIS IS WHERE THE TARDIS TOOK US—IT'LL HAVE TO DO!
AMY, PLEASE—THIS REALLY ISN'T NECESSARY—
I KNOW YOU'LL HAVE FUN—IF YOU JUST LET YOURSELVES.
YOU'RE MY BOYS!
HER BOYS...

—SKIP AHEAD A FEW HOURS IN THE *TARDIS!* JUST TO THE END OF THE NIGHT, BEFORE AMY GETS DONE SIGHTSEEING.

A PERFECTLY ROUTINE TIME JUMP—NOT EVEN A JUMP REALLY, MORE OF A TIME HOP!

WHAT COULD GO WRONG?

WHAT COULD GO *WRONG?* OH, I DON'T KNOW, HOW ABOUT—

—COMING BACK TO MY WIFE *36 YEARS* TOO LATE?

AGAIN?

OH, COME ON RORY! WHEN ARE YOU GOING TO LET THAT GO? THAT WAS—

—I WAS GOING TO SAY 200 YEARS AGO, BUT I SUPPOSE IT'S BEEN SOMEWHAT SHORTER FOR YOU, SO—

LET IT GO? YOUR WHOLE HISTORY WITH AMY IS YOU SHOWING UP *YEARS LATE!*

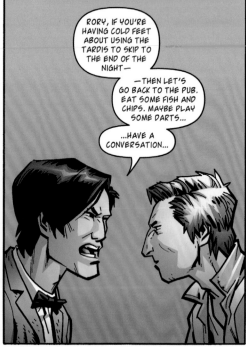

RORY, IF YOU'RE HAVING COLD FEET ABOUT USING THE TARDIS TO SKIP TO THE END OF THE NIGHT—

—THEN LET'S GO BACK TO THE PUB. EAT SOME FISH AND CHIPS. MAYBE PLAY SOME DARTS...

...HAVE A CONVERSATION...

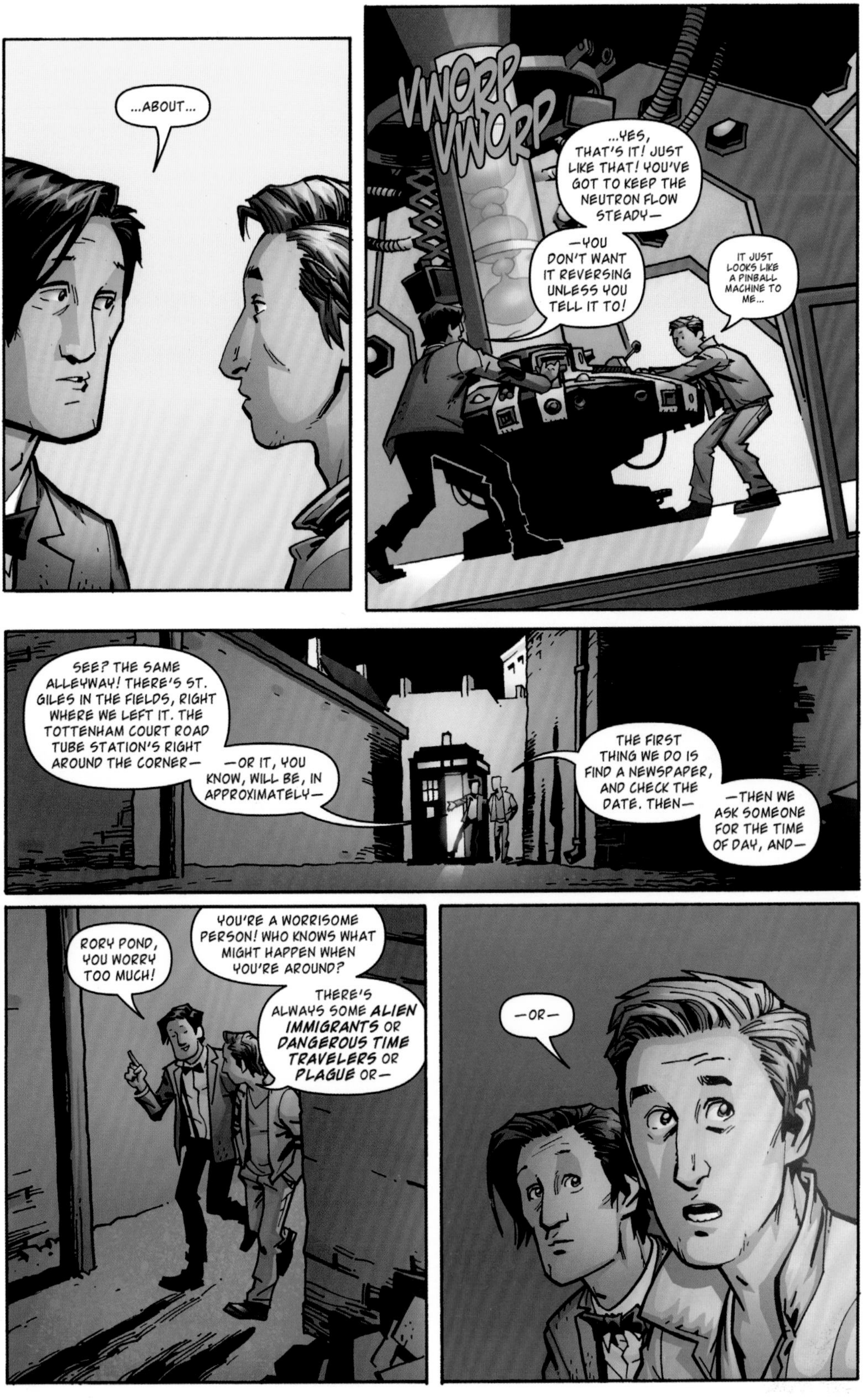
...ABOUT...
VWORP VWORP
...YES, THAT'S IT! JUST LIKE THAT! YOU'VE GOT TO KEEP THE NEUTRON FLOW STEADY—
—YOU DON'T WANT IT REVERSING UNLESS YOU TELL IT TO!
IT JUST LOOKS LIKE A PINBALL MACHINE TO ME...
SEE? THE SAME ALLEYWAY! THERE'S ST. GILES IN THE FIELDS, RIGHT WHERE WE LEFT IT. THE TOTTENHAM COURT ROAD TUBE STATION'S RIGHT AROUND THE CORNER—
—OR IT, YOU KNOW, WILL BE, IN APPROXIMATELY—
THE FIRST THING WE DO IS FIND A NEWSPAPER, AND CHECK THE DATE. THEN—
—THEN WE ASK SOMEONE FOR THE TIME OF DAY, AND—
RORY POND, YOU WORRY TOO MUCH!
YOU'RE A WORRISOME PERSON! WHO KNOWS WHAT MIGHT HAPPEN WHEN YOU'RE AROUND?
THERE'S ALWAYS SOME ALIEN IMMIGRANTS OR DANGEROUS TIME TRAVELERS OR PLAGUE OR—
—OR—

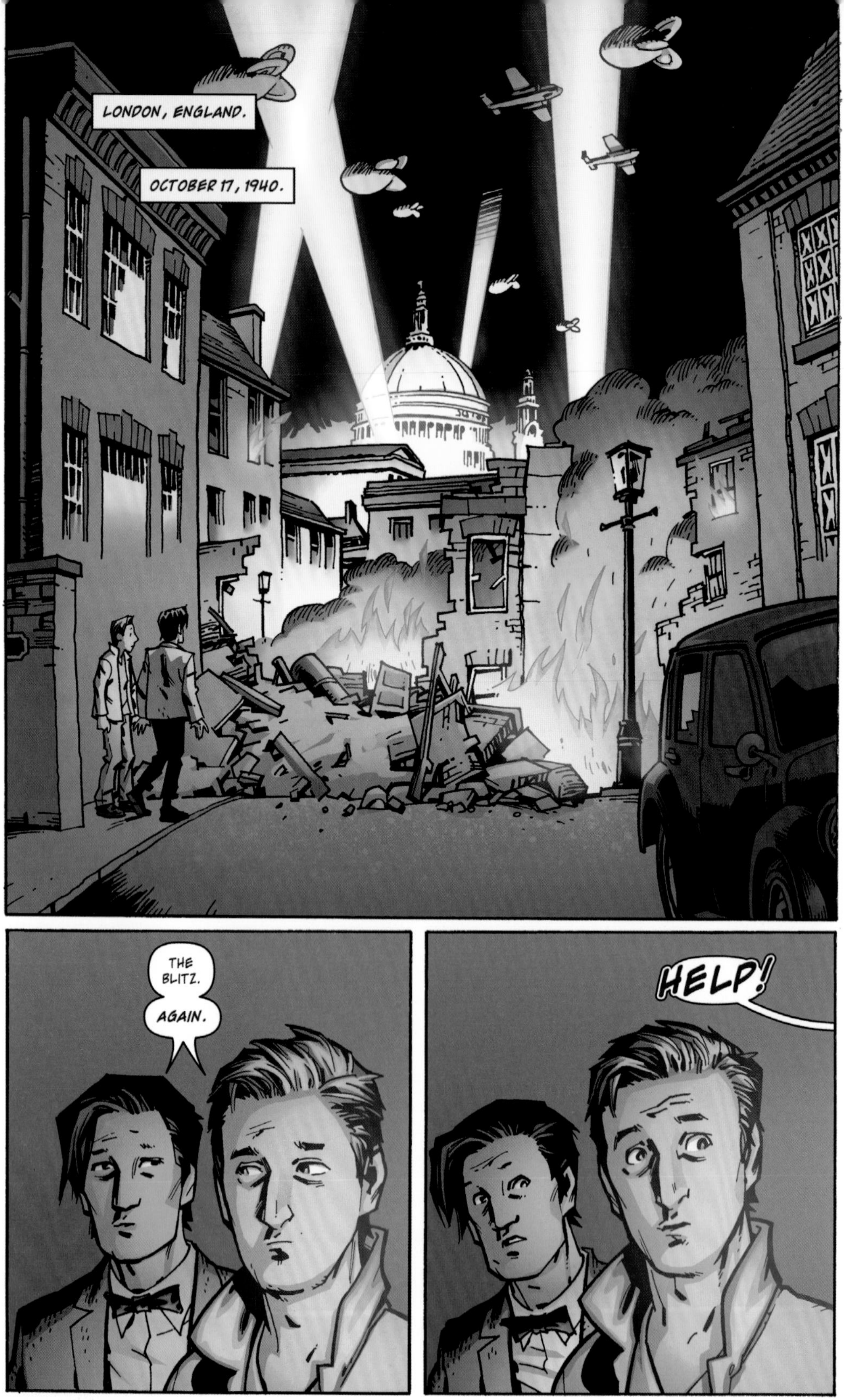
LONDON, ENGLAND.
OCTOBER 17, 1940.
THE BLITZ.
AGAIN.
HELP!

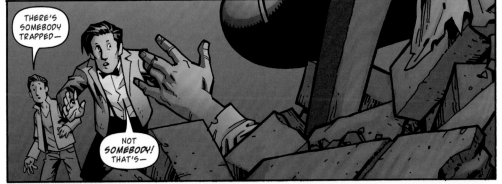

THERE'S SOMEBODY TRAPPED—

NOT SOMEBODY! THAT'S—

—IAN FLEMING!

THE GUY WHO CREATED *JAMES BOND?*

THE GUY WHO WILL CREATE JAMES BOND—IN ABOUT TEN YEARS—

—IF HE LIVES THROUGH TONIGHT!

BUT... WHAT'S IAN FLEMING DOING HERE?

IN WORLD WAR II, HE WASN'T A NOVELIST YET—

—HE WAS A *SPY!* HE'S PROBABLY HERE DOING, YOU KNOW, SPY THINGS!

NO, I MEAN—WHAT ARE THE ODDS THAT HE'D BE *RIGHT HERE* WHEN WE SHOW UP?

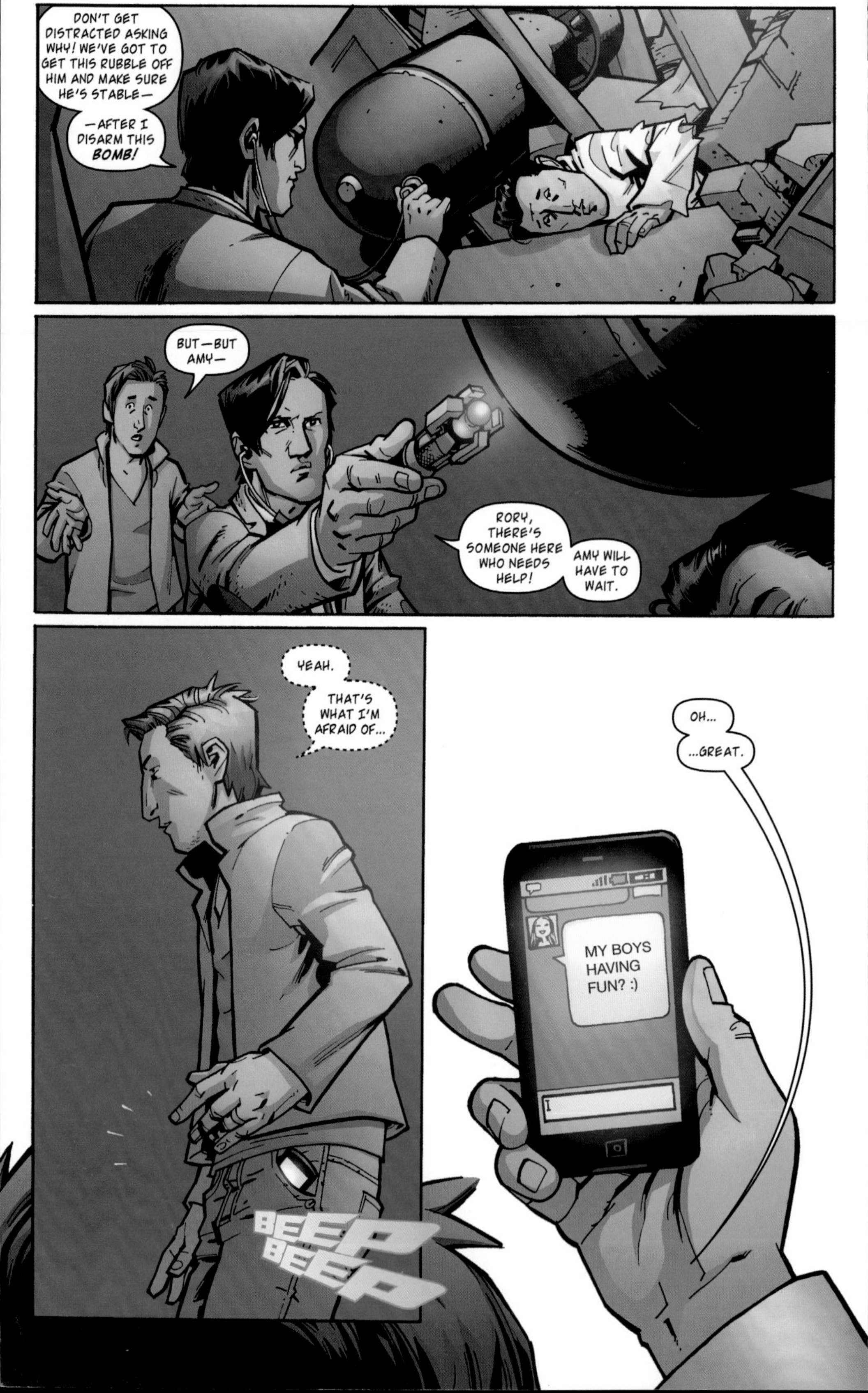
DON'T GET DISTRACTED ASKING WHY! WE'VE GOT TO GET THIS RUBBLE OFF HIM AND MAKE SURE HE'S STABLE—
—AFTER I DISARM THIS BOMB!
BUT—BUT AMY—
RORY, THERE'S SOMEONE HERE WHO NEEDS HELP!
AMY WILL HAVE TO WAIT.
YEAH.
THAT'S WHAT I'M AFRAID OF...
BEEP BEEP
MY BOYS HAVING FUN? :)
OH...
...GREAT.

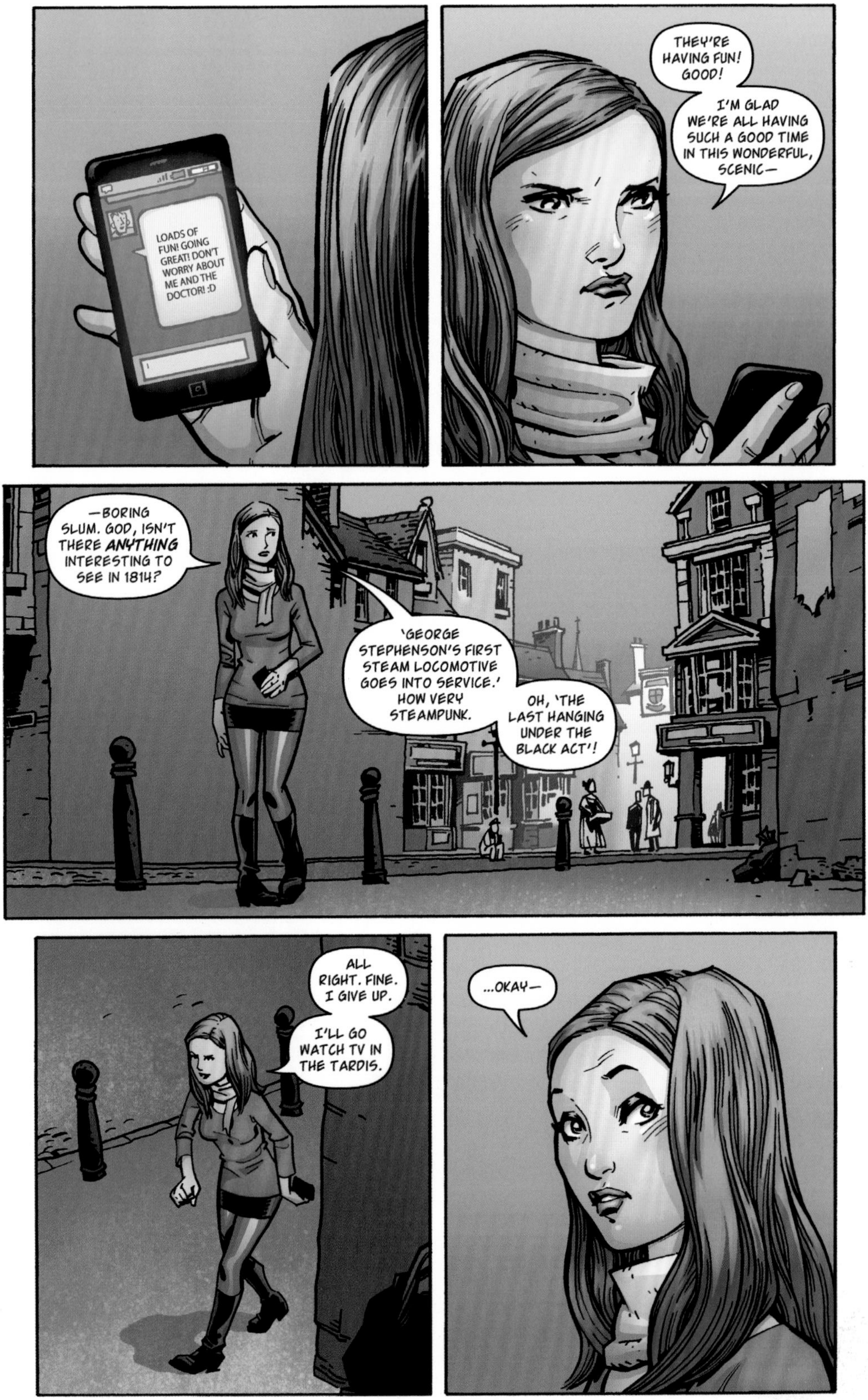
LOADS OF FUN! GOING GREAT! DON'T WORRY ABOUT ME AND THE DOCTOR! :D
THEY'RE HAVING FUN! GOOD!
I'M GLAD WE'RE ALL HAVING SUCH A GOOD TIME IN THIS WONDERFUL, SCENIC—
—BORING SLUM. GOD, ISN'T THERE ANYTHING INTERESTING TO SEE IN 1814?
'GEORGE STEPHENSON'S FIRST STEAM LOCOMOTIVE GOES INTO SERVICE.' HOW VERY STEAMPUNK.
OH, 'THE LAST HANGING UNDER THE BLACK ACT'!
ALL RIGHT. FINE. I GIVE UP.
I'LL GO WATCH TV IN THE TARDIS.
...OKAY—

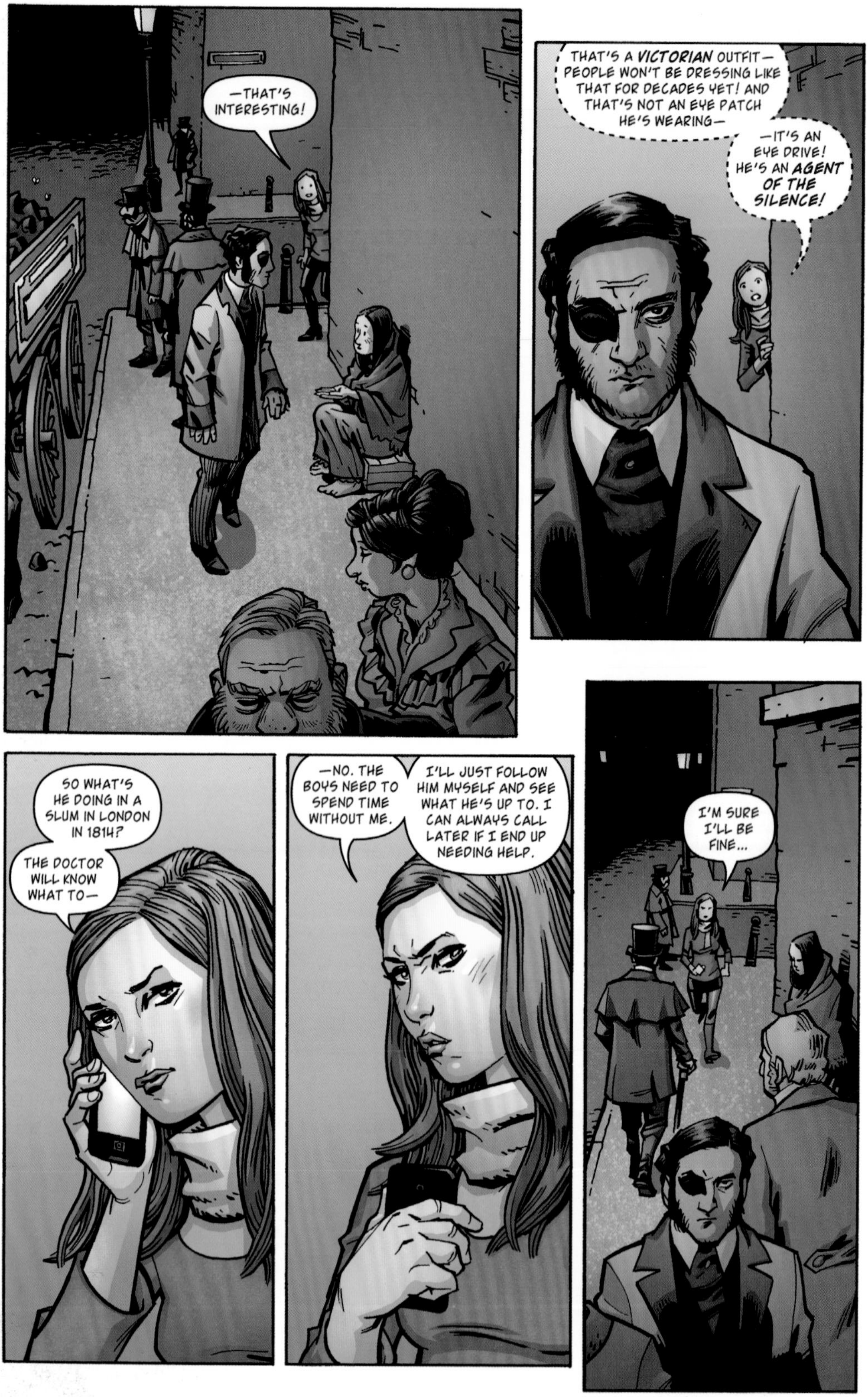
—THAT'S INTERESTING!
THAT'S A VICTORIAN OUTFIT— PEOPLE WON'T BE DRESSING LIKE THAT FOR DECADES YET! AND THAT'S NOT AN EYE PATCH HE'S WEARING—
—IT'S AN EYE DRIVE! HE'S AN AGENT OF THE SILENCE!
SO WHAT'S HE DOING IN A SLUM IN LONDON IN 1814?
THE DOCTOR WILL KNOW WHAT TO—
—NO. THE BOYS NEED TO SPEND TIME WITHOUT ME.
I'LL JUST FOLLOW HIM MYSELF AND SEE WHAT HE'S UP TO. I CAN ALWAYS CALL LATER IF I END UP NEEDING HELP.
I'M SURE I'LL BE FINE...

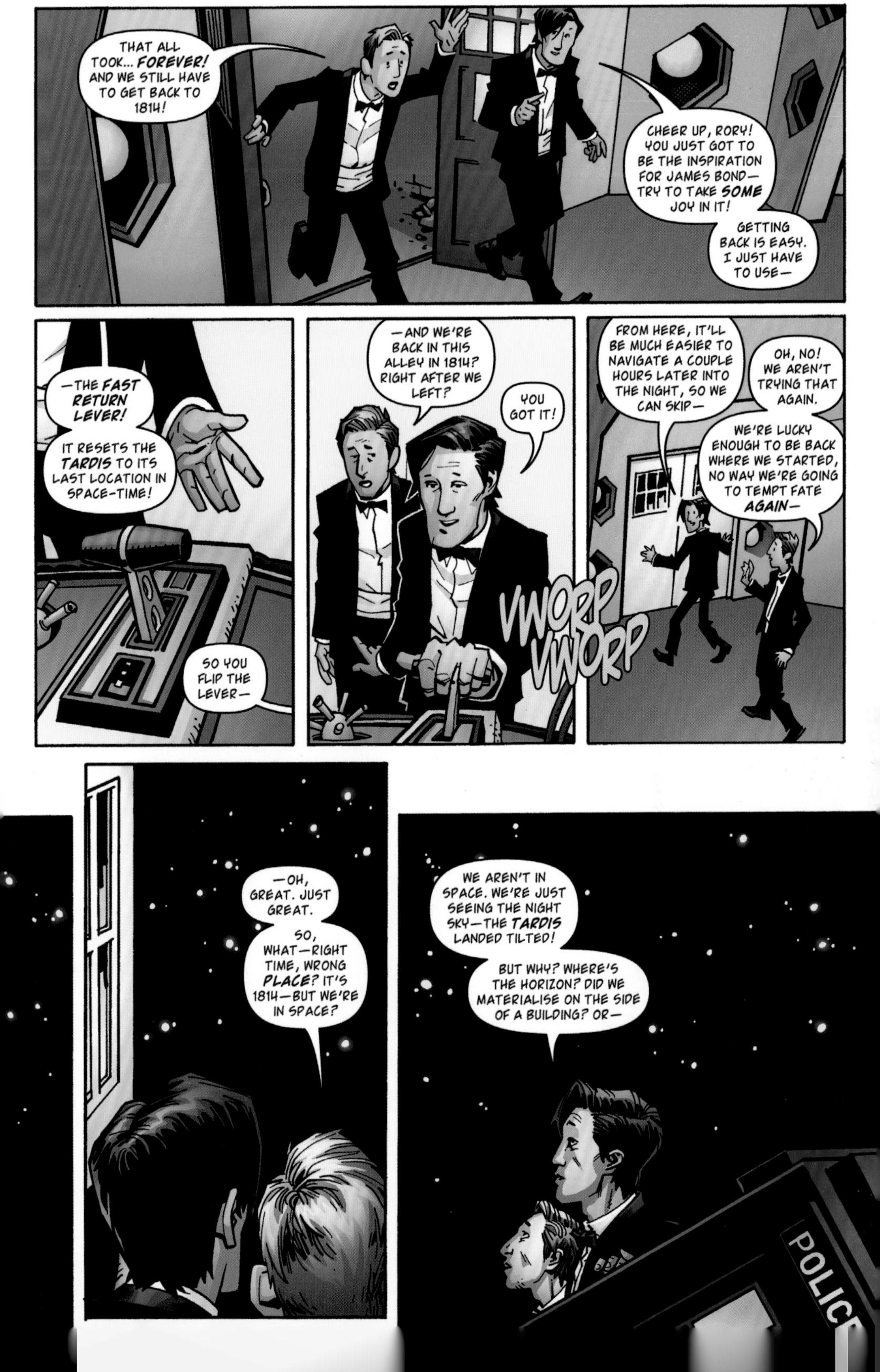
THAT ALL TOOK... FOREVER! AND WE STILL HAVE TO GET BACK TO 1814!
CHEER UP, RORY! YOU JUST GOT TO BE THE INSPIRATION FOR JAMES BOND— TRY TO TAKE SOME JOY IN IT!
GETTING BACK IS EASY. I JUST HAVE TO USE—
—THE FAST RETURN LEVER!
IT RESETS THE TARDIS TO ITS LAST LOCATION IN SPACE-TIME!
SO YOU FLIP THE LEVER—
—AND WE'RE BACK IN THIS ALLEY IN 1814? RIGHT AFTER WE LEFT?
YOU GOT IT!
VWORP VWORP
FROM HERE, IT'LL BE MUCH EASIER TO NAVIGATE A COUPLE HOURS LATER INTO THE NIGHT, SO WE CAN SKIP—
OH, NO! WE AREN'T TRYING THAT AGAIN.
WE'RE LUCKY ENOUGH TO BE BACK WHERE WE STARTED, NO WAY WE'RE GOING TO TEMPT FATE AGAIN—
—OH, GREAT. JUST GREAT.
SO, WHAT—RIGHT TIME, WRONG PLACE? IT'S 1814—BUT WE'RE IN SPACE?
WE AREN'T IN SPACE. WE'RE JUST SEEING THE NIGHT SKY—THE TARDIS LANDED TILTED!
BUT WHY? WHERE'S THE HORIZON? DID WE MATERIALISE ON THE SIDE OF A BUILDING? OR—
POLIC

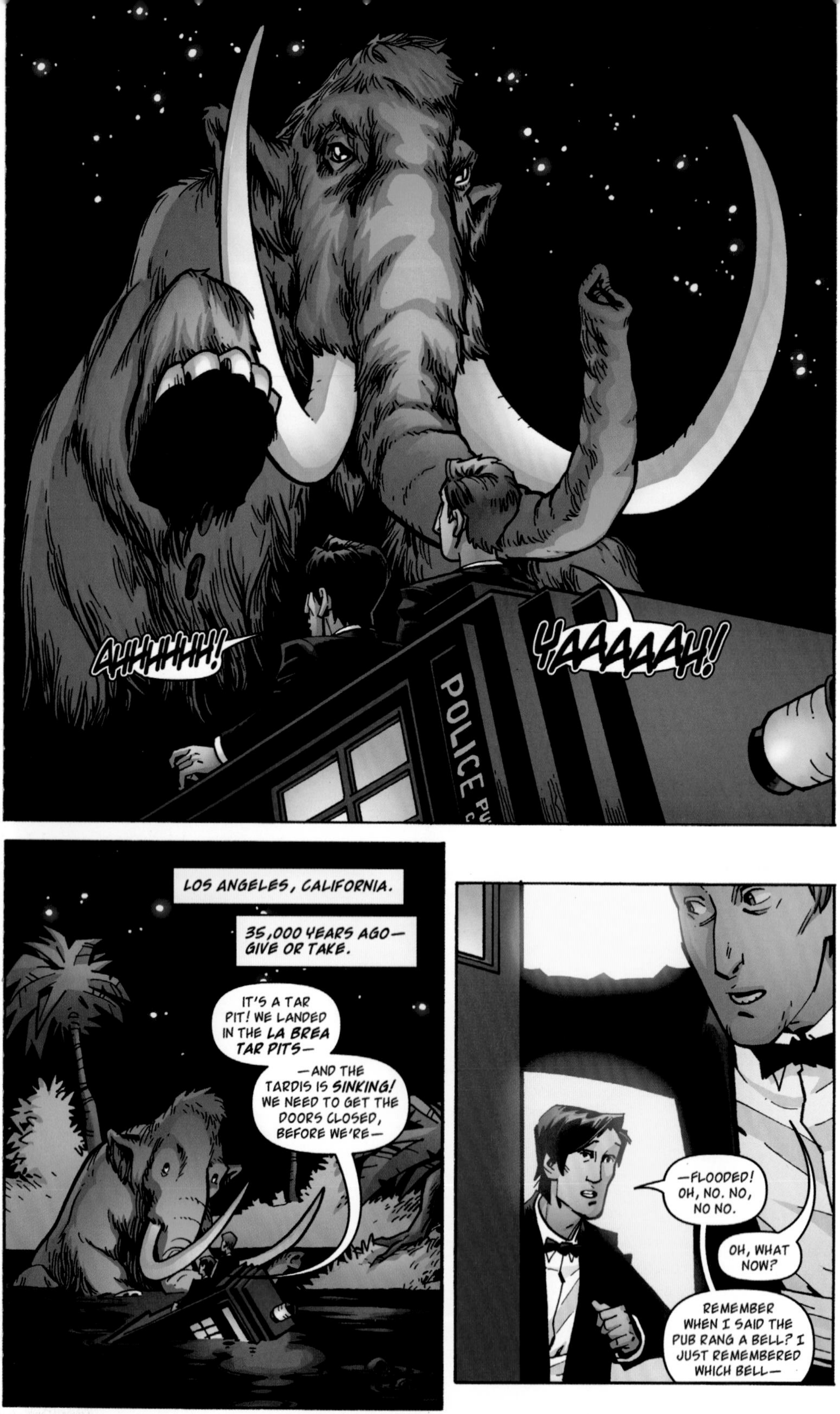
AHHHHHH!
YAAAAAH!
POLICE
LOS ANGELES, CALIFORNIA.
35,000 YEARS AGO— GIVE OR TAKE.
IT'S A TAR PIT! WE LANDED IN THE LA BREA TAR PITS—
—AND THE TARDIS IS SINKING! WE NEED TO GET THE DOORS CLOSED, BEFORE WE'RE—
—FLOODED! OH, NO. NO, NO NO.
OH, WHAT NOW?
REMEMBER WHEN I SAID THE PUB RANG A BELL? I JUST REMEMBERED WHICH BELL—

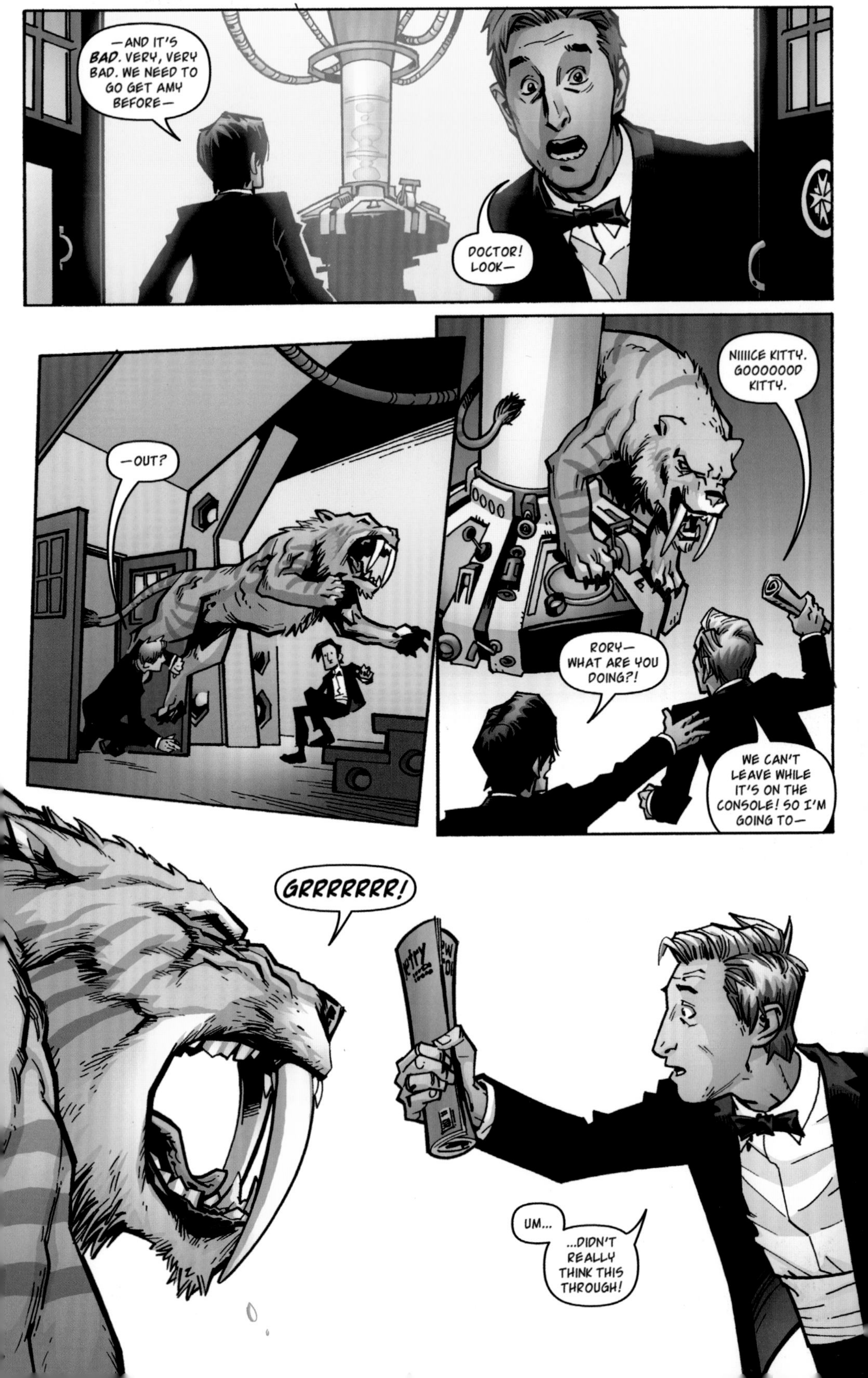
—AND IT'S BAD. VERY, VERY BAD. WE NEED TO GO GET AMY BEFORE—
DOCTOR! LOOK—
—OUT?
NIIIICE KITTY. GOOOOOOD KITTY.
RORY— WHAT ARE YOU DOING?!
WE CAN'T LEAVE WHILE IT'S ON THE CONSOLE! SO I'M GOING TO—
GRRRRRRR!
UM...
...DIDN'T REALLY THINK THIS THROUGH!

WHAP

MEW?

RORY—

—YOU JUST HIT A SABERTOOTH WITH A MAGAZINE!

I THOUGHT IT WAS GOING TO—UH—SABERBITE ME!

IT'S OFF THE CONSOLE—COULD YOU GET US OUT OF THE TAR PIT AND BACK TO AMY? I'LL GO—UH, CATCH IT OR SOMETHING?

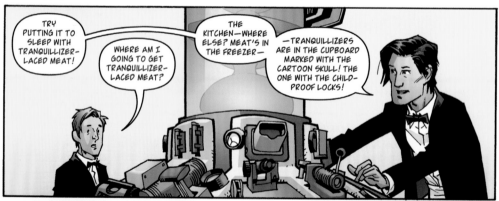

TRY PUTTING IT TO SLEEP WITH TRANQUILLIZER-LACED MEAT!

WHERE AM I GOING TO GET TRANQUILLIZER-LACED MEAT?

THE KITCHEN—WHERE ELSE? MEAT'S IN THE FREEZER—

—TRANQUILLIZERS ARE IN THE CUPBOARD MARKED WITH THE CARTOON SKULL! THE ONE WITH THE CHILD-PROOF LOCKS!

'PERFECTLY ROUTINE'—I SHOULD'VE FIGURED THAT'S DOCTOR-ESE FOR 'EXCEEDINGLY DANGEROUS'...

...I HOPE AMY'S OKAY.

AND TRY NOT TO DIE FOR ONCE!

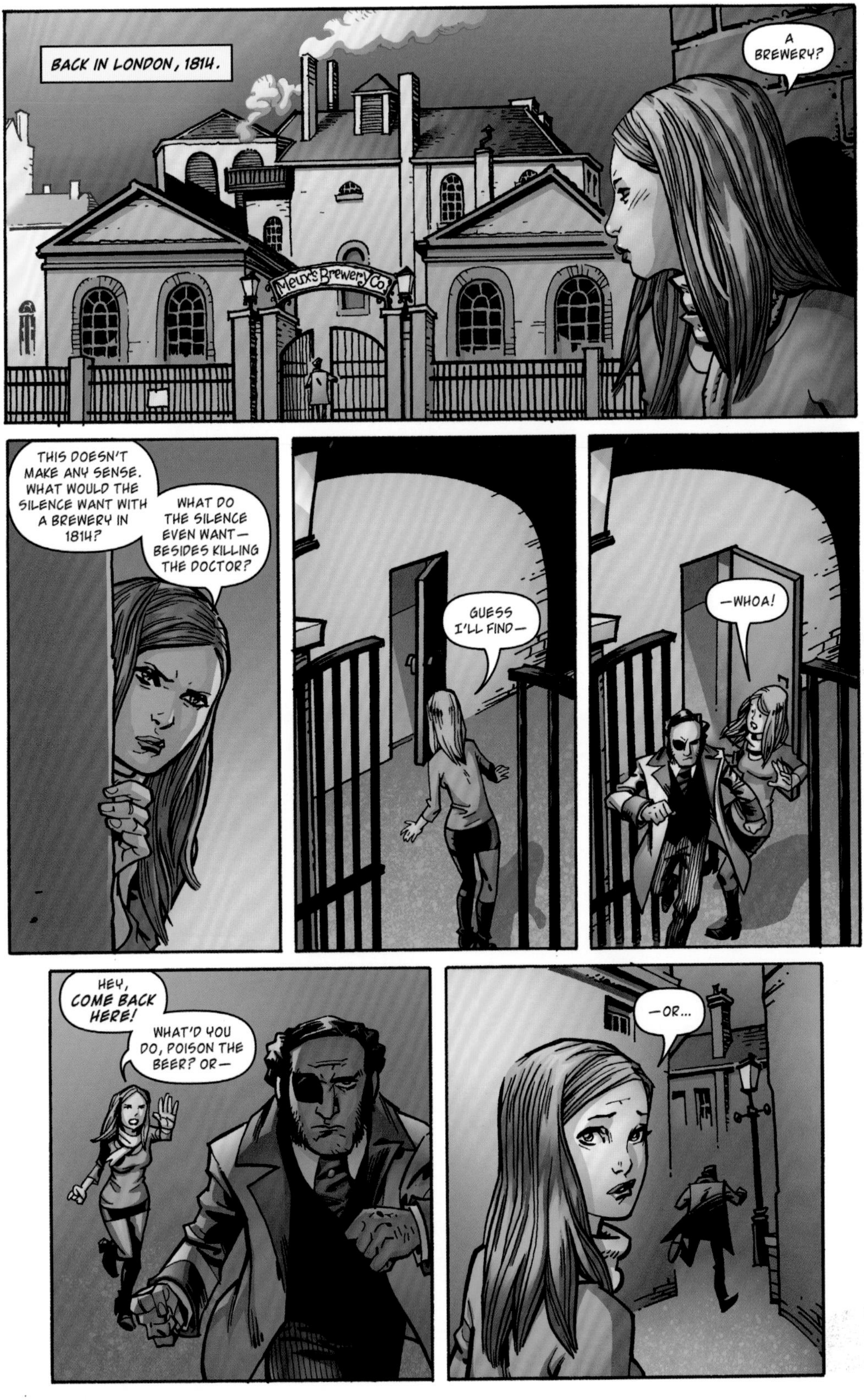

BACK IN LONDON, 1814.
A BREWERY?
Meux's Brewery Co.
THIS DOESN'T MAKE ANY SENSE. WHAT WOULD THE SILENCE WANT WITH A BREWERY IN 1814?
WHAT DO THE SILENCE EVEN WANT—BESIDES KILLING THE DOCTOR?
GUESS I'LL FIND—
—WHOA!
HEY, COME BACK HERE!
WHAT'D YOU DO, POISON THE BEER? OR—
—OR...

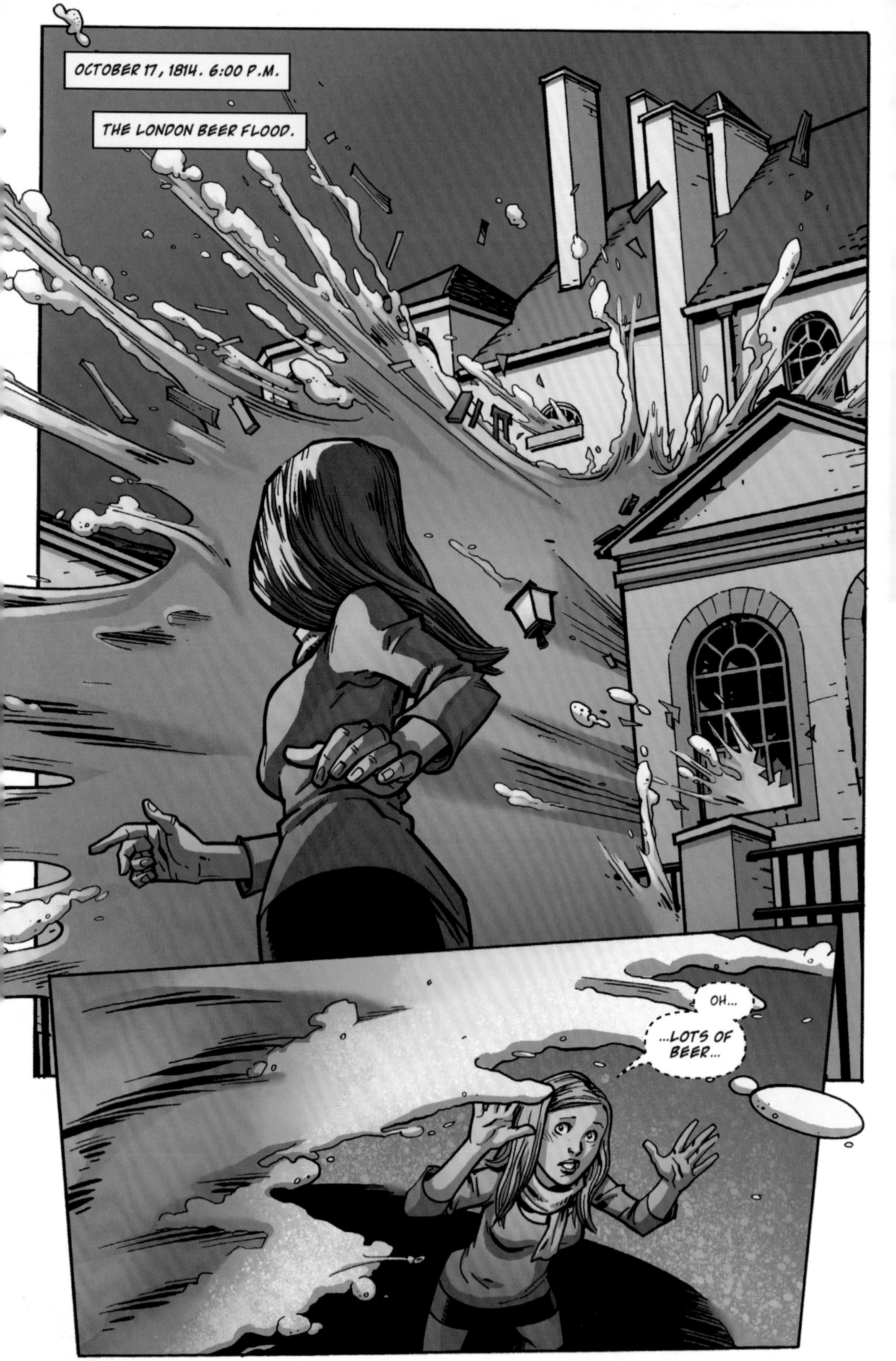
OCTOBER 17, 1814. 6:00 P.M.
THE LONDON BEER FLOOD.
OH...
...LOTS OF BEER...

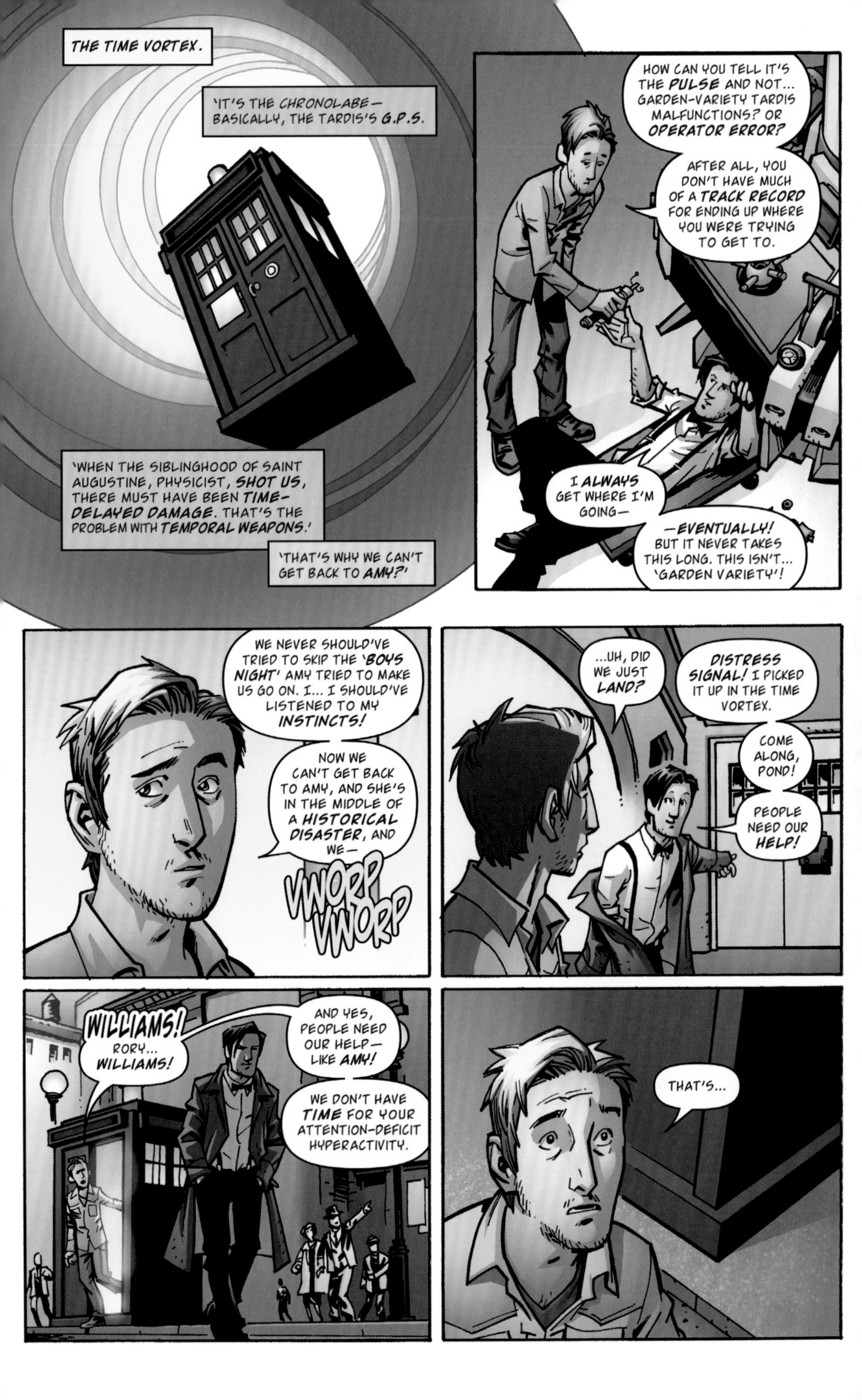
THE TIME VORTEX.
'IT'S THE CHRONOLABE— BASICALLY, THE TARDIS'S G.P.S.
'WHEN THE SIBLINGHOOD OF SAINT AUGUSTINE, PHYSICIST, SHOT US, THERE MUST HAVE BEEN TIME-DELAYED DAMAGE. THAT'S THE PROBLEM WITH TEMPORAL WEAPONS.'
'THAT'S WHY WE CAN'T GET BACK TO AMY?'
HOW CAN YOU TELL IT'S THE PULSE AND NOT... GARDEN-VARIETY TARDIS MALFUNCTIONS? OR OPERATOR ERROR?
AFTER ALL, YOU DON'T HAVE MUCH OF A TRACK RECORD FOR ENDING UP WHERE YOU WERE TRYING TO GET TO.
I ALWAYS GET WHERE I'M GOING—
—EVENTUALLY! BUT IT NEVER TAKES THIS LONG. THIS ISN'T... 'GARDEN VARIETY'!
WE NEVER SHOULD'VE TRIED TO SKIP THE 'BOYS NIGHT' AMY TRIED TO MAKE US GO ON. I... I SHOULD'VE LISTENED TO MY INSTINCTS!
NOW WE CAN'T GET BACK TO AMY, AND SHE'S IN THE MIDDLE OF A HISTORICAL DISASTER, AND WE—
VWORP VWORP
...UH, DID WE JUST LAND?
DISTRESS SIGNAL! I PICKED IT UP IN THE TIME VORTEX.
COME ALONG, POND!
PEOPLE NEED OUR HELP!
WILLIAMS! RORY... WILLIAMS!
AND YES, PEOPLE NEED OUR HELP— LIKE AMY!
WE DON'T HAVE TIME FOR YOUR ATTENTION-DEFICIT HYPERACTIVITY.
THAT'S...

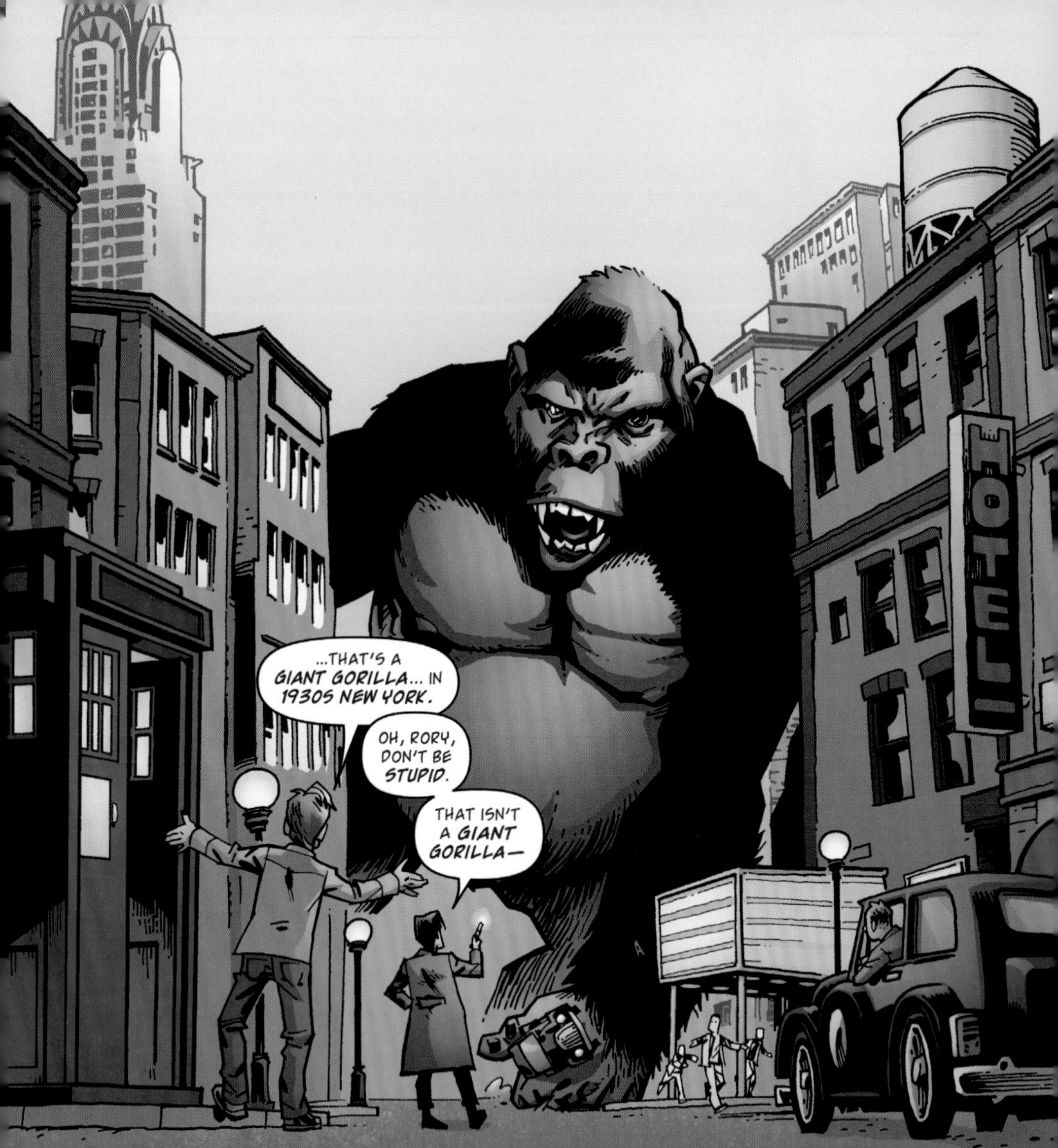
...THAT'S A GIANT GORILLA... IN 1930S NEW YORK.
OH, RORY, DON'T BE STUPID.
THAT ISN'T A GIANT GORILLA—
HOTEL

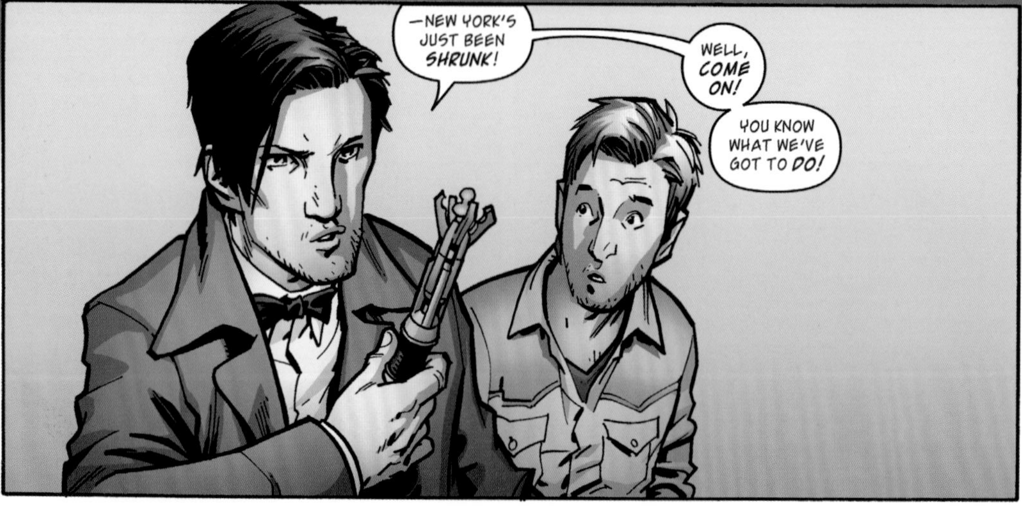
—NEW YORK'S JUST BEEN SHRUNK!
WELL, COME ON!
YOU KNOW WHAT WE'VE GOT TO DO!

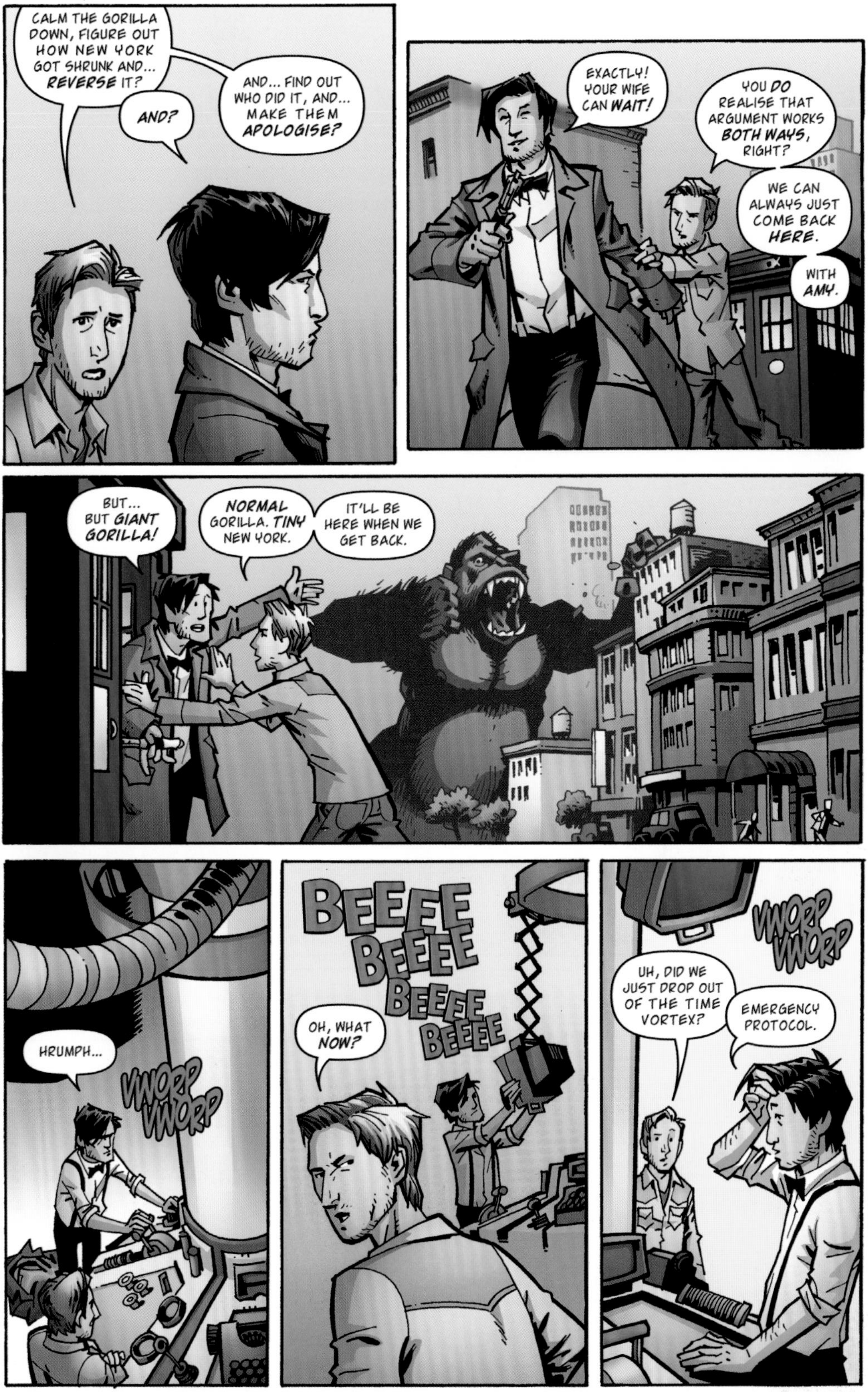
CALM THE GORILLA DOWN, FIGURE OUT HOW NEW YORK GOT SHRUNK AND... REVERSE IT?
AND?
AND... FIND OUT WHO DID IT, AND... MAKE THEM APOLOGISE?
EXACTLY! YOUR WIFE CAN WAIT!
YOU DO REALISE THAT ARGUMENT WORKS BOTH WAYS, RIGHT?
WE CAN ALWAYS JUST COME BACK HERE.
WITH AMY.
BUT... BUT GIANT GORILLA!
NORMAL GORILLA. TINY NEW YORK.
IT'LL BE HERE WHEN WE GET BACK.
HRUMPH...
VWORP VWORP
BEEEE BEEEE BEEEE BEEEE
OH, WHAT NOW?
VWORP VWORP
UH, DID WE JUST DROP OUT OF THE TIME VORTEX?
EMERGENCY PROTOCOL.

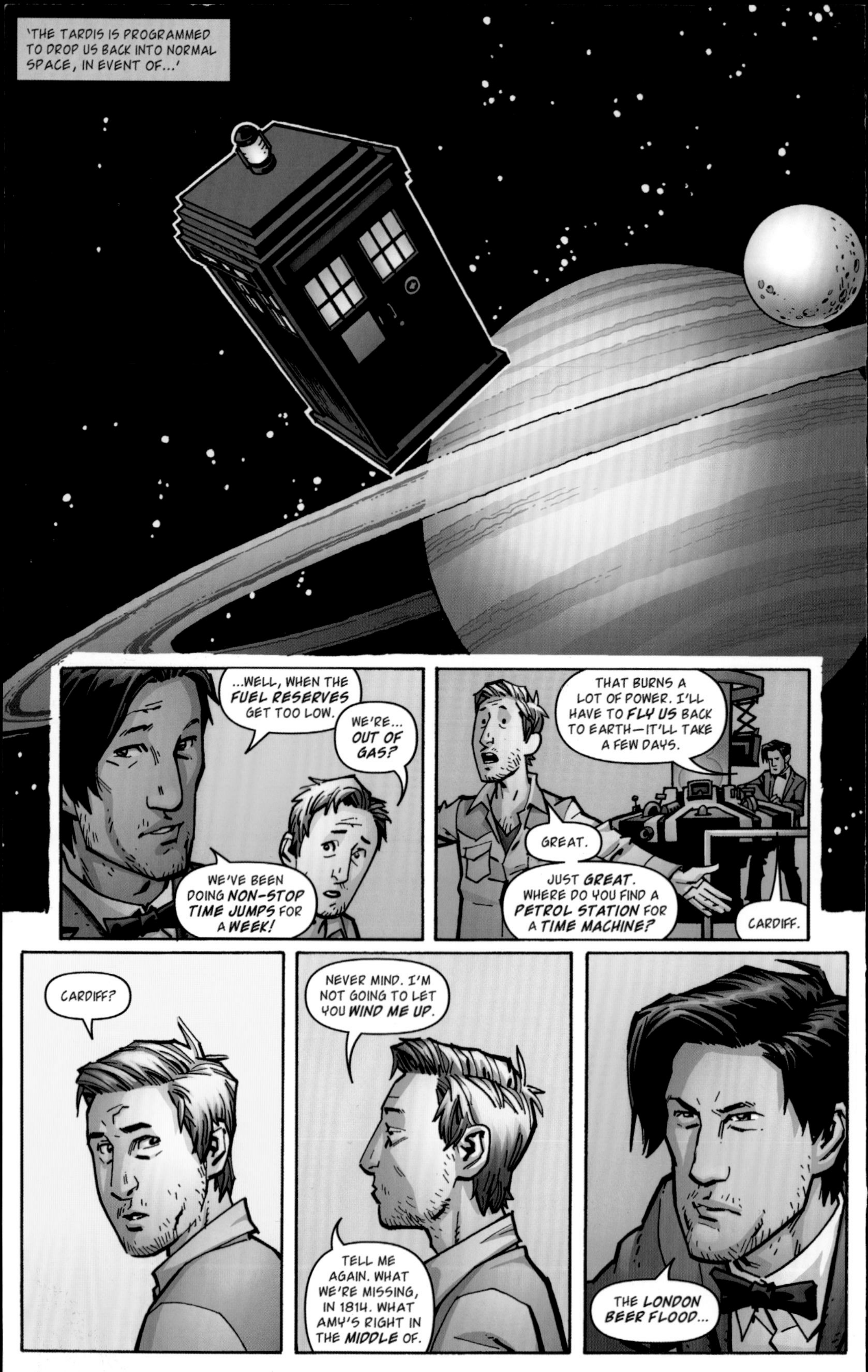
'THE TARDIS IS PROGRAMMED TO DROP US BACK INTO NORMAL SPACE, IN EVENT OF...'
...WELL, WHEN THE FUEL RESERVES GET TOO LOW.
WE'RE... OUT OF GAS?
WE'VE BEEN DOING NON-STOP TIME JUMPS FOR A WEEK!
THAT BURNS A LOT OF POWER. I'LL HAVE TO FLY US BACK TO EARTH—IT'LL TAKE A FEW DAYS.
GREAT.
JUST GREAT. WHERE DO YOU FIND A PETROL STATION FOR A TIME MACHINE?
CARDIFF.
CARDIFF?
NEVER MIND. I'M NOT GOING TO LET YOU WIND ME UP.
TELL ME AGAIN. WHAT WE'RE MISSING, IN 1814. WHAT AMY'S RIGHT IN THE MIDDLE OF.
THE LONDON BEER FLOOD...

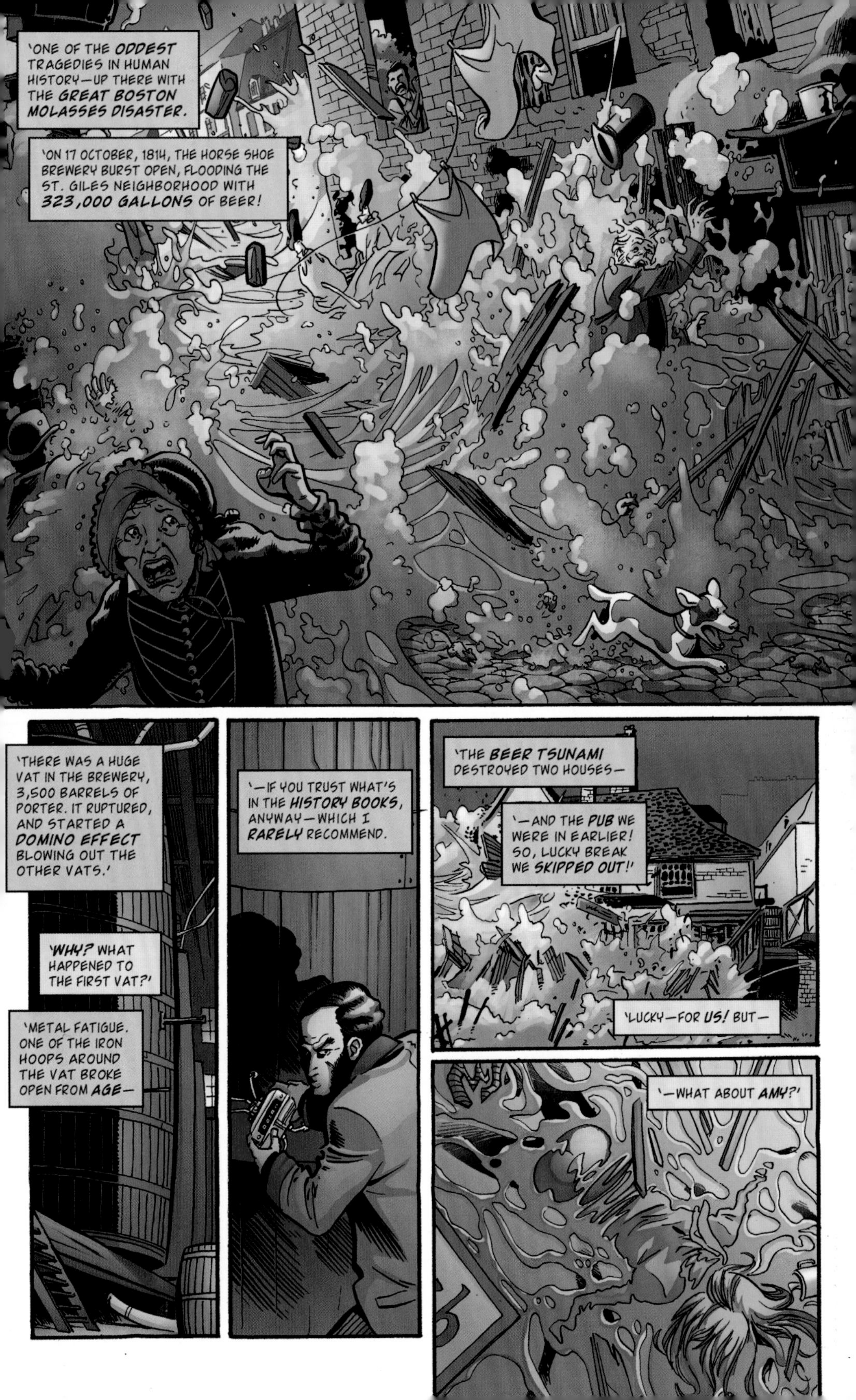
'ONE OF THE ODDEST TRAGEDIES IN HUMAN HISTORY—UP THERE WITH THE GREAT BOSTON MOLASSES DISASTER.
'ON 17 OCTOBER, 1814, THE HORSE SHOE BREWERY BURST OPEN, FLOODING THE ST. GILES NEIGHBORHOOD WITH 323,000 GALLONS OF BEER!
'THERE WAS A HUGE VAT IN THE BREWERY, 3,500 BARRELS OF PORTER. IT RUPTURED, AND STARTED A DOMINO EFFECT BLOWING OUT THE OTHER VATS.'
'WHY? WHAT HAPPENED TO THE FIRST VAT?'
'METAL FATIGUE. ONE OF THE IRON HOOPS AROUND THE VAT BROKE OPEN FROM AGE—
'—IF YOU TRUST WHAT'S IN THE HISTORY BOOKS, ANYWAY—WHICH I RARELY RECOMMEND.
'THE BEER TSUNAMI DESTROYED TWO HOUSES—
'—AND THE PUB WE WERE IN EARLIER! SO, LUCKY BREAK WE SKIPPED OUT!'
'LUCKY—FOR US! BUT—
'—WHAT ABOUT AMY?'

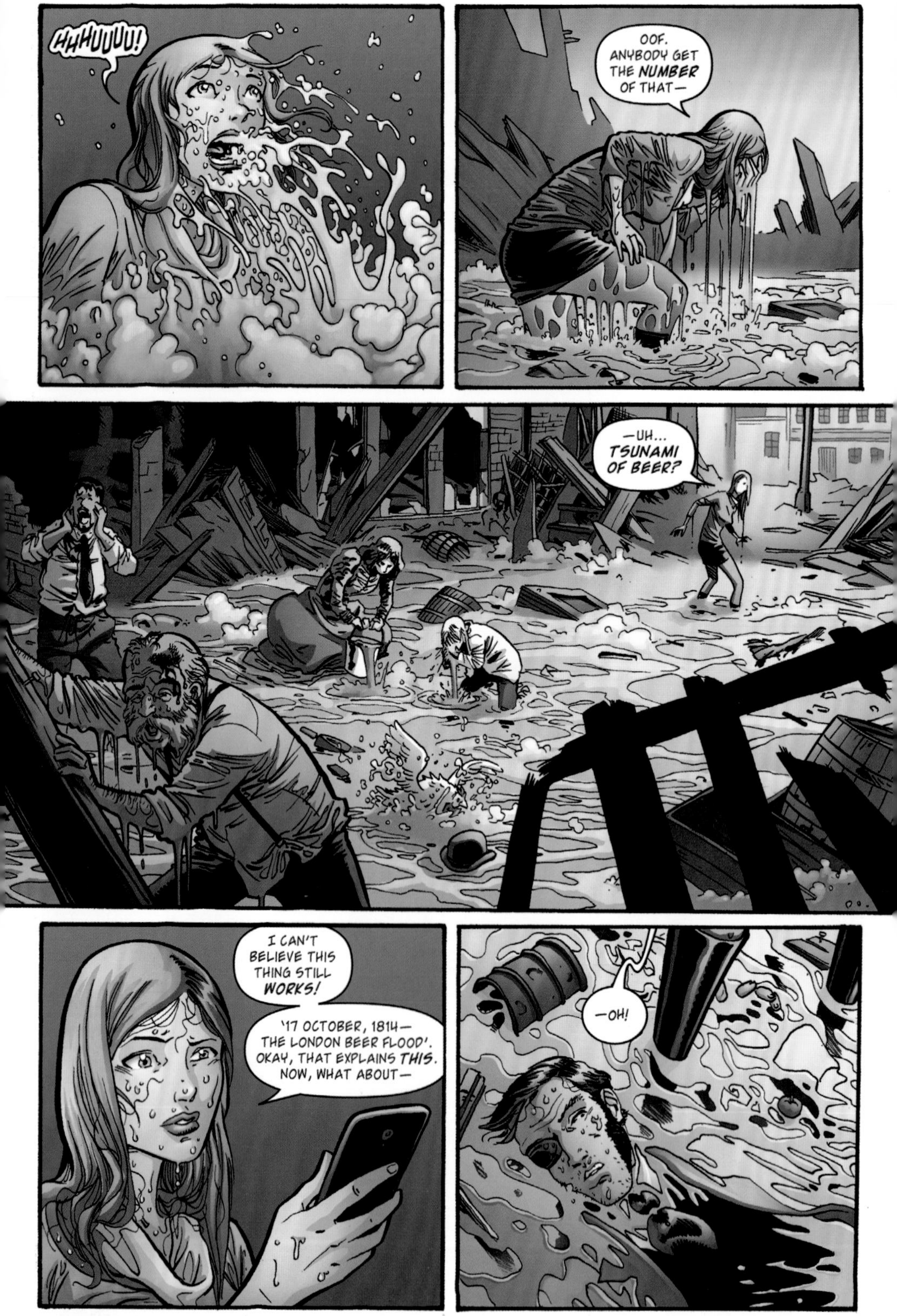
UHHUUUU!
OOF. ANYBODY GET THE NUMBER OF THAT—
—UH... TSUNAMI OF BEER?
I CAN'T BELIEVE THIS THING STILL WORKS!
'17 OCTOBER, 1814— THE LONDON BEER FLOOD'. OKAY, THAT EXPLAINS THIS. NOW, WHAT ABOUT—
—OH!

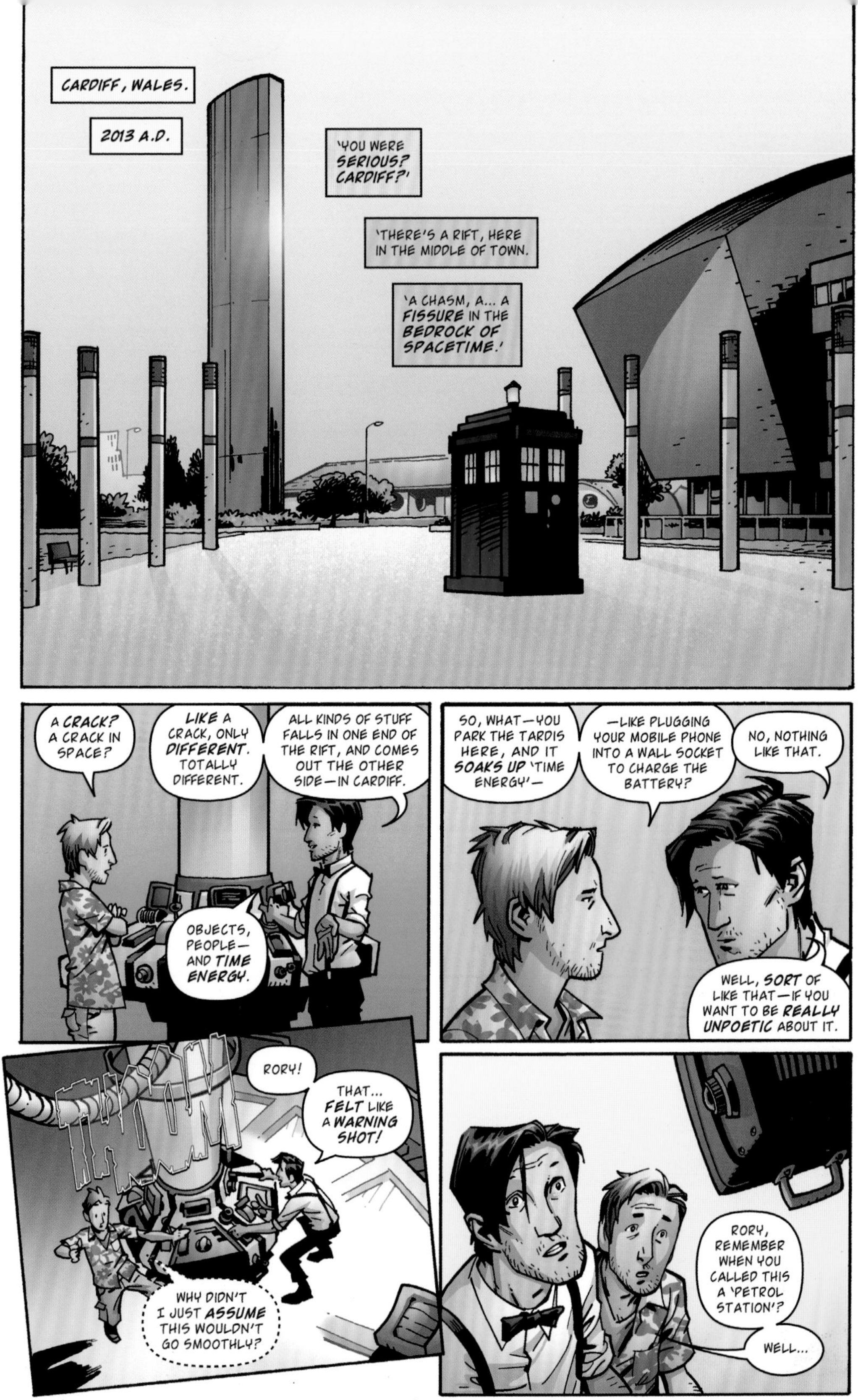
CARDIFF, WALES.
2013 A.D.
'YOU WERE SERIOUS? CARDIFF?'
'THERE'S A RIFT, HERE IN THE MIDDLE OF TOWN.
'A CHASM, A... A FISSURE IN THE BEDROCK OF SPACETIME.'
A CRACK? A CRACK IN SPACE?
LIKE A CRACK, ONLY DIFFERENT. TOTALLY DIFFERENT.
ALL KINDS OF STUFF FALLS IN ONE END OF THE RIFT, AND COMES OUT THE OTHER SIDE—IN CARDIFF.
OBJECTS, PEOPLE— AND TIME ENERGY.
SO, WHAT—YOU PARK THE TARDIS HERE, AND IT SOAKS UP 'TIME ENERGY'—
—LIKE PLUGGING YOUR MOBILE PHONE INTO A WALL SOCKET TO CHARGE THE BATTERY?
NO, NOTHING LIKE THAT.
WELL, SORT OF LIKE THAT—IF YOU WANT TO BE REALLY UNPOETIC ABOUT IT.
RORY!
THAT... FELT LIKE A WARNING SHOT!
WHY DIDN'T I JUST ASSUME THIS WOULDN'T GO SMOOTHLY?
RORY, REMEMBER WHEN YOU CALLED THIS A 'PETROL STATION'?
WELL...

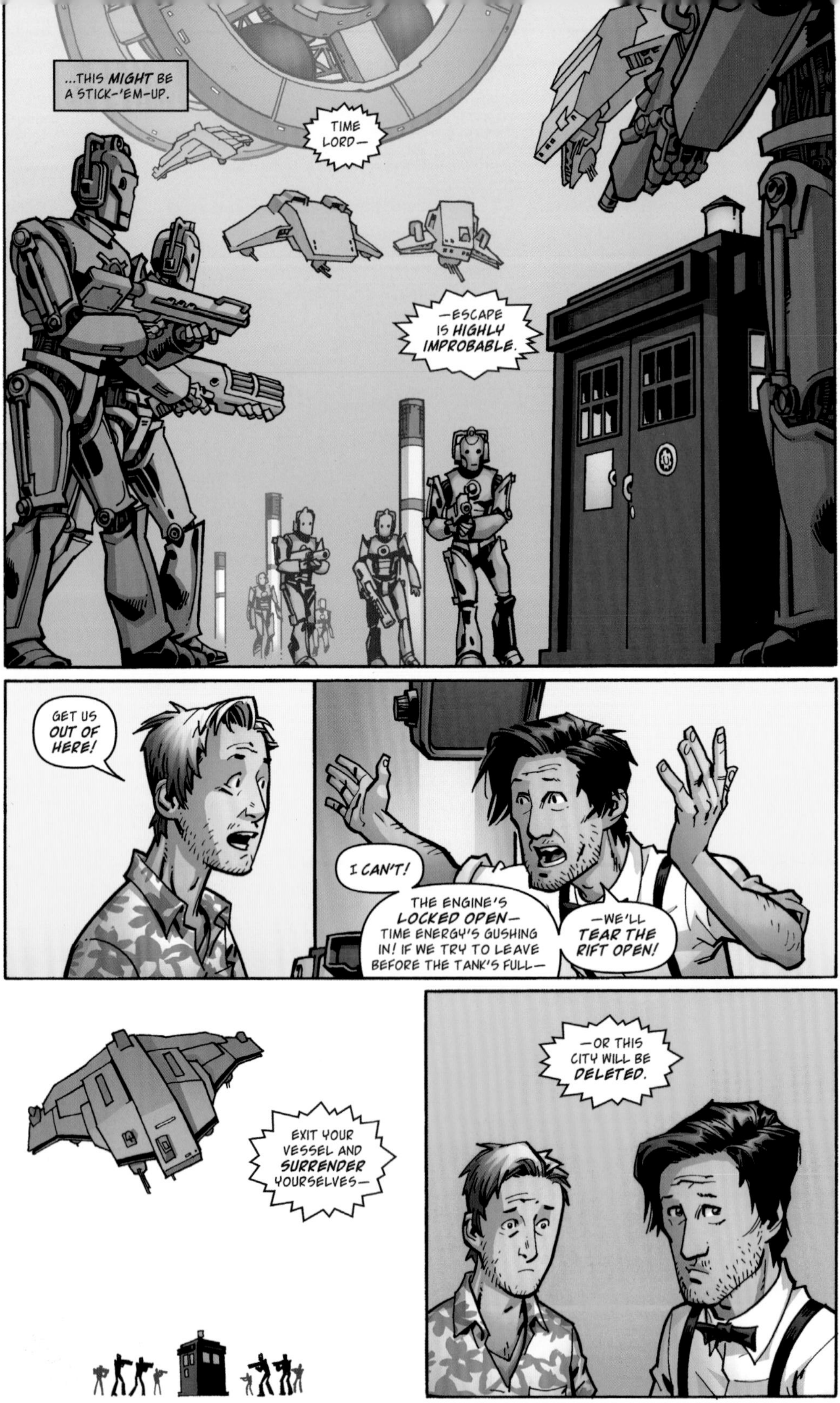

...THIS MIGHT BE A STICK-'EM-UP.
TIME LORD—
—ESCAPE IS HIGHLY IMPROBABLE.
GET US OUT OF HERE!
I CAN'T!
THE ENGINE'S LOCKED OPEN— TIME ENERGY'S GUSHING IN! IF WE TRY TO LEAVE BEFORE THE TANK'S FULL—
—WE'LL TEAR THE RIFT OPEN!
EXIT YOUR VESSEL AND SURRENDER YOURSELVES—
—OR THIS CITY WILL BE DELETED.

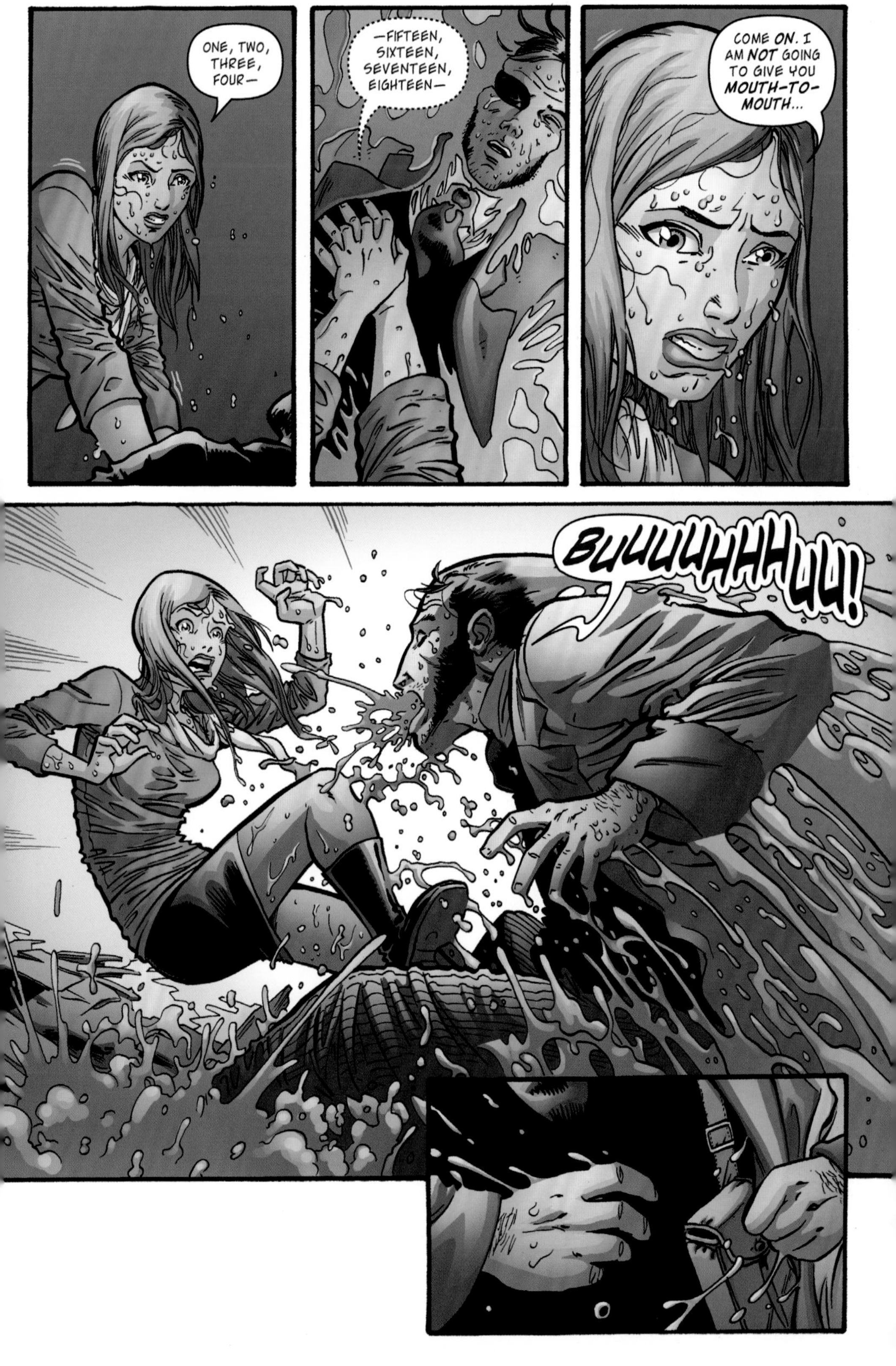
ONE, TWO, THREE, FOUR—
—FIFTEEN, SIXTEEN, SEVENTEEN, EIGHTEEN—
COME ON. I AM NOT GOING TO GIVE YOU MOUTH-TO-MOUTH...
BUUUUHHHUU!

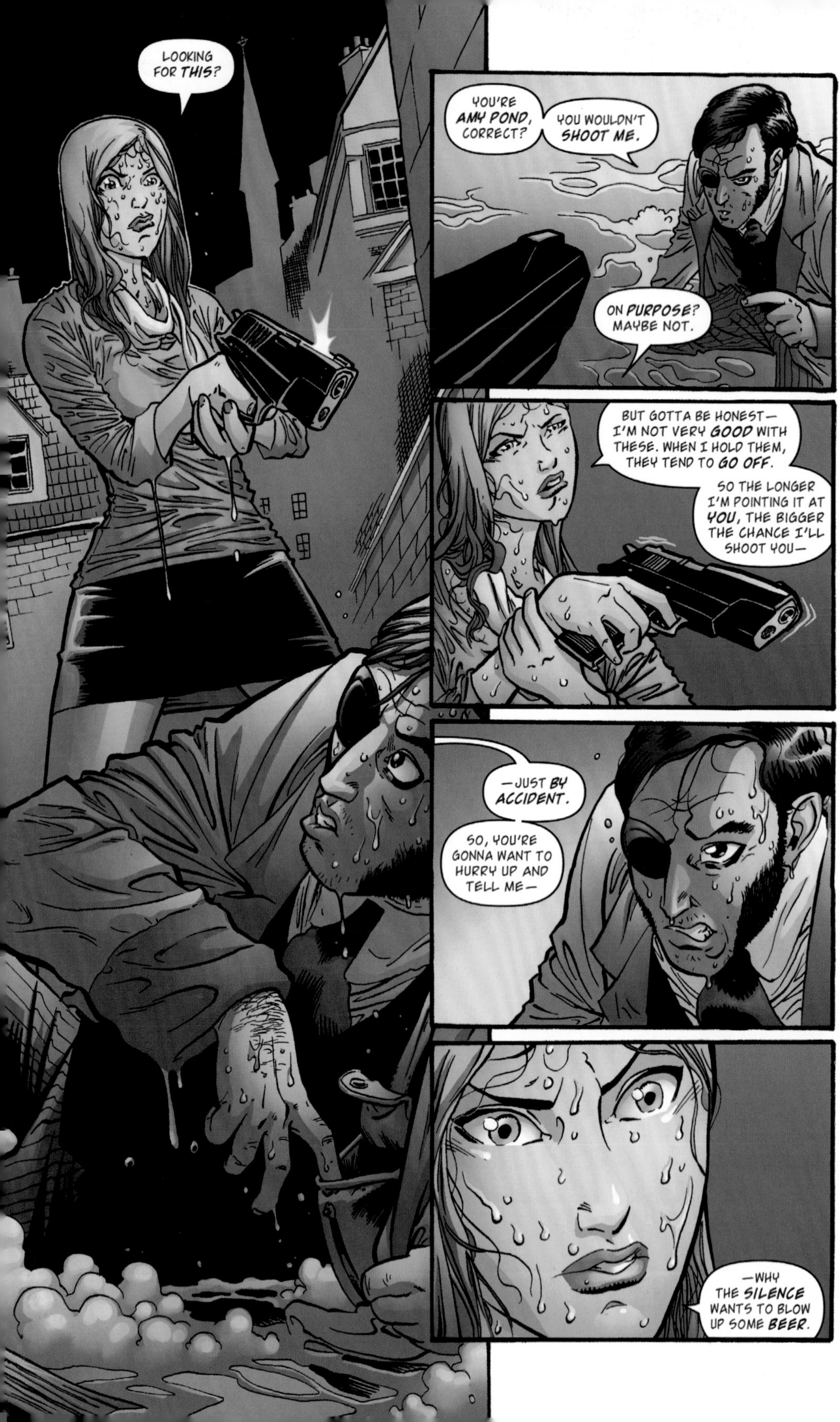
LOOKING FOR THIS?
YOU'RE AMY POND, CORRECT?
YOU WOULDN'T SHOOT ME.
ON PURPOSE? MAYBE NOT.
BUT GOTTA BE HONEST— I'M NOT VERY GOOD WITH THESE. WHEN I HOLD THEM, THEY TEND TO GO OFF.
SO THE LONGER I'M POINTING IT AT YOU, THE BIGGER THE CHANCE I'LL SHOOT YOU—
—JUST BY ACCIDENT.
SO, YOU'RE GONNA WANT TO HURRY UP AND TELL ME—
—WHY THE SILENCE WANTS TO BLOW UP SOME BEER.

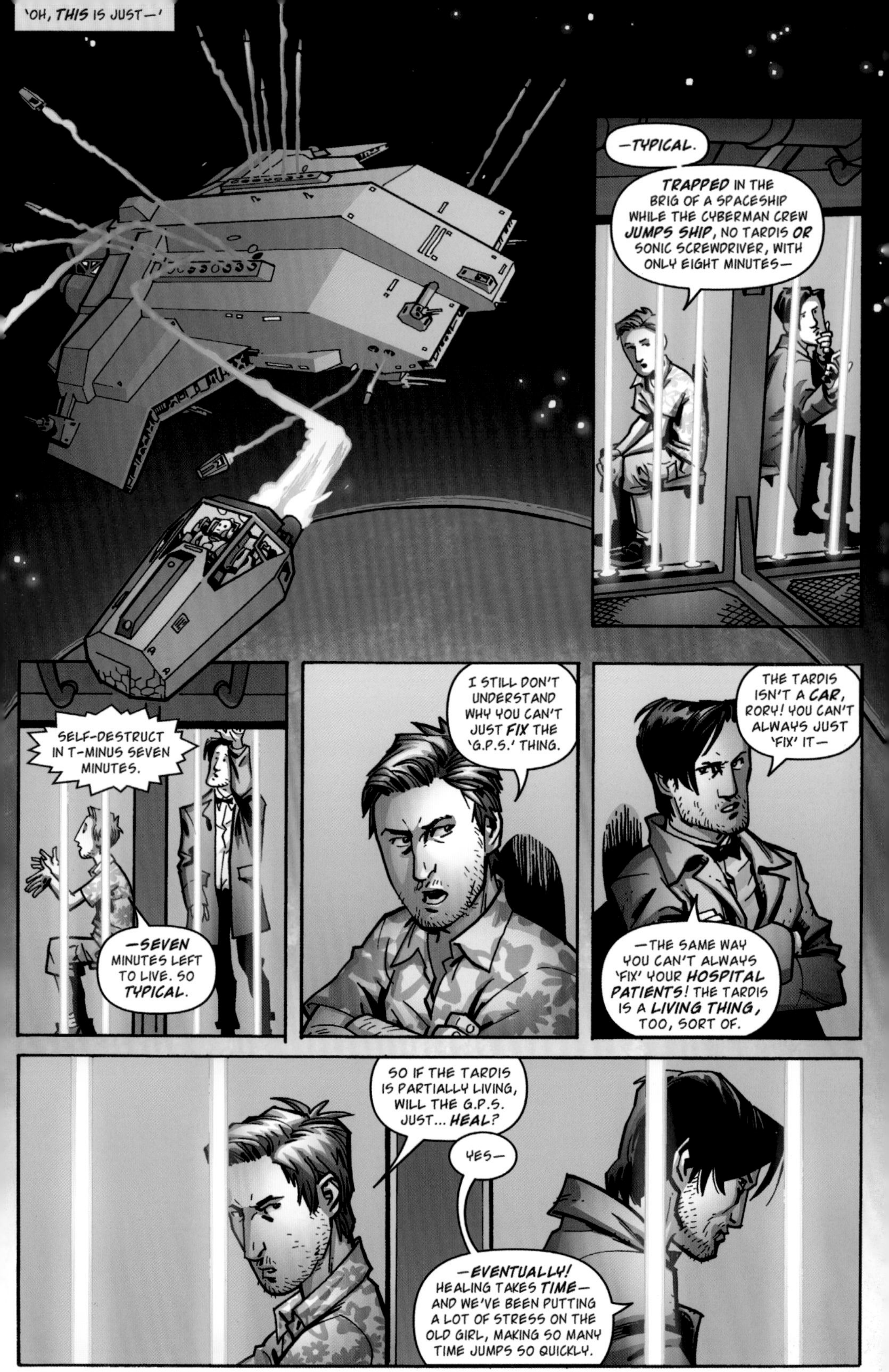
'OH, THIS IS JUST—'
—TYPICAL.
TRAPPED IN THE BRIG OF A SPACESHIP WHILE THE CYBERMAN CREW JUMPS SHIP, NO TARDIS OR SONIC SCREWDRIVER, WITH ONLY EIGHT MINUTES—
SELF-DESTRUCT IN T-MINUS SEVEN MINUTES.
—SEVEN MINUTES LEFT TO LIVE. SO TYPICAL.
I STILL DON'T UNDERSTAND WHY YOU CAN'T JUST FIX THE 'G.P.S.' THING.
THE TARDIS ISN'T A CAR, RORY! YOU CAN'T ALWAYS JUST 'FIX' IT—
—THE SAME WAY YOU CAN'T ALWAYS 'FIX' YOUR HOSPITAL PATIENTS! THE TARDIS IS A LIVING THING, TOO, SORT OF.
SO IF THE TARDIS IS PARTIALLY LIVING, WILL THE G.P.S. JUST... HEAL?
YES—
—EVENTUALLY! HEALING TAKES TIME—AND WE'VE BEEN PUTTING A LOT OF STRESS ON THE OLD GIRL, MAKING SO MANY TIME JUMPS SO QUICKLY.

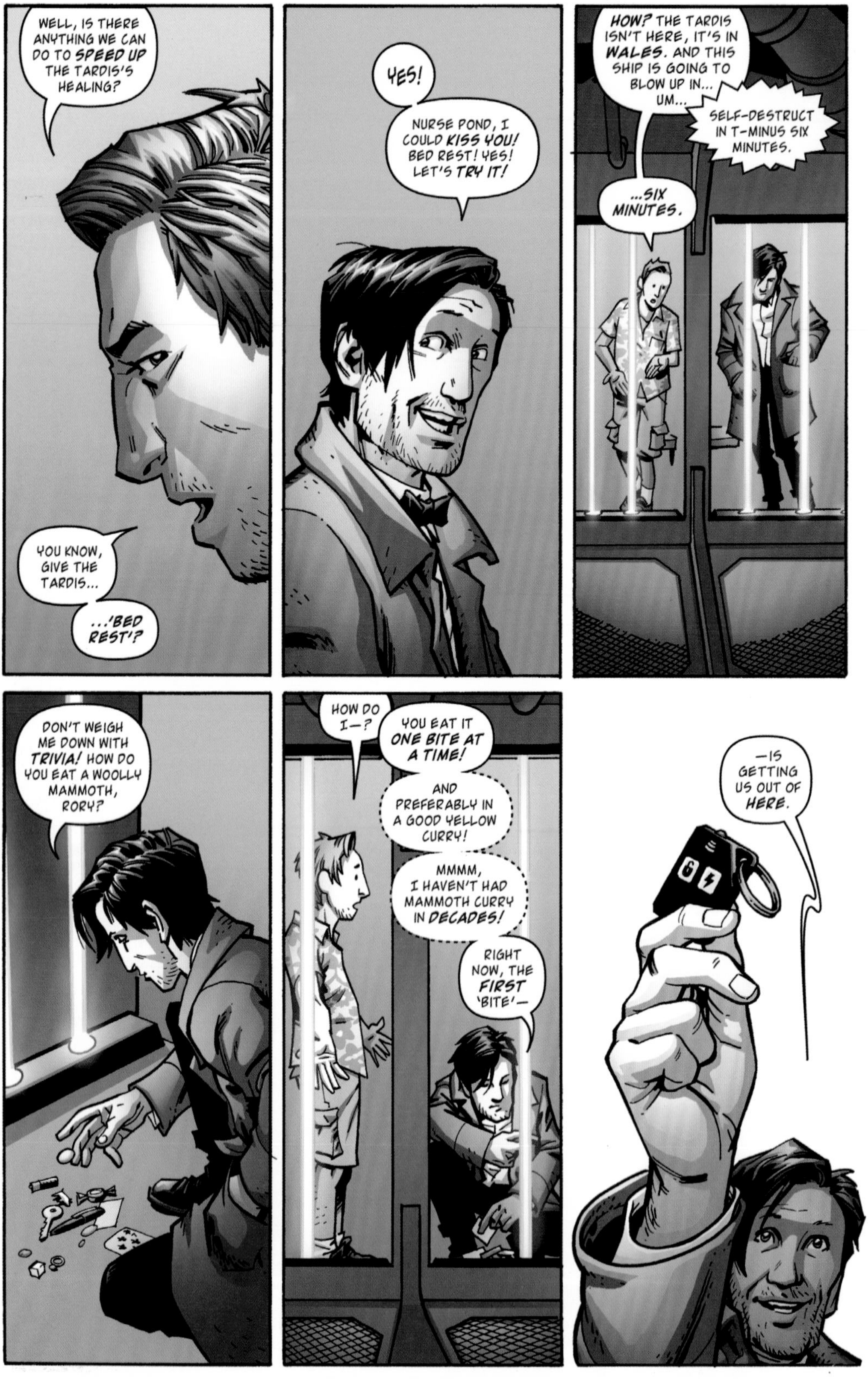
WELL, IS THERE ANYTHING WE CAN DO TO SPEED UP THE TARDIS'S HEALING?
YOU KNOW, GIVE THE TARDIS...
...'BED REST'?
YES!
NURSE POND, I COULD KISS YOU! BED REST! YES! LET'S TRY IT!
HOW? THE TARDIS ISN'T HERE, IT'S IN WALES. AND THIS SHIP IS GOING TO BLOW UP IN... UM...
SELF-DESTRUCT IN T-MINUS SIX MINUTES.
...SIX MINUTES.
DON'T WEIGH ME DOWN WITH TRIVIA! HOW DO YOU EAT A WOOLLY MAMMOTH, RORY?
HOW DO I—?
YOU EAT IT ONE BITE AT A TIME!
AND PREFERABLY IN A GOOD YELLOW CURRY!
MMMM, I HAVEN'T HAD MAMMOTH CURRY IN DECADES!
RIGHT NOW, THE FIRST 'BITE'—
—IS GETTING US OUT OF HERE.

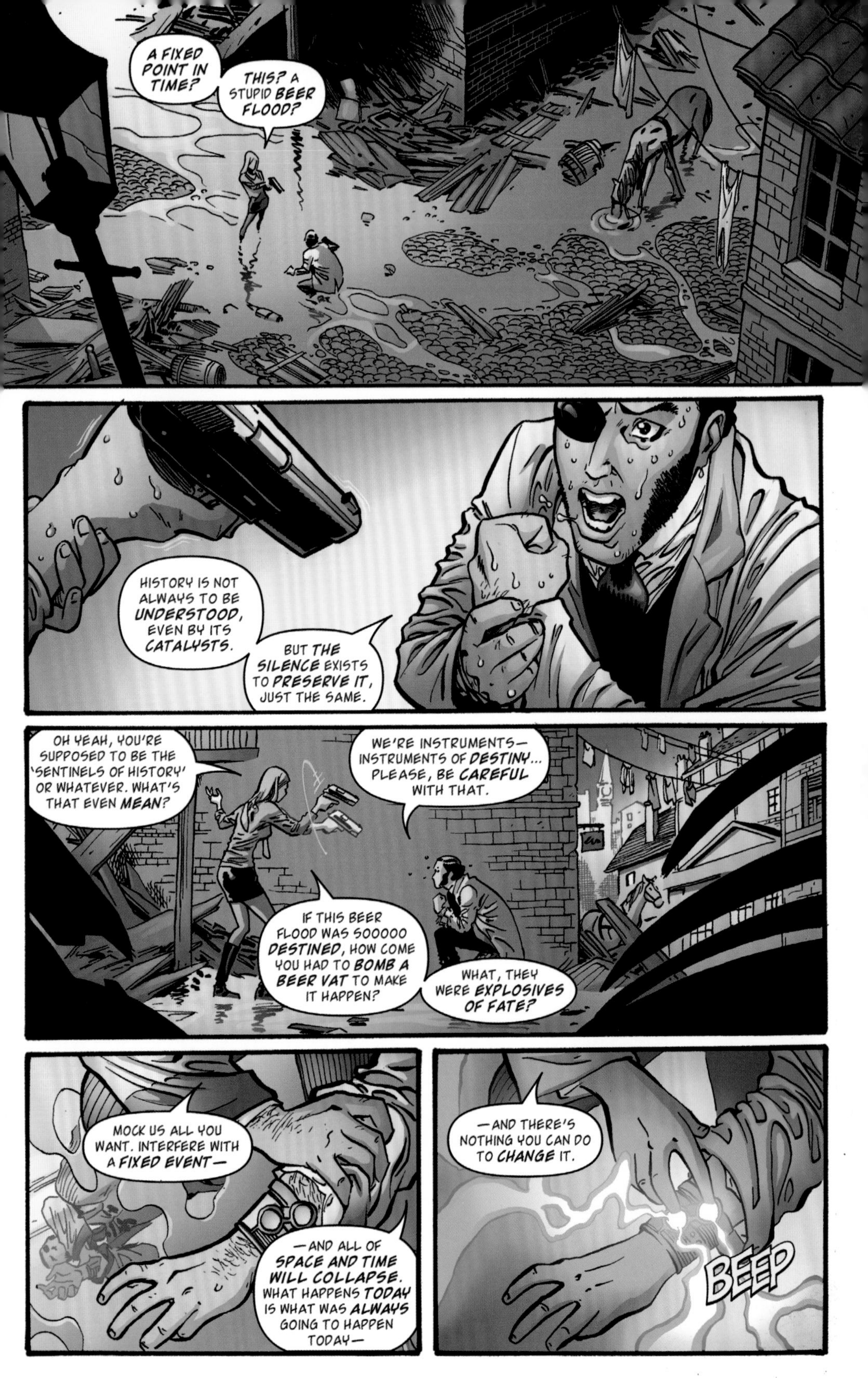
A FIXED POINT IN TIME?
THIS? A STUPID BEER FLOOD?
HISTORY IS NOT ALWAYS TO BE UNDERSTOOD, EVEN BY ITS CATALYSTS.
BUT THE SILENCE EXISTS TO PRESERVE IT, JUST THE SAME.
OH YEAH, YOU'RE SUPPOSED TO BE THE 'SENTINELS OF HISTORY' OR WHATEVER. WHAT'S THAT EVEN MEAN?
WE'RE INSTRUMENTS— INSTRUMENTS OF DESTINY... PLEASE, BE CAREFUL WITH THAT.
IF THIS BEER FLOOD WAS SOOOOO DESTINED, HOW COME YOU HAD TO BOMB A BEER VAT TO MAKE IT HAPPEN?
WHAT, THEY WERE EXPLOSIVES OF FATE?
MOCK US ALL YOU WANT. INTERFERE WITH A FIXED EVENT—
—AND ALL OF SPACE AND TIME WILL COLLAPSE. WHAT HAPPENS TODAY IS WHAT WAS ALWAYS GOING TO HAPPEN TODAY—
—AND THERE'S NOTHING YOU CAN DO TO CHANGE IT.
BEEP

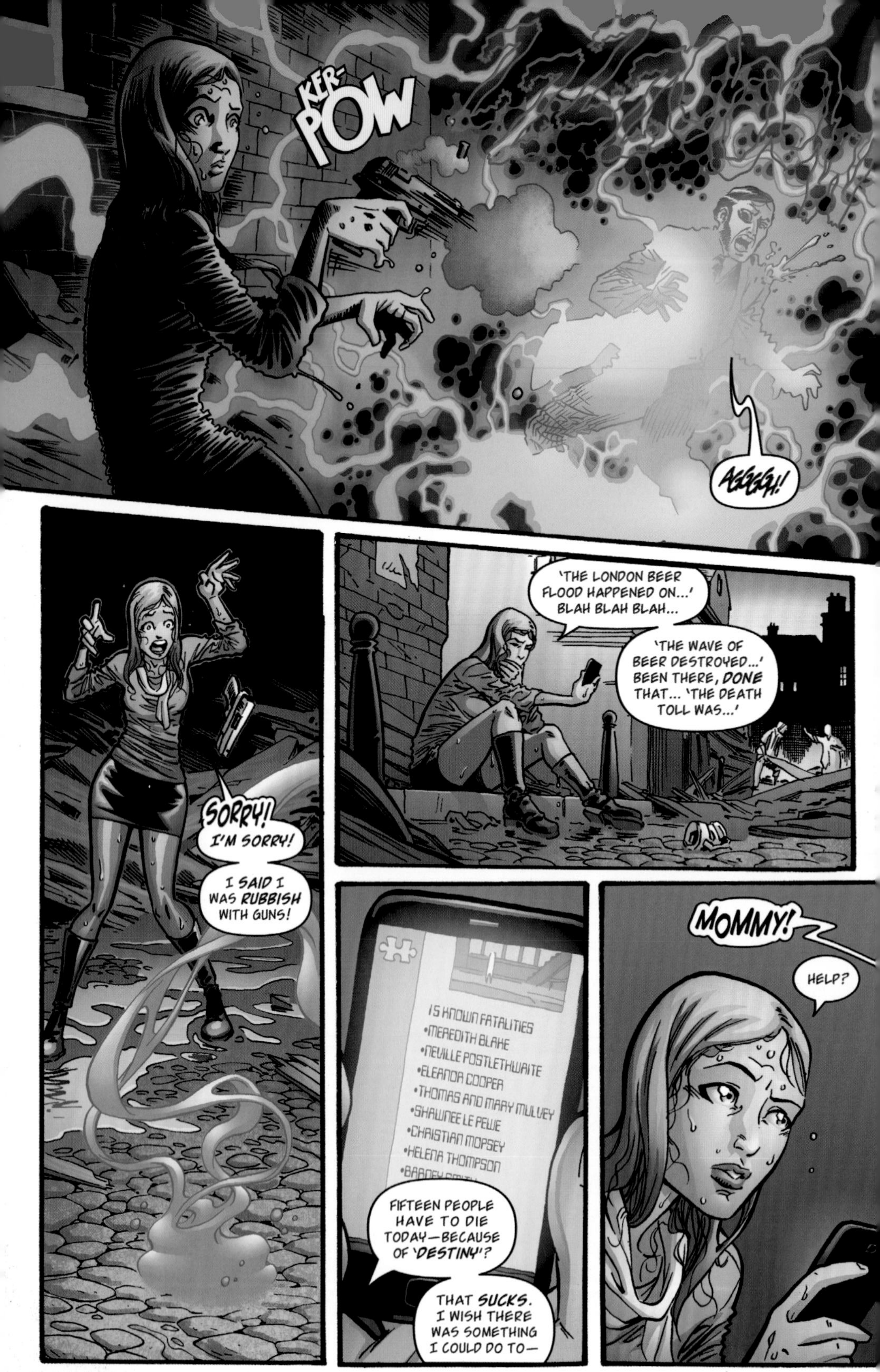
KER-POW
AGGGH!
SORRY! I'M SORRY!
I SAID I WAS RUBBISH WITH GUNS!
'THE LONDON BEER FLOOD HAPPENED ON...' BLAH BLAH BLAH...
'THE WAVE OF BEER DESTROYED...' BEEN THERE, DONE THAT... 'THE DEATH TOLL WAS...'
15 KNOWN FATALITIES
•MEREDITH BLAKE
•NEVILLE POSTLETHWAITE
•ELEANOR COOPER
•THOMAS AND MARY MULVEY
•SHAWNEE LE PEWE
•CHRISTIAN MOPSEY
•HELENA THOMPSON
FIFTEEN PEOPLE HAVE TO DIE TODAY—BECAUSE OF 'DESTINY'?
THAT SUCKS. I WISH THERE WAS SOMETHING I COULD DO TO—
MOMMY!
HELP?

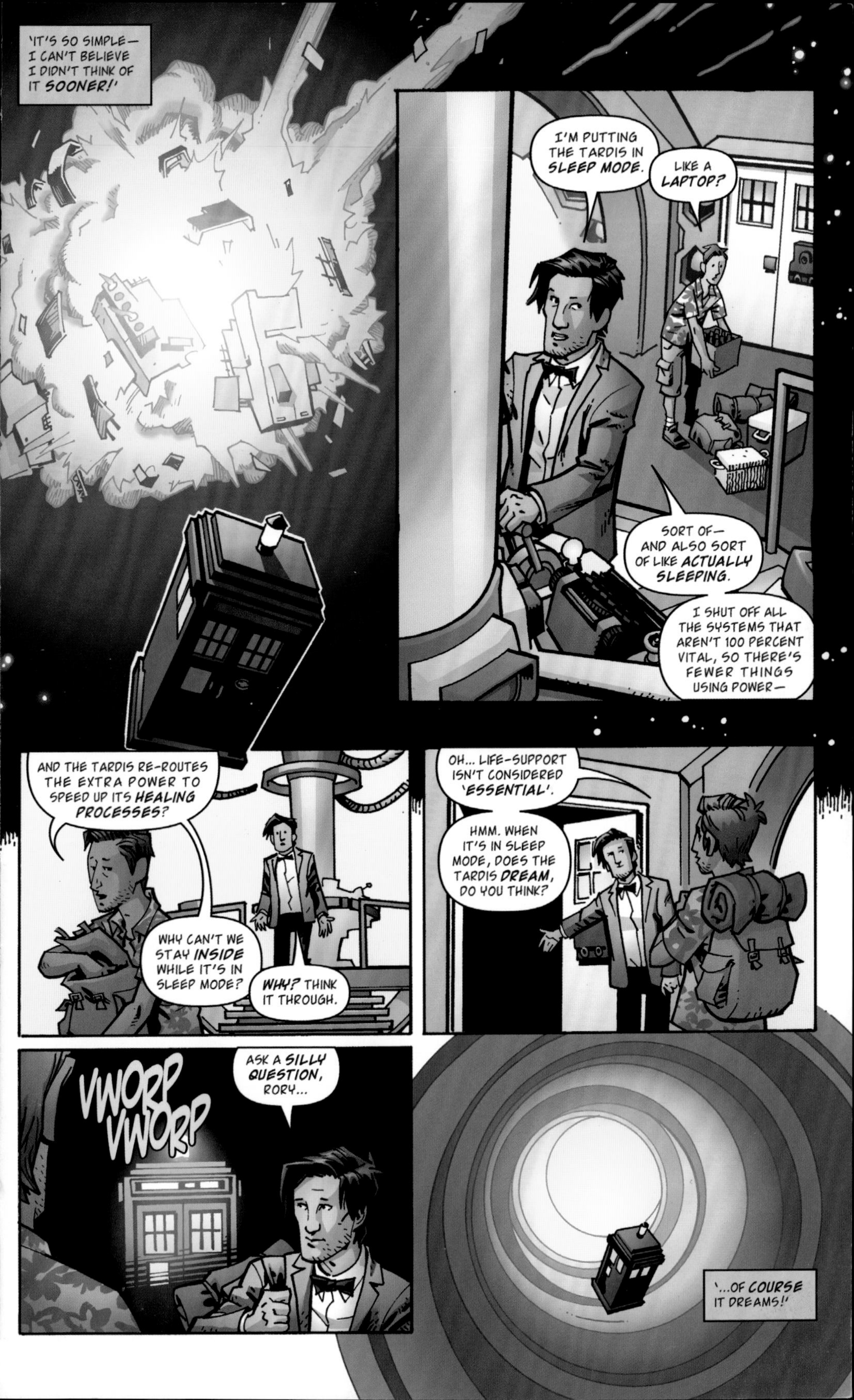

'IT'S SO SIMPLE— I CAN'T BELIEVE I DIDN'T THINK OF IT SOONER!'
I'M PUTTING THE TARDIS IN SLEEP MODE.
LIKE A LAPTOP?
SORT OF— AND ALSO SORT OF LIKE ACTUALLY SLEEPING.
I SHUT OFF ALL THE SYSTEMS THAT AREN'T 100 PERCENT VITAL, SO THERE'S FEWER THINGS USING POWER—
AND THE TARDIS RE-ROUTES THE EXTRA POWER TO SPEED UP ITS HEALING PROCESSES?
WHY CAN'T WE STAY INSIDE WHILE IT'S IN SLEEP MODE?
WHY? THINK IT THROUGH.
OH... LIFE-SUPPORT ISN'T CONSIDERED 'ESSENTIAL'.
HMM. WHEN IT'S IN SLEEP MODE, DOES THE TARDIS DREAM, DO YOU THINK?
VWORP VWORP
ASK A SILLY QUESTION, RORY...
'...OF COURSE IT DREAMS!'

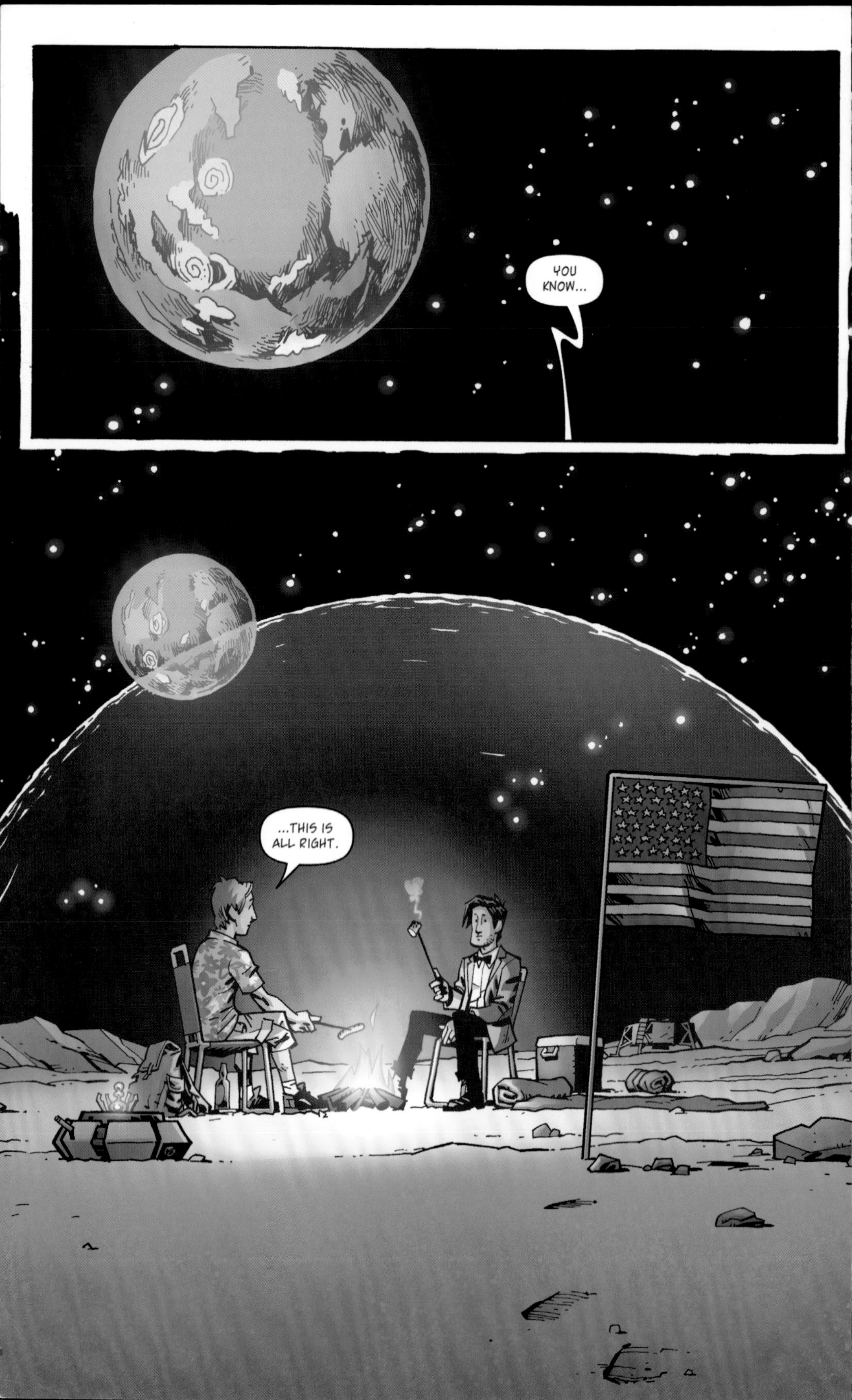
YOU KNOW...
...THIS IS ALL RIGHT.

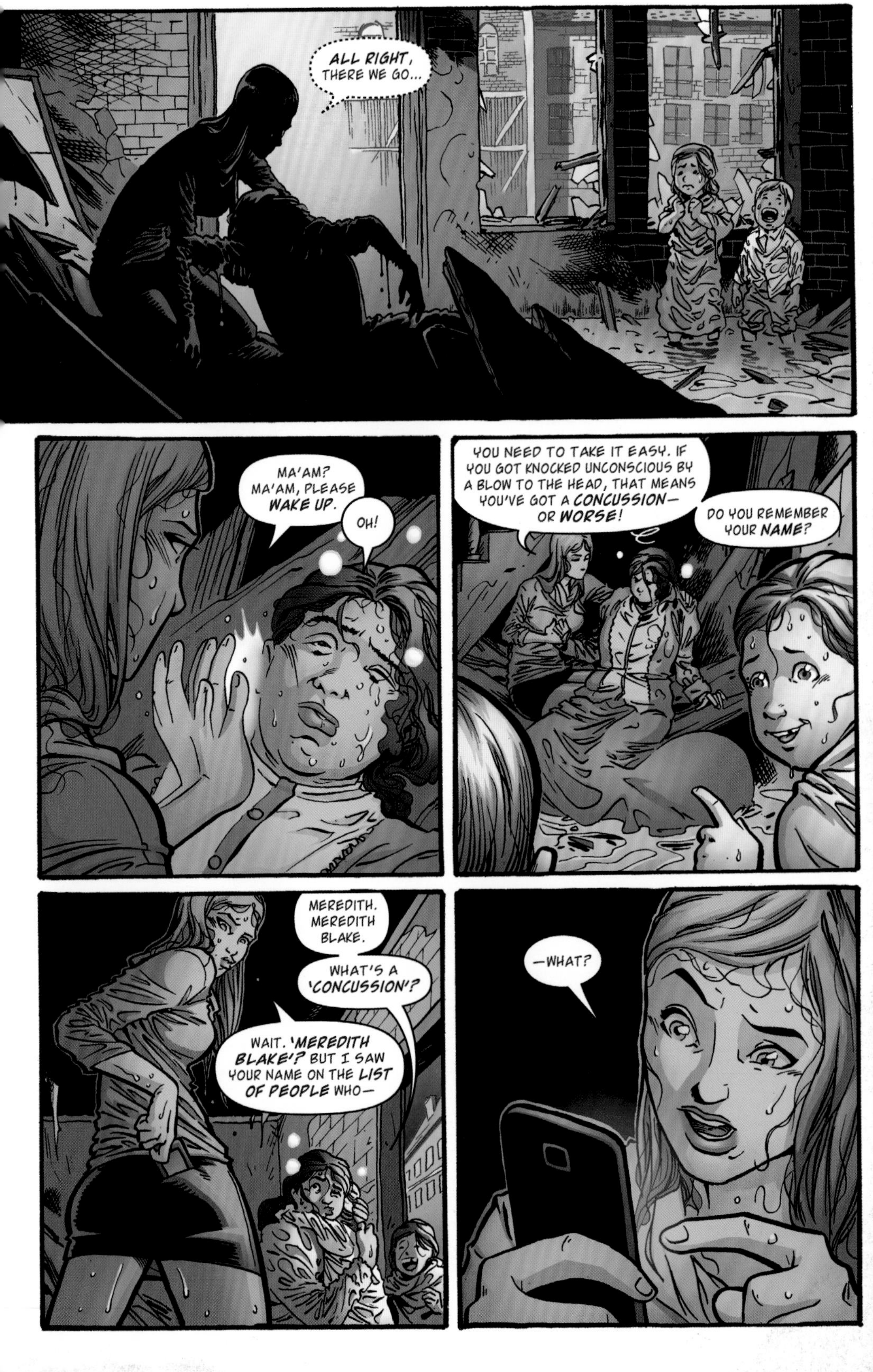
ALL RIGHT, THERE WE GO...
MA'AM? MA'AM, PLEASE WAKE UP.
OH!
YOU NEED TO TAKE IT EASY. IF YOU GOT KNOCKED UNCONSCIOUS BY A BLOW TO THE HEAD, THAT MEANS YOU'VE GOT A CONCUSSION— OR WORSE!
DO YOU REMEMBER YOUR NAME?
MEREDITH. MEREDITH BLAKE.
WHAT'S A 'CONCUSSION'?
WAIT. 'MEREDITH BLAKE'? BUT I SAW YOUR NAME ON THE LIST OF PEOPLE WHO—
—WHAT?

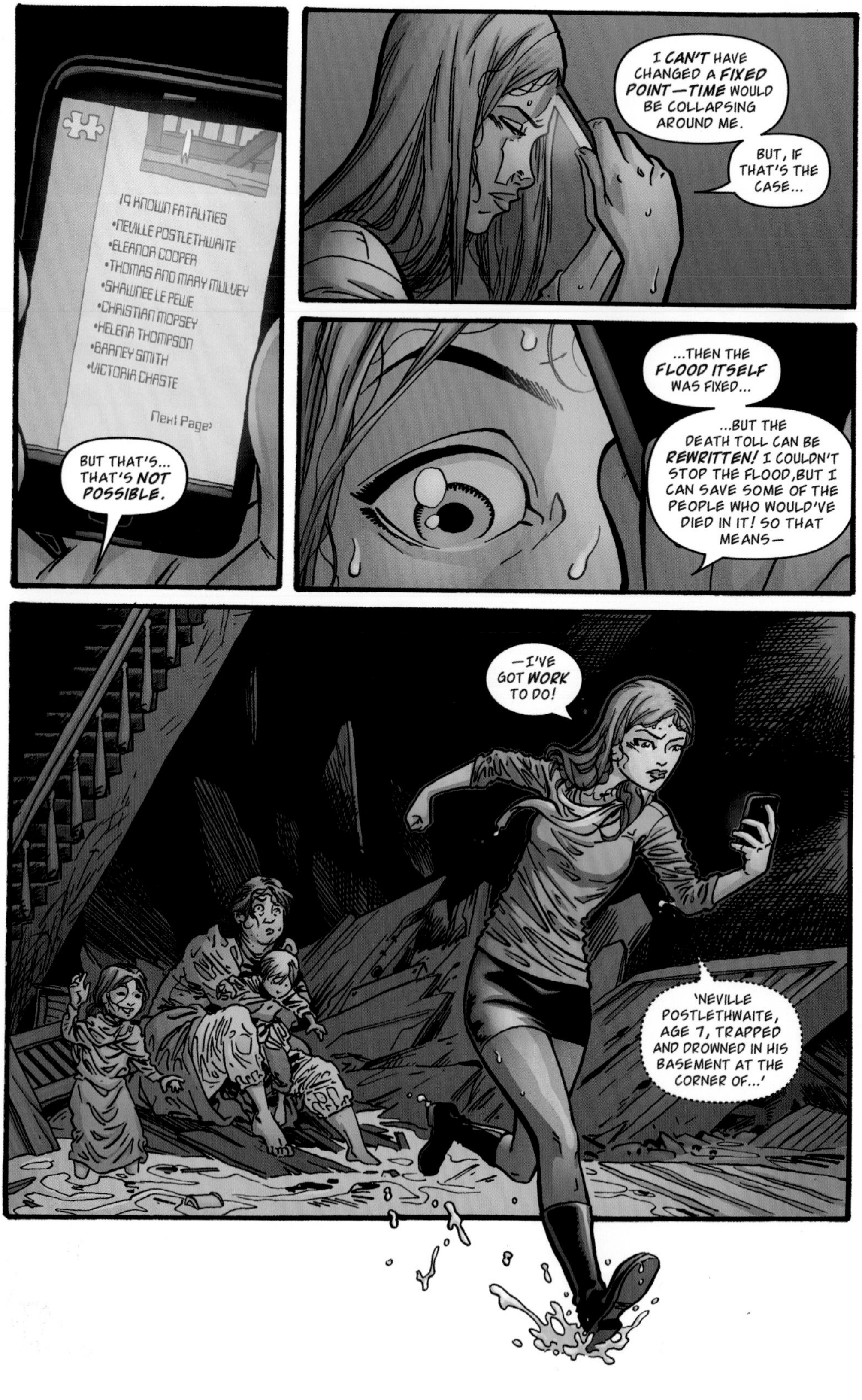

19 KNOWN FATALITIES
•NEVILLE POSTLETHWAITE
•ELEANOR COOPER
•THOMAS AND MARY MULVEY
•SHAWNEE LE PEWE
•CHRISTIAN MOPSEY
•HELENA THOMPSON
•BARNEY SMITH
•VICTORIA CHASTE
Next Page›
BUT THAT'S... THAT'S NOT POSSIBLE.
I CAN'T HAVE CHANGED A FIXED POINT—TIME WOULD BE COLLAPSING AROUND ME.
BUT, IF THAT'S THE CASE...
...THEN THE FLOOD ITSELF WAS FIXED...
...BUT THE DEATH TOLL CAN BE REWRITTEN! I COULDN'T STOP THE FLOOD,BUT I CAN SAVE SOME OF THE PEOPLE WHO WOULD'VE DIED IN IT! SO THAT MEANS—
—I'VE GOT WORK TO DO!
'NEVILLE POSTLETHWAITE, AGE 7, TRAPPED AND DROWNED IN HIS BASEMENT AT THE CORNER OF...'

VWORP VWORP

IT'S BACK. THAT'S... *GOOD*, RIGHT?

IT'S *EXCELLENT*—

—NOW WE WON'T *DIE ON THE MOON* WHEN THE AIR-SHELL RUNS OUT OF POWER.

BUT... IS IT *FIXED*? OR *HEALED*, OR WHATEVER?

NO WAY TO KNOW JUST BY *LOOKING* AT IT. THE ONLY WAY TO BE SURE IS—

—TO TAKE HER FOR A *SPIN*.

VWORP VWORP

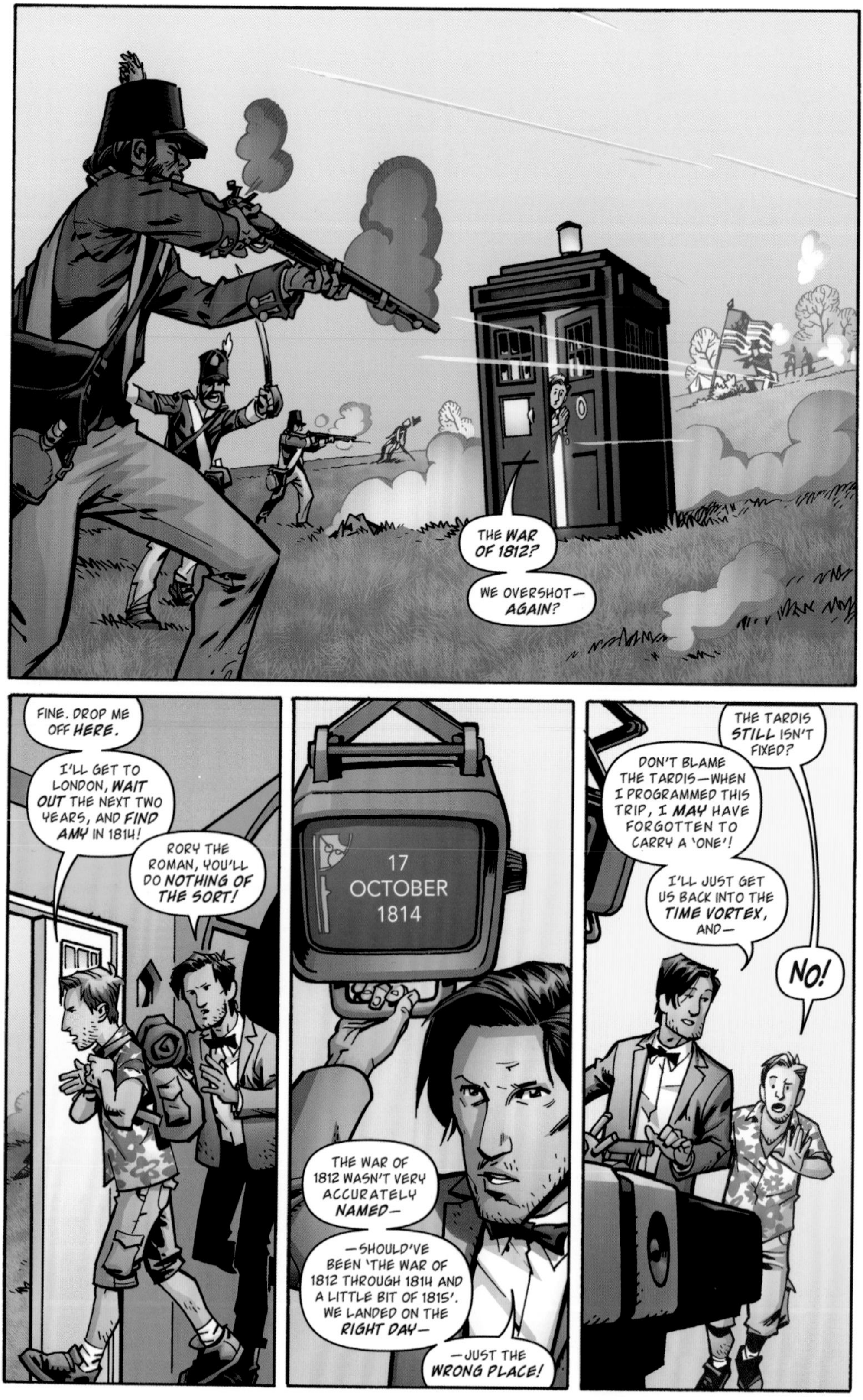
THE WAR OF 1812?
WE OVERSHOT—AGAIN?
FINE. DROP ME OFF HERE.
I'LL GET TO LONDON, WAIT OUT THE NEXT TWO YEARS, AND FIND AMY IN 1814!
RORY THE ROMAN, YOU'LL DO NOTHING OF THE SORT!
17 OCTOBER 1814
THE WAR OF 1812 WASN'T VERY ACCURATELY NAMED—
—SHOULD'VE BEEN 'THE WAR OF 1812 THROUGH 1814 AND A LITTLE BIT OF 1815'. WE LANDED ON THE RIGHT DAY—
—JUST THE WRONG PLACE!
THE TARDIS STILL ISN'T FIXED?
DON'T BLAME THE TARDIS—WHEN I PROGRAMMED THIS TRIP, I MAY HAVE FORGOTTEN TO CARRY A 'ONE'!
I'LL JUST GET US BACK INTO THE TIME VORTEX, AND—
NO!

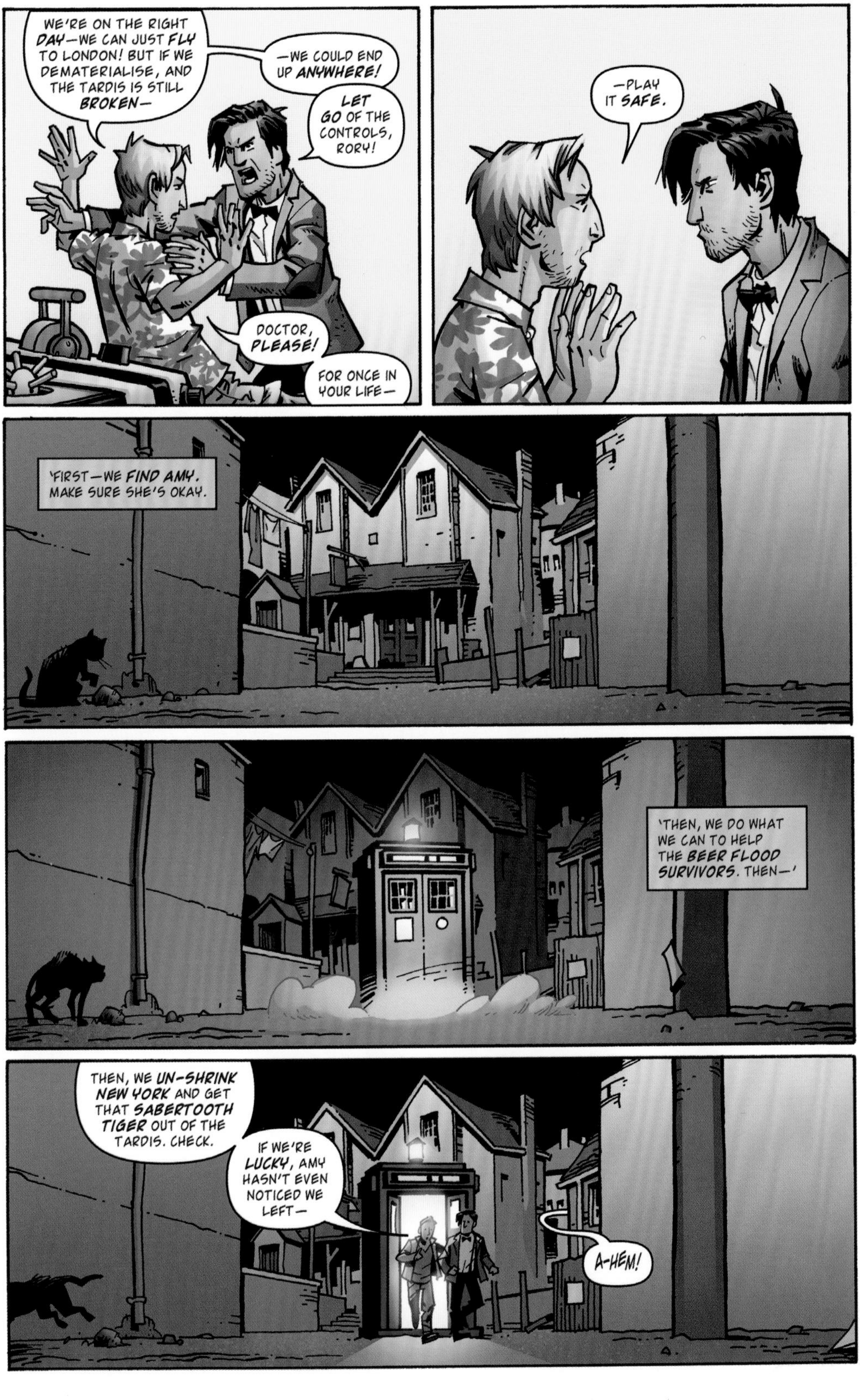
WE'RE ON THE RIGHT DAY—WE CAN JUST FLY TO LONDON! BUT IF WE DEMATERIALISE, AND THE TARDIS IS STILL BROKEN—
—WE COULD END UP ANYWHERE!
LET GO OF THE CONTROLS, RORY!
DOCTOR, PLEASE!
FOR ONCE IN YOUR LIFE—
—PLAY IT SAFE.
'FIRST—WE FIND AMY. MAKE SURE SHE'S OKAY.
'THEN, WE DO WHAT WE CAN TO HELP THE BEER FLOOD SURVIVORS. THEN—'
THEN, WE UN-SHRINK NEW YORK AND GET THAT SABERTOOTH TIGER OUT OF THE TARDIS. CHECK.
IF WE'RE LUCKY, AMY HASN'T EVEN NOTICED WE LEFT—
A-HEM!

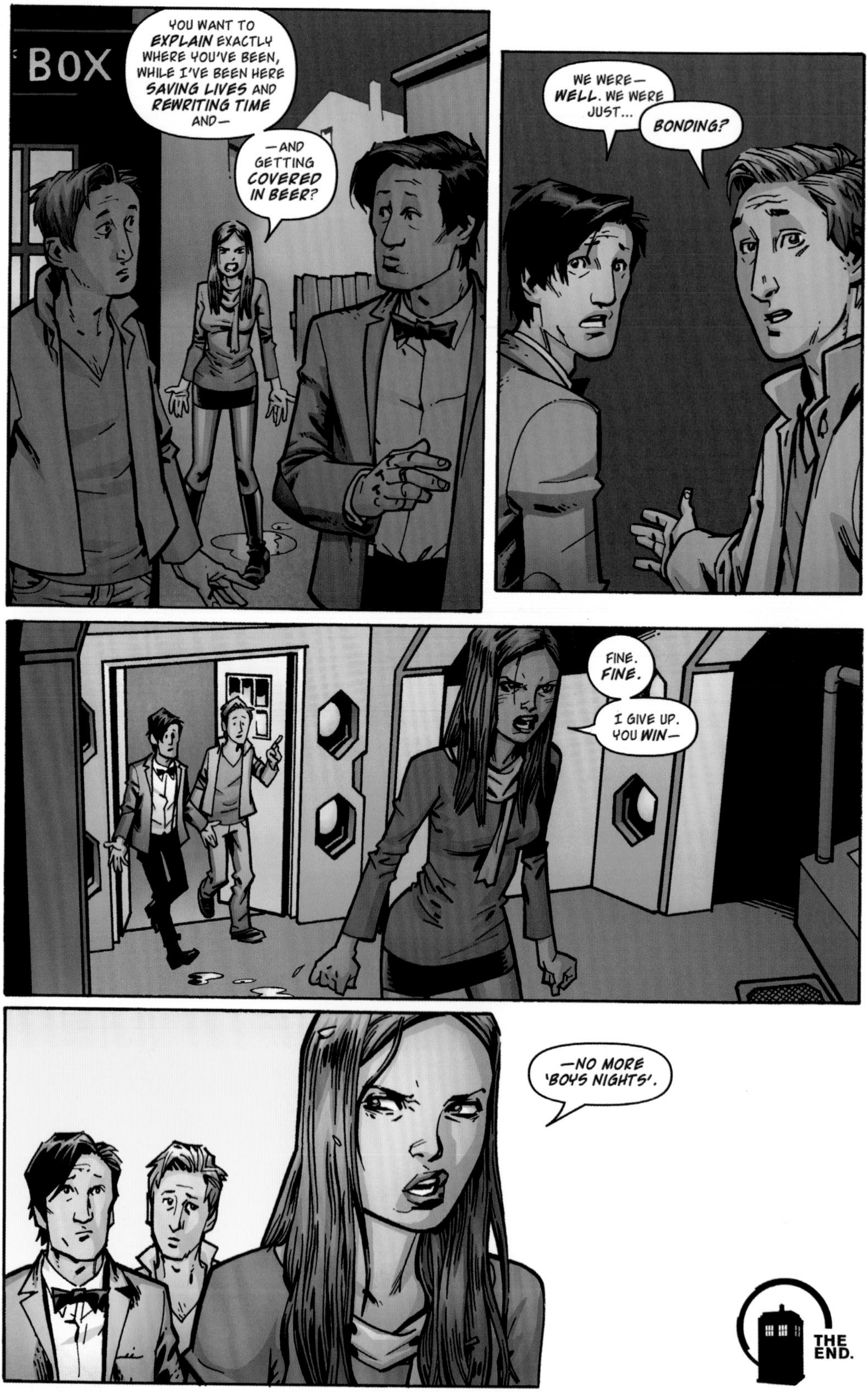
BOX
YOU WANT TO EXPLAIN EXACTLY WHERE YOU'VE BEEN, WHILE I'VE BEEN HERE SAVING LIVES AND REWRITING TIME AND—
—AND GETTING COVERED IN BEER?
WE WERE— WELL. WE WERE JUST...
BONDING?
FINE. FINE.
I GIVE UP. YOU WIN—
—NO MORE 'BOYS NIGHTS'.
THE END.

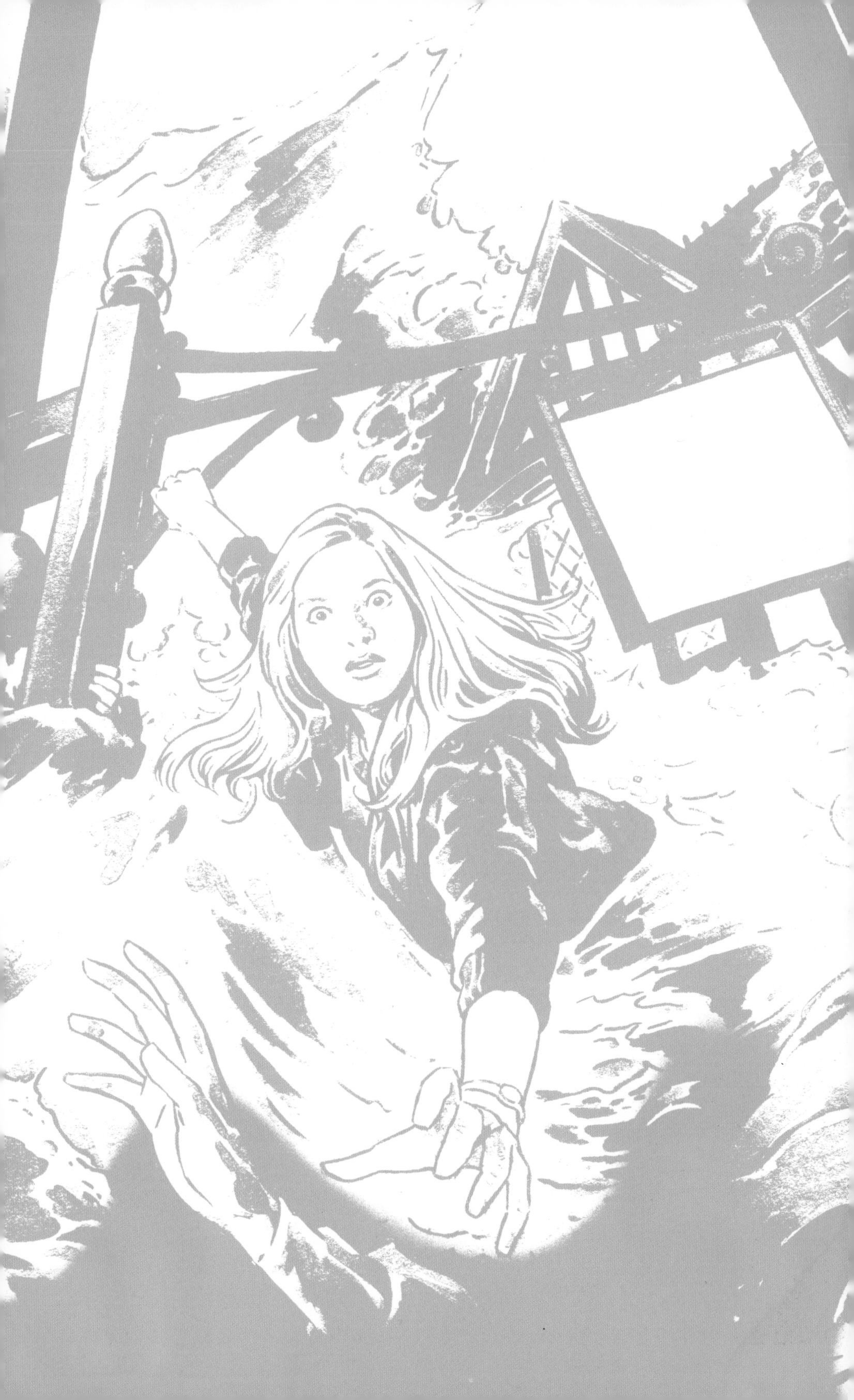

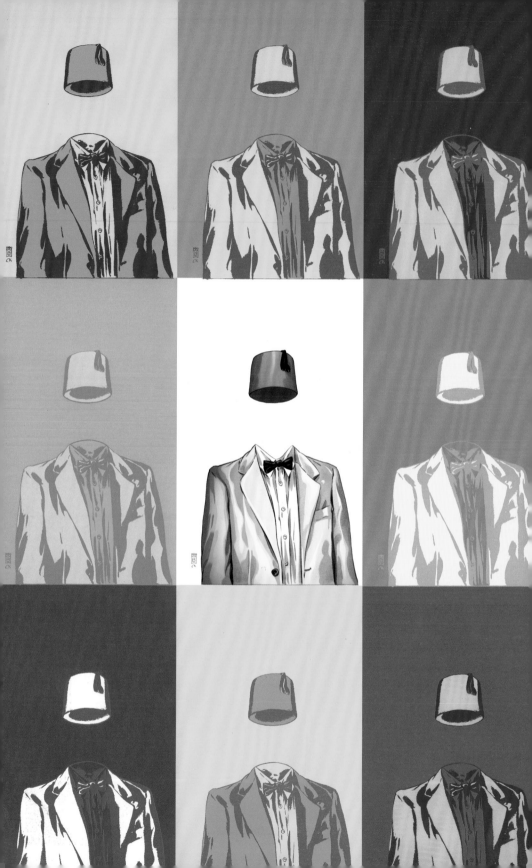

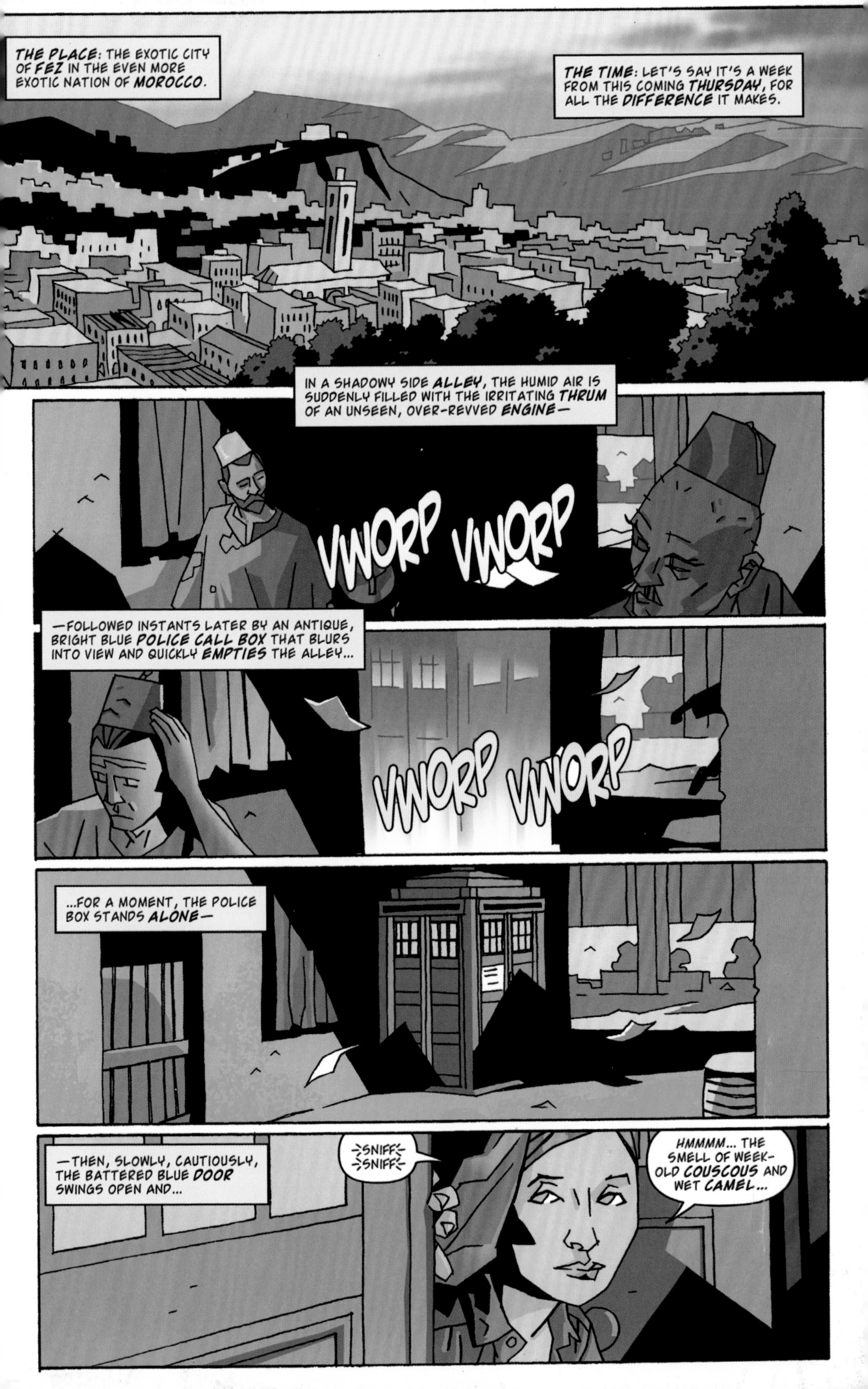
THE PLACE: THE EXOTIC CITY OF FEZ IN THE EVEN MORE EXOTIC NATION OF MOROCCO.
THE TIME: LET'S SAY IT'S A WEEK FROM THIS COMING THURSDAY, FOR ALL THE DIFFERENCE IT MAKES.
IN A SHADOWY SIDE ALLEY, THE HUMID AIR IS SUDDENLY FILLED WITH THE IRRITATING THRUM OF AN UNSEEN, OVER-REVVED ENGINE—
VWORP VWORP
—FOLLOWED INSTANTS LATER BY AN ANTIQUE, BRIGHT BLUE POLICE CALL BOX THAT BLURS INTO VIEW AND QUICKLY EMPTIES THE ALLEY...
VWORP VWORP
...FOR A MOMENT, THE POLICE BOX STANDS ALONE—
—THEN, SLOWLY, CAUTIOUSLY, THE BATTERED BLUE DOOR SWINGS OPEN AND...
SNIFF SNIFF
HMMMM... THE SMELL OF WEEK-OLD COUSCOUS AND WET CAMEL...

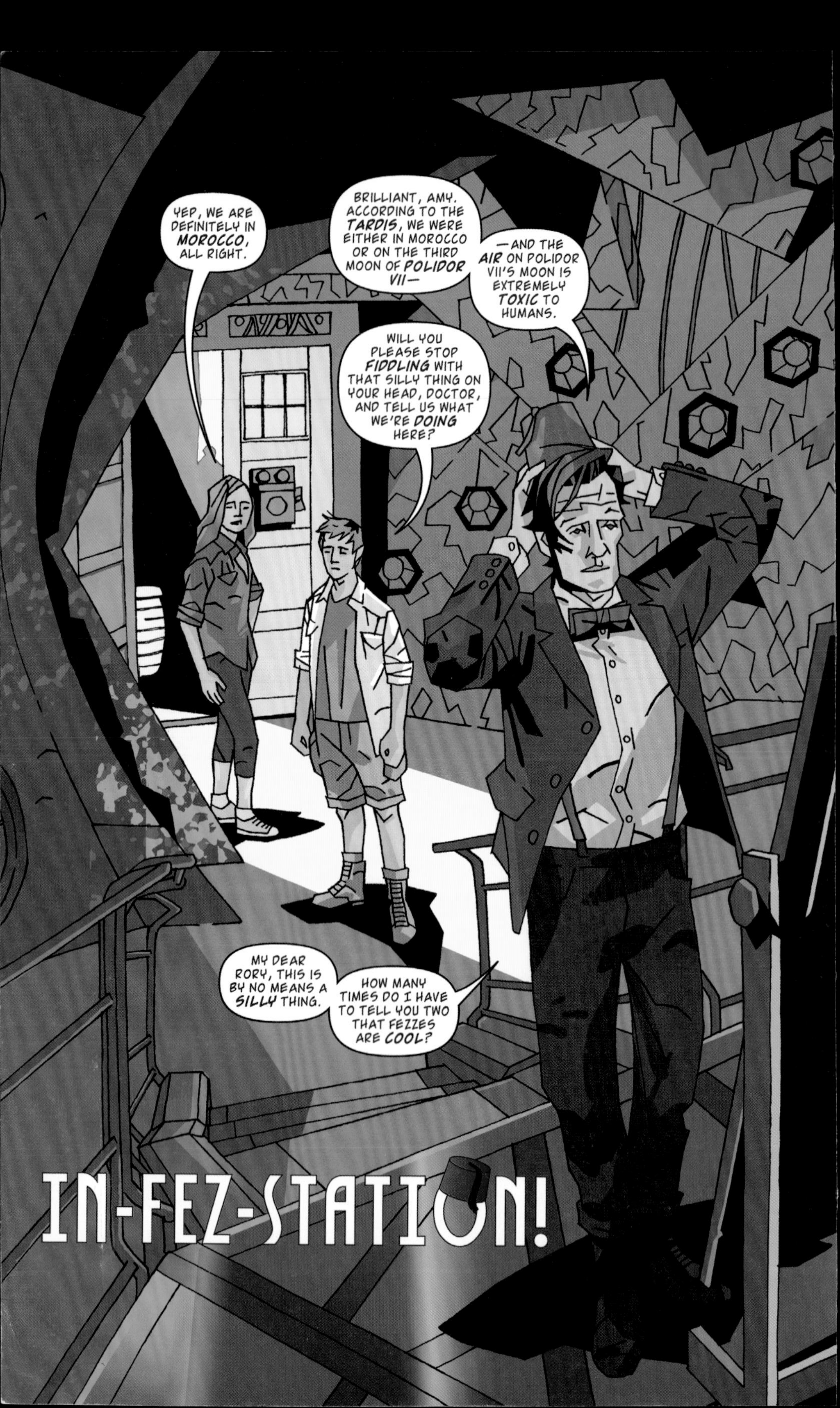
YEP, WE ARE DEFINITELY IN MOROCCO, ALL RIGHT.
BRILLIANT, AMY. ACCORDING TO THE TARDIS, WE WERE EITHER IN MOROCCO OR ON THE THIRD MOON OF POLIDOR VII—
—AND THE AIR ON POLIDOR VII'S MOON IS EXTREMELY TOXIC TO HUMANS.
WILL YOU PLEASE STOP FIDDLING WITH THAT SILLY THING ON YOUR HEAD, DOCTOR, AND TELL US WHAT WE'RE DOING HERE?
MY DEAR RORY, THIS IS BY NO MEANS A SILLY THING.
HOW MANY TIMES DO I HAVE TO TELL YOU TWO THAT FEZZES ARE COOL?
IN-FEZ-STATION!

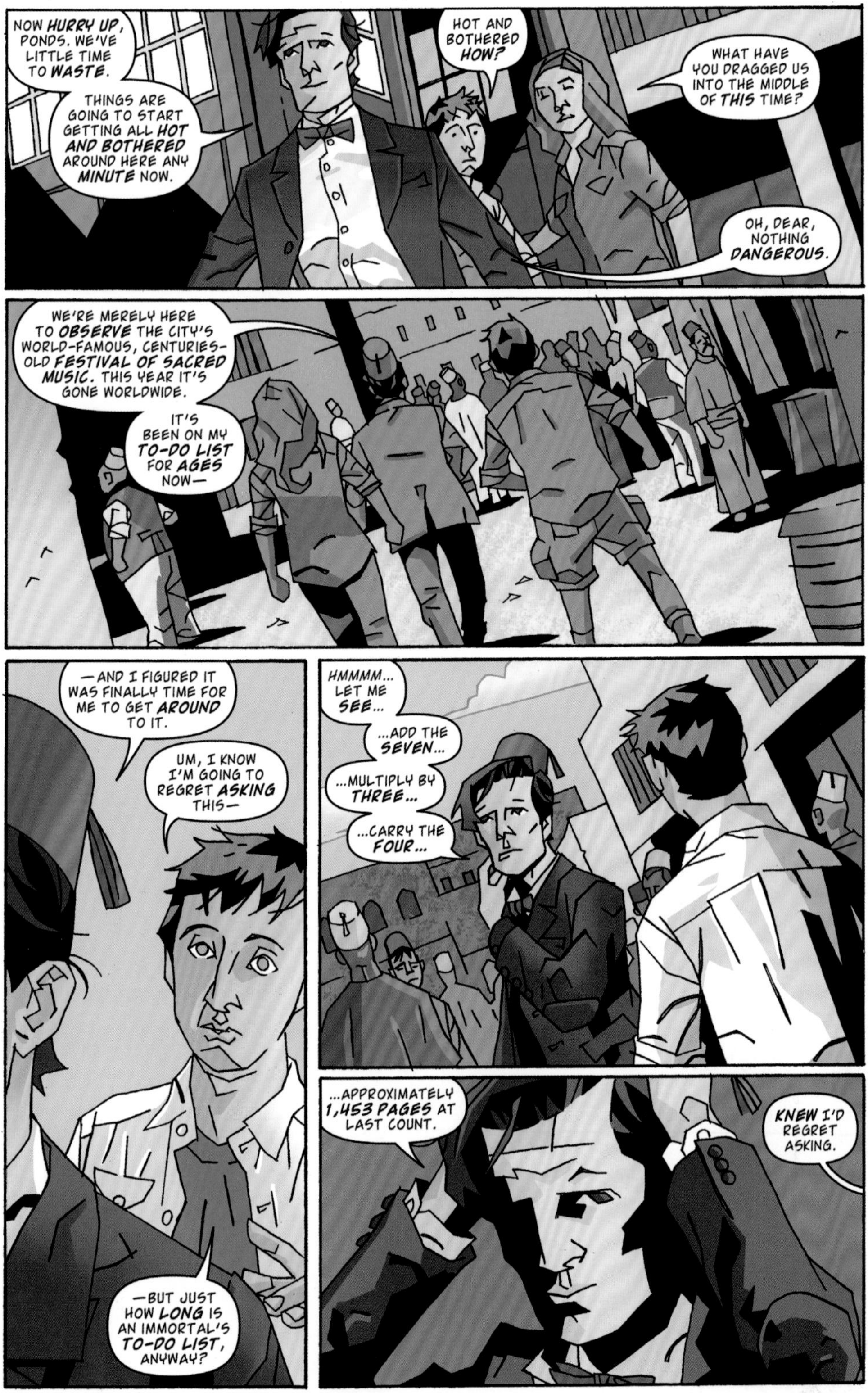
NOW HURRY UP, PONDS. WE'VE LITTLE TIME TO WASTE.
THINGS ARE GOING TO START GETTING ALL HOT AND BOTHERED AROUND HERE ANY MINUTE NOW.
HOT AND BOTHERED HOW?
WHAT HAVE YOU DRAGGED US INTO THE MIDDLE OF THIS TIME?
OH, DEAR, NOTHING DANGEROUS.
WE'RE MERELY HERE TO OBSERVE THE CITY'S WORLD-FAMOUS, CENTURIES-OLD FESTIVAL OF SACRED MUSIC. THIS YEAR IT'S GONE WORLDWIDE.
IT'S BEEN ON MY TO-DO LIST FOR AGES NOW—
—AND I FIGURED IT WAS FINALLY TIME FOR ME TO GET AROUND TO IT.
UM, I KNOW I'M GOING TO REGRET ASKING THIS—
—BUT JUST HOW LONG IS AN IMMORTAL'S TO-DO LIST, ANYWAY?
HMMMM... LET ME SEE...
...ADD THE SEVEN...
...MULTIPLY BY THREE...
...CARRY THE FOUR...
...APPROXIMATELY 1,453 PAGES AT LAST COUNT.
KNEW I'D REGRET ASKING.

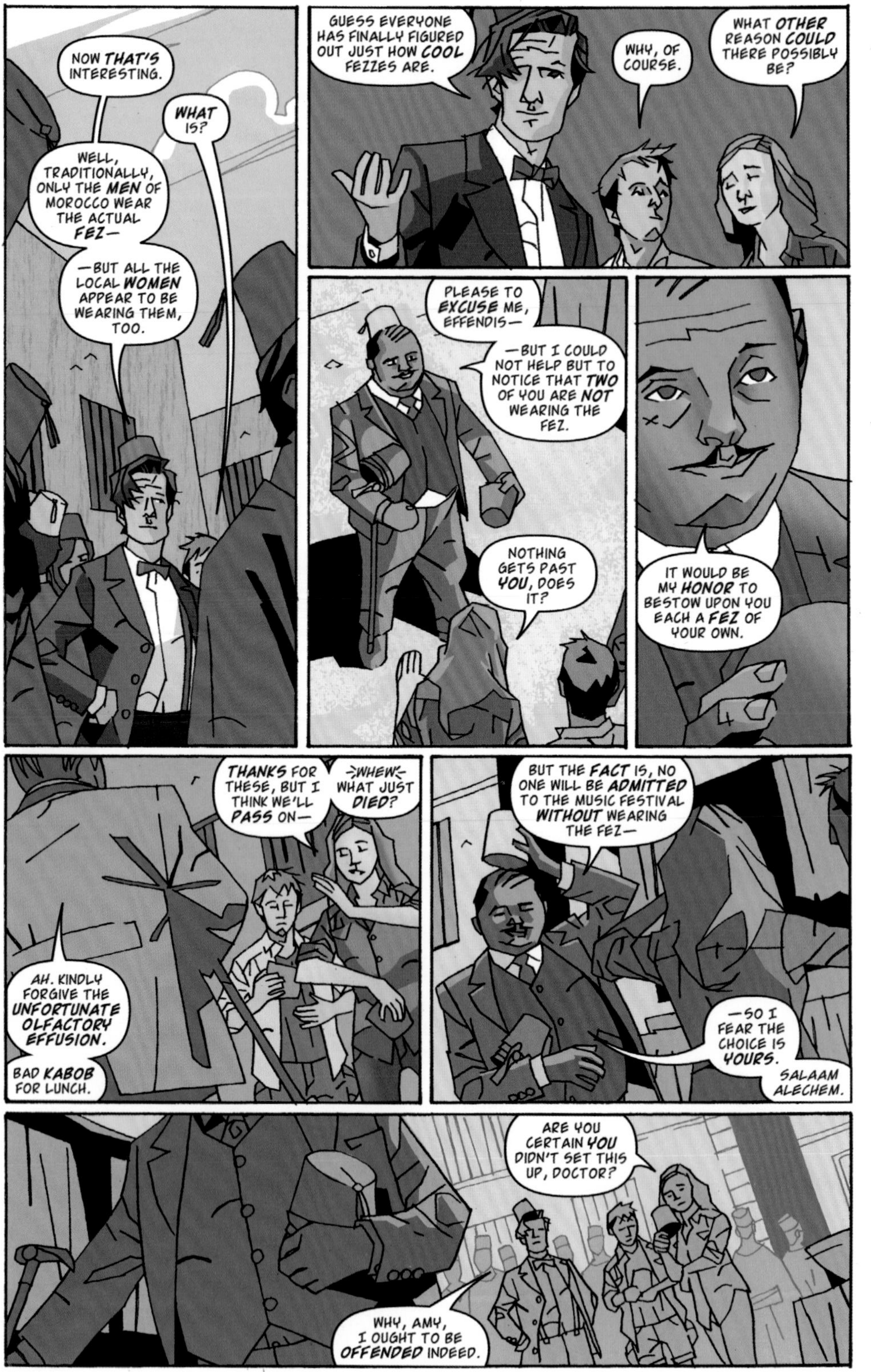
NOW THAT'S INTERESTING.
WHAT IS?
WELL, TRADITIONALLY, ONLY THE MEN OF MOROCCO WEAR THE ACTUAL FEZ—
—BUT ALL THE LOCAL WOMEN APPEAR TO BE WEARING THEM, TOO.
GUESS EVERYONE HAS FINALLY FIGURED OUT JUST HOW COOL FEZZES ARE.
WHY, OF COURSE.
WHAT OTHER REASON COULD THERE POSSIBLY BE?
PLEASE TO EXCUSE ME, EFFENDIS—
—BUT I COULD NOT HELP BUT TO NOTICE THAT TWO OF YOU ARE NOT WEARING THE FEZ.
NOTHING GETS PAST YOU, DOES IT?
IT WOULD BE MY HONOR TO BESTOW UPON YOU EACH A FEZ OF YOUR OWN.
THANKS FOR THESE, BUT I THINK WE'LL PASS ON—
WHEW! WHAT JUST DIED?
AH. KINDLY FORGIVE THE UNFORTUNATE OLFACTORY EFFUSION.
BAD KABOB FOR LUNCH.
BUT THE FACT IS, NO ONE WILL BE ADMITTED TO THE MUSIC FESTIVAL WITHOUT WEARING THE FEZ—
—SO I FEAR THE CHOICE IS YOURS.
SALAAM ALECHEM.
ARE YOU CERTAIN YOU DIDN'T SET THIS UP, DOCTOR?
WHY, AMY, I OUGHT TO BE OFFENDED INDEED.

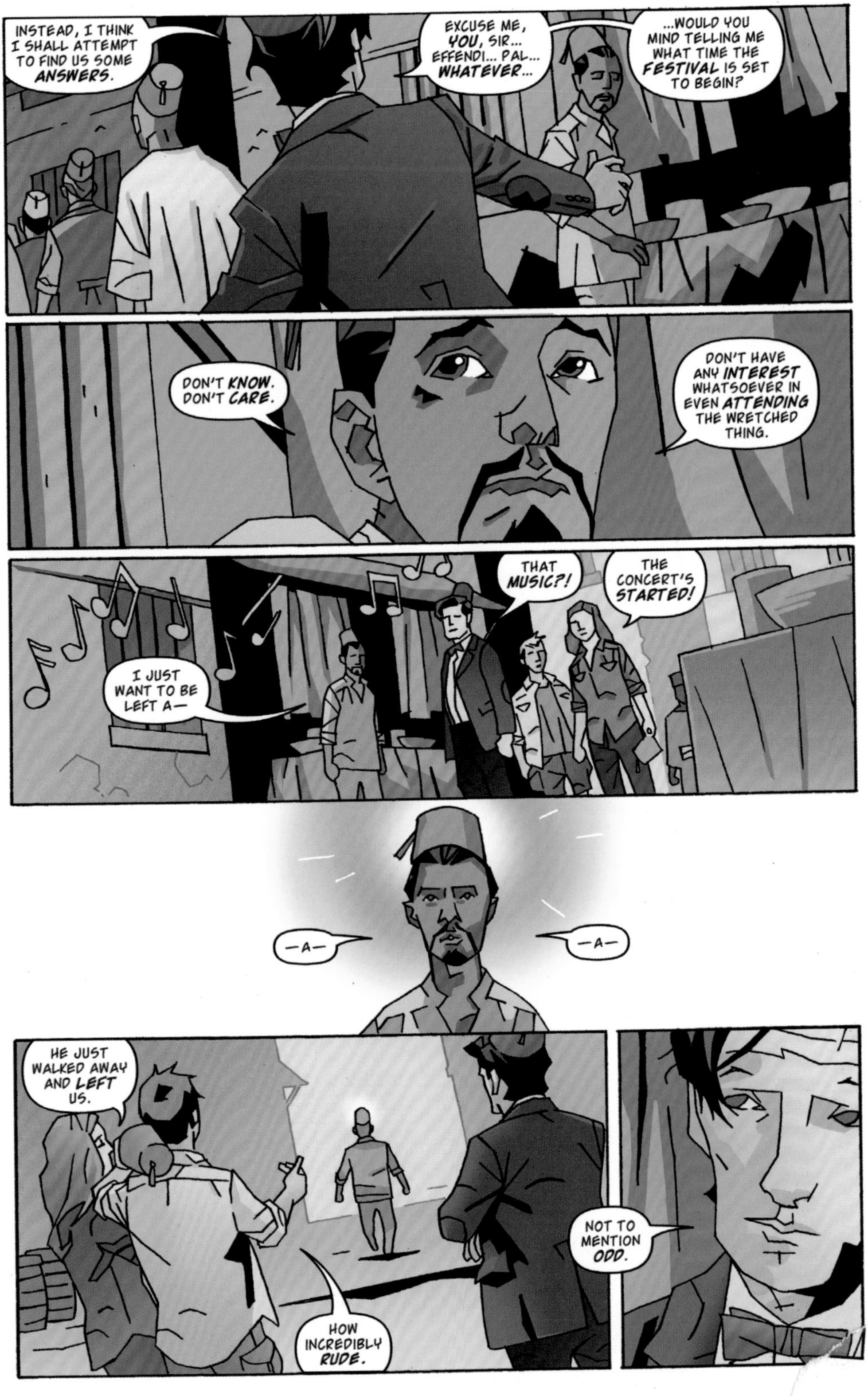
INSTEAD, I THINK I SHALL ATTEMPT TO FIND US SOME ANSWERS.
EXCUSE ME, YOU, SIR... EFFENDI... PAL... WHATEVER...
...WOULD YOU MIND TELLING ME WHAT TIME THE FESTIVAL IS SET TO BEGIN?
DON'T KNOW. DON'T CARE.
DON'T HAVE ANY INTEREST WHATSOEVER IN EVEN ATTENDING THE WRETCHED THING.
THAT MUSIC?!
THE CONCERT'S STARTED!
I JUST WANT TO BE LEFT A—
—A—
—A—
HE JUST WALKED AWAY AND LEFT US.
HOW INCREDIBLY RUDE.
NOT TO MENTION ODD.

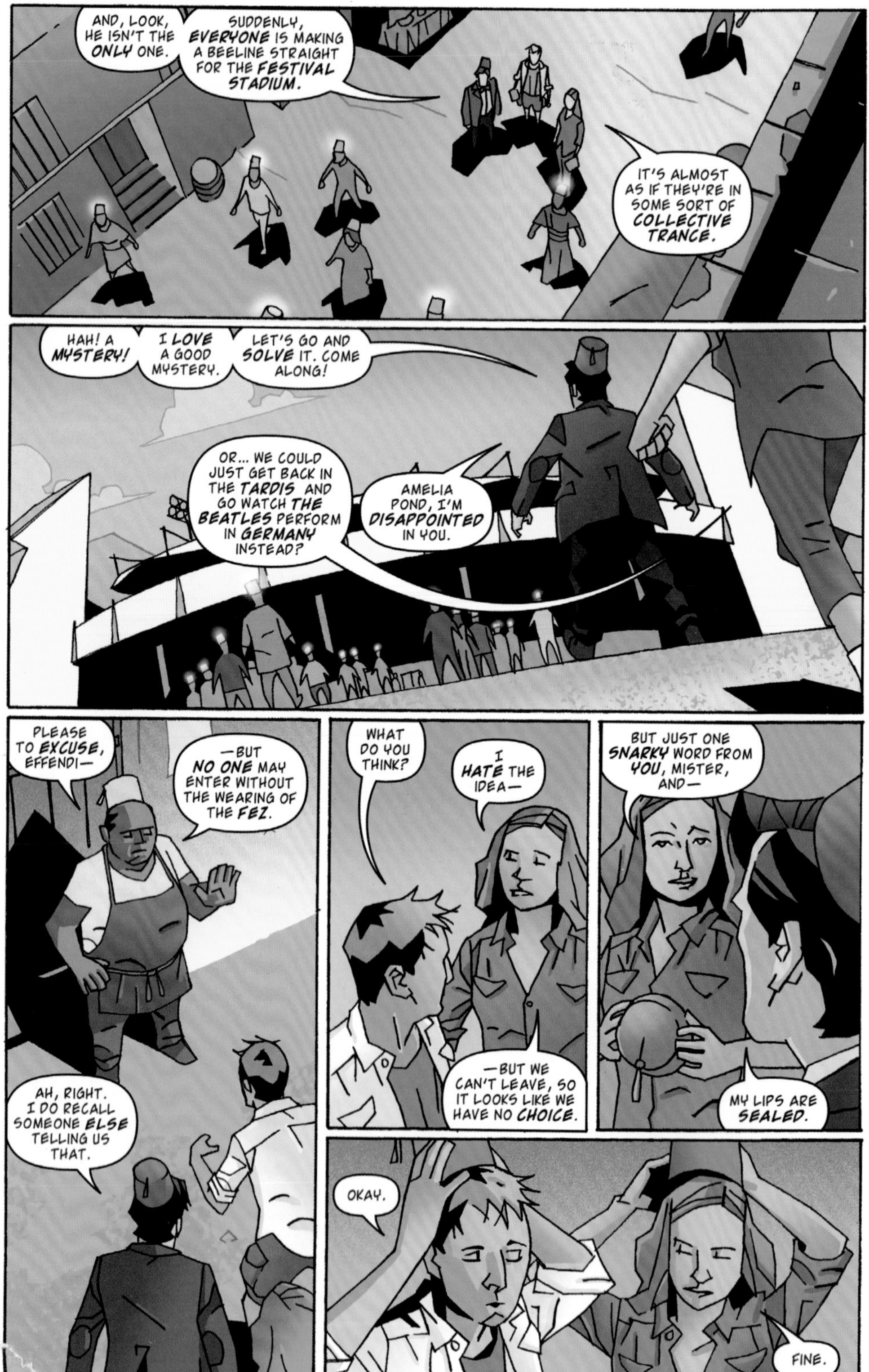
AND, LOOK, HE ISN'T THE ONLY ONE.
SUDDENLY, EVERYONE IS MAKING A BEELINE STRAIGHT FOR THE FESTIVAL STADIUM.
IT'S ALMOST AS IF THEY'RE IN SOME SORT OF COLLECTIVE TRANCE.
HAH! A MYSTERY!
I LOVE A GOOD MYSTERY.
LET'S GO AND SOLVE IT. COME ALONG!
OR... WE COULD JUST GET BACK IN THE TARDIS AND GO WATCH THE BEATLES PERFORM IN GERMANY INSTEAD?
AMELIA POND, I'M DISAPPOINTED IN YOU.
PLEASE TO EXCUSE, EFFENDI—
—BUT NO ONE MAY ENTER WITHOUT THE WEARING OF THE FEZ.
AH, RIGHT. I DO RECALL SOMEONE ELSE TELLING US THAT.
WHAT DO YOU THINK?
I HATE THE IDEA—
—BUT WE CAN'T LEAVE, SO IT LOOKS LIKE WE HAVE NO CHOICE.
BUT JUST ONE SNARKY WORD FROM YOU, MISTER, AND—
MY LIPS ARE SEALED.
OKAY.
FINE.

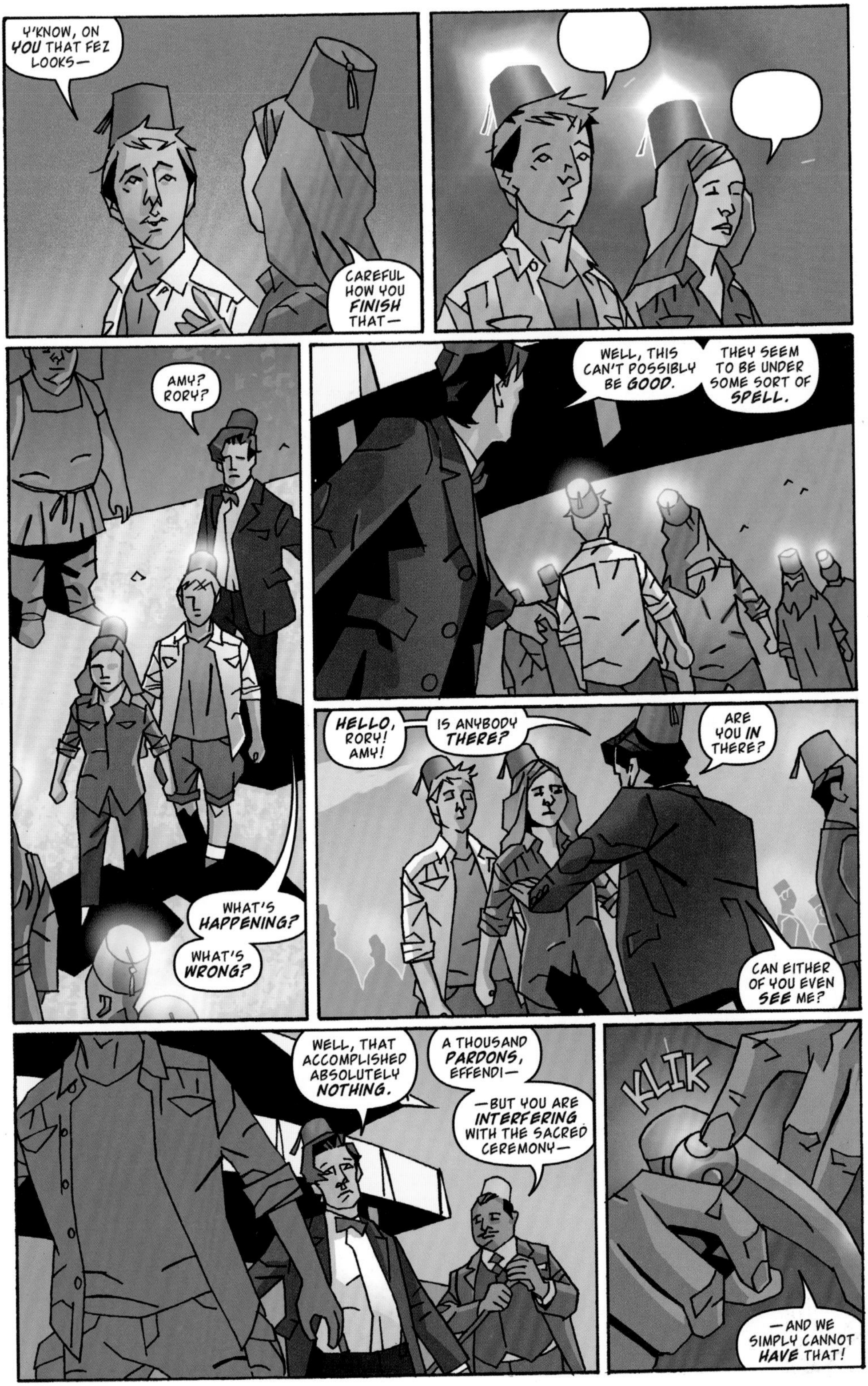

Y'KNOW, ON YOU THAT FEZ LOOKS—
CAREFUL HOW YOU FINISH THAT—
AMY? RORY?
WHAT'S HAPPENING?
WHAT'S WRONG?
WELL, THIS CAN'T POSSIBLY BE GOOD.
THEY SEEM TO BE UNDER SOME SORT OF SPELL.
HELLO, RORY! AMY!
IS ANYBODY THERE?
ARE YOU IN THERE?
CAN EITHER OF YOU EVEN SEE ME?
WELL, THAT ACCOMPLISHED ABSOLUTELY NOTHING.
A THOUSAND PARDONS, EFFENDI—
—BUT YOU ARE INTERFERING WITH THE SACRED CEREMONY—
KLIK
—AND WE SIMPLY CANNOT HAVE THAT!

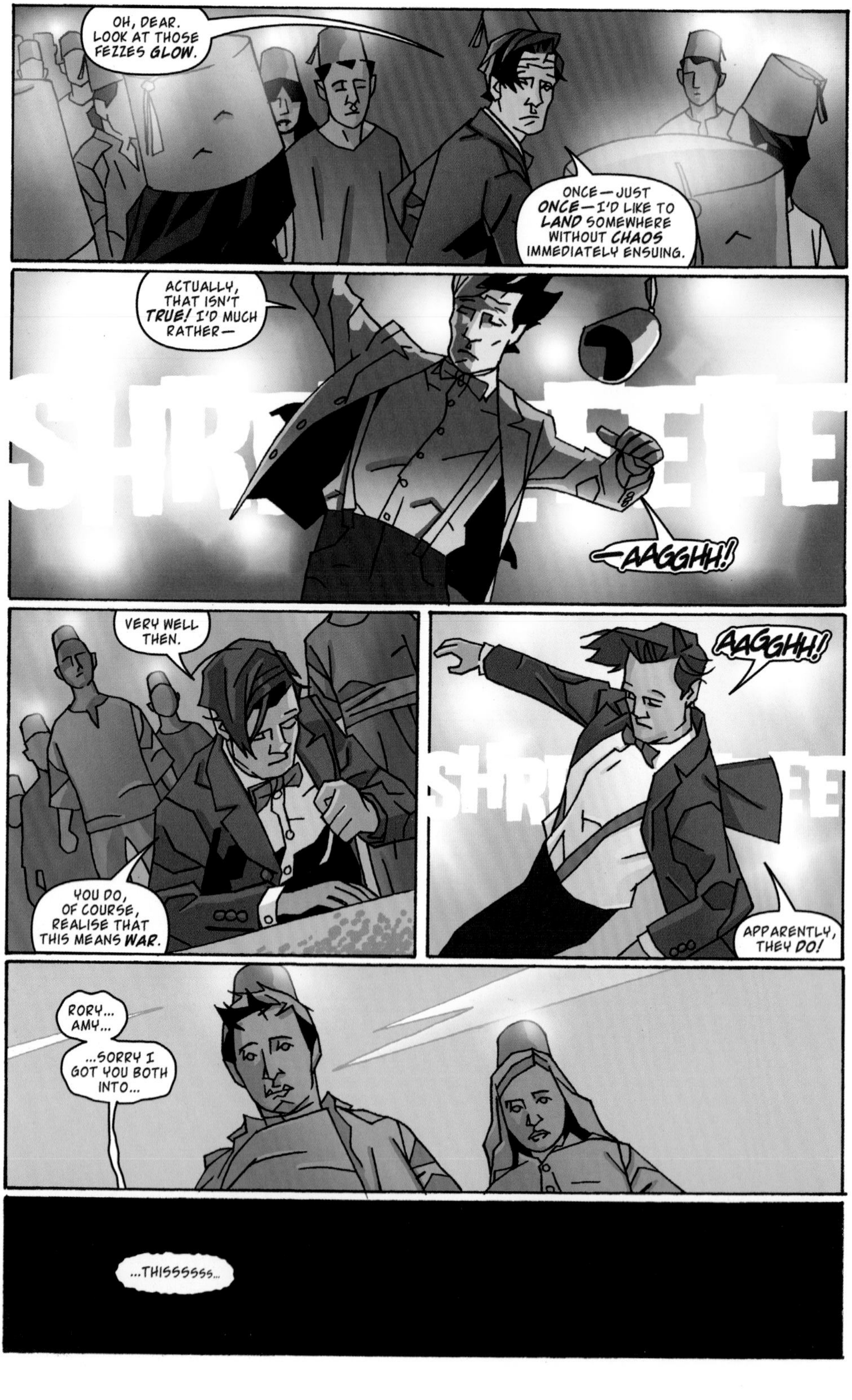

OH, DEAR. LOOK AT THOSE FEZZES GLOW.
ONCE—JUST ONCE—I'D LIKE TO LAND SOMEWHERE WITHOUT CHAOS IMMEDIATELY ENSUING.
ACTUALLY, THAT ISN'T TRUE! I'D MUCH RATHER—
—AAGGHH!
VERY WELL THEN.
YOU DO, OF COURSE, REALISE THAT THIS MEANS WAR.
AAGGHH!
APPARENTLY, THEY DO!
RORY... AMY...
...SORRY I GOT YOU BOTH INTO...
...THISSSSSS...

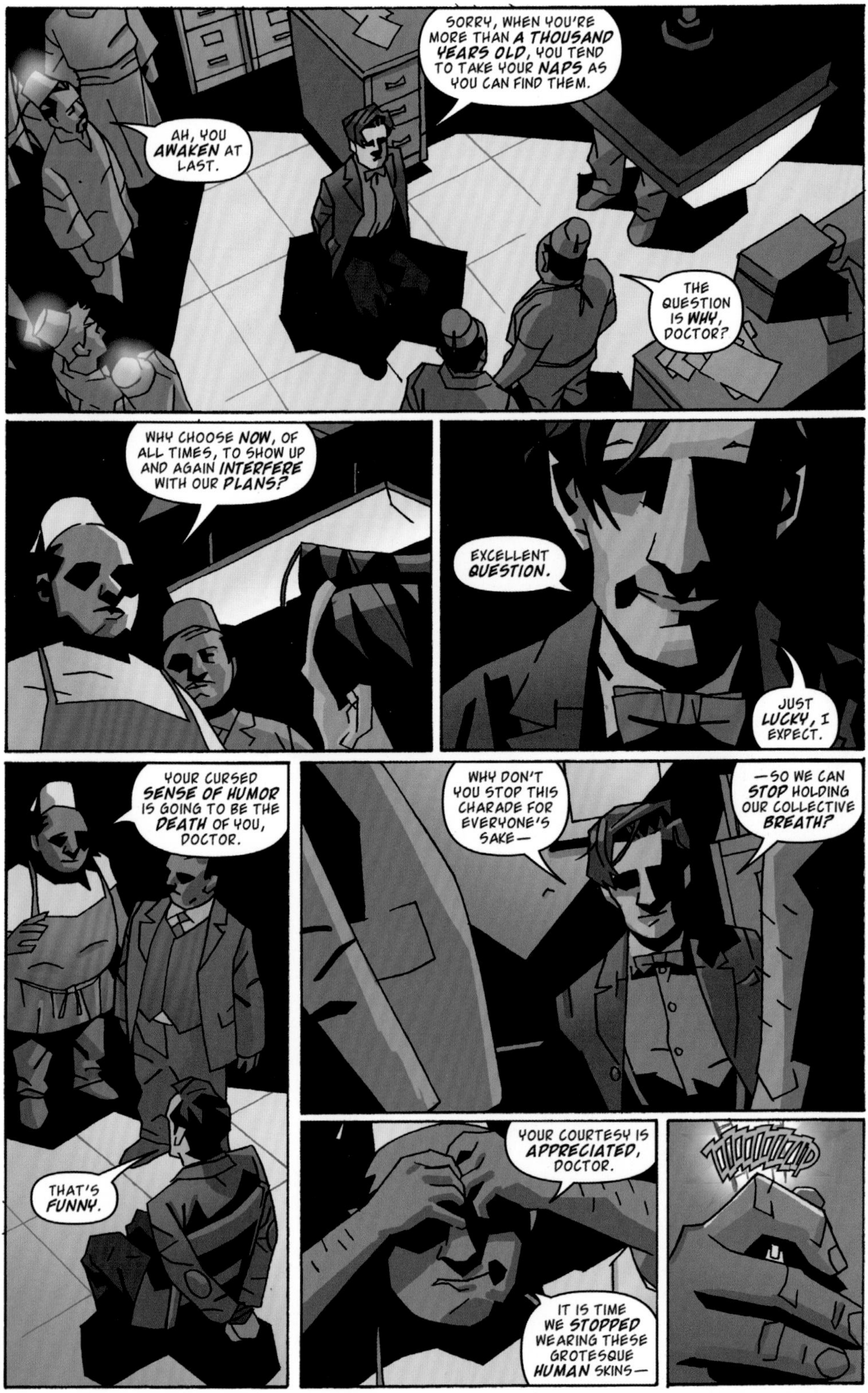
AH, YOU AWAKEN AT LAST.
SORRY, WHEN YOU'RE MORE THAN A THOUSAND YEARS OLD, YOU TEND TO TAKE YOUR NAPS AS YOU CAN FIND THEM.
THE QUESTION IS WHY, DOCTOR?
WHY CHOOSE NOW, OF ALL TIMES, TO SHOW UP AND AGAIN INTERFERE WITH OUR PLANS?
EXCELLENT QUESTION.
JUST LUCKY, I EXPECT.
YOUR CURSED SENSE OF HUMOR IS GOING TO BE THE DEATH OF YOU, DOCTOR.
THAT'S FUNNY.
WHY DON'T YOU STOP THIS CHARADE FOR EVERYONE'S SAKE—
—SO WE CAN STOP HOLDING OUR COLLECTIVE BREATH?
YOUR COURTESY IS APPRECIATED, DOCTOR.
IT IS TIME WE STOPPED WEARING THESE GROTESQUE HUMAN SKINS—

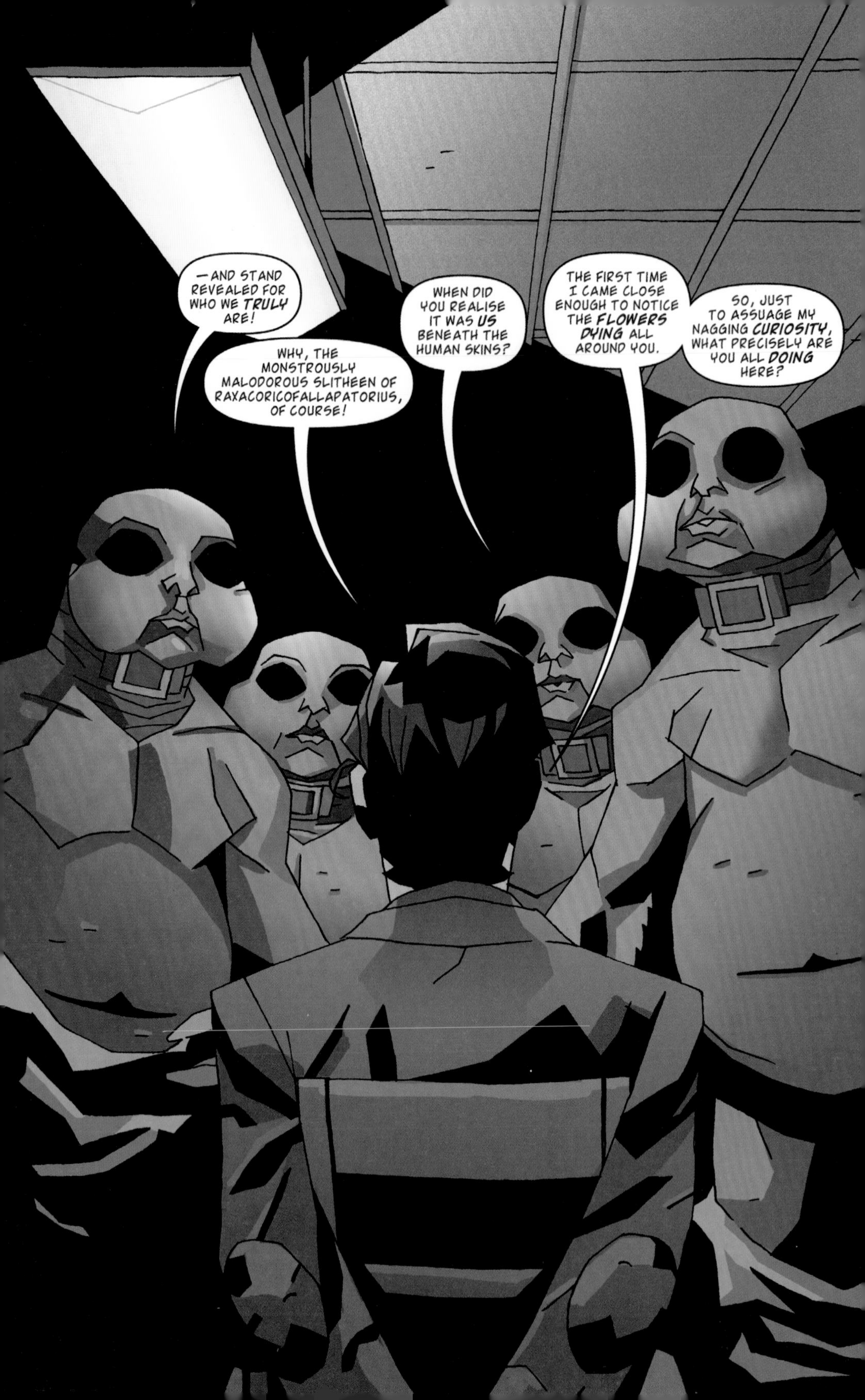
—AND STAND REVEALED FOR WHO WE TRULY ARE!
WHY, THE MONSTROUSLY MALODOROUS SLITHEEN OF RAXACORICOFALLAPATORIUS, OF COURSE!
WHEN DID YOU REALISE IT WAS US BENEATH THE HUMAN SKINS?
THE FIRST TIME I CAME CLOSE ENOUGH TO NOTICE THE FLOWERS DYING ALL AROUND YOU.
SO, JUST TO ASSUAGE MY NAGGING CURIOSITY, WHAT PRECISELY ARE YOU ALL DOING HERE?

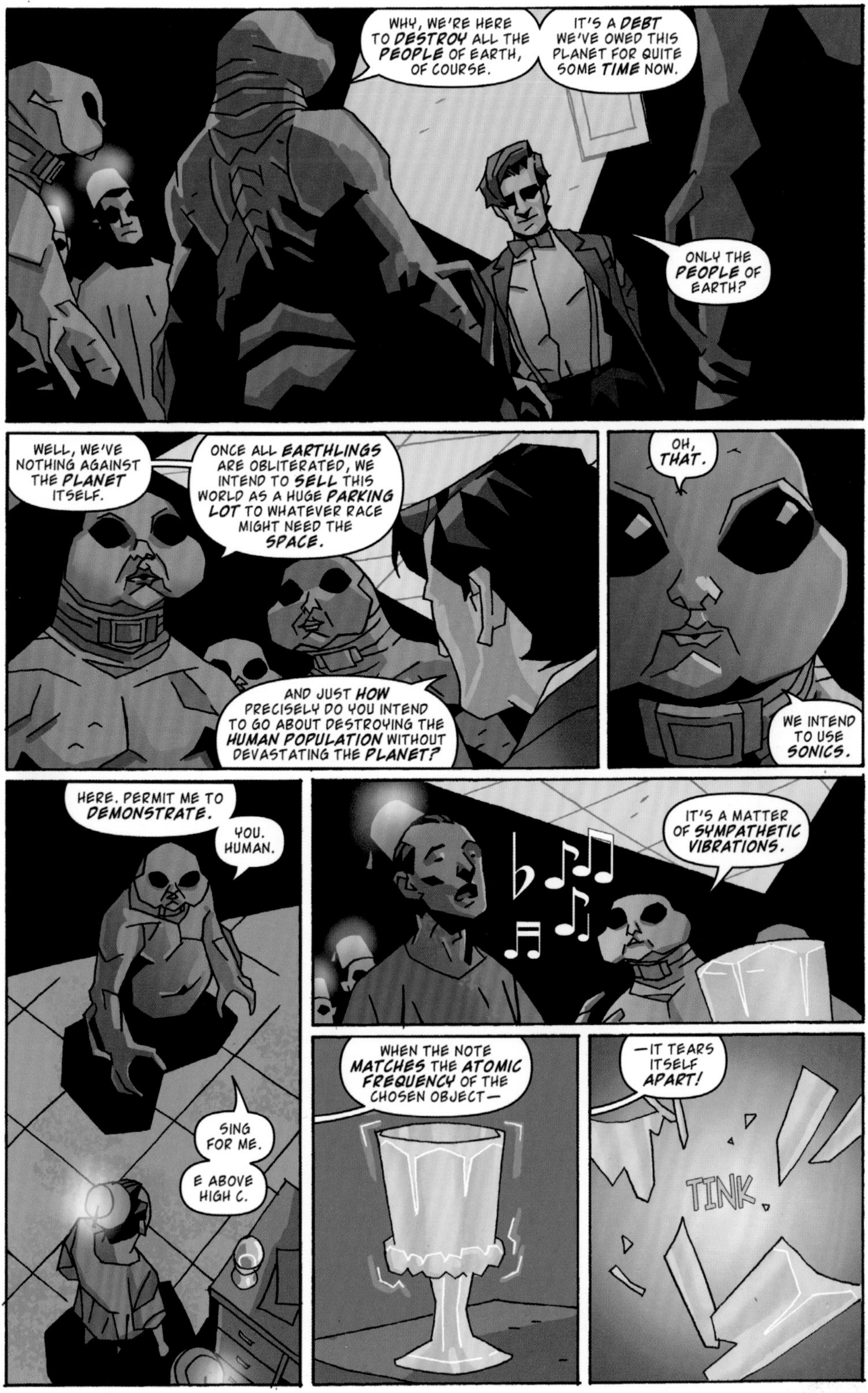
WHY, WE'RE HERE TO DESTROY ALL THE PEOPLE OF EARTH, OF COURSE.
IT'S A DEBT WE'VE OWED THIS PLANET FOR QUITE SOME TIME NOW.
ONLY THE PEOPLE OF EARTH?
WELL, WE'VE NOTHING AGAINST THE PLANET ITSELF.
ONCE ALL EARTHLINGS ARE OBLITERATED, WE INTEND TO SELL THIS WORLD AS A HUGE PARKING LOT TO WHATEVER RACE MIGHT NEED THE SPACE.
AND JUST HOW PRECISELY DO YOU INTEND TO GO ABOUT DESTROYING THE HUMAN POPULATION WITHOUT DEVASTATING THE PLANET?
OH, THAT.
WE INTEND TO USE SONICS.
HERE. PERMIT ME TO DEMONSTRATE.
YOU. HUMAN.
SING FOR ME.
E ABOVE HIGH C.
IT'S A MATTER OF SYMPATHETIC VIBRATIONS.
WHEN THE NOTE MATCHES THE ATOMIC FREQUENCY OF THE CHOSEN OBJECT—
—IT TEARS ITSELF APART!
TINK

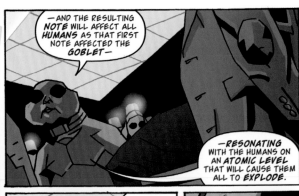

WE'RE USING THE FEZZES TO *CONTROL* THE MINDS OF EVERY *HUMAN* WE CAN IDENTIFY WHO HAS A LEGITIMATE *SINGING VOICE.*

IN A FEW *MOMENTS,* ALL ACROSS THIS *WORLD,* WE SHALL USE OUR MIND-CONTROL TO *FORCE* OUR SUBSERVIENT HUMANS TO SING IN *UNISON*—

—AND THE RESULTING *NOTE* WILL AFFECT ALL *HUMANS* AS THAT FIRST NOTE AFFECTED THE *GOBLET*—

—*RESONATING* WITH THE HUMANS ON AN *ATOMIC LEVEL* THAT WILL CAUSE THEM ALL TO *EXPLODE.*

A *MESSY* FORM OF REVENGE, GRANTED—

—BUT REALLY RATHER *EFFECTIVE.*

FASCINATING *THEORY*—

—BUT YOU'RE MAKING A TERRIBLE *MISTAKE.*

NOT *THIS* TIME.

JUST *SIT* THERE FOR A FEW MORE *MINUTES* AND YOU'LL SEE.

SERIOUSLY... YOU DON'T WANT TO *DO* THIS.

WE'VE NEVER WANTED ANYTHING *MORE.*

LET THE SYMPHONY *COMMENCE.*

KLIK

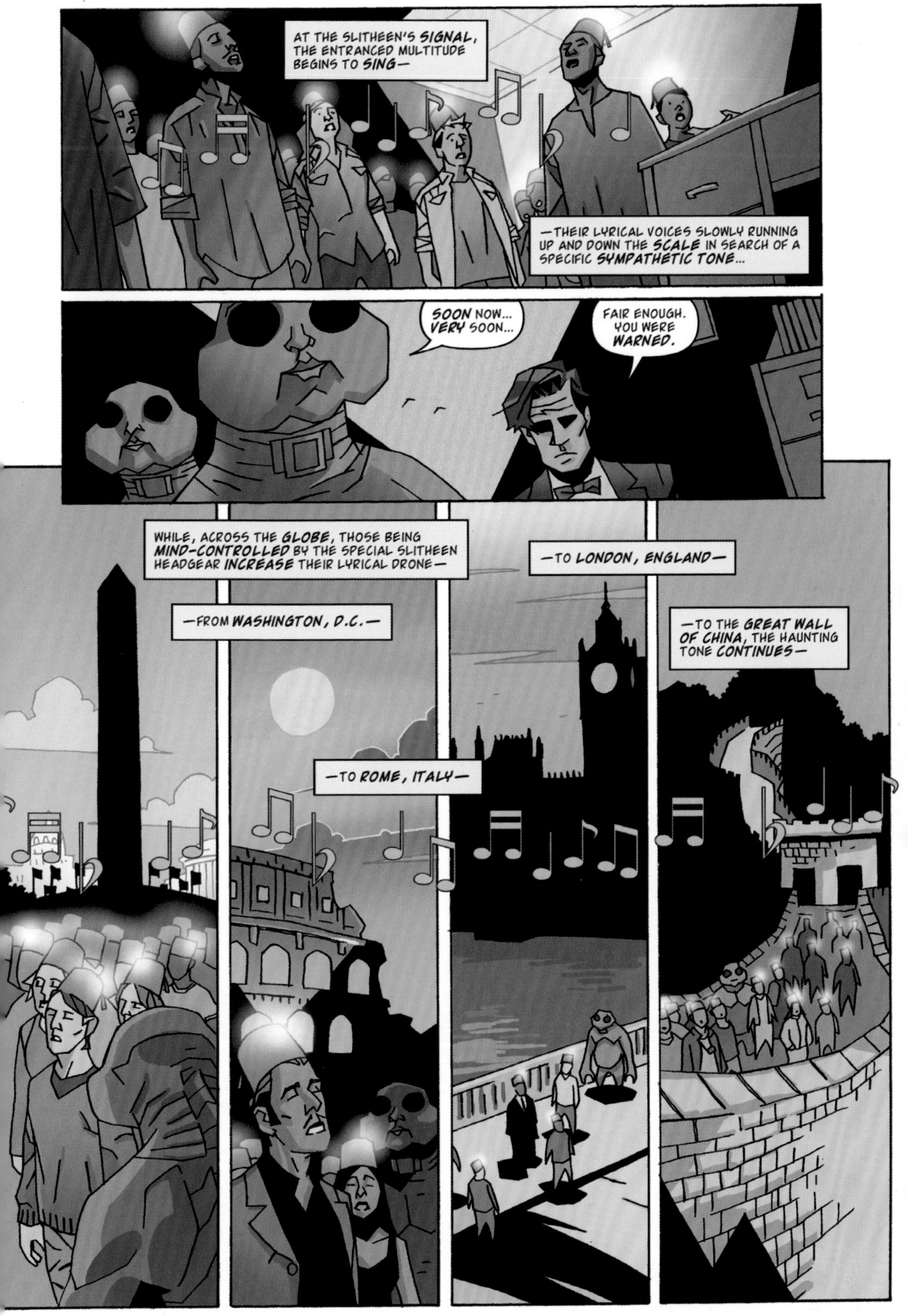
AT THE SLITHEEN'S SIGNAL, THE ENTRANCED MULTITUDE BEGINS TO SING—
—THEIR LYRICAL VOICES SLOWLY RUNNING UP AND DOWN THE SCALE IN SEARCH OF A SPECIFIC SYMPATHETIC TONE...
SOON NOW... VERY SOON...
FAIR ENOUGH. YOU WERE WARNED.
WHILE, ACROSS THE GLOBE, THOSE BEING MIND-CONTROLLED BY THE SPECIAL SLITHEEN HEADGEAR INCREASE THEIR LYRICAL DRONE—
—FROM WASHINGTON, D.C.—
—TO ROME, ITALY—
—TO LONDON, ENGLAND—
—TO THE GREAT WALL OF CHINA, THE HAUNTING TONE CONTINUES—

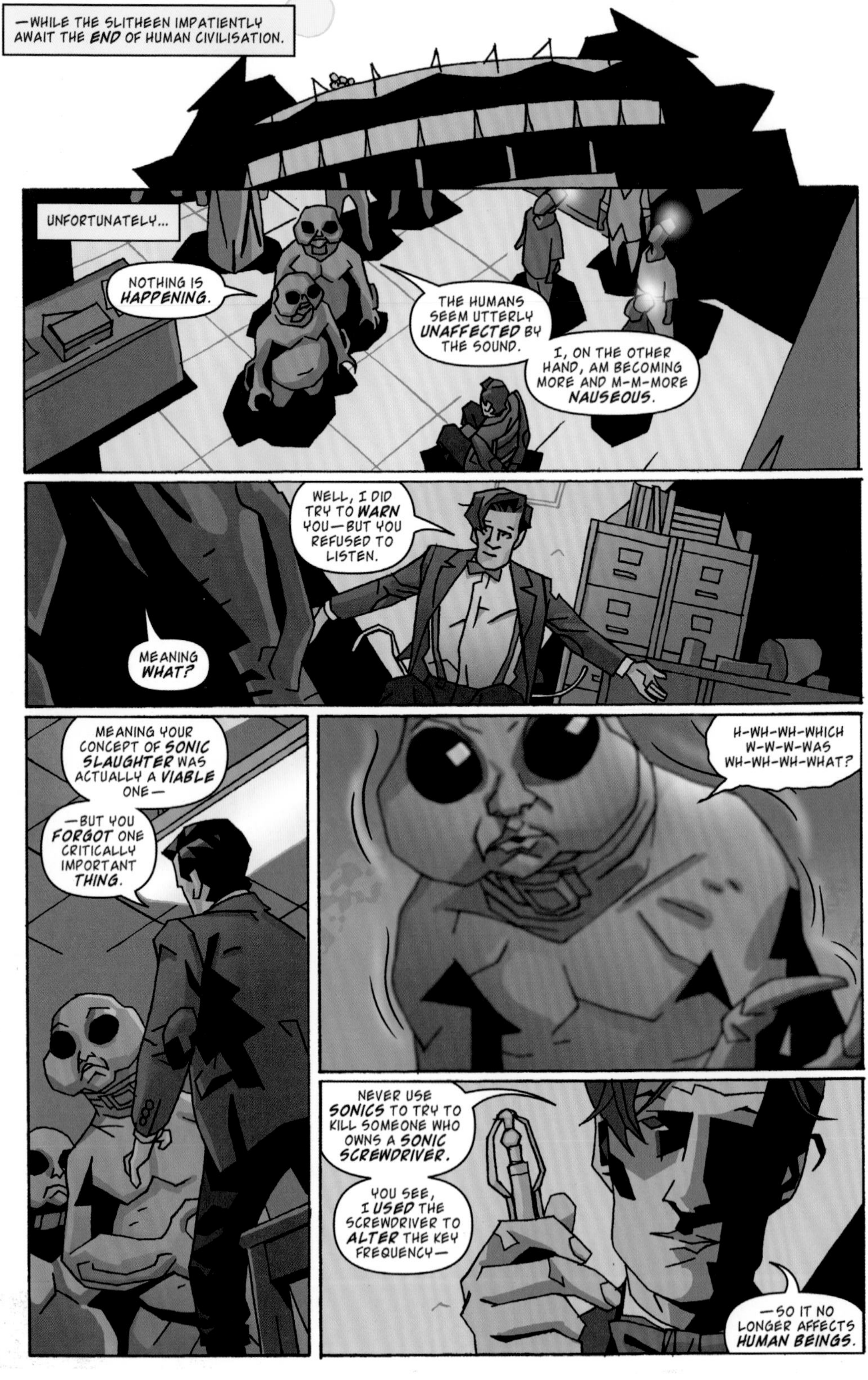
—WHILE THE SLITHEEN IMPATIENTLY AWAIT THE END OF HUMAN CIVILISATION.
UNFORTUNATELY...
NOTHING IS HAPPENING.
THE HUMANS SEEM UTTERLY UNAFFECTED BY THE SOUND.
I, ON THE OTHER HAND, AM BECOMING MORE AND M-M-MORE NAUSEOUS.
WELL, I DID TRY TO WARN YOU—BUT YOU REFUSED TO LISTEN.
MEANING WHAT?
MEANING YOUR CONCEPT OF SONIC SLAUGHTER WAS ACTUALLY A VIABLE ONE—
—BUT YOU FORGOT ONE CRITICALLY IMPORTANT THING.
H-WH-WH-WHICH W-W-W-WAS WH-WH-WH-WHAT?
NEVER USE SONICS TO TRY TO KILL SOMEONE WHO OWNS A SONIC SCREWDRIVER.
YOU SEE, I USED THE SCREWDRIVER TO ALTER THE KEY FREQUENCY—
—SO IT NO LONGER AFFECTS HUMAN BEINGS.

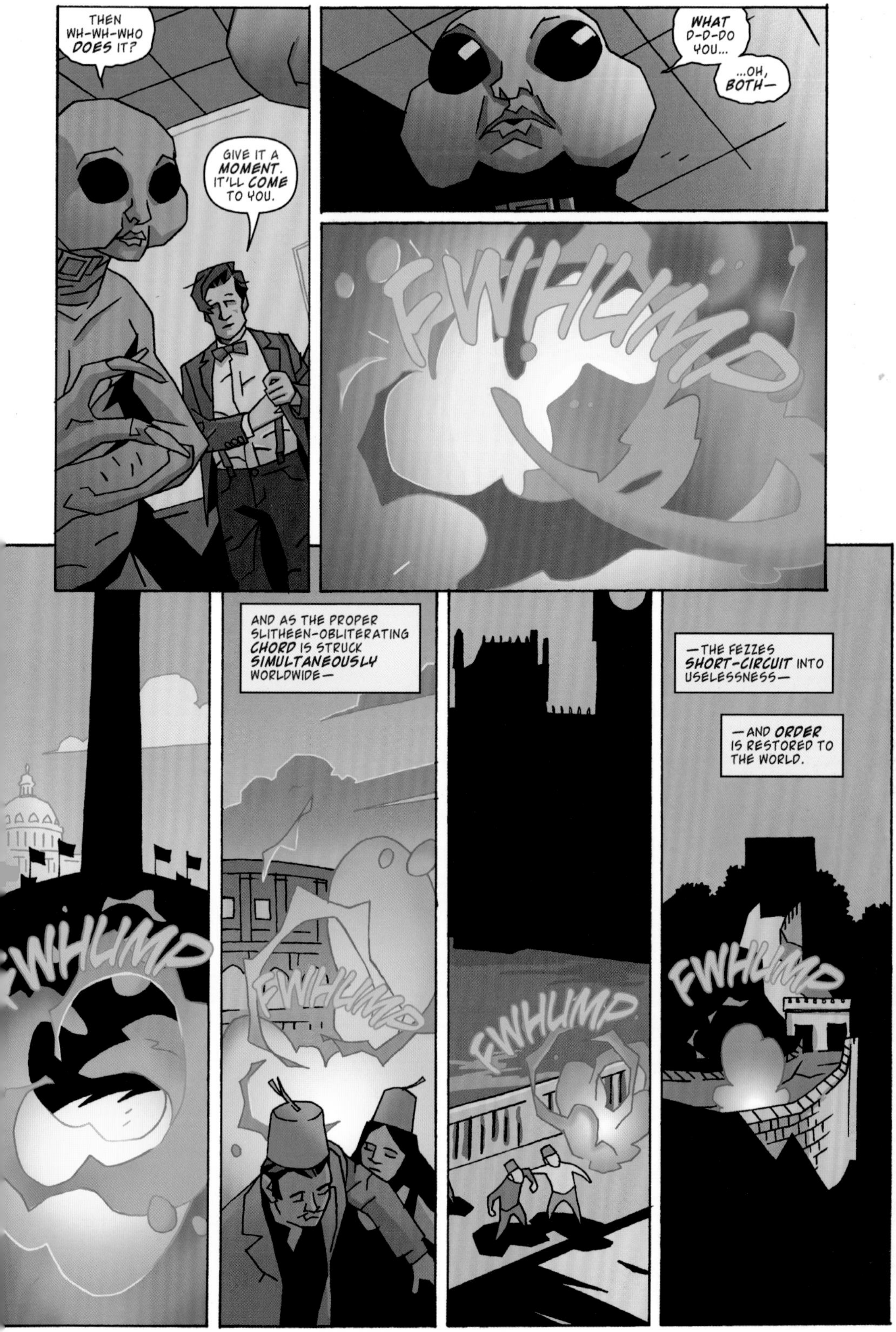
THEN WH-WH-WHO DOES IT?
GIVE IT A MOMENT. IT'LL COME TO YOU.
WHAT D-D-DO YOU...
...OH, BOTH—
FWHUMP
FWHUMP
AND AS THE PROPER SLITHEEN-OBLITERATING CHORD IS STRUCK SIMULTANEOUSLY WORLDWIDE—
FWHUMP
FWHUMP
—THE FEZZES SHORT-CIRCUIT INTO USELESSNESS—
—AND ORDER IS RESTORED TO THE WORLD.
FWHUMP

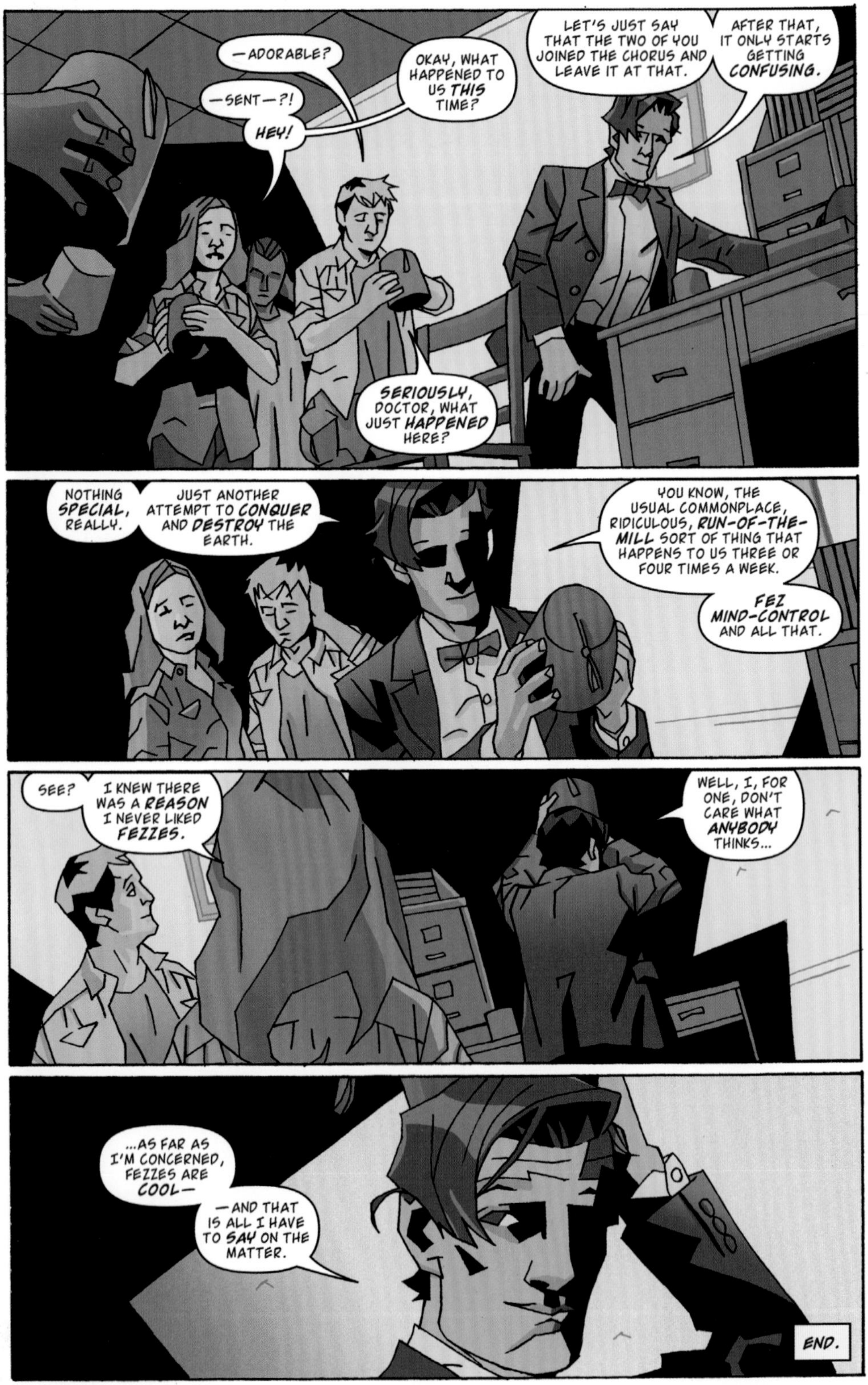
—ADORABLE?
—SENT—?!
HEY!
OKAY, WHAT HAPPENED TO US THIS TIME?
LET'S JUST SAY THAT THE TWO OF YOU JOINED THE CHORUS AND LEAVE IT AT THAT.
AFTER THAT, IT ONLY STARTS GETTING CONFUSING.
SERIOUSLY, DOCTOR, WHAT JUST HAPPENED HERE?
NOTHING SPECIAL, REALLY.
JUST ANOTHER ATTEMPT TO CONQUER AND DESTROY THE EARTH.
YOU KNOW, THE USUAL COMMONPLACE, RIDICULOUS, RUN-OF-THE-MILL SORT OF THING THAT HAPPENS TO US THREE OR FOUR TIMES A WEEK.
FEZ MIND-CONTROL AND ALL THAT.
SEE?
I KNEW THERE WAS A REASON I NEVER LIKED FEZZES.
WELL, I, FOR ONE, DON'T CARE WHAT ANYBODY THINKS...
...AS FAR AS I'M CONCERNED, FEZZES ARE COOL—
—AND THAT IS ALL I HAVE TO SAY ON THE MATTER.
END.

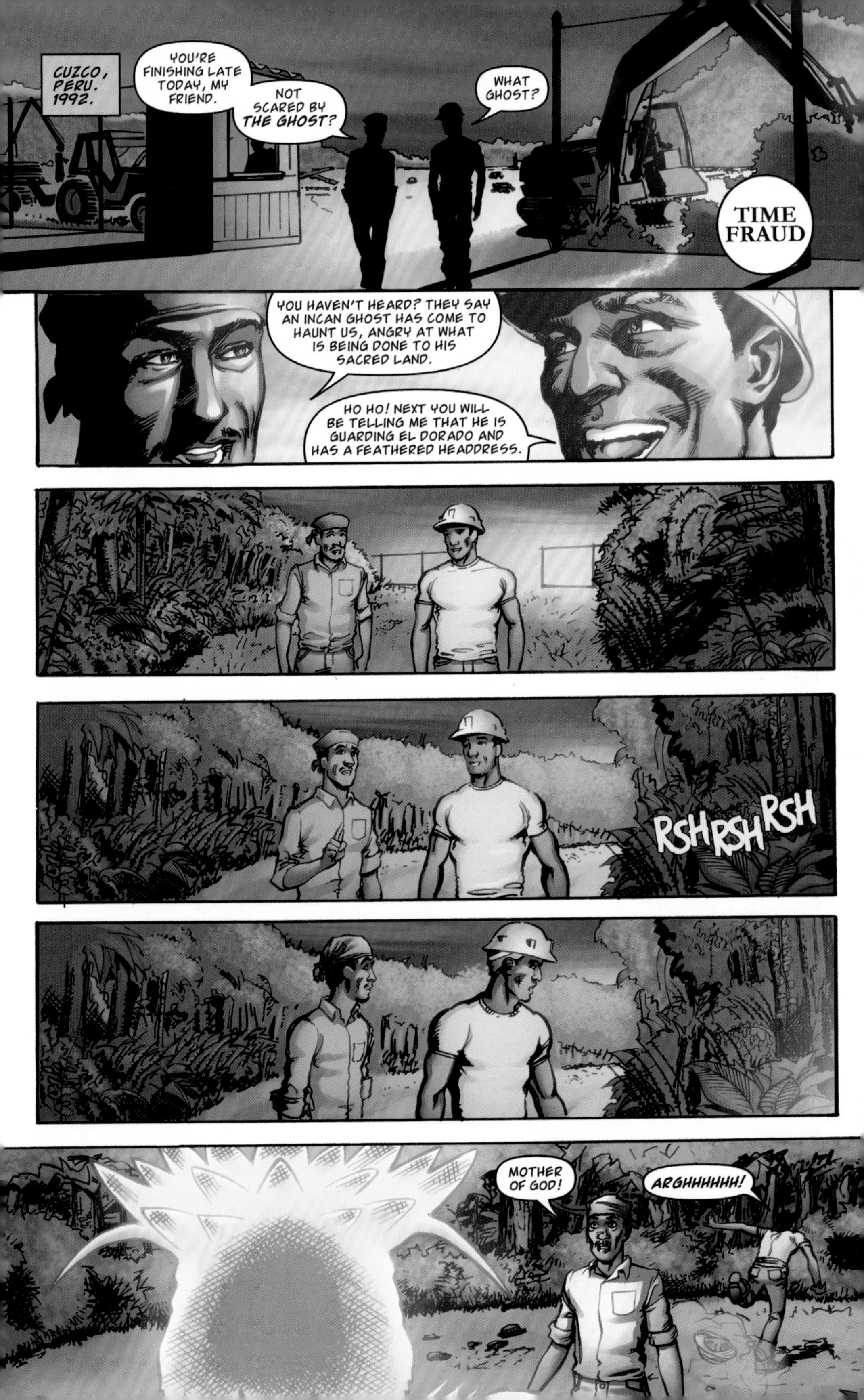
CUZCO, PERU. 1992.
YOU'RE FINISHING LATE TODAY, MY FRIEND.
NOT SCARED BY THE GHOST?
WHAT GHOST?
TIME FRAUD
YOU HAVEN'T HEARD? THEY SAY AN INCAN GHOST HAS COME TO HAUNT US, ANGRY AT WHAT IS BEING DONE TO HIS SACRED LAND.
HO HO! NEXT YOU WILL BE TELLING ME THAT HE IS GUARDING EL DORADO AND HAS A FEATHERED HEADDRESS.
RSH RSH RSH
MOTHER OF GOD!
ARGHHHHHH!

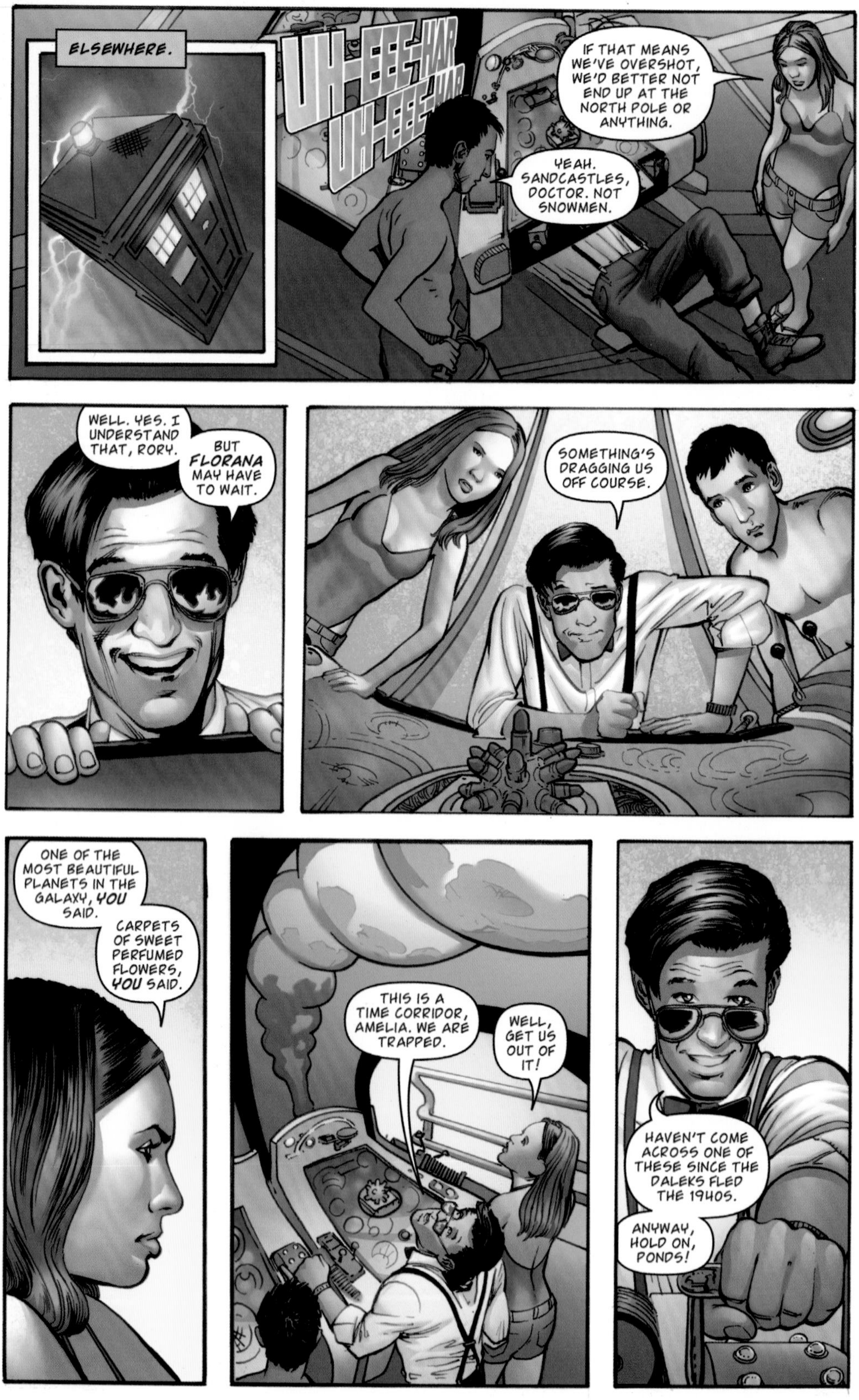

ELSEWHERE.
UH-EEE-HAR UH-EEE-HAR
IF THAT MEANS WE'VE OVERSHOT, WE'D BETTER NOT END UP AT THE NORTH POLE OR ANYTHING.
YEAH. SANDCASTLES, DOCTOR. NOT SNOWMEN.
WELL. YES. I UNDERSTAND THAT, RORY.
BUT **FLORANA** MAY HAVE TO WAIT.
SOMETHING'S DRAGGING US OFF COURSE.
ONE OF THE MOST BEAUTIFUL PLANETS IN THE GALAXY, **YOU** SAID.
CARPETS OF SWEET PERFUMED FLOWERS, **YOU** SAID.
THIS IS A TIME CORRIDOR, AMELIA. WE ARE TRAPPED.
WELL, GET US OUT OF IT!
HAVEN'T COME ACROSS ONE OF THESE SINCE THE DALEKS FLED THE 1940S.
ANYWAY, HOLD ON, PONDS!

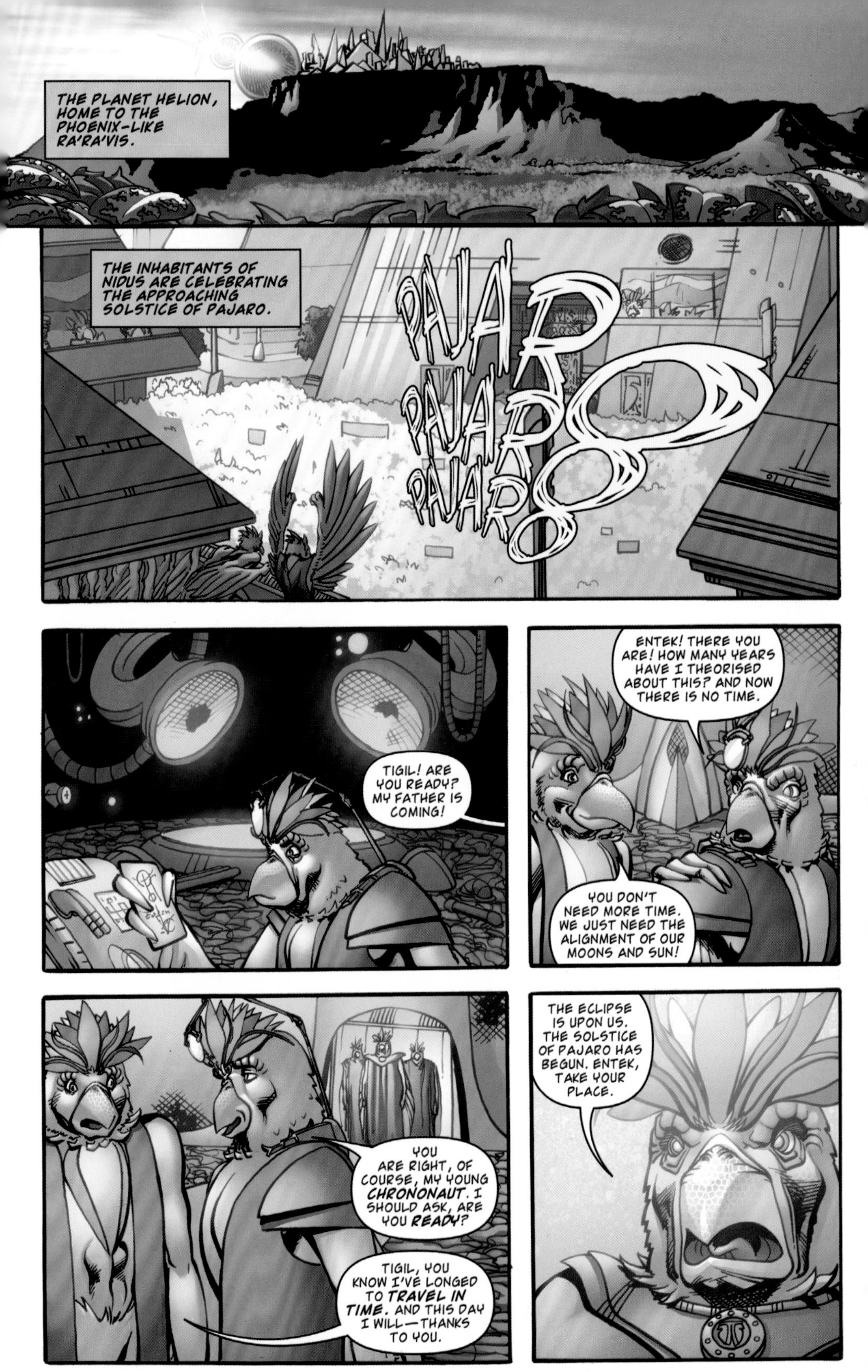
THE PLANET HELION, HOME TO THE PHOENIX-LIKE RA'RA'VIS.
THE INHABITANTS OF NIDUS ARE CELEBRATING THE APPROACHING SOLSTICE OF PAJARO.
PAJARO PAJARO PAJARO
TIGIL! ARE YOU READY? MY FATHER IS COMING!
ENTEK! THERE YOU ARE! HOW MANY YEARS HAVE I THEORISED ABOUT THIS? AND NOW THERE IS NO TIME.
YOU DON'T NEED MORE TIME. WE JUST NEED THE ALIGNMENT OF OUR MOONS AND SUN!
YOU ARE RIGHT, OF COURSE, MY YOUNG **CHRONONAUT**. I SHOULD ASK, ARE YOU **READY**?
TIGIL, YOU KNOW I'VE LONGED TO **TRAVEL IN TIME**. AND THIS DAY I WILL—THANKS TO YOU.
THE ECLIPSE IS UPON US. THE SOLSTICE OF PAJARO HAS BEGUN. ENTEK, TAKE YOUR PLACE.

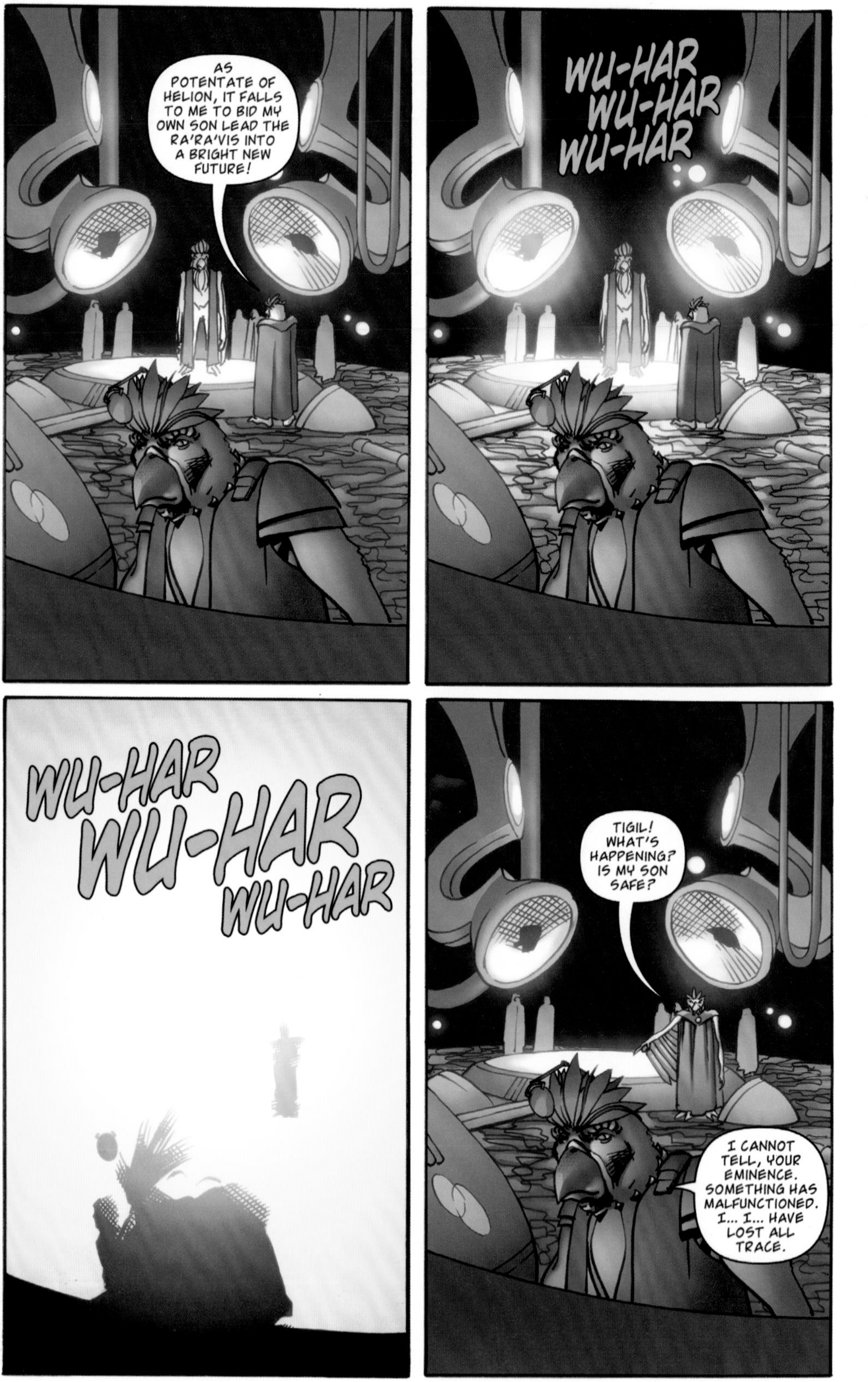
AS POTENTATE OF HELION, IT FALLS TO ME TO BID MY OWN SON LEAD THE RA'RA'VIS INTO A BRIGHT NEW FUTURE!
WU-HAR WU-HAR WU-HAR
WU-HAR WU-HAR WU-HAR
TIGIL! WHAT'S HAPPENING? IS MY SON SAFE?
I CANNOT TELL, YOUR EMINENCE. SOMETHING HAS MALFUNCTIONED. I... I... HAVE LOST ALL TRACE.

CUZCO, PERU. 1992.

WHAT DOES A TIME CORRIDOR LOOK LIKE? HAS IT GOT ROUNDELS?

I AM CERTAINLY LOVING THIS *HEAT!* IS THERE A POOL?

NO. NO POOL. JUST PONDS. AND NO RIVER. WELL, THE AMAZON. BUT NOT *THAT* RIVER.

SAW SOME EXILLON MARKINGS NEAR HERE ONCE, TOO.

THIS WAY!

THIS IS AN OUTRAGE! YOU MUST HAVE RUN EVERY VARIATION OF YOUR MODEL. MY SON... MY *SON!*

I WAS CERTAIN I HAD, YOUR EMINENCE. I ASSURE YOU I WOULD NEVER HAVE ENDANGERED ENTEK. I... MUST HAVE OVERREACHED MYSELF. MY CALCULATIONS MUST HAVE BEEN WRONG.

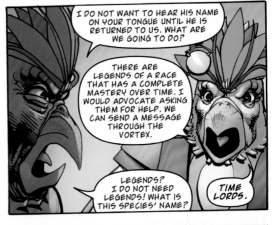

I DO NOT WANT TO HEAR HIS NAME ON YOUR TONGUE UNTIL HE IS RETURNED TO US. WHAT ARE WE GOING TO DO?

THERE ARE LEGENDS OF A RACE THAT HAS A COMPLETE MASTERY OVER TIME. I WOULD ADVOCATE ASKING THEM FOR HELP. WE CAN SEND A MESSAGE THROUGH THE VORTEX.

LEGENDS? I DO NOT NEED LEGENDS! WHAT IS THIS SPECIES' NAME?

TIME LORDS.

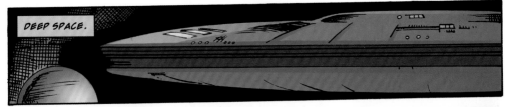

DEEP SPACE.

TAKE ME TO YOUR LEADER!

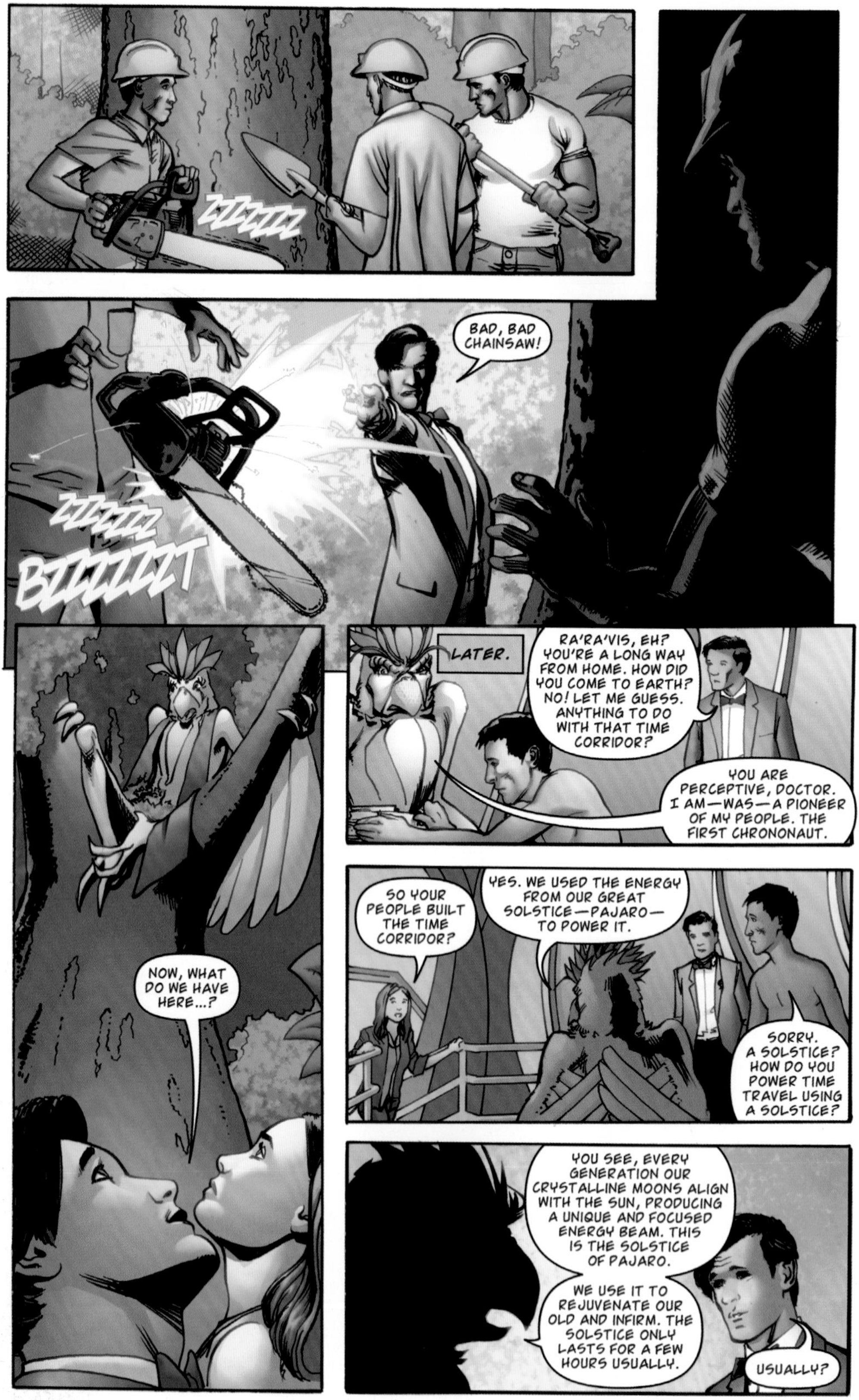
ZZZZZZ
BAD, BAD CHAINSAW!
ZZZZZZ
BZZZZZZT
NOW, WHAT DO WE HAVE HERE...?
LATER.
RA'RA'VIS, EH? YOU'RE A LONG WAY FROM HOME. HOW DID YOU COME TO EARTH? NO! LET ME GUESS. ANYTHING TO DO WITH THAT TIME CORRIDOR?
YOU ARE PERCEPTIVE, DOCTOR. I AM—WAS—A PIONEER OF MY PEOPLE. THE FIRST CHRONONAUT.
SO YOUR PEOPLE BUILT THE TIME CORRIDOR?
YES. WE USED THE ENERGY FROM OUR GREAT SOLSTICE—PAJARO—TO POWER IT.
SORRY. A SOLSTICE? HOW DO YOU POWER TIME TRAVEL USING A SOLSTICE?
YOU SEE, EVERY GENERATION OUR CRYSTALLINE MOONS ALIGN WITH THE SUN, PRODUCING A UNIQUE AND FOCUSED ENERGY BEAM. THIS IS THE SOLSTICE OF PAJARO.
WE USE IT TO REJUVENATE OUR OLD AND INFIRM. THE SOLSTICE ONLY LASTS FOR A FEW HOURS USUALLY.
USUALLY?

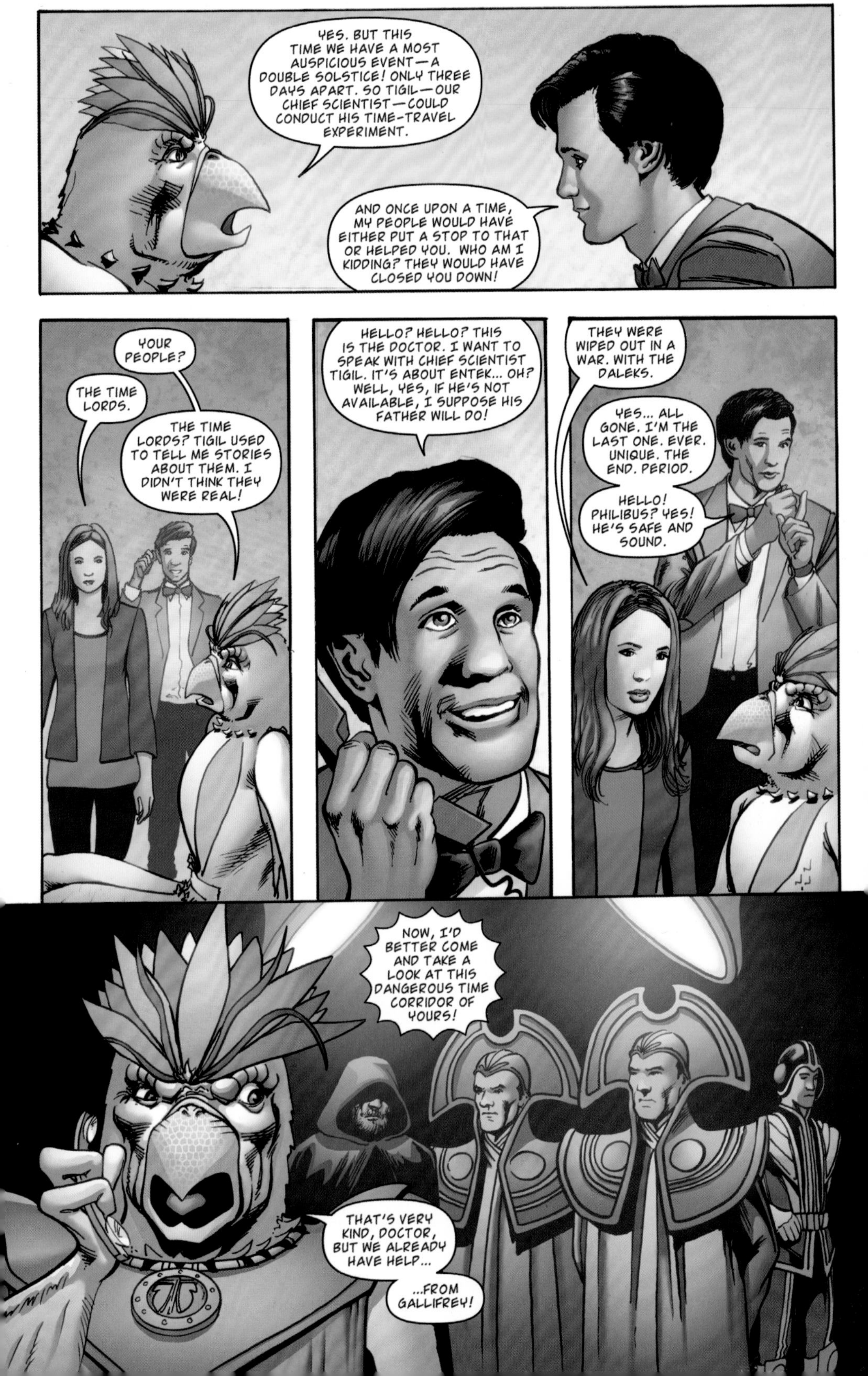
YES. BUT THIS TIME WE HAVE A MOST AUSPICIOUS EVENT—A DOUBLE SOLSTICE! ONLY THREE DAYS APART. SO TIGIL—OUR CHIEF SCIENTIST—COULD CONDUCT HIS TIME-TRAVEL EXPERIMENT.
AND ONCE UPON A TIME, MY PEOPLE WOULD HAVE EITHER PUT A STOP TO THAT OR HELPED YOU. WHO AM I KIDDING? THEY WOULD HAVE CLOSED YOU DOWN!
YOUR PEOPLE?
THE TIME LORDS.
THE TIME LORDS? TIGIL USED TO TELL ME STORIES ABOUT THEM. I DIDN'T THINK THEY WERE REAL!
HELLO? HELLO? THIS IS THE DOCTOR. I WANT TO SPEAK WITH CHIEF SCIENTIST TIGIL. IT'S ABOUT ENTEK... OH? WELL, YES, IF HE'S NOT AVAILABLE, I SUPPOSE HIS FATHER WILL DO!
THEY WERE WIPED OUT IN A WAR. WITH THE DALEKS.
YES... ALL GONE. I'M THE LAST ONE. EVER. UNIQUE. THE END. PERIOD.
HELLO! PHILIBUS? YES! HE'S SAFE AND SOUND.
NOW, I'D BETTER COME AND TAKE A LOOK AT THIS DANGEROUS TIME CORRIDOR OF YOURS!
THAT'S VERY KIND, DOCTOR, BUT WE ALREADY HAVE HELP...
...FROM GALLIFREY!

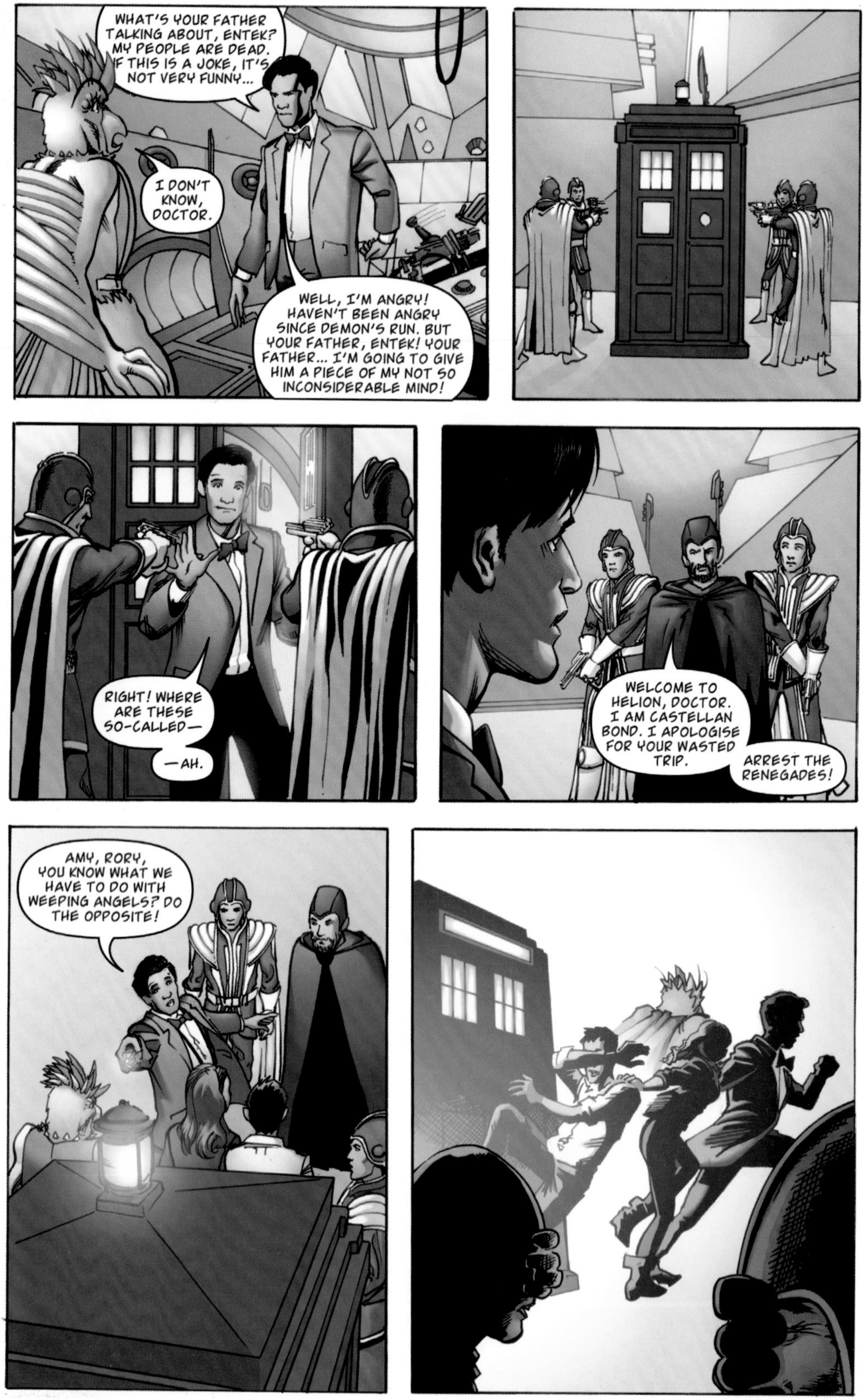
WHAT'S YOUR FATHER TALKING ABOUT, ENTEK? MY PEOPLE ARE DEAD. IF THIS IS A JOKE, IT'S NOT VERY FUNNY...
I DON'T KNOW, DOCTOR.
WELL, I'M ANGRY! HAVEN'T BEEN ANGRY SINCE DEMON'S RUN. BUT YOUR FATHER, ENTEK! YOUR FATHER... I'M GOING TO GIVE HIM A PIECE OF MY NOT SO INCONSIDERABLE MIND!
RIGHT! WHERE ARE THESE SO-CALLED—
—AH.
WELCOME TO HELION, DOCTOR. I AM CASTELLAN BOND. I APOLOGISE FOR YOUR WASTED TRIP.
ARREST THE RENEGADES!
AMY, RORY, YOU KNOW WHAT WE HAVE TO DO WITH WEEPING ANGELS? DO THE OPPOSITE!

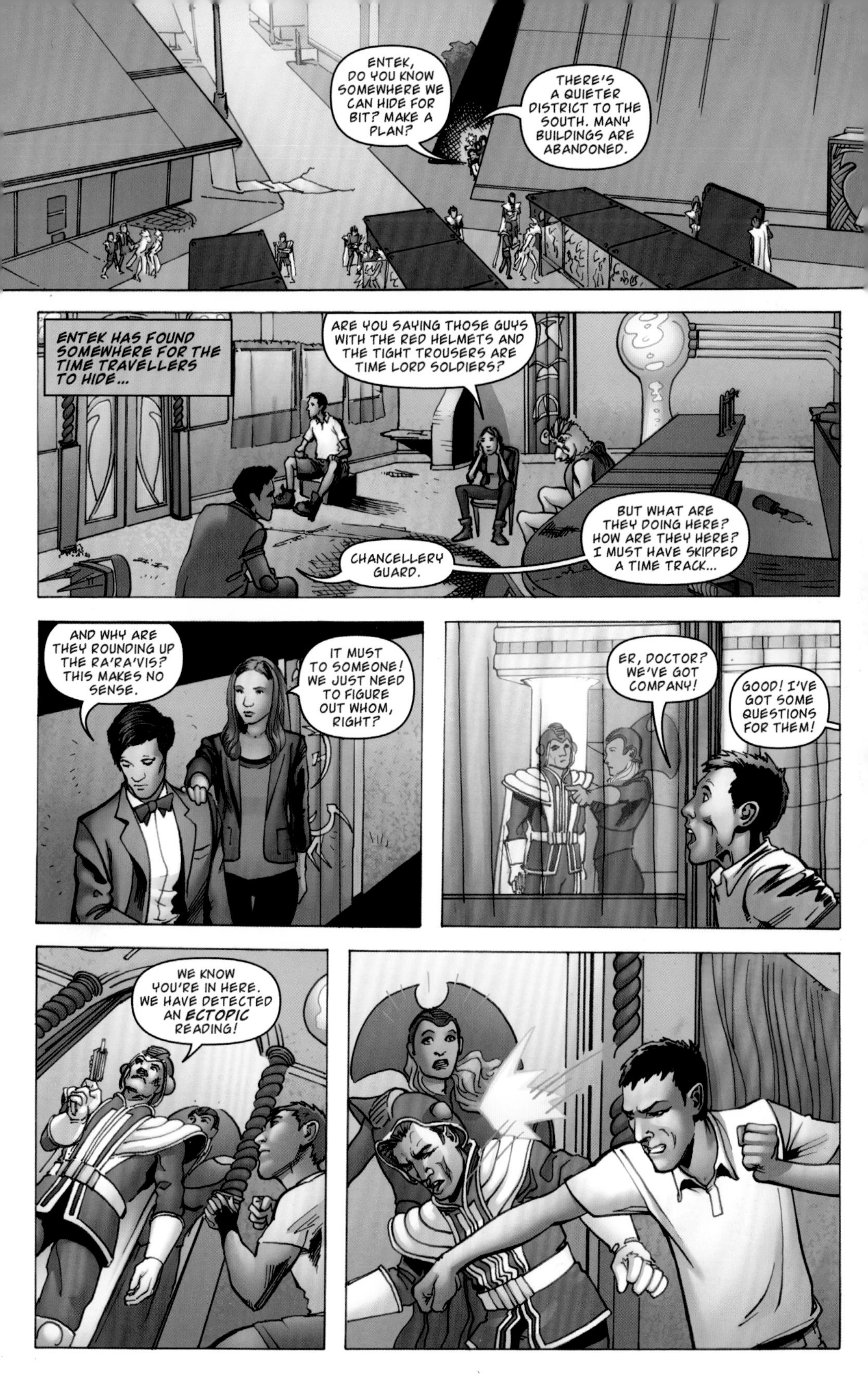

ENTEK, DO YOU KNOW SOMEWHERE WE CAN HIDE FOR BIT? MAKE A PLAN?
THERE'S A QUIETER DISTRICT TO THE SOUTH. MANY BUILDINGS ARE ABANDONED.
ENTEK HAS FOUND SOMEWHERE FOR THE TIME TRAVELLERS TO HIDE...
ARE YOU SAYING THOSE GUYS WITH THE RED HELMETS AND THE TIGHT TROUSERS ARE TIME LORD SOLDIERS?
CHANCELLERY GUARD.
BUT WHAT ARE THEY DOING HERE? HOW ARE THEY HERE? I MUST HAVE SKIPPED A TIME TRACK...
AND WHY ARE THEY ROUNDING UP THE RA'RA'VIS? THIS MAKES NO SENSE.
IT MUST TO SOMEONE! WE JUST NEED TO FIGURE OUT WHOM, RIGHT?
ER, DOCTOR? WE'VE GOT COMPANY!
GOOD! I'VE GOT SOME QUESTIONS FOR THEM!
WE KNOW YOU'RE IN HERE. WE HAVE DETECTED AN ECTOPIC READING!

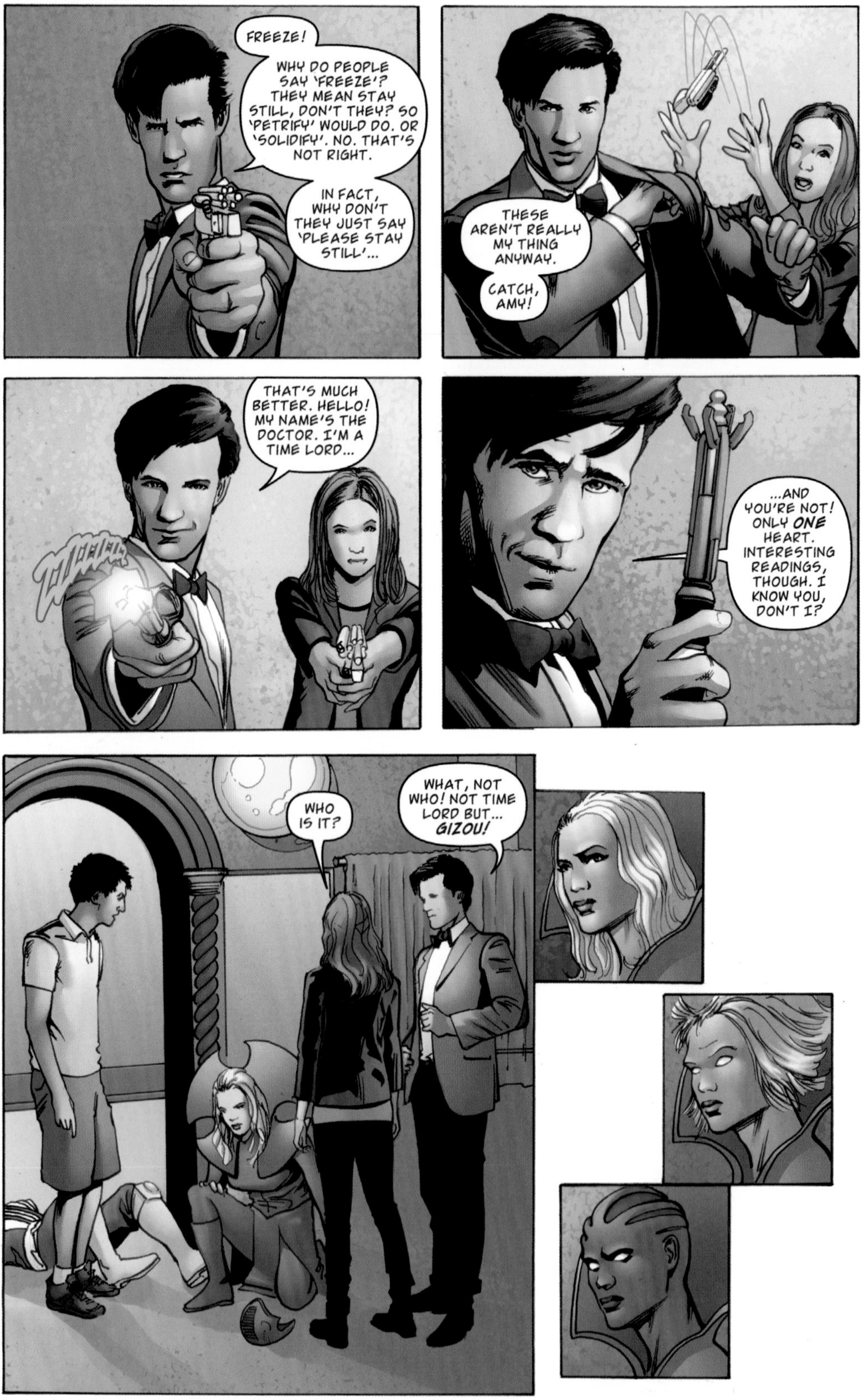
FREEZE!
WHY DO PEOPLE SAY 'FREEZE'? THEY MEAN STAY STILL, DON'T THEY? SO 'PETRIFY' WOULD DO. OR 'SOLIDIFY'. NO. THAT'S NOT RIGHT.
IN FACT, WHY DON'T THEY JUST SAY 'PLEASE STAY STILL'...
THESE AREN'T REALLY MY THING ANYWAY.
CATCH, AMY!
THAT'S MUCH BETTER. HELLO! MY NAME'S THE DOCTOR. I'M A TIME LORD...
...AND YOU'RE NOT! ONLY ONE HEART. INTERESTING READINGS, THOUGH. I KNOW YOU, DON'T I?
WHO IS IT?
WHAT, NOT WHO! NOT TIME LORD BUT... GIZOU!

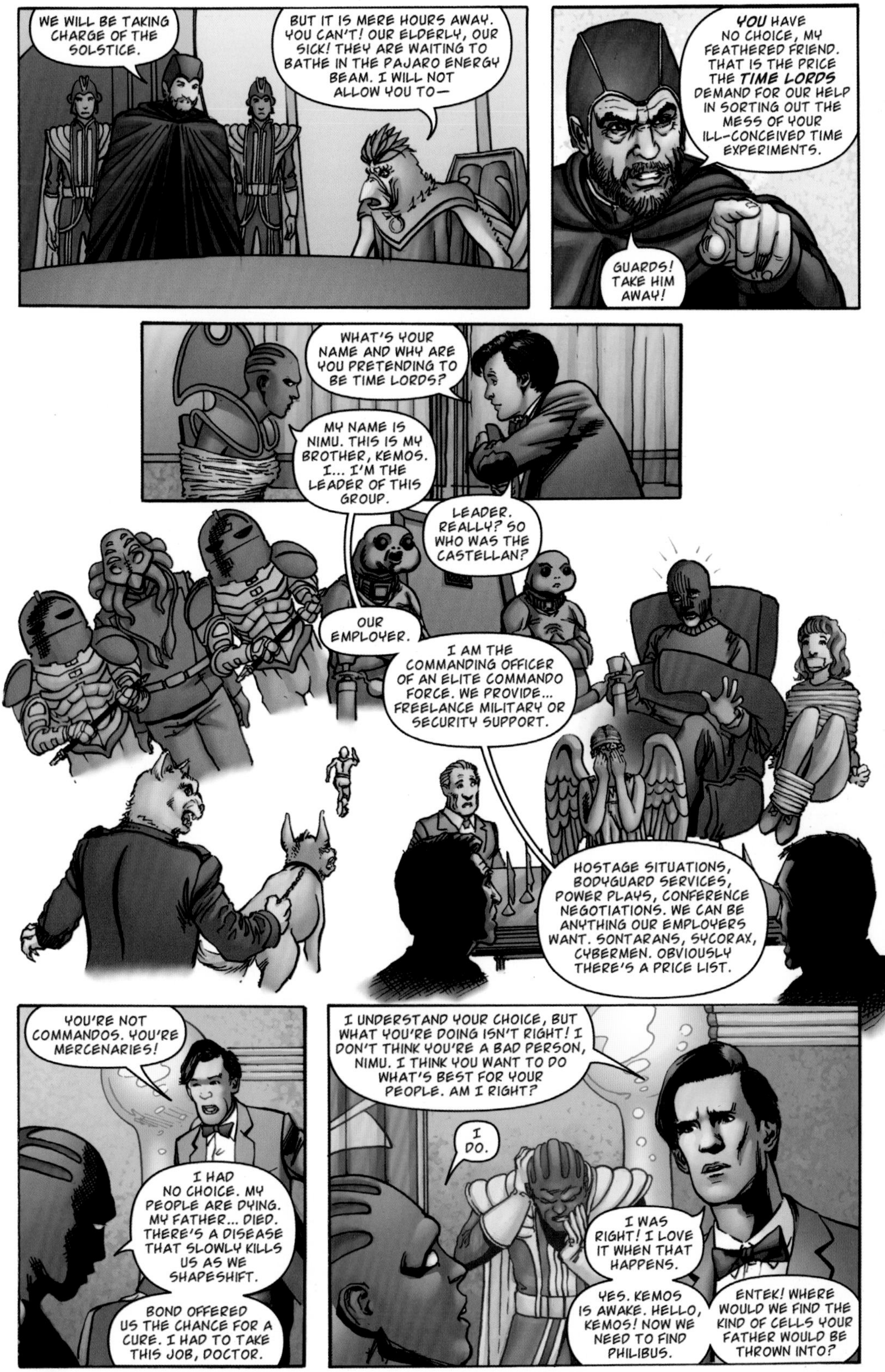
WE WILL BE TAKING CHARGE OF THE SOLSTICE.
BUT IT IS MERE HOURS AWAY. YOU CAN'T! OUR ELDERLY, OUR SICK! THEY ARE WAITING TO BATHE IN THE PAJARO ENERGY BEAM. I WILL NOT ALLOW YOU TO—
YOU HAVE NO CHOICE, MY FEATHERED FRIEND. THAT IS THE PRICE THE TIME LORDS DEMAND FOR OUR HELP IN SORTING OUT THE MESS OF YOUR ILL-CONCEIVED TIME EXPERIMENTS.
GUARDS! TAKE HIM AWAY!
WHAT'S YOUR NAME AND WHY ARE YOU PRETENDING TO BE TIME LORDS?
MY NAME IS NIMU. THIS IS MY BROTHER, KEMOS. I... I'M THE LEADER OF THIS GROUP.
LEADER. REALLY? SO WHO WAS THE CASTELLAN?
OUR EMPLOYER.
I AM THE COMMANDING OFFICER OF AN ELITE COMMANDO FORCE. WE PROVIDE... FREELANCE MILITARY OR SECURITY SUPPORT.
HOSTAGE SITUATIONS, BODYGUARD SERVICES, POWER PLAYS, CONFERENCE NEGOTIATIONS. WE CAN BE ANYTHING OUR EMPLOYERS WANT. SONTARANS, SYCORAX, CYBERMEN. OBVIOUSLY THERE'S A PRICE LIST.
YOU'RE NOT COMMANDOS. YOU'RE MERCENARIES!
I HAD NO CHOICE. MY PEOPLE ARE DYING. MY FATHER... DIED. THERE'S A DISEASE THAT SLOWLY KILLS US AS WE SHAPESHIFT.
BOND OFFERED US THE CHANCE FOR A CURE. I HAD TO TAKE THIS JOB, DOCTOR.
I UNDERSTAND YOUR CHOICE, BUT WHAT YOU'RE DOING ISN'T RIGHT! I DON'T THINK YOU'RE A BAD PERSON, NIMU. I THINK YOU WANT TO DO WHAT'S BEST FOR YOUR PEOPLE. AM I RIGHT?
I DO.
I WAS RIGHT! I LOVE IT WHEN THAT HAPPENS.
YES. KEMOS IS AWAKE. HELLO, KEMOS! NOW WE NEED TO FIND PHILIBUS.
ENTEK! WHERE WOULD WE FIND THE KIND OF CELLS YOUR FATHER WOULD BE THROWN INTO?

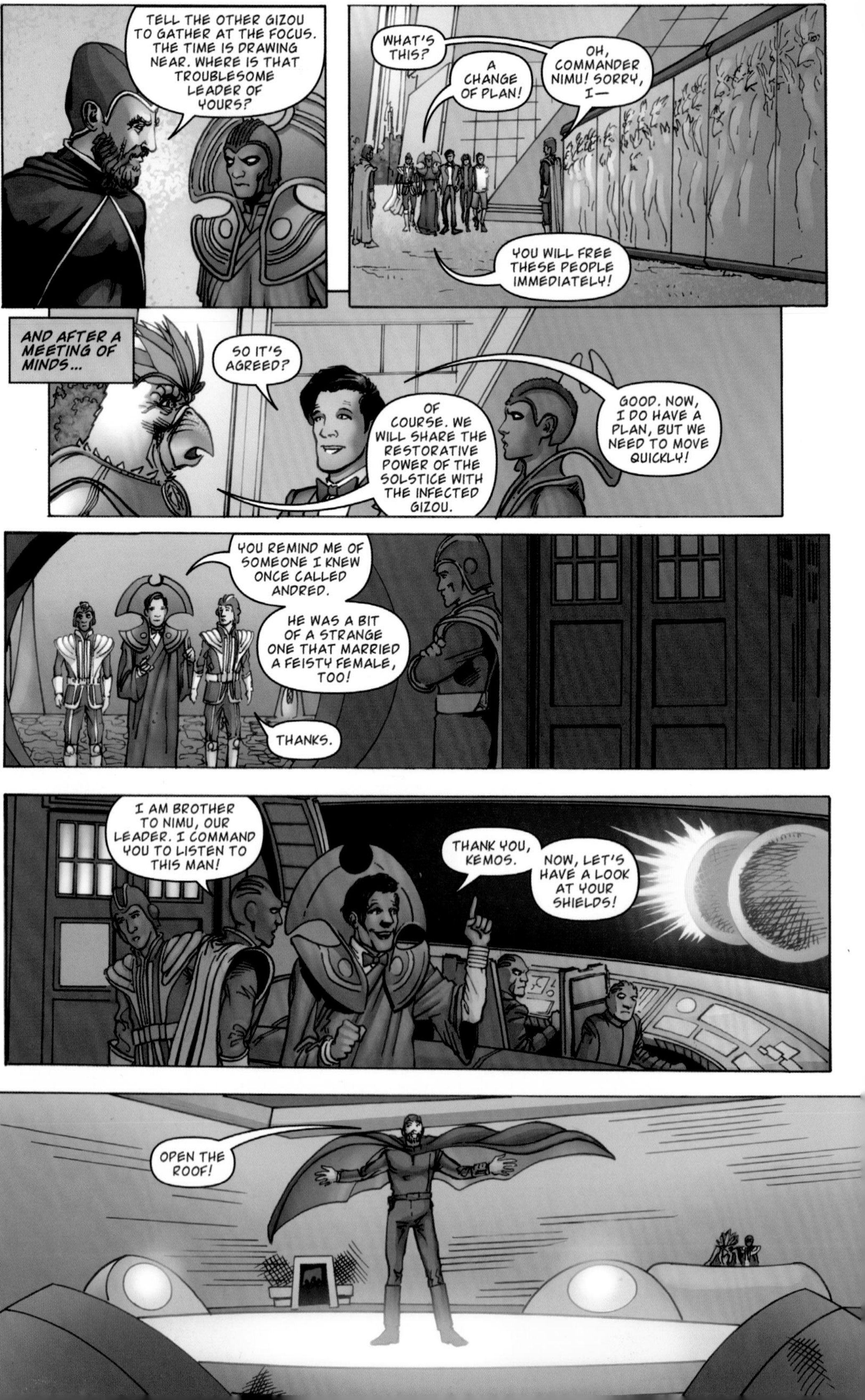
TELL THE OTHER GIZOU TO GATHER AT THE FOCUS. THE TIME IS DRAWING NEAR. WHERE IS THAT TROUBLESOME LEADER OF YOURS?
WHAT'S THIS?
OH, COMMANDER NIMU! SORRY, I—
A CHANGE OF PLAN!
YOU WILL FREE THESE PEOPLE IMMEDIATELY!
AND AFTER A MEETING OF MINDS...
SO IT'S AGREED?
OF COURSE. WE WILL SHARE THE RESTORATIVE POWER OF THE SOLSTICE WITH THE INFECTED GIZOU.
GOOD. NOW, I DO HAVE A PLAN, BUT WE NEED TO MOVE QUICKLY!
YOU REMIND ME OF SOMEONE I KNEW ONCE CALLED ANDRED.
HE WAS A BIT OF A STRANGE ONE THAT MARRIED A FEISTY FEMALE, TOO!
THANKS.
I AM BROTHER TO NIMU, OUR LEADER. I COMMAND YOU TO LISTEN TO THIS MAN!
THANK YOU, KEMOS.
NOW, LET'S HAVE A LOOK AT YOUR SHIELDS!
OPEN THE ROOF!

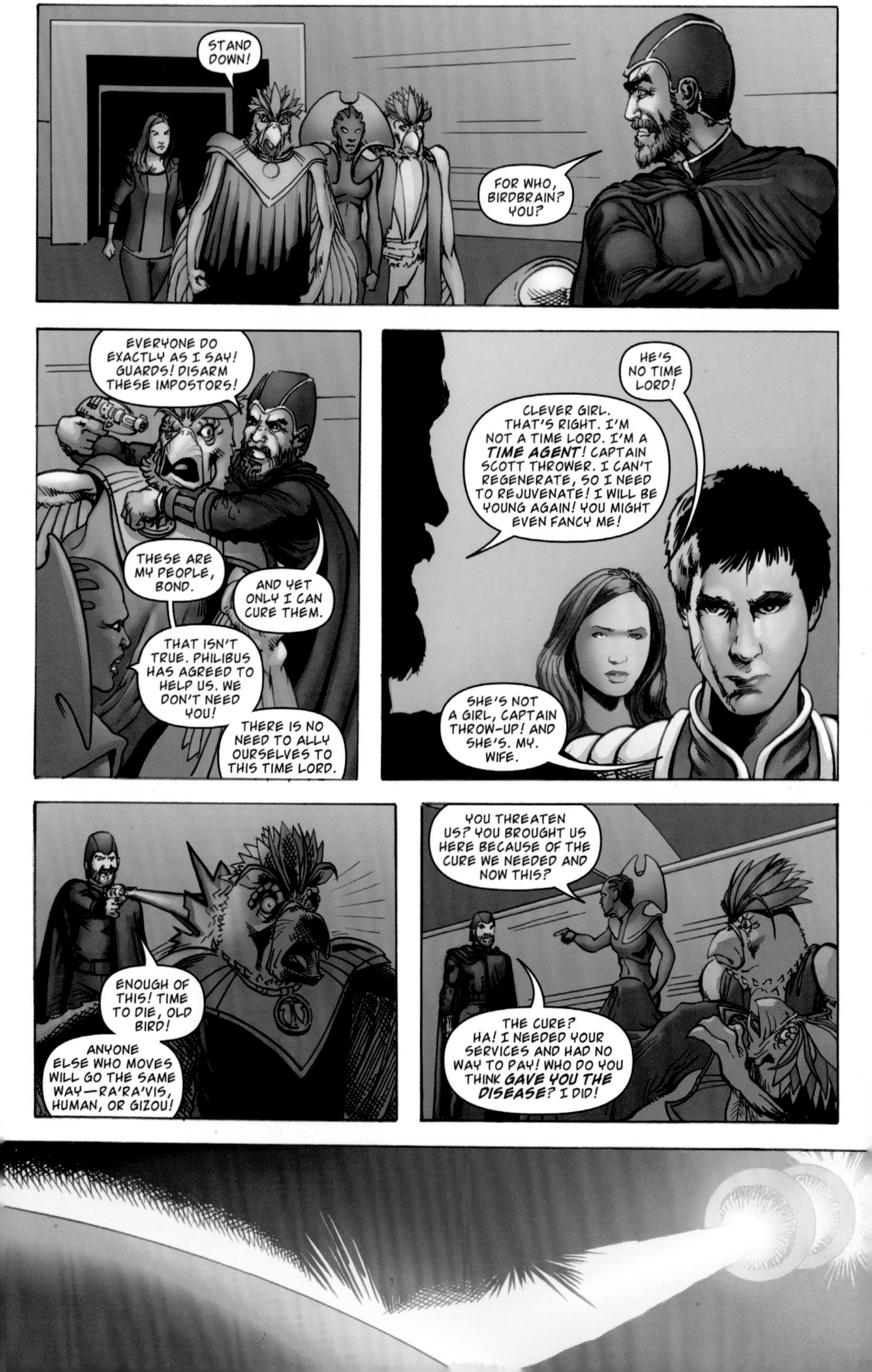
STAND DOWN!
FOR WHO, BIRDBRAIN? YOU?
EVERYONE DO EXACTLY AS I SAY! GUARDS! DISARM THESE IMPOSTORS!
THESE ARE MY PEOPLE, BOND.
AND YET ONLY I CAN CURE THEM.
THAT ISN'T TRUE. PHILIBUS HAS AGREED TO HELP US. WE DON'T NEED YOU!
THERE IS NO NEED TO ALLY OURSELVES TO THIS TIME LORD.
HE'S NO TIME LORD!
CLEVER GIRL. THAT'S RIGHT. I'M NOT A TIME LORD. I'M A TIME AGENT! CAPTAIN SCOTT THROWER. I CAN'T REGENERATE, SO I NEED TO REJUVENATE! I WILL BE YOUNG AGAIN! YOU MIGHT EVEN FANCY ME!
SHE'S NOT A GIRL, CAPTAIN THROW-UP! AND SHE'S. MY. WIFE.
ENOUGH OF THIS! TIME TO DIE, OLD BIRD!
ANYONE ELSE WHO MOVES WILL GO THE SAME WAY—RA'RA'VIS, HUMAN, OR GIZOU!
YOU THREATEN US? YOU BROUGHT US HERE BECAUSE OF THE CURE WE NEEDED AND NOW THIS?
THE CURE? HA! I NEEDED YOUR SERVICES AND HAD NO WAY TO PAY! WHO DO YOU THINK GAVE YOU THE DISEASE? I DID!

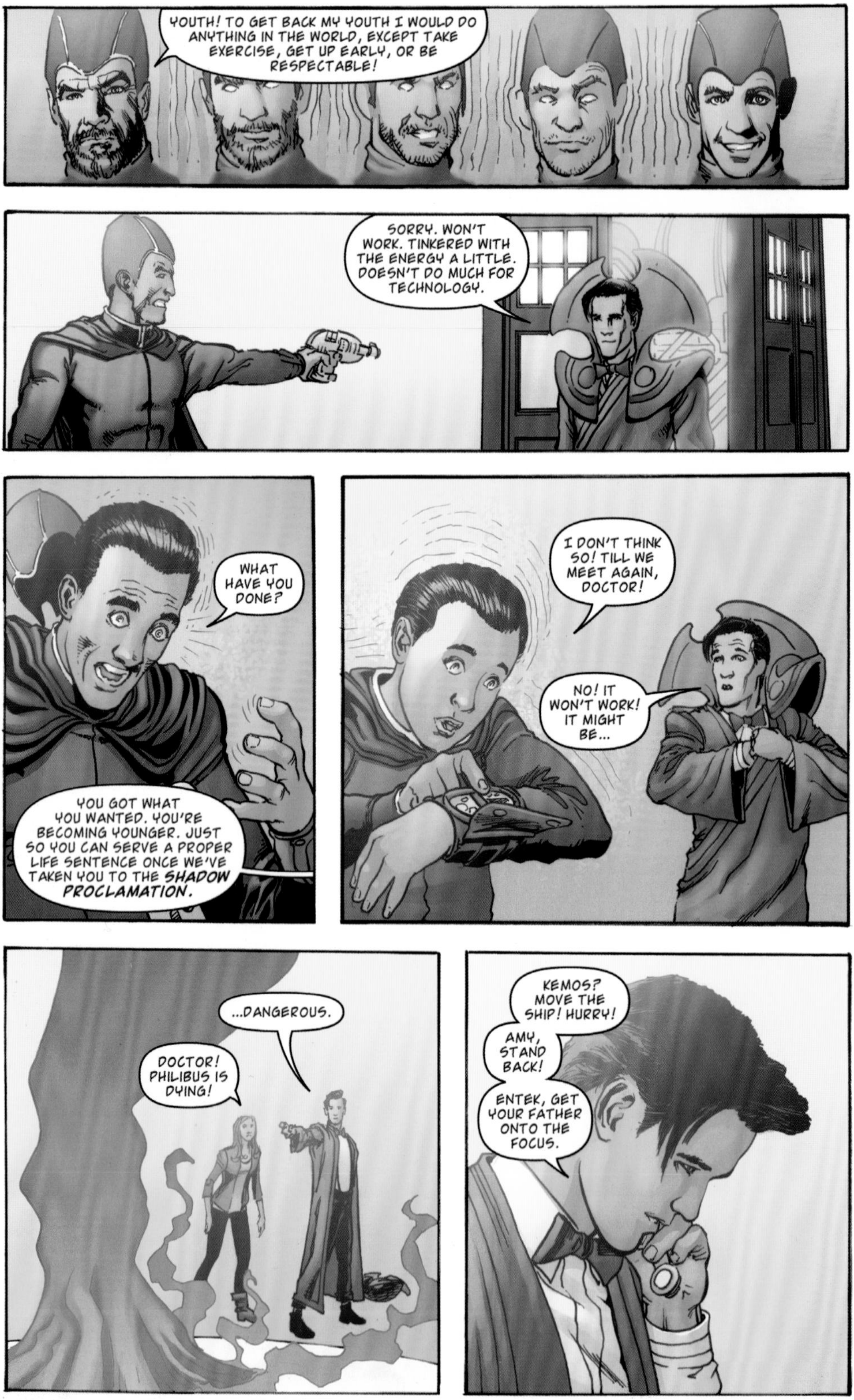
YOUTH! TO GET BACK MY YOUTH I WOULD DO ANYTHING IN THE WORLD, EXCEPT TAKE EXERCISE, GET UP EARLY, OR BE RESPECTABLE!
SORRY. WON'T WORK. TINKERED WITH THE ENERGY A LITTLE. DOESN'T DO MUCH FOR TECHNOLOGY.
WHAT HAVE YOU DONE?
YOU GOT WHAT YOU WANTED. YOU'RE BECOMING YOUNGER. JUST SO YOU CAN SERVE A PROPER LIFE SENTENCE ONCE WE'VE TAKEN YOU TO THE SHADOW PROCLAMATION.
I DON'T THINK SO! TILL WE MEET AGAIN, DOCTOR!
NO! IT WON'T WORK! IT MIGHT BE...
...DANGEROUS.
DOCTOR! PHILIBUS IS DYING!
KEMOS? MOVE THE SHIP! HURRY!
AMY, STAND BACK!
ENTEK, GET YOUR FATHER ONTO THE FOCUS.

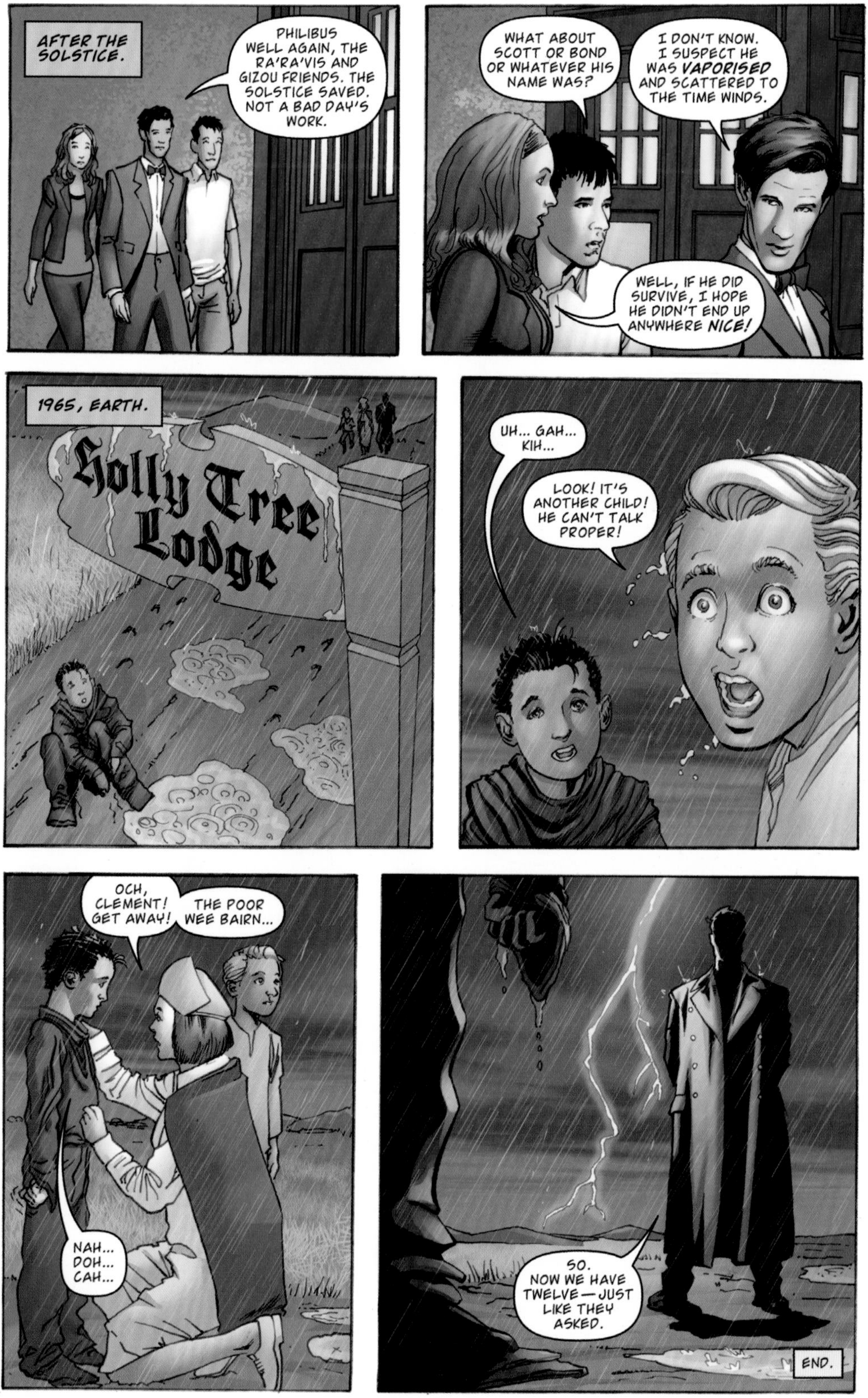
AFTER THE SOLSTICE.
PHILIBUS WELL AGAIN, THE RA'RA'VIS AND GIZOU FRIENDS. THE SOLSTICE SAVED. NOT A BAD DAY'S WORK.
WHAT ABOUT SCOTT OR BOND OR WHATEVER HIS NAME WAS?
I DON'T KNOW. I SUSPECT HE WAS VAPORISED AND SCATTERED TO THE TIME WINDS.
WELL, IF HE DID SURVIVE, I HOPE HE DIDN'T END UP ANYWHERE NICE!
1965, EARTH.
Holly Tree Lodge
UH... GAH... KIH...
LOOK! IT'S ANOTHER CHILD! HE CAN'T TALK PROPER!
OCH, CLEMENT! GET AWAY!
THE POOR WEE BAIRN...
NAH... DOH... CAH...
SO. NOW WE HAVE TWELVE—JUST LIKE THEY ASKED.
END.

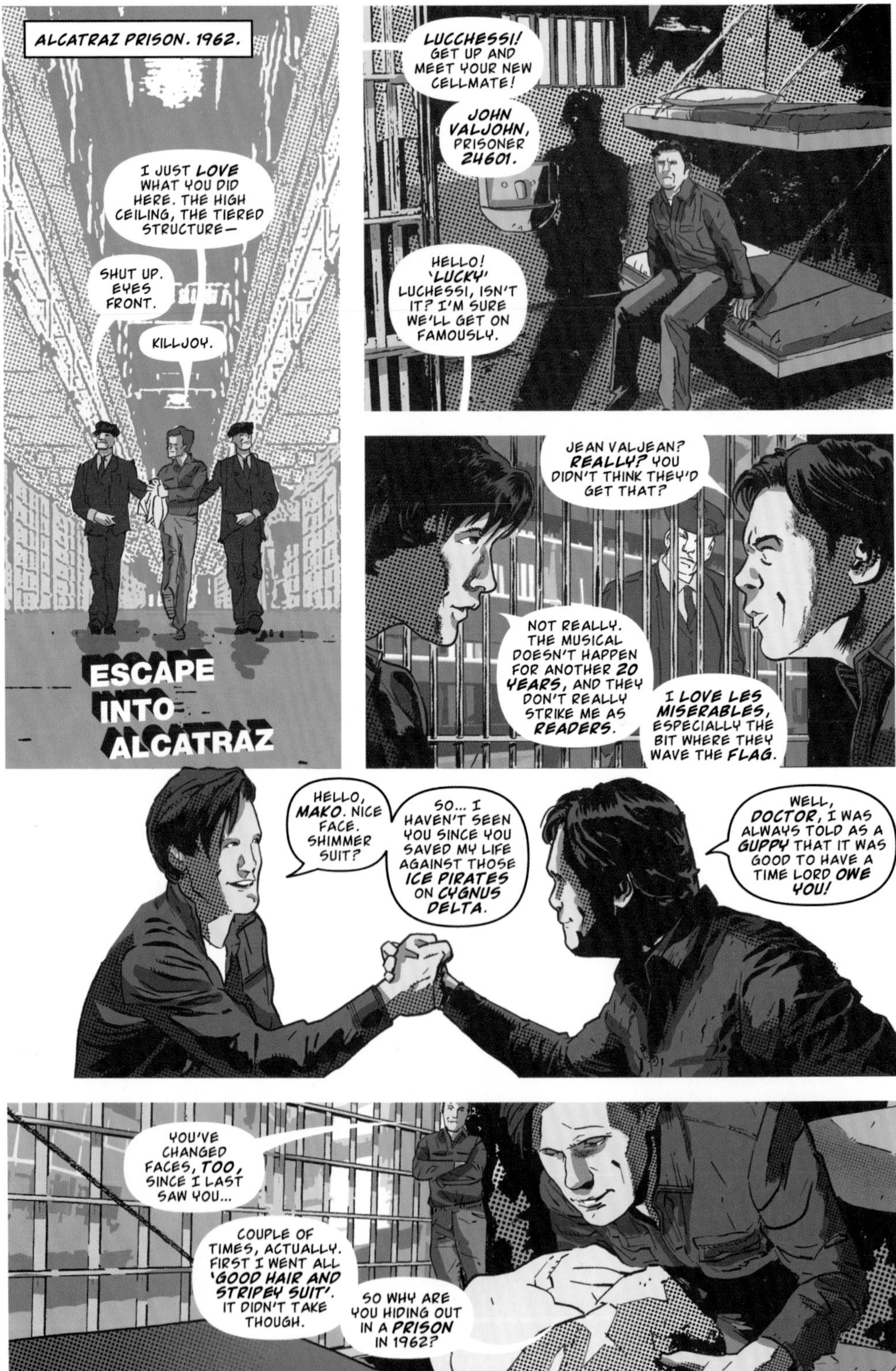
ALCATRAZ PRISON. 1962.
I JUST LOVE WHAT YOU DID HERE. THE HIGH CEILING, THE TIERED STRUCTURE—
SHUT UP. EYES FRONT.
KILLJOY.
ESCAPE INTO ALCATRAZ
LUCCHESSI! GET UP AND MEET YOUR NEW CELLMATE!
JOHN VALJOHN, PRISONER 24601.
HELLO! 'LUCKY' LUCHESSI, ISN'T IT? I'M SURE WE'LL GET ON FAMOUSLY.
JEAN VALJEAN? REALLY? YOU DIDN'T THINK THEY'D GET THAT?
NOT REALLY. THE MUSICAL DOESN'T HAPPEN FOR ANOTHER 20 YEARS, AND THEY DON'T REALLY STRIKE ME AS READERS.
I LOVE LES MISERABLES, ESPECIALLY THE BIT WHERE THEY WAVE THE FLAG.
HELLO, MAKO. NICE FACE. SHIMMER SUIT?
SO... I HAVEN'T SEEN YOU SINCE YOU SAVED MY LIFE AGAINST THOSE ICE PIRATES ON CYGNUS DELTA.
WELL, DOCTOR, I WAS ALWAYS TOLD AS A GUPPY THAT IT WAS GOOD TO HAVE A TIME LORD OWE YOU!
YOU'VE CHANGED FACES, TOO, SINCE I LAST SAW YOU...
COUPLE OF TIMES, ACTUALLY. FIRST I WENT ALL 'GOOD HAIR AND STRIPEY SUIT'. IT DIDN'T TAKE THOUGH.
SO WHY ARE YOU HIDING OUT IN A PRISON IN 1962?

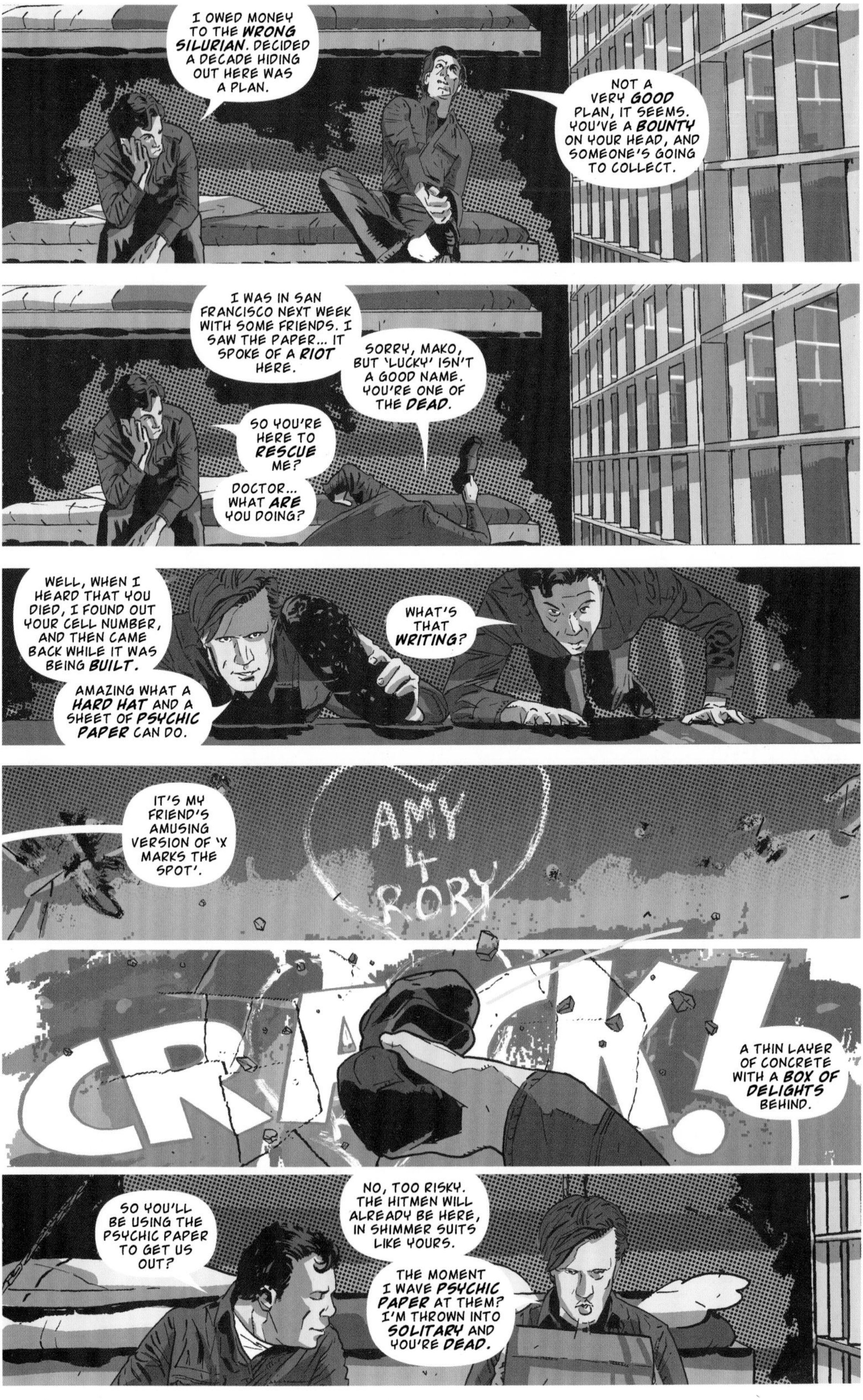
I OWED MONEY TO THE WRONG SILURIAN. DECIDED A DECADE HIDING OUT HERE WAS A PLAN.
NOT A VERY GOOD PLAN, IT SEEMS. YOU'VE A BOUNTY ON YOUR HEAD, AND SOMEONE'S GOING TO COLLECT.
I WAS IN SAN FRANCISCO NEXT WEEK WITH SOME FRIENDS. I SAW THE PAPER... IT SPOKE OF A RIOT HERE.
SORRY, MAKO, BUT 'LUCKY' ISN'T A GOOD NAME. YOU'RE ONE OF THE DEAD.
SO YOU'RE HERE TO RESCUE ME?
DOCTOR... WHAT ARE YOU DOING?
WELL, WHEN I HEARD THAT YOU DIED, I FOUND OUT YOUR CELL NUMBER, AND THEN CAME BACK WHILE IT WAS BEING BUILT.
AMAZING WHAT A HARD HAT AND A SHEET OF PSYCHIC PAPER CAN DO.
WHAT'S THAT WRITING?
IT'S MY FRIEND'S AMUSING VERSION OF 'X MARKS THE SPOT'.
AMY 4 RORY
CRACK!
A THIN LAYER OF CONCRETE WITH A BOX OF DELIGHTS BEHIND.
SO YOU'LL BE USING THE PSYCHIC PAPER TO GET US OUT?
NO, TOO RISKY. THE HITMEN WILL ALREADY BE HERE, IN SHIMMER SUITS LIKE YOURS.
THE MOMENT I WAVE PSYCHIC PAPER AT THEM? I'M THROWN INTO SOLITARY AND YOU'RE DEAD.

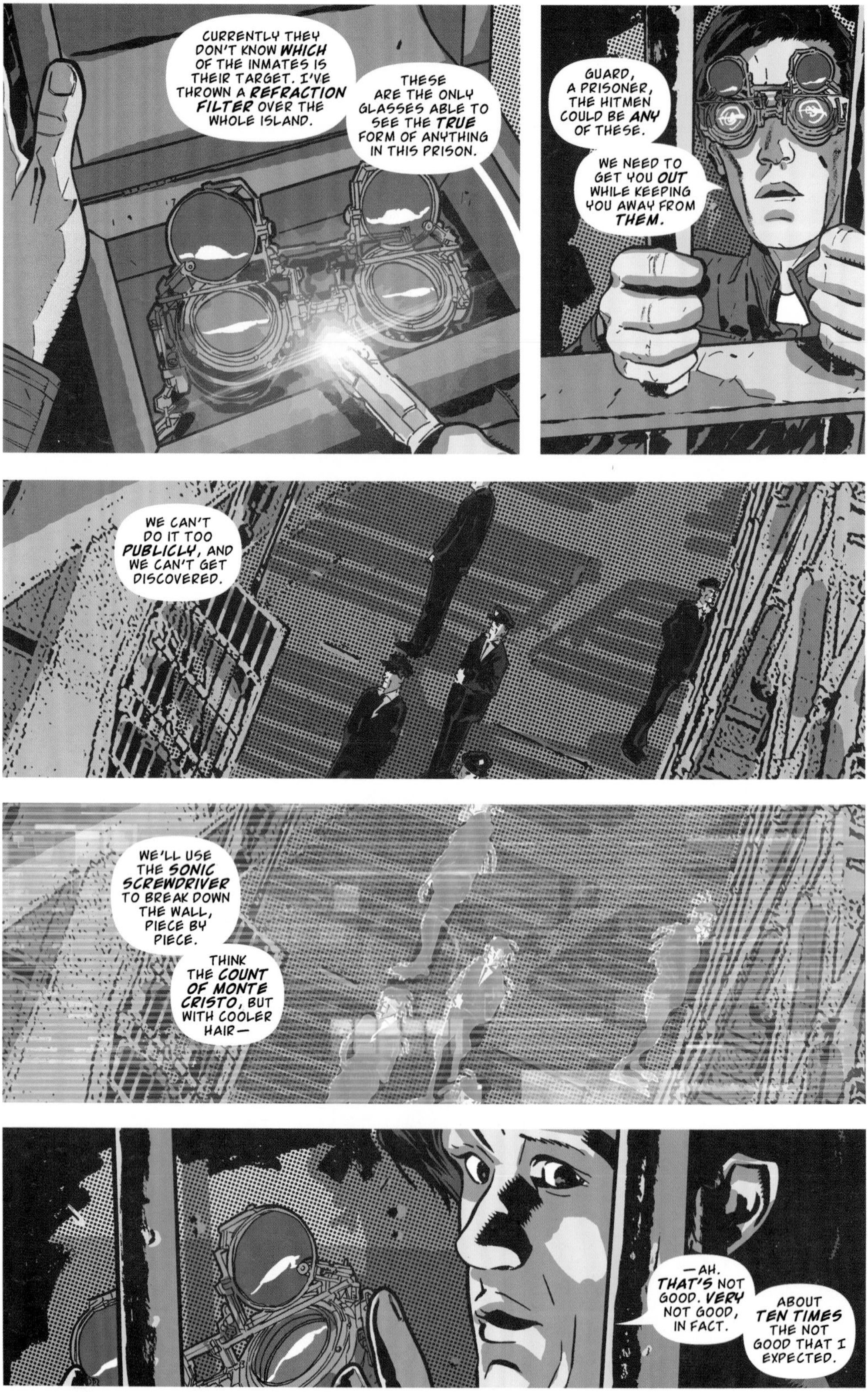
CURRENTLY THEY DON'T KNOW WHICH OF THE INMATES IS THEIR TARGET. I'VE THROWN A REFRACTION FILTER OVER THE WHOLE ISLAND.
THESE ARE THE ONLY GLASSES ABLE TO SEE THE TRUE FORM OF ANYTHING IN THIS PRISON.
GUARD, A PRISONER, THE HITMEN COULD BE ANY OF THESE.
WE NEED TO GET YOU OUT WHILE KEEPING YOU AWAY FROM THEM.
WE CAN'T DO IT TOO PUBLICLY, AND WE CAN'T GET DISCOVERED.
WE'LL USE THE SONIC SCREWDRIVER TO BREAK DOWN THE WALL, PIECE BY PIECE.
THINK THE COUNT OF MONTE CRISTO, BUT WITH COOLER HAIR—
—AH. THAT'S NOT GOOD. VERY NOT GOOD, IN FACT.
ABOUT TEN TIMES THE NOT GOOD THAT I EXPECTED.

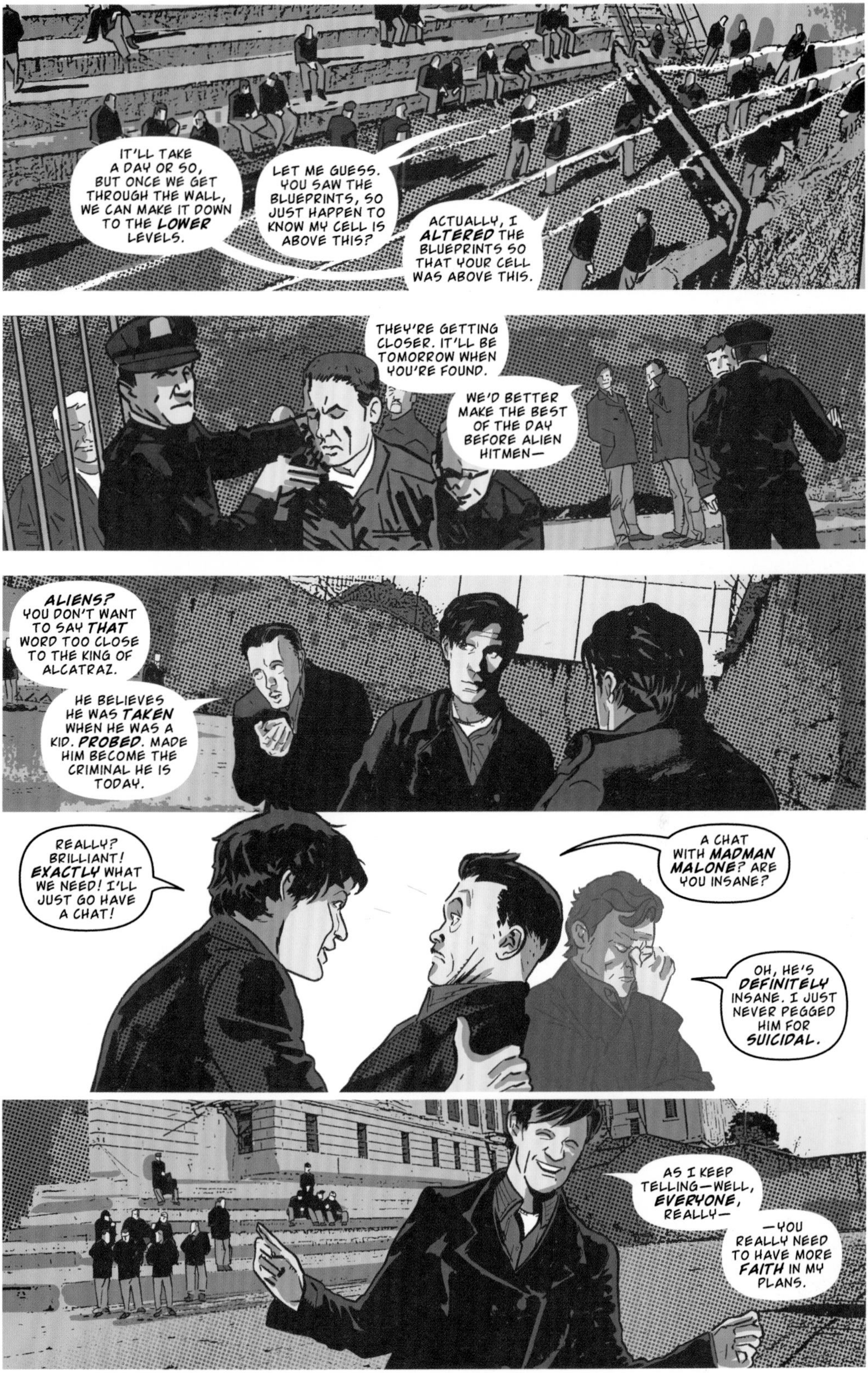
IT'LL TAKE A DAY OR SO, BUT ONCE WE GET THROUGH THE WALL, WE CAN MAKE IT DOWN TO THE LOWER LEVELS.
LET ME GUESS. YOU SAW THE BLUEPRINTS, SO JUST HAPPEN TO KNOW MY CELL IS ABOVE THIS?
ACTUALLY, I ALTERED THE BLUEPRINTS SO THAT YOUR CELL WAS ABOVE THIS.
THEY'RE GETTING CLOSER. IT'LL BE TOMORROW WHEN YOU'RE FOUND.
WE'D BETTER MAKE THE BEST OF THE DAY BEFORE ALIEN HITMEN—
ALIENS? YOU DON'T WANT TO SAY THAT WORD TOO CLOSE TO THE KING OF ALCATRAZ.
HE BELIEVES HE WAS TAKEN WHEN HE WAS A KID. PROBED. MADE HIM BECOME THE CRIMINAL HE IS TODAY.
REALLY? BRILLIANT! EXACTLY WHAT WE NEED! I'LL JUST GO HAVE A CHAT!
A CHAT WITH MADMAN MALONE? ARE YOU INSANE?
OH, HE'S DEFINITELY INSANE. I JUST NEVER PEGGED HIM FOR SUICIDAL.
AS I KEEP TELLING—WELL, EVERYONE, REALLY—
—YOU REALLY NEED TO HAVE MORE FAITH IN MY PLANS.

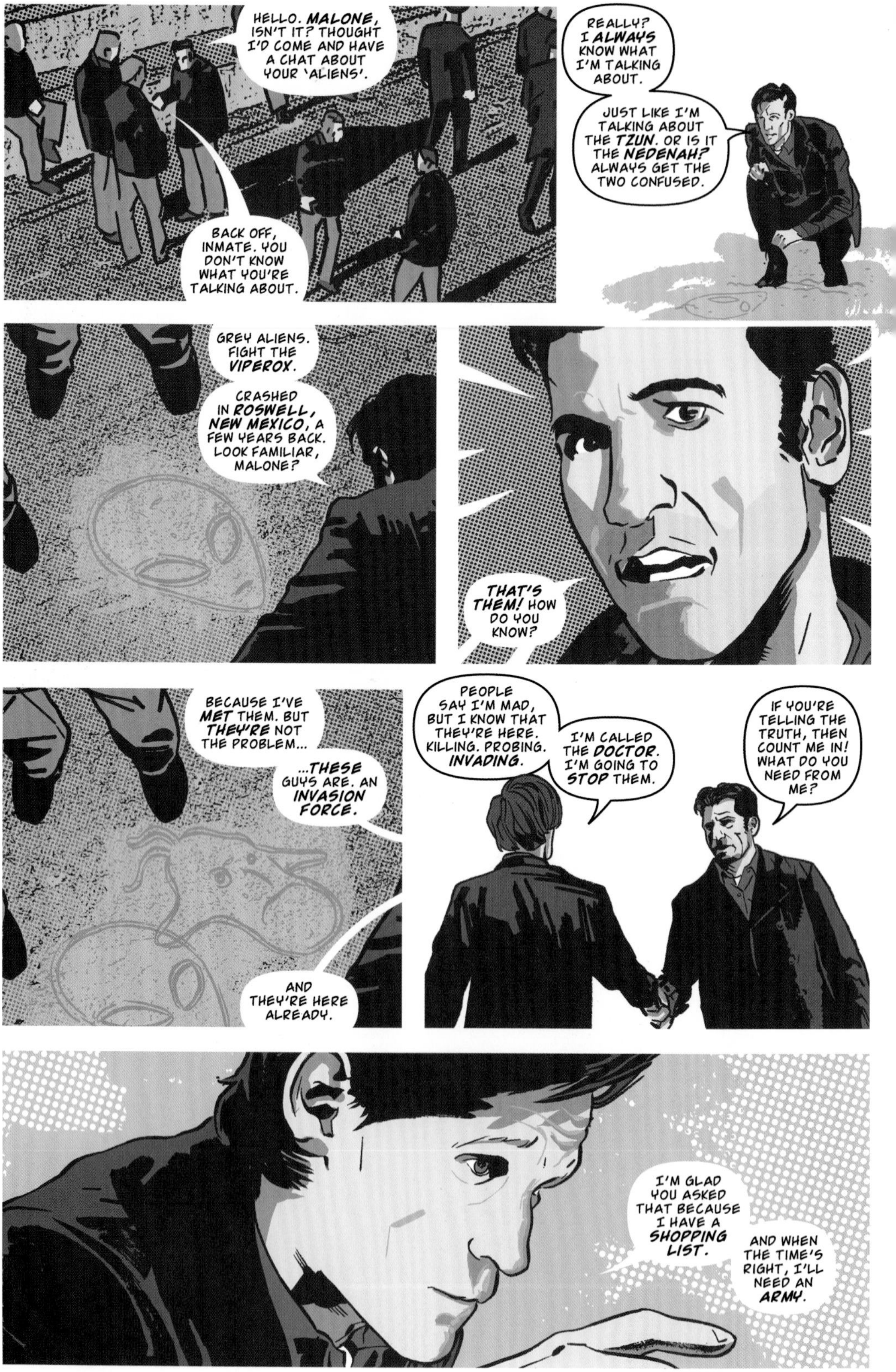
HELLO. MALONE, ISN'T IT? THOUGHT I'D COME AND HAVE A CHAT ABOUT YOUR 'ALIENS'.
BACK OFF, INMATE. YOU DON'T KNOW WHAT YOU'RE TALKING ABOUT.
REALLY? I ALWAYS KNOW WHAT I'M TALKING ABOUT.
JUST LIKE I'M TALKING ABOUT THE TZUN. OR IS IT THE NEDENAH? ALWAYS GET THE TWO CONFUSED.
GREY ALIENS. FIGHT THE VIPEROX.
CRASHED IN ROSWELL, NEW MEXICO, A FEW YEARS BACK. LOOK FAMILIAR, MALONE?
THAT'S THEM! HOW DO YOU KNOW?
BECAUSE I'VE MET THEM. BUT THEY'RE NOT THE PROBLEM...
...THESE GUYS ARE. AN INVASION FORCE.
AND THEY'RE HERE ALREADY.
PEOPLE SAY I'M MAD, BUT I KNOW THAT THEY'RE HERE. KILLING. PROBING. INVADING.
I'M CALLED THE DOCTOR. I'M GOING TO STOP THEM.
IF YOU'RE TELLING THE TRUTH, THEN COUNT ME IN! WHAT DO YOU NEED FROM ME?
I'M GLAD YOU ASKED THAT BECAUSE I HAVE A SHOPPING LIST.
AND WHEN THE TIME'S RIGHT, I'LL NEED AN ARMY.

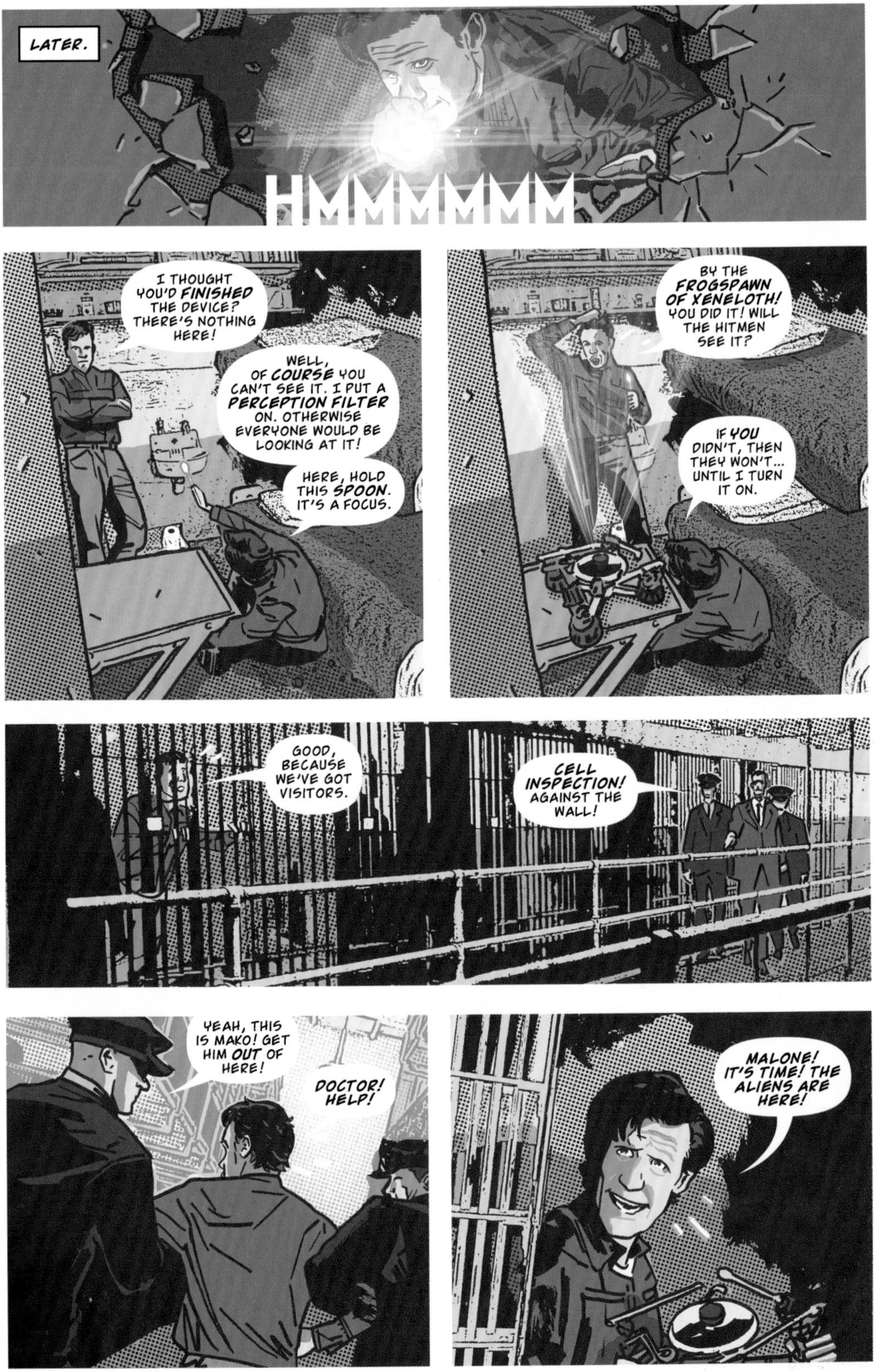
LATER.
HMMMMMMM
I THOUGHT YOU'D FINISHED THE DEVICE? THERE'S NOTHING HERE!
WELL, OF COURSE YOU CAN'T SEE IT. I PUT A PERCEPTION FILTER ON. OTHERWISE EVERYONE WOULD BE LOOKING AT IT!
HERE, HOLD THIS SPOON. IT'S A FOCUS.
BY THE FROGSPAWN OF XENELOTH! YOU DID IT! WILL THE HITMEN SEE IT?
IF YOU DIDN'T, THEN THEY WON'T... UNTIL I TURN IT ON.
GOOD, BECAUSE WE'VE GOT VISITORS.
CELL INSPECTION! AGAINST THE WALL!
YEAH, THIS IS MAKO! GET HIM OUT OF HERE!
DOCTOR! HELP!
MALONE! IT'S TIME! THE ALIENS ARE HERE!

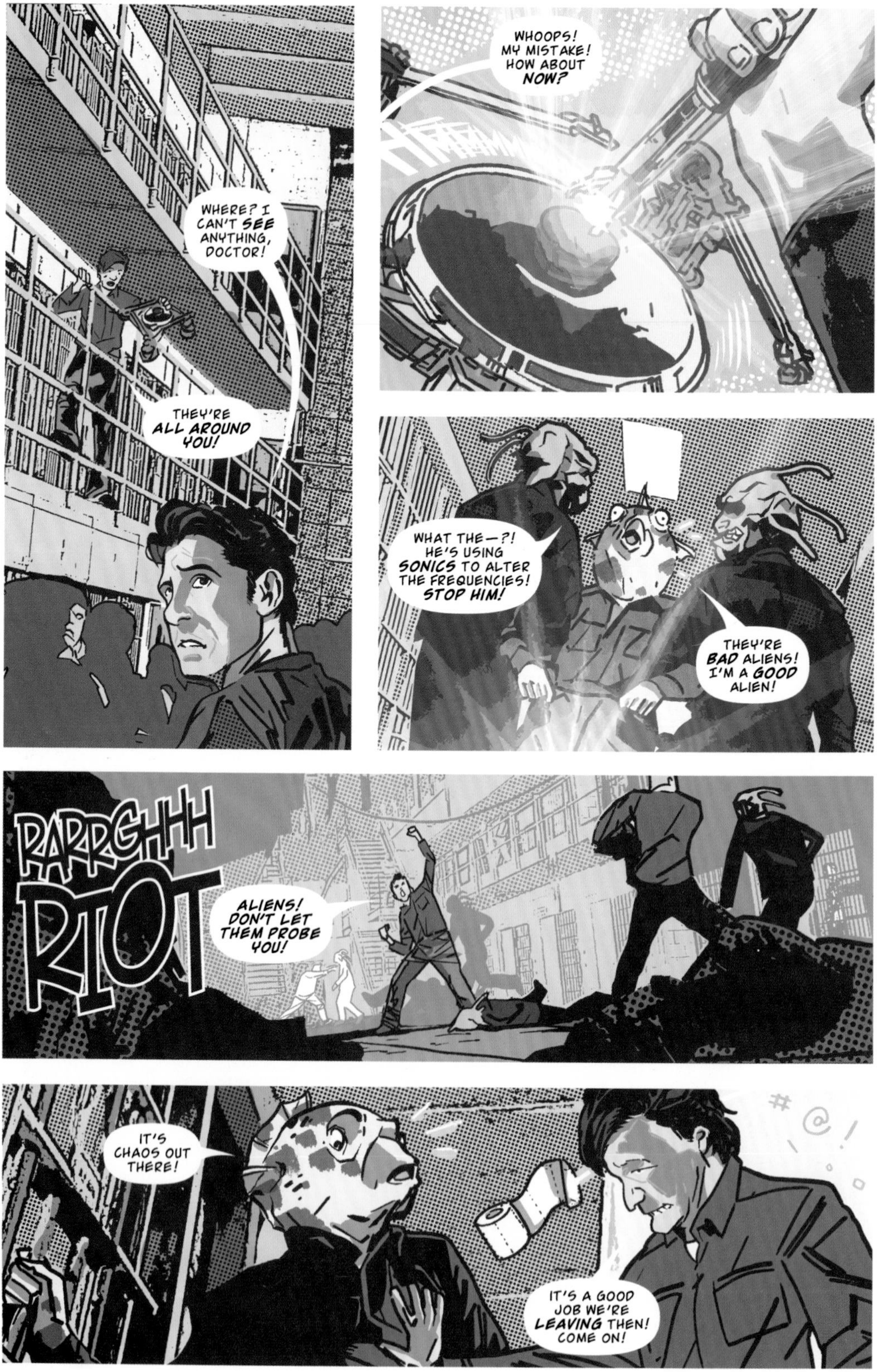
WHERE? I CAN'T SEE ANYTHING, DOCTOR!
THEY'RE ALL AROUND YOU!
WHOOPS! MY MISTAKE! HOW ABOUT NOW?
WHAT THE—?! HE'S USING SONICS TO ALTER THE FREQUENCIES! STOP HIM!
THEY'RE BAD ALIENS! I'M A GOOD ALIEN!
RARRGHHH
RIOT
ALIENS! DON'T LET THEM PROBE YOU!
IT'S CHAOS OUT THERE!
IT'S A GOOD JOB WE'RE LEAVING THEN! COME ON!

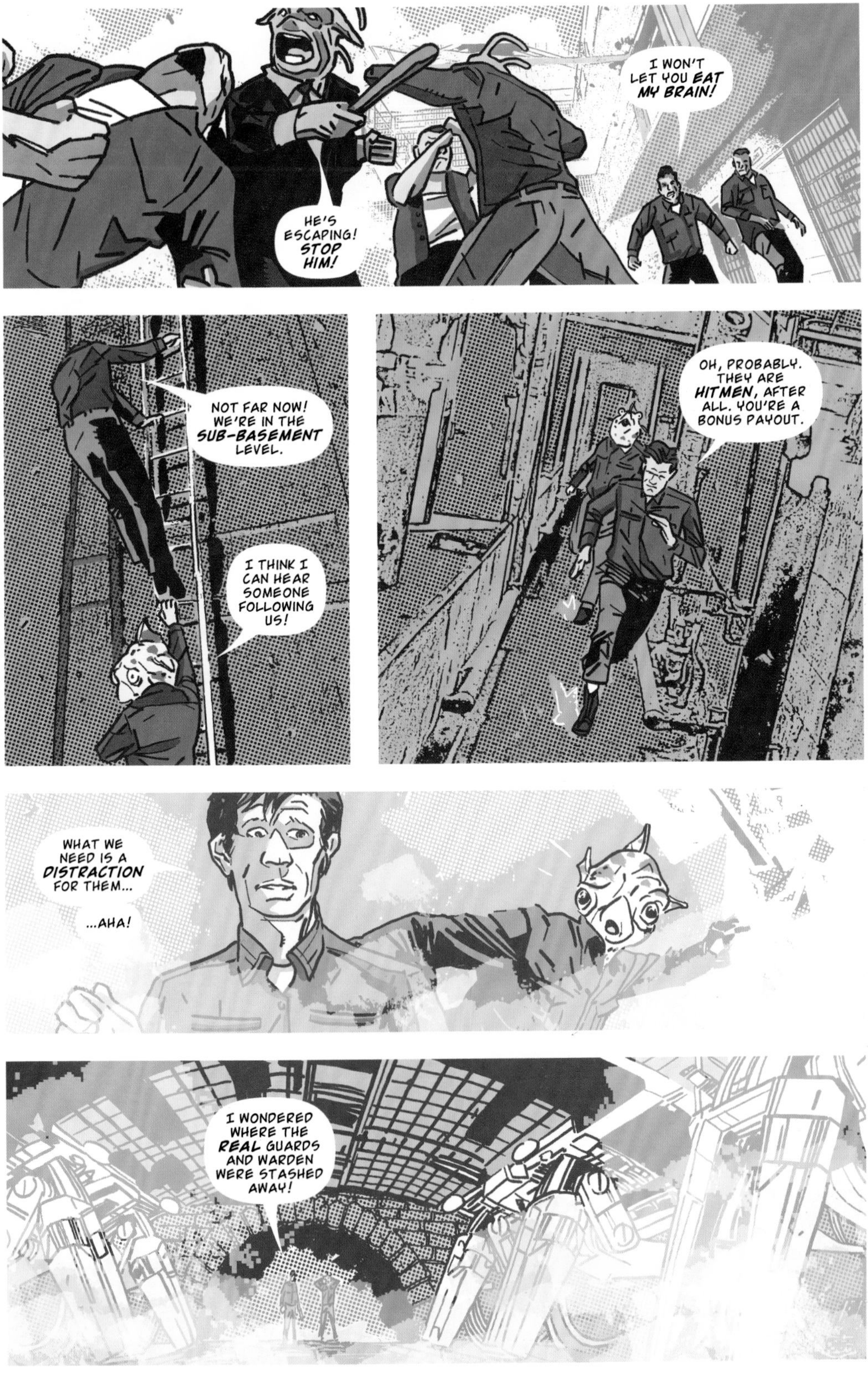

HE'S ESCAPING! STOP HIM!
I WON'T LET YOU EAT MY BRAIN!
NOT FAR NOW! WE'RE IN THE SUB-BASEMENT LEVEL.
I THINK I CAN HEAR SOMEONE FOLLOWING US!
OH, PROBABLY. THEY ARE HITMEN, AFTER ALL. YOU'RE A BONUS PAYOUT.
WHAT WE NEED IS A DISTRACTION FOR THEM...
...AHA!
I WONDERED WHERE THE REAL GUARDS AND WARDEN WERE STASHED AWAY!

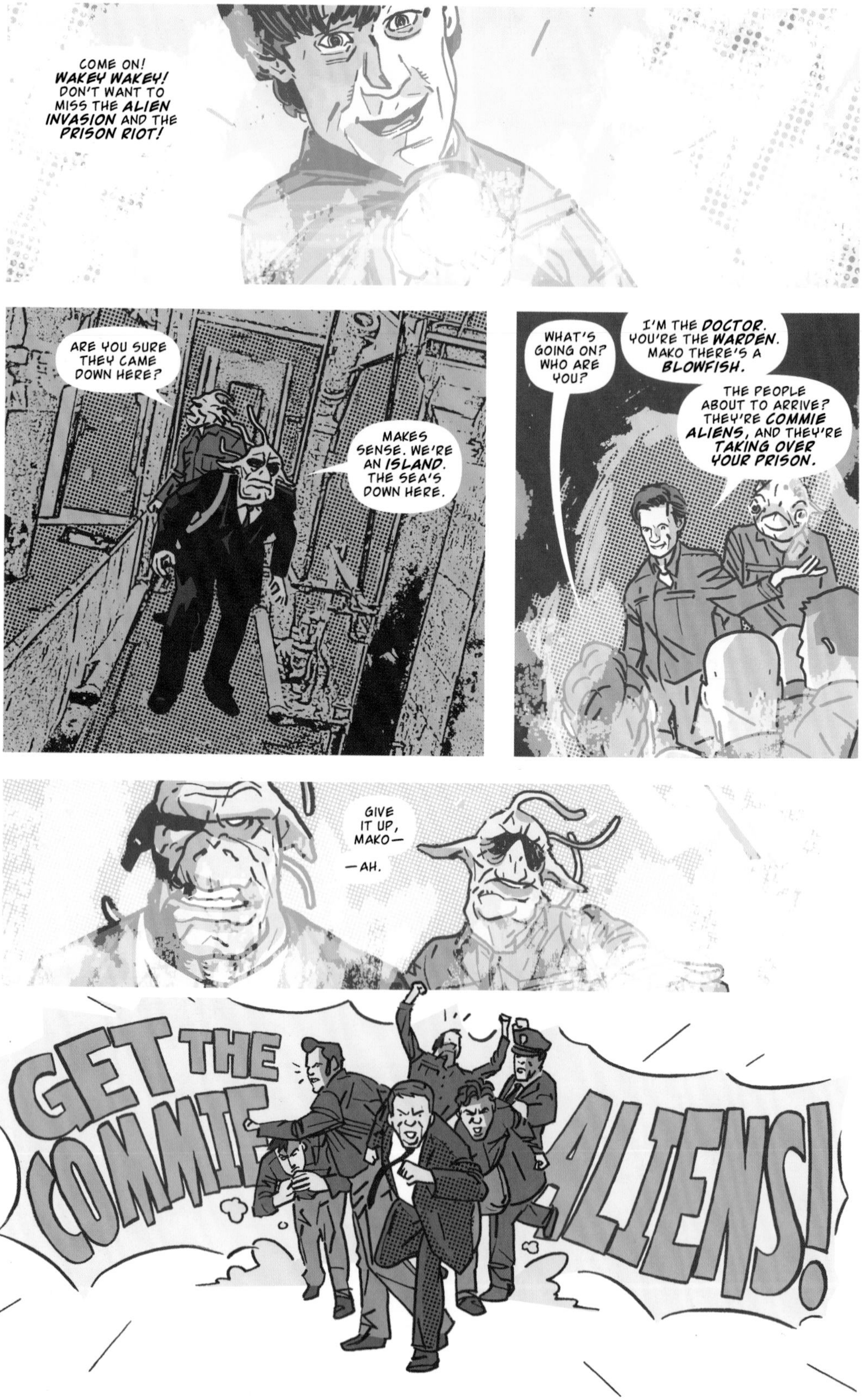
COME ON! WAKEY WAKEY! DON'T WANT TO MISS THE ALIEN INVASION AND THE PRISON RIOT!
ARE YOU SURE THEY CAME DOWN HERE?
MAKES SENSE. WE'RE AN ISLAND. THE SEA'S DOWN HERE.
WHAT'S GOING ON? WHO ARE YOU?
I'M THE DOCTOR. YOU'RE THE WARDEN. MAKO THERE'S A BLOWFISH.
THE PEOPLE ABOUT TO ARRIVE? THEY'RE COMMIE ALIENS, AND THEY'RE TAKING OVER YOUR PRISON.
GIVE IT UP, MAKO—
—AH.
GET THE COMMIE ALIENS!

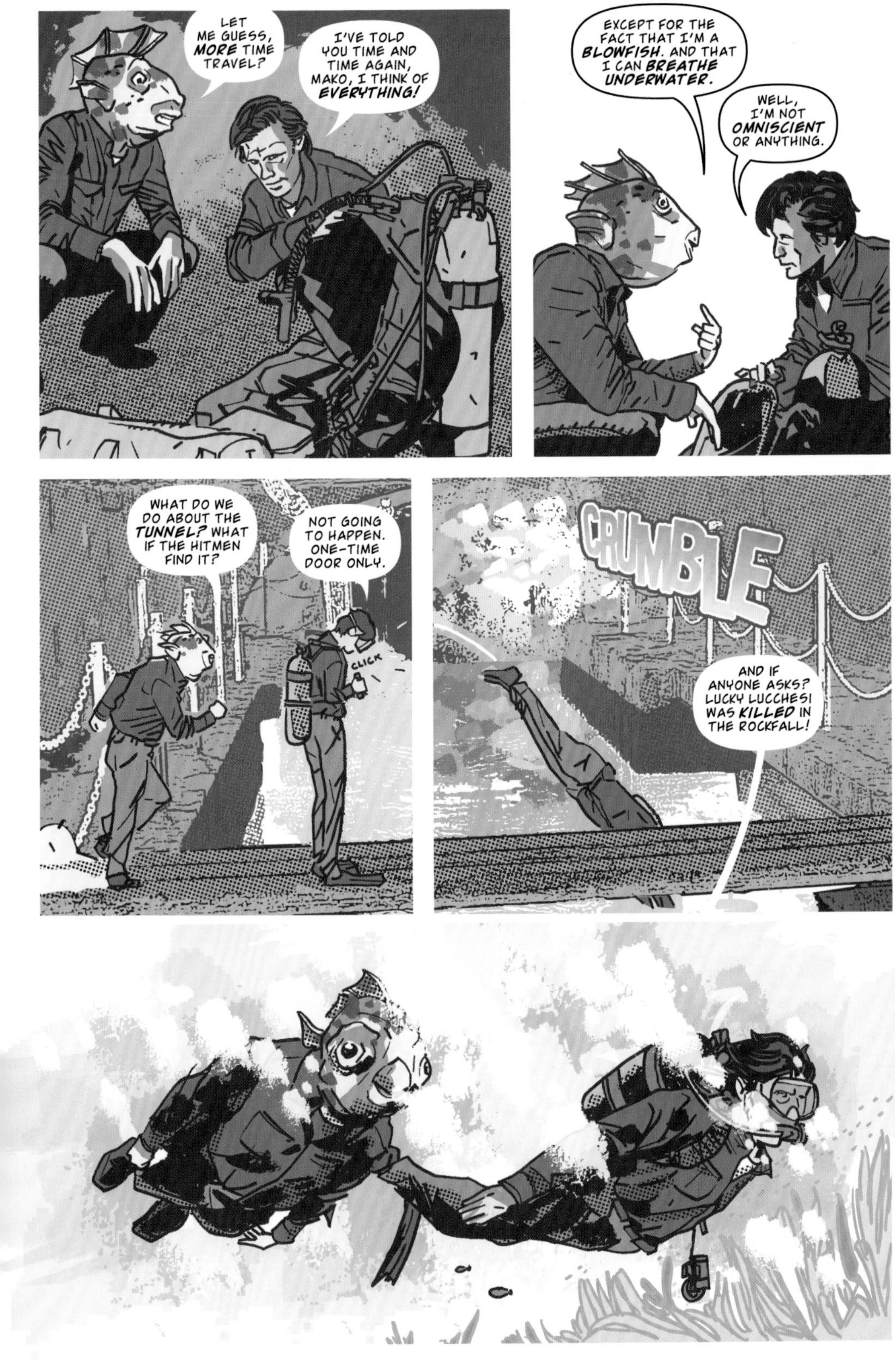
LET ME GUESS, MORE TIME TRAVEL?
I'VE TOLD YOU TIME AND TIME AGAIN, MAKO, I THINK OF EVERYTHING!
EXCEPT FOR THE FACT THAT I'M A BLOWFISH. AND THAT I CAN BREATHE UNDERWATER.
WELL, I'M NOT OMNISCIENT OR ANYTHING.
WHAT DO WE DO ABOUT THE TUNNEL? WHAT IF THE HITMEN FIND IT?
NOT GOING TO HAPPEN. ONE-TIME DOOR ONLY.
CLICK
CRUMBLE
AND IF ANYONE ASKS? LUCKY LUCCHESI WAS KILLED IN THE ROCKFALL!

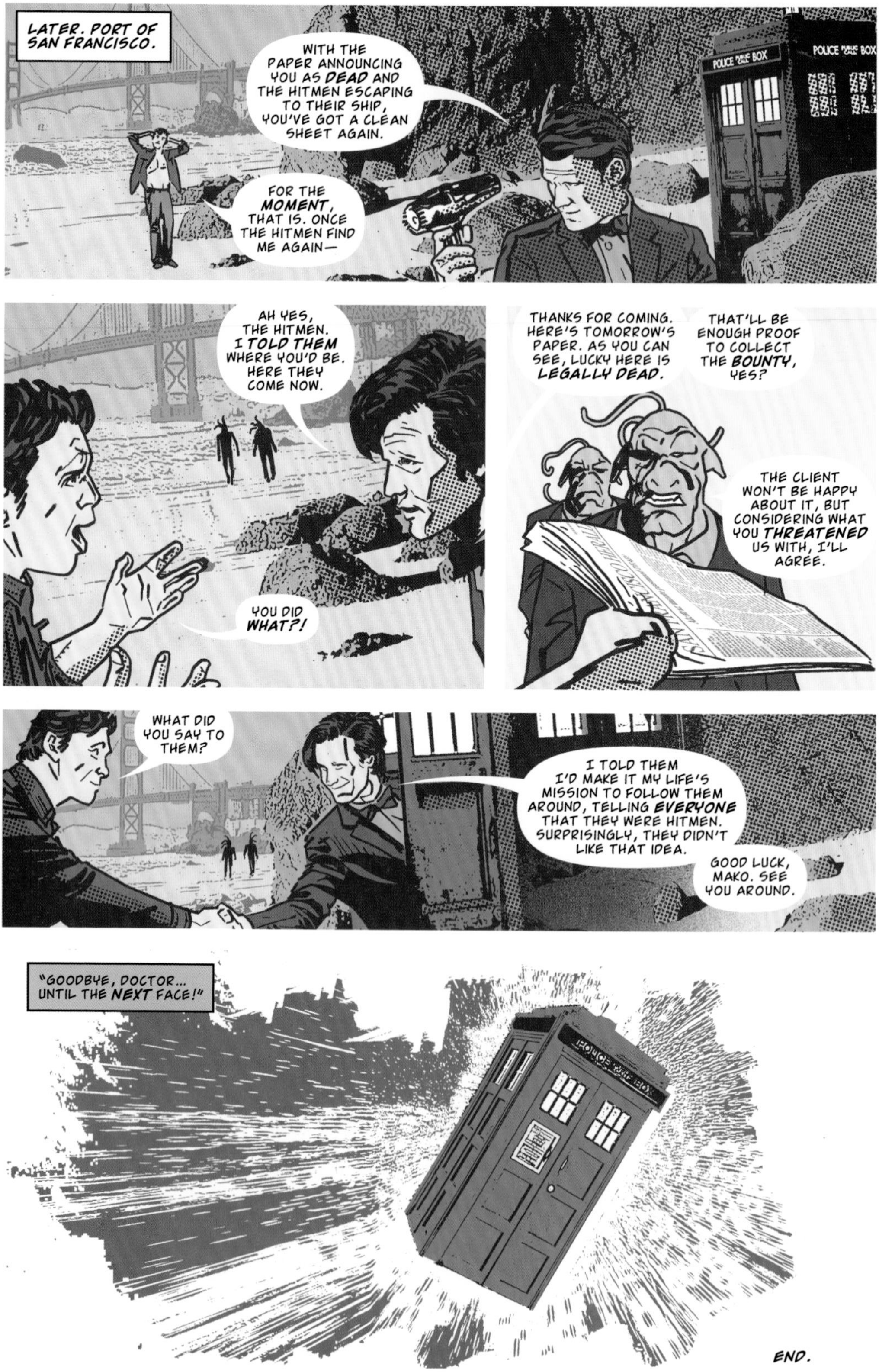
LATER. PORT OF SAN FRANCISCO.
POLICE PUBLIC CALL BOX
WITH THE PAPER ANNOUNCING YOU AS DEAD AND THE HITMEN ESCAPING TO THEIR SHIP, YOU'VE GOT A CLEAN SHEET AGAIN.
FOR THE MOMENT, THAT IS. ONCE THE HITMEN FIND ME AGAIN—
AH YES, THE HITMEN. I TOLD THEM WHERE YOU'D BE. HERE THEY COME NOW.
YOU DID WHAT?!
THANKS FOR COMING. HERE'S TOMORROW'S PAPER. AS YOU CAN SEE, LUCKY HERE IS LEGALLY DEAD.
THAT'LL BE ENOUGH PROOF TO COLLECT THE BOUNTY, YES?
THE CLIENT WON'T BE HAPPY ABOUT IT, BUT CONSIDERING WHAT YOU THREATENED US WITH, I'LL AGREE.
WHAT DID YOU SAY TO THEM?
I TOLD THEM I'D MAKE IT MY LIFE'S MISSION TO FOLLOW THEM AROUND, TELLING EVERYONE THAT THEY WERE HITMEN. SURPRISINGLY, THEY DIDN'T LIKE THAT IDEA.
GOOD LUCK, MAKO. SEE YOU AROUND.
"GOODBYE, DOCTOR... UNTIL THE NEXT FACE!"
END.

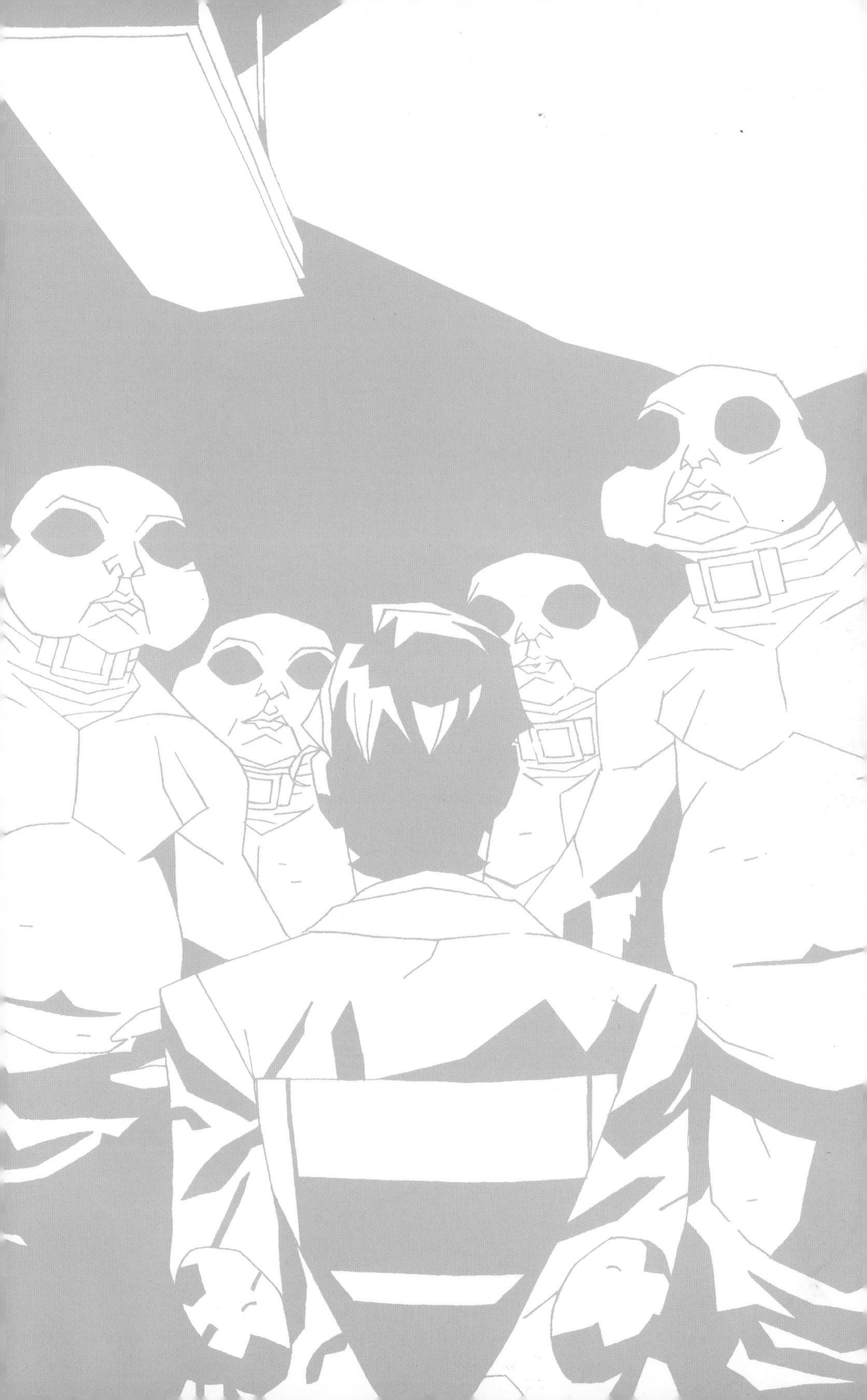

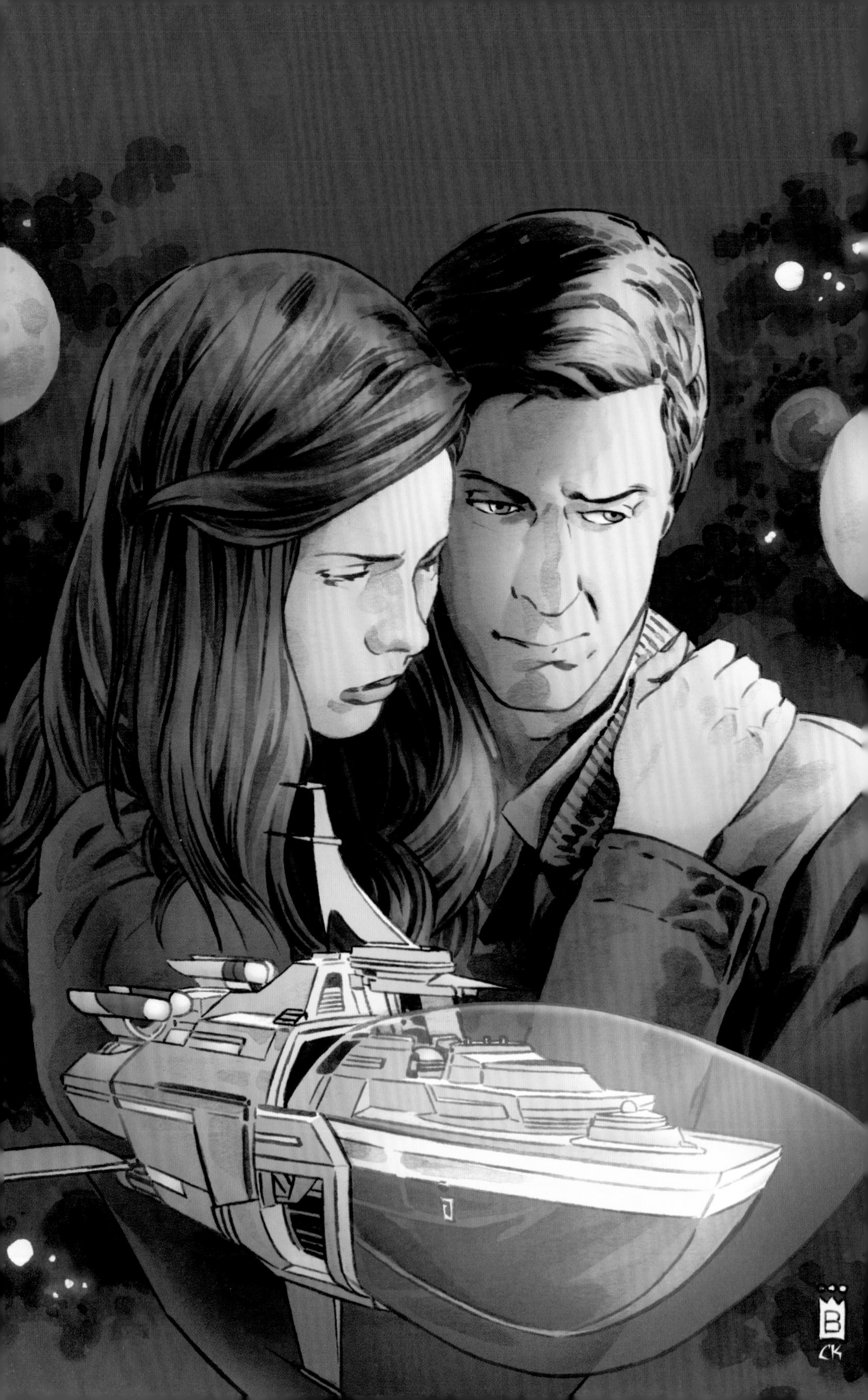

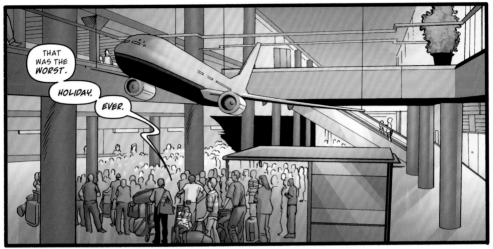

THAT WAS THE WORST.

HOLIDAY.

EVER.

THE HOTEL LOOKED REALLY NICE IN THE BROCHURE...

OH, SURE, IT LOOKED *AMAZING.* SHAME THAT WAS JUST AN *ARTIST'S INTERPRETATION*—

—BECAUSE THEY HADN'T ACTUALLY FINISHED *BUILDING* IT YET!

STILL, AT LEAST WE GOT TO ENJOY THE SPANISH SUN—

IT RAINED!

EXOTIC FOOD—

SOGGY FISH AND CHIPS IN A FAKE ENGLISH PUB!

WELL, AT LEAST WE'LL BE HOME SOON, EH?

WE REGRET TO INFORM PASSENGERS THAT ALL COMMERCIAL FLIGHTS FROM MAJORCA ARE DELAYED INDEFINITELY.

PLEASE WAIT FOR FURTHER ANNOUNCEMENTS.

ARGH! WE'VE ALREADY BEEN STUCK HERE FOR *FIVE HOURS!*

IF THEY DON'T LET ME ON A PLANE *RIGHT NOW* I'M GONNA—

ONE SIDE PEOPLE!

MAKE A HOLE!

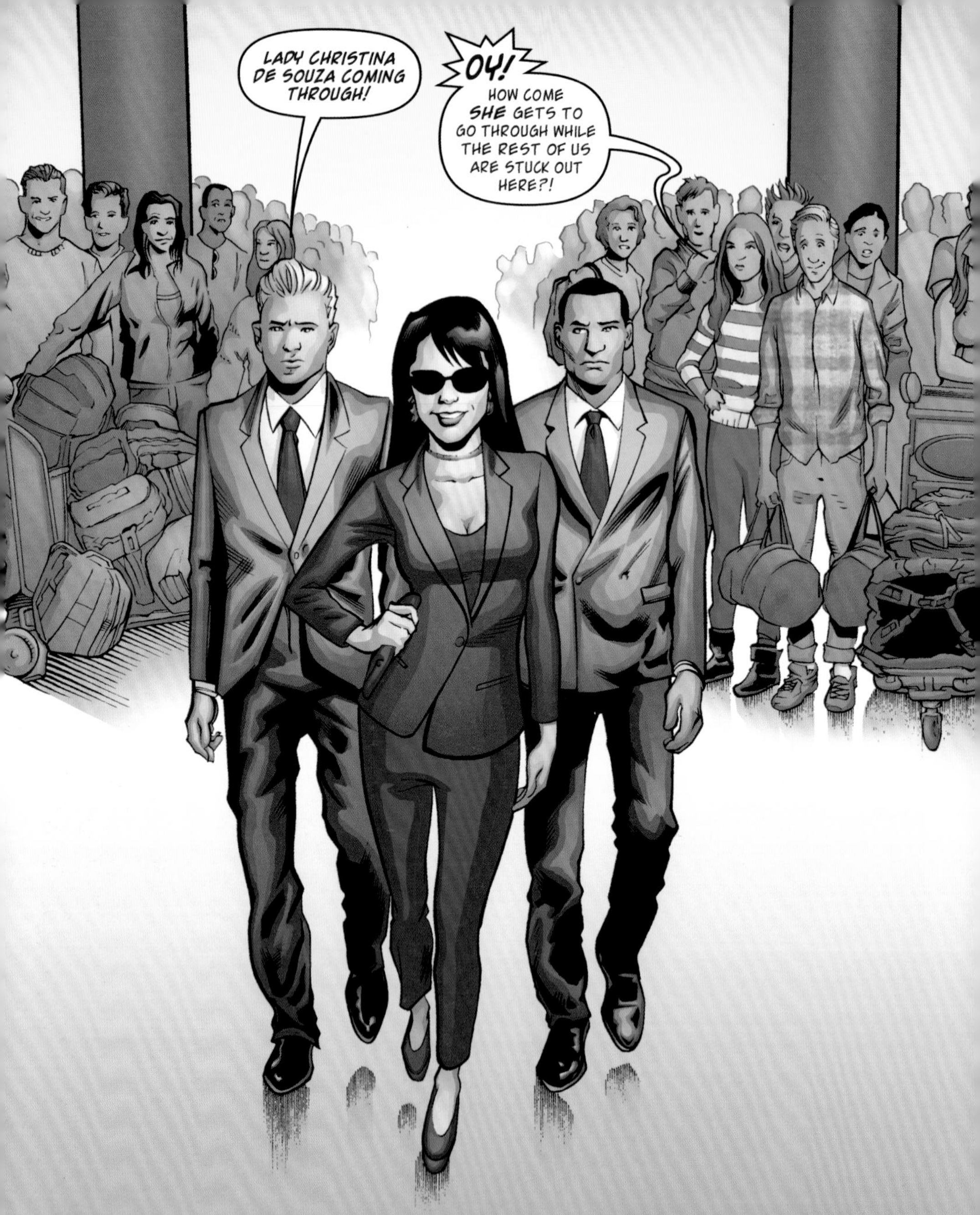
LADY CHRISTINA DE SOUZA COMING THROUGH!
OY!
HOW COME SHE GETS TO GO THROUGH WHILE THE REST OF US ARE STUCK OUT HERE?!

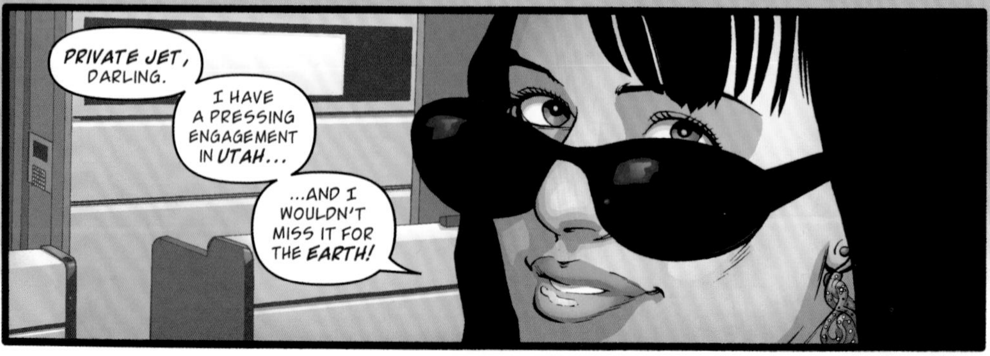
PRIVATE JET, DARLING.
I HAVE A PRESSING ENGAGEMENT IN UTAH...
...AND I WOULDN'T MISS IT FOR THE EARTH!

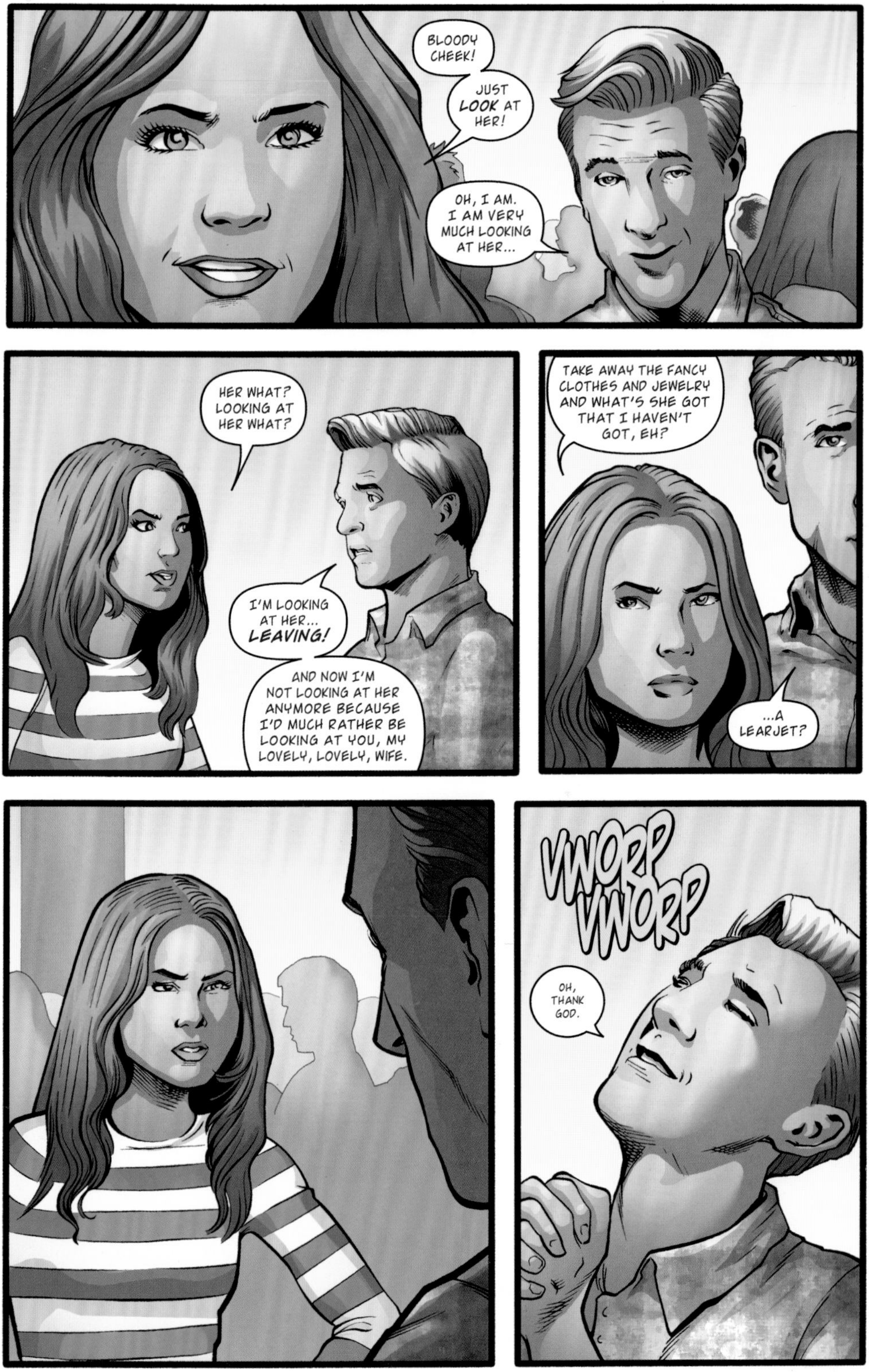
BLOODY CHEEK!
JUST LOOK AT HER!
OH, I AM. I AM VERY MUCH LOOKING AT HER...
HER WHAT? LOOKING AT HER WHAT?
I'M LOOKING AT HER... LEAVING!
AND NOW I'M NOT LOOKING AT HER ANYMORE BECAUSE I'D MUCH RATHER BE LOOKING AT YOU, MY LOVELY, LOVELY, WIFE.
TAKE AWAY THE FANCY CLOTHES AND JEWELRY AND WHAT'S SHE GOT THAT I HAVEN'T GOT, EH?
...A LEARJET?
VWORP VWORP
OH, THANK GOD.

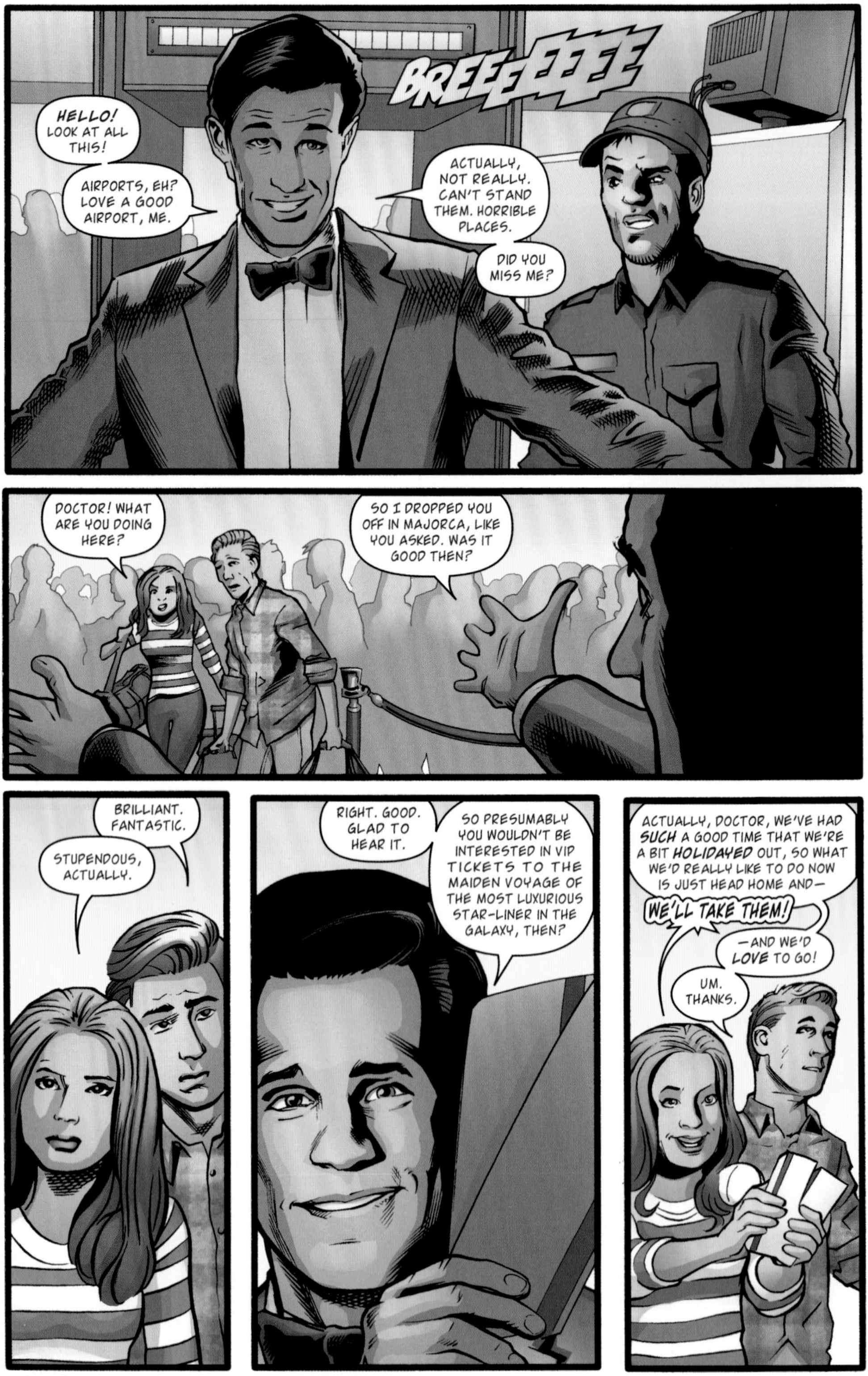
BREEEEEEE
HELLO! LOOK AT ALL THIS!
AIRPORTS, EH? LOVE A GOOD AIRPORT, ME.
ACTUALLY, NOT REALLY. CAN'T STAND THEM. HORRIBLE PLACES.
DID YOU MISS ME?
DOCTOR! WHAT ARE YOU DOING HERE?
SO I DROPPED YOU OFF IN MAJORCA, LIKE YOU ASKED. WAS IT GOOD THEN?
BRILLIANT. FANTASTIC.
STUPENDOUS, ACTUALLY.
RIGHT. GOOD. GLAD TO HEAR IT.
SO PRESUMABLY YOU WOULDN'T BE INTERESTED IN VIP TICKETS TO THE MAIDEN VOYAGE OF THE MOST LUXURIOUS STAR-LINER IN THE GALAXY, THEN?
ACTUALLY, DOCTOR, WE'VE HAD SUCH A GOOD TIME THAT WE'RE A BIT HOLIDAYED OUT, SO WHAT WE'D REALLY LIKE TO DO NOW IS JUST HEAD HOME AND—
WE'LL TAKE THEM!
—AND WE'D LOVE TO GO!
UM. THANKS.

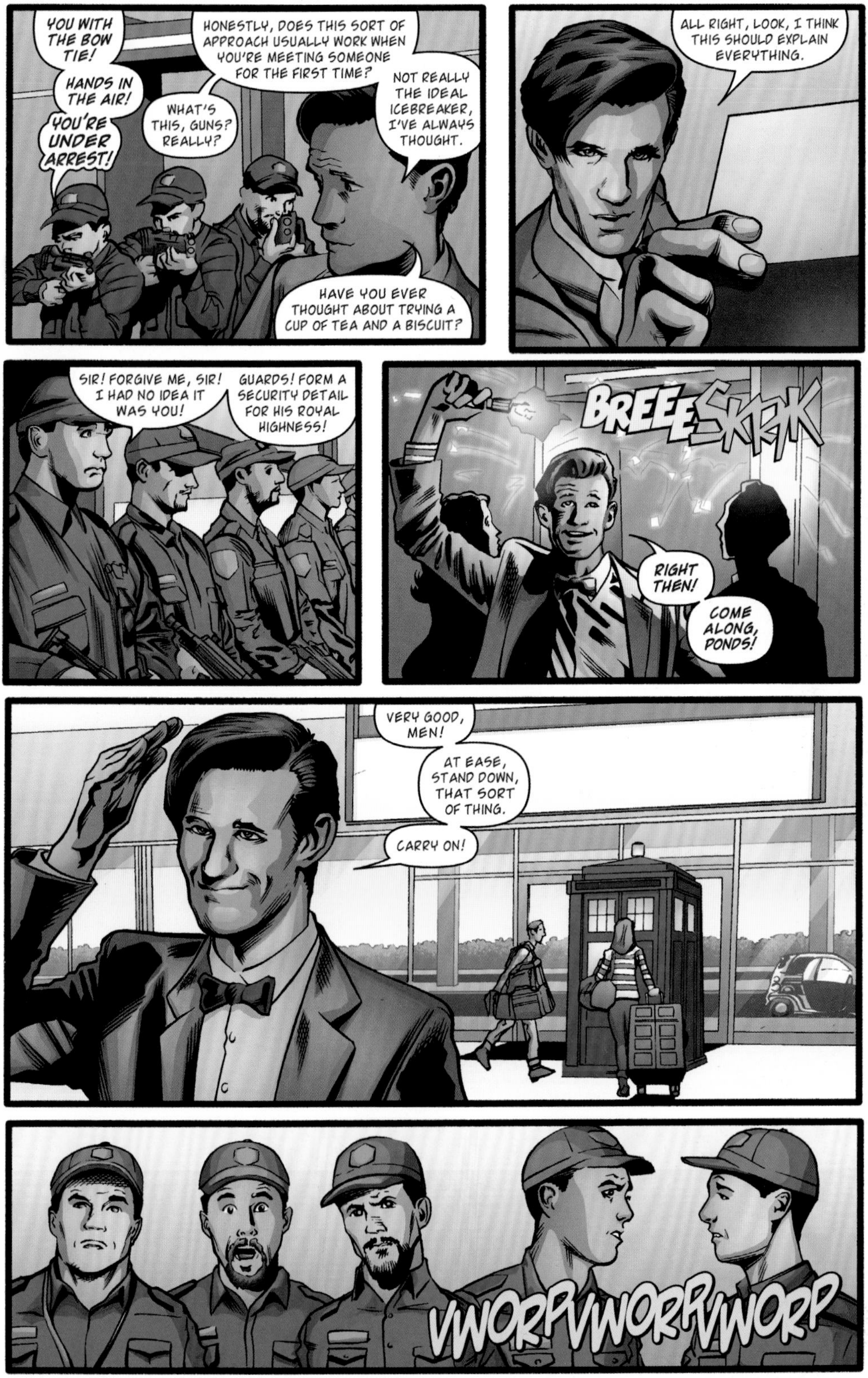
YOU WITH THE BOW TIE!
HANDS IN THE AIR!
YOU'RE UNDER ARREST!
HONESTLY, DOES THIS SORT OF APPROACH USUALLY WORK WHEN YOU'RE MEETING SOMEONE FOR THE FIRST TIME?
WHAT'S THIS, GUNS? REALLY?
NOT REALLY THE IDEAL ICEBREAKER, I'VE ALWAYS THOUGHT.
HAVE YOU EVER THOUGHT ABOUT TRYING A CUP OF TEA AND A BISCUIT?
ALL RIGHT, LOOK, I THINK THIS SHOULD EXPLAIN EVERYTHING.
SIR! FORGIVE ME, SIR! I HAD NO IDEA IT WAS YOU!
GUARDS! FORM A SECURITY DETAIL FOR HIS ROYAL HIGHNESS!
BREEESKRK
RIGHT THEN!
COME ALONG, PONDS!
VERY GOOD, MEN!
AT EASE, STAND DOWN, THAT SORT OF THING.
CARRY ON!
VWORPVWORPVWORP

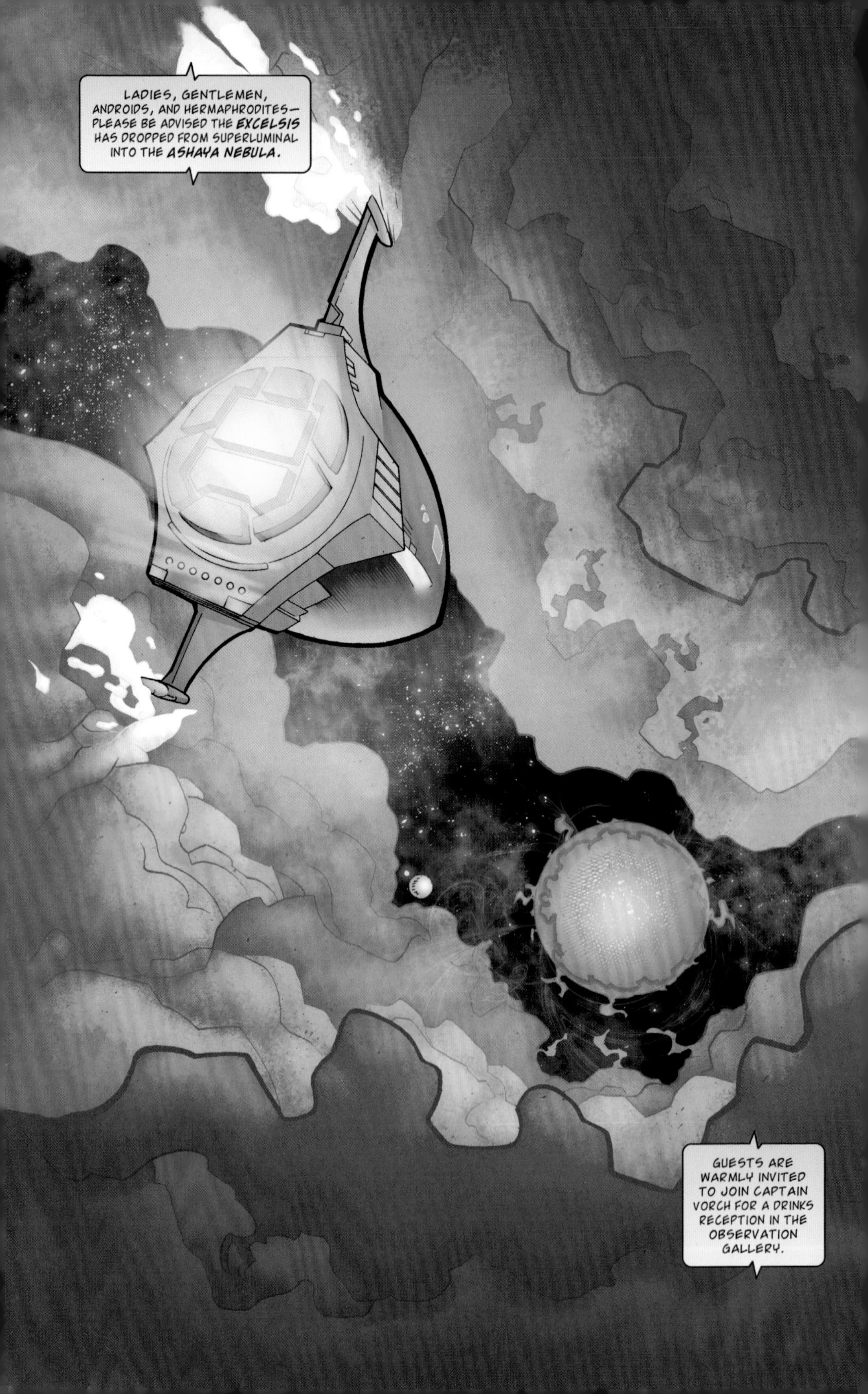

LADIES, GENTLEMEN, ANDROIDS, AND HERMAPHRODITES—PLEASE BE ADVISED THE *EXCELSIS* HAS DROPPED FROM SUPERLUMINAL INTO THE *ASHAYA NEBULA*.
GUESTS ARE WARMLY INVITED TO JOIN CAPTAIN VORCH FOR A DRINKS RECEPTION IN THE OBSERVATION GALLERY.

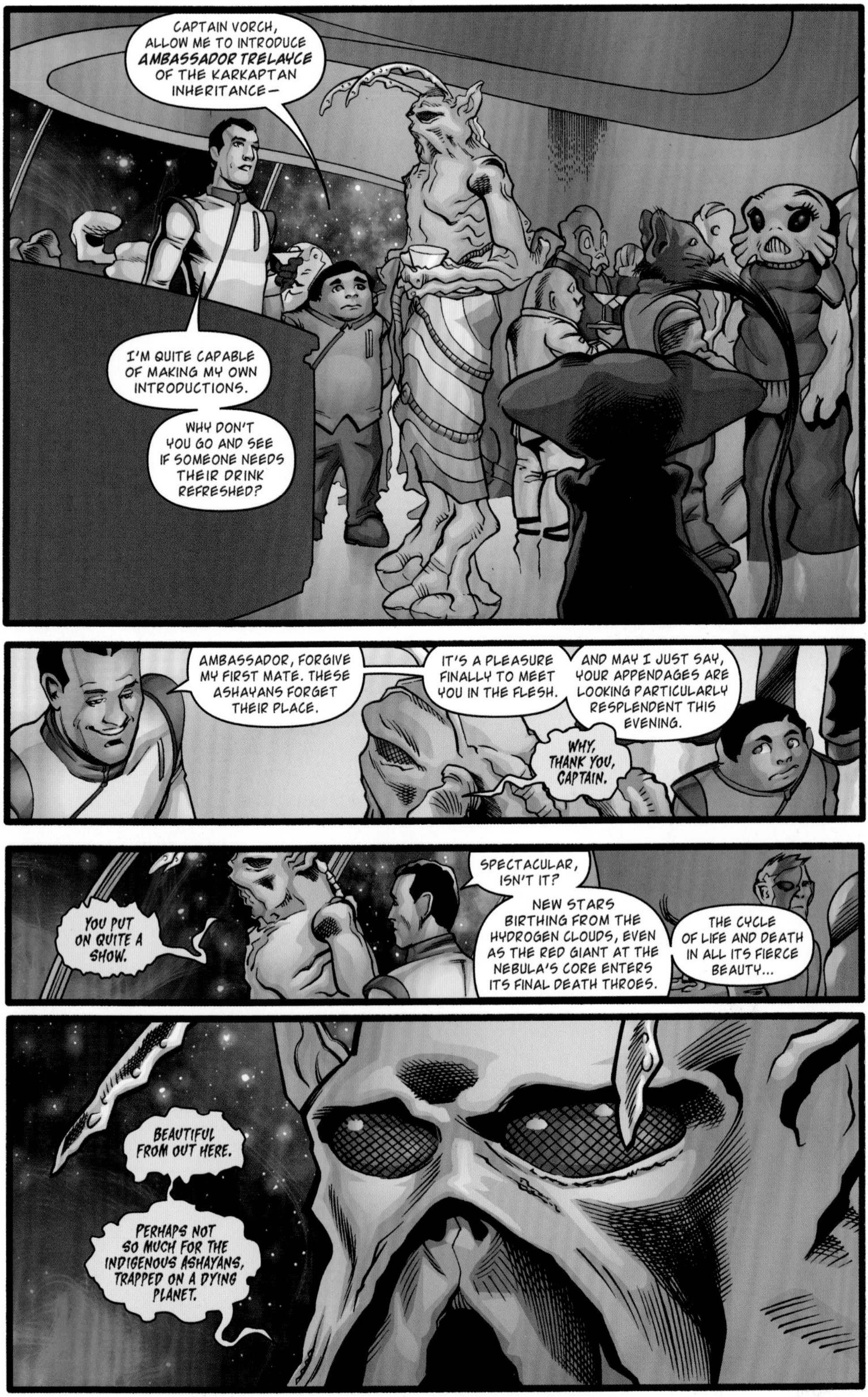
CAPTAIN VORCH, ALLOW ME TO INTRODUCE AMBASSADOR TRELAYCE OF THE KARKAPTAN INHERITANCE—
I'M QUITE CAPABLE OF MAKING MY OWN INTRODUCTIONS.
WHY DON'T YOU GO AND SEE IF SOMEONE NEEDS THEIR DRINK REFRESHED?
AMBASSADOR, FORGIVE MY FIRST MATE. THESE ASHAYANS FORGET THEIR PLACE.
IT'S A PLEASURE FINALLY TO MEET YOU IN THE FLESH.
AND MAY I JUST SAY, YOUR APPENDAGES ARE LOOKING PARTICULARLY RESPLENDENT THIS EVENING.
WHY, THANK YOU, CAPTAIN.
YOU PUT ON QUITE A SHOW.
SPECTACULAR, ISN'T IT?
NEW STARS BIRTHING FROM THE HYDROGEN CLOUDS, EVEN AS THE RED GIANT AT THE NEBULA'S CORE ENTERS ITS FINAL DEATH THROES.
THE CYCLE OF LIFE AND DEATH IN ALL ITS FIERCE BEAUTY...
BEAUTIFUL FROM OUT HERE.
PERHAPS NOT SO MUCH FOR THE INDIGENOUS ASHAYANS, TRAPPED ON A DYING PLANET.

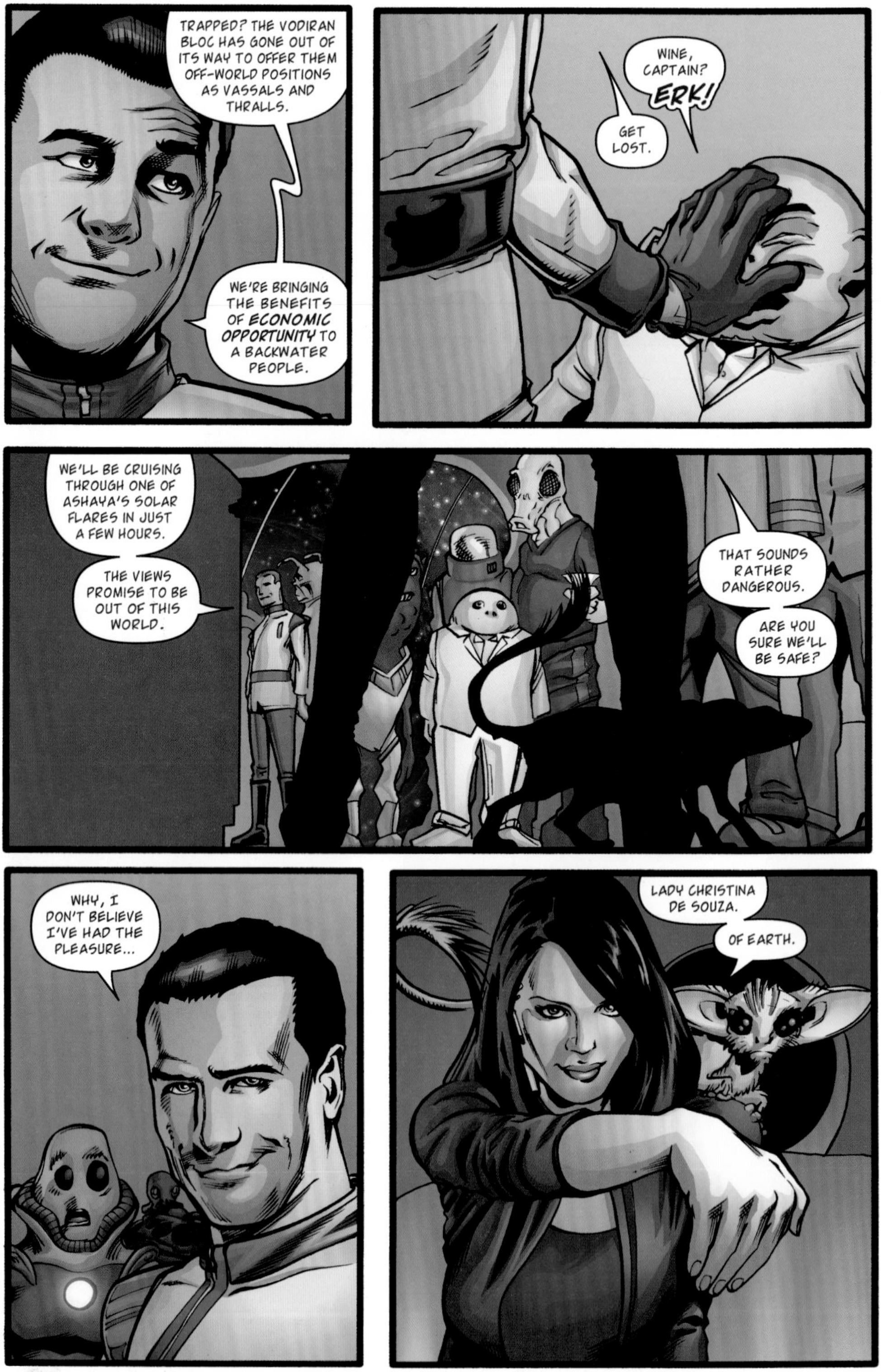
TRAPPED? THE VODIRAN BLOC HAS GONE OUT OF ITS WAY TO OFFER THEM OFF-WORLD POSITIONS AS VASSALS AND THRALLS.
WE'RE BRINGING THE BENEFITS OF ECONOMIC OPPORTUNITY TO A BACKWATER PEOPLE.
WINE, CAPTAIN?
ERK!
GET LOST.
WE'LL BE CRUISING THROUGH ONE OF ASHAYA'S SOLAR FLARES IN JUST A FEW HOURS.
THE VIEWS PROMISE TO BE OUT OF THIS WORLD.
THAT SOUNDS RATHER DANGEROUS.
ARE YOU SURE WE'LL BE SAFE?
WHY, I DON'T BELIEVE I'VE HAD THE PLEASURE...
LADY CHRISTINA DE SOUZA.
OF EARTH.

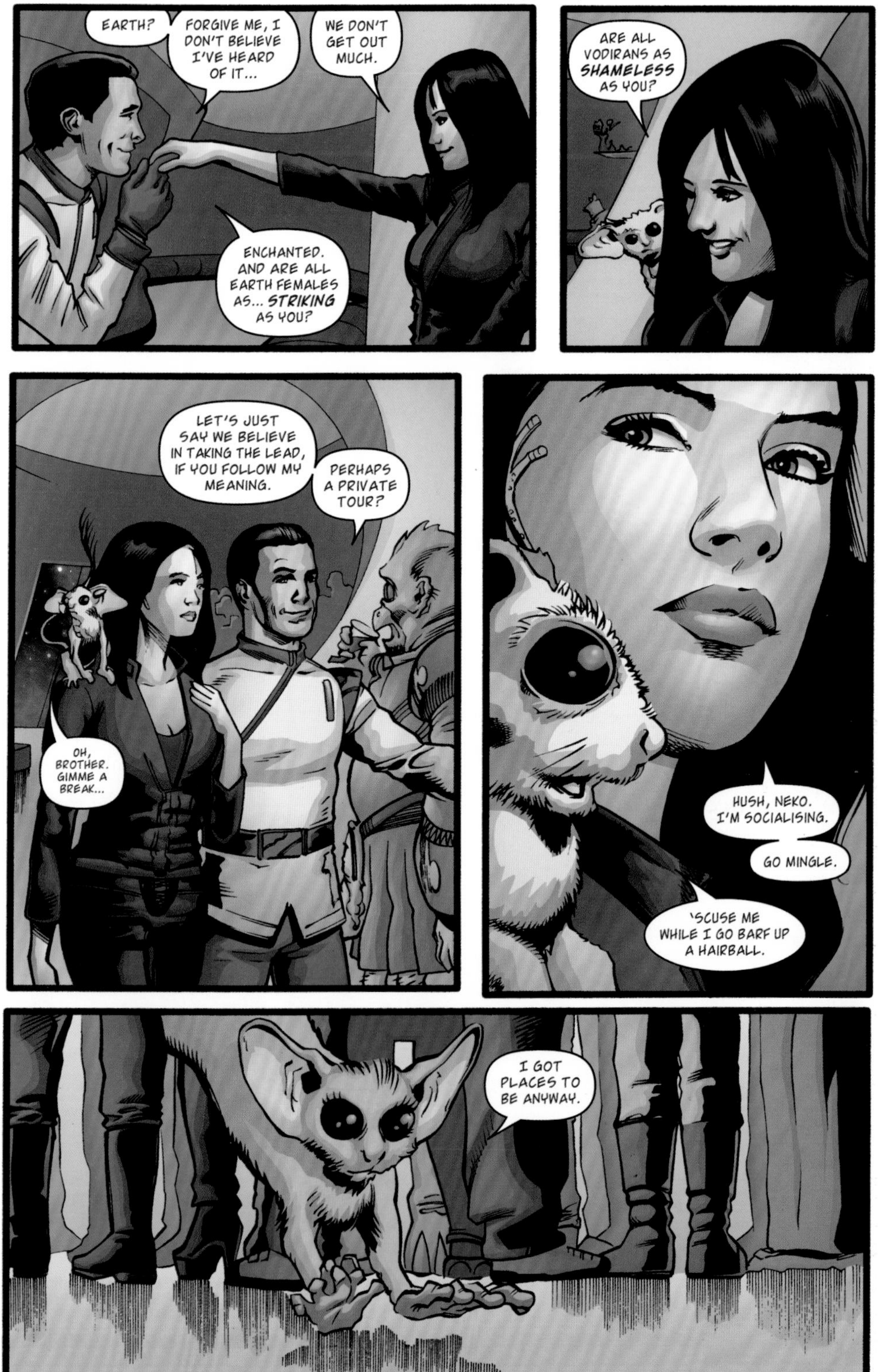
EARTH?
FORGIVE ME, I DON'T BELIEVE I'VE HEARD OF IT...
WE DON'T GET OUT MUCH.
ENCHANTED. AND ARE ALL EARTH FEMALES AS... STRIKING AS YOU?
ARE ALL VODIRANS AS SHAMELESS AS YOU?
LET'S JUST SAY WE BELIEVE IN TAKING THE LEAD, IF YOU FOLLOW MY MEANING.
PERHAPS A PRIVATE TOUR?
OH, BROTHER. GIMME A BREAK...
HUSH, NEKO. I'M SOCIALISING.
GO MINGLE.
'SCUSE ME WHILE I GO BARF UP A HAIRBALL.
I GOT PLACES TO BE ANYWAY.

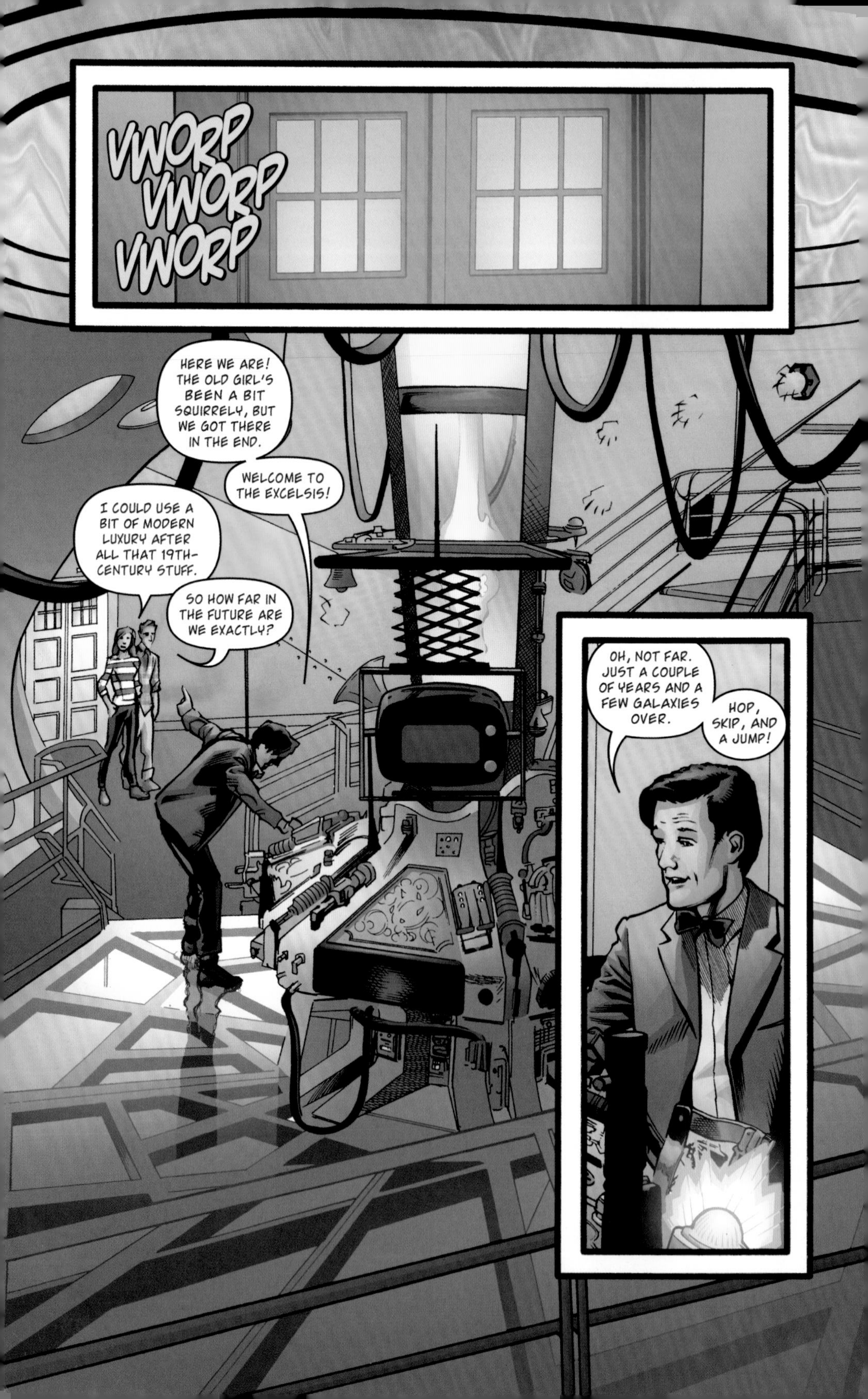
VWORP VWORP VWORP
HERE WE ARE! THE OLD GIRL'S BEEN A BIT SQUIRRELY, BUT WE GOT THERE IN THE END.
WELCOME TO THE EXCELSIS!
I COULD USE A BIT OF MODERN LUXURY AFTER ALL THAT 19TH-CENTURY STUFF.
SO HOW FAR IN THE FUTURE ARE WE EXACTLY?
OH, NOT FAR. JUST A COUPLE OF YEARS AND A FEW GALAXIES OVER.
HOP, SKIP, AND A JUMP!

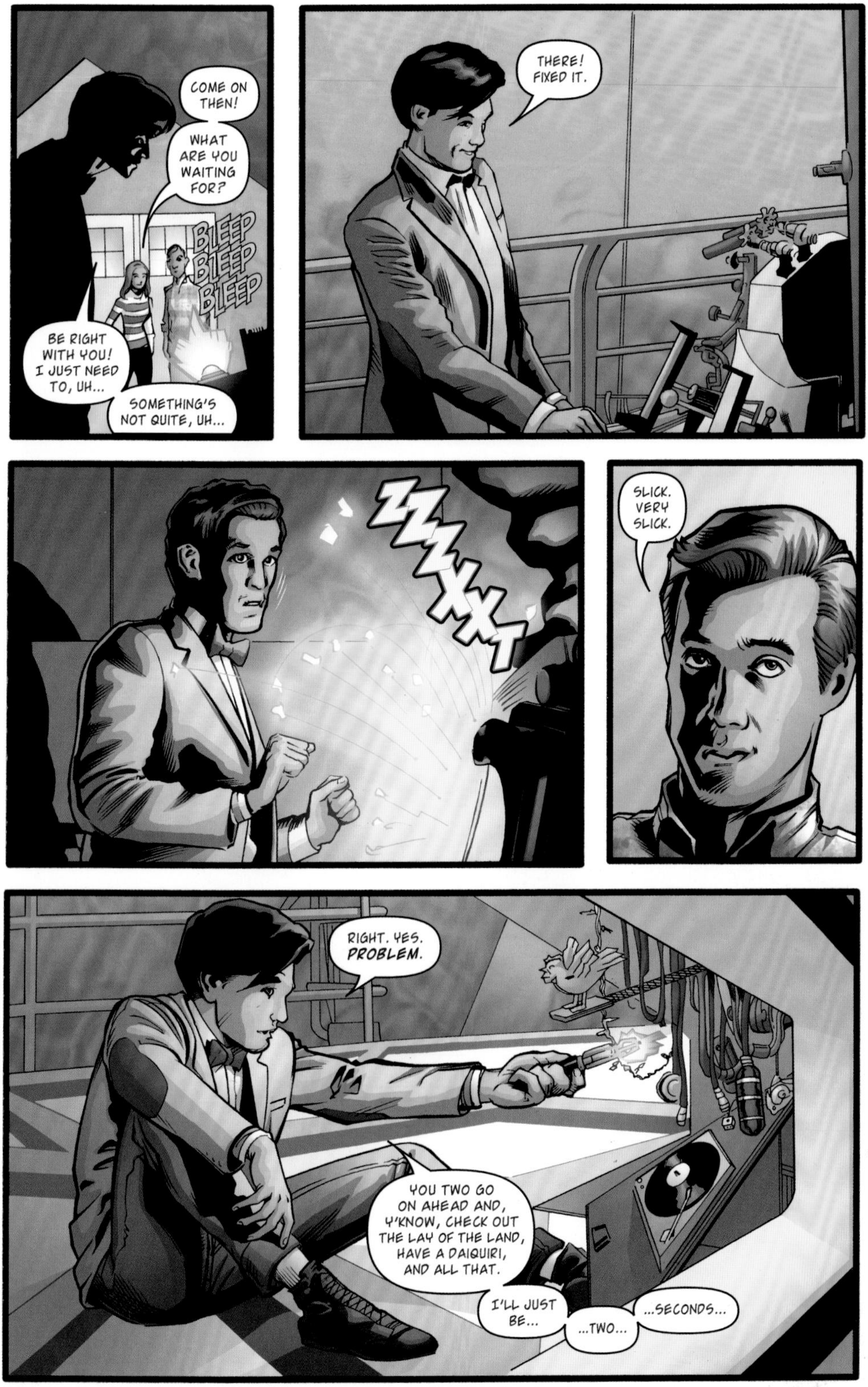
COME ON THEN!
WHAT ARE YOU WAITING FOR?
BLEEP BLEEP BLEEP
BE RIGHT WITH YOU! I JUST NEED TO, UH...
SOMETHING'S NOT QUITE, UH...
THERE! FIXED IT.
ZZZXXT
SLICK. VERY SLICK.
RIGHT. YES. PROBLEM.
YOU TWO GO ON AHEAD AND, Y'KNOW, CHECK OUT THE LAY OF THE LAND, HAVE A DAIQUIRI, AND ALL THAT.
I'LL JUST BE...
...TWO...
...SECONDS...

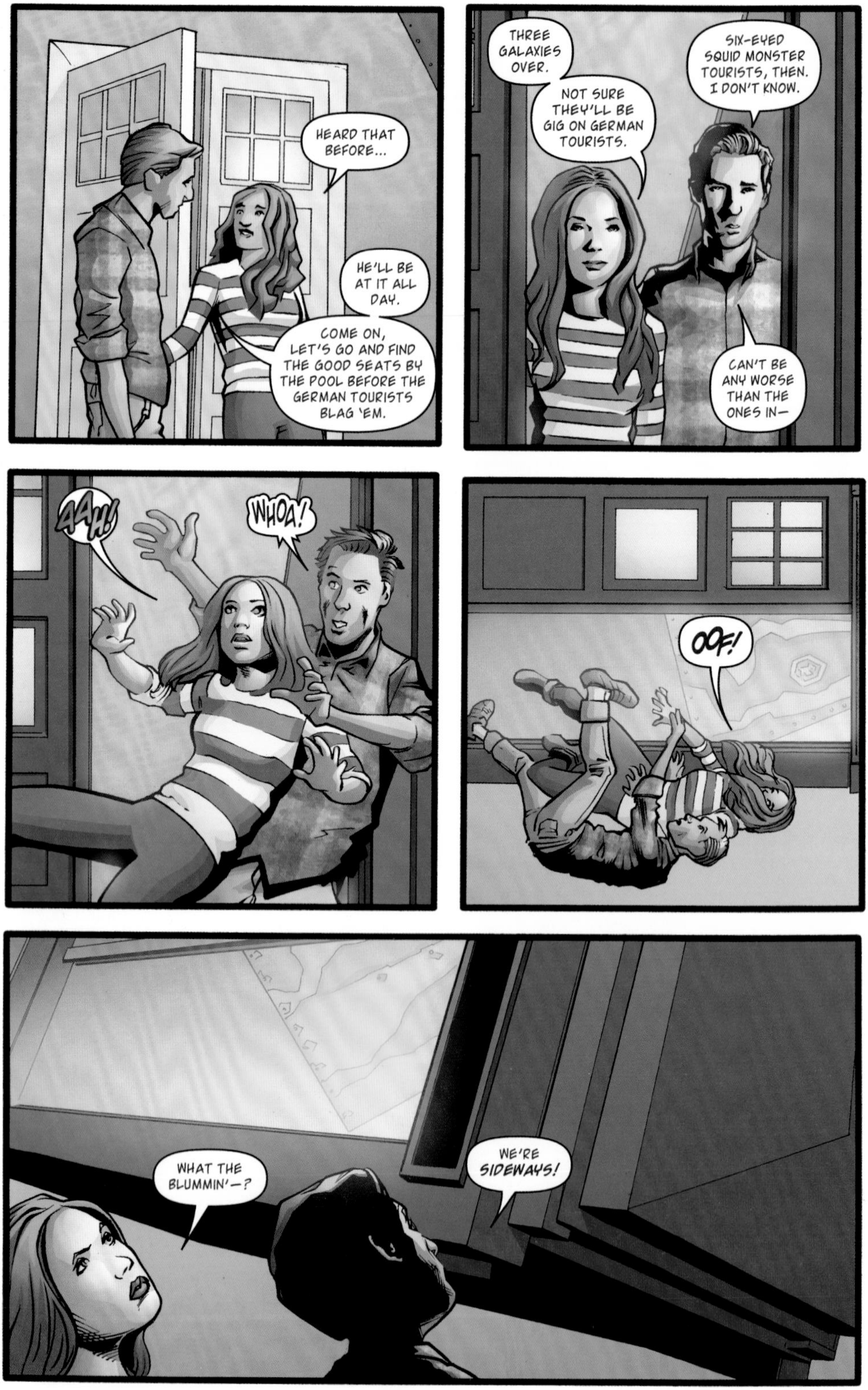
HEARD THAT BEFORE...
HE'LL BE AT IT ALL DAY.
COME ON, LET'S GO AND FIND THE GOOD SEATS BY THE POOL BEFORE THE GERMAN TOURISTS BLAG 'EM.
THREE GALAXIES OVER.
NOT SURE THEY'LL BE GIG ON GERMAN TOURISTS.
SIX-EYED SQUID MONSTER TOURISTS, THEN. I DON'T KNOW.
CAN'T BE ANY WORSE THAN THE ONES IN—
AAH!
WHOA!
OOF!
WHAT THE BLUMMIN'—?
WE'RE *SIDEWAYS!*

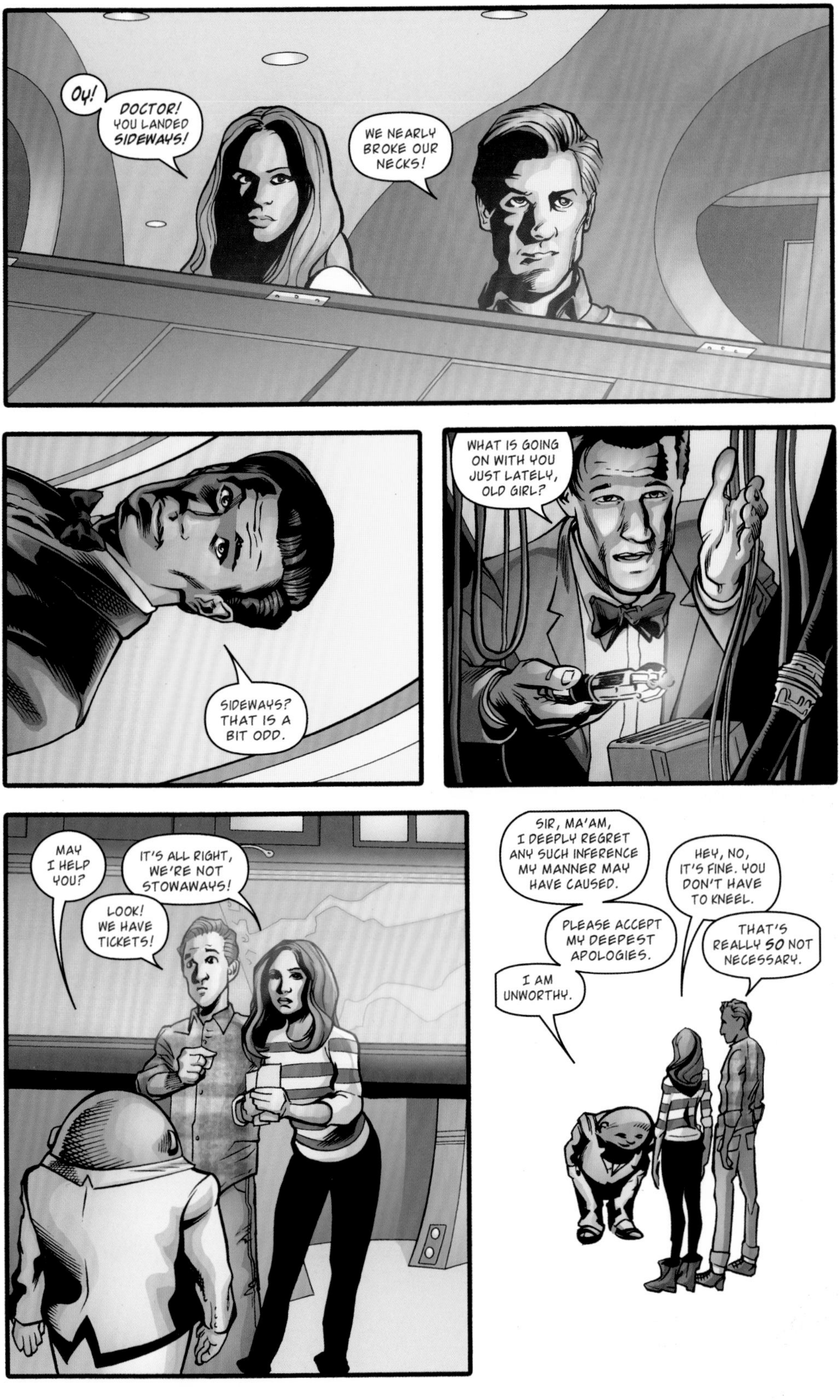
OY!
DOCTOR! YOU LANDED SIDEWAYS!
WE NEARLY BROKE OUR NECKS!
SIDEWAYS? THAT IS A BIT ODD.
WHAT IS GOING ON WITH YOU JUST LATELY, OLD GIRL?
MAY I HELP YOU?
IT'S ALL RIGHT, WE'RE NOT STOWAWAYS!
LOOK! WE HAVE TICKETS!
SIR, MA'AM, I DEEPLY REGRET ANY SUCH INFERENCE MY MANNER MAY HAVE CAUSED.
PLEASE ACCEPT MY DEEPEST APOLOGIES.
I AM UNWORTHY.
HEY, NO, IT'S FINE. YOU DON'T HAVE TO KNEEL.
THAT'S REALLY SO NOT NECESSARY.

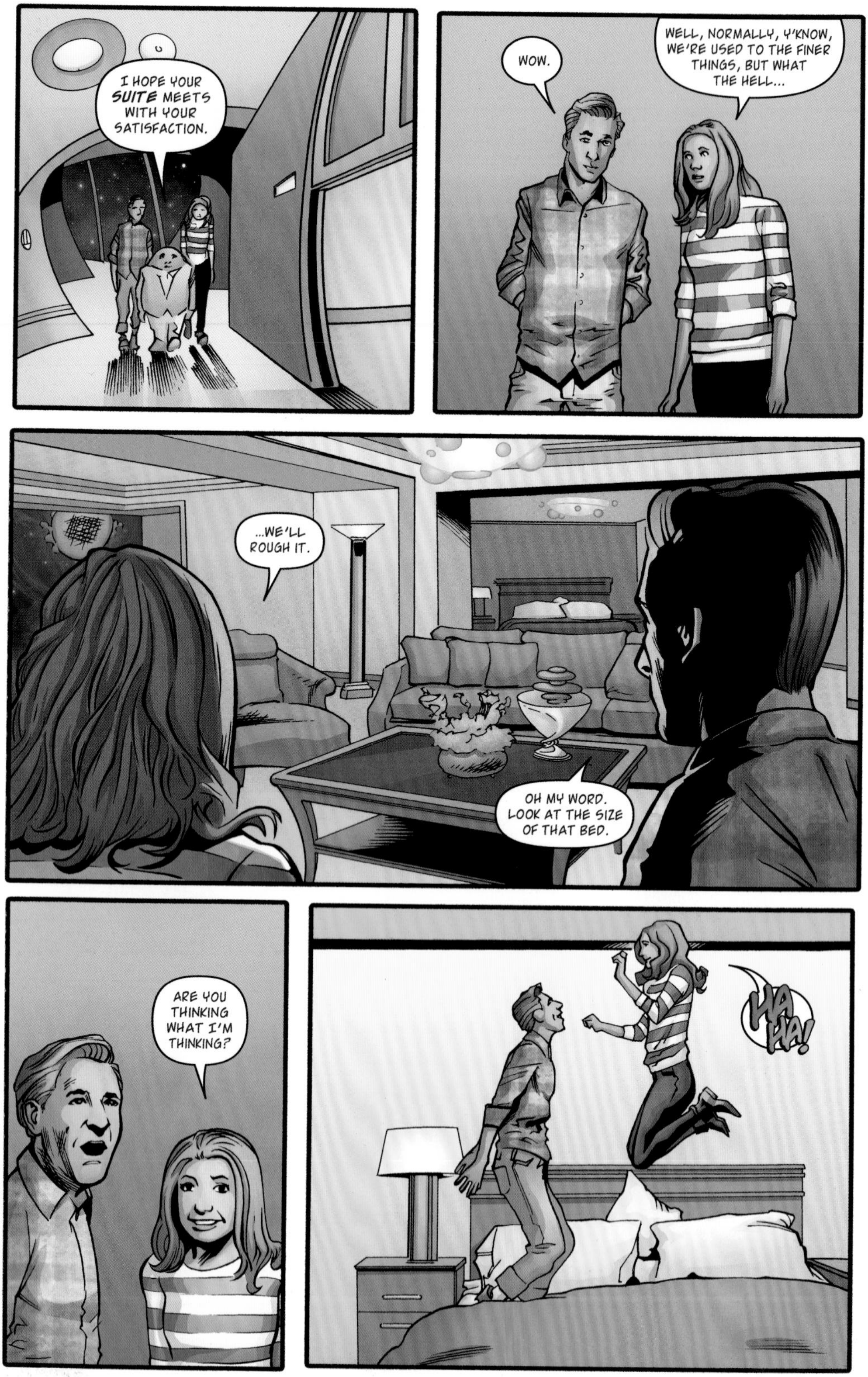
I HOPE YOUR SUITE MEETS WITH YOUR SATISFACTION.
WOW.
WELL, NORMALLY, Y'KNOW, WE'RE USED TO THE FINER THINGS, BUT WHAT THE HELL...
...WE'LL ROUGH IT.
OH MY WORD. LOOK AT THE SIZE OF THAT BED.
ARE YOU THINKING WHAT I'M THINKING?
HA HA!

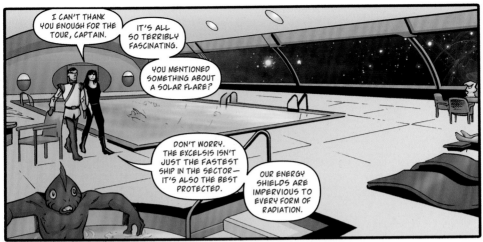

I CAN'T THANK YOU ENOUGH FOR THE TOUR, CAPTAIN.

IT'S ALL SO TERRIBLY FASCINATING.

YOU MENTIONED SOMETHING ABOUT A SOLAR FLARE?

DON'T WORRY. THE EXCELSIS ISN'T JUST THE FASTEST SHIP IN THE SECTOR— IT'S ALSO THE BEST PROTECTED.

OUR ENERGY SHIELDS ARE IMPERVIOUS TO EVERY FORM OF RADIATION.

EXCEPT VISIBLE LIGHT, OF COURSE.

WELL, WE WANT OUR GUESTS TO ENJOY THE VIEW...

...AND WORK ON THEIR TANS.

SPEAKING OF WHICH, PERHAPS YOU'D LIKE TO SLIP INTO SOMETHING MORE REVEALING—

HOW DO THEY WORK?

I'M SORRY?

THE SHIELDS.

FORGIVE ME, I'D FEEL SAFER IF I KNEW MORE ABOUT THEM.

THE EXCELSIS IS POWERED BY A REFRACTION DRIVE. ZERO-POINT ENERGY, FOCUSED THROUGH THE LARGEST DIAMOND IN THE GALAXY.

A DIAMOND, YOU SAY.

HOW INTERESTING.

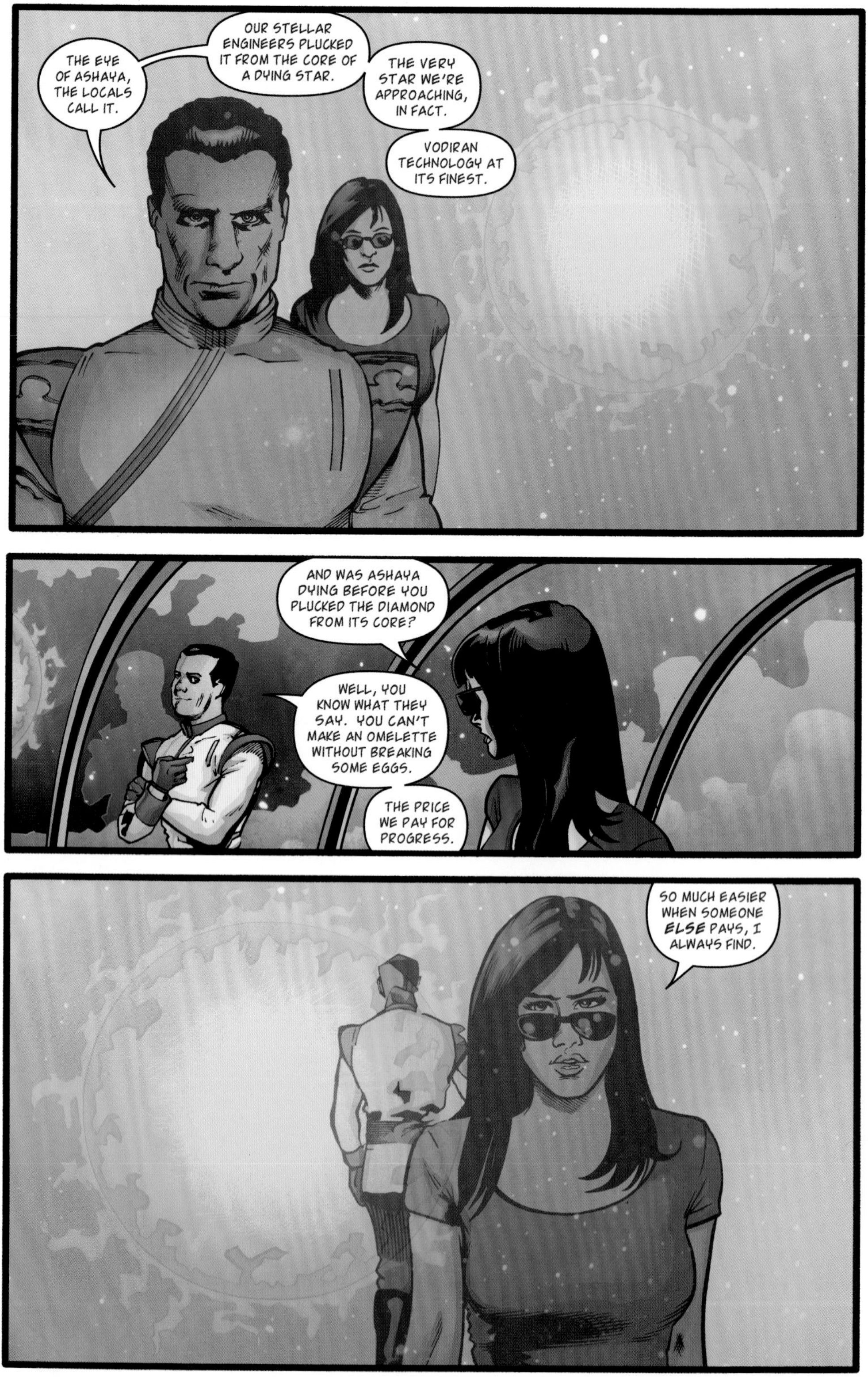
THE EYE OF ASHAYA, THE LOCALS CALL IT.
OUR STELLAR ENGINEERS PLUCKED IT FROM THE CORE OF A DYING STAR.
THE VERY STAR WE'RE APPROACHING, IN FACT.
VODIRAN TECHNOLOGY AT ITS FINEST.
AND WAS ASHAYA DYING BEFORE YOU PLUCKED THE DIAMOND FROM ITS CORE?
WELL, YOU KNOW WHAT THEY SAY. YOU CAN'T MAKE AN OMELETTE WITHOUT BREAKING SOME EGGS.
THE PRICE WE PAY FOR PROGRESS.
SO MUCH EASIER WHEN SOMEONE ELSE PAYS, I ALWAYS FIND.

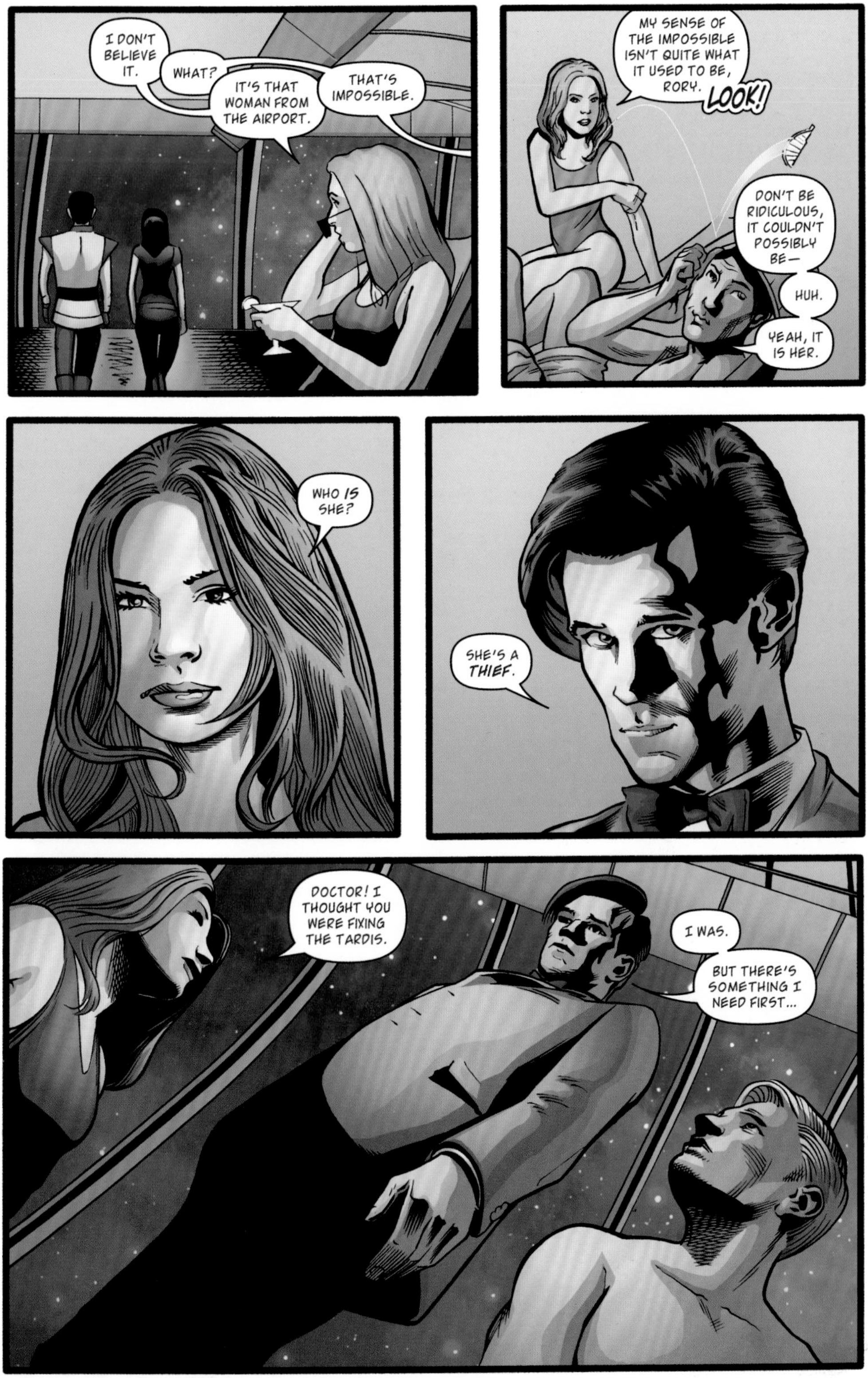
I DON'T BELIEVE IT.
WHAT?
IT'S THAT WOMAN FROM THE AIRPORT.
THAT'S IMPOSSIBLE.
MY SENSE OF THE IMPOSSIBLE ISN'T QUITE WHAT IT USED TO BE, RORY.
LOOK!
DON'T BE RIDICULOUS, IT COULDN'T POSSIBLY BE—
HUH.
YEAH, IT IS HER.
WHO IS SHE?
SHE'S A THIEF.
DOCTOR! I THOUGHT YOU WERE FIXING THE TARDIS.
I WAS.
BUT THERE'S SOMETHING I NEED FIRST...

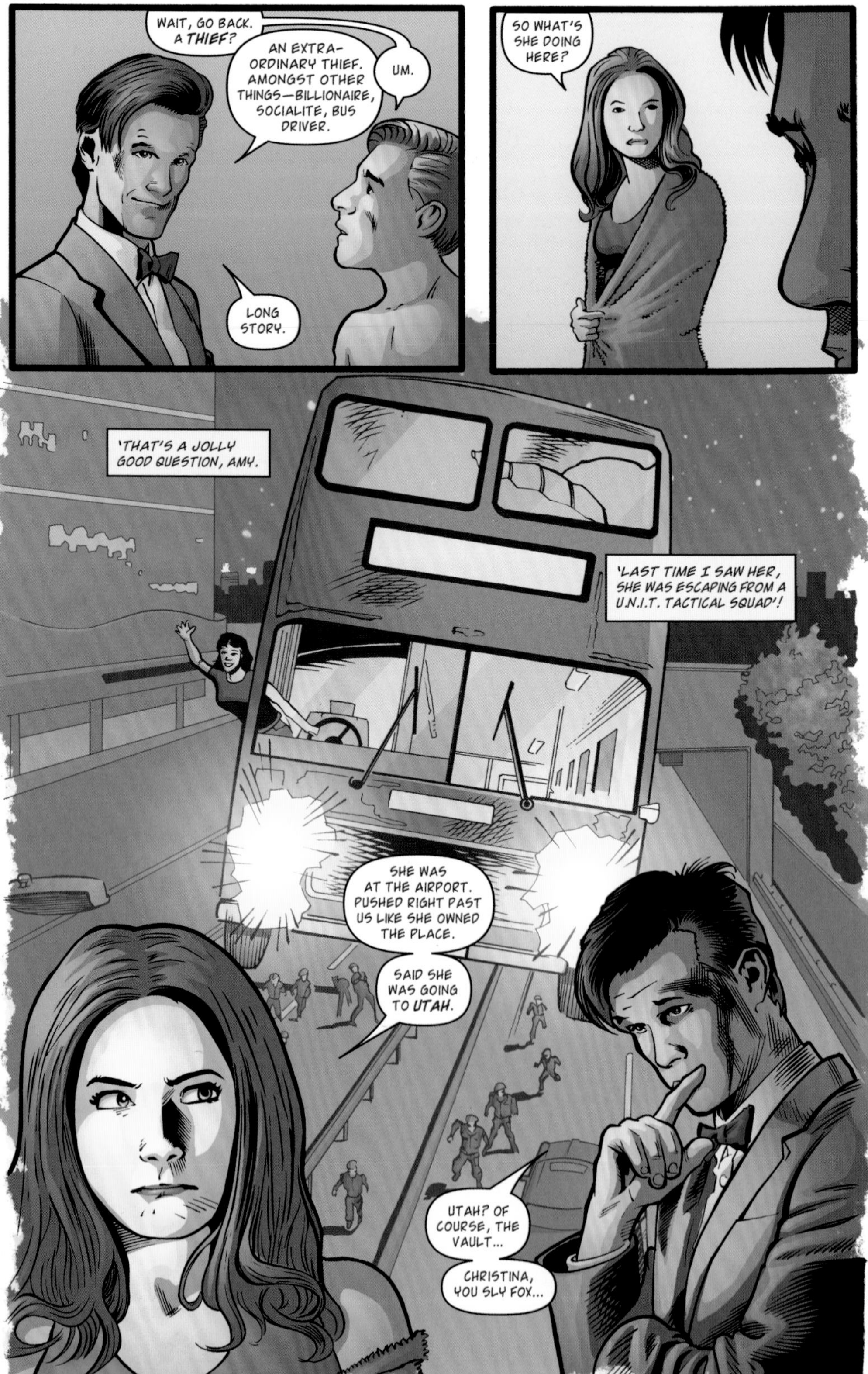
WAIT, GO BACK. A THIEF?
AN EXTRA-ORDINARY THIEF. AMONGST OTHER THINGS—BILLIONAIRE, SOCIALITE, BUS DRIVER.
UM.
LONG STORY.
SO WHAT'S SHE DOING HERE?
'THAT'S A JOLLY GOOD QUESTION, AMY.
'LAST TIME I SAW HER, SHE WAS ESCAPING FROM A U.N.I.T. TACTICAL SQUAD'!
SHE WAS AT THE AIRPORT. PUSHED RIGHT PAST US LIKE SHE OWNED THE PLACE.
SAID SHE WAS GOING TO UTAH.
UTAH? OF COURSE, THE VAULT...
CHRISTINA, YOU SLY FOX...

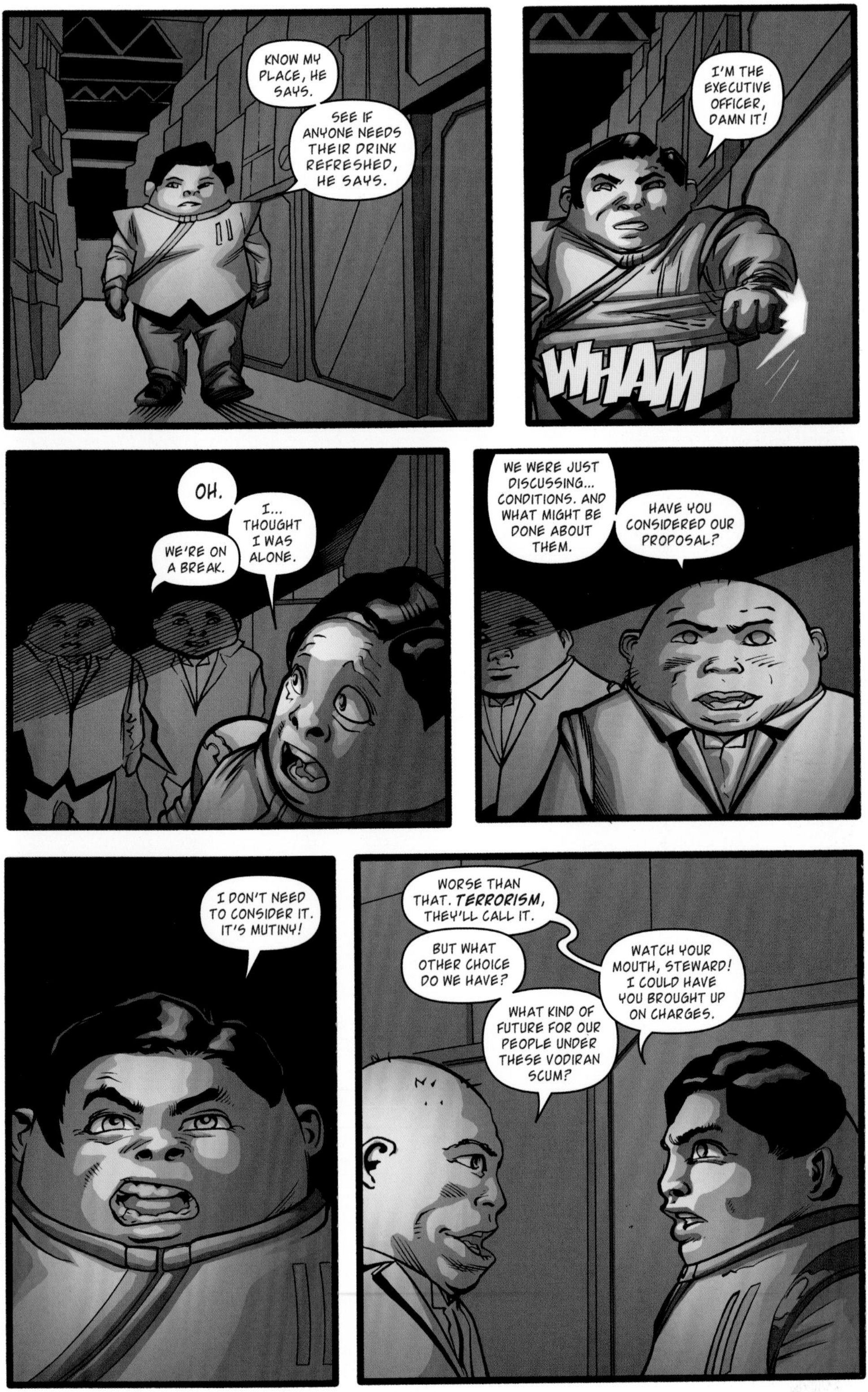
KNOW MY PLACE, HE SAYS.
SEE IF ANYONE NEEDS THEIR DRINK REFRESHED, HE SAYS.
I'M THE EXECUTIVE OFFICER, DAMN IT!
WHAM
OH.
I... THOUGHT I WAS ALONE.
WE'RE ON A BREAK.
WE WERE JUST DISCUSSING... CONDITIONS. AND WHAT MIGHT BE DONE ABOUT THEM.
HAVE YOU CONSIDERED OUR PROPOSAL?
I DON'T NEED TO CONSIDER IT. IT'S MUTINY!
WORSE THAN THAT. TERRORISM, THEY'LL CALL IT.
BUT WHAT OTHER CHOICE DO WE HAVE?
WHAT KIND OF FUTURE FOR OUR PEOPLE UNDER THESE VODIRAN SCUM?
WATCH YOUR MOUTH, STEWARD! I COULD HAVE YOU BROUGHT UP ON CHARGES.

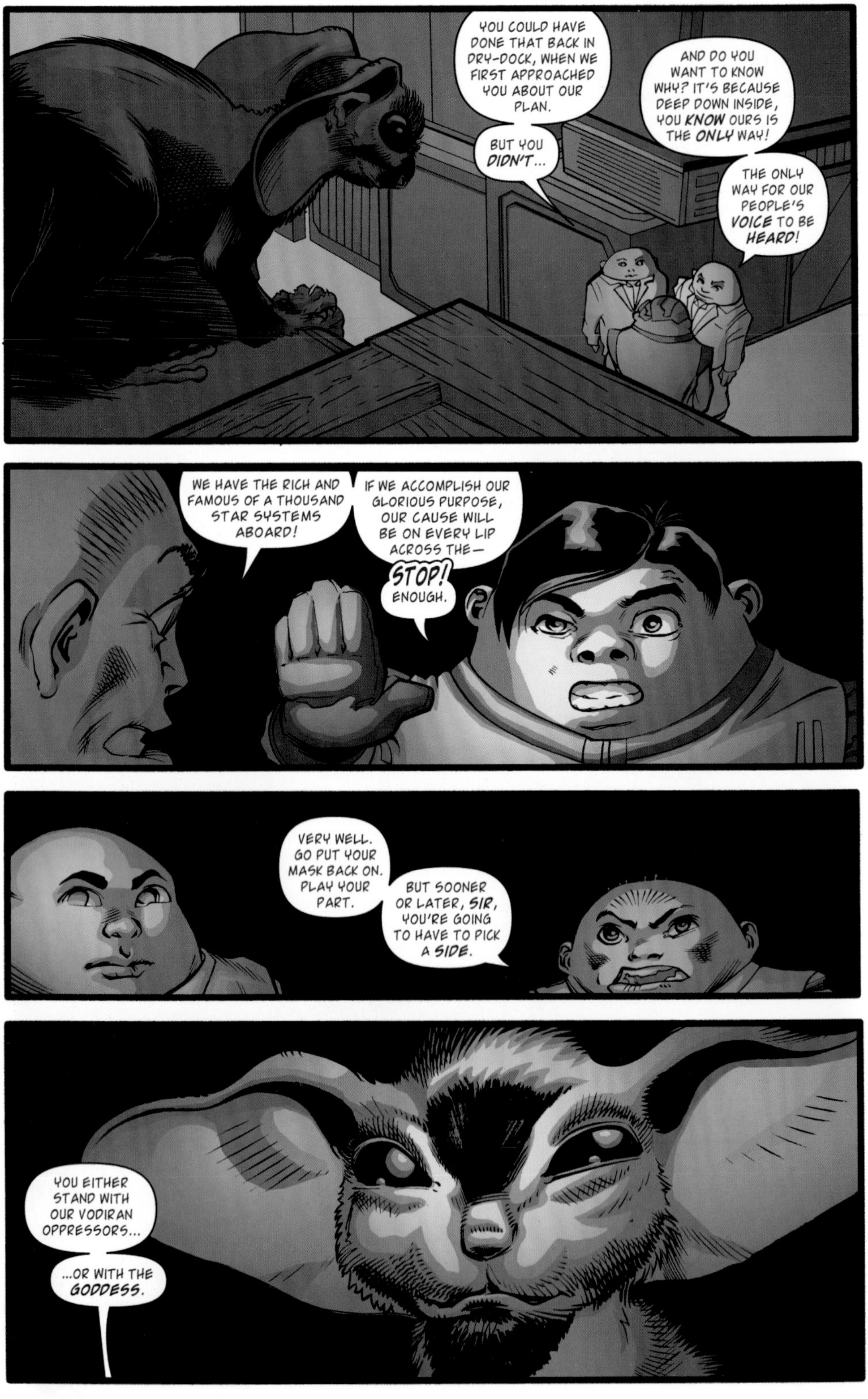
YOU COULD HAVE DONE THAT BACK IN DRY-DOCK, WHEN WE FIRST APPROACHED YOU ABOUT OUR PLAN.
BUT YOU DIDN'T...
AND DO YOU WANT TO KNOW WHY? IT'S BECAUSE DEEP DOWN INSIDE, YOU KNOW OURS IS THE ONLY WAY!
THE ONLY WAY FOR OUR PEOPLE'S VOICE TO BE HEARD!
WE HAVE THE RICH AND FAMOUS OF A THOUSAND STAR SYSTEMS ABOARD!
IF WE ACCOMPLISH OUR GLORIOUS PURPOSE, OUR CAUSE WILL BE ON EVERY LIP ACROSS THE—
STOP! ENOUGH.
VERY WELL. GO PUT YOUR MASK BACK ON. PLAY YOUR PART.
BUT SOONER OR LATER, SIR, YOU'RE GOING TO HAVE TO PICK A SIDE.
YOU EITHER STAND WITH OUR VODIRAN OPPRESSORS...
...OR WITH THE GODDESS.

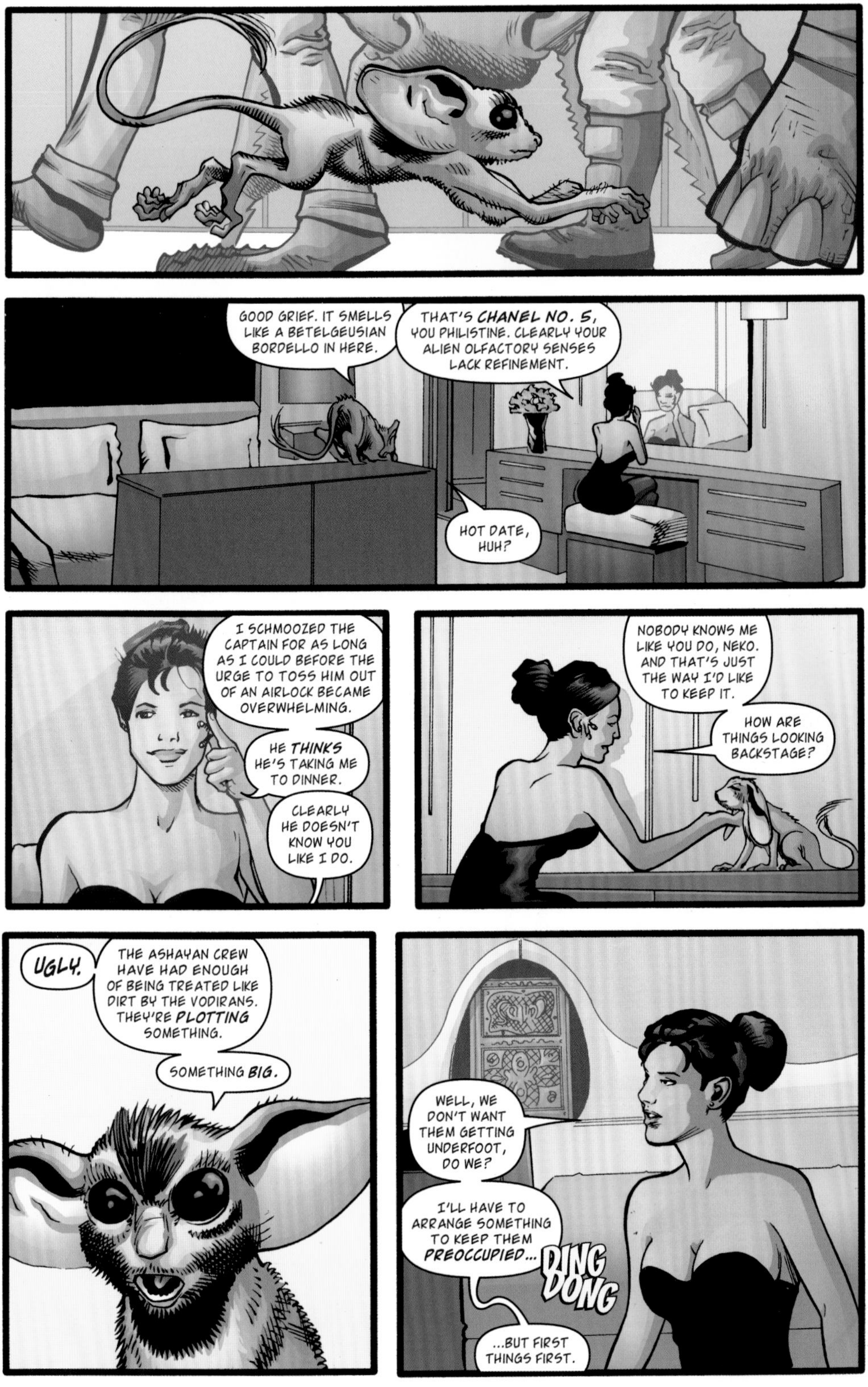
GOOD GRIEF. IT SMELLS LIKE A BETELGEUSIAN BORDELLO IN HERE.
THAT'S CHANEL NO. 5, YOU PHILISTINE. CLEARLY YOUR ALIEN OLFACTORY SENSES LACK REFINEMENT.
HOT DATE, HUH?
I SCHMOOZED THE CAPTAIN FOR AS LONG AS I COULD BEFORE THE URGE TO TOSS HIM OUT OF AN AIRLOCK BECAME OVERWHELMING.
HE THINKS HE'S TAKING ME TO DINNER.
CLEARLY HE DOESN'T KNOW YOU LIKE I DO.
NOBODY KNOWS ME LIKE YOU DO, NEKO. AND THAT'S JUST THE WAY I'D LIKE TO KEEP IT.
HOW ARE THINGS LOOKING BACKSTAGE?
UGLY.
THE ASHAYAN CREW HAVE HAD ENOUGH OF BEING TREATED LIKE DIRT BY THE VODIRANS. THEY'RE PLOTTING SOMETHING.
SOMETHING BIG.
WELL, WE DON'T WANT THEM GETTING UNDERFOOT, DO WE?
I'LL HAVE TO ARRANGE SOMETHING TO KEEP THEM PREOCCUPIED...
DING DONG
...BUT FIRST THINGS FIRST.

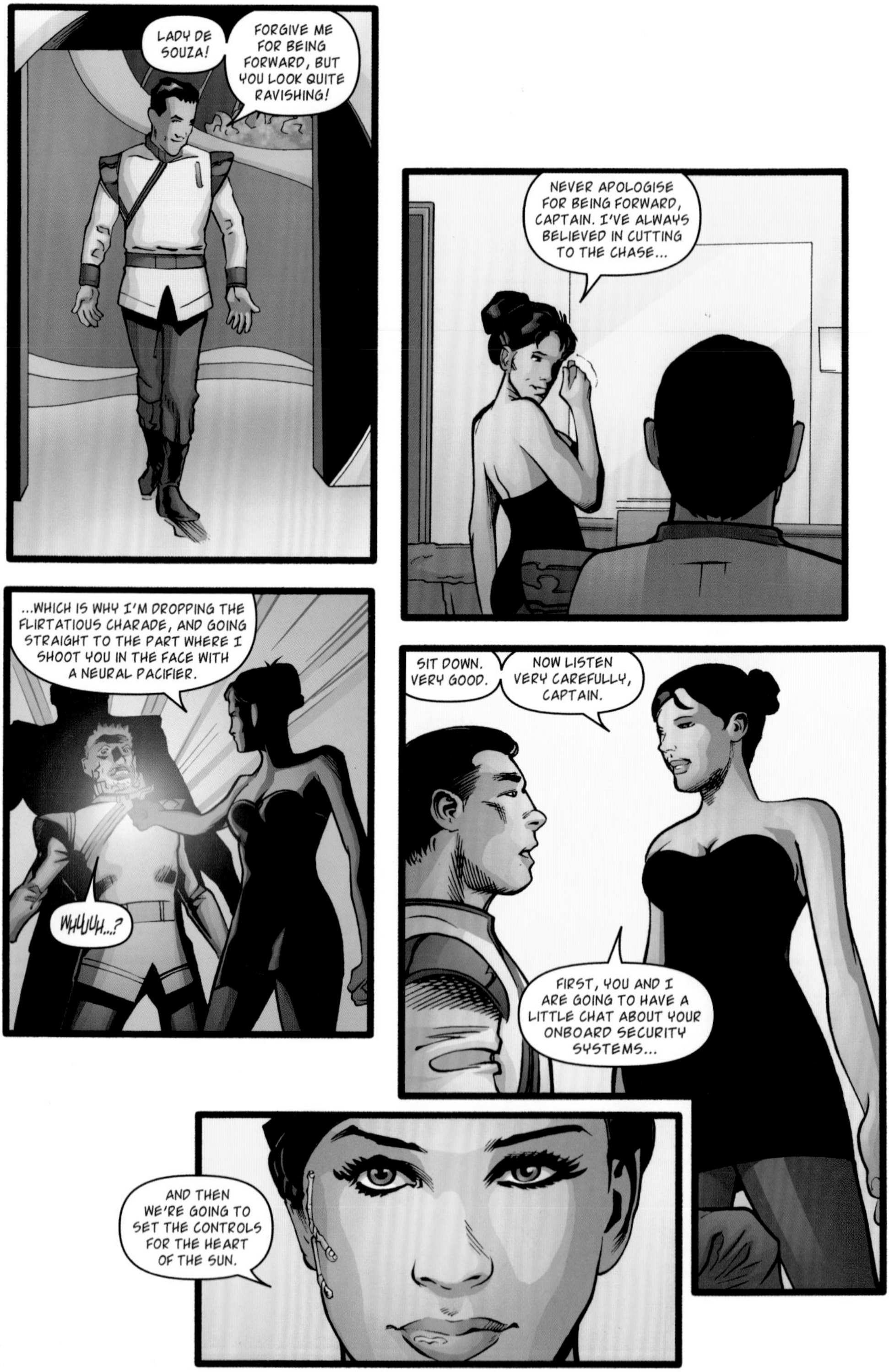
LADY DE SOUZA!
FORGIVE ME FOR BEING FORWARD, BUT YOU LOOK QUITE RAVISHING!
NEVER APOLOGISE FOR BEING FORWARD, CAPTAIN. I'VE ALWAYS BELIEVED IN CUTTING TO THE CHASE...
...WHICH IS WHY I'M DROPPING THE FLIRTATIOUS CHARADE, AND GOING STRAIGHT TO THE PART WHERE I SHOOT YOU IN THE FACE WITH A NEURAL PACIFIER.
WHUUUH...?
SIT DOWN. VERY GOOD.
NOW LISTEN VERY CAREFULLY, CAPTAIN.
FIRST, YOU AND I ARE GOING TO HAVE A LITTLE CHAT ABOUT YOUR ONBOARD SECURITY SYSTEMS...
AND THEN WE'RE GOING TO SET THE CONTROLS FOR THE HEART OF THE SUN.

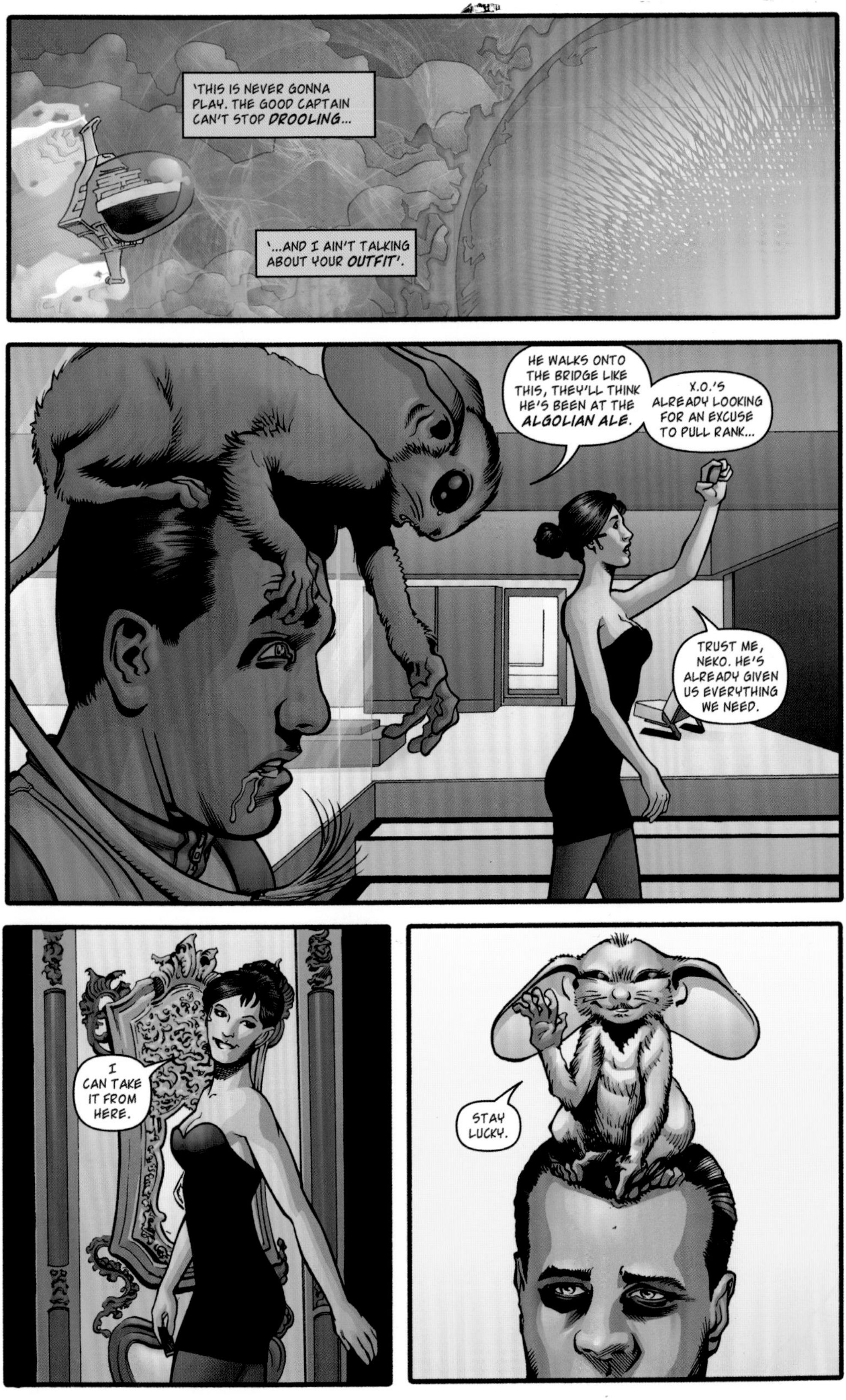
'THIS IS NEVER GONNA PLAY. THE GOOD CAPTAIN CAN'T STOP DROOLING...
'...AND I AIN'T TALKING ABOUT YOUR OUTFIT'.
HE WALKS ONTO THE BRIDGE LIKE THIS, THEY'LL THINK HE'S BEEN AT THE ALGOLIAN ALE.
X.O.'S ALREADY LOOKING FOR AN EXCUSE TO PULL RANK...
TRUST ME, NEKO. HE'S ALREADY GIVEN US EVERYTHING WE NEED.
I CAN TAKE IT FROM HERE.
STAY LUCKY.

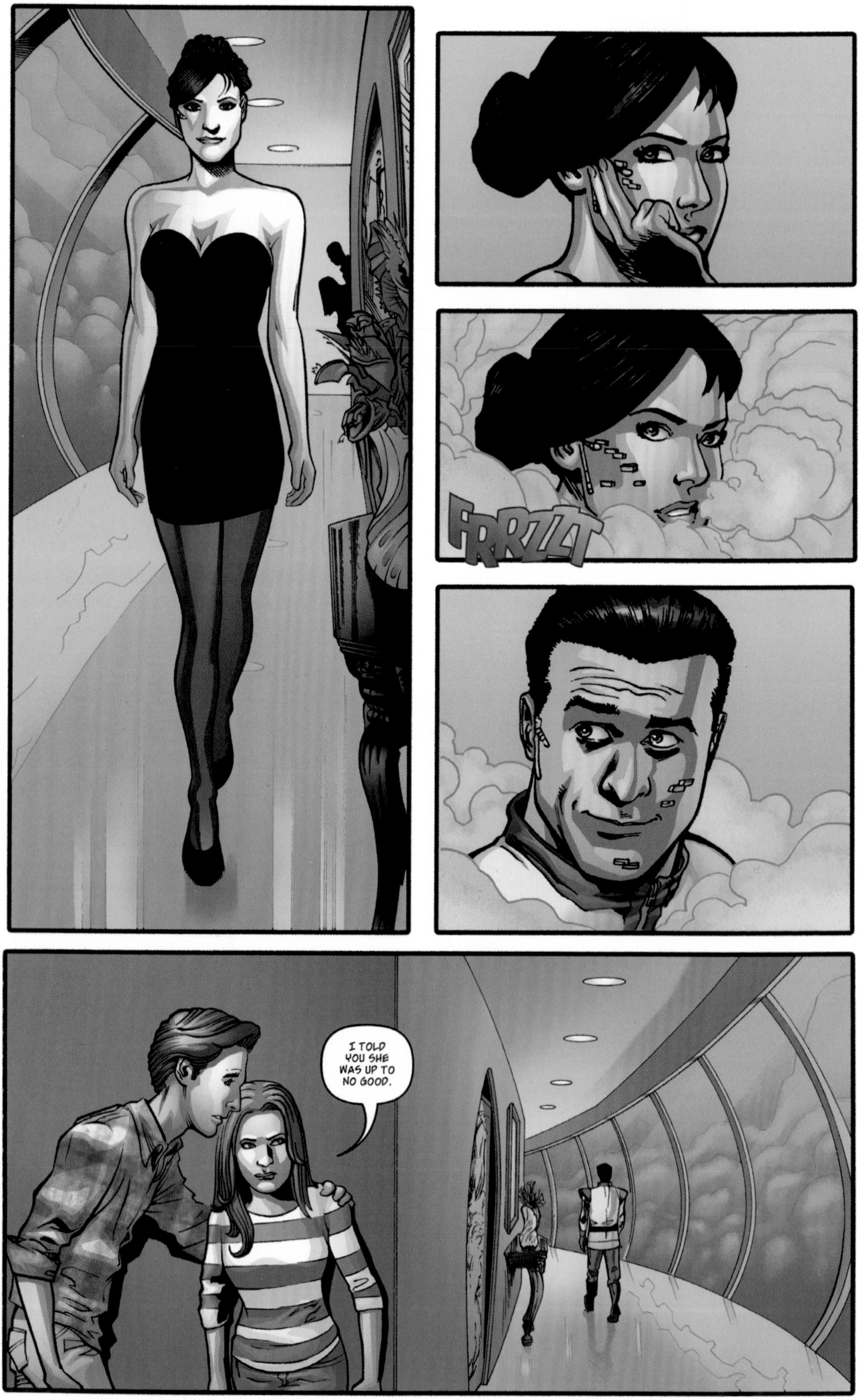
FRRZZZT
I TOLD YOU SHE WAS UP TO NO GOOD.

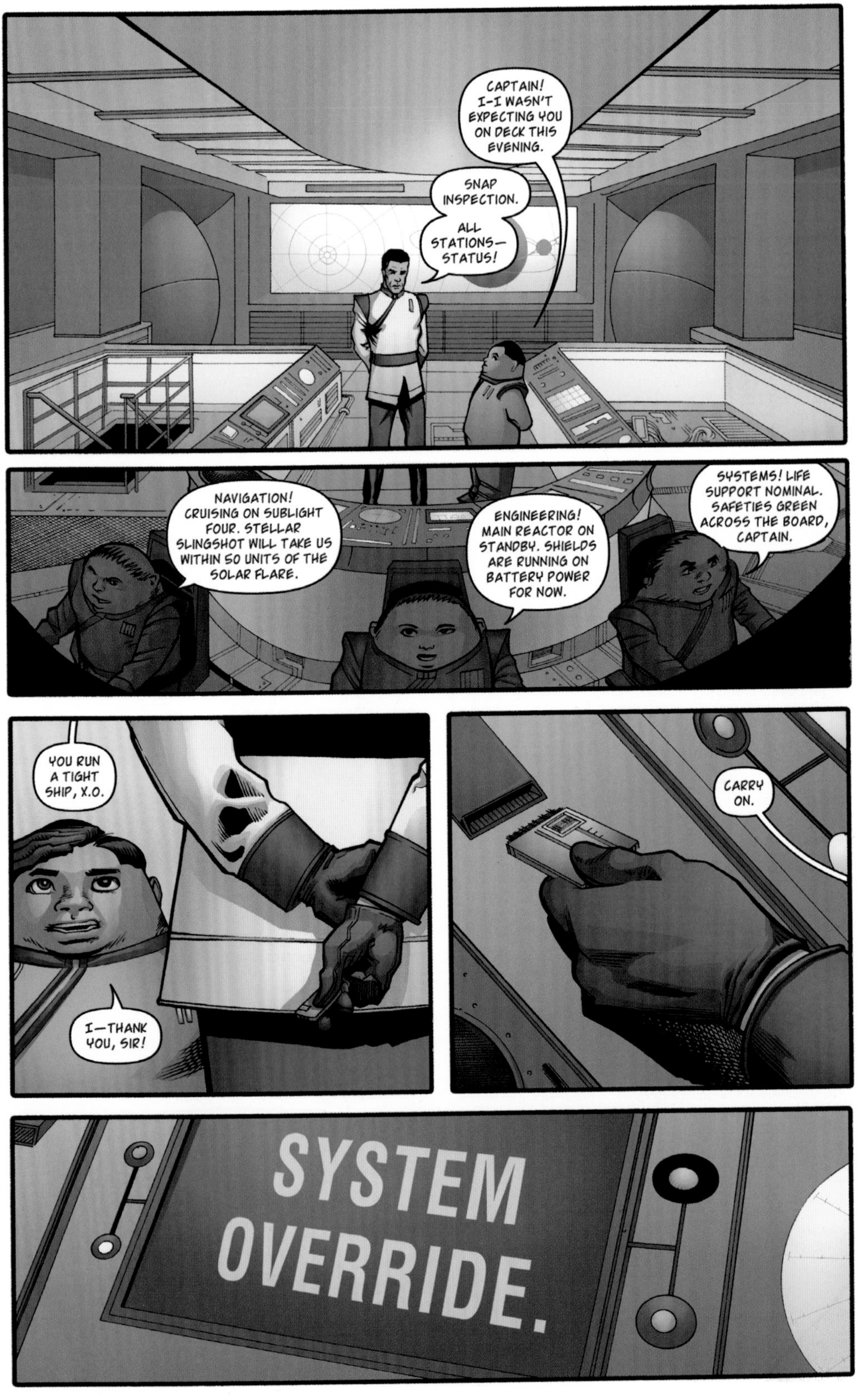
CAPTAIN! I-I WASN'T EXPECTING YOU ON DECK THIS EVENING.
SNAP INSPECTION.
ALL STATIONS—STATUS!
NAVIGATION! CRUISING ON SUBLIGHT FOUR. STELLAR SLINGSHOT WILL TAKE US WITHIN 50 UNITS OF THE SOLAR FLARE.
ENGINEERING! MAIN REACTOR ON STANDBY. SHIELDS ARE RUNNING ON BATTERY POWER FOR NOW.
SYSTEMS! LIFE SUPPORT NOMINAL. SAFETIES GREEN ACROSS THE BOARD, CAPTAIN.
YOU RUN A TIGHT SHIP, X.O.
I—THANK YOU, SIR!
CARRY ON.
SYSTEM OVERRIDE.

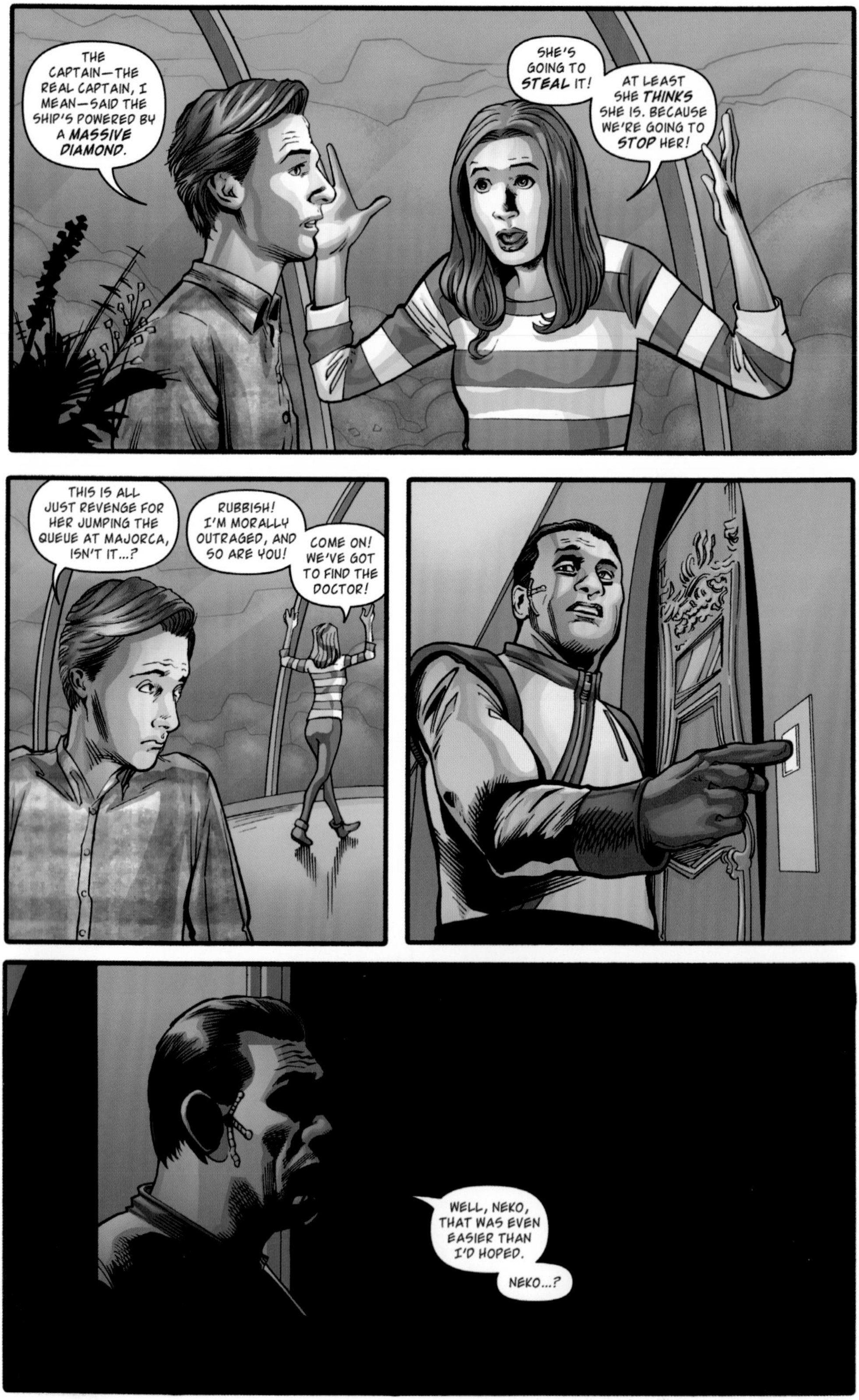
THE CAPTAIN—THE REAL CAPTAIN, I MEAN—SAID THE SHIP'S POWERED BY A MASSIVE DIAMOND.
SHE'S GOING TO STEAL IT!
AT LEAST SHE THINKS SHE IS. BECAUSE WE'RE GOING TO STOP HER!
THIS IS ALL JUST REVENGE FOR HER JUMPING THE QUEUE AT MAJORCA, ISN'T IT...?
RUBBISH! I'M MORALLY OUTRAGED, AND SO ARE YOU!
COME ON! WE'VE GOT TO FIND THE DOCTOR!
WELL, NEKO, THAT WAS EVEN EASIER THAN I'D HOPED.
NEKO...?

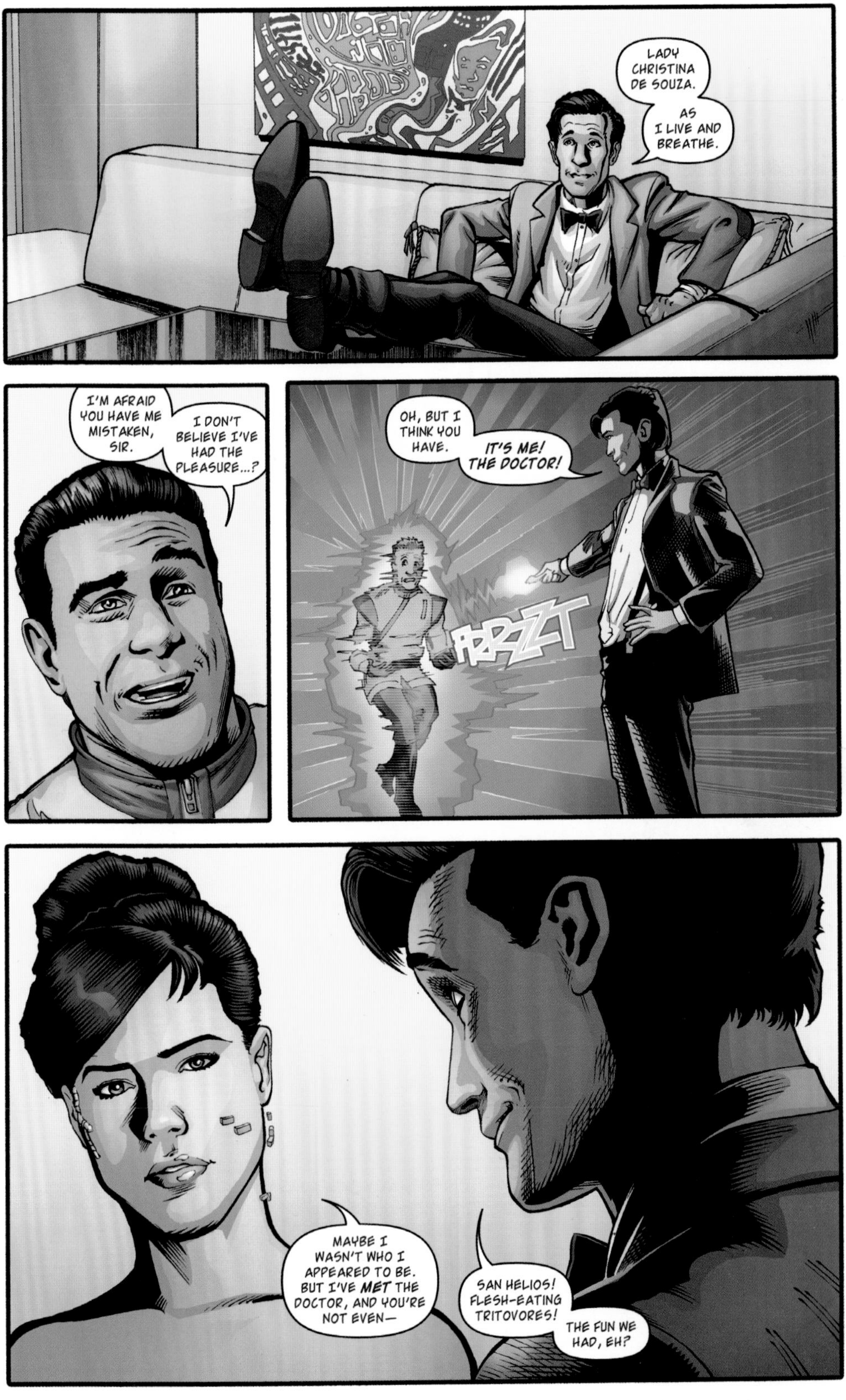
LADY CHRISTINA DE SOUZA.
AS I LIVE AND BREATHE.
I'M AFRAID YOU HAVE ME MISTAKEN, SIR.
I DON'T BELIEVE I'VE HAD THE PLEASURE...?
OH, BUT I THINK YOU HAVE.
IT'S ME! THE DOCTOR!
FRRZZT
MAYBE I WASN'T WHO I APPEARED TO BE. BUT I'VE MET THE DOCTOR, AND YOU'RE NOT EVEN—
SAN HELIOS! FLESH-EATING TRITOVORES!
THE FUN WE HAD, EH?

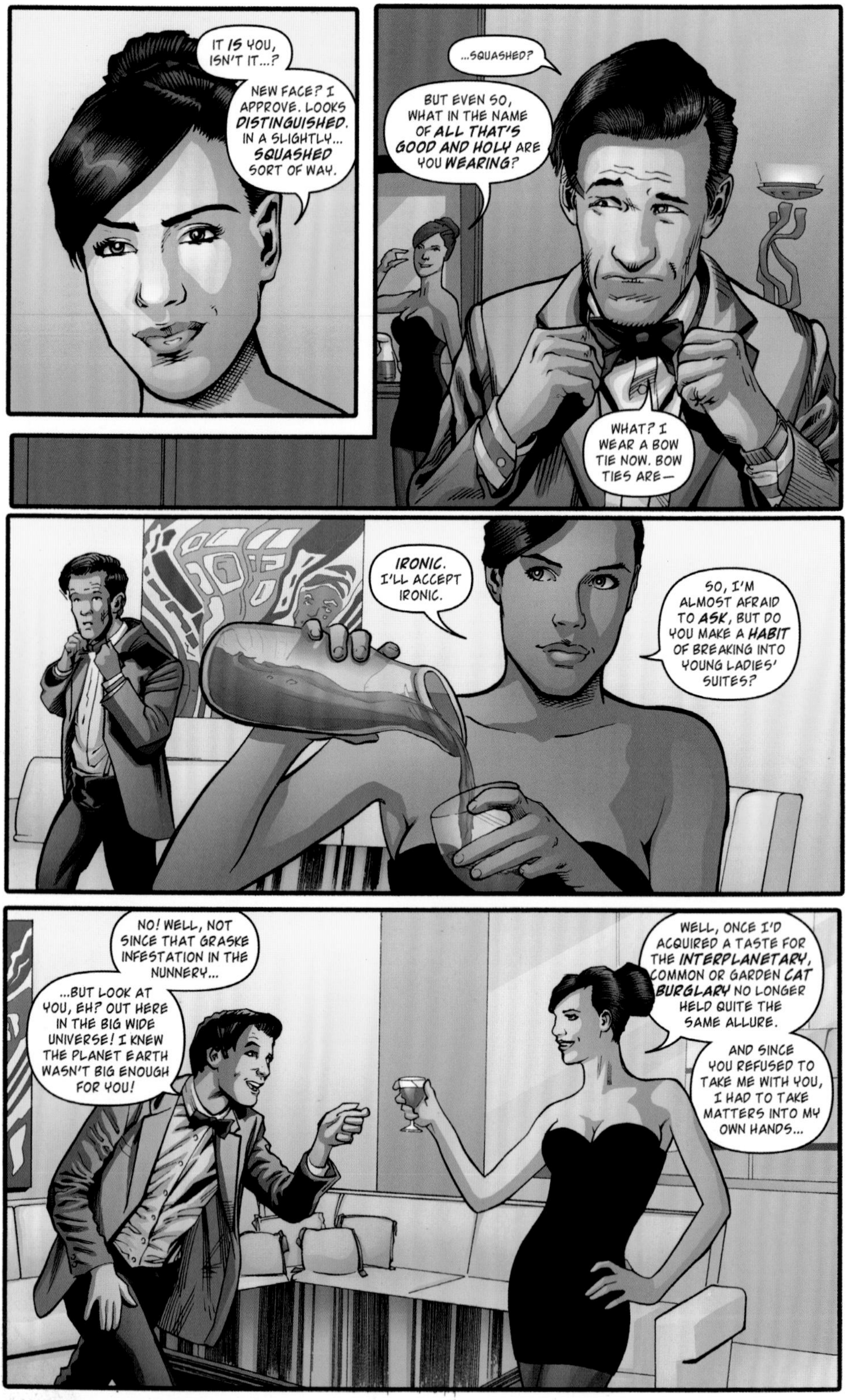

IT IS YOU, ISN'T IT...?
NEW FACE? I APPROVE. LOOKS DISTINGUISHED. IN A SLIGHTLY... SQUASHED SORT OF WAY.
...SQUASHED?
BUT EVEN SO, WHAT IN THE NAME OF ALL THAT'S GOOD AND HOLY ARE YOU WEARING?
WHAT? I WEAR A BOW TIE NOW. BOW TIES ARE—
IRONIC. I'LL ACCEPT IRONIC.
SO, I'M ALMOST AFRAID TO ASK, BUT DO YOU MAKE A HABIT OF BREAKING INTO YOUNG LADIES' SUITES?
NO! WELL, NOT SINCE THAT GRASKE INFESTATION IN THE NUNNERY...
...BUT LOOK AT YOU, EH? OUT HERE IN THE BIG WIDE UNIVERSE! I KNEW THE PLANET EARTH WASN'T BIG ENOUGH FOR YOU!
WELL, ONCE I'D ACQUIRED A TASTE FOR THE INTERPLANETARY, COMMON OR GARDEN CAT BURGLARY NO LONGER HELD QUITE THE SAME ALLURE.
AND SINCE YOU REFUSED TO TAKE ME WITH YOU, I HAD TO TAKE MATTERS INTO MY OWN HANDS...

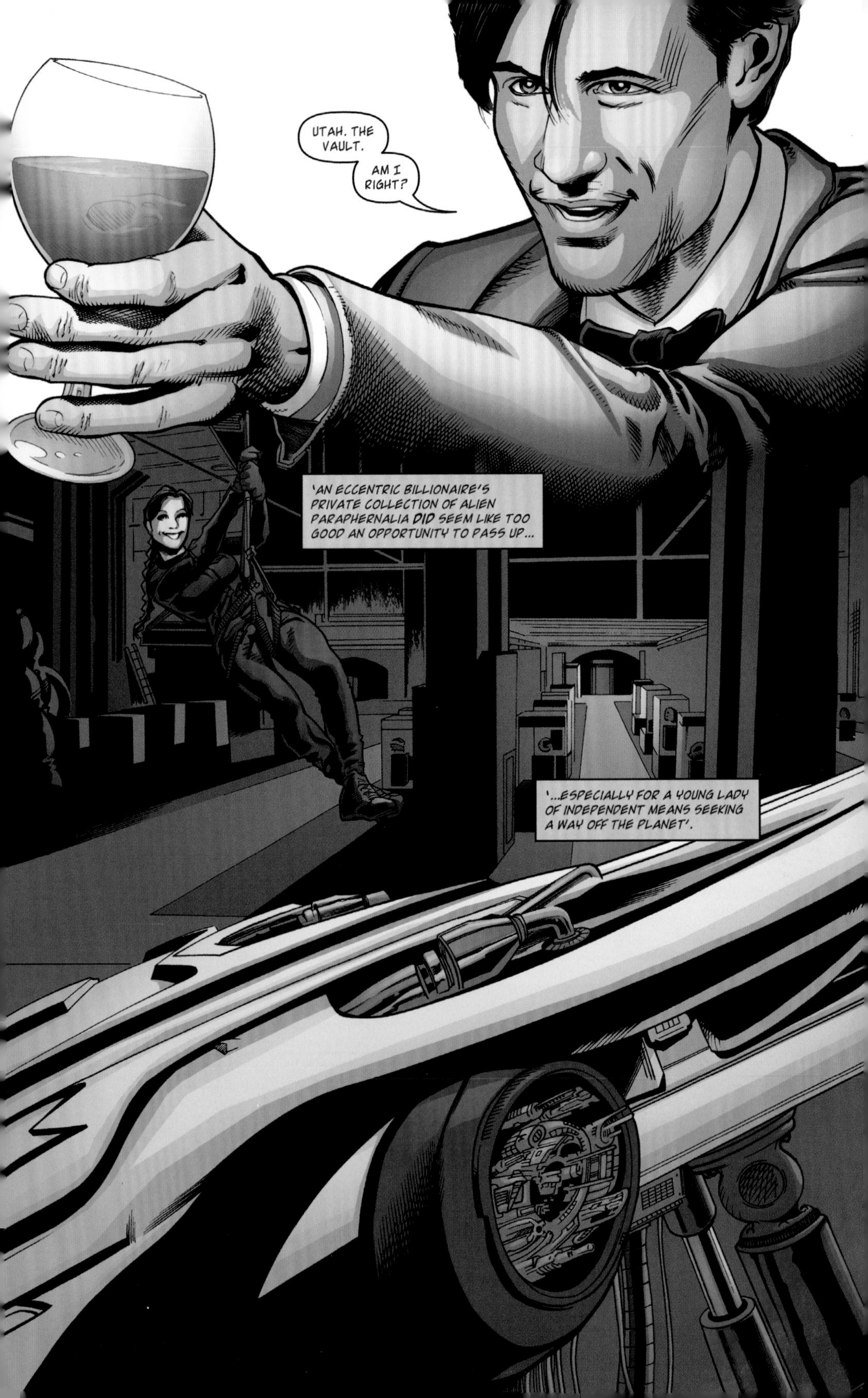
UTAH. THE VAULT.
AM I RIGHT?
'AN ECCENTRIC BILLIONAIRE'S PRIVATE COLLECTION OF ALIEN PARAPHERNALIA DID SEEM LIKE TOO GOOD AN OPPORTUNITY TO PASS UP...
'...ESPECIALLY FOR A YOUNG LADY OF INDEPENDENT MEANS SEEKING A WAY OFF THE PLANET'.

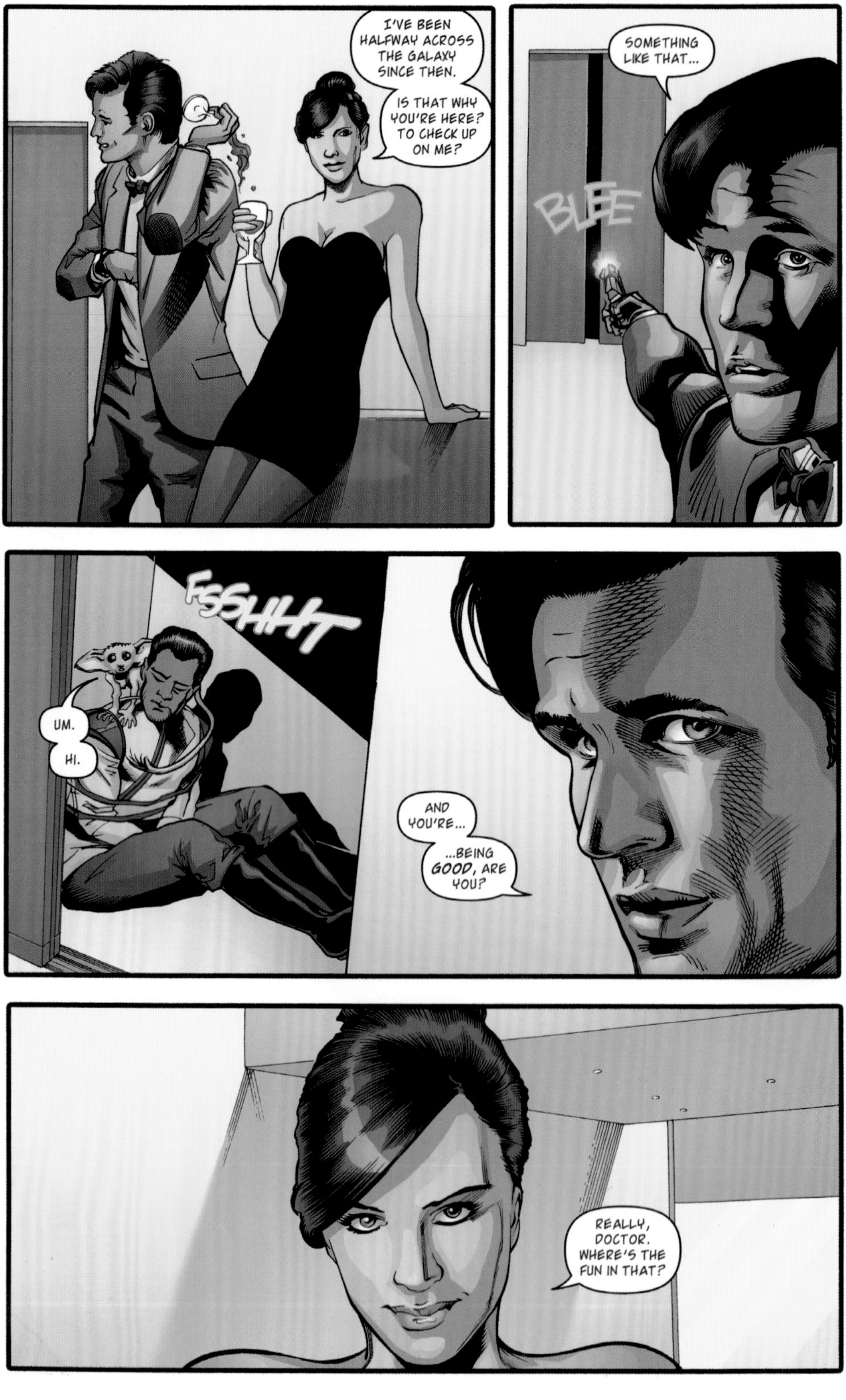
I'VE BEEN HALFWAY ACROSS THE GALAXY SINCE THEN.
IS THAT WHY YOU'RE HERE? TO CHECK UP ON ME?
SOMETHING LIKE THAT...
BLEE
FSSHHT
UM.
HI.
AND YOU'RE...
...BEING GOOD, ARE YOU?
REALLY, DOCTOR. WHERE'S THE FUN IN THAT?

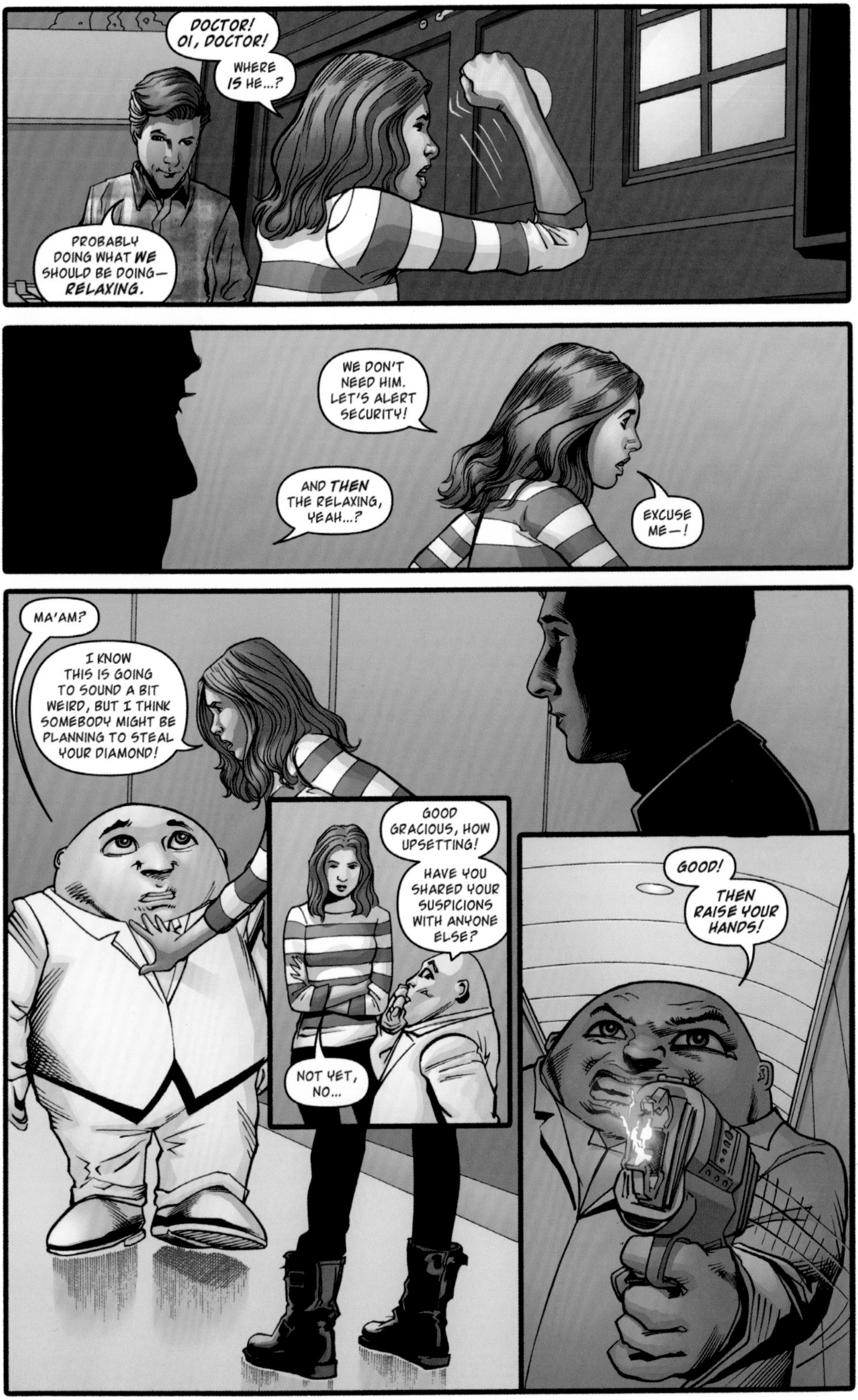

DOCTOR! OI, DOCTOR!
WHERE IS HE...?
PROBABLY DOING WHAT WE SHOULD BE DOING— RELAXING.
WE DON'T NEED HIM. LET'S ALERT SECURITY!
AND THEN THE RELAXING, YEAH...?
EXCUSE ME—!
MA'AM?
I KNOW THIS IS GOING TO SOUND A BIT WEIRD, BUT I THINK SOMEBODY MIGHT BE PLANNING TO STEAL YOUR DIAMOND!
GOOD GRACIOUS, HOW UPSETTING!
HAVE YOU SHARED YOUR SUSPICIONS WITH ANYONE ELSE?
NOT YET, NO...
GOOD!
THEN RAISE YOUR HANDS!

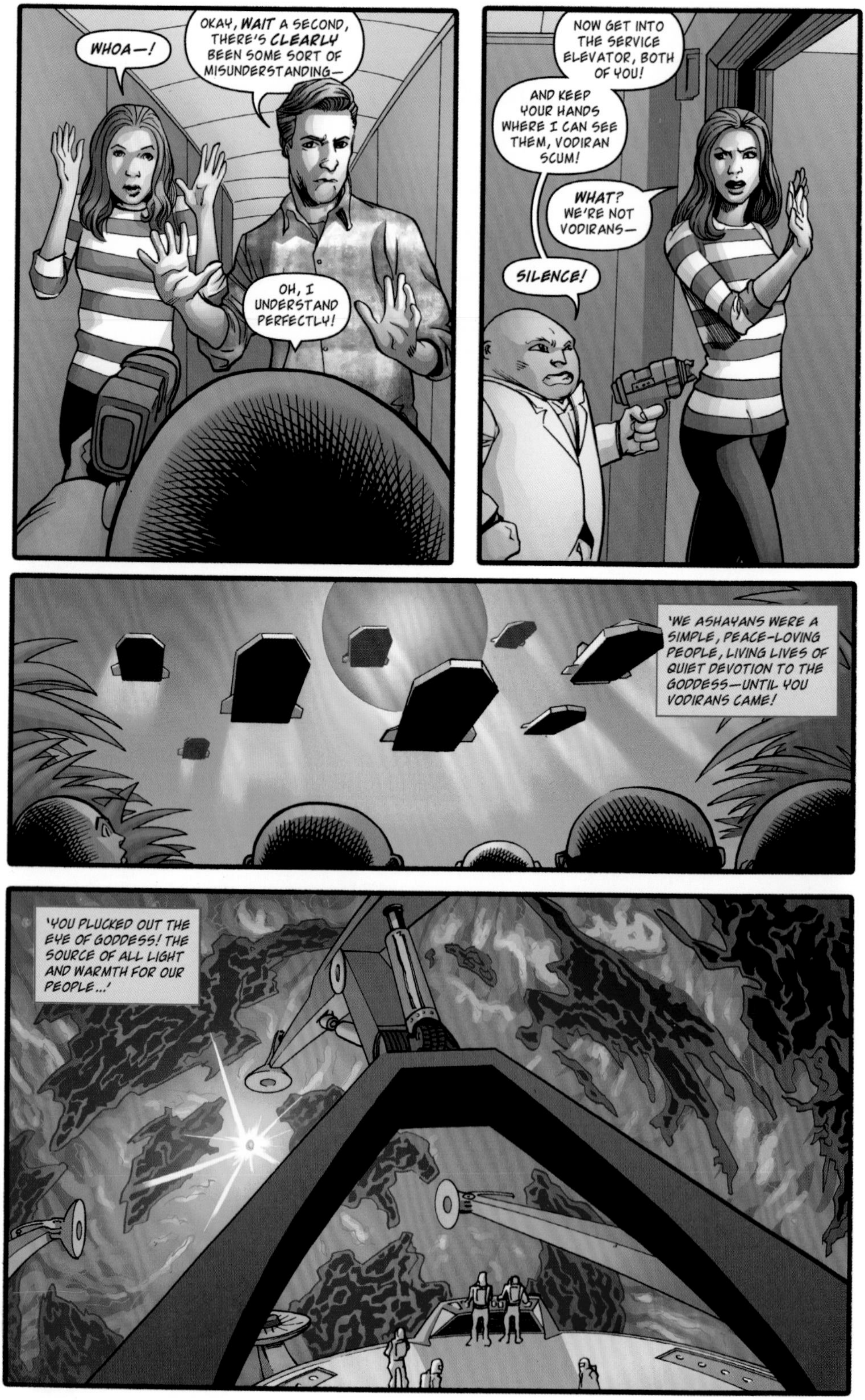
WHOA—!
OKAY, WAIT A SECOND, THERE'S CLEARLY BEEN SOME SORT OF MISUNDERSTANDING—
OH, I UNDERSTAND PERFECTLY!
NOW GET INTO THE SERVICE ELEVATOR, BOTH OF YOU!
AND KEEP YOUR HANDS WHERE I CAN SEE THEM, VODIRAN SCUM!
WHAT? WE'RE NOT VODIRANS—
SILENCE!
'WE ASHAYANS WERE A SIMPLE, PEACE-LOVING PEOPLE, LIVING LIVES OF QUIET DEVOTION TO THE GODDESS—UNTIL YOU VODIRANS CAME!
'YOU PLUCKED OUT THE EYE OF GODDESS! THE SOURCE OF ALL LIGHT AND WARMTH FOR OUR PEOPLE...'

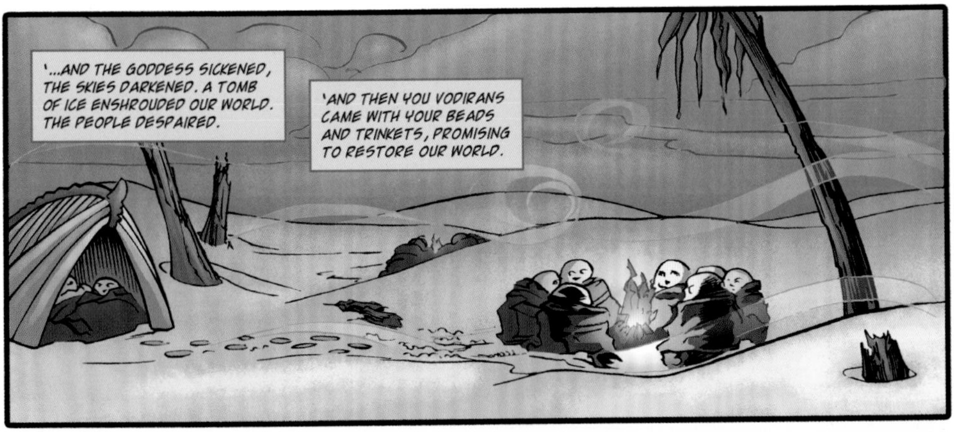
'...AND THE GODDESS SICKENED, THE SKIES DARKENED. A TOMB OF ICE ENSHROUDED OUR WORLD. THE PEOPLE DESPAIRED.
'AND THEN YOU VODIRANS CAME WITH YOUR BEADS AND TRINKETS, PROMISING TO RESTORE OUR WORLD.

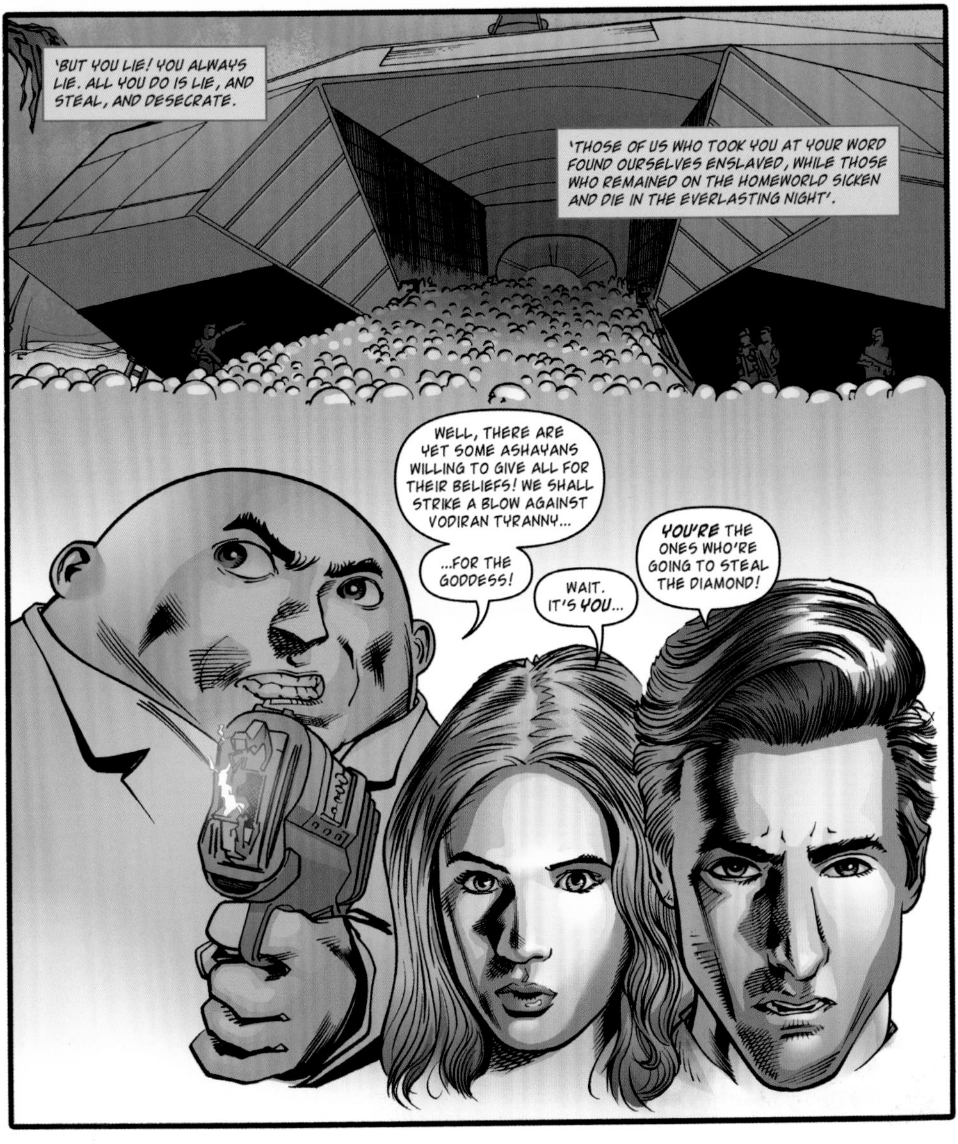
'BUT YOU LIE! YOU ALWAYS LIE. ALL YOU DO IS LIE, AND STEAL, AND DESECRATE.
'THOSE OF US WHO TOOK YOU AT YOUR WORD FOUND OURSELVES ENSLAVED, WHILE THOSE WHO REMAINED ON THE HOMEWORLD SICKEN AND DIE IN THE EVERLASTING NIGHT'.
WELL, THERE ARE YET SOME ASHAYANS WILLING TO GIVE ALL FOR THEIR BELIEFS! WE SHALL STRIKE A BLOW AGAINST VODIRAN TYRANNY...
...FOR THE GODDESS!
WAIT. IT'S YOU...
YOU'RE THE ONES WHO'RE GOING TO STEAL THE DIAMOND!

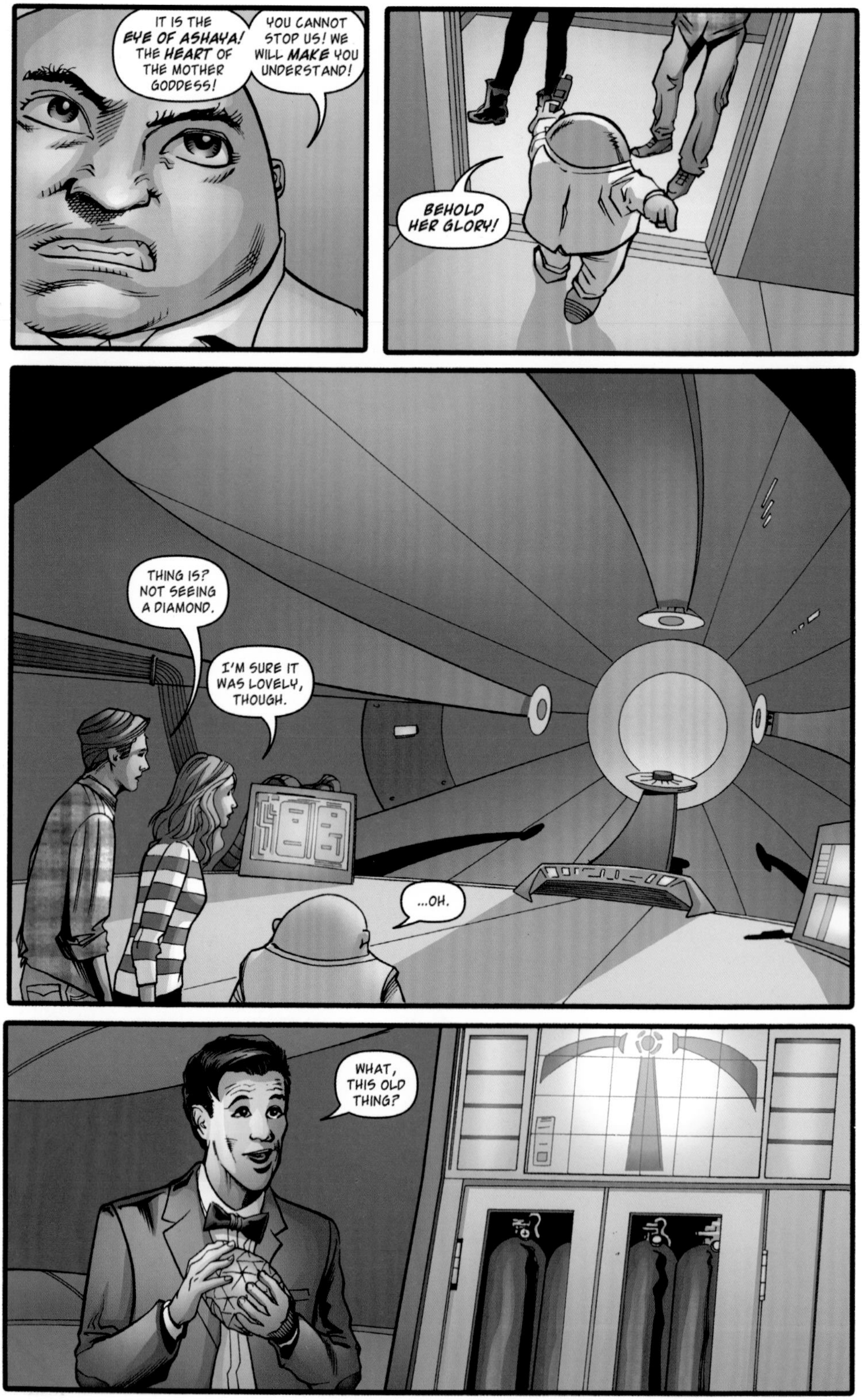
IT IS THE EYE OF ASHAYA! THE HEART OF THE MOTHER GODDESS!
YOU CANNOT STOP US! WE WILL MAKE YOU UNDERSTAND!
BEHOLD HER GLORY!
THING IS? NOT SEEING A DIAMOND.
I'M SURE IT WAS LOVELY, THOUGH.
...OH.
WHAT, THIS OLD THING?

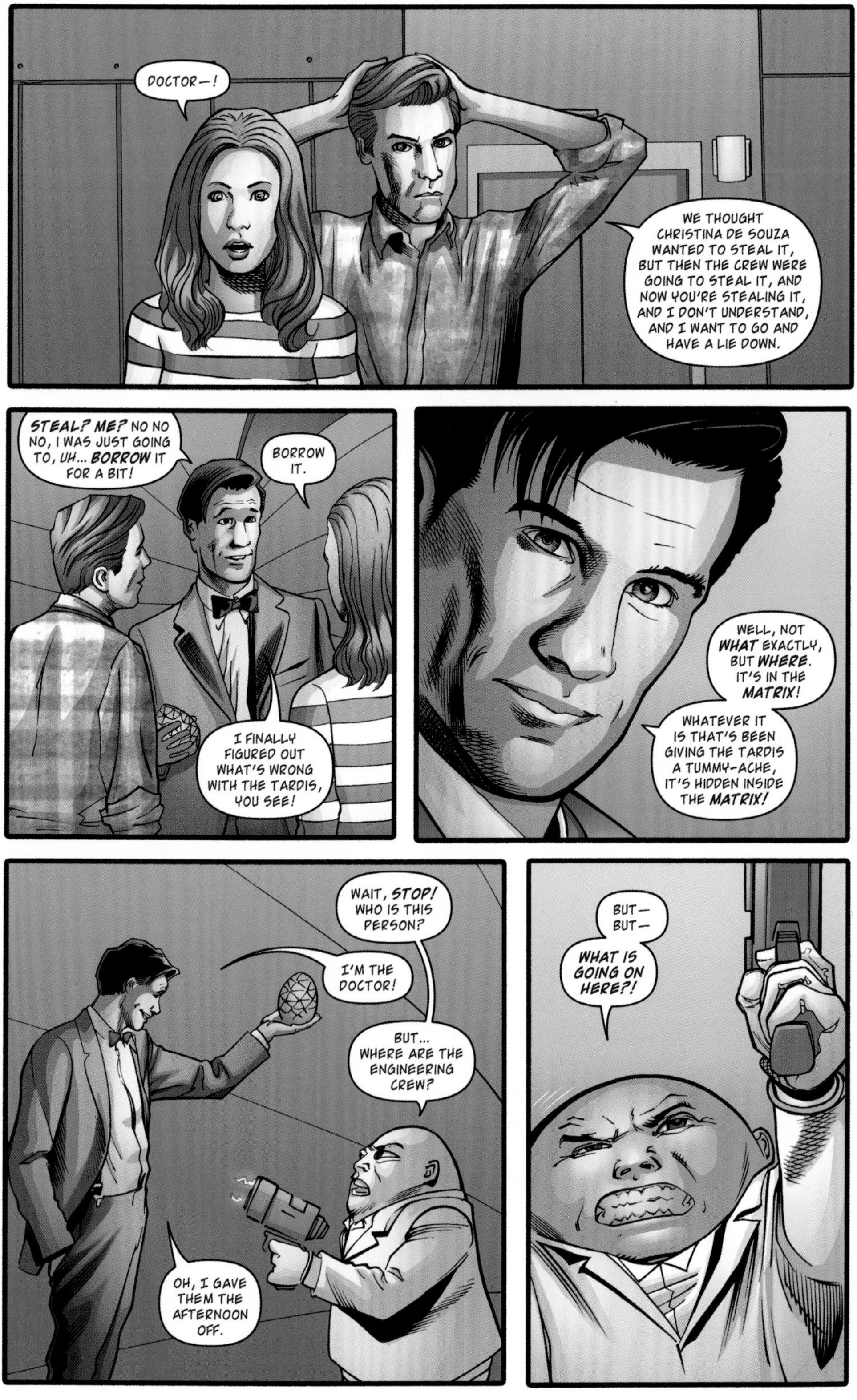
DOCTOR—!
WE THOUGHT CHRISTINA DE SOUZA WANTED TO STEAL IT, BUT THEN THE CREW WERE GOING TO STEAL IT, AND NOW YOU'RE STEALING IT, AND I DON'T UNDERSTAND, AND I WANT TO GO AND HAVE A LIE DOWN.
STEAL? ME? NO NO NO, I WAS JUST GOING TO, UH... BORROW IT FOR A BIT!
BORROW IT.
I FINALLY FIGURED OUT WHAT'S WRONG WITH THE TARDIS, YOU SEE!
WELL, NOT WHAT EXACTLY, BUT WHERE. IT'S IN THE MATRIX!
WHATEVER IT IS THAT'S BEEN GIVING THE TARDIS A TUMMY-ACHE, IT'S HIDDEN INSIDE THE MATRIX!
WAIT, STOP! WHO IS THIS PERSON?
I'M THE DOCTOR!
BUT... WHERE ARE THE ENGINEERING CREW?
OH, I GAVE THEM THE AFTERNOON OFF.
BUT— BUT—
WHAT IS GOING ON HERE?!

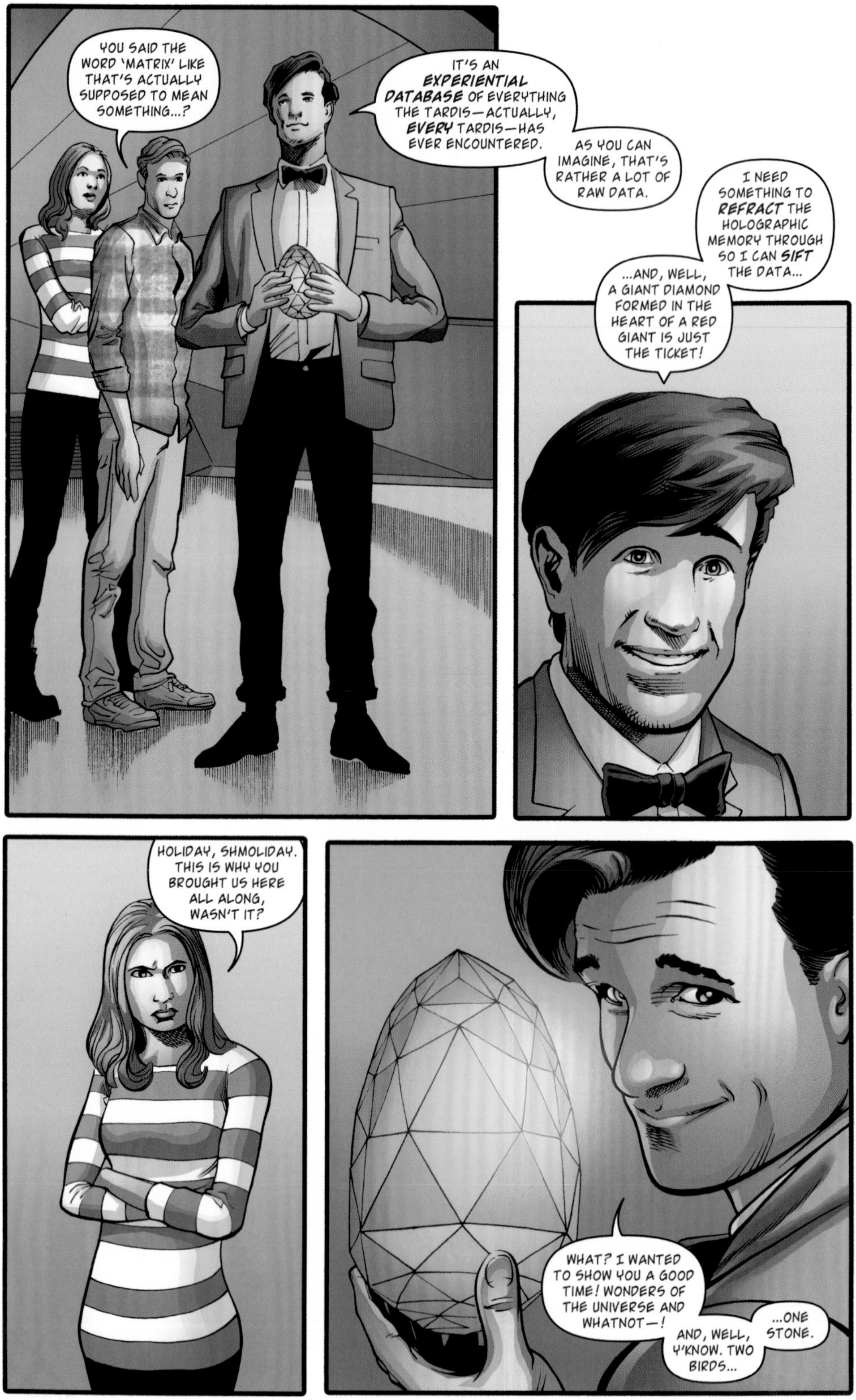
YOU SAID THE WORD 'MATRIX' LIKE THAT'S ACTUALLY SUPPOSED TO MEAN SOMETHING...?
IT'S AN EXPERIENTIAL DATABASE OF EVERYTHING THE TARDIS—ACTUALLY, EVERY TARDIS—HAS EVER ENCOUNTERED.
AS YOU CAN IMAGINE, THAT'S RATHER A LOT OF RAW DATA.
I NEED SOMETHING TO REFRACT THE HOLOGRAPHIC MEMORY THROUGH SO I CAN SIFT THE DATA...
...AND, WELL, A GIANT DIAMOND FORMED IN THE HEART OF A RED GIANT IS JUST THE TICKET!
HOLIDAY, SHMOLIDAY. THIS IS WHY YOU BROUGHT US HERE ALL ALONG, WASN'T IT?
WHAT? I WANTED TO SHOW YOU A GOOD TIME! WONDERS OF THE UNIVERSE AND WHATNOT—!
AND, WELL, Y'KNOW. TWO BIRDS...
...ONE STONE.

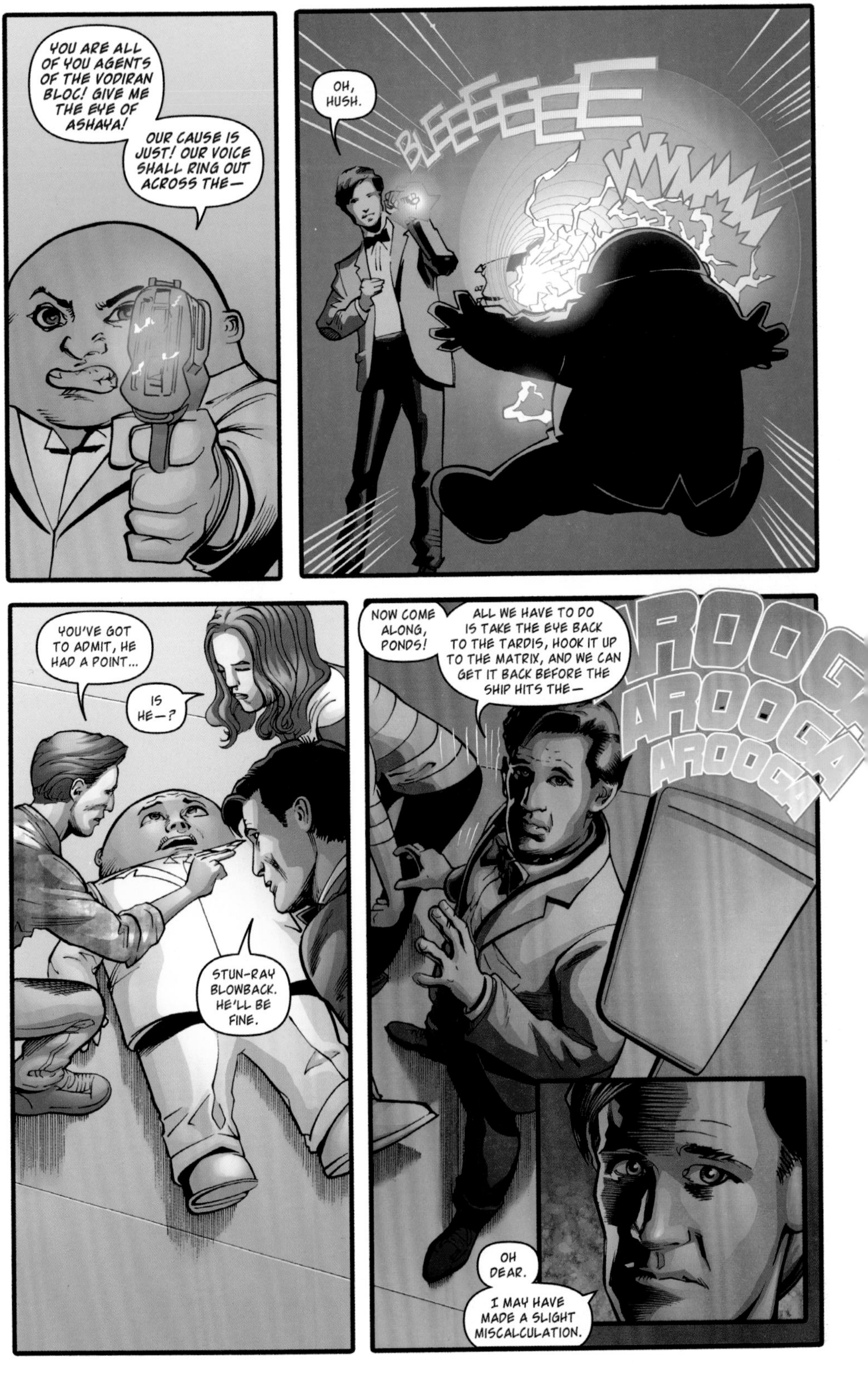
YOU ARE ALL OF YOU AGENTS OF THE VODIRAN BLOC! GIVE ME THE EYE OF ASHAYA!
OUR CAUSE IS JUST! OUR VOICE SHALL RING OUT ACROSS THE—
OH, HUSH.
YOU'VE GOT TO ADMIT, HE HAD A POINT...
IS HE—?
STUN-RAY BLOWBACK. HE'LL BE FINE.
NOW COME ALONG, PONDS!
ALL WE HAVE TO DO IS TAKE THE EYE BACK TO THE TARDIS, HOOK IT UP TO THE MATRIX, AND WE CAN GET IT BACK BEFORE THE SHIP HITS THE—
AROOGA
AROOGA
OH DEAR.
I MAY HAVE MADE A SLIGHT MISCALCULATION.

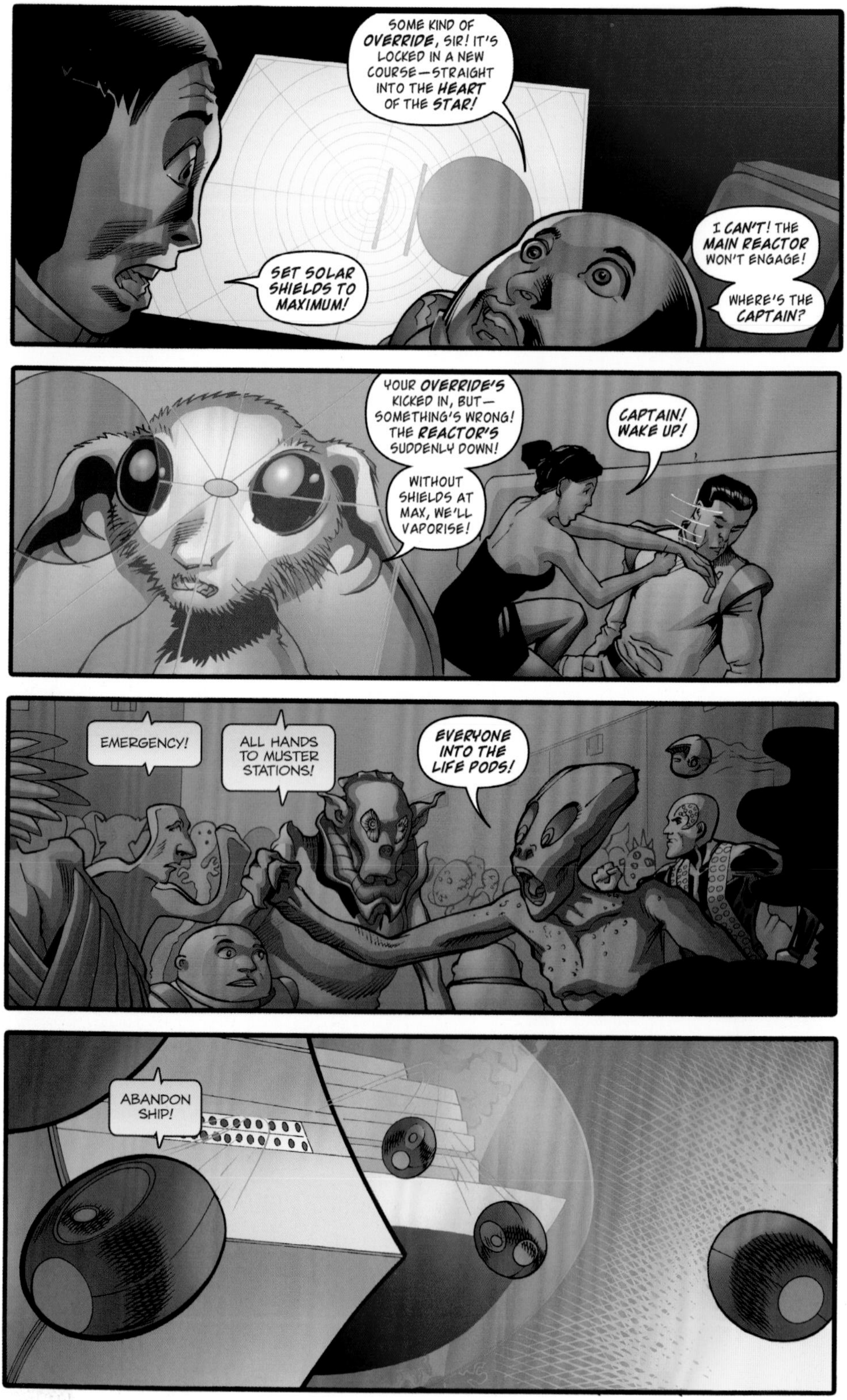
SOME KIND OF OVERRIDE, SIR! IT'S LOCKED IN A NEW COURSE—STRAIGHT INTO THE HEART OF THE STAR!
SET SOLAR SHIELDS TO MAXIMUM!
I CAN'T! THE MAIN REACTOR WON'T ENGAGE!
WHERE'S THE CAPTAIN?
YOUR OVERRIDE'S KICKED IN, BUT—SOMETHING'S WRONG! THE REACTOR'S SUDDENLY DOWN!
WITHOUT SHIELDS AT MAX, WE'LL VAPORISE!
CAPTAIN! WAKE UP!
EMERGENCY!
ALL HANDS TO MUSTER STATIONS!
EVERYONE INTO THE LIFE PODS!
ABANDON SHIP!

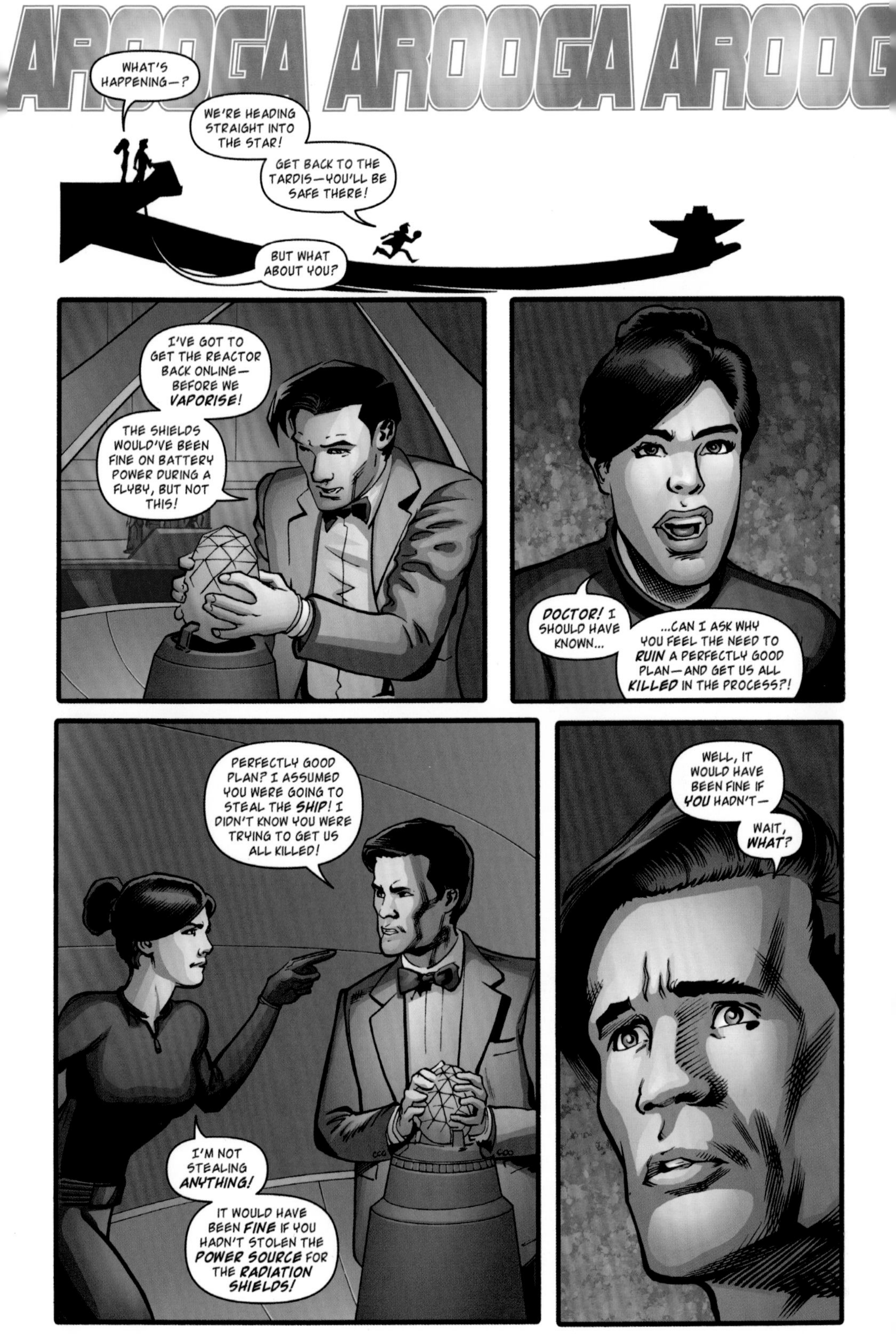
AROOGA AROOGA AROOG
WHAT'S HAPPENING—?
WE'RE HEADING STRAIGHT INTO THE STAR!
GET BACK TO THE TARDIS—YOU'LL BE SAFE THERE!
BUT WHAT ABOUT YOU?
I'VE GOT TO GET THE REACTOR BACK ONLINE—BEFORE WE VAPORISE!
THE SHIELDS WOULD'VE BEEN FINE ON BATTERY POWER DURING A FLYBY, BUT NOT THIS!
DOCTOR! I SHOULD HAVE KNOWN...
...CAN I ASK WHY YOU FEEL THE NEED TO RUIN A PERFECTLY GOOD PLAN—AND GET US ALL KILLED IN THE PROCESS?!
PERFECTLY GOOD PLAN? I ASSUMED YOU WERE GOING TO STEAL THE SHIP! I DIDN'T KNOW YOU WERE TRYING TO GET US ALL KILLED!
I'M NOT STEALING ANYTHING!
IT WOULD HAVE BEEN FINE IF YOU HADN'T STOLEN THE POWER SOURCE FOR THE RADIATION SHIELDS!
WELL, IT WOULD HAVE BEEN FINE IF YOU HADN'T—
WAIT, WHAT?

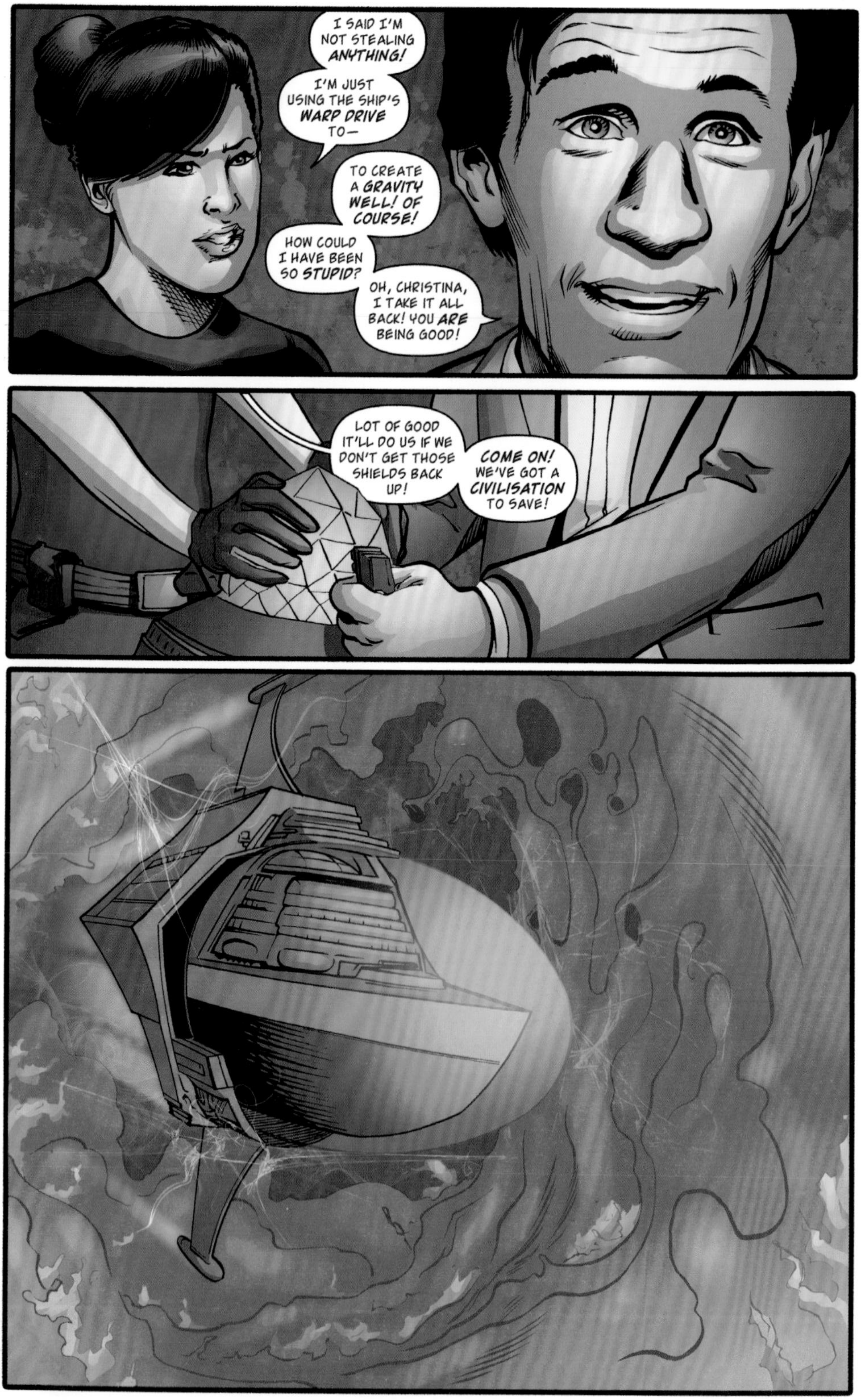

I SAID I'M NOT STEALING ANYTHING!
I'M JUST USING THE SHIP'S WARP DRIVE TO—
TO CREATE A GRAVITY WELL! OF COURSE!
HOW COULD I HAVE BEEN SO STUPID?
OH, CHRISTINA, I TAKE IT ALL BACK! YOU ARE BEING GOOD!
LOT OF GOOD IT'LL DO US IF WE DON'T GET THOSE SHIELDS BACK UP!
COME ON! WE'VE GOT A CIVILISATION TO SAVE!

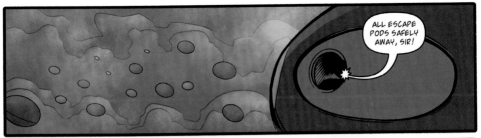

ALL ESCAPE PODS SAFELY AWAY, SIR!

WHAT ABOUT THE *EXCELSIS?*

ENTERING THE STELLAR CORE NOW, SIR!

SHIELDS ARE BACK AT MAXIMUM! BUT I'M GETTING SOME STRANGE READINGS...

...THEY'VE ACTIVATED *THE WARP DRIVE*, BUT... THE SHIP'S *NOT MOVING!*

IT'S CREATING A GRAVITY WELL!

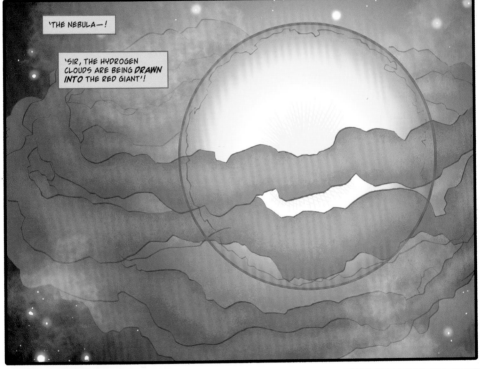

'THE NEBULA—!

'SIR, THE HYDROGEN CLOUDS ARE BEING *DRAWN INTO* THE RED GIANT'!

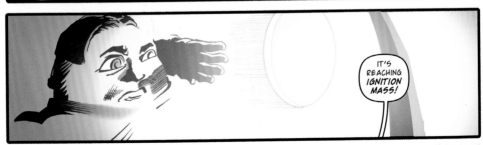

IT'S REACHING *IGNITION MASS!*

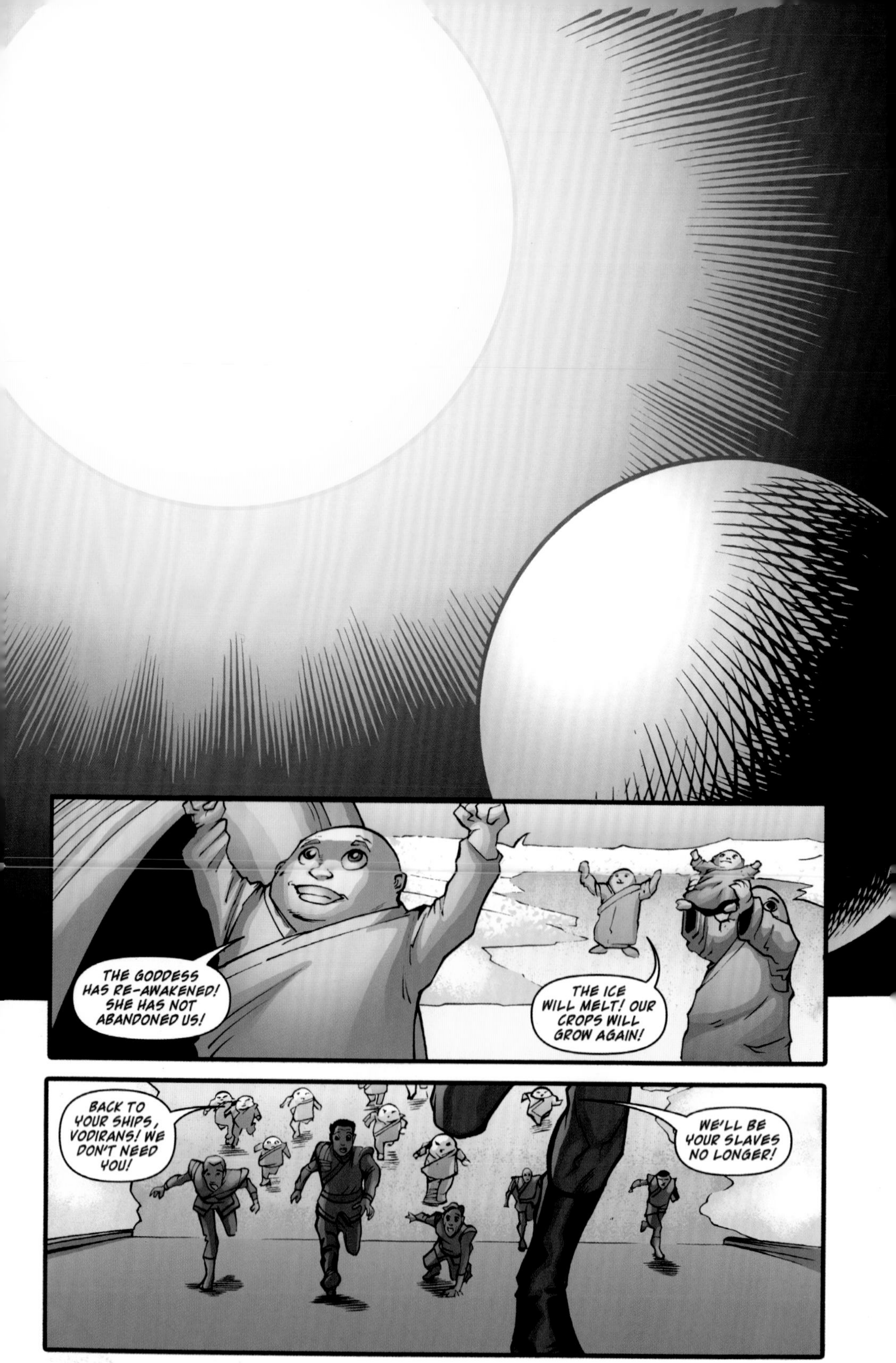
THE GODDESS HAS RE-AWAKENED! SHE HAS NOT ABANDONED US!
THE ICE WILL MELT! OUR CROPS WILL GROW AGAIN!
BACK TO YOUR SHIPS, VODIRANS! WE DON'T NEED YOU!
WE'LL BE YOUR SLAVES NO LONGER!

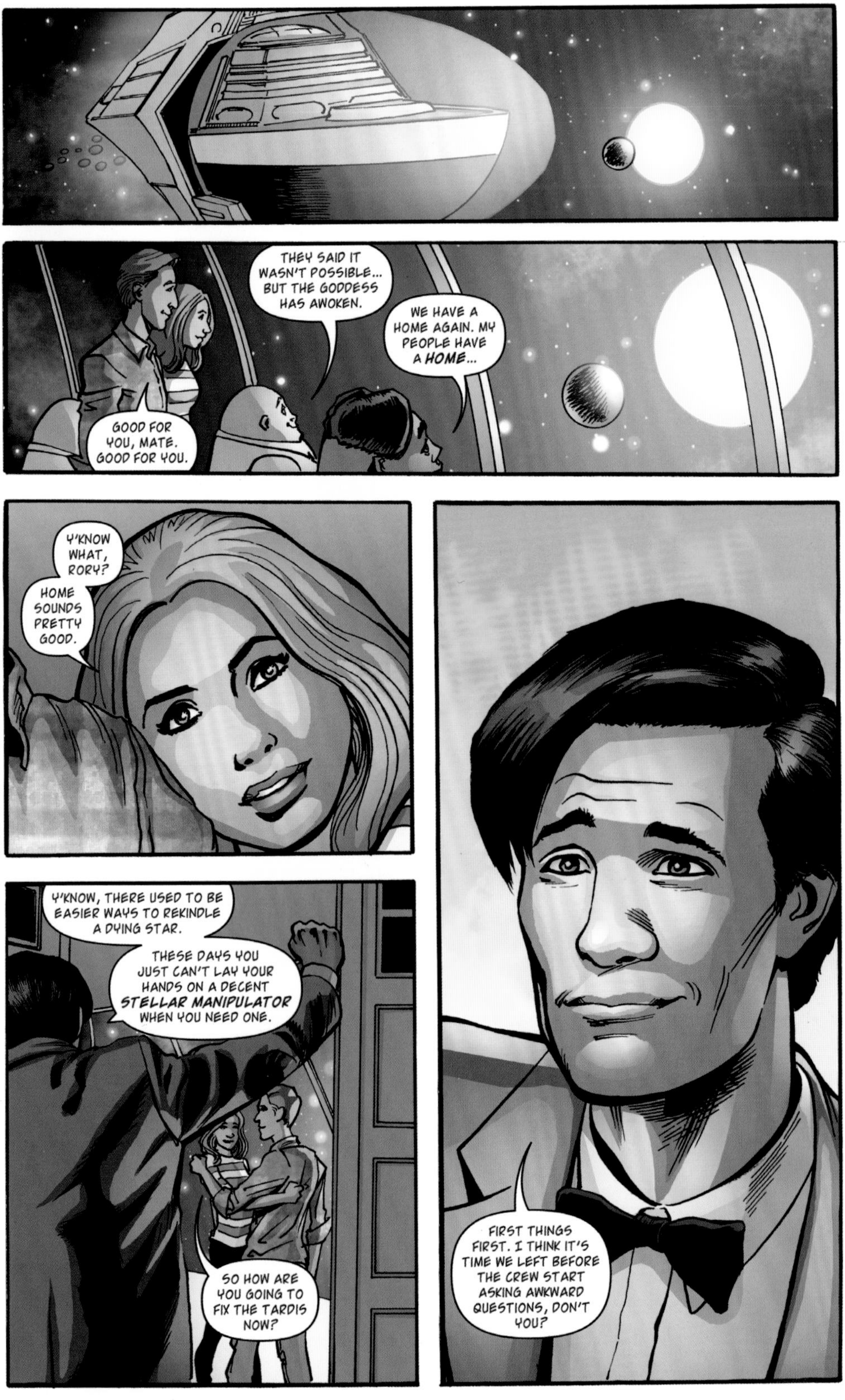
THEY SAID IT WASN'T POSSIBLE... BUT THE GODDESS HAS AWOKEN.
WE HAVE A HOME AGAIN. MY PEOPLE HAVE A HOME...
GOOD FOR YOU, MATE. GOOD FOR YOU.
Y'KNOW WHAT, RORY?
HOME SOUNDS PRETTY GOOD.
Y'KNOW, THERE USED TO BE EASIER WAYS TO REKINDLE A DYING STAR.
THESE DAYS YOU JUST CAN'T LAY YOUR HANDS ON A DECENT STELLAR MANIPULATOR WHEN YOU NEED ONE.
SO HOW ARE YOU GOING TO FIX THE TARDIS NOW?
FIRST THINGS FIRST. I THINK IT'S TIME WE LEFT BEFORE THE CREW START ASKING AWKWARD QUESTIONS, DON'T YOU?

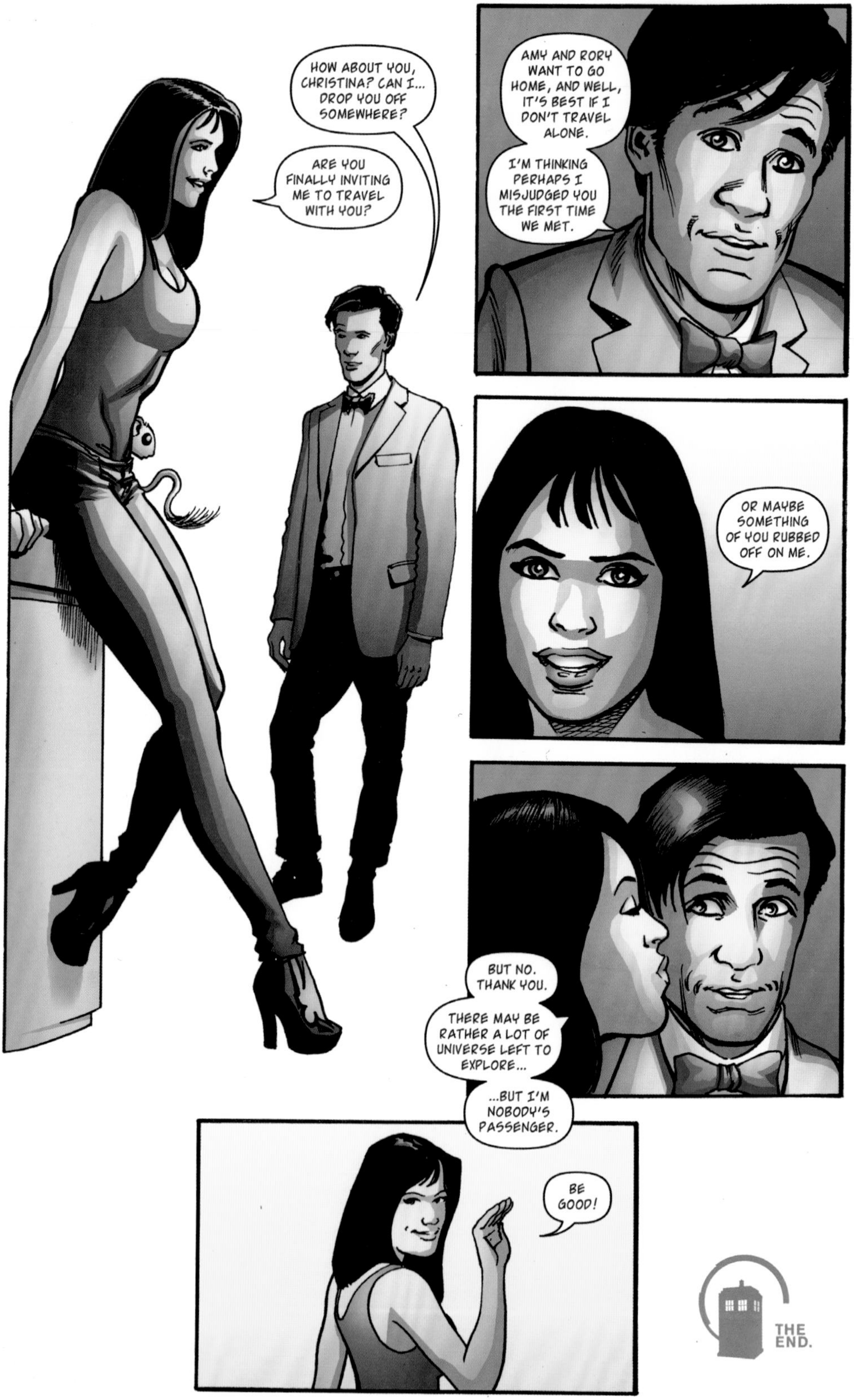
HOW ABOUT YOU, CHRISTINA? CAN I... DROP YOU OFF SOMEWHERE?
ARE YOU FINALLY INVITING ME TO TRAVEL WITH YOU?
AMY AND RORY WANT TO GO HOME, AND WELL, IT'S BEST IF I DON'T TRAVEL ALONE.
I'M THINKING PERHAPS I MISJUDGED YOU THE FIRST TIME WE MET.
OR MAYBE SOMETHING OF YOU RUBBED OFF ON ME.
BUT NO. THANK YOU.
THERE MAY BE RATHER A LOT OF UNIVERSE LEFT TO EXPLORE...
...BUT I'M NOBODY'S PASSENGER.
BE GOOD!
THE END.

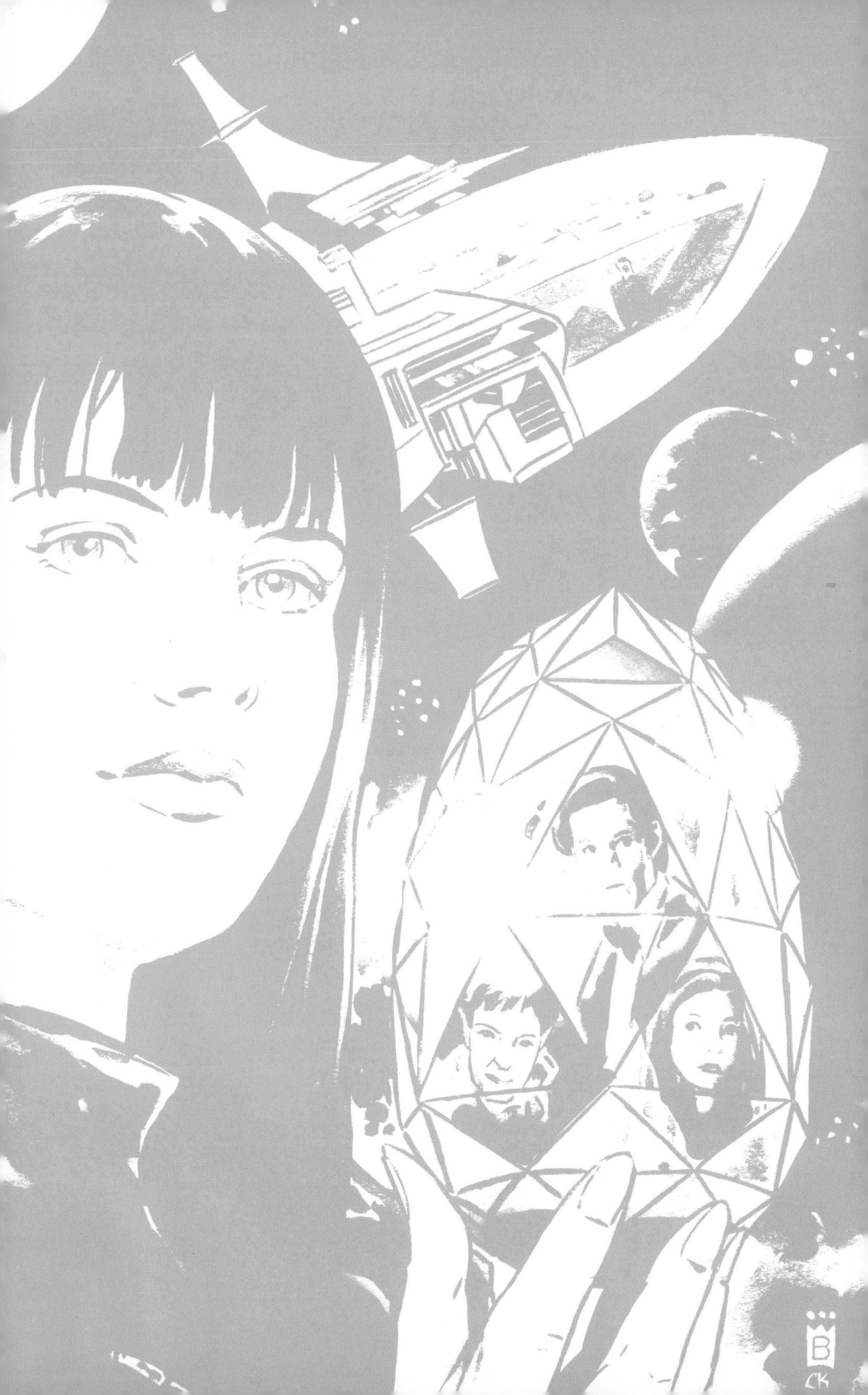
B
CK

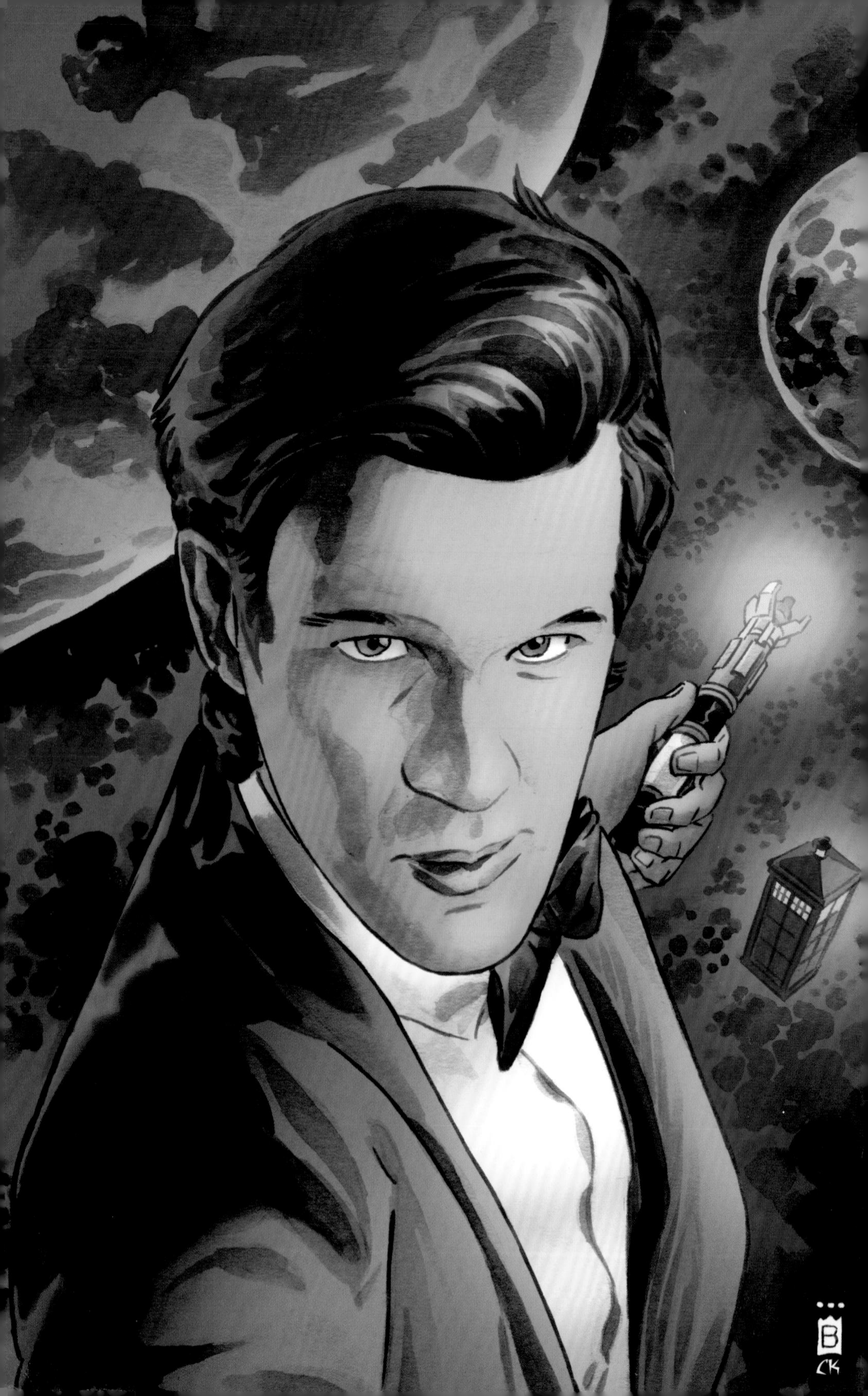

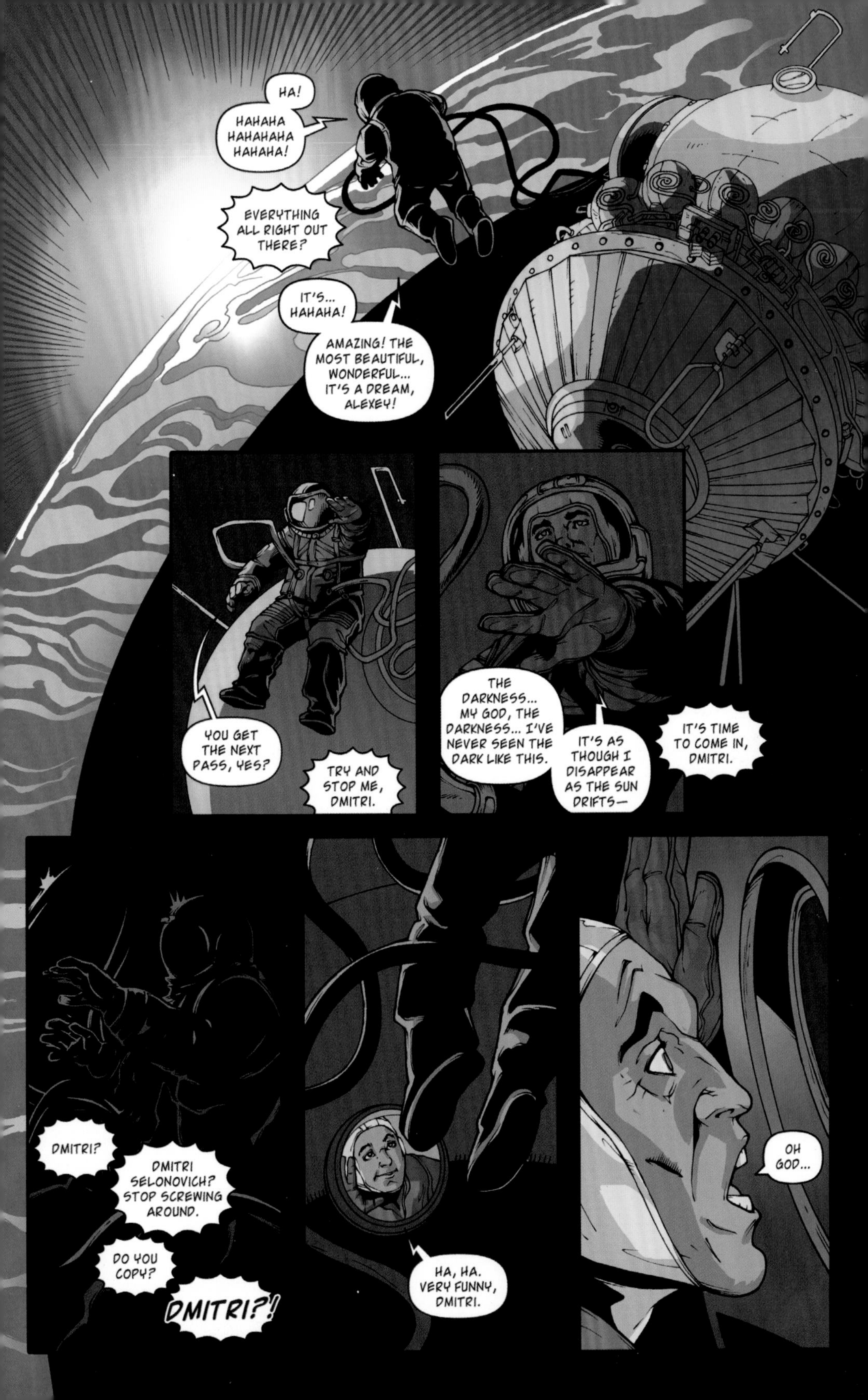
HA!
HAHAHA HAHAHAHA HAHAHA!
EVERYTHING ALL RIGHT OUT THERE?
IT'S... HAHAHA!
AMAZING! THE MOST BEAUTIFUL, WONDERFUL... IT'S A DREAM, ALEXEY!
YOU GET THE NEXT PASS, YES?
TRY AND STOP ME, DMITRI.
THE DARKNESS... MY GOD, THE DARKNESS... I'VE NEVER SEEN THE DARK LIKE THIS.
IT'S AS THOUGH I DISAPPEAR AS THE SUN DRIFTS—
IT'S TIME TO COME IN, DMITRI.
DMITRI?
DMITRI SELONOVICH? STOP SCREWING AROUND.
DO YOU COPY?
DMITRI?!
HA, HA. VERY FUNNY, DMITRI.
OH GOD...

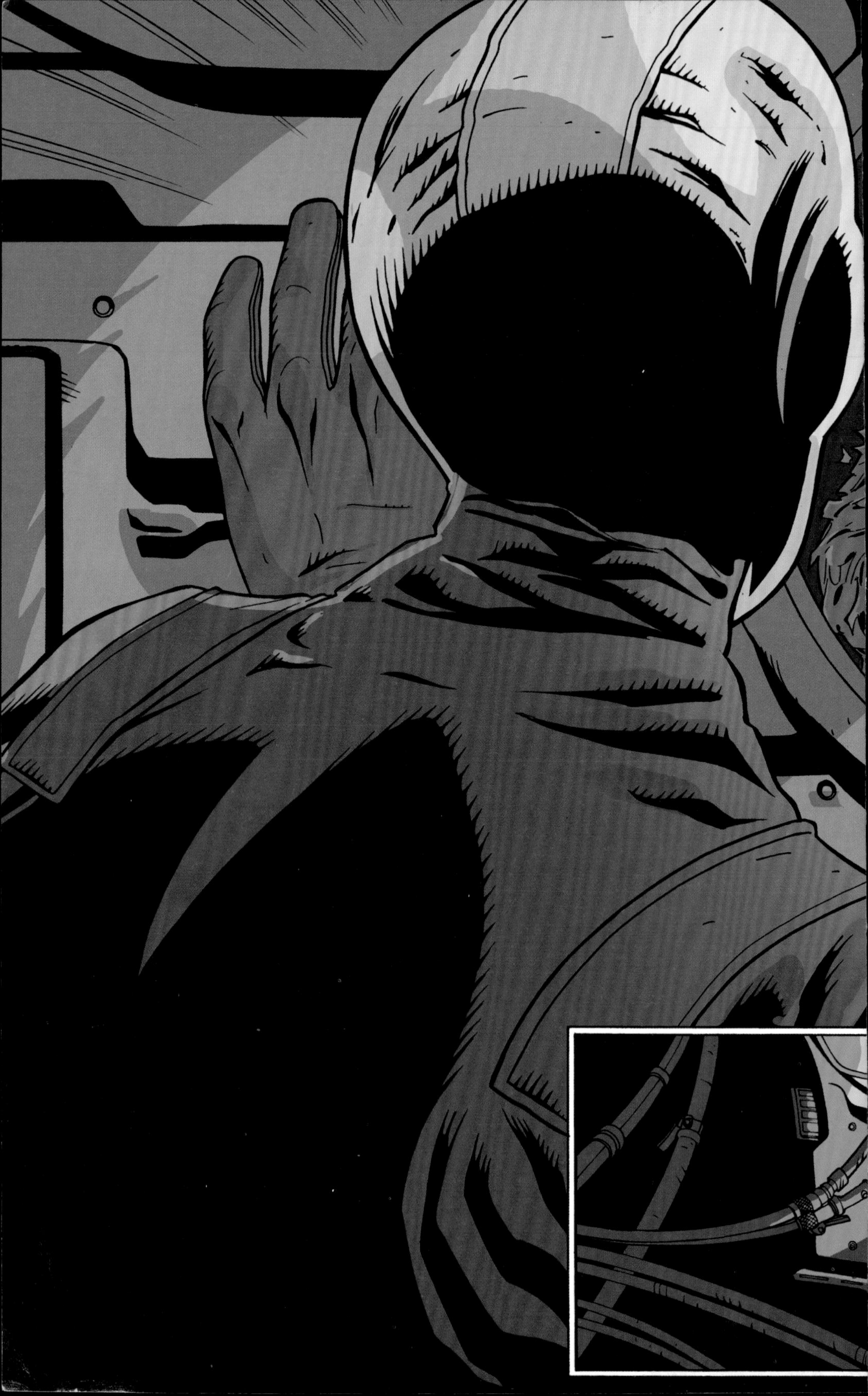

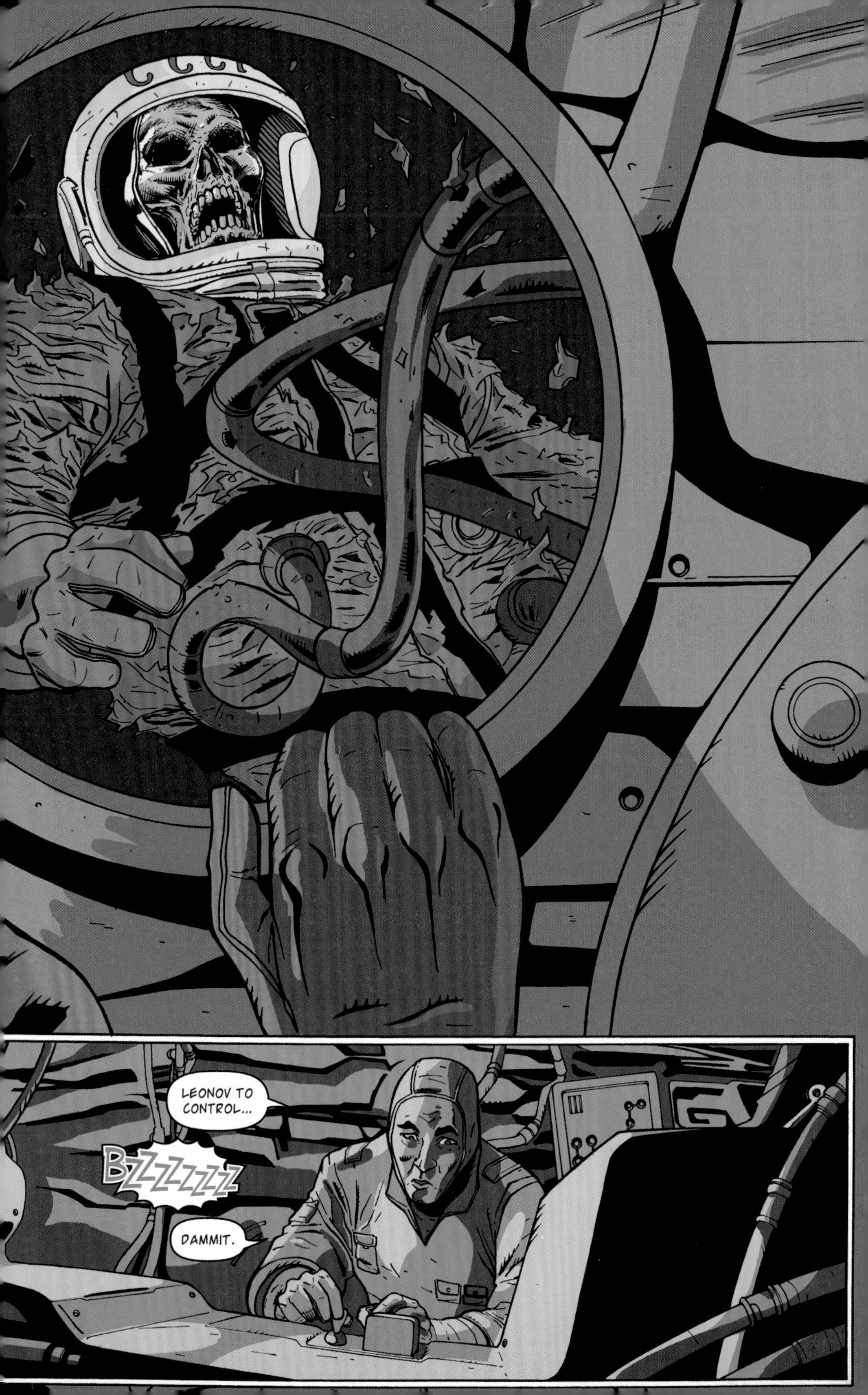
LEONOV TO CONTROL...
BZZZZZZZZ
DAMMIT.

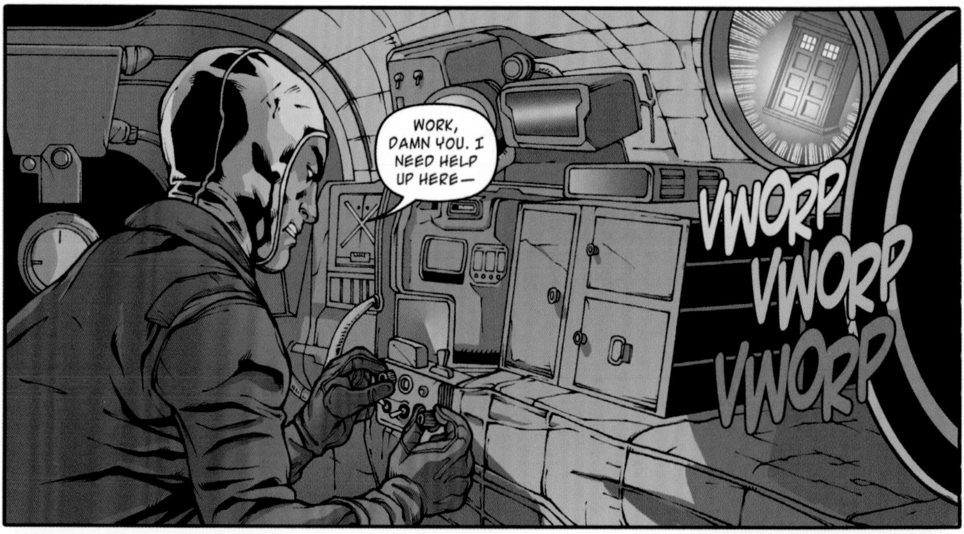
WORK, DAMN YOU. I NEED HELP UP HERE—
VWORP VWORP VWORP

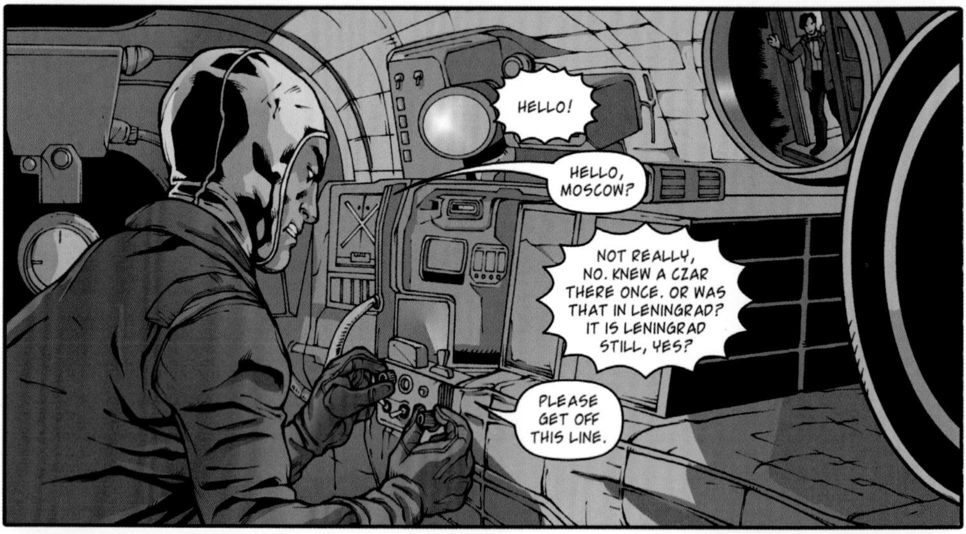
HELLO!
HELLO, MOSCOW?
NOT REALLY, NO. KNEW A CZAR THERE ONCE. OR WAS THAT IN LENINGRAD? IT IS LENINGRAD STILL, YES?
PLEASE GET OFF THIS LINE.

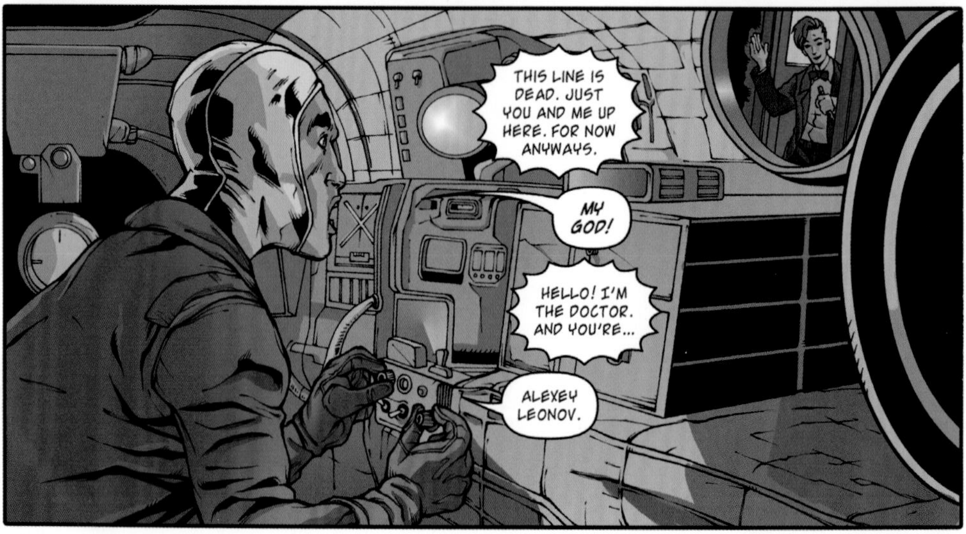
THIS LINE IS DEAD. JUST YOU AND ME UP HERE. FOR NOW ANYWAYS.
MY GOD!
HELLO! I'M THE DOCTOR. AND YOU'RE...
ALEXEY LEONOV.

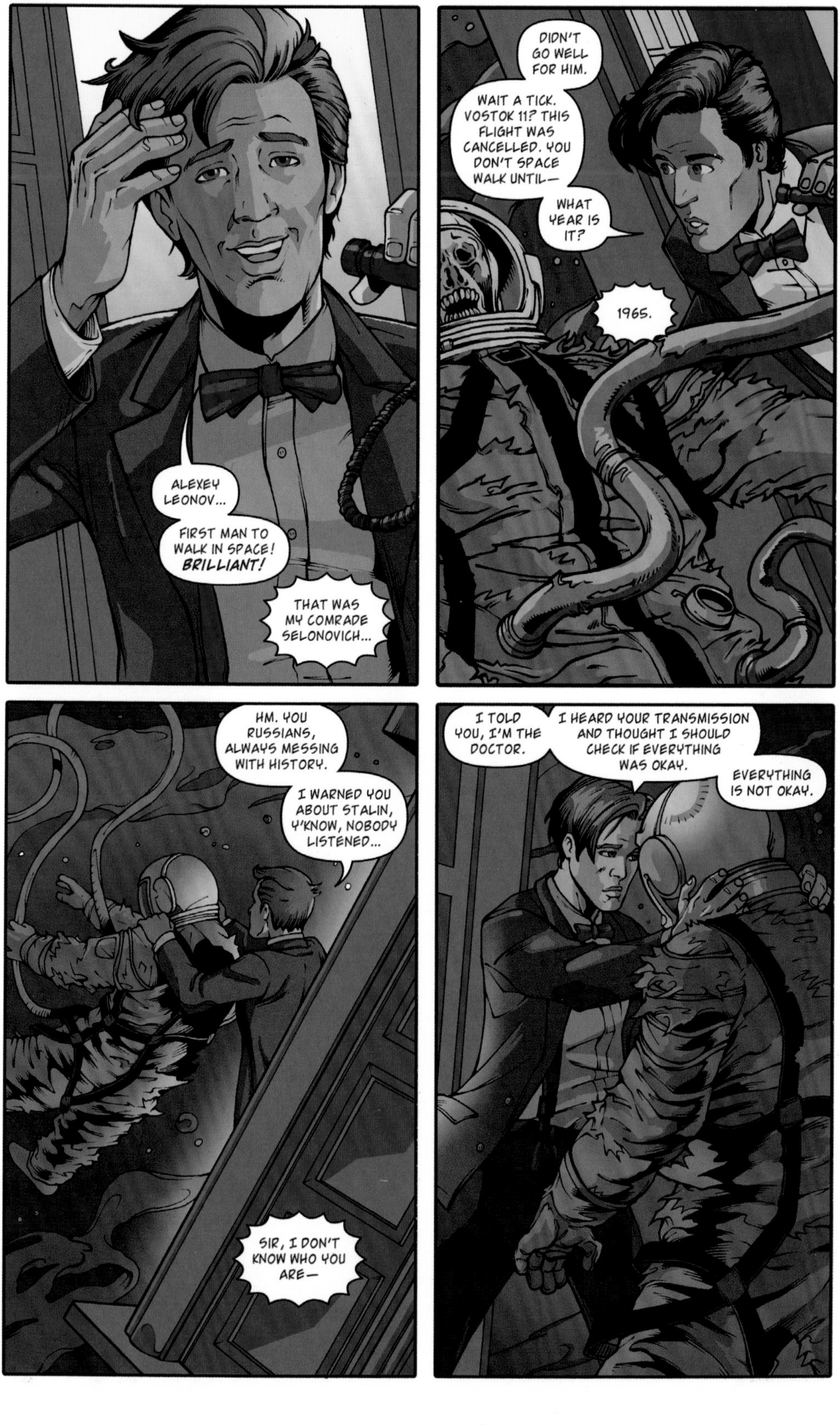
ALEXEY LEONOV...
FIRST MAN TO WALK IN SPACE! BRILLIANT!
THAT WAS MY COMRADE SELONOVICH...
DIDN'T GO WELL FOR HIM.
WAIT A TICK. VOSTOK 11? THIS FLIGHT WAS CANCELLED. YOU DON'T SPACE WALK UNTIL—
WHAT YEAR IS IT?
1965.
HM. YOU RUSSIANS, ALWAYS MESSING WITH HISTORY.
I WARNED YOU ABOUT STALIN, Y'KNOW, NOBODY LISTENED...
SIR, I DON'T KNOW WHO YOU ARE—
I TOLD YOU, I'M THE DOCTOR.
I HEARD YOUR TRANSMISSION AND THOUGHT I SHOULD CHECK IF EVERYTHING WAS OKAY.
EVERYTHING IS NOT OKAY.

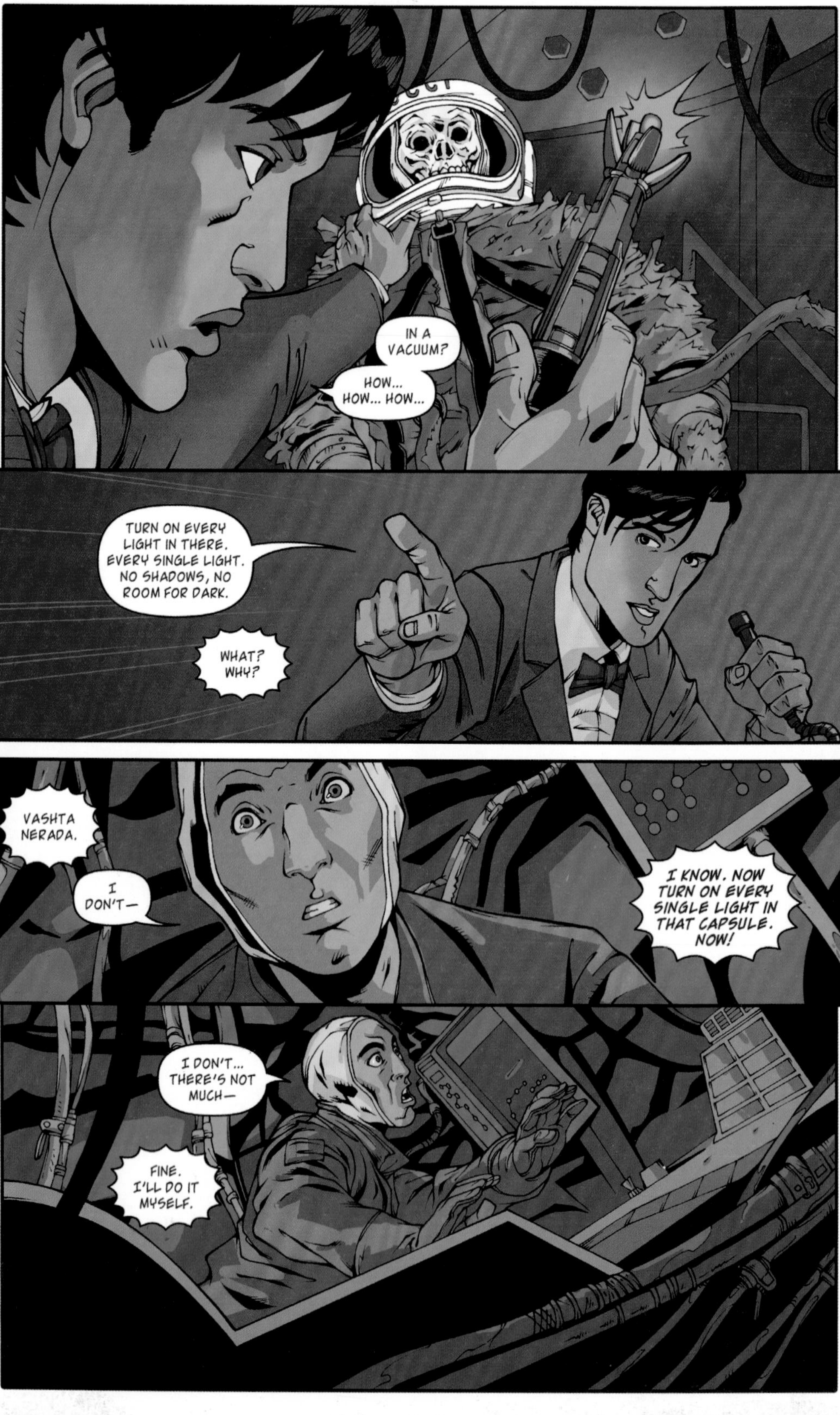

IN A VACUUM?
HOW... HOW... HOW...
TURN ON EVERY LIGHT IN THERE. EVERY SINGLE LIGHT. NO SHADOWS, NO ROOM FOR DARK.
WHAT? WHY?
VASHTA NERADA.
I DON'T—
I KNOW. NOW TURN ON EVERY SINGLE LIGHT IN THAT CAPSULE. NOW!
I DON'T... THERE'S NOT MUCH—
FINE. I'LL DO IT MYSELF.

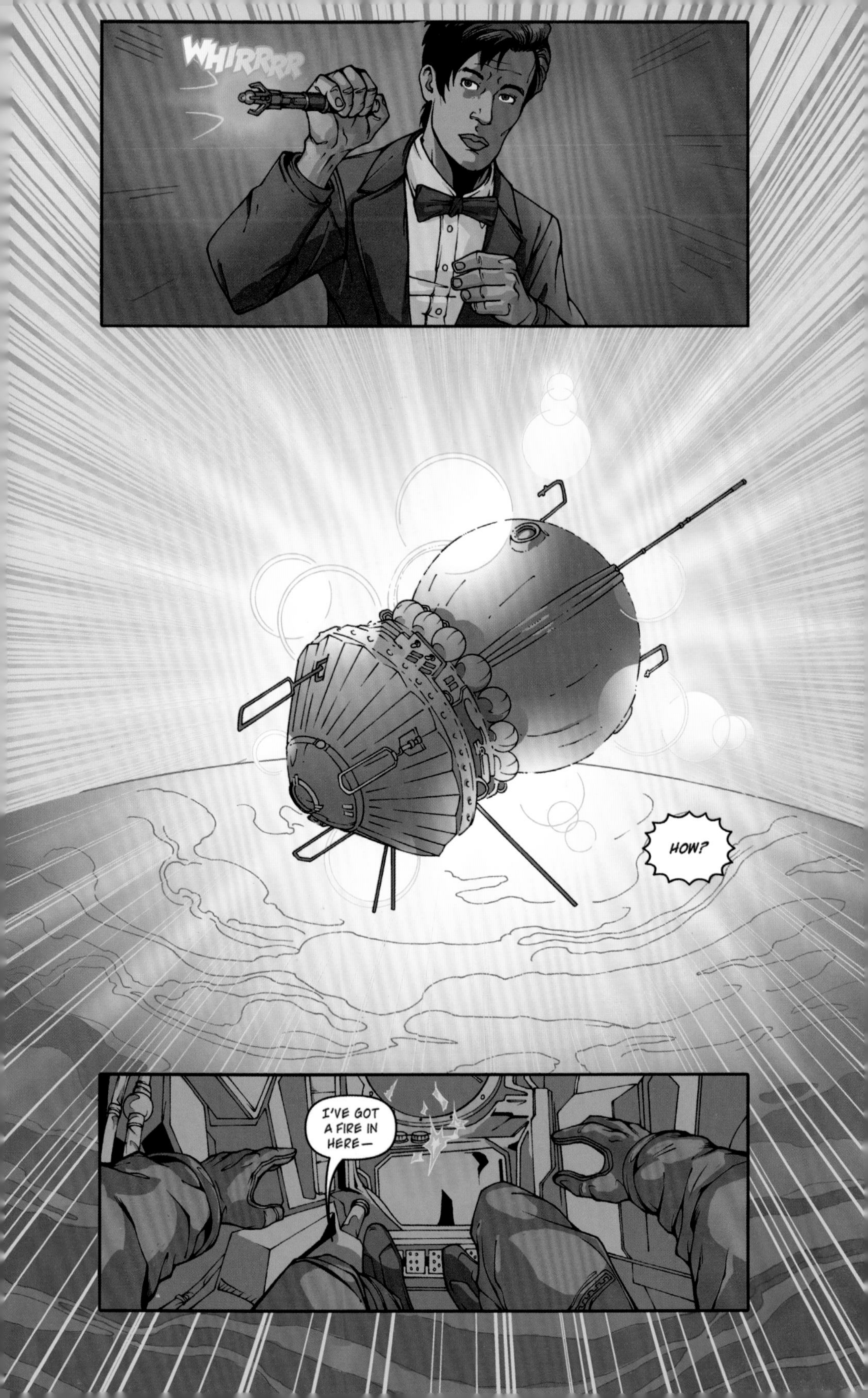
WHIRRRR
HOW?
I'VE GOT A FIRE IN HERE—

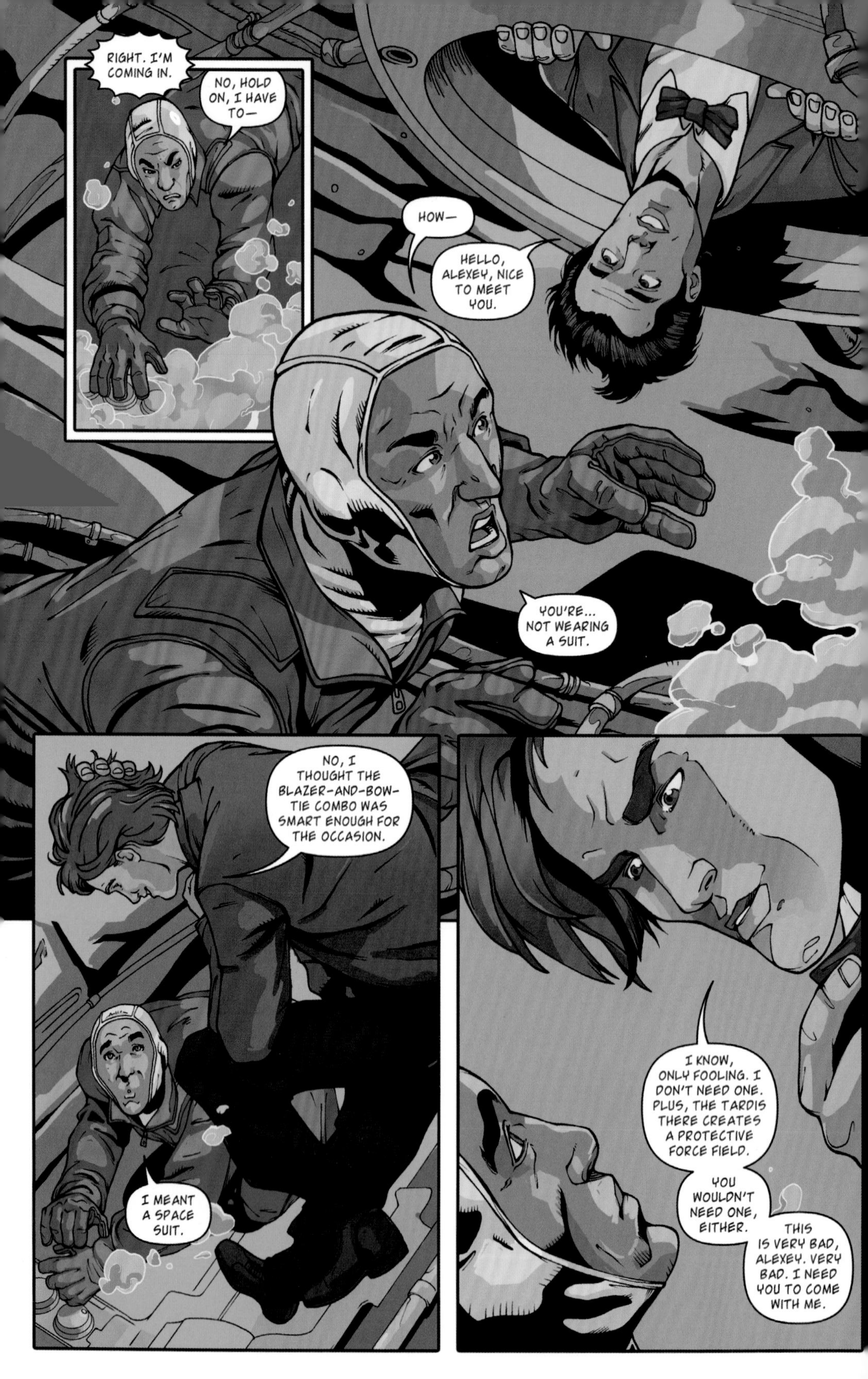
RIGHT. I'M COMING IN.
NO, HOLD ON, I HAVE TO—
HOW—
HELLO, ALEXEY, NICE TO MEET YOU.
YOU'RE... NOT WEARING A SUIT.
NO, I THOUGHT THE BLAZER-AND-BOW-TIE COMBO WAS SMART ENOUGH FOR THE OCCASION.
I MEANT A SPACE SUIT.
I KNOW, ONLY FOOLING. I DON'T NEED ONE. PLUS, THE TARDIS THERE CREATES A PROTECTIVE FORCE FIELD.
YOU WOULDN'T NEED ONE, EITHER.
THIS IS VERY BAD, ALEXEY. VERY BAD. I NEED YOU TO COME WITH ME.

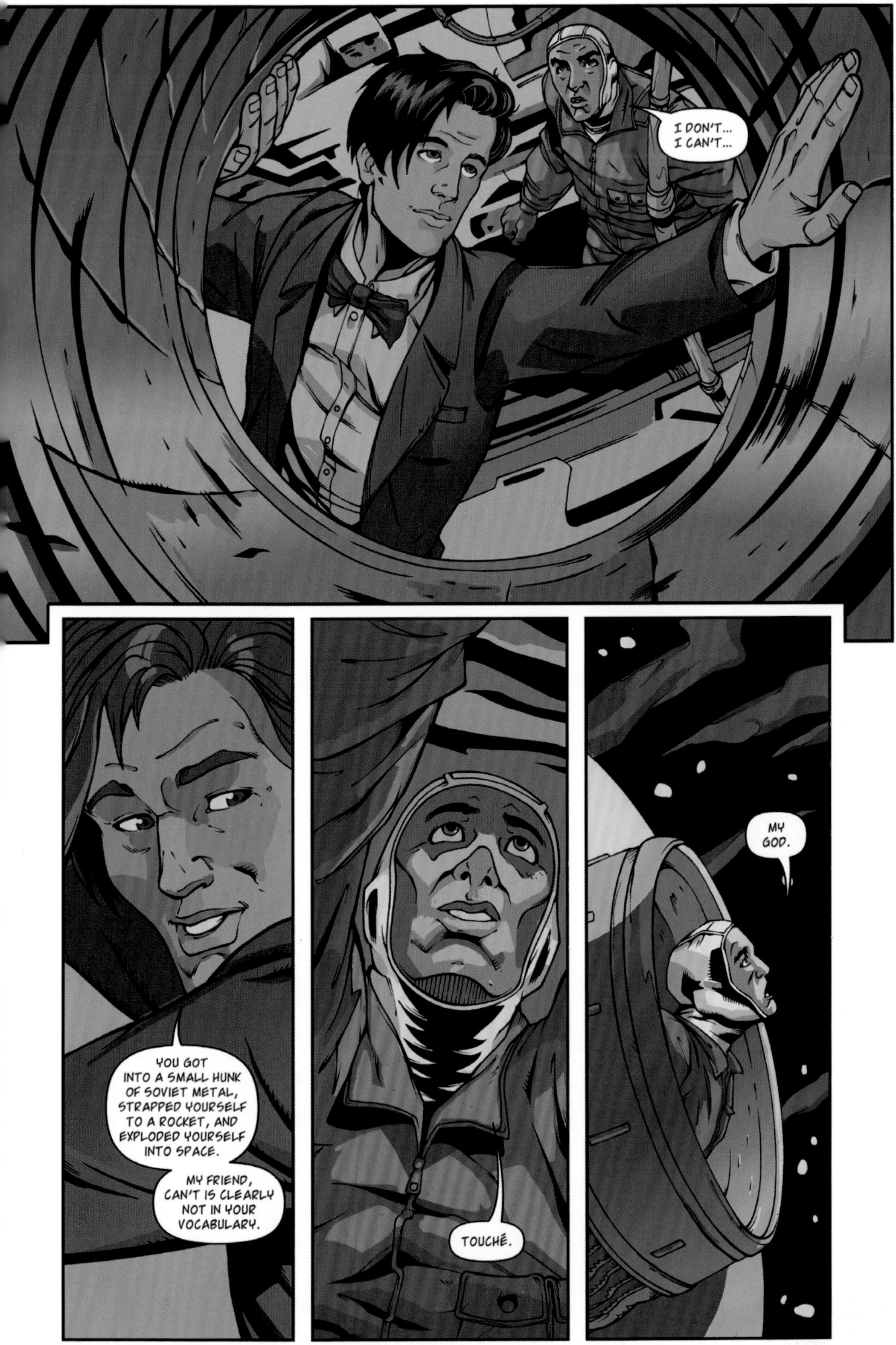
I DON'T...
I CAN'T...
YOU GOT INTO A SMALL HUNK OF SOVIET METAL, STRAPPED YOURSELF TO A ROCKET, AND EXPLODED YOURSELF INTO SPACE.
MY FRIEND, CAN'T IS CLEARLY NOT IN YOUR VOCABULARY.
TOUCHÉ.
MY GOD.

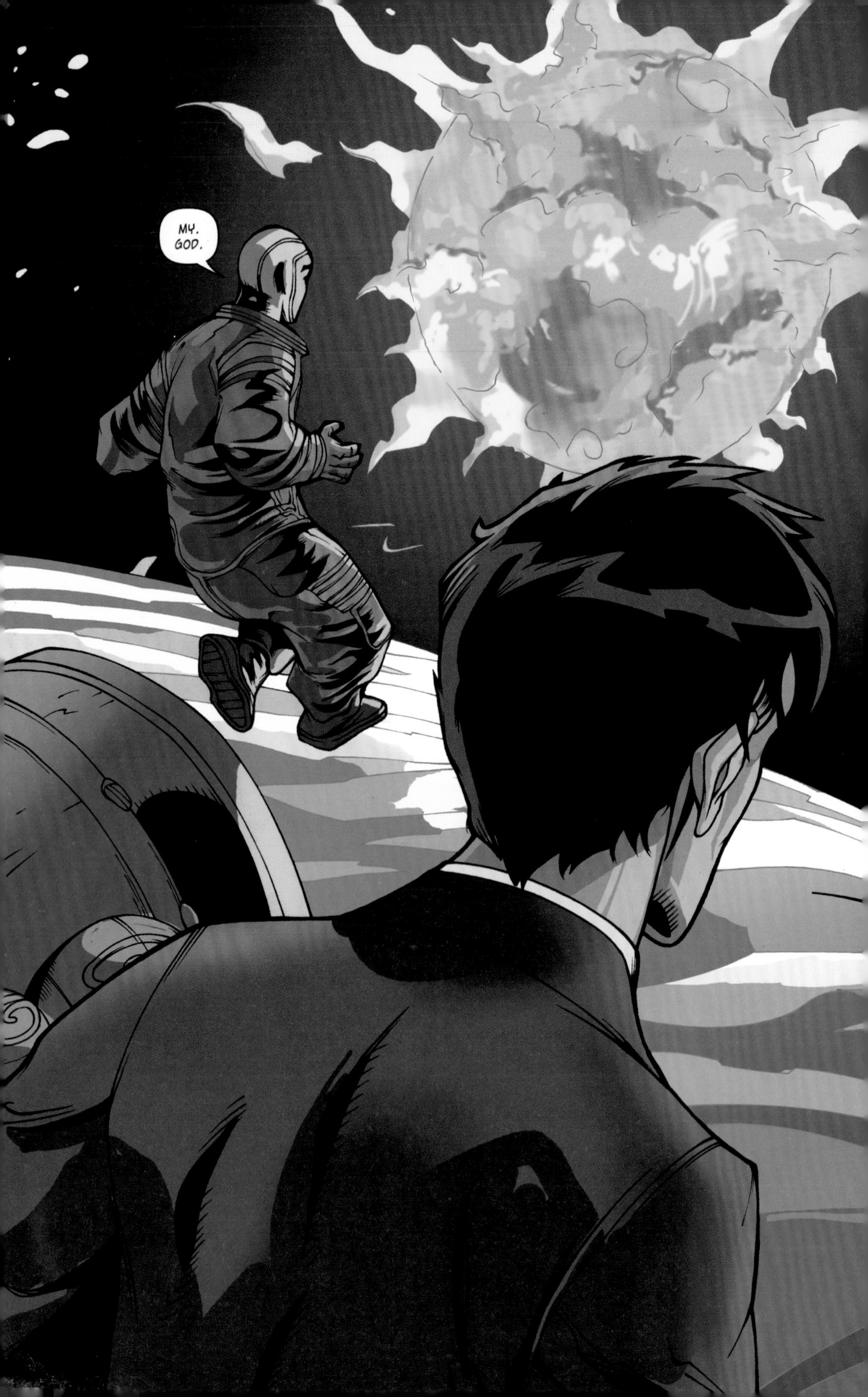
MY. GOD.

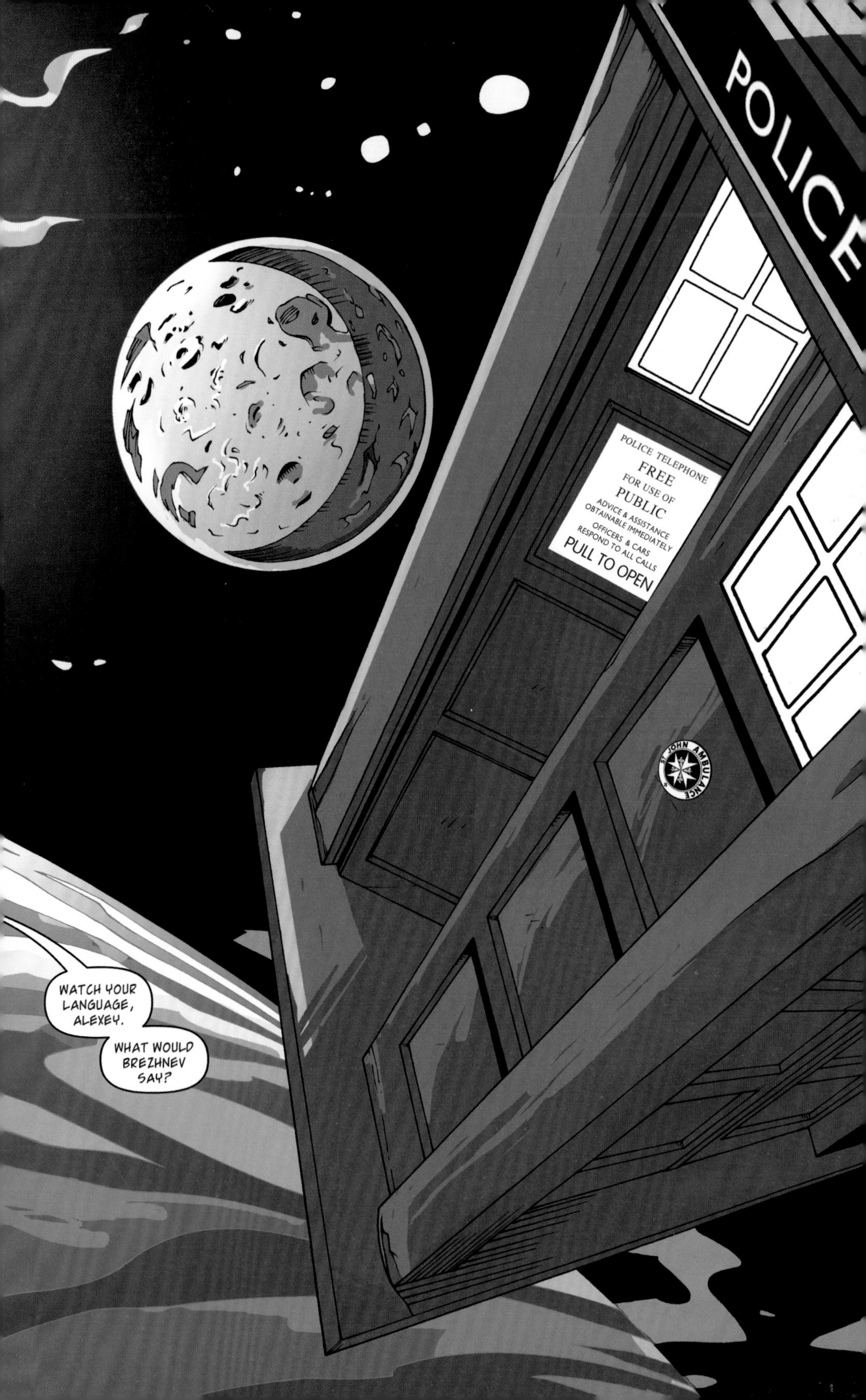
POLICE
POLICE TELEPHONE
FREE
FOR USE OF
PUBLIC
ADVICE & ASSISTANCE
OBTAINABLE IMMEDIATELY
OFFICERS & CARS
RESPOND TO ALL CALLS
PULL TO OPEN
ST JOHN AMBULANCE
WATCH YOUR LANGUAGE, ALEXEY.
WHAT WOULD BREZHNEV SAY?

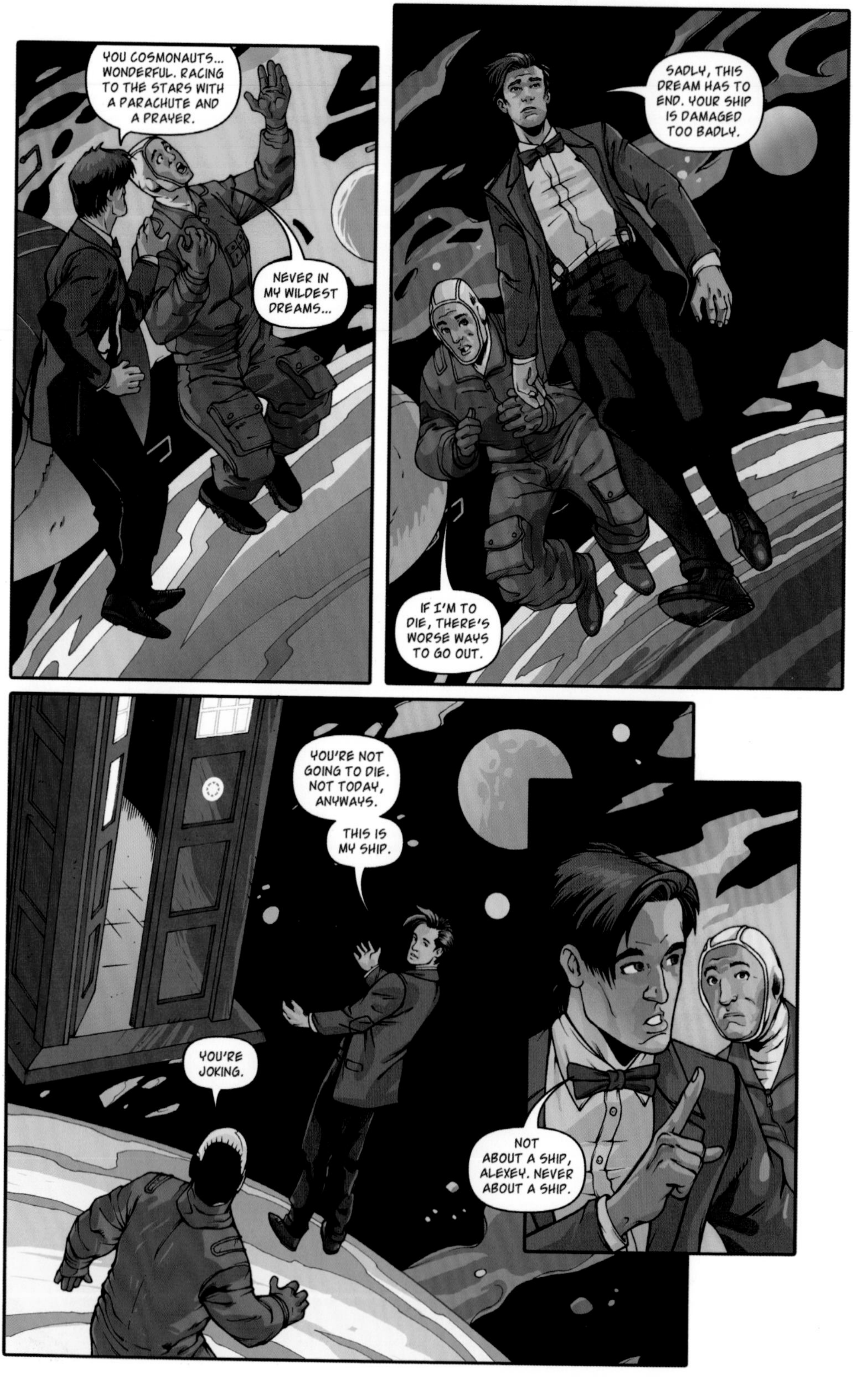
YOU COSMONAUTS... WONDERFUL. RACING TO THE STARS WITH A PARACHUTE AND A PRAYER.
NEVER IN MY WILDEST DREAMS...
SADLY, THIS DREAM HAS TO END. YOUR SHIP IS DAMAGED TOO BADLY.
IF I'M TO DIE, THERE'S WORSE WAYS TO GO OUT.
YOU'RE NOT GOING TO DIE. NOT TODAY, ANYWAYS.
THIS IS MY SHIP.
YOU'RE JOKING.
NOT ABOUT A SHIP, ALEXEY. NEVER ABOUT A SHIP.

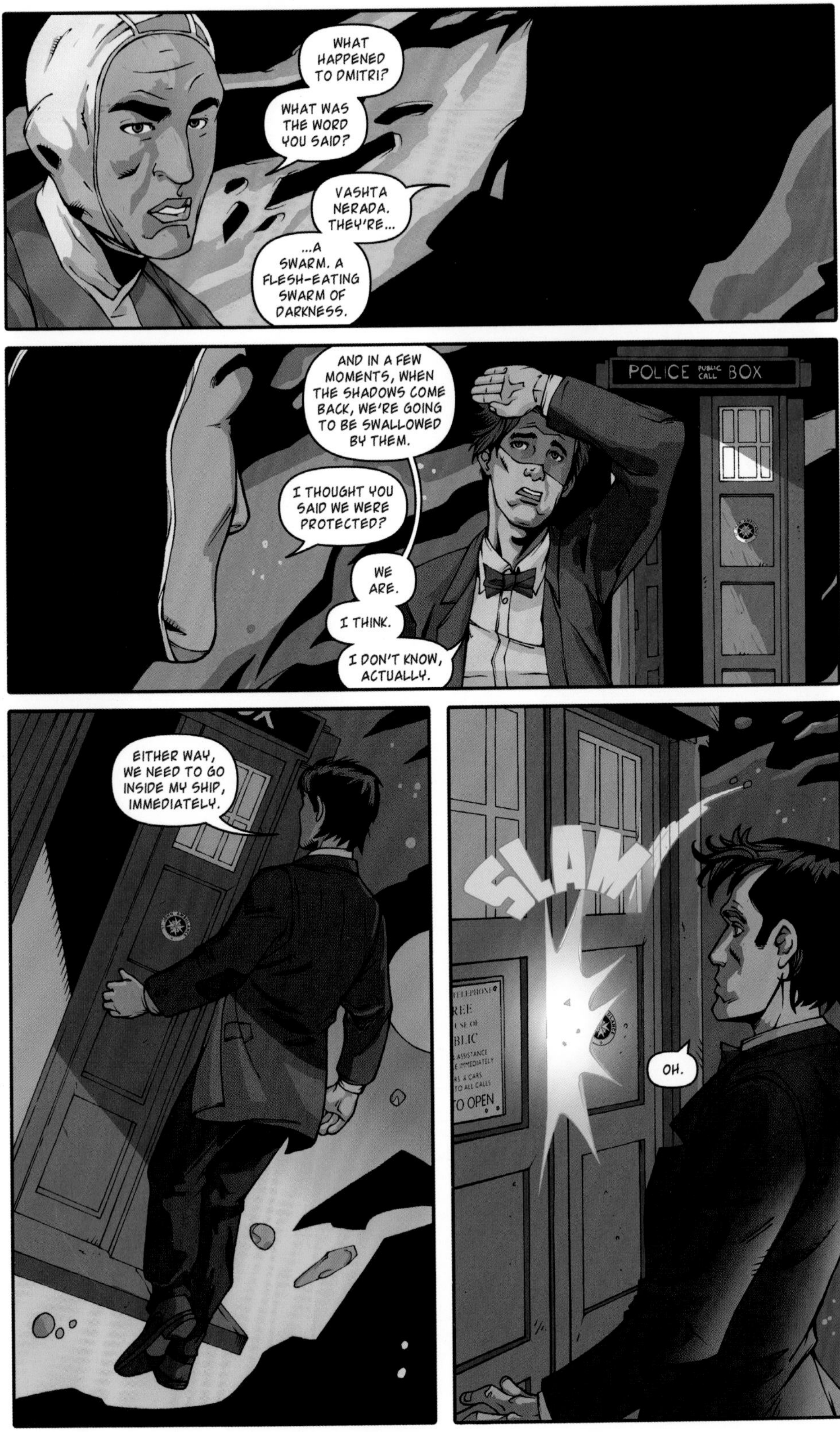
WHAT HAPPENED TO DMITRI?
WHAT WAS THE WORD YOU SAID?
VASHTA NERADA. THEY'RE...
...A SWARM. A FLESH-EATING SWARM OF DARKNESS.
POLICE PUBLIC CALL BOX
AND IN A FEW MOMENTS, WHEN THE SHADOWS COME BACK, WE'RE GOING TO BE SWALLOWED BY THEM.
I THOUGHT YOU SAID WE WERE PROTECTED?
WE ARE.
I THINK.
I DON'T KNOW, ACTUALLY.
EITHER WAY, WE NEED TO GO INSIDE MY SHIP, IMMEDIATELY.
SLAM!
OH.

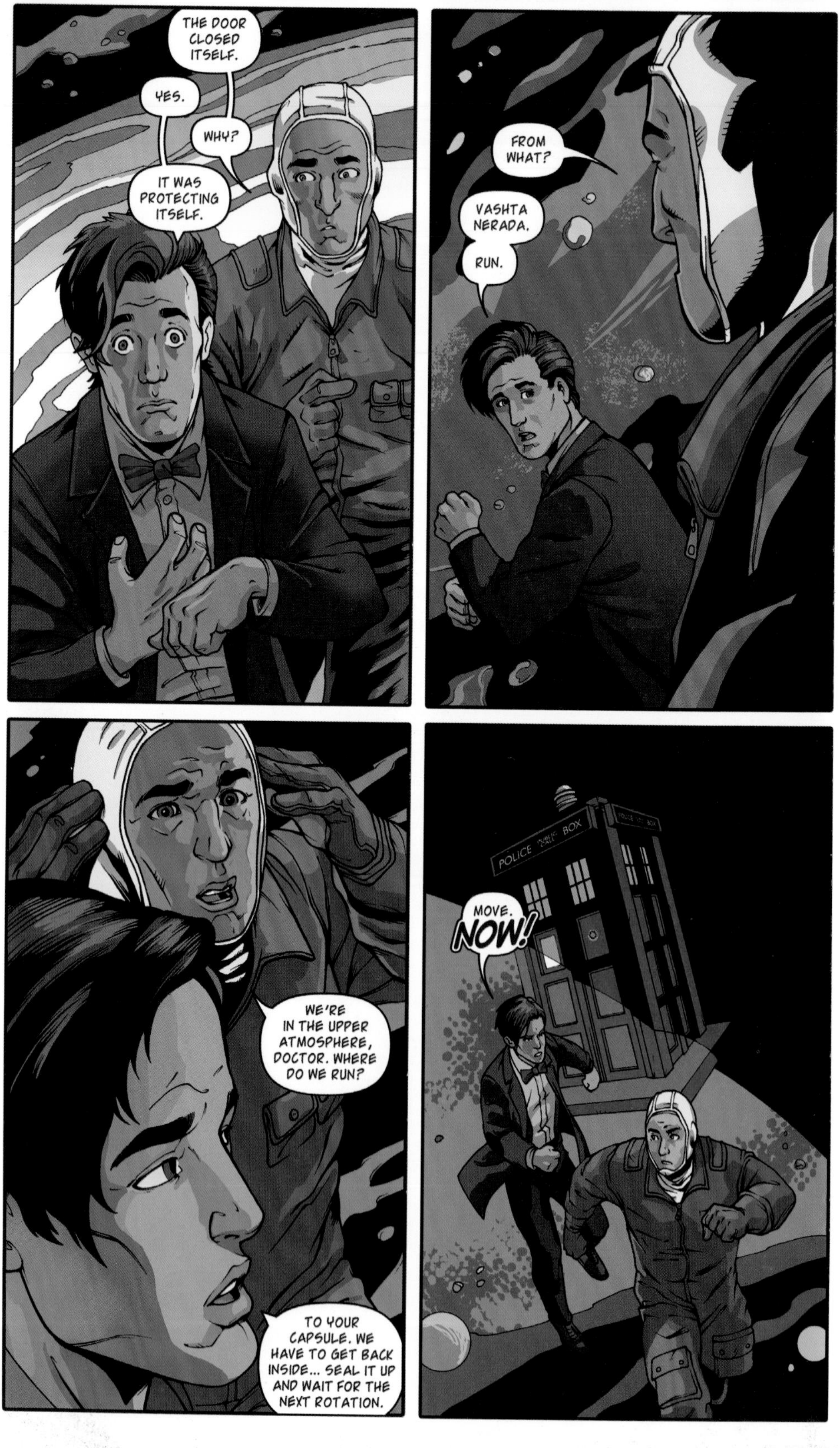
THE DOOR CLOSED ITSELF.
YES.
WHY?
IT WAS PROTECTING ITSELF.
FROM WHAT?
VASHTA NERADA.
RUN.
WE'RE IN THE UPPER ATMOSPHERE, DOCTOR. WHERE DO WE RUN?
TO YOUR CAPSULE. WE HAVE TO GET BACK INSIDE... SEAL IT UP AND WAIT FOR THE NEXT ROTATION.
POLICE PUBLIC CALL BOX
MOVE. NOW!

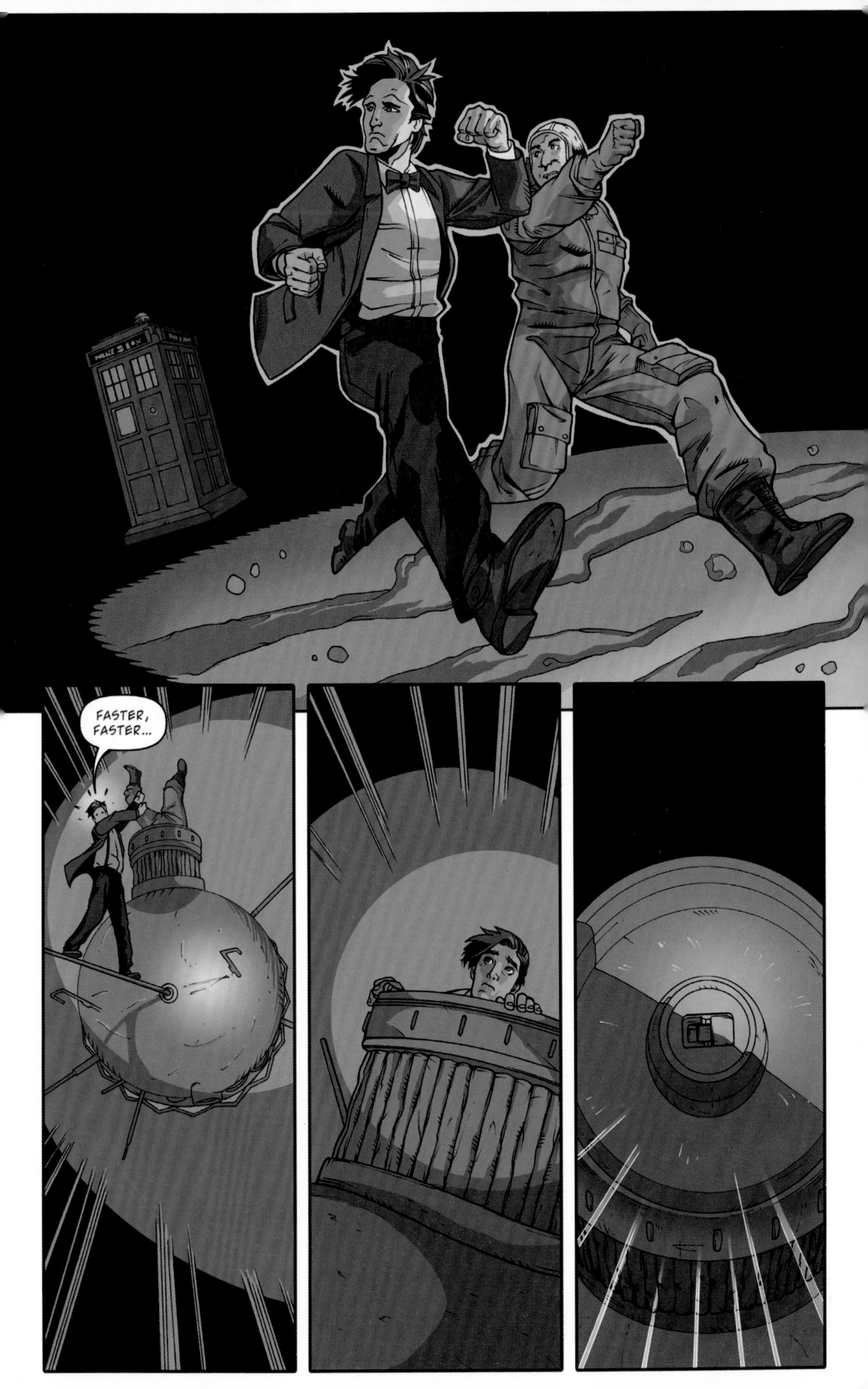
FASTER, FASTER...

WHIRRRR
COME ON, COME ON...
DOCTOR?
JUST A SECOND...
WHIRRRR
THE FIRE, IT MUST'VE CAUSED A SHORT... THE LIGHTS—

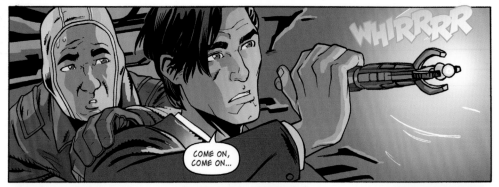

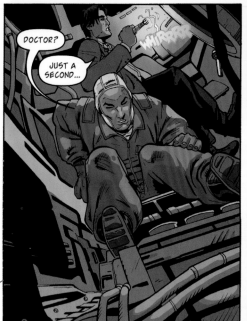

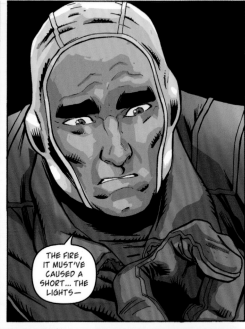

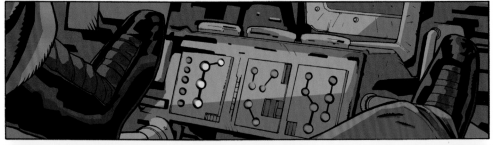

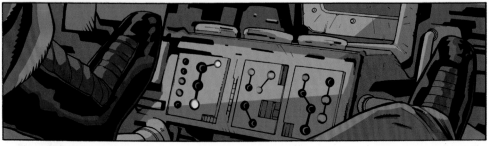

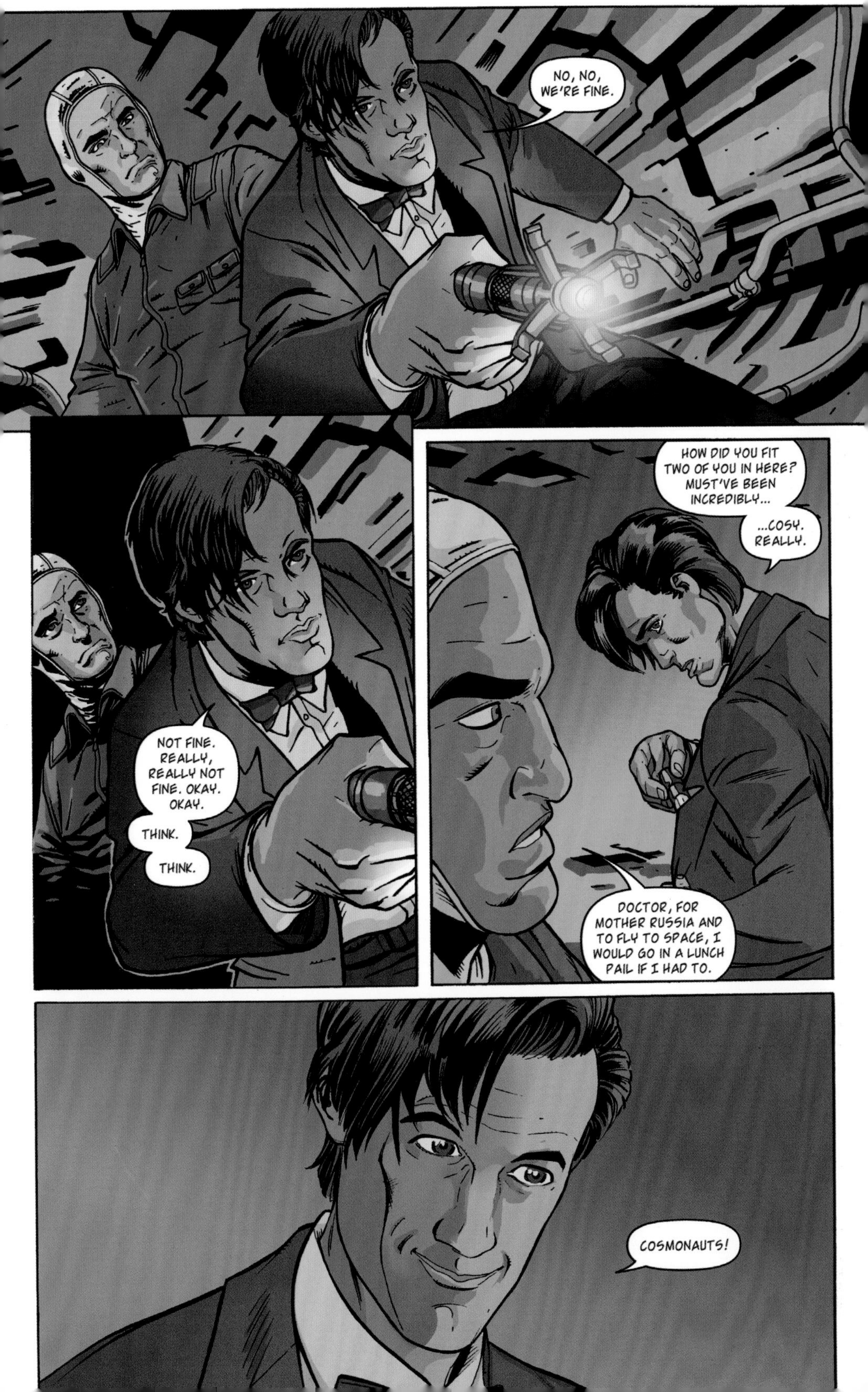
NO, NO, WE'RE FINE.
NOT FINE. REALLY, REALLY NOT FINE. OKAY. OKAY.
THINK.
THINK.
HOW DID YOU FIT TWO OF YOU IN HERE? MUST'VE BEEN INCREDIBLY...
...COSY. REALLY.
DOCTOR, FOR MOTHER RUSSIA AND TO FLY TO SPACE, I WOULD GO IN A LUNCH PAIL IF I HAD TO.
COSMONAUTS!

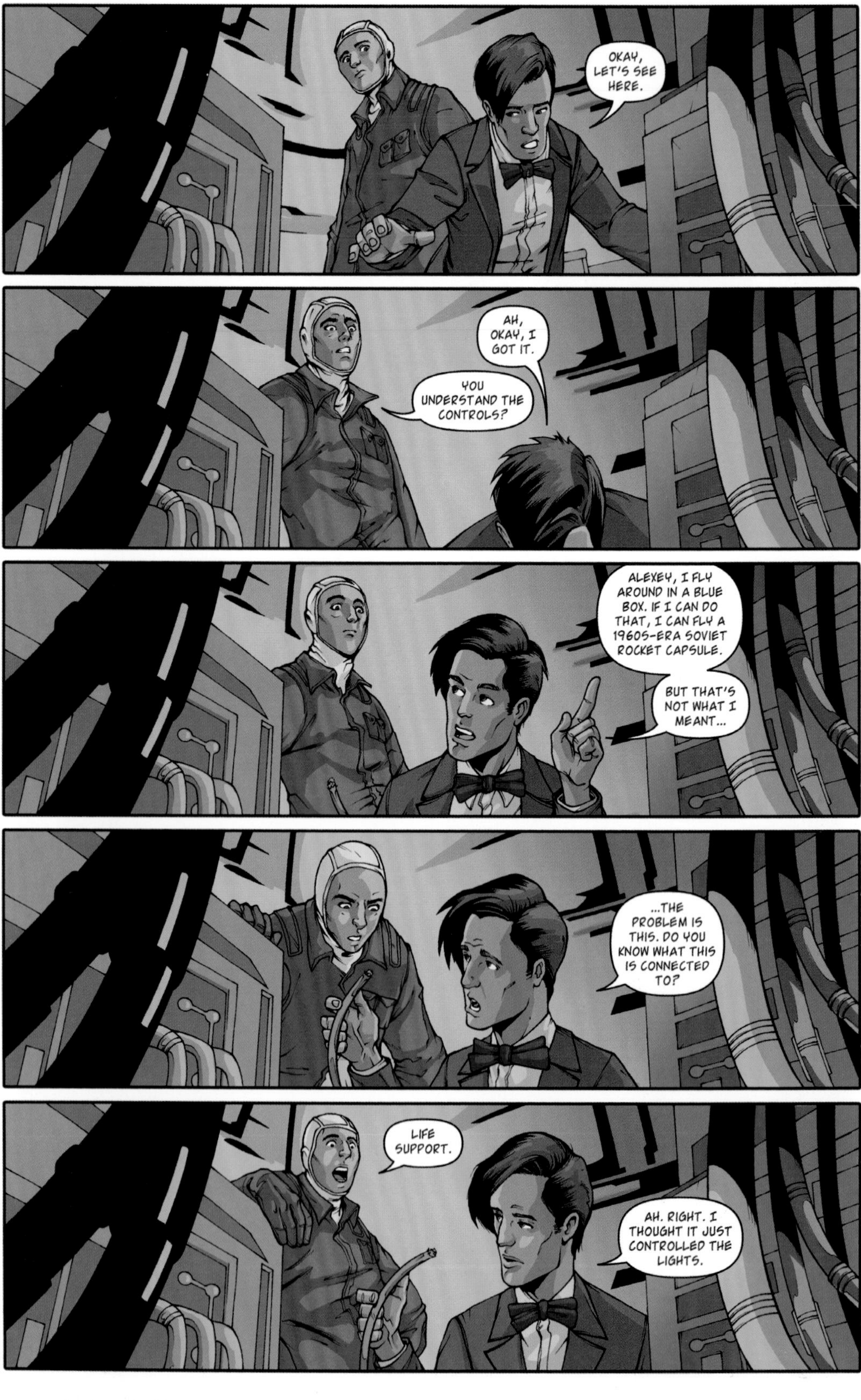
OKAY, LET'S SEE HERE.
AH, OKAY, I GOT IT.
YOU UNDERSTAND THE CONTROLS?
ALEXEY, I FLY AROUND IN A BLUE BOX. IF I CAN DO THAT, I CAN FLY A 1960S-ERA SOVIET ROCKET CAPSULE.
BUT THAT'S NOT WHAT I MEANT...
...THE PROBLEM IS THIS. DO YOU KNOW WHAT THIS IS CONNECTED TO?
LIFE SUPPORT.
AH. RIGHT. I THOUGHT IT JUST CONTROLLED THE LIGHTS.

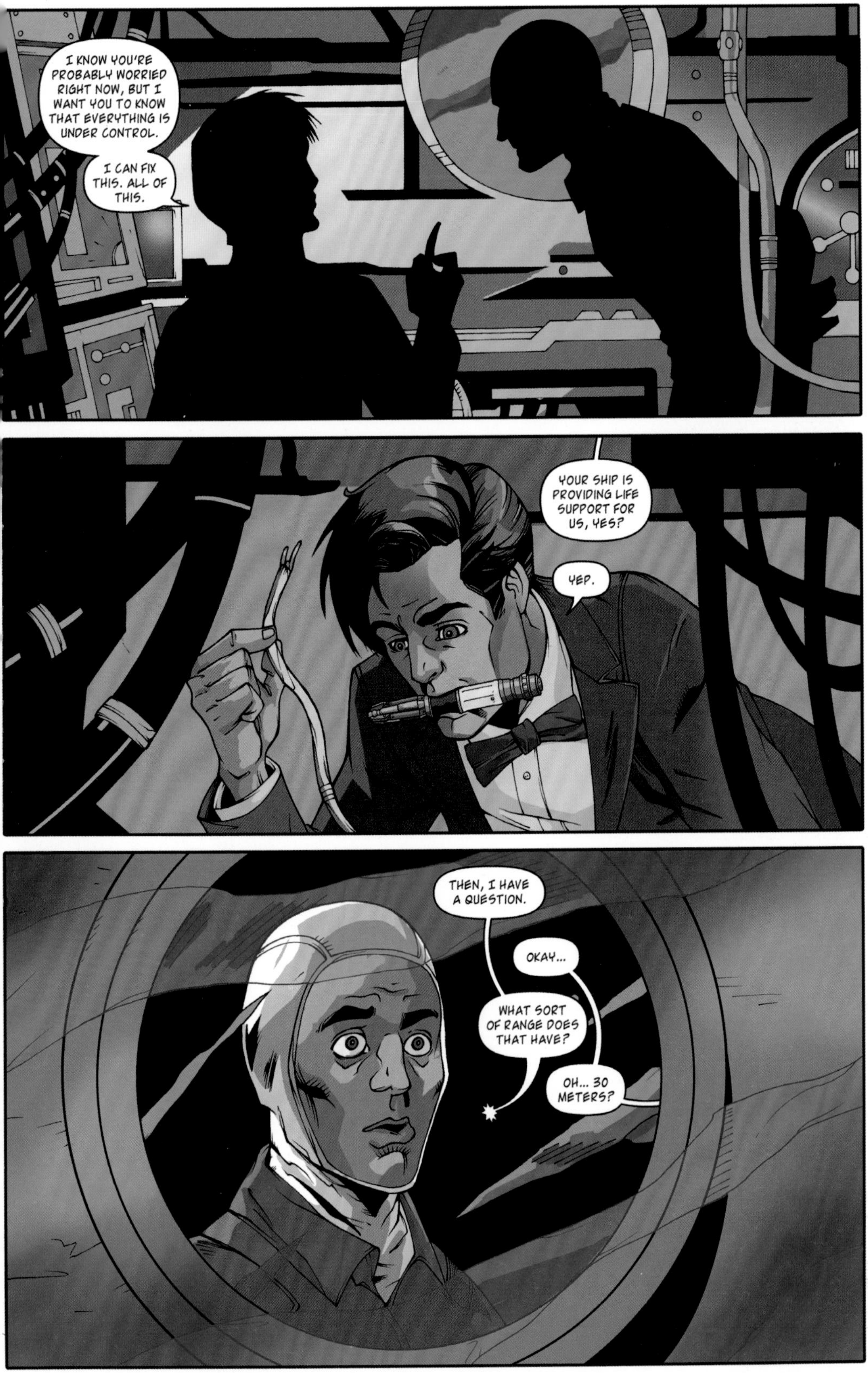
I KNOW YOU'RE PROBABLY WORRIED RIGHT NOW, BUT I WANT YOU TO KNOW THAT EVERYTHING IS UNDER CONTROL.
I CAN FIX THIS. ALL OF THIS.
YOUR SHIP IS PROVIDING LIFE SUPPORT FOR US, YES?
YEP.
THEN, I HAVE A QUESTION.
OKAY...
WHAT SORT OF RANGE DOES THAT HAVE?
OH... 30 METERS?

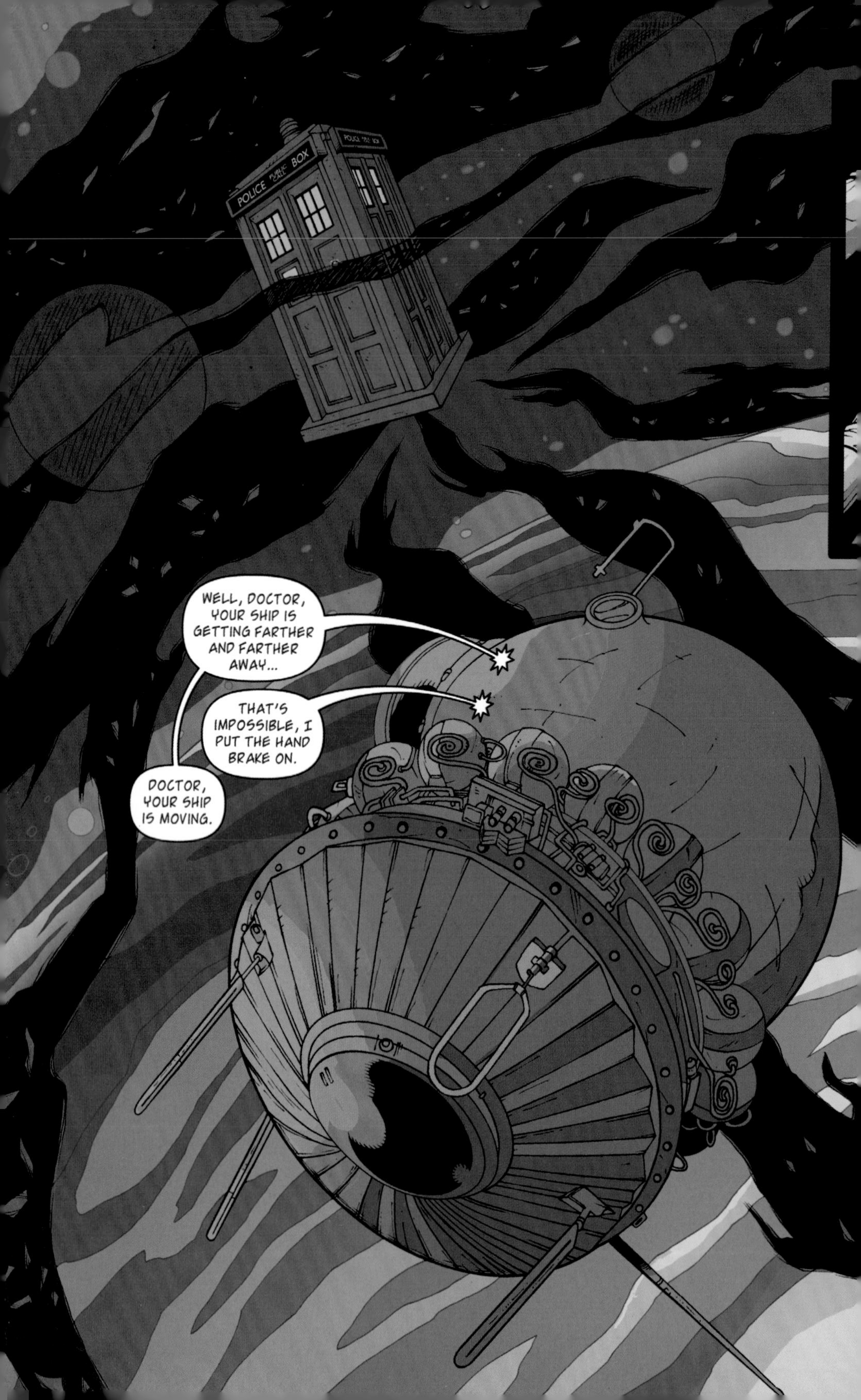
WELL, DOCTOR, YOUR SHIP IS GETTING FARTHER AND FARTHER AWAY...
THAT'S IMPOSSIBLE, I PUT THE HAND BRAKE ON.
DOCTOR, YOUR SHIP IS MOVING.

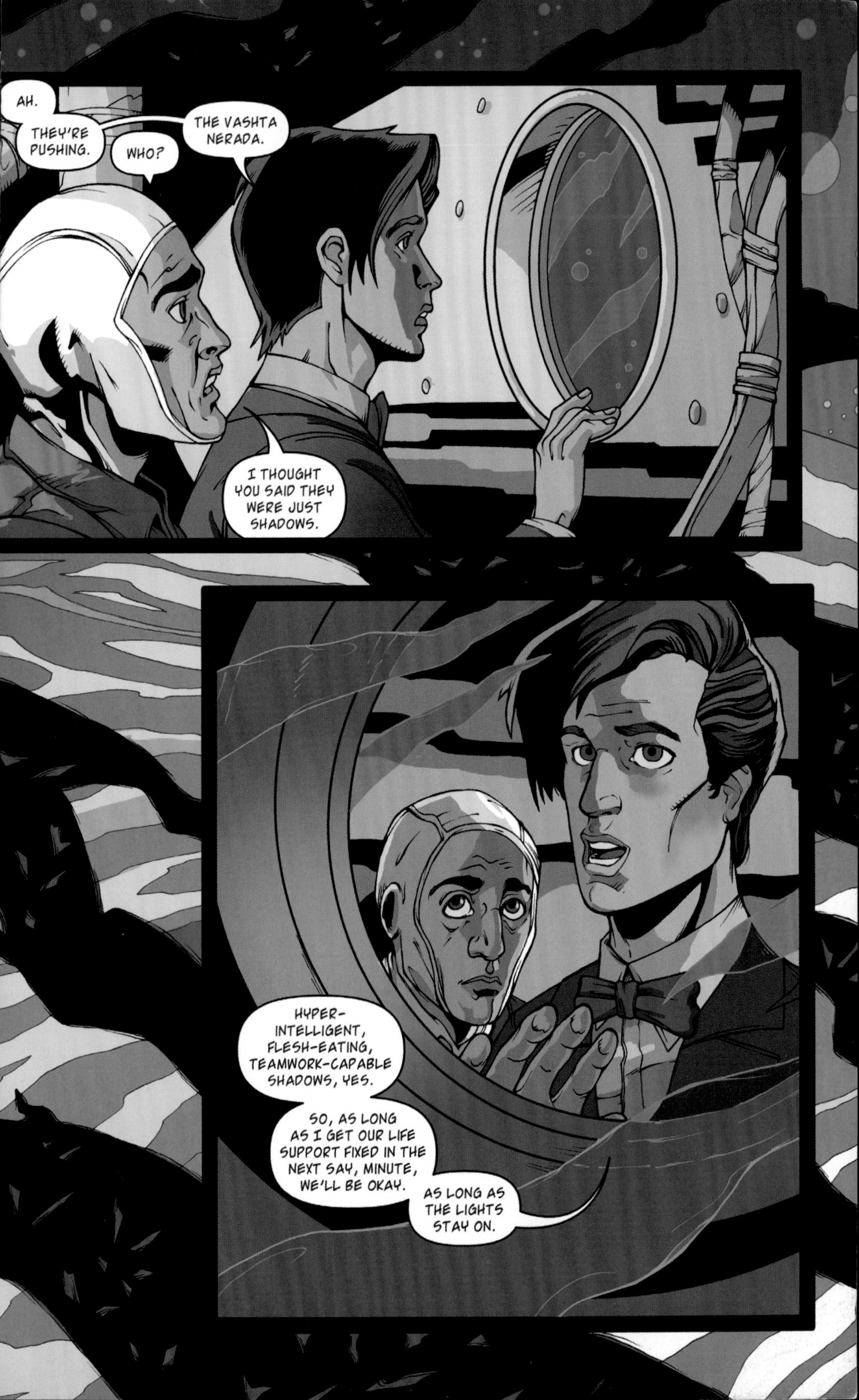
AH.
THEY'RE PUSHING.
WHO?
THE VASHTA NERADA.
I THOUGHT YOU SAID THEY WERE JUST SHADOWS.
HYPER-INTELLIGENT, FLESH-EATING, TEAMWORK-CAPABLE SHADOWS, YES.
SO, AS LONG AS I GET OUR LIFE SUPPORT FIXED IN THE NEXT SAY, MINUTE, WE'LL BE OKAY.
AS LONG AS THE LIGHTS STAY ON.

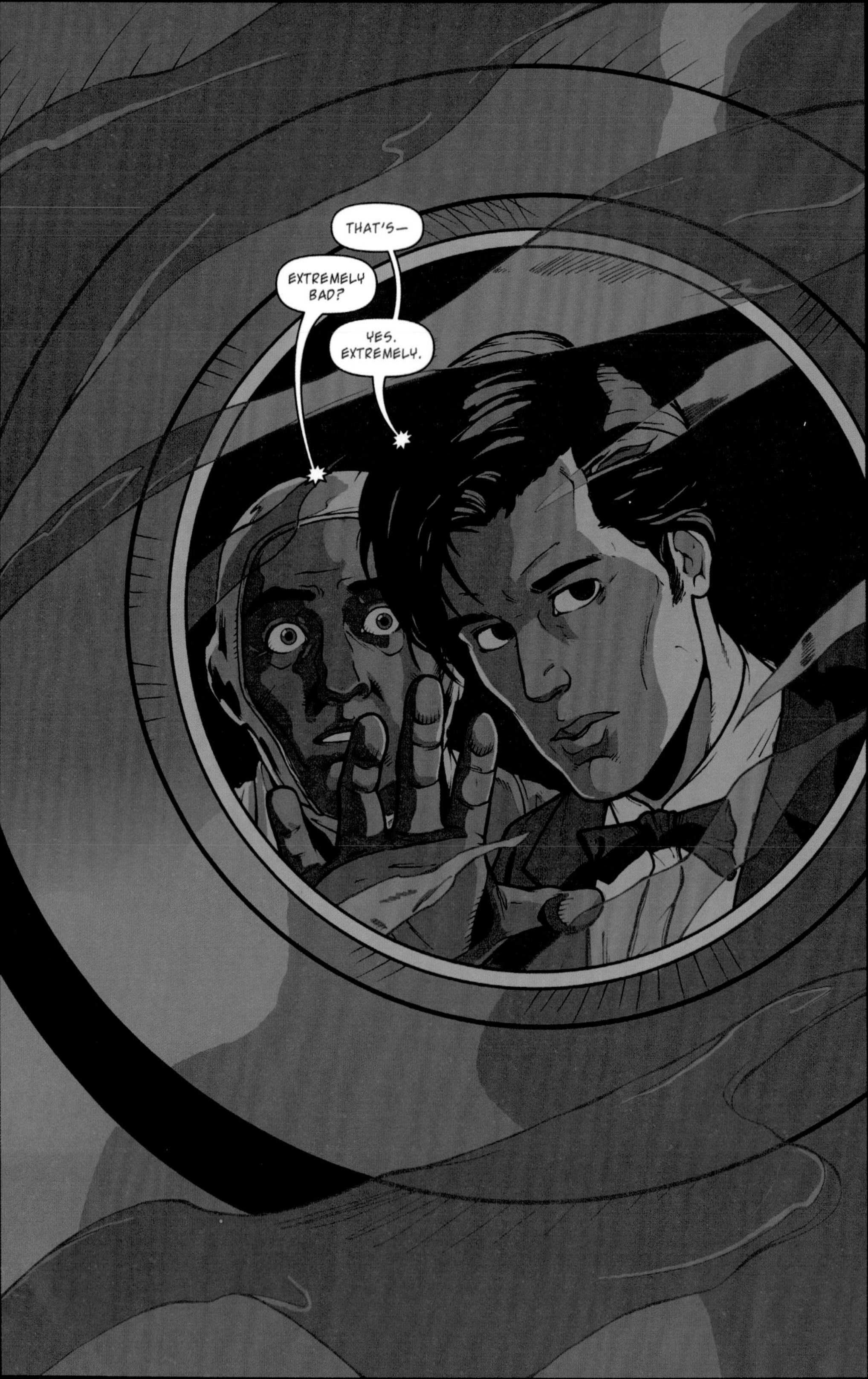
THAT'S—
EXTREMELY BAD?
YES. EXTREMELY.

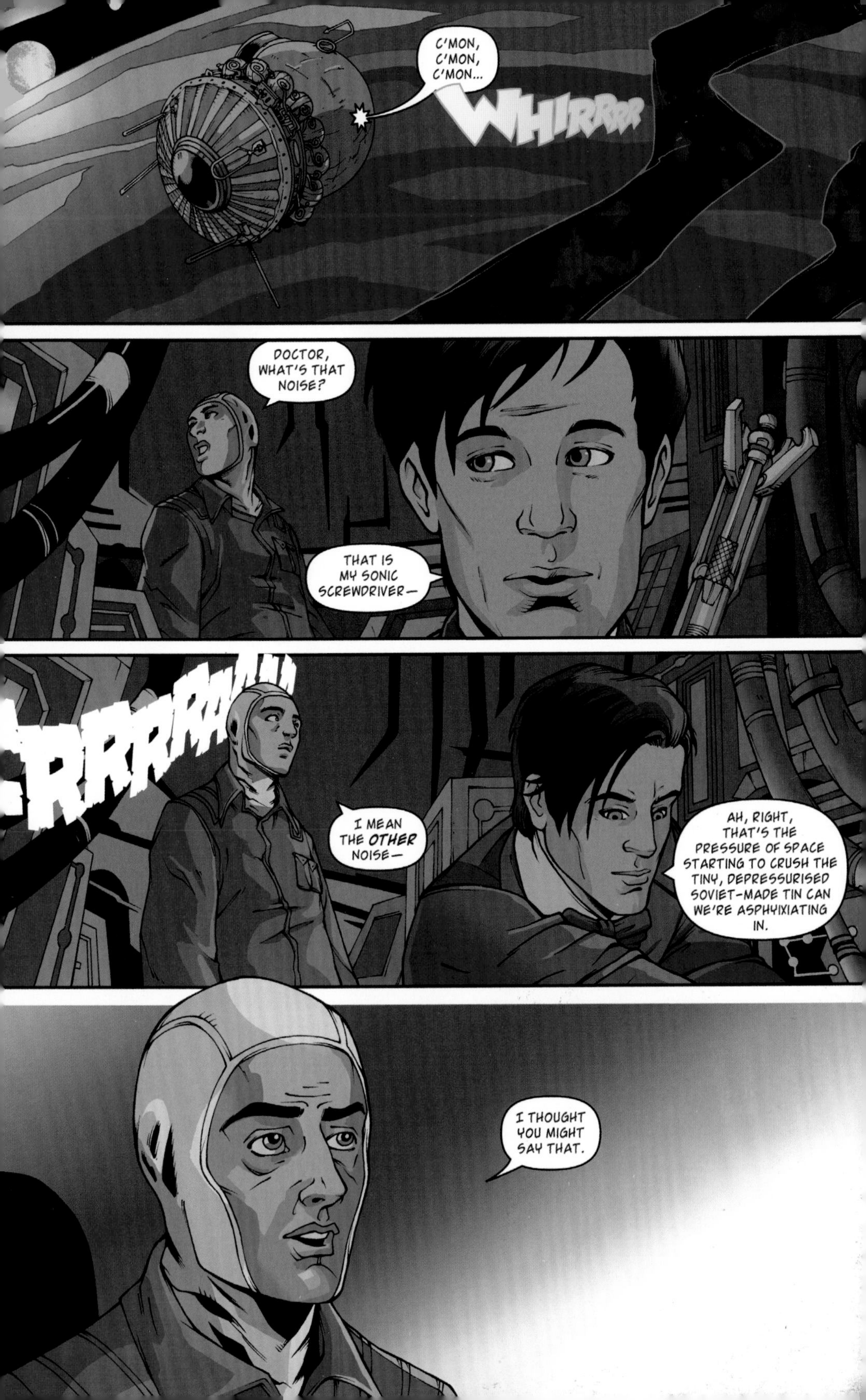
C'MON, C'MON, C'MON...
WHIRRRR
DOCTOR, WHAT'S THAT NOISE?
THAT IS MY SONIC SCREWDRIVER—
I MEAN THE *OTHER* NOISE—
AH, RIGHT, THAT'S THE PRESSURE OF SPACE STARTING TO CRUSH THE TINY, DEPRESSURISED SOVIET-MADE TIN CAN WE'RE ASPHYIXIATING IN.
I THOUGHT YOU MIGHT SAY THAT.

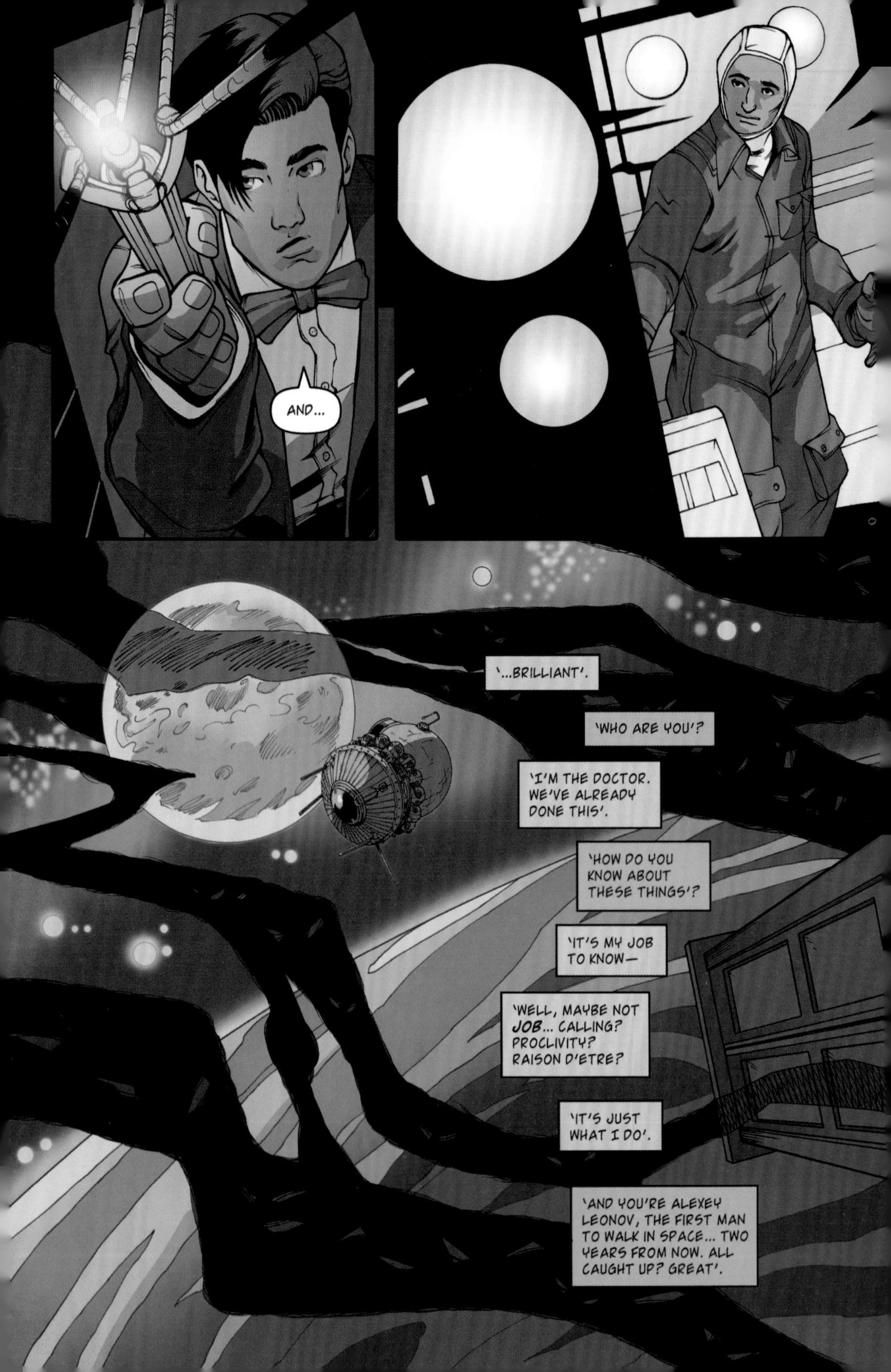

AND...
'...BRILLIANT'.
'WHO ARE YOU'?
'I'M THE DOCTOR. WE'VE ALREADY DONE THIS'.
'HOW DO YOU KNOW ABOUT THESE THINGS'?
'IT'S MY JOB TO KNOW—
'WELL, MAYBE NOT *JOB*... CALLING? PROCLIVITY? RAISON D'ETRE?
'IT'S JUST WHAT I DO'.
'AND YOU'RE ALEXEY LEONOV, THE FIRST MAN TO WALK IN SPACE... TWO YEARS FROM NOW. ALL CAUGHT UP? GREAT'.

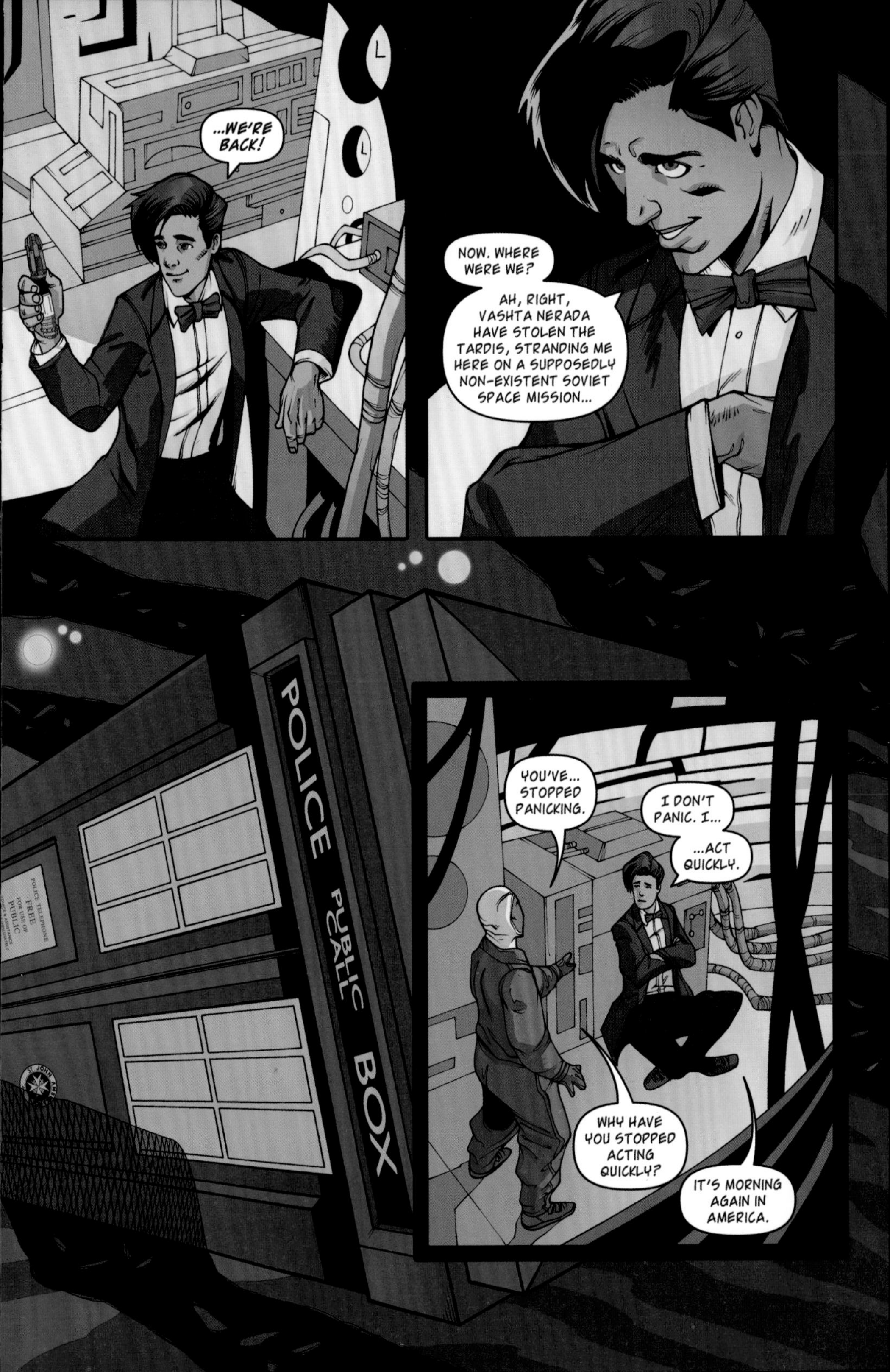
...WE'RE BACK!
NOW. WHERE WERE WE?
AH, RIGHT, VASHTA NERADA HAVE STOLEN THE TARDIS, STRANDING ME HERE ON A SUPPOSEDLY NON-EXISTENT SOVIET SPACE MISSION...
POLICE PUBLIC CALL BOX
POLICE TELEPHONE FREE FOR USE OF PUBLIC
YOU'VE... STOPPED PANICKING.
I DON'T PANIC. I...
...ACT QUICKLY.
WHY HAVE YOU STOPPED ACTING QUICKLY?
IT'S MORNING AGAIN IN AMERICA.

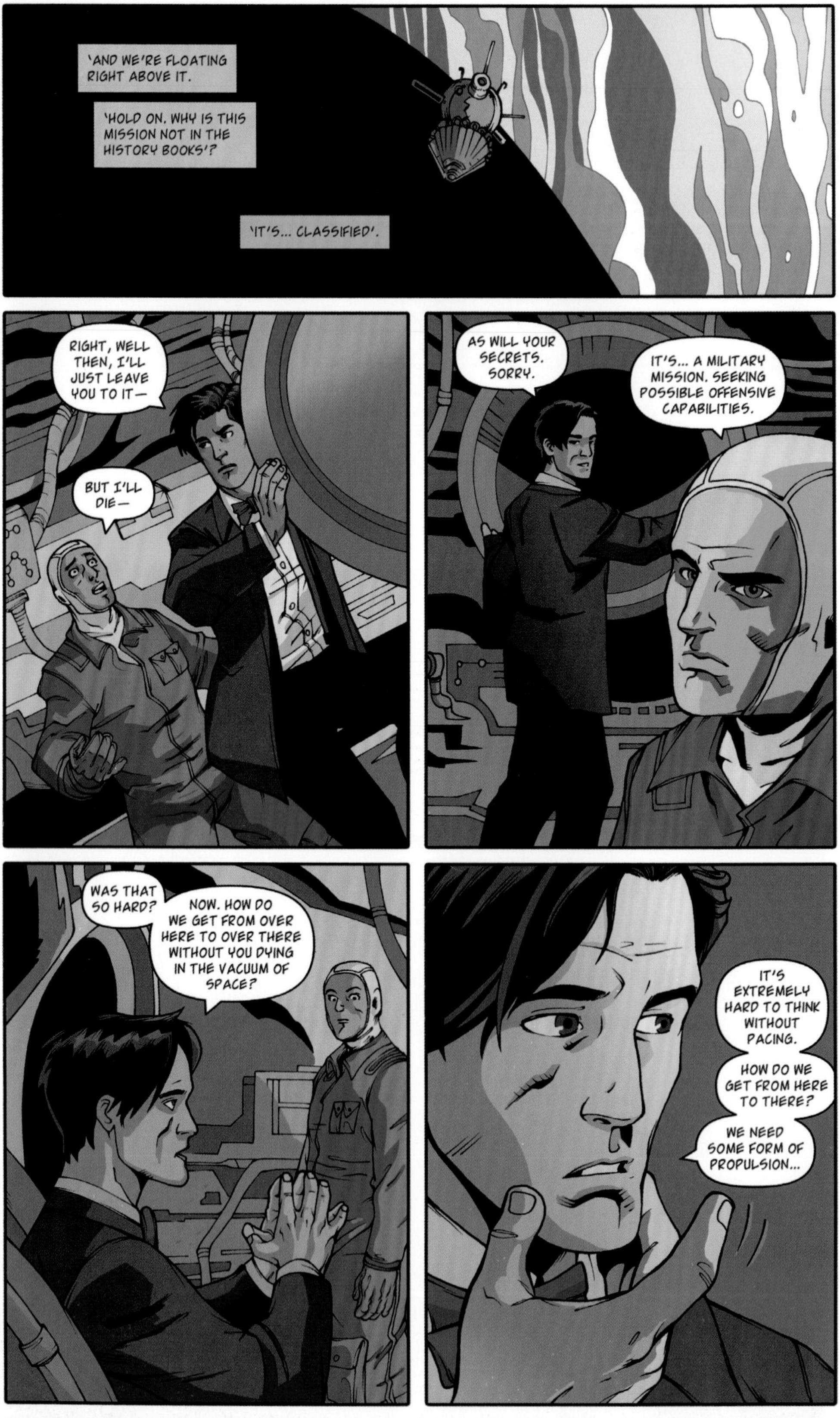
'AND WE'RE FLOATING RIGHT ABOVE IT.
'HOLD ON. WHY IS THIS MISSION NOT IN THE HISTORY BOOKS'?
'IT'S... CLASSIFIED'.
RIGHT, WELL THEN, I'LL JUST LEAVE YOU TO IT—
BUT I'LL DIE—
AS WILL YOUR SECRETS. SORRY.
IT'S... A MILITARY MISSION. SEEKING POSSIBLE OFFENSIVE CAPABILITIES.
WAS THAT SO HARD?
NOW. HOW DO WE GET FROM OVER HERE TO OVER THERE WITHOUT YOU DYING IN THE VACUUM OF SPACE?
IT'S EXTREMELY HARD TO THINK WITHOUT PACING.
HOW DO WE GET FROM HERE TO THERE?
WE NEED SOME FORM OF PROPULSION...

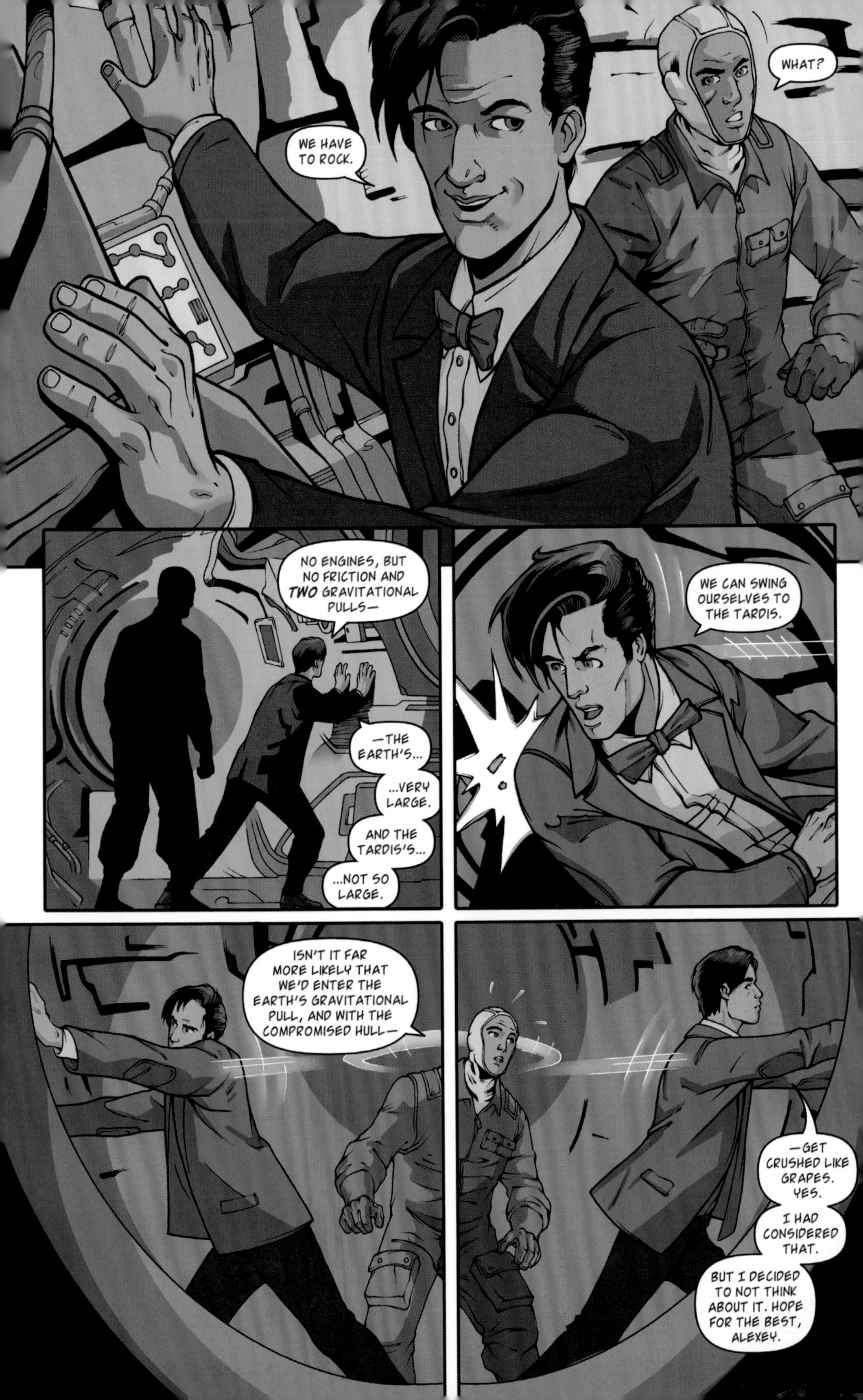

WHAT?
WE HAVE TO ROCK.
NO ENGINES, BUT NO FRICTION AND *TWO* GRAVITATIONAL PULLS—
—THE EARTH'S...
...VERY LARGE.
AND THE TARDIS'S...
...NOT SO LARGE.
WE CAN SWING OURSELVES TO THE TARDIS.
ISN'T IT FAR MORE LIKELY THAT WE'D ENTER THE EARTH'S GRAVITATIONAL PULL, AND WITH THE COMPROMISED HULL—
—GET CRUSHED LIKE GRAPES. YES.
I HAD CONSIDERED THAT.
BUT I DECIDED TO NOT THINK ABOUT IT. HOPE FOR THE BEST, ALEXEY.

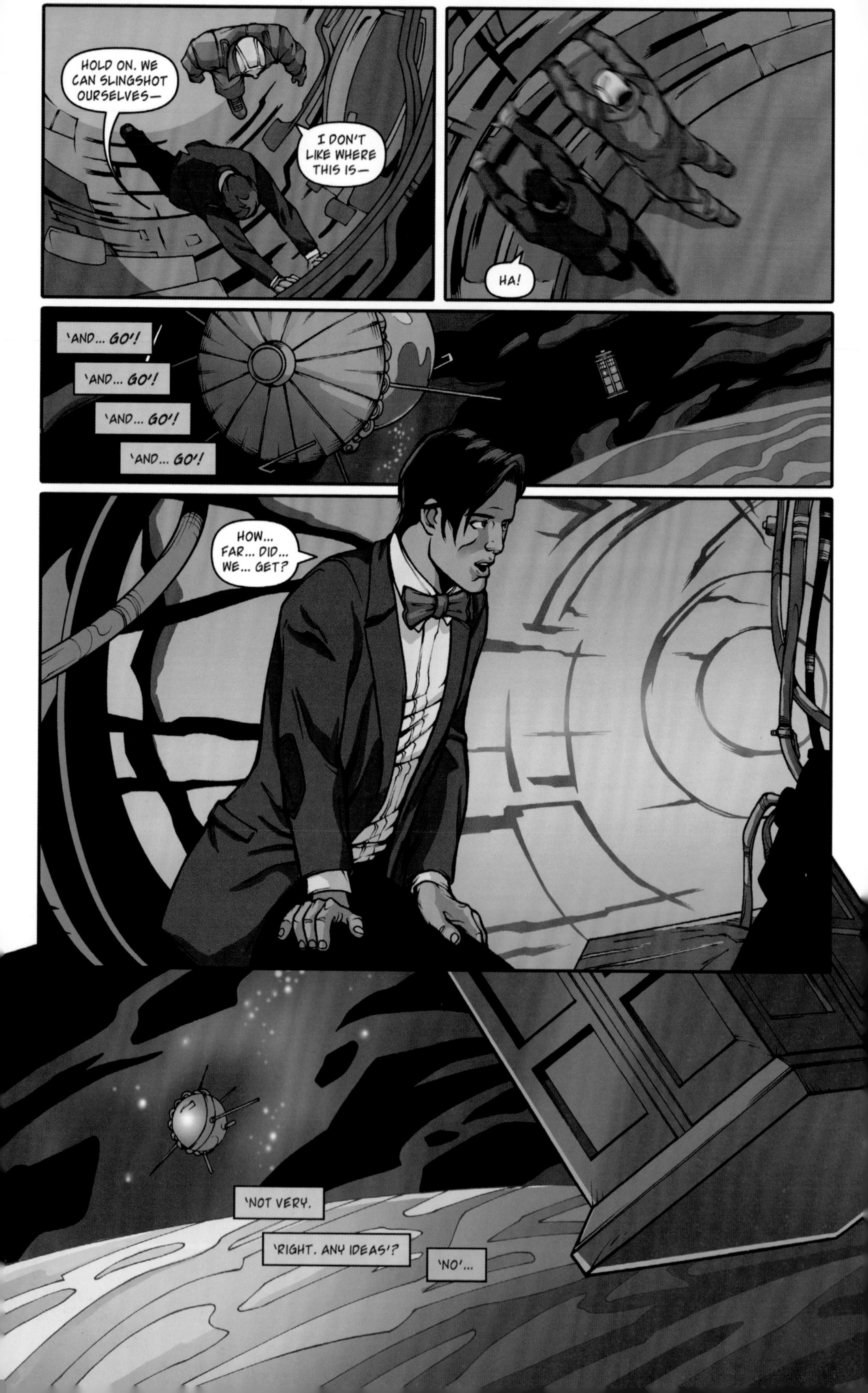
HOLD ON. WE CAN SLINGSHOT OURSELVES—
I DON'T LIKE WHERE THIS IS—
HA!
'AND... GO'!
'AND... GO'!
'AND... GO'!
'AND... GO'!
HOW... FAR... DID... WE... GET?
'NOT VERY.
'RIGHT. ANY IDEAS'?
'NO'...

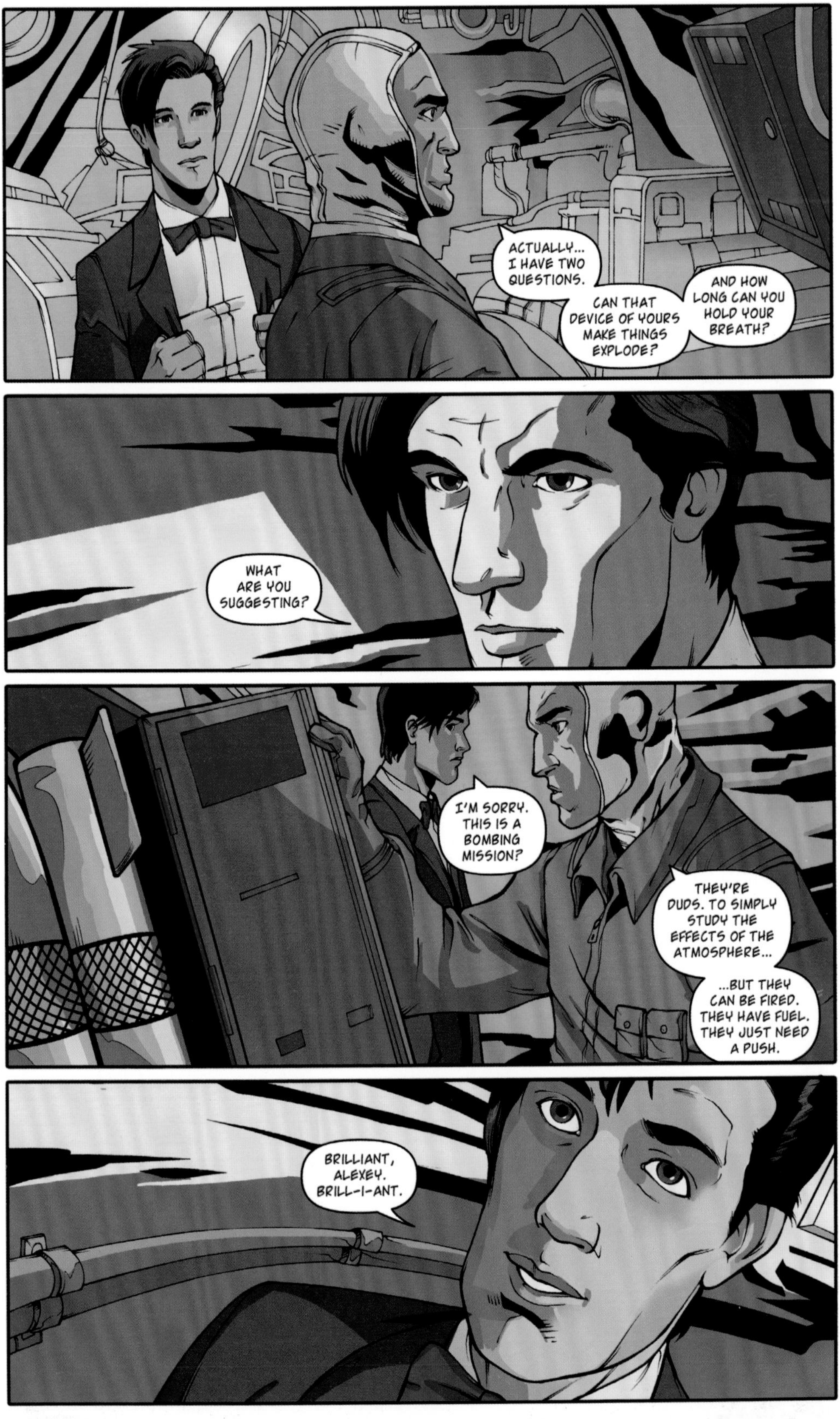
ACTUALLY... I HAVE TWO QUESTIONS.
CAN THAT DEVICE OF YOURS MAKE THINGS EXPLODE?
AND HOW LONG CAN YOU HOLD YOUR BREATH?
WHAT ARE YOU SUGGESTING?
I'M SORRY. THIS IS A BOMBING MISSION?
THEY'RE DUDS. TO SIMPLY STUDY THE EFFECTS OF THE ATMOSPHERE...
...BUT THEY CAN BE FIRED. THEY HAVE FUEL. THEY JUST NEED A PUSH.
BRILLIANT, ALEXEY. BRILL-I-ANT.

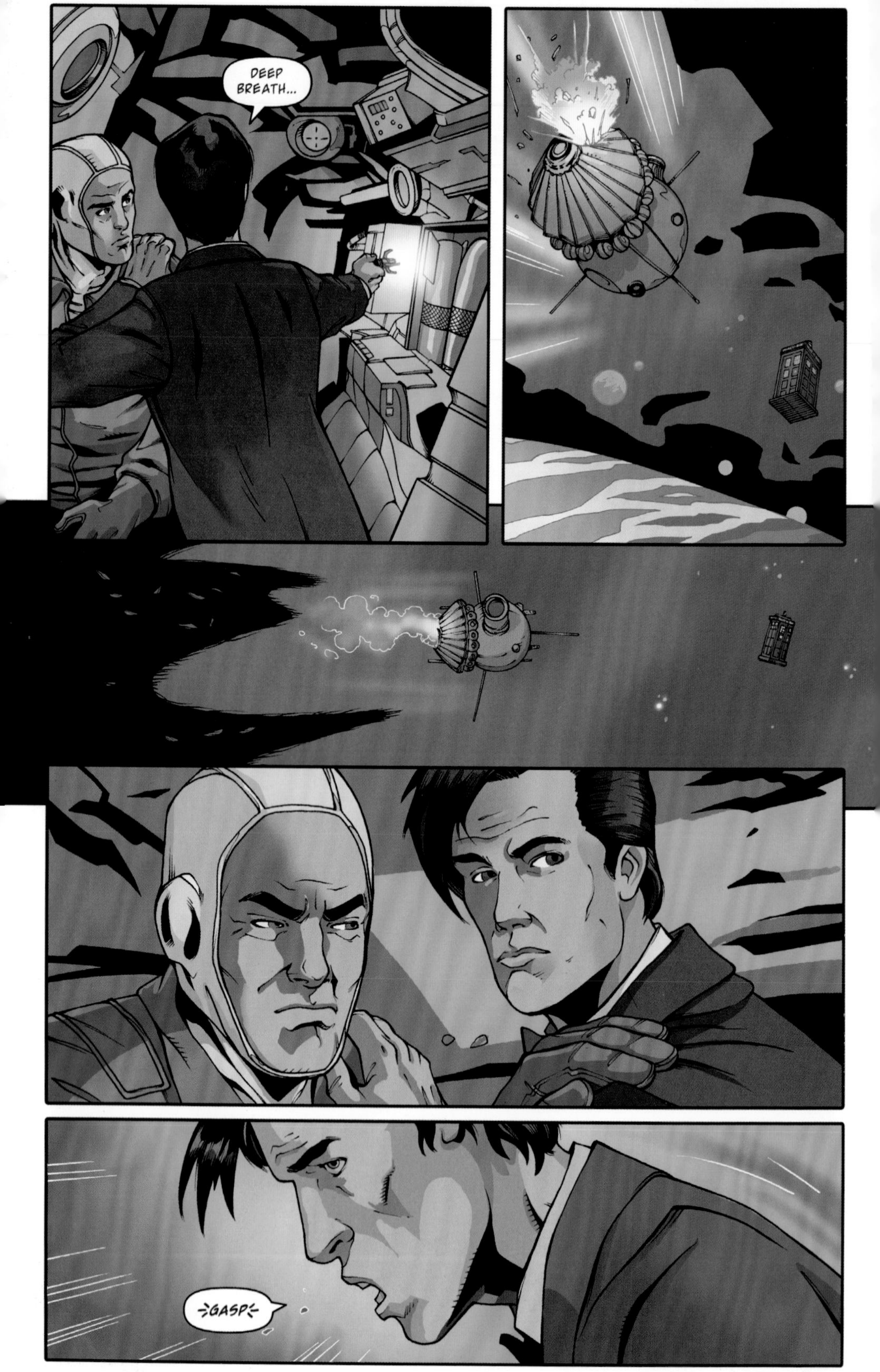
DEEP BREATH...
GASP

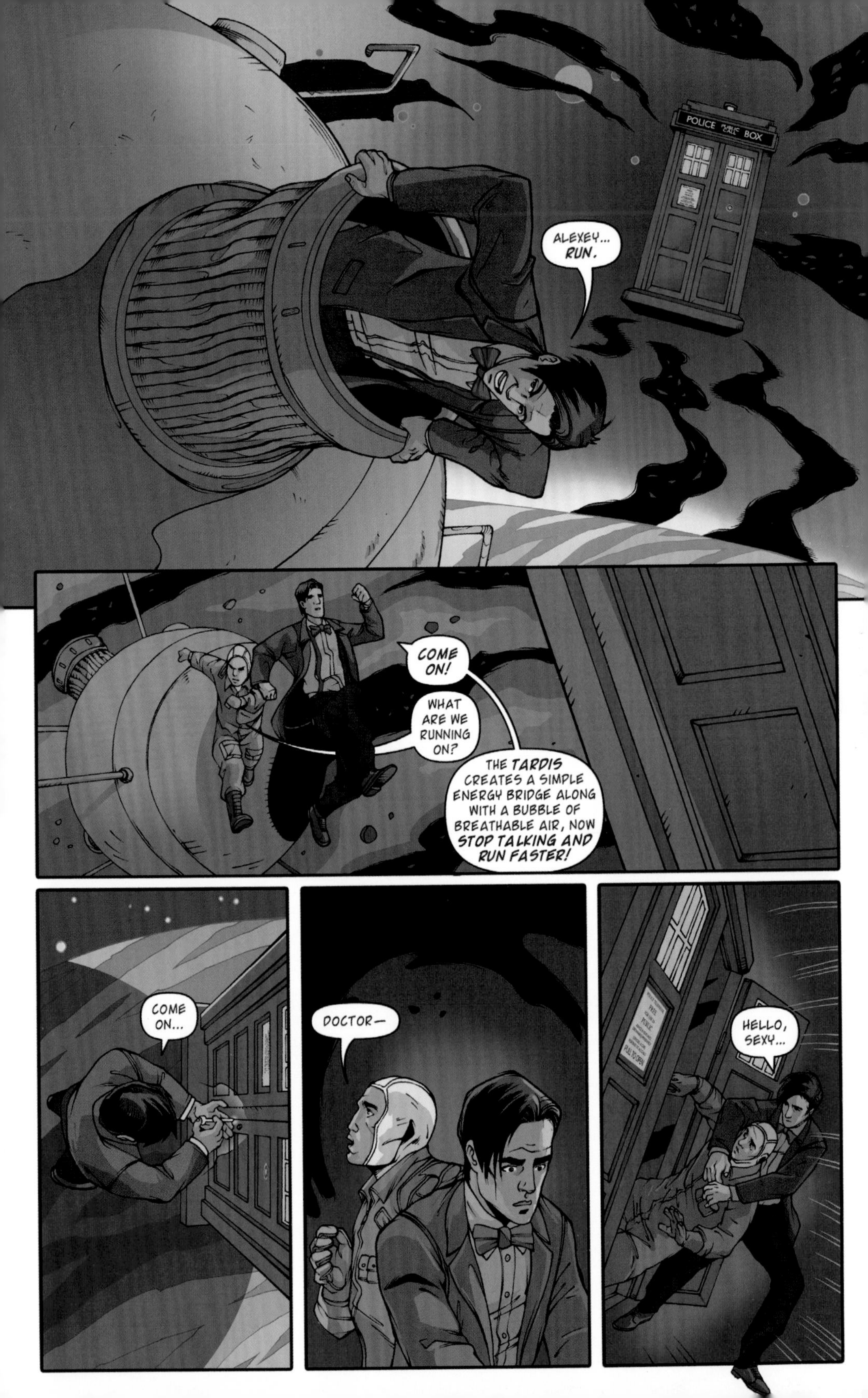
POLICE PUBLIC CALL BOX
ALEXEY... RUN.
COME ON!
WHAT ARE WE RUNNING ON?
THE TARDIS CREATES A SIMPLE ENERGY BRIDGE ALONG WITH A BUBBLE OF BREATHABLE AIR, NOW STOP TALKING AND RUN FASTER!
COME ON...
DOCTOR—
HELLO, SEXY...

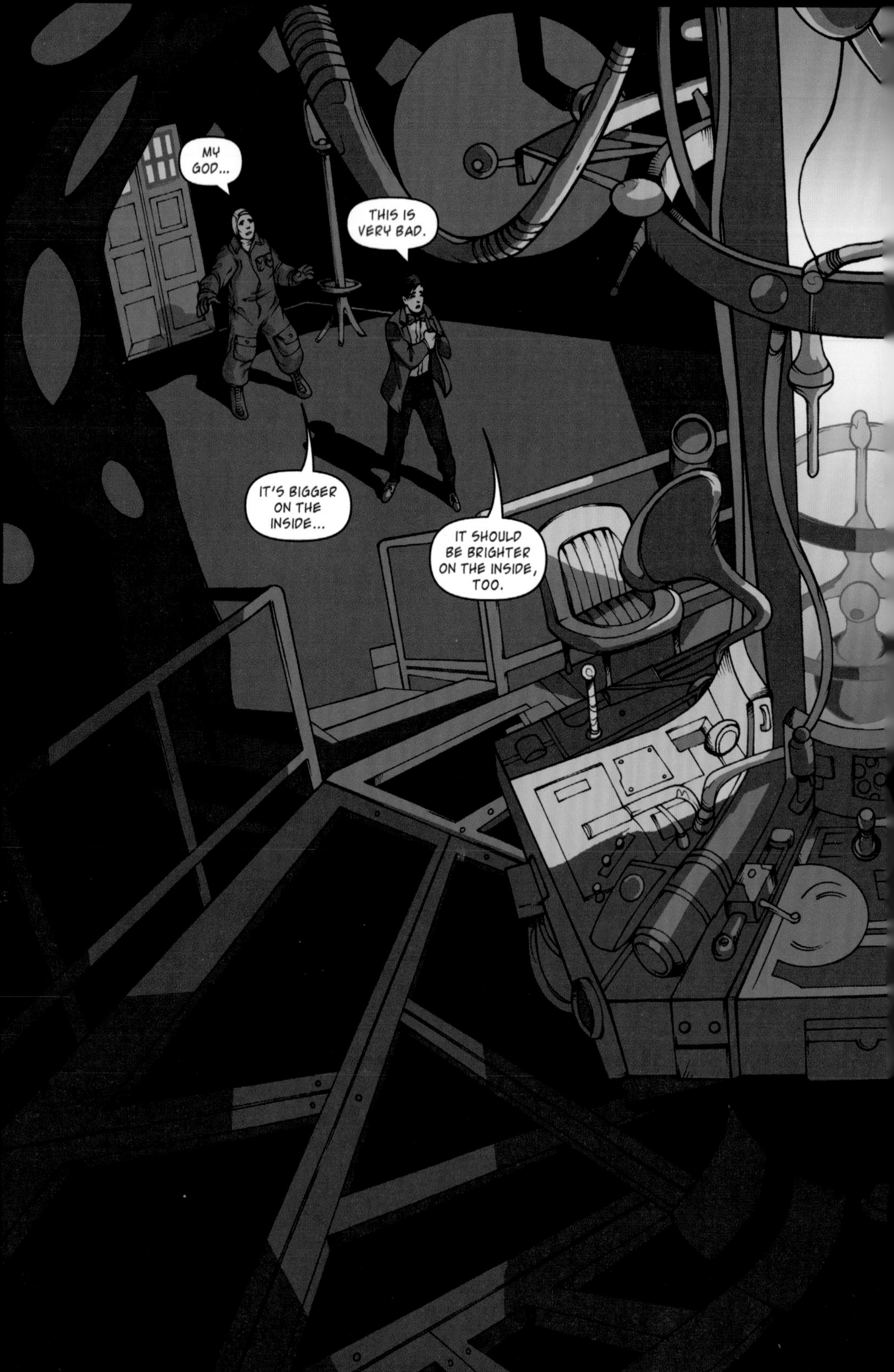
MY GOD...
THIS IS VERY BAD.
IT'S BIGGER ON THE INSIDE...
IT SHOULD BE BRIGHTER ON THE INSIDE, TOO.

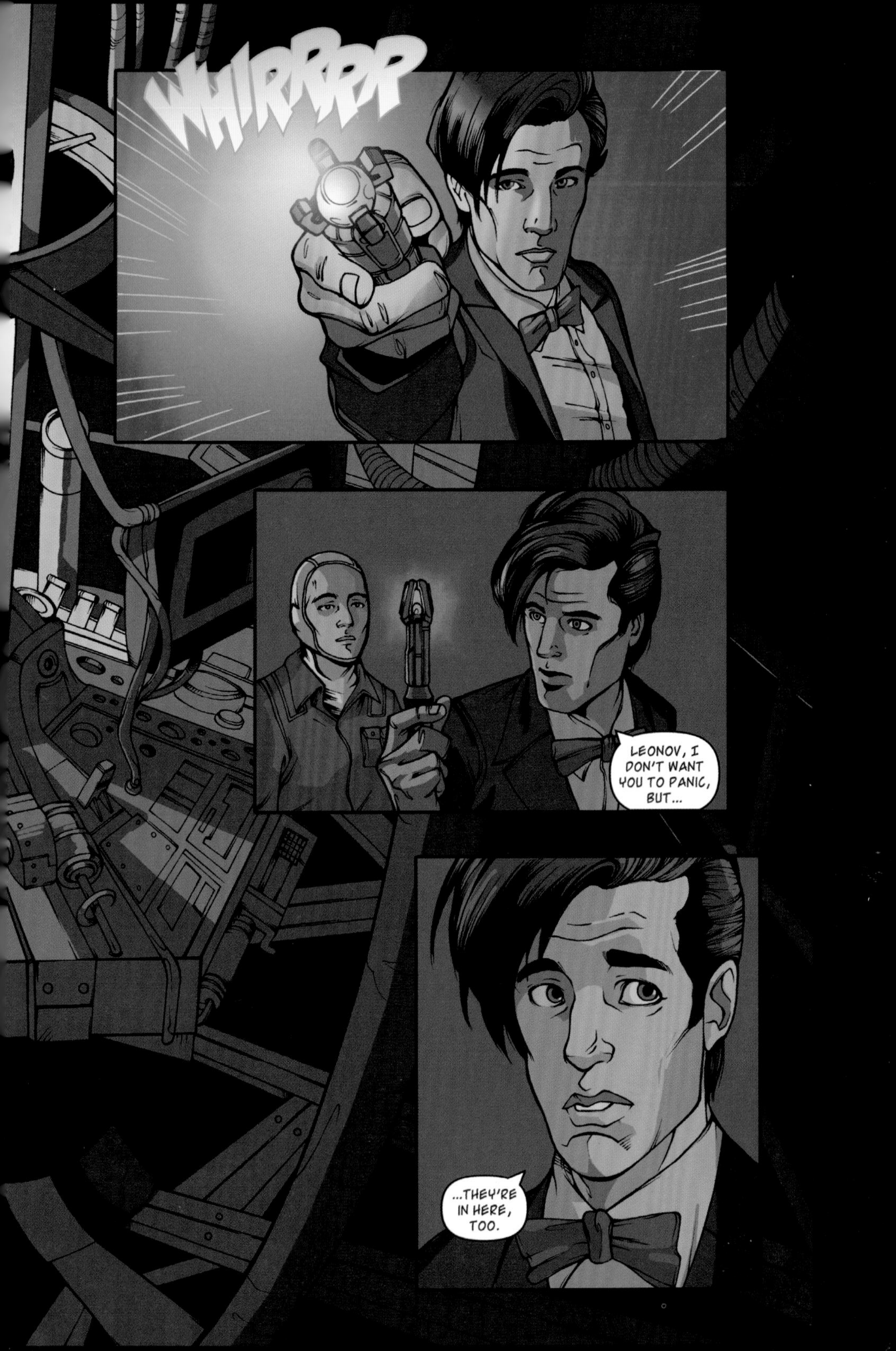
WHIRRRP
LEONOV, I DON'T WANT YOU TO PANIC, BUT...
...THEY'RE IN HERE, TOO.

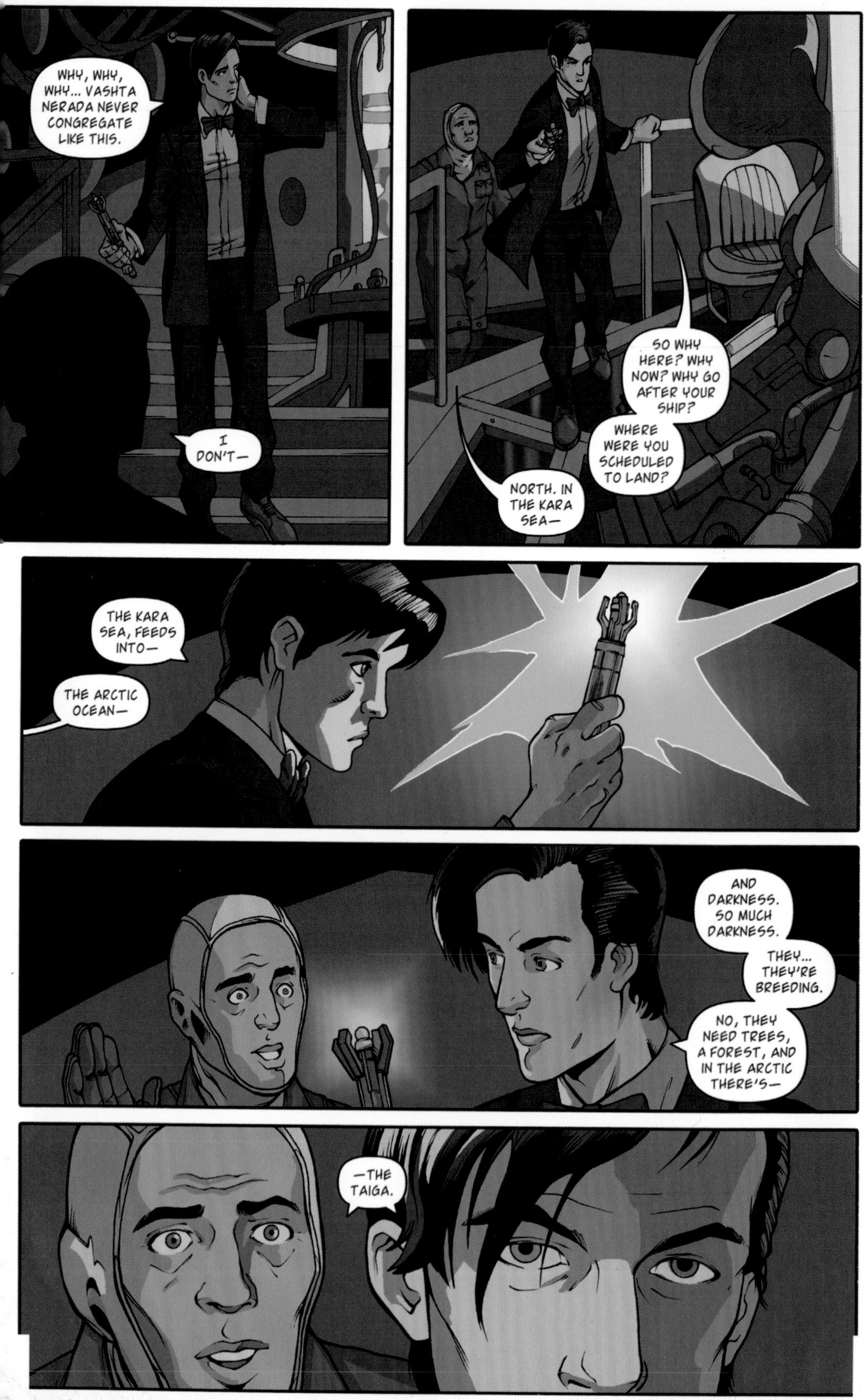
WHY, WHY, WHY... VASHTA NERADA NEVER CONGREGATE LIKE THIS.
I DON'T—
SO WHY HERE? WHY NOW? WHY GO AFTER YOUR SHIP?
WHERE WERE YOU SCHEDULED TO LAND?
NORTH. IN THE KARA SEA—
THE KARA SEA, FEEDS INTO—
THE ARCTIC OCEAN—
AND DARKNESS. SO MUCH DARKNESS.
THEY... THEY'RE BREEDING.
NO, THEY NEED TREES, A FOREST, AND IN THE ARCTIC THERE'S—
—THE TAIGA.

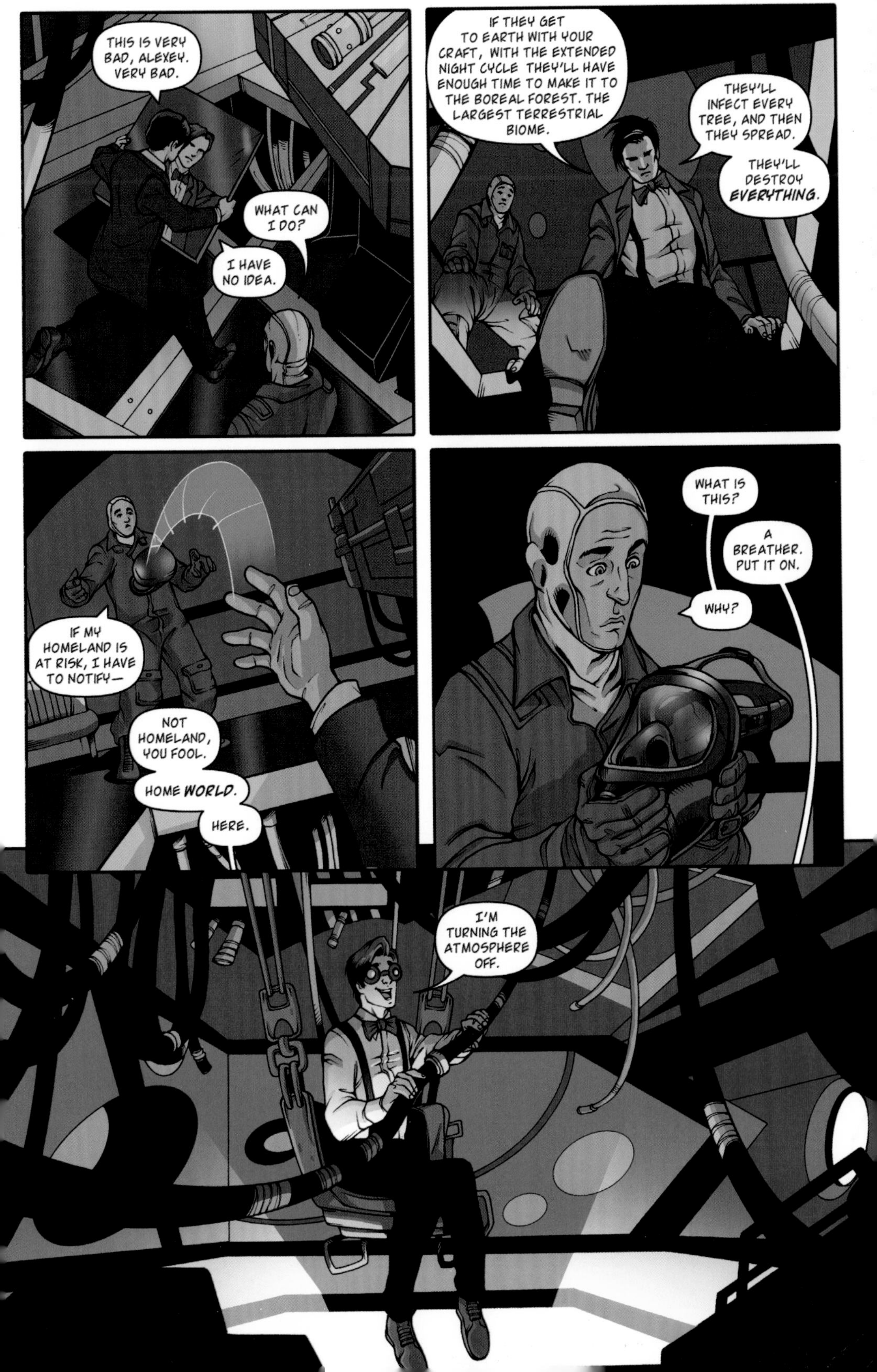
THIS IS VERY BAD, ALEXEY. VERY BAD.
WHAT CAN I DO?
I HAVE NO IDEA.
IF THEY GET TO EARTH WITH YOUR CRAFT, WITH THE EXTENDED NIGHT CYCLE THEY'LL HAVE ENOUGH TIME TO MAKE IT TO THE BOREAL FOREST. THE LARGEST TERRESTRIAL BIOME.
THEY'LL INFECT EVERY TREE, AND THEN THEY SPREAD.
THEY'LL DESTROY EVERYTHING.
IF MY HOMELAND IS AT RISK, I HAVE TO NOTIFY—
NOT HOMELAND, YOU FOOL.
HOME WORLD.
HERE.
WHAT IS THIS?
A BREATHER. PUT IT ON.
WHY?
I'M TURNING THE ATMOSPHERE OFF.

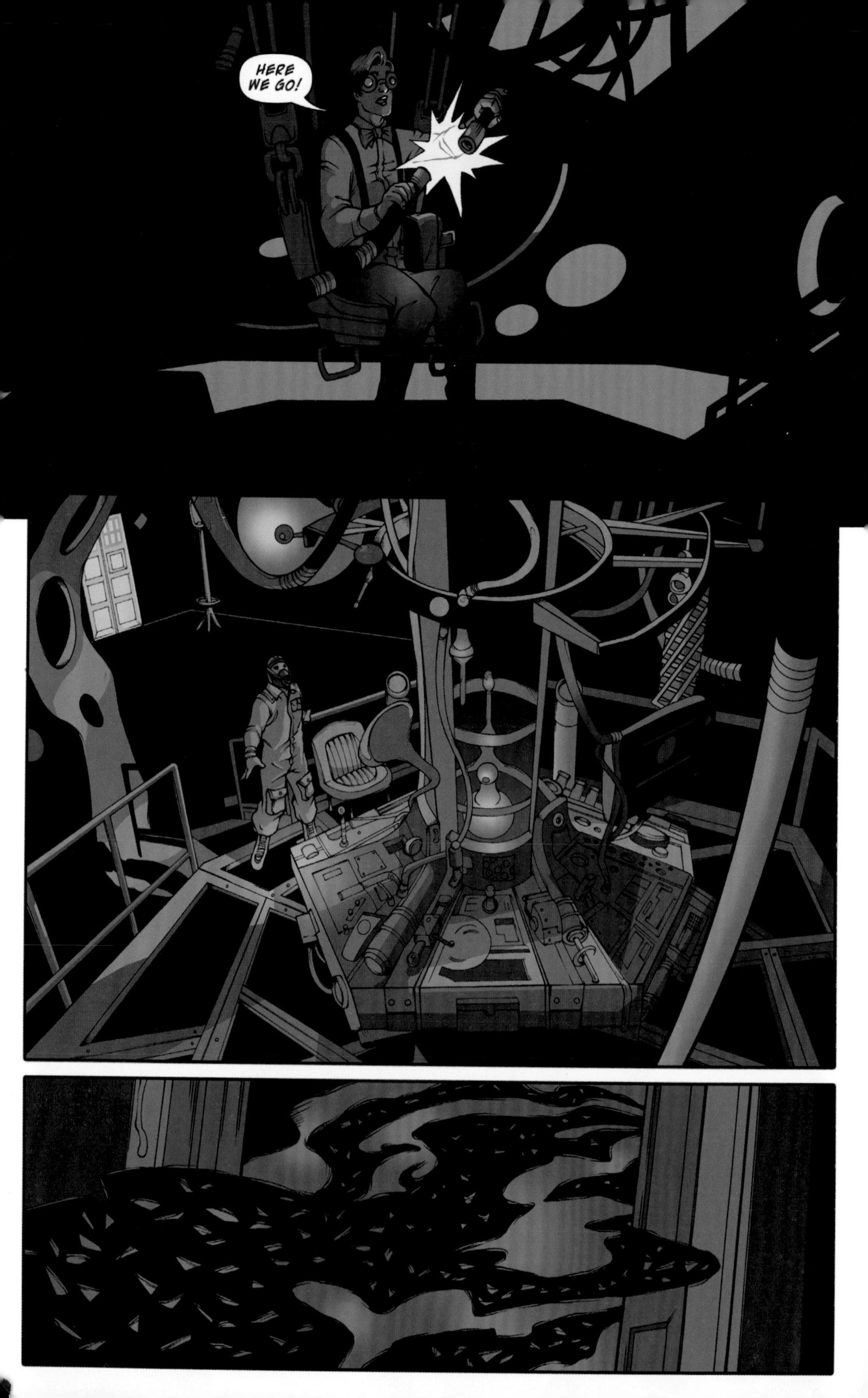
HERE WE GO!

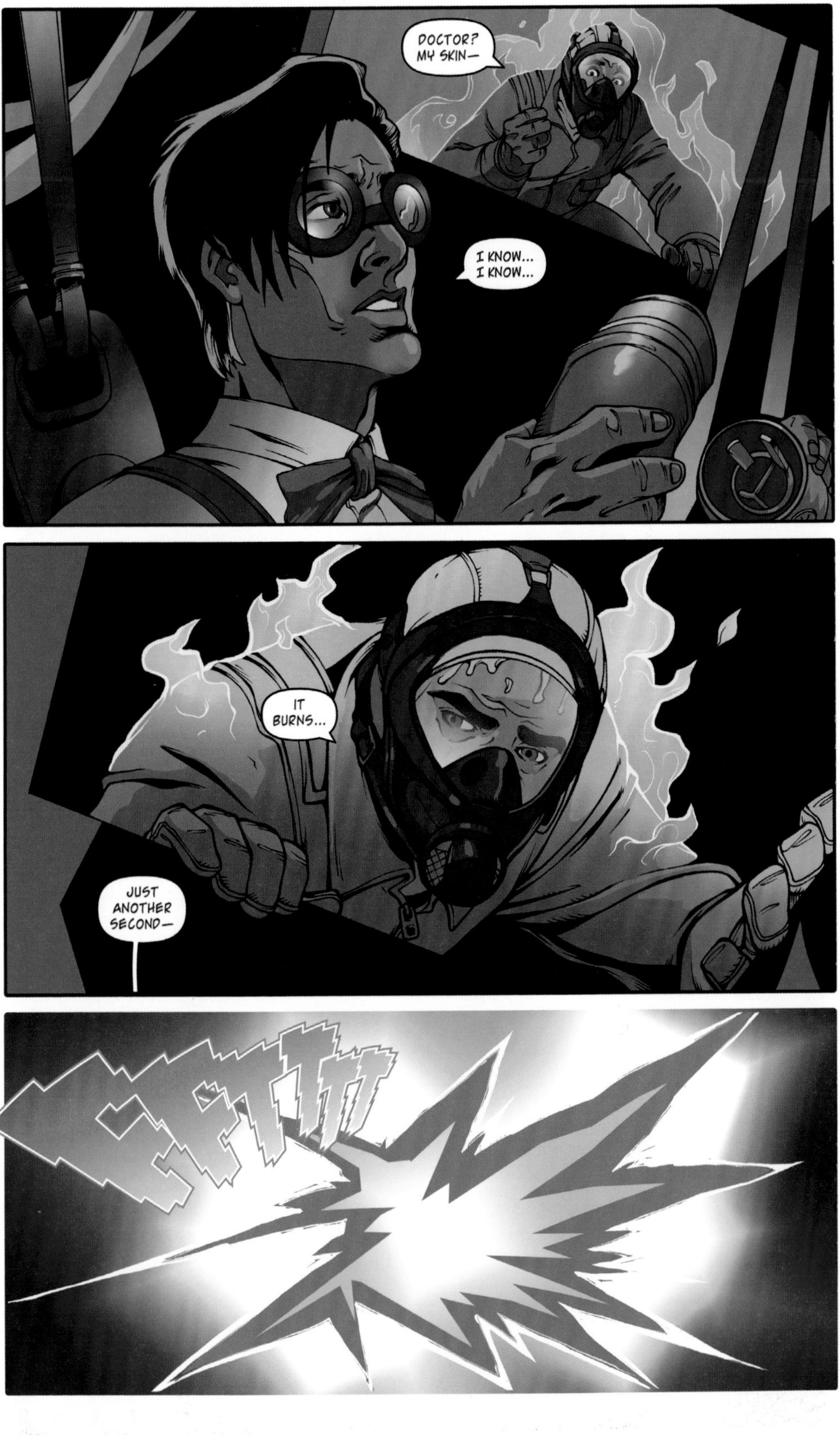
DOCTOR? MY SKIN—
I KNOW... I KNOW...
IT BURNS...
JUST ANOTHER SECOND—

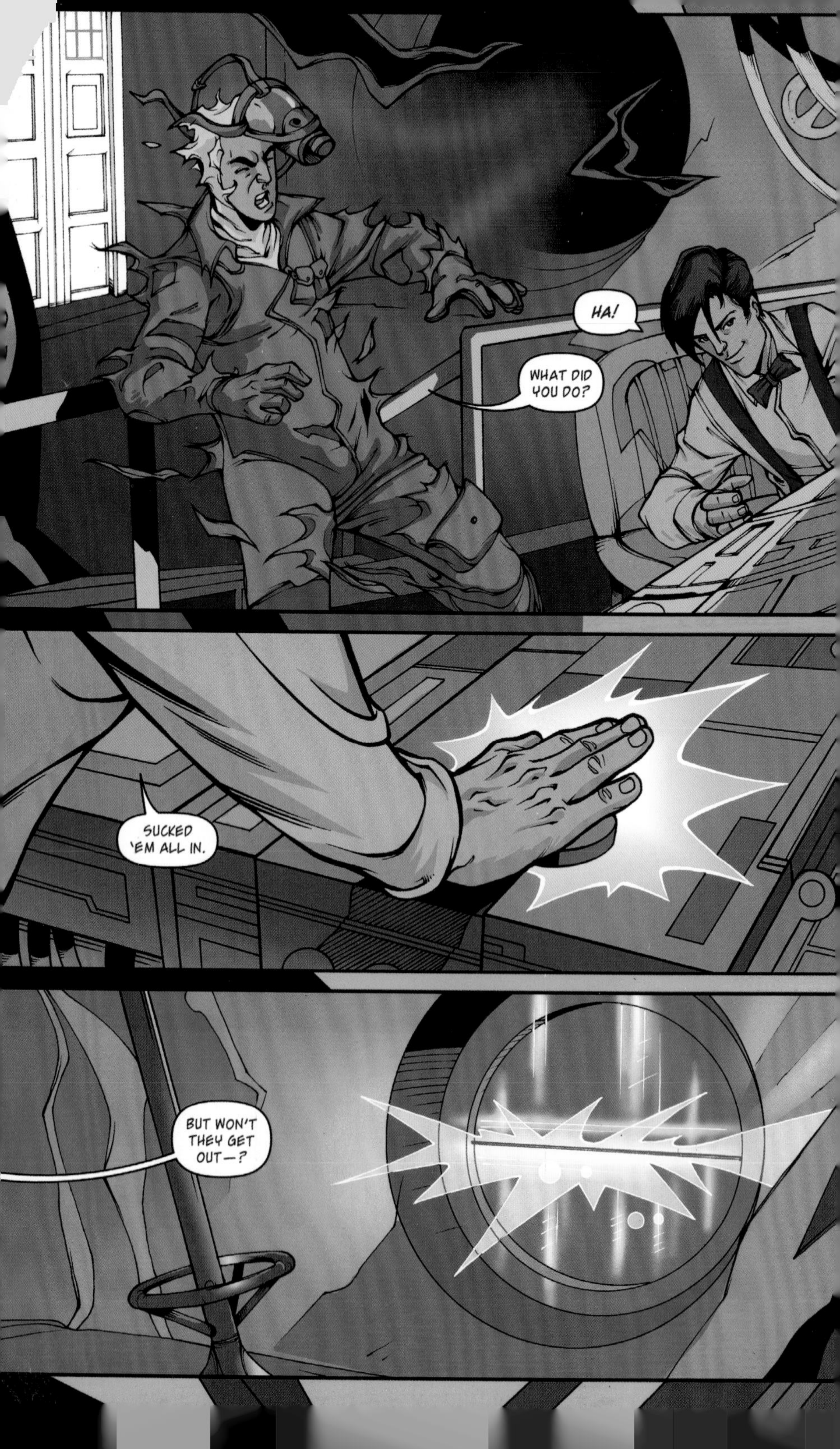
HA!
WHAT DID YOU DO?
SUCKED 'EM ALL IN.
BUT WON'T THEY GET OUT—?

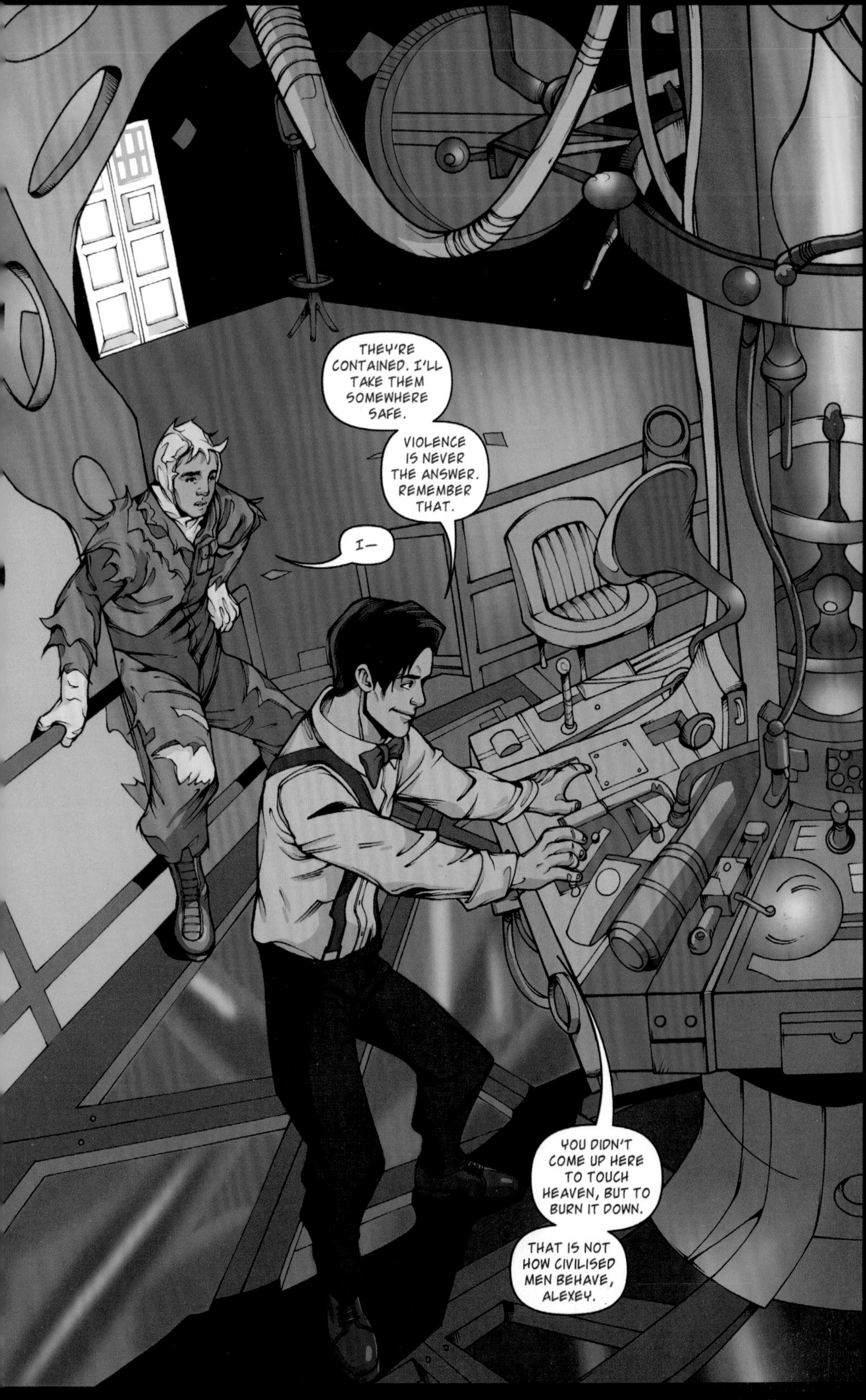
THEY'RE CONTAINED. I'LL TAKE THEM SOMEWHERE SAFE.
VIOLENCE IS NEVER THE ANSWER. REMEMBER THAT.
I—
YOU DIDN'T COME UP HERE TO TOUCH HEAVEN, BUT TO BURN IT DOWN.
THAT IS NOT HOW CIVILISED MEN BEHAVE, ALEXEY.

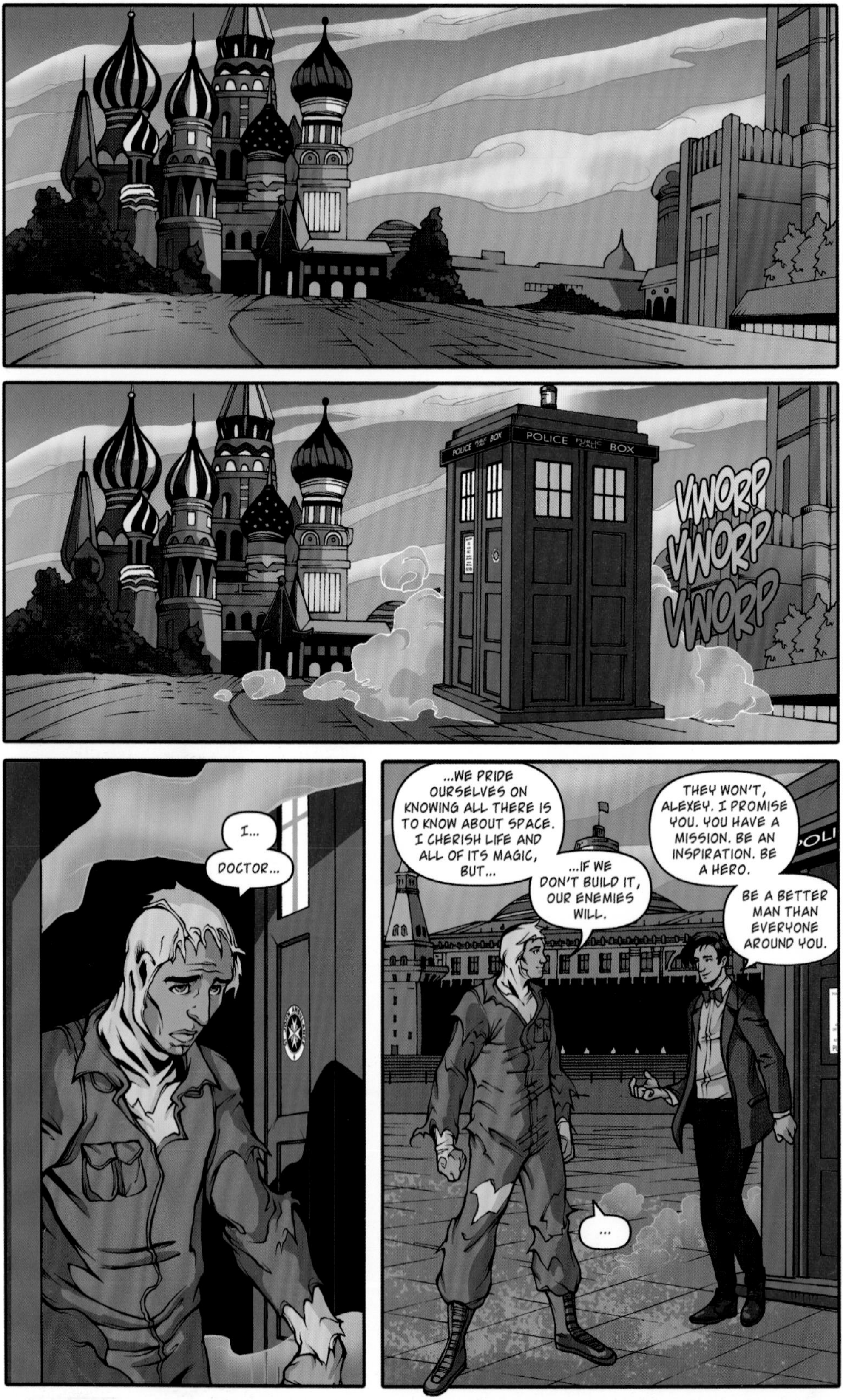
POLICE PUBLIC CALL BOX
VWORP VWORP VWORP
I...
DOCTOR...
...WE PRIDE OURSELVES ON KNOWING ALL THERE IS TO KNOW ABOUT SPACE. I CHERISH LIFE AND ALL OF ITS MAGIC, BUT...
...IF WE DON'T BUILD IT, OUR ENEMIES WILL.
THEY WON'T, ALEXEY. I PROMISE YOU. YOU HAVE A MISSION. BE AN INSPIRATION. BE A HERO.
BE A BETTER MAN THAN EVERYONE AROUND YOU.
...

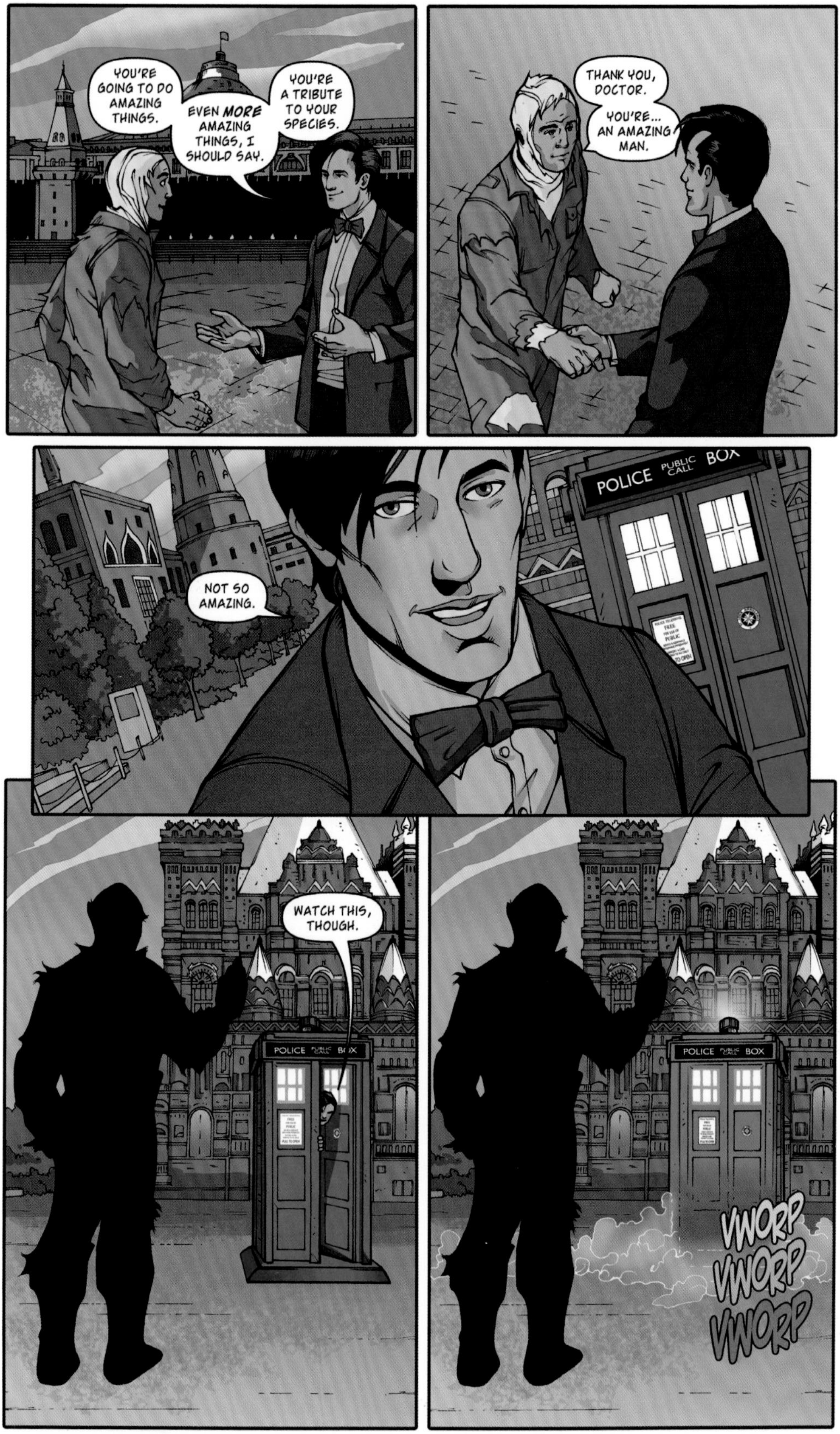
YOU'RE GOING TO DO AMAZING THINGS.
EVEN MORE AMAZING THINGS, I SHOULD SAY.
YOU'RE A TRIBUTE TO YOUR SPECIES.
THANK YOU, DOCTOR.
YOU'RE... AN AMAZING MAN.
POLICE PUBLIC CALL BOX
NOT SO AMAZING.
WATCH THIS, THOUGH.
POLICE PUBLIC CALL BOX
POLICE PUBLIC CALL BOX
VWORP VWORP VWORP

BY CONVENTION 15 OF THE SHADOW PROCLAMATION, I OFFER YOU THE CHANCE TO DISPERSE AND CEASE HOSTILITIES TOWARDS THIS PLANET.

IF YOU AGREE TO MY TERMS, I WILL RELEASE YOU, AND I ASSURE YOU NO HARM WILL COME TO YOU.

I'LL TAKE YOU TO A NEW HOME WORLD, SOMEWHERE YOU CAN THRIVE AND LIVE, AND NOT KILL ANYBODY.

NO?

I... FIGURED AS MUCH.

SLAM

REMOVE PROTECTIVE FAILSAFES.

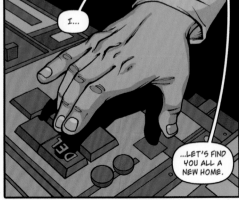

I...

...LET'S FIND YOU ALL A NEW HOME.

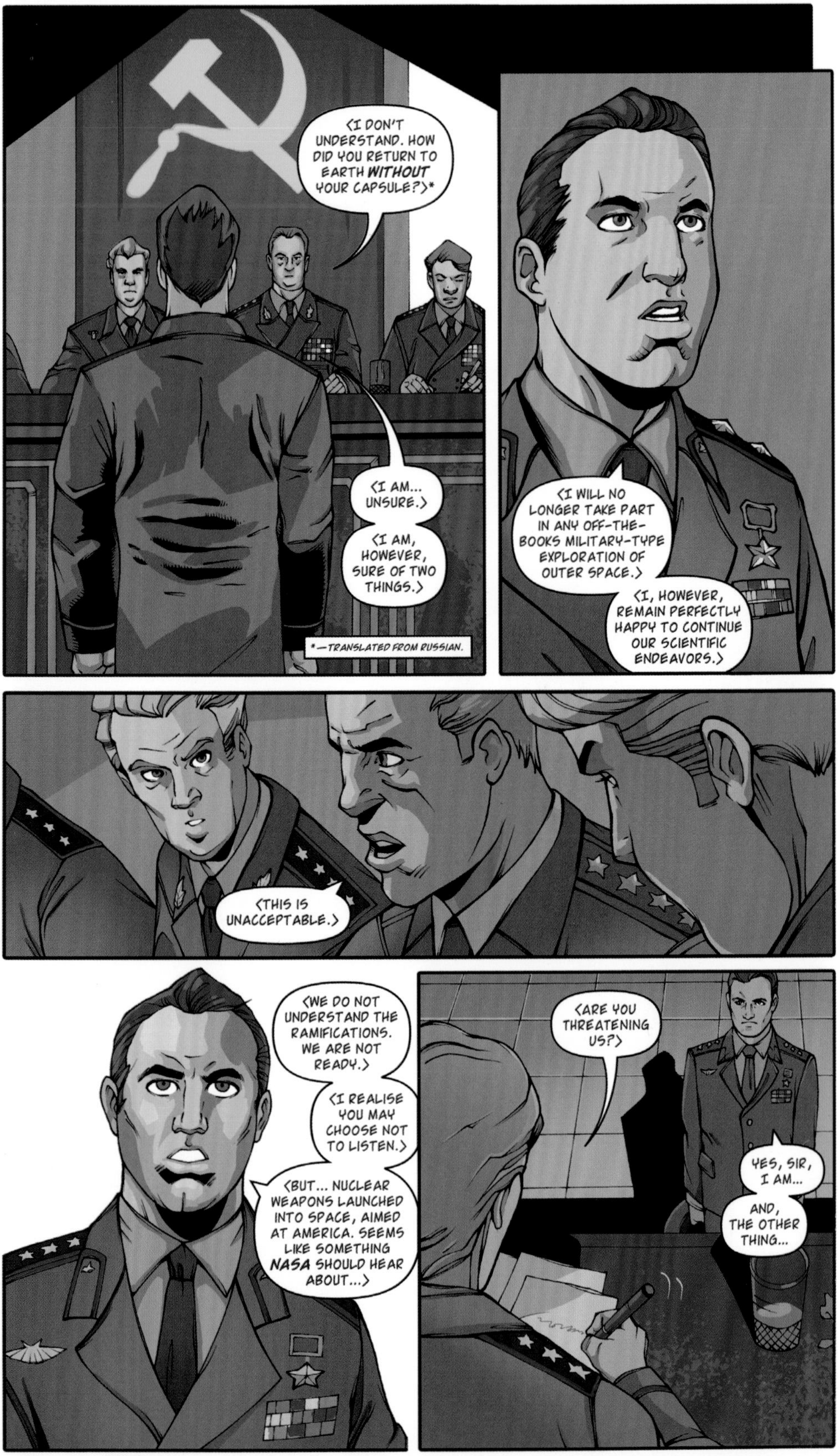

<I DON'T UNDERSTAND. HOW DID YOU RETURN TO EARTH WITHOUT YOUR CAPSULE?>*
<I AM... UNSURE.>
<I AM, HOWEVER, SURE OF TWO THINGS.>
*—TRANSLATED FROM RUSSIAN.
<I WILL NO LONGER TAKE PART IN ANY OFF-THE-BOOKS MILITARY-TYPE EXPLORATION OF OUTER SPACE.>
<I, HOWEVER, REMAIN PERFECTLY HAPPY TO CONTINUE OUR SCIENTIFIC ENDEAVORS.>
<THIS IS UNACCEPTABLE.>
<WE DO NOT UNDERSTAND THE RAMIFICATIONS. WE ARE NOT READY.>
<I REALISE YOU MAY CHOOSE NOT TO LISTEN.>
<BUT... NUCLEAR WEAPONS LAUNCHED INTO SPACE, AIMED AT AMERICA. SEEMS LIKE SOMETHING NASA SHOULD HEAR ABOUT...>
<ARE YOU THREATENING US?>
YES, SIR, I AM...
AND, THE OTHER THING...

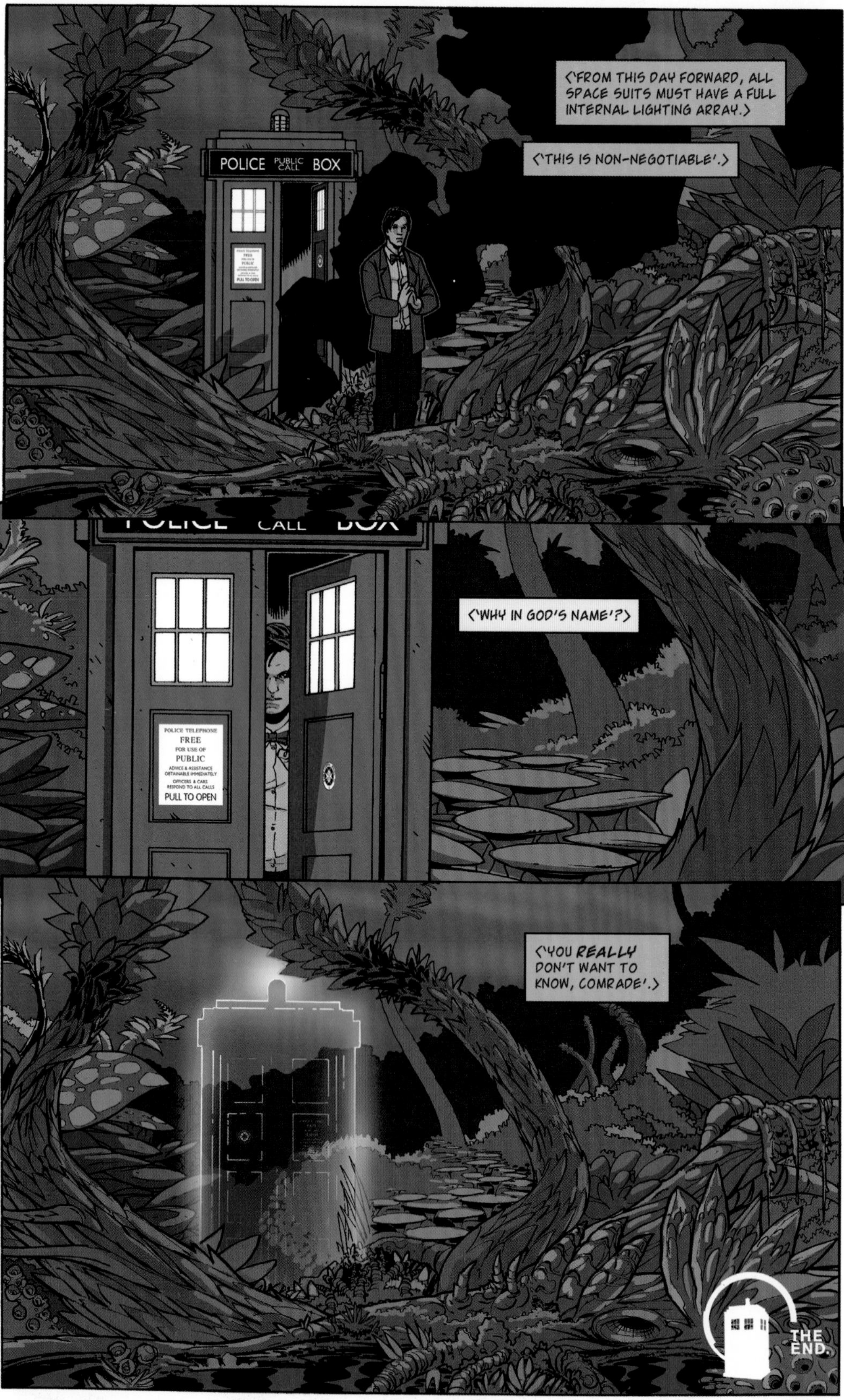
<'FROM THIS DAY FORWARD, ALL SPACE SUITS MUST HAVE A FULL INTERNAL LIGHTING ARRAY.>
<'THIS IS NON-NEGOTIABLE'.>
POLICE PUBLIC CALL BOX
<'WHY IN GOD'S NAME'?>
POLICE TELEPHONE
FREE
FOR USE OF
PUBLIC
ADVICE & ASSISTANCE OBTAINABLE IMMEDIATELY
OFFICERS & CARS RESPOND TO ALL CALLS
PULL TO OPEN
<'YOU ***REALLY*** DON'T WANT TO KNOW, COMRADE'.>
THE END.

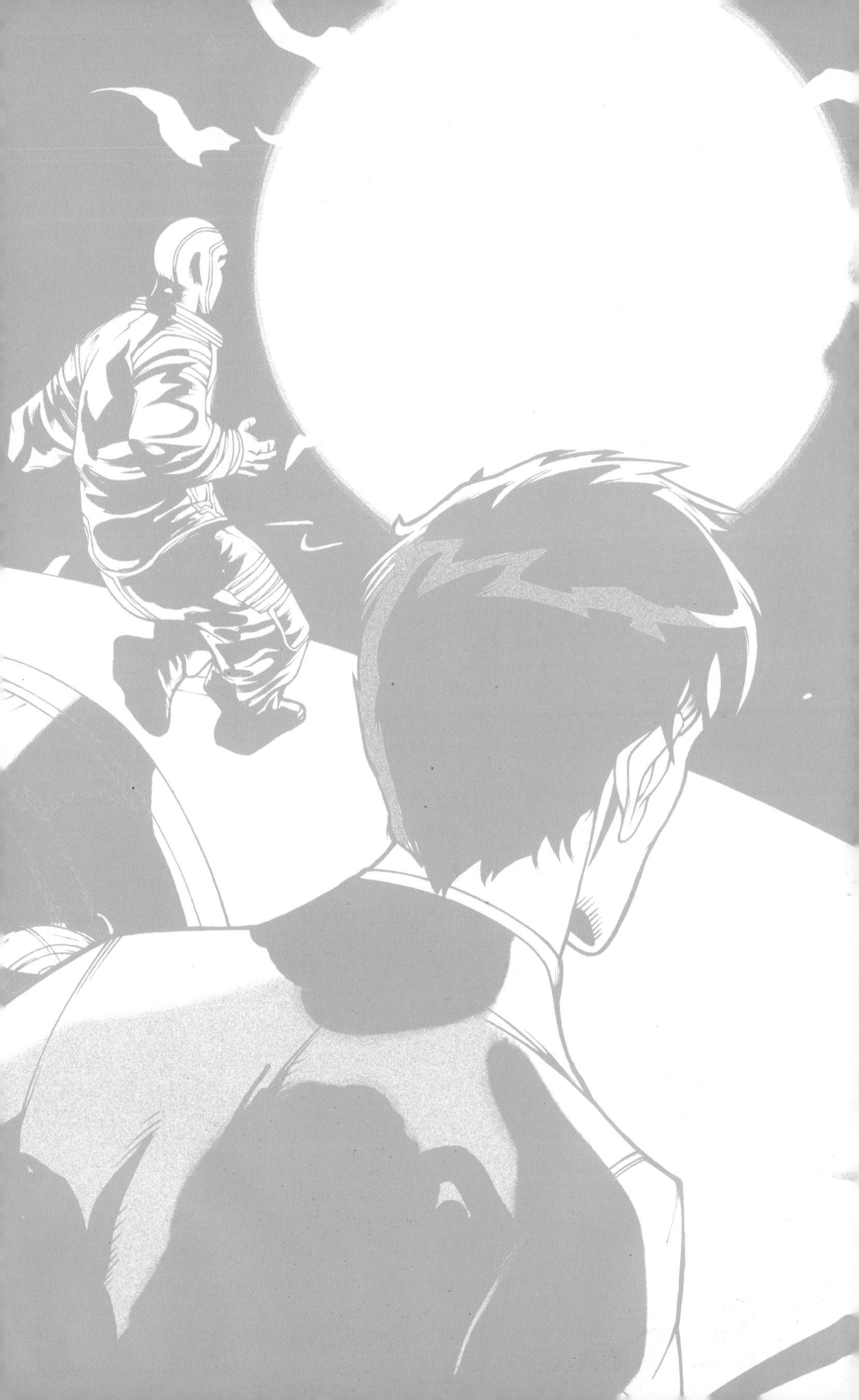

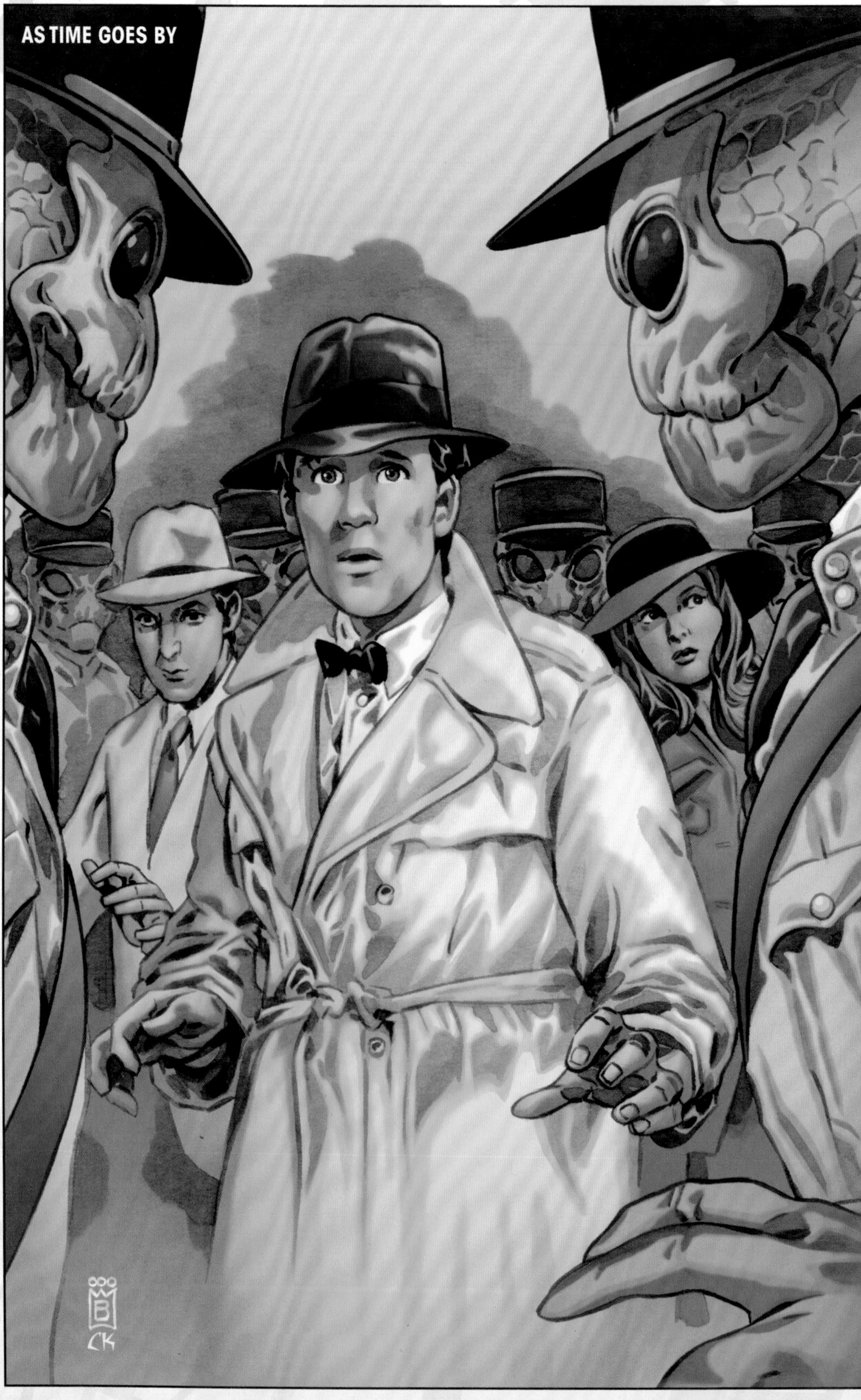
AS TIME GOES BY

AS TIME GOES BY

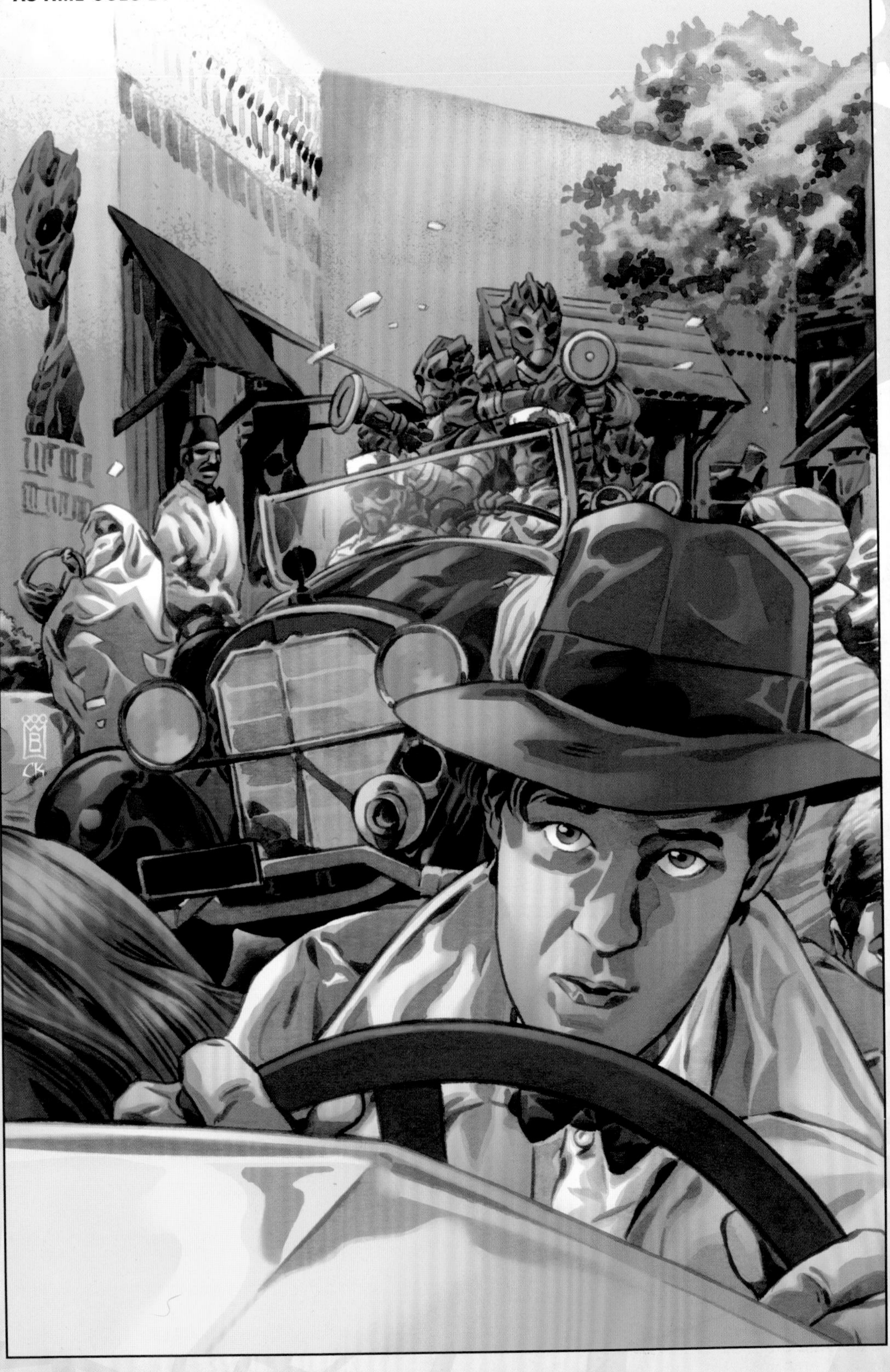

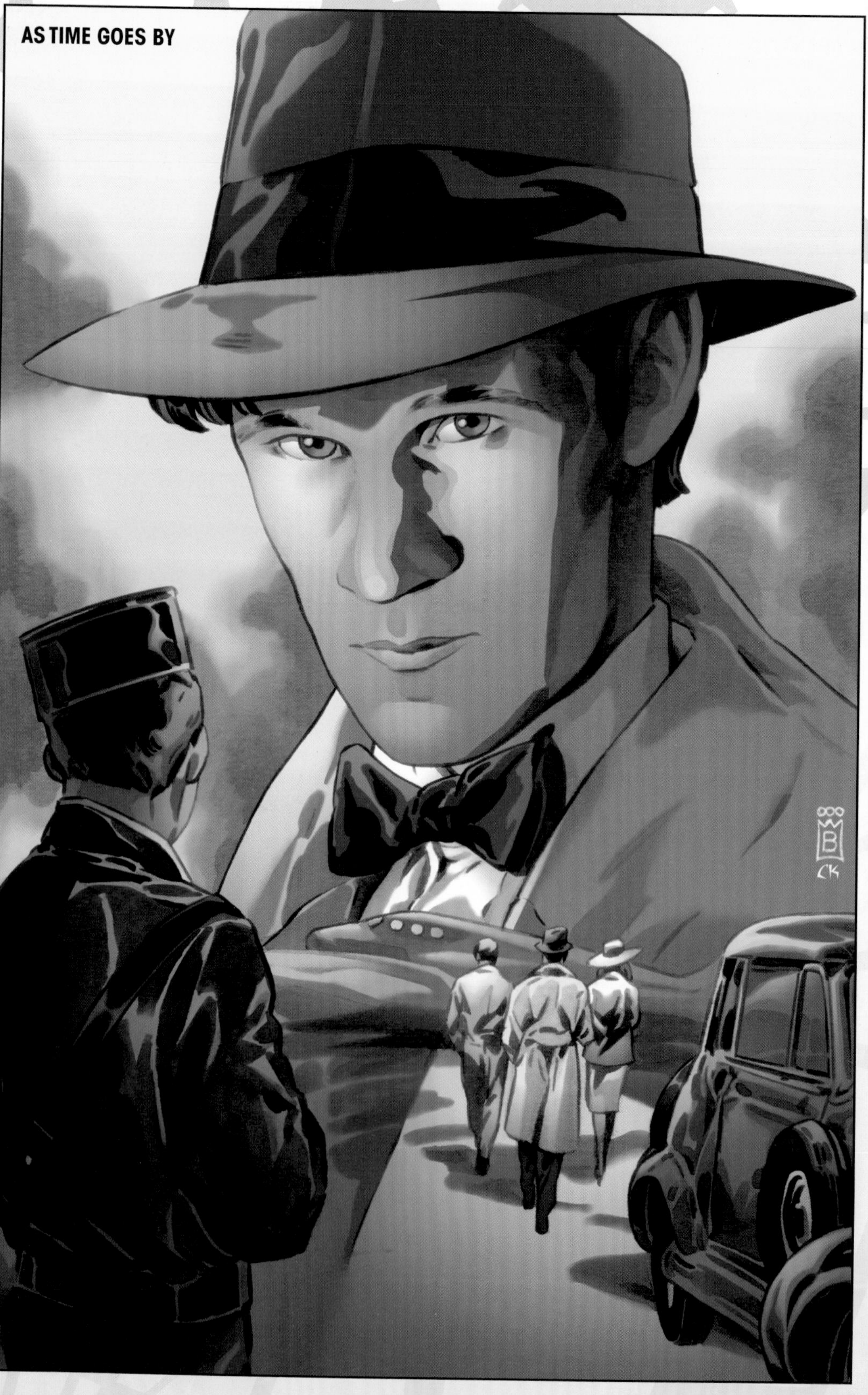
AS TIME GOES BY

THE HYPOTHETICAL GENTLEMAN

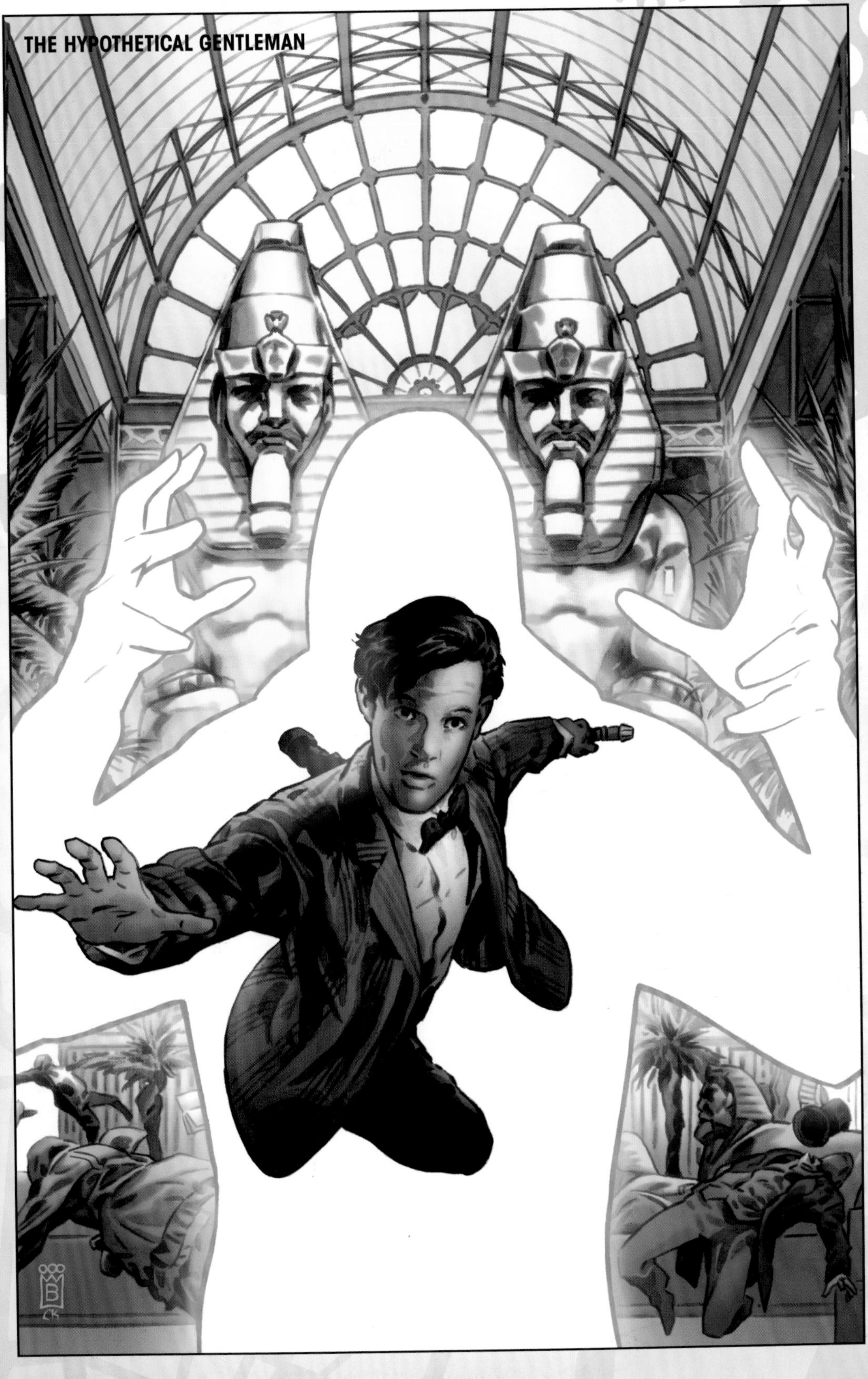

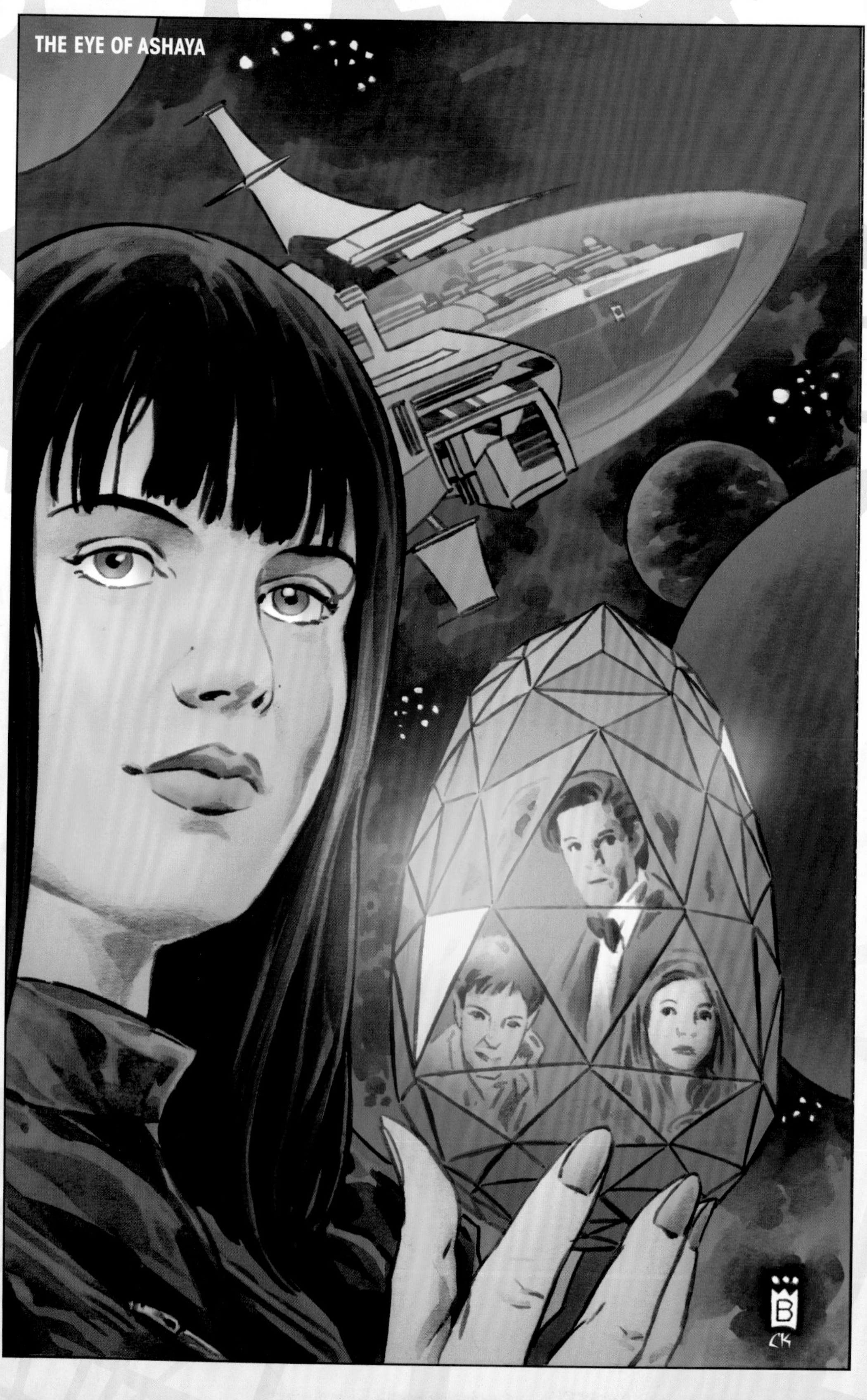
THE EYE OF ASHAYA
CK

SPACE ODDITY

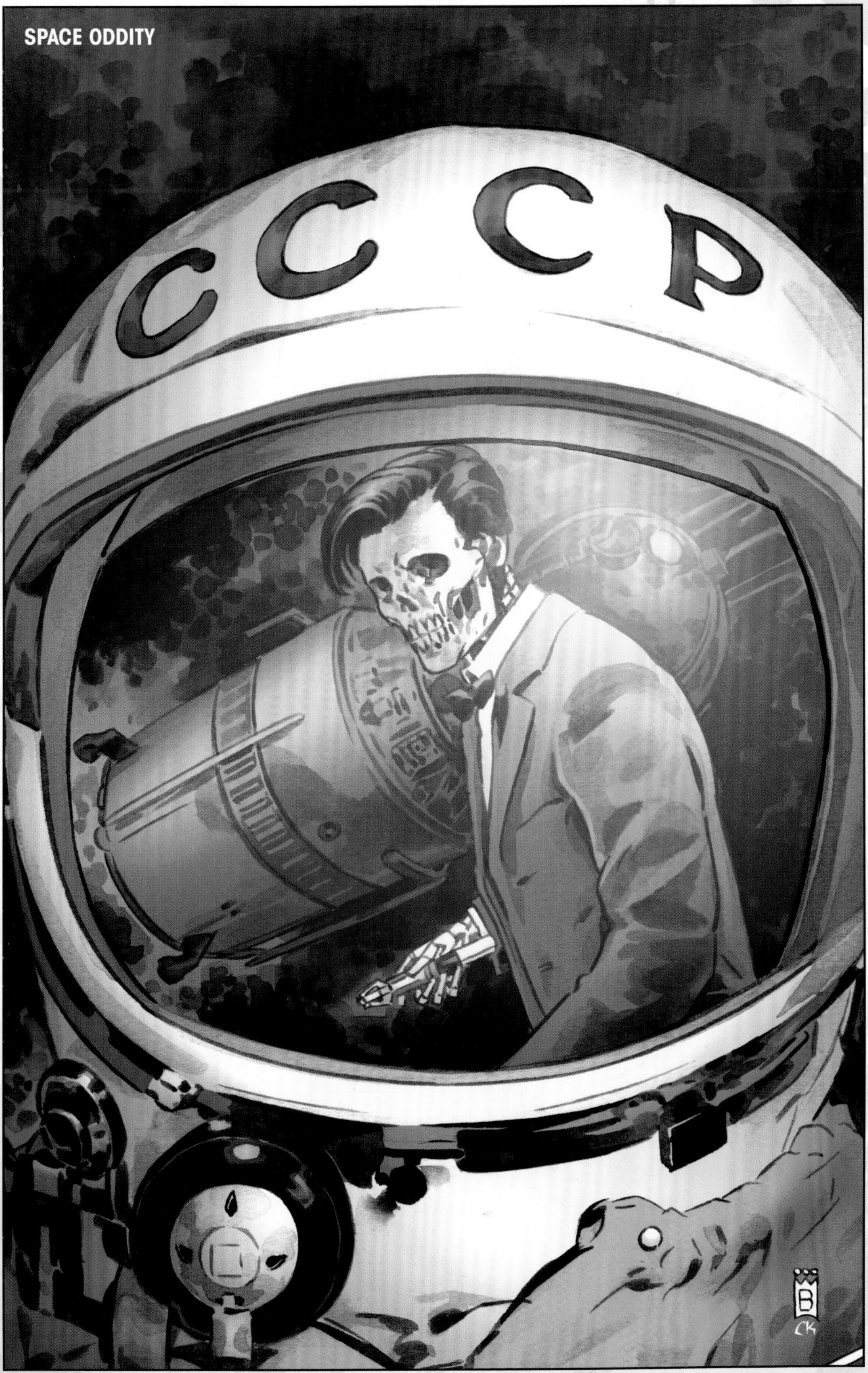
CCCP

THE TRIUMPHANT FIRST
AND SECOND COLLECTIONS!
AVAILABLE NOW!

DOCTOR WHO: THE TWELFTH DOCTOR
VOL. 1: TERRORFORMER

ISBN: 9781782761778
ON SALE NOW - $19.99 / $22.95 CAN

DOCTOR WHO: THE TWELFTH DOCTOR
VOL. 2: FRACTURES

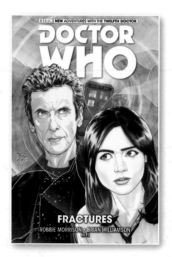

ISBN: 9781782763017
ON SALE NOW - $19.99 / $25.99 CAN

DOCTOR WHO: THE TWELFTH DOCTOR
VOL. 3: HYPERION

ISBN: 9781782767473
COMING SOON - $19.99 / $25.99 CAN

DOCTOR WHO: THE TENTH DOCTOR
VOL. 1: REVOLUTIONS OF TERROR

ISBN: 9781782761730
ON SALE NOW - $19.99 / $22.95 CAN

DOCTOR WHO: THE TENTH DOCTOR
VOL. 2: THE WEEPING ANGELS OF MONS

ISBN: 9781782761754
ON SALE NOW - $19.99 / $25.99 CAN

DOCTOR WHO: THE TENTH DOCTOR
VOL. 3: THE FOUNTAINS OF FOREVER

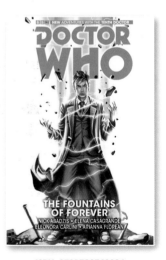

ISBN: 9781782763024
COMING SOON - $19.99 / $25.99 CAN

For information on how to subscribe to our great Doctor Who titles, or to purchase them digitally for your favorite device, visit:

WWW.TITAN-COMICS.COM

COMPLETE YOUR COLLECTION!
ELEVENTH DOCTOR VOL. 1 AND 2
AVAILABLE NOW!

**DOCTOR WHO: THE ELEVENTH DOCTOR
VOL. 1: AFTER LIFE**

**DOCTOR WHO: THE ELEVENTH DOCTOR
VOL. 2: SERVE YOU**

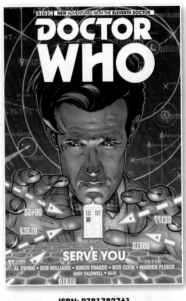

**ISBN: 9781782761747
ON SALE NOW - $19.99 / $22.95 CAN**

**ISBN: 9781782761
ON SALE NOW - $19.99 / $25.99 CAN**

COMING SOON!
DOCTOR WHO: THE NINTH DOCTOR
VOL. 1: WEAPONS OF PAST
DESTRUCTION

**COLLECTS DOCTOR WHO:
THE NINTH DOCTOR MINISERIES #1-#5
COMING SOON $19.99 / $25.99 CAN**

ISBN: 9781782763369

AVAILABLE IN ALL GOOD COMIC STORES,
BOOK STORES, AND DIGITAL PROVIDERS!

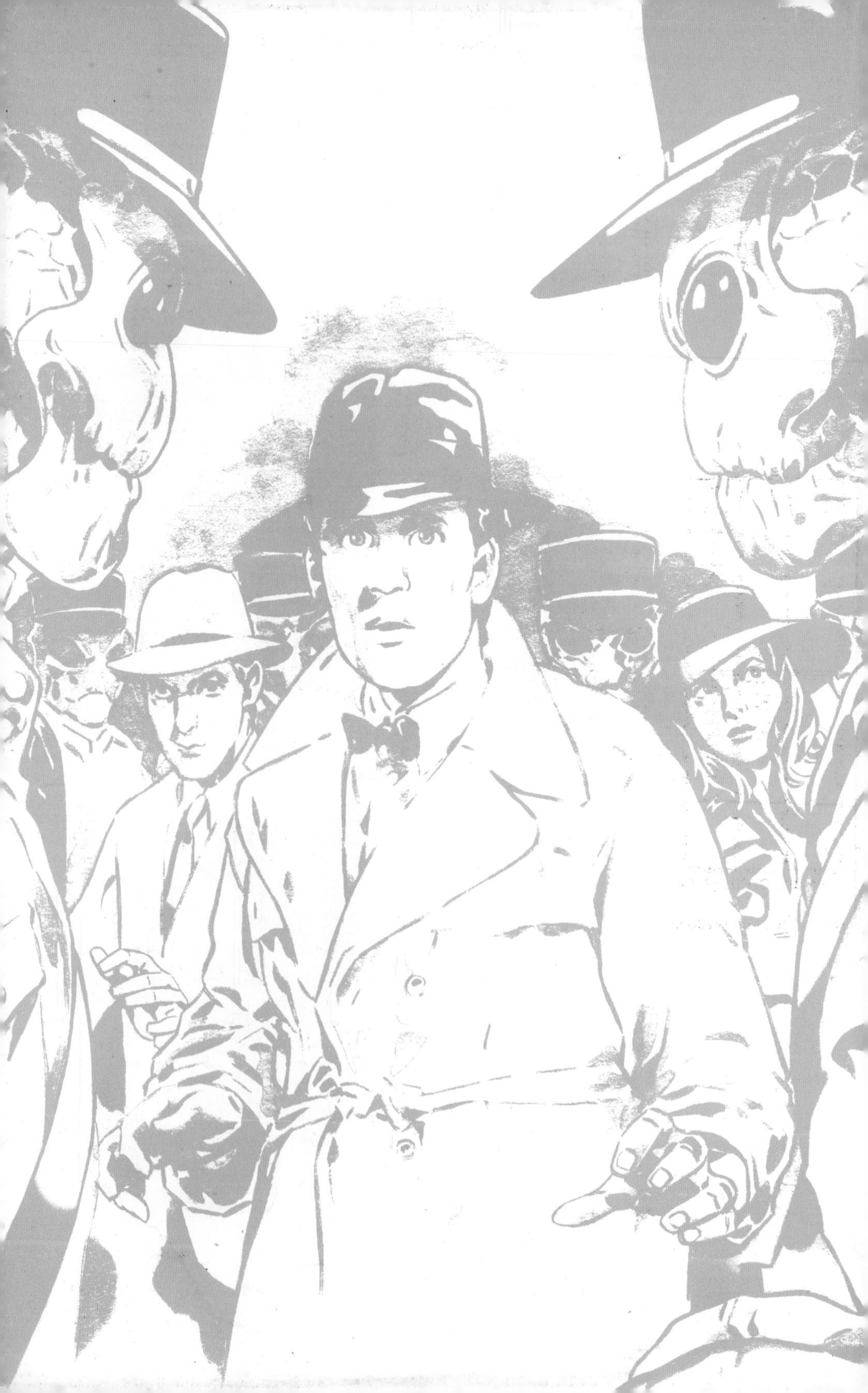